The Great American Mosaic

Volume 1
African American Experience

Volume 2
American Indian Experience

Volume 3
Asian American and Pacific Islander Experience

Volume 4
Latino American Experience

The Great American Mosaic

An Exploration of Diversity in Primary Documents

Gary Y. Okihiro, General Editor

Volume 3
Asian American and Pacific Islander Experience

Emily Moberg Robinson, Volume Editor

GREENWOOD

AN IMPRINT OF ABC-CLIO, LLC
Santa Barbara, California • Denver, Colorado • Oxford, England

Library of Congress Cataloging-in-Publication Data

The great American mosaic: an exploration of diversity in primary documents/Gary Y. Okihiro, general editor.
   volumes cm
Contents: Volume 1. African American Experience/Lionel C. Bascom, volume editor.
ISBN 978-1-61069-612-8 (hardback : acid-free paper)—ISBN
978-1-61069-613-5 (ebook) 1. Cultural pluralism—United States—History—Sources. 2. United States—Race relations—History—Sources. 3. United States—Ethnic relations—History—Sources. 4. Minorities—United States—History—Sources. 5. United States—History—Sources. I. Okihiro, Gary Y., 1945- II. Bascom, Lionel C.
E184.A1G826 2014
305.800973—dc23   2014007428

ISBN: 978-1-61069-612-8
EISBN: 978-1-61069-613-5

18 17 16 15 14   1 2 3 4 5

This book is also available on the World Wide Web as an eBook.
Visit www.abc-clio.com for details.

Greenwood
An Imprint of ABC-CLIO, LLC

ABC-CLIO, LLC
130 Cremona Drive, P.O. Box 1911
Santa Barbara, California 93116-1911

This book is printed on acid-free paper ∞
Manufactured in the United States of America

Contents

American Samoans

Bangladeshi Americans

Cambodian Americans

Chinese Americans

Filipino Americans

Guamanian Americans

Native Hawaiian Americans

Indonesian Americans

Japanese Americans

Korean Americans

Lao Americans

Malaysian Americans

Pakistani Americans

Sri Lankan Americans

Thai Americans

Vietnamese Americans

Multiheritage Asian Americans

General Introduction

Peoples of color—African Americans, Asian and Pacific Islander Americans, Latinas/Latinos, and Native Americans—were not always included within the American mosaic. In fact, throughout much of the nation's history, peoples of color were not members or citizens of these United States. In 1787, John Jay, a Founding Father and a leading designer of the nation-state, declared in "Concerning the Dangers from Foreign Force and Influence," essays that were part of *The Federalist* papers, that Americans are "one united people—a people descended from the same ancestors, speaking the same language, professing the same religion, attached to the same principles of government, very similar in their manners and customs."

Jay's "one united people" were Europeans, foreigners, who called themselves "persons" and "whites" in the new nation's Constitution, laws, and census. Those not included within that racialized, nationalized category or "the citizen race" in the words of U.S. Supreme Court chief justice Roger Taney in *Dred Scott v. Sandford* (1857), were of "another and different class of persons" and they represented "foreign dangers," threatening disunity and conflict. It is the experiences of those peoples that *The Great American Mosaic: An Exploration of Diversity in Primary Documents* covers in its four volumes. Volume 1 provides a collection of documents exploring the African American experience; Volume 2, the American Indian experience; Volume 3, the Asian American and Pacific Islander experience; and Volume 4, the Latino experience.

Standard narratives of the nation routinely excluded peoples of color. Only around the mid-20th century did U.S. history textbooks reflect more fully the nation's diversity, highlighting especially the presence of African Americans. Still, the architecture of American history remains white at its core; Native Americans, including American Indians and Pacific Islanders, formed the environment and background for white expansion and settlement, and African and Asian Americans and Latinas/Latinos played minor notes in an anthem devoted to the European nation.

Indeed, the nation, since the English invasion and colonization of America in the 17th century, systematically excluded peoples of color from the privileges and protections accorded Taney's "citizen race." "We, the people" of the U.S. Constitution was never intended to embrace nonwhites; that exclusion is the foundational premise upon which the nation was conceived. Conversely, the inclusion of peoples of color democratized the nation and was truly revolutionary. The American Revolution, by contrast, was not transformative in that the new nation was an extension of the original white settler colonialism that infringed upon these shores.

American Indians

To the invaders, American Indians were impediments to their freedom, especially embodied in the concept of "free" land. Conquest and expulsion were the means of American Indian alienation whereby English foreigners became natives on their sovereign estates, and the land's natives became aliens. The English-drawn border of 1763, despite its porous nature, was indicative of that demarcation, that segregation of "citizens" from "aliens."

The postcolonial nation acknowledged that arrangement in the Treaty of Greenville (1795), which recognized Indian sovereignty in territories not claimed by the United States. In *Worcester v. Georgia* (1832), the U.S. Supreme Court declared the Cherokee nation to be a "foreign state," a condition reaffirmed by Chief Justice Taney in his *Dred Scott* (1857) majority opinion. As Taney wrote, the United States signed treaties with American Indian nations, "under subjection to the white race," and, accordingly, in the United States whites were the "citizen race" and American Indians were "aliens."

That exclusion shifted with the white flood, which by the late 19th century had engulfed the entire continent from sea to shining sea. Following the final bloody wars of conquest waged mainly against Indians of the Great Plains, the U.S. census of 1890 declared in that year, which saw the massacre of Indian men, women, and children at Wounded Knee, that the entire continent had been filled (by whites). President Theodore Roosevelt called those lands, memorably, the "red wastes," and other men called them "virgin land." There were no more frontiers for manly probing and capture.

Conquest achieved, the Dawes Act (1887) sought to dissolve Indian nations and assimilate American Indians as individuals. Soon thereafter, the U.S. Supreme Court affirmed, in *Lone Wolf v. Hitchcock* (1903), the plenary powers of Congress over Indian nations because they constituted "domestic dependent nations." The assimilation continued with U.S. citizenship bestowed in 1924 on those born after that year, and, in 1940, on all American Indians.

Following a brief interlude during the New Deal of the 1930s, the attempt to absorb American Indians politically and culturally continued into the 1950s, when Dillon Myer, as chief of the Bureau of Indian Affairs, pursued the policy called appropriately "termination." Myer had experience with termination, having administered the concentration camps for Japanese Americans as the War Relocation Authority's director during World War II.

American Indians, thus, were at first excluded as "foreign" nations and peoples, and, after conquest, were assimilated and rendered domestic dependencies and dependents.

African Americans

Like American Indians, African Americans were "aliens" excluded from community membership. In 1669, a Virginia colony jury ruled that Anthony Johnson was "a Negroe and by consequence an alien." Race determined citizenship. The postcolonial nation and its founding

Constitution (1787) specified that African Americans were not "persons" but "three fifths of all other Persons" and thereby failed to qualify for full representation in the Congress.

In fact, as Chief Justice Taney held in *Dred Scott* (1857): "Negroes of the African race" and their descendants "are not included, and were not intended to be included, under the word 'citizens' in the Constitution, and can therefore claim none of the rights and privileges which that instrument provides for and secures to citizens of the United States." Moreover, Taney pointed out, from the republic's founding, the 1790 Naturalization Act limited citizenship to "free white persons," making clear the distinction between the "citizen race" or whites and "persons of color" or those "not included in the word citizens."

That separation dissolved with the Thirteenth (1865), Fourteenth (1868), and Fifteenth (1870) Amendments to the U.S. Constitution, which, respectively, ended slavery, extended citizenship to all persons born in the United States, and enfranchised men regardless of "race, color, or previous condition of servitude." In 1870, Congress extended to Africans the right of naturalization. African American citizens, although without full equality under Jim Crow, transformed the complexion of the "citizen race" and, thus, the nation. The change was a radical break with the past; it was, in fact, revolutionary.

Still, racial segregation was the primary instrument of the state to secure African American political and economic dependency, and Jim Crow, as was affirmed by *Plessy v. Ferguson* (1896), ruled the land until *Brown v. Board of Education* (1954), which integrated public schools. In *Plessy*, the U.S. Supreme Court ruled that racial segregation in private businesses, conducted under the doctrine of "separate but equal," fulfilled the Fourteenth Amendment's equal protection clause. States routinely denied African American men and, after 1920, women access to the ballot through property and literacy requirements from the end of Reconstruction in the 1870s to the Voting Rights Act of 1965.

Latinas/Latinos

Mexican Americans were a people made through conquest, much like American Indians. In the 1820s and 1830s, Americans, many of them owning slaves, settled in the Mexican province of Texas. These white Protestant settlers, never comfortable in a Catholic republic that sought to end slavery, shook off Mexican control in 1836. In 1845, the United States admitted Texas as a state, an action that helped precipitate the Mexican American War (1846–1848). Driven by Manifest Destiny, an expansionist doctrine that proclaimed the God-given right of the United States to expand across the North American continent, the U.S. government, after defeating Mexico, demanded the cession of almost half of Mexico's territory, land that later formed the entire states of California, Nevada, and Utah, as well as portions of Colorado, Wyoming, Arizona, and New Mexico. The Treaty of Guadalupe Hidalgo (1848), which ended the war, granted U.S. citizenship to Mexican residents of the ceded lands, and Mexicans were thus rendered "white" by treaty. At the same time, many Mexican Americans lost their farms and land, like American Indians, and were widely denied equality in employment, housing, and education on the basis of race, class, and culture.

Judicial decisions commonly cited the contradiction between Mexican whiteness by treaty and Mexicans as a mestizo and "mongrel" race by scientific and common opinion. Further, courts decided, in accordance with the one-drop rule, that is, one drop of nonwhite blood meant a person was considered nonwhite, that children of whites and nonwhites were "colored." This principle was applied in such cases as *In re Camille* (1880), involving a white father and American Indian mother, and *In re Young* (1912), involving a white father and Japanese mother. Still, as *In re Rodriguez* (1897), the courts were compelled to rule that Mexican Americans were white and thus citizens. At the same time, whiteness in theory disallowed Mexican American claims of racial discrimination in practice, such as the right to a trial of their peers, which, if granted, would end instances of all-Anglo juries ruling on Mexican Americans.

The state segregated Mexican American children in inferior schools on the basis of language and "migrant farming patterns," as was affirmed by a Texas court in *Independent School District v. Salvatierra* (1930). Mexicans emerged from the white race in the 1930 U.S. census and appeared as "Mexicans." The enumeration facilitated the expulsion to Mexico of about half a million Mexican and Mexican Americans from the United States during the Great Depression, when their labor was no longer required. That removal complemented the 1935 Filipino Repatriation Act, which offered Filipino Americans, like Mexican American migrant laborers, free passage to the Philippines.

Asian and Pacific Islander Americans

The 1790 Naturalization Act, which limited U.S. citizenship to "free white persons," excluded Pacific Islanders and Asians, like American Indians and African Americans, from the "citizen race." In the 1850s, California's supreme court chief judge Hugh Murray affirmed the distinction between "a free white citizen of this State" and American Indians, Africans, Pacific Islanders, and Asians, those "not of white blood," in Murray's words. Unlike Native Americans, including American Indians and Pacific Islanders, whose utility to the nation involved mainly their land, Asians were employed, like African and Mexican Americans, as laborers.

As persons "not of white blood," Pacific Islander and Asian men served as slaves and servants to whites; appealed to whites and antislavery societies for manumission; married American Indian, African American, and Mexican women; were counted in the U.S. census as colored and mulatto; fought in African American units in the Civil War; and were buried in colored cemeteries. Like Mexicans, Asians and Pacific Islanders served employers as migrant laborers, mainly in agriculture but also in mines and on railroads; formed unions irrespective of race; and married and produced bicultural children.

Unique among people of color in the United States was the persistent condition of Asians as "aliens ineligible to citizenship" under the 1790 Naturalization Act. Mexicans by treaty and African Americans and American Indians through law acquired U.S. citizenship, albeit absent its full rights and privileges. Unable to naturalize, Asians and Pacific Islanders gained U.S. citizenship by birth under the Fourteenth Amendment. Chinese acquired the right to naturalization in 1943, South Asians and Filipinos in 1946, and Japanese and Koreans not until 1952. Accordingly, the United States denied Asians naturalization rights for more than 160 years, from 1790 to 1952.

Tempering those acts of inclusion were immigration quotas imposed on Asians and Pacific Islanders. Starting in 1929, under the Johnson-Reed Immigrant Act (1924), Congress assigned an annual quota of 100 each to those immigrating from Australia and Melanesia, Bhutan, China, India, Iran, Iraq, Japan, Micronesia, Nepal, New Zealand, Oman, Sāmoa, and Thailand.

The law gave to Turkey, straddling Europe and Asia, a quota of 226. Likewise, the law assigned to African nations, from Egypt to South Africa, annual quotas of 100.

European countries, by contrast, which supplied the "citizen race," received quotas of 1,181 (Denmark), 2,377 (Norway), 3,153 (Netherlands), 5,802 (Italy), 17,853 (Irish Free State), 25,957 (Germany), and 65,721 (Great Britain and Northern Ireland). In force until 1965, the Johnson-Reed Act established the nation's first comprehensive, restrictive immigration policy. The act also served to define the nation, its citizens, and its peoples—called a race—by excluding those who were deemed unworthy or even dangerous. In that sense, immigration is a matter of national defense and homeland security.

Imperialism

Conquest did not end with the filling of the continent. The nation, in the late 19th century, extended its imperial reach overseas to the Caribbean and Pacific. Peoples indigenous to and settled upon those territories thereby became Americans, though not fully. After the Spanish-American War of 1898, Puerto Ricans and Filipinos, natives of unincorporated territories, followed divergent paths; Puerto Ricans became U.S. citizens in 1917, and Filipino nationals became Asian aliens in 1934. Contrarily, Hawaiians and Alaska's indigenous peoples, natives of incorporated territories, became U.S. citizens, whereas those in the unincorporated territories of Guam, where "America's day begins," are U.S. citizens while those in American Sāmoa are nationals.

American Mosaic

Founding Father John Jay's "one united people" diversified with the nation's expansion. European immigration during the late 19th century was unlike the usual flow from Great Britain and northern Europe. These new immigrants came from southern and eastern Europe and brought with them different religions, languages, and cultures. Nonetheless, most, through Americanization and assimilation, became members of the white, citizen race.

Peoples of color were not counted among that number at first, and when they became Americans and citizens, they transformed the nation and its peoples from a people descended from the same ancestors to an American mosaic. Racism and segregation, nonetheless, deferred dreams and attenuated the achievement of that revolution. As the documents in these four volumes testify, however, peoples of color are more than minor figures in the nation's narrative; they are central to it, and the documents collected in these volumes shed new light on that history, revealing a more complex, diverse, and troubled American past.

These documents expand upon the standard narratives of nation, which have, for the most part, excluded and marginalized peoples of color. They offer a fuller, more comprehensive understanding of these United States, and are of great consequence for all Americans. They are also important for peoples of color. As Frantz Fanon pointed out in his *The Wretched of the Earth* (1961), colonization denies a people their past, leading to "estrangement" from their history and culture. Freedom requires a recuperation of "the whole body of efforts made by a people in the sphere of thought to describe, justify, and praise the action through which that people has created itself and keeps itself in existence" (p. 233).

We, the people, and descendants of the nation's branching genealogy possess the ability and share the responsibility to shape a more inclusive, equitable, and democratic future.

Gary Y. Okihiro

Volume Introduction

Asian American and Pacific Islander Experience, volume 3 of *The Great American Mosaic: An Exploration of Diversity in Primary Documents*, is a collection of more than 150 primary source documents illustrating the life and history of Asian Americans and Pacific Islanders in the United States. Dating from the early 19th century to today, the documents in the collection cover multiple geographic areas of the country and represent a diverse range of perspectives on religion, ethnicity, gender, sexuality, class, immigration, politics, and family and community life. Each document is preceded by a short introduction providing information on its author as well as a brief discussion of the historical and cultural context in which it was written. The collection includes a wide variety of document types, among them interviews, poems, personal essays, eulogies, rap lyrics, recipes, novel selections, and movie script excerpts. It emphasizes contemporary voices, highlighting new forms of media such as blog posts and e-zine articles.

Volume Organization and Document Types

The volume is divided into 21 sections, and documents are organized chronologically within each section. The documents in the first apply to Asian Americans in general; the documents in the final section are written by multiheritage Asian Americans; and the middle sections are organized by ethnicity. Care has been taken to include more recent groups of Asian Americans, especially immigrants from Southeast Asia, Pakistan, and the Himalayas. Although they presently make up a small percentage of the overall Asian American population, their histories, immigration experiences, and growing communities add both familiar and new elements to contemporary Asian America.

Most of the documents are written by Asian and Pacific Americans; however, some of the sources, especially ones dating from the 19th century, represent outsider perspectives. It is difficult to find English-language sources written by early Chinese immigrants: most of the male laborers were illiterate, and the women, many of whom were brought to America against their will, overwhelmingly left no written record. There are a few exceptions, however. Nineteenth-century Japanese sailor Joseph Heco (born Hizoko Hamada) published a diary chronicling his years living in the United States and describing his 1858 naturalization. The *Golden Hills'*

News is a second unusual source: the first Chinese-language newspaper published in the United States; it provides insight into mid-19th-century merchant life in San Francisco's Chinatown.

These kinds of documents are rare, however. Scholars must supplement them, using the words of the non-Chinese to fill out the historical context and paint a fuller picture of early Chinese American experiences. Therefore, the editors have included a variety of both antagonistic and benevolent Anglo American perspectives on their Chinese American counterparts. Speeches given by xenophobic labor organizers and pieces of legislation like the Chinese Exclusion Act of 1882 contributed to the hostile environment in which Chinese Americans lived. In contrast, white missionaries like Donaldina Cameron, the head of a Chinese prostitute rescue organization, and Marian Bokee, a teacher in a Chinatown mission school, wrote much more sympathetic and nuanced descriptions of the Chinese Americans among whom they lived and worked. At the same time, these well-meaning people were not immune to mainstream assumptions about the inferiority of Chinese culture. Even the most supportive accounts bemoan the plight of the helpless Chinese man struggling with his inherent backward, heathen, and unmanly propensities. This perspective closely corresponds to the authors' romanticized visions of the redemptive role played by virtuous and heroic white missionaries in godless Chinatown. It is necessary to pay close attention to such biases when using outsider accounts to learn about a group.

In addition to these Anglo American first-person documents, the volume also includes excerpts of several court cases, ordinances, and laws, all of which, up until fairly recently, have been composed and enacted by white politicians and judges. The editors have been careful to incorporate both restrictive legislation, meant to exclude and discriminate against Asian and Pacific Americans, as well as legislation meant to rectify past injustices and safeguard their constitutional rights as residents and citizens.

Scope

There is considerable debate over whether Pacific Islanders, including Native Americans, should be categorized as Asian American. Some scholars argue that in terms of ethnicity, history, socioeconomic situation, and experience with colonialism, Pacific Islanders are more closely aligned with Native Americans. However, for a few reasons, *Asian American and Pacific Islander Experience* includes Native Hawaiians, American Samoans, and Guamanians, all Pacific Islanders under the aegis of the United States. First, because there is no definitive consensus on the issue, the editors have decided to err on the side of inclusivity. Second, in part due to the high levels of intermarriage and the prevalence of mixed-race identity, particularly in Hawaii, many Pacific Islanders themselves identify as Asian American. All of the contemporary contributors to this volume have chosen to be included. Nevertheless, for generations the relationship between Asian American settlers and Pacific Islander natives has been fraught with ethnic tension, colonialist mentalities, economic exploitation, and power imbalances. The editors have tried to reflect this reality in the documents selected.

Themes

Although the documents in this volume are arranged chronologically within the ethnic group sections, several themes have emerged that cross ethnicity and time period. The impact of the immigration experience on the formation of individual and community identity is one major theme running through the volume. Early Asian immigrants struggled to enter an increasingly xenophobic and restrictive nation. Transcripts of United States Immigration Service interviews of successful—and unsuccessful—prospective Chinese immigrants, like Yee Wing Thing and Huey Fong, paint a vivid picture of their struggles and strategies to become Asian Americans. Many other immigrants fled deprivation, persecution, and war; their move to the United States was not by choice. Pang Xiong Sirirathasuk Sikoun, whose brothers were killed by the Pathet Lao in the 1960s; Vatey Seng, who escaped from Cambodia during Pol Pot's regime in the 1970s; and Prem Tamang, who fled Nepalese Maoists in the 1980s, are three examples of people whose lives in the United States were shadowed by harrowing experiences in their homeland. Still others came as war brides, marrying American servicemen and often moving to an environment with little social or cultural support. Two documents in particular reflect on these experiences: Yayoi Winfrey's essay on her mother, a Japanese woman who married an African American pilot; and Daniel Clark's interview with his grandmother, who moved from Okinawa to rural West Virginia with her American husband. The diverse stories contained in this volume raise the question of how different experiences affect immigrants' lives in the United States: their desire and ability to Americanize, the effects of trauma on their communities, and the legacy of their histories for their children and grandchildren.

A second major theme spanning ethnic categories in this volume is cultural preservation. Maintaining a certain level of cultural continuity and homogeneity is a matter of great concern to immigrant and ethnic communities, both to sustain ties with the homeland, and to create a cohesive identity in a new land. Cultural preservation takes many forms, from the retention of language skills, to the perpetuation of traditional gender roles and family hierarchies, to the upholding of religious beliefs and practices. All these are fought for tenaciously by some—and are contested, adapted, redefined, and abandoned by others. Inevitably, however, the complicated process of preserving homeland culture in the United States results in the creation of something new. Definitively nonhomogeneous communities spanning multiple generations, at once familiar and unfamiliar, emerge over the years, and with them Asian America evolves.

Several authors included in this document collection discuss their deliberate and concrete attempts to create tangible links to their past. Sifu Cheung Shu Pui mourns the loss of Chinese language and holidays in his immigrant neighborhood, but he teaches folk arts, including kung fu and the lion dance, in the hope that at least a small part of his cultural heritage may be passed down to American-born children. For similar reasons, Charlene Gima learns traditional Okinawan Bon dances in Hawaii. In addition, the importance of food, itself an intriguing physical link to identities, has surfaced in a number of documents. Sheng Yang cultivates and cooks with Hmong herbs and vegetables brought over from Laos; she buys her chickens from Hmong farmers, who raise and butcher them using long-established techniques. For Sara Sarasohn, who is half Japanese, certain foods provide an emotional connection to her mother's family and history. When Jae Ran Kim, a Korean American adoptee, learns to cook Korean food, she gets a small sense—a taste—of the culture she missed growing up in a white household.

Asian American families attempt to maintain cultural cohesiveness in more intangible ways as well. These efforts are continually challenged by both external and internal forces, resulting in the evolution of the family structure over time. For example, in early Chinese

American communities, the very definition of family was complicated and constantly being reinvented. Laws restricting Chinese women from immigrating to the United States created bachelor societies of uncles and brothers in Chinatowns. The Chinese Exclusion Act of 1882 resulted in the construction of complex—and fictitious—kin networks of paper relatives. Eddie Fung's mother came over as the paper wife of his uncle, who then divorced her so she could marry his brother, her (real) husband. Fung's adopted brothers came over as paper sons of his uncle, and never changed their names back to "Fung" after they reached the United States. Fung himself thought nothing of this convoluted arrangement "because it was so common in Chinatown." Moreover, extended family networks take on great importance in transnational families, who often do not feel deeply rooted in either country. This is as true today as it was in the 19th century. Shymala Dason writes about modern-day reverse migration, describing immigrants whose family ties in their land of origin remain so strong and compelling that they leave the United States and return home.

Conflict between maintaining traditional ways and adapting to American mainstream culture often centers on this transforming family structure and is manifested very clearly in friction over the second generation's courtship and marriage choices. Kerala-born Mary T. Mathew discusses how she and her daughters navigate between American and Indian social mores, particularly with respect to dating. In their poetry, Indian American Ainee Fatima and Hmong American Noukou Thao explore the tension between their parents' expectations for them to enter arranged marriages and their own conflicted desires to choose a spouse or please their families. Desi essayist Sweta Vikram denounces the pressure for South Asian Americans to select "fair-skinned" spouses.

Negotiating traditional—and evolving—gender roles, especially for women, plays an integral part in the Asian American family dynamic. In their own ways, Apolonia Dangzalan and Maggie Gee challenged their contemporaries' views on working Asian American women: Dangzalan by embracing her uncommon status as a Depression-era Filipina entrepreneur, and Gee by joining the elite World War II Women Airforce Service Pilots, one of only two Chinese Americans to be accepted. Chloe Sun writes about how the place of women in Chinese American churches is circumscribed by religious and ethnic assumptions and how she and other women are breaking through these boundaries and creating new spaces for themselves.

Asian American religion is a particularly interesting phenomenon because it functions both as a means of assimilation and as a means of maintaining ethnic identity. Although it originated in Western missionary efforts in Asia and in American Chinatowns, Asian American Christianity has emerged over the past few decades as its own movement, self-consciously distinct from mainstream Christianity. Seminary professor Fumitaka Matsuoka's benediction for the Students of Color graduation ceremony illustrates how the Asian American community's experience with racism colors their interpretation of Christ's message and the Christian mission; and Joy Wong asserts that her identity as an evangelical Christian is inseparable from her identity as an Asian American woman. Both these positions mark a deliberate departure from earlier (white) missionary philosophies, which held that Christian identity was nearly synonymous with American cultural identity, and that Asian history and culture must be erased for converts to become true Christians.

Indigenous Asian religions also evolve, once imported to the United States. Japanese Shin Buddhism has steadily transformed into Japanese American Shin Buddhism, incorporating religious forms and practices adopted from Protestant Christianity. In his graphic-novel version of the Hindu epic *Ramayana*, Sanjay Patel retells an ancient story to engage and appeal to young people today; and Rajiv Srinivasan struggles with how to reconcile his Hindu faith with his job in the United States military. Defying stereotypes, assumptions, and expectations from all sides, Asma Hasan spiritedly calls herself a "Muslim feminist cowgirl." Religious evolution does not go uncontested, of course. Debates over authenticity are emotionally charged, especially because change represents a challenge to first-generation immigrant authority. Farah Akbar writes about the attempts of second-generation Bangladeshi Americans to mesh their Muslim faith with their American sensibilities—attempts strongly resisted by traditional imams. Similarly, the Hindu American Foundation's position paper criticizes the "mainstreaming" and "Westernizing" of yoga, which increasingly denudes the practice of its fundamental religious significance. Cultural, ethnic, and religious identities are inextricably intertwined; adaptations and changes in one affect the rest.

Finally, many of the documents in this volume explore what happens when obvious ethnic delineations break down, challenging what it means to be "legitimately" Asian American. Race and ethnicity have always been fluid categories, and legal definitions do not always keep pace with public perception. The United States Naturalization Act of 1790 restricted naturalization to "free white" immigrants. Initially aimed specifically at African American slaves, the Naturalization Act was used half a century later to prevent Chinese immigrants from becoming citizens. However, Japanese immigrants were not officially defined as nonwhite until 1922 (Joseph Heco, the Japanese sailor who came to the United States in 1837, took advantage of this loophole). In 1923, the Supreme Court ruled that, geographic and scientific definitions notwithstanding, Indians were not white "in the common understanding." *United States* v. *Bhagat Singh Thind* retroactively stripped naturalized Indian immigrants of their citizenship and subjected them to the racially restrictive Alien Land Laws. The fluctuating laws codifying racial and ethnic categories signify the malleable characters of race and ethnicity themselves.

Biracial and multiracial Asian Americans further complicate these categories. Historically rejected by both Asian and non-Asian communities alike, mixed-race people were labeled morally and physically deficient by 19th-century sociologists and dismissed as insufficiently Asian by 20th-century activists, especially when physical appearances made it possible for them to pass as white. Multiracial Asian Americans have long challenged these stereotypes: as early as the 1890s, Edith Maude Eaton was exploring her own Chinese American identity in short stories and novels that condemned American racism and exclusion. A century later, many multiracial Asian Americans adopted the Hawaiian word "hapa" as a term of pride, claiming and celebrating their diverse heritage while simultaneously acknowledging their continuing struggles to be accepted as legitimate members of *any* ethnic community.

Today, a new generation of Asian Americans pushes the boundaries of ethnic identification and definition. Simone Fujita, whose high school Asian American peers did not accept her because of her African American ancestry, finds a place for herself in college. Blogger Jade Keller muses about what it means to be "authentically" Asian, and about her and her children's place in the Thai American community. Because the editors believe these perspectives are unique and important, and to avoid forcing people into monolithic ethnic categories that do not acknowledge other parts of their identity, these documents appear in their own "Multiheritage Asian Americans" category.

The *Asian American and Pacific Islander Experience* volume also features many adopted Asian Americans. Up until at least the late 1980s, adoptive parents were encouraged to raise their children as if they shared the same history; the adopted child's own cultural and ethnic heritage was erased in an effort to encourage total assimilation. For many Asian American adoptees, this precipitated deep identity crises once they were old enough to realize they were not white like their parents and siblings (the vast majority of adoptive families are white), especially as they had little or no contact with any Asian Americans who could have helped ease them through this transition. In response to this absence of family and community resources, Vietnamese adoptees Tuan Schneider and Trista Goldberg both travel to Vietnam as adults, looking for connections with their birth country and biological families. Jenny Ryun Foster, adopted from Korea as an infant, also journeys back to her birth country, where she discovers that although Americans see her as Asian, Koreans see her as American. And, finally, there is the singular story of Scott Fujita, the adopted white son of a Japanese American father. Raised in a Japanese American family, Fujita grew up celebrating Japanese holidays, eating Japanese food, learning about Japanese art and history, and listening to the internment stories of his grandparents and father. He considers himself to be half Japanese American.

Taken together, the documents in this volume raise philosophical questions: What does it mean to be Asian American? Is it dependent on ethnic heritage? Is it dependent on a common history of experienced "otherness" in the United States? Or is it dependent on a deliberate embrace of particular cultural practices? More than a dozen ethnic groups are represented in this volume alone, and there are at least 20 more in Asia itself. Each group speaks its own language or dialect, practices its own religion, and creates its own art forms; each group remembers its own distinct history, both in the homeland and in the United States. Thus, locating a common, unifying Asian American identity is difficult from the beginning. It becomes even more challenging when you compare Asian immigrants with established Asian American families; when you take into account people with multiple racial and ethnic backgrounds; when you look at people who reject their communities' definitions of traditional gender roles, religious beliefs and practices, and sexuality—and when you include those who perhaps were never a part of these communities to begin with.

The documents in this volume do not provide an easy definition of what it means to be Asian American. Instead, the editors have included as many different perspectives as possible in an effort to present a picture of an ever-evolving kaleidoscope of individuals, families, and groups—a collection of people who are continually redefining "Asian America."

Emily Moberg Robinson

Brief Guide to Primary Sources

Primary sources are original, direct, firsthand stories, personal experiences, testimony, and viewpoints that are created during the time period involved. They may include such forms as diaries, journals, letters, personal narratives, government records, graffiti, laws, court cases, plays, novels, poems, architectural plans, maps, memoirs, autobiographies, sound recordings, songs, advertisements, photographs, paintings, prints, speeches, and other material objects. The sources become the raw material that historians, or other scholars, use to create their works in book or article form. Secondary sources are interpretations, which are often made using myriad primary sources.

Primary sources provide readers with a wealth of firsthand information that gets them close to the actual experiences of the historical time period, people, and events. Firsthand material offers a window to a particular time and place, viewpoints, and eyewitness accounts that supplement information and facts typically provided in textbooks and other secondary sources. Primary sources offer readers the raw material of history that has not been analyzed and interpreted.

How to Read and Reflect on Primary Documents

Primary sources in written form, as illustrated by the document selections included in *The Great American Mosaic: An Exploration of Diversity in Primary Documents*, were produced at a particular historical moment and for a particular purpose. These volumes are intended to provide an outlet for the voices of people of color whose experiences and viewpoints are often overlooked or downplayed in the larger American history narrative. Some of these documents were written by an author conscious of a larger audience or with the expectation that they would be published; others were written for personal reasons without the expectation that others would read them. Some documents were intended to persuade, inform, or entertain. Note that documents are based on the particular viewpoints, experiences, and memories of the writer and can reflect selective memories, mistaken information, or deception. The reader is left to evaluate the relevance, reliability, and value of the information and to take into account the analysis and interpretations of secondary sources. The documents in *The Great American Mosaic* provide readers with a variety of firsthand content, ranging from creation myths to legislation to reflections on historical events that provide insights into the experiences of people of color in the United States.

What Questions Should You Ask as You Read?

- Who wrote or produced the document, and what do we know about him or her?
- When and where was the source written or produced, and how does it fit into the timeline of the events and period described?
- Where was the source written or produced? Does that material portray cultural, social, or religious values? What form did it take originally?
- Why was the source material written or produced? What was its creator's intention or purpose? What is the overall tone of the source material?
- Who was the intended audience? How was the document used, and how widely distributed or read was it?
- Overall, how do we evaluate the relevance, reliability, and value of the content? What might the author have left out, intentionally or not?

General Asian American

Page Law
(1875)

Most Chinese immigrants in the mid- to late 19th century financed their trip using the credit-ticket system. Under this arrangement, American hiring agencies advanced money for the steamship passage; the immigrant would pay back this loan with the wages he earned in the United States. In part because most laborers earned enough to pay off the loan but not enough to send back to China for a wife, a gender imbalance soon developed in the Chinese American community—along with burgeoning prostitution and sex-trafficking industries in American Chinatowns. At the same time, the American Progressive movement was advocating the regulation of morality, family, and sexuality, especially in immigrant and working-class communities. All these factors, coupled with growing racial and labor antagonism toward the Chinese, contributed to the passage of the Page Law in 1875.

The Page Law prohibited certain classes of immigrants from coming to the United States. One clause limited contract laborers from Asia (the Chinese Exclusion Act would codify this

more thoroughly in 1882), another clause prohibited convicts, and a third denied entry to Asian prostitutes. Plantation owners and farmers seeking cheap labor managed to circumvent most of the proscriptions on "coolie" laborers, and, in fact, between 1875 and 1882 the number of Chinese immigrants to the United States reached a historic high. However, the clause prohibiting prostitutes effectively halted Asian female immigration, particularly women from China: immigration officials generally did not distinguish between women coming over as brides of Chinese Americans and women coming over as prostitutes.

The Page Law created an even more extreme demographic imbalance among Chinese Americans (and, paradoxically, exacerbated the problem of prostitution). Chinatowns remained primarily bachelor societies, and the stereotype of the Chinese man as a sexual predator threatening white womanhood was cemented in the imaginations of mainstream Americans. The gender imbalance in the Chinese American

1

community would not be rectified until World War II, when the War Brides Act enabled Chinese American soldiers to marry women they met while stationed overseas.

FORTY-THIRD CONGRESS. SESS. II. CH. 141. 1875.

CHAP. 141.-An act supplementary to the acts in relation to immigration.

Be it enacted by the Senate and House of Representatives of the United States of America in Congress assembled, That in determining whether the immigration of any subject of China, Japan, or any Oriental country, to the United States, is free and voluntary, as provided by section two thousand one hundred and sixty-two of the Revised Code, title "Immigration," it shall be the duty of the consul-general or consul of the United States residing at the port from which it is proposed to convey such subjects, in any vessels enrolled or licensed in the United States, or any port within the same, before delivering to the masters of any such vessels the permit or certificate provided for in such section, to ascertain whether such immigrant has entered into a contract or agreement for a term of service within the United States, for lewd and immoral purposes; and if there be such contract or agreement, the said consul-general or consul shall not deliver the required permit or certificate.

SEC. 2. That if any citizen of the United States, or other person amenable to the laws of the United States shall take, or cause to be taken or transported, to or from the United States any subject of China, Japan, or any Oriental country, without their free and voluntary consent, for the purpose of holding them to a term of service, such citizen or other person shall be liable to be indicted therefore, and, on conviction of such offense, shall be punished by a fine not exceeding two thousand dollars and be imprisoned not exceeding one year; and all contracts and agreements for a term of service of such persons in the United States, whether made in advance or in pursuance of such illegal importation, and whether such importation shall have been in American or other vessels, are hereby declared void.

SEC. 3. That the importation into the United States of women for the purposes of prostitution is hereby forbidden; and all contracts and agreements in relation thereto, made in advance or in pursuance of such illegal importation and purposes, are hereby declared void; and whoever shall knowingly and willfully import, or cause any importation of, women into the United States for the purposes of prostitution, or shall knowingly or willfully hold, or attempt to hold, any woman to such purposes, in pursuance of such illegal importation and contract or agreement, shall be deemed guilty of a felony, and, on conviction thereof, shall be imprisoned not exceeding five years and pay a fine not exceeding five thousand dollars.

SEC. 4. That if any person shall knowlingly and willfully contract, or attempt to contract, in advance or in pursuance of such illegal importation, to supply to another the labor of any cooly or other person brought into the United States in violation of section two thousand one hundred and fifty-eight of the Revised Statutes, or of any other section of the laws prohibiting the cooly-trade or of this act, such person shall be deemed guilty of a felony, and, upon conviction thereof, in any United States court, shall be fined in a sum not exceeding five hundred dollars and imprisoned for a term not exceeding one year.

SEC. 5. That it shall be unlawful for aliens of the following classes to immigrate into the United States, namely, persons who are undergoing a sentence for conviction in their own country of felonious crimes other than political or growing out of or the result of such political offenses, or whose sentence has been remitted on condition of their emigration, and women "imported for the purposes of prostitution." Every vessel arriving in the United States may be inspected under the direction of the collector of the port at which it arrives, if he shall have reason to believe that any such obnoxious persons are on board; and the officer making such inspection shall certify the result thereof to the master or other person in charge of such vessel, designating in such certificate the person or persons, if any there be, ascertained by him to be of either of the classes whose importation is hereby forbidden. When such inspection is required by the collector as aforesaid, it shall be unlawful without his permission, for any alien to leave any such vessel arriving in the United States from a foreign country until the inspection shall have been had and the result certified as herein provided; and at no time thereafter shall any alien certified to by the inspecting officer as being of either of the classes whose immigration is forbidden by this section, be allowed to land in the United States, except in obedience to a judicial process issued pursuant to law. If any person shall feel aggrieved by the certificate of such inspecting officer stating him or her to be within either of the classes whose immigration is forbidden by this section, and shall apply for release or other remedy to any proper court or judge, then it shall be the duty of the collector at said port of entry to detain said vessel until a hearing and determination of the matter are had, to the end that if the said inspector shall be found to be in accordance with this section and sustained, the obnoxious person or persons shall be returned on board of said vessel, and shall not thereafter be permitted to land, unless the master, owner or consignee of the vessel shall give bond and security, to be approved by the court or judge hearing the cause, in the sum of five hundred dollars for each such person permitted to land, conditioned for the return of such person, within six months from the date thereof, to the country whence his or her emigration shall have taken place, or unless the vessel bringing such obnoxious person or persons shall be forfeited, in which event the proceeds of such forfeiture shall be paid over to the collector of the port of arrival, and applied by him, as far as necessary, to the return of such person or persons to his or her own country within the said period of six months. And for all violations of this act, the vessel, by the acts, omissions, or connivance of the owners, master, or other custodian, or the consignees of which the same are committed, shall be liable to forfeiture, and may be proceeded against as in cases of frauds against the revenue laws, for which forfeiture is prescribed by existing law.

Approved March 3, 1875.

Source: The Page Law of 1875 (An act supplementary to the acts in relation to immigration). U.S. Statutes at Large 18 (1875): 477. 43rd Cong., Sess. II, Chap. 131.

National Origins Act

(1924)

In the years after World War I, the United States retreated into itself, rejecting international involvement and attempting to resurrect a mythical golden age of (racially, politically, socially) pure American history. To this end, Congress passed the Immigration Act of 1924, also known as the Johnson-Reed Act, or National Origins Act. A new quota was set for immigrants entering the United States each year: 2 percent of the total of each national group (including immigrants and natural-born citizens) living in the United States, as reported in the 1890 census.

This quota was aimed at restricting southern and eastern European immigrants, especially Jews; none of these groups had come to the United States in statistically significant numbers until after 1900. However, the National Origins Act also barred entry to all aliens ineligible for citizenship—thus halting Asian immigration altogether. This bar affected the Japanese in particular because most other Asians had already been excluded by nation-specific pieces of legislation. The Japanese government protested the National Origins Act, claiming it violated the terms of the Gentlemen's Agreement (an informal set of treaties between the United States and Japan curtailing Japanese immigration). But the United States was more interested in creating a racially homogenous nation than in maintaining strong ties with Japan, and the legislation passed. Not until the 1965 Immigration and Nationality Act would the United States open its doors to all of Asia.

The following excerpt from the National Origins Act lays out the main quota system, establishes the specific exclusion clause, and calls for the prosecution of people who bring over illegal aliens. It also includes a description of people unfit to immigrate, the category in which Asian immigrants found themselves.

AN ACT

To limit the immigration of aliens into the United States, and for other purposes.

Be it enacted by the Senate and House of Representatives of the United States of America in Congress assembled, That this Act may be cited as the "Immigration Act of 1924" . . .

Application for Immigration Visa.

Sec. 7. (a) Every immigrant applying for an immigration visa shall make application therefor in duplicate in such form as shall be by regulations prescribed . . .

(d) In the application the immigrant shall also state (to such extent as shall be by regulations prescribed) whether or not he is a member of each class of individuals excluded from admission to the United States under the immigration laws, and such classes shall be stated on the blank in such form as shall be by regulations prescribed, and the immigrant shall answer separately as to each class.

(e) If the immigrant is unable to state that he does not come within any of the excluded classes, but claims to be for any legal reason exempt from exclusion, he shall state fully in the application the grounds for such alleged exemption. . . .

Numerical Limitations.

Sec. 11. (a) The annual quota of any nationality shall be 2 per centum of the number of foreign-born individuals of such nationality resident in continental United States as determined by the United States census of 1890, but the minimum quota of any nationality shall be 100.

(b) The annual quota of any nationality for the fiscal year beginning July 1, 1927, and for each fiscal year thereafter, shall be a number which bears the same ratio to 150,000 as the number of inhabitants in continental United States in 1920 having that national origin (ascertained as hereinafter provided in this section) bears to the number of inhabitants in continental United States in 1920, but the minimum quota of any nationality shall be 100 . . .

Exclusion from United States.

Sec. 13.

(c) **No alien ineligible to citizenship shall be admitted to the United States** unless such alien (1) is admissible as a non-quota immigrant under the provisions of subdivision (b), (d), or (e) of section 4, or (2) is the wife, or the unmarried child under 18 years of age, of an immigrant admissible under such subdivision (d), and is accompanying or following to join him, or (3) is not an immigrant as defined in section 3. . . .

Deportation.

Sec. 14. Any alien who at any time after entering the United States is found to have been at the time of entry not entitled under this Act to enter the United States, or to have remained therein for a longer time than permitted under this Act or regulations made thereunder, shall be taken into custody and deported in the same manner as provided for in sections 19 and 20 of the Immigration Act of 1917: Provided, That the Secretary of Labor may, under such conditions and restrictions as to support and care as he may deem necessary, permit permanently to remain in the United States, any alien child who, when under sixteen years of age was heretofore temporarily admitted to the United States and who is now within the United States and either of whose parents is a citizen of the United States. . . .

Penalty for Illegal Transportation.

Sec. 16. (a) It shall be unlawful for any person, including any transportation company, or the owner, master, agent, charter, or consignee of any vessel, to bring to the United States by water from any place outside thereof (other than foreign contiguous territory) (1) any immigrant who does not have an unexpired immigration visa, or (2) any quota immigrant having an immigration visa the visa in which specifies him as a non-quota immigrant.

(b) If it appears to the satisfaction of the Secretary of Labor that any immigrant has been so brought, such person, or transportation company, or the master, agent, owner, charterer, or consignee of any such vessel, shall pay to the collector of customs of the customs district in which the port of arrival is located the sum of $1,000 for each immigrant so brought, and in addition a sum equal to that paid by such immigrant for his transportation from the initial point of departure, indicated in his ticket, to the port of arrival, such latter sum to be delivered by the collector of customs to the immigrant on whose account assessed. No vessel shall be granted clearance pending the determination of the liability to the payment of such sums, or while such sums remain unpaid, except that clearance may be granted prior to the determination of such question upon the deposit of an amount sufficient to cover such sums, or of a bond with sufficient surety to secure the payment thereof approved by the collector of customs. . . .

Steamship Fines under 1917 Act.

Sec. 26. Section 9 of the Immigration Act of 1917 is amended to read as follows:

"Sec. 9. That it shall be unlawful for any person, including any transportation company other than railway lines entering the United States from foreign contiguous territory, or the owner, master, agent, or consignee of any vessel to bring to the United States either from a foreign country or any insular possession of the United States any **alien afflicted with idiocy, insanity, imbecility, feeble-mindedness, epilepsy, constitutional psychopathic inferiority, chronic alcoholism, tuberculosis in any form, or a loathsome or dangerous contagious disease,** and if it shall appear to the satisfaction of the Secretary of Labor that any alien so brought to the United States was afflicted with any of the said diseases or disabilities at the time of foreign embarkation, and that the existence of such disease or disability might have been detected by means of a competent medical examination at such time, such person or transportation company, or the master, agent, owner, or consignee of any such vessel shall pay to the collector of customs of the customs district in which the port of arrival is located the sum of $1,000, and in addition a sum equal to that paid by such alien for his transportation from the initial point of departure, indicated in his ticket, to the port of arrival for each and every violation of the provisions of this section, such latter sum to be delivered by the collector of customs to the alien on whose account assessed. . . .

General Definitions.

Sec. 28. As used in this Act—

(c) The term "ineligible to citizenship," when used in reference to any individual, includes an individual who is debarred from becoming a citizen of the United States under section 2169 of the Revised Statutes, or under section 14 of the Act entitled "An Act to execute certain treaty stipulations relating to Chinese," approved May 6, 1882, or under section 1996, 1997, or 1998 of the Revised Statutes, as amended, or under section 2 of the Act entitled "An Act to authorize the President to increase temporarily the Military Establishment of the United States," approved May 18, 1917, as amended, or under law amendatory of, supplementary to, or in substitution for, any of such sections. . . .

Saving Clause in Event of Unconstitutionality.

Sec. 32. If any provision of this Act, or the application thereof to any person or circumstances, is held invalid, the remainder of the Act, and the application of such provision to other persons or circumstances, shall not be affected thereby.

Approved, May 26, 1924.

Source: The National Origins Act of 1924. U.S. Statutes at Large 43 (1924): 153. 68th Cong., Sess. I, Chp. 190.

War Brides Act

(1945)

The first War Brides Act, Public Law 271, temporarily allowed American soldiers to bring their foreign wives to the United States. The federal government amended the act in 1946 and 1947, extending the deadline, and the 1947 Soldier Brides Act allowed the wives to enter the United States regardless of racial background. Although temporary, the War Brides Act was the first step in legal recognition of marriages between American GIs and foreign wives. In 1952, the McCarran-Walter Act ended the harsh immigration restrictions of the 1924 National Origins Act and lifted the ban on naturalization for Asians, clearing the way for foreign military wives. Military brides became the foundation for a new wave of post-1965 immigrants from Asia. They were the largest group of women to ever arrive from Asia.

AN ACT

To expedite the admission to the United States of alien spouses and alien minor children of citizen members of the United States armed forces.

Be it enacted by the Senate and House of Representatives of the United States of America in Congress assembled, That notwithstanding any of the several clauses of section 3 of the Act of February 5, 1917, excluding physically and mentally defective aliens, and notwithstanding the documentary requirements of any of the immigration laws or regulations, Executive orders, or Presidential proclamations issued thereunder, alien spouses or alien children of United States citizens serving in, or having an honorable discharge certificate from the armed forces of the United States during the Second World War shall, if otherwise admissible under the immigration laws and if application for admission is made within three years of the effective date of this Act, be admitted to the United States: *Provided,* That the time of arrival in accordance with the provisions of section 16 of the Act of February 5, 1917, and if found suffering from any disability which would be the basis for a ground of exclusion except for the provision of this Act, the Immigration and Naturalization Service shall forthwith notify the appropriate public medical officer of the local community to which the alien is destined: *Provided further,* That the provisions of this Act shall not affect the duties of the United States Public Health Service so far as they relate to quarantinable diseases.

Sec. 2. Regardless of section 9 of the Immigration Act of 1924, any alien admitted under section 1 of this Act shall be deemed to be a nonquota immigrant as defined in section 4 (a) of the Immigration Act of 1924.

Sec. 3. Any alien admitted under section 1 of this Act who at any time returns to the United States after a temporary absence abroad shall not be excluded because of the disability or disabilities that existed at the time of that admission.

Sec. 4. No fine or penalty shall be imposed under the Act of February 4, 1917, except those arising under section 14, because of the transportation to the United States of any alien admitted under this Act.

Sec. 5. For the purpose of this Act, the Second World War shall be deemed to have commenced on December 7, 1941, and to have ceased a joint resolution of Congress.

Approved December 28, 1945.

Source: War Brides Act of 1945. U.S. Statutes at Large 59 (1945) 659. 79th Congress, H.R. 4857; Pub.L. 79–271.

McCarran-Walter Act

(1952)

The 1952 Immigration and Nationality Act, also known as the McCarran-Walter Act after Senator Pat McCarran (D-Nevada) and Congressman Francis Walter (D-Pennsylvania), overturned the Chinese Exclusion Act of 1882. However, the McCarran-Walter Act was largely symbolic. It was passed in response to communist expansion in Asia—American leaders hoped that abolishing racist legislation would make democracy more appealing to nations that might otherwise be seduced by communist egalitarianism. In reality, the McCarran-Walter Act upheld the restrictive racial restrictions created by the Immigration Act of 1924, strictly limiting immigration based on racial and national quotas and favoring European immigrants. The act granted only a token quota for Asian immigrants: it limited immigrants from the Asia-Pacific Triangle, which it described as all countries from India to Japan and all the Pacific islands north of Australia, to a maximum of 2,000 a year, and each country within the triangle was limited to 100 immigrants.

AN ACT

To revise the laws relating to immigration, naturalization, and nationality; and for other purposes.

Be it enacted by the Senate and House of Representatives of the United States of America in Congress assembled, That this Act, divided into titles, chapters, and sections according to the following table of contents, may be cited as the "Immigration and Nationality Act".

Determination of Quota to which an Immigrant is Chargeable

Sec. 202.

(b) With reference to determination of the quota to which shall be chargeable an immigrant who is attributable by as much as one-half of his ancestry to a people or peoples indigenous to the Asia-Pacific triangle comprising all quota areas and all colonies and other dependent areas situate wholly east of the meridian sixty degrees east of

Greenwich, wholly west of the meridian one hundred and sixty-five degrees west, and wholly north of the parallel twenty-five degrees south latitude—

(1) there is hereby established, in addition to quotas for separate quota areas comprising independent countries, self-governing dominions, and territories under the international trusteeship system of the United Nations situate wholly within said Asia-Pacific triangle, an Asia-Pacific quota of one hundred annually, which quota shall not be subject to the provisions of subsection (e);

(2) such immigrant born within a separate quota area situate wholly within such Asia-Pacific triangle shall not be chargeable to the Asia-Pacific quota, but shall be chargeable to the quota for the separate quota area in which he was born;

(3) such immigrant born within a colony or other dependent area situate wholly within said Asia-Pacific triangle shall be chargeable to the Asia-Pacific quota;

(4) such immigrant born outside the Asia-Pacific triangle who is attributable by as much as one-half of his ancestry to a people or peoples indigenous to not more than one separate quota area, situate wholly within the Asia-Pacific triangle, shall be chargeable to the quota of that quota area;

(5) such immigrant born outside the Asia-Pacific triangle who is attributable by as much as one-half of his ancestry to one or more colonies or other dependent areas situate wholly within the Asia-Pacific triangle, shall be chargeable to the Asia-Pacific quota;

(6) such immigrant born outside the Asia-Pacific triangle who is attributable by as much as one-half of his ancestry to peoples indigenous to two or more separate quota areas situate wholly within the Asia-Pacific triangle, or to a quota area or areas and one or more colonies and other dependent areas situate wholly therein, shall be chargeable to the Asia-Pacific quota.

(c) Any immigrant born in a colony or other component or dependent area of a governing country for which no separate or specific quota has been established, unless a nonquota immigrant as provided in section 101 (a) (27) of this Act, shall be chargeable to the quota of the governing country, except that (1) not more than one hundred persons born in any one such colony or other component or dependent area overseas from the governing country shall be chargeable to the quota of its governing country in any one year, and (2) any such immigrant, if attributable by as much as one-half of his ancestry to a people or peoples indigenous to the Asia-Pacific triangle, shall be chargeable to a quota as provided in subsection (b) of this section.

(d) The provision of an immigration quota for a quota area shall not constitute recognition by the United States of the political transfer of territory from one country to another, or recognition of a government not recognized by the United States.

(e) After the determination of quotas has been made as provided in section 201, revision of the quotas shall be made by the Secretary of State, the Secretary of Commerce, and the Attorney General, jointly, whenever necessary, to provide for any change of boundaries resulting in transfer of territory from one sovereignty to another, a change of administrative arrangements of a colony or other dependent area, or any other political change, requiring a change in the list of quota areas or of the territorial limits thereof, but any increase in the number of minimum quota areas above twenty within the Asia-Pacific triangle shall result in a proportionate decrease in each minimum quota of such area in order that the sum total of all minimum quotas within the Asia-Pacific triangle shall not exceed two thousand. In the case of any change in the territorial limits of quota areas, not requiring a change in the quotas for such areas, the Secretary of State shall, upon recognition of such change, issue appropriate instructions to all consular offices concerning the change in the territorial limits of the quota area involved.

Source: McCarran-Walter Act of 1952. U.S. Statutes at Large 66 (1952): 82; 163–282.

Asian American Movement: Documents Illustrating the San Francisco State Strike
(1968–1969)

The 1960s and 1970s were a time of unprecedented social protest and upheaval. Young people all over the world spoke out, marched, and protested against war, racism, sexism, poverty, and exploitation, sometimes with violent results. Many American students were involved in a variety of movements, like the anti–Vietnam War protests and the fight to save the International Hotel in San Francisco, and in community organizations, like the Black Panther Party. The San Francisco State strike, originating at San Francisco State University, was one of the earliest multiracial movements and marked the beginning of a concerted Asian American movement.

The strike—the longest student strike in U.S. history—began in November 1968 and lasted for 167 days. In March 1968, the Black Students Union, the Mexican American Student Confederation, the Philippine American Collegiate Endeavor, the Intercollegiate Chinese for Social Action, the Latin American Students Organization, and the Student Kouncil of Intertribal Nations formed the Third World Liberation Front (TWLF). A few months later, the San Francisco State University chapter of the Asian American Political Alliance, a student group formed in May at the University of California–Berkeley, joined the TWLF. The students demanded a separate Third World College that would be run by faculty of color and provide an education relevant to their communities' issues and needs. The protest spread quickly to Berkeley, where students of color initiated their own strike. Although the students did not win all their demands, their protests led (first at San Francisco State and then at Berkeley) to the establishment of ethnic studies as a legitimate field of academic study.

The following six excerpts from documents related to the San Francisco State strike illustrate the students' struggle for equal rights and the end of racism. Among others, they include the Third World Liberation Front's strike demands (including the demand to reinstate George Murray, a lecturer fired by the English department for participating in the Black Panther Party), an excerpt taken from a Chinese American student organization brochure, and a compilation of statistics published by the Research Organizing Cooperative of San Francisco on injuries inflicted by the police on arrested strikers (and innocent bystanders) between December 2, 1968, and January 30, 1969.

1. THIRD WORLD LIBERATION FRONT, "SAN FRANCISCO STATE UNIVERSITY TWLF STRIKE DEMANDS" (1968)

1. That a School of Ethnic Studies for the ethnic groups involved in the Third World be set up with the students in each particular ethnic organization having the authority and control of the hiring and retention of any faculty member, director, and administrator, as well as the curriculum in a specific area of study.

2. That 50 faculty positions be appropriated to the School of Ethnic Studies, 20 would be for the Black Studies Program.

3. That in the Spring semester, the College fulfill its commitment to the non-white students by admitting those that apply.

4. That in the Fall of 1969, all applications of non-white students be accepted.

5. That George Murray and any other faculty person chosen by non-white people as their teacher be retained in their position.

Source: Third World Liberation Front. "San Francisco State University TWLF Strike Demands." 1968. *Stand Up: An Archive Collection of the Bay Area Asian American Movement, 1968–1974*, edited and compiled by Asian Community Center Archive Group. Berkeley: Eastwind Books of Berkeley, 2009. http://aam1968.blogspot.com/2008/01/san-francisco-state-strike-1968-twlf.html.

2. PHILIPPINE-AMERICAN COLLEGIATE ENDEAVOR (PACE), "STATE OF THE PHILIPPINE-AMERICAN COLLEGIATE ENDEAVOR PHILOSOPHY AND GOALS" (1968)

"We seek . . . simply to function as human beings, to control our own lives. Initially, following the myth of the American Dream, we worked to attend predominantly white colleges, but we have learned through direct analysis that it is impossible for our people, so-called minorities, to function as human beings, in a racist society in which white always come first . . . So we have decided to fuse ourselves with the masses of Third World people, which are the majority of the world's peoples, to create, through struggle, a new humanity, a new humanism, a New World Consciousness, and within that context collectively control our own destinies."

Source: Philippine-American Collegiate Endeavor (PACE), "State of the Philippine-American Collegiate Endeavor Philosophy and Goals," 1968. *Stand Up: An Archive Collection of the Bay Area Asian American Movement, 1968–1974*, edited and compiled by Asian Community Center Archive Group. Berkeley: Eastwind Books of Berkeley, 2009. http://aam1968.blogspot.com/2008/01/philippine-american-collegiate-endeavor.html.

3. "INTERCOLLEGIATE CHINESE FOR SOCIAL ACTION" (1968)

S. F. State, a community college, exists in a moral vacuum, oblivious to the community it purports to serve. It does not reflect the pluralistic society that is San Francisco—it does not begin to serve the 300,000 non-white people who live in this urban community in poverty, ignorance, despair. The Chinese ghetto, Chinatown, is a case in point.

1. S. F. State has a Chinese language department that isolates the "Chinese Experience" as a cultural phenomenon in language that 83% of the Chinese in the U. S. don't speak. Realistically, we can expect that a Chinese woman living in the ghetto, who speaks Cantonese, cannot explain to the scholar that she is dying of tuberculosis because she speaks a "street language" while the scholar mutters a classical poetry in Mandarin. S. F. State does not teach Cantonese.

2. Chinatown is a *ghetto* in San Francisco, there are approximately 50,000 Chinese of whom the vast majority live in Chinatown. It is an area of old buildings, narrow streets & alleys, and the effluvia of a great many people packed into a very small space. At present, more than 5,000 new Chinese immigrants stream into this overpopulated ghetto each year, an area already blessed with a birthrate that is rising, and will rise more. Tuberculosis is endemic, rents are high and constantly rising, city services are inadequate to provide reasonable sanitation, and space is at such a premium as to resemble the Malthusian ratio at in most extreme. There are no adequate courses in any department of school at S. F. State that even begin to deal with the problems of the Chinese people in their exclusionary and racist environment."

Source: "Intercollegiate Chinese for Social Action," 1968. *Stand Up: An Archive Collection of the Bay Area Asian American Movement, 1968–1974*, edited and compiled by Asian Community Center Archive Group, 46. Berkeley: Eastwind Books of Berkeley, 2009. http://aam1968.blogspot.com/2007/12/blog-post_3620.html.

4. RESEARCH ORGANIZING COOPERATIVE OF SAN FRANCISCO, "SFSU TWLF STRIKE INJURIES FROM POLICE BRUTALITY" (1969)

NUMBER TYPE OF INJURY

1   Ruptured spleen (removed)
2   Fractured skull

2 Concussion

15 Forehead, skull lacerations

3 Nose broken, bloodied

1 Fractured eye orbit

7 Eyes maced

2 Other eye damage (e. g., black)

6 Facial lacerations, swelling

18 Other head damage (bump, swelling, contusion)

8 Stomach badly clubbed, scratched or kicked

2 Broken, contused, fractured ribs

3 Broken fingers, thumb

1 Broken, fractured leg

1 Arm broken, fractured from surgery

1 Arm infected from surgery

1 Kidney infection

4 Other groin area damaged

2 Respiratory Infection

1 Contused lung

7 Other rib area damage (soreness)

12 Back, neck (clubbing, choking, welts, burns)

4 Blood vessel damage (massive bruises only)

15 Hand, arm, foot, leg laceration, swelling, lumps

5 Limb, finger, toe sprain, wrenched, contused

13 General bumps, bruises, soreness only

1 Nausea

80 Total number injured arrestees (many had more than one injury)

These do not include: (1) injuries sustained between November 6 and December 1; (2) injuries not reported; and (3) injuries to people who were not arrested. There might well be more of the latter than there were injured arrestees; it is impossible to tell how many.

Source: Research Organizing Cooperative of San Francisco. "SFSU TWLF Strike Injuries from Police Brutality," 1969. *Stand Up: An Archive Collection of the Bay Area Asian American Movement, 1968–1974*, edited and compiled by Asian Community Center Archive Group. Berkeley: Eastwind Books of Berkeley, 2009, 31. http://aam1968.blogspot.com/2008/01/sfsu-twlf-strike-injuries-from-police.html.

5. ASIAN AMERICAN POLITICAL ALLIANCE, "AAPA PERSPECTIVES" (1969)

"The Asian American Political Alliance is people. It is a people's alliance to effect social and political changes. We believe that the American society is historically racist and one which has systematically employed social discrimination and economic imperialism, both domestically and internationally, exploiting all non-white people in the process of building up their affluent society.

"They did so at the expense of all of us. Uncontrolled capitalism has pushed all of the non-white people into a social position so that only manual jobs with subhuman pay are open to them. Consequently, we have been psychologically so conditioned by the blue-eye—blond—hair standard that many of us have lost our perspective, We can only survive if "we know our place"—-shut up and accept what we are given, We resent this kind of domination and we are determined to change.

"The goal of AAPA is political education and advancement of the movement among Asian people, so that they may make all decisions that affect their own lives, in a society that never asks people to do so. AAPA is not an isolated group, and should never profess to be such. Its only legitimacy and value is in the effects it has on many people, not just a small group of people. In the same vein, AAPA is not meant to isolate Asians from other people; it is unhealthy as well as unwise to do such a thing. AAPA must constantly expand and grow, and reach out to other people and groups. At the same time, AAPA must meet the needs of its own members and deal with its own problems.

"In the past political organizations have tended to subject themselves to rigid, traditional levels of structure in which a few make the decisions, present them to the body, and the body can vote either "yes" or "no." This hierarchic organization, however, is only a manifestation of the elite control, primeval structure mentality in which you are not capable of making your own decisions, an idea drilled into you. from the foundations of this society.

"AAPA is only what the people make it. We have adopted a structure which better fits the needs and goals of our alliance, not a structure to which we have to adjust ourselves. Furthermore, there is no membership in AAPA in the strict sense of the word. There are workers who for common interests join together with one or more people to intensify the effectiveness of an action

"Since May, 1968, AAPA has grown from a small group of students and community workers to a powerhouse for Asian thought and action. AAPA is now a member of the Third World Liberation Front, Asian Association, and Asian Coalition. Some past activities of Berkeley AAPA include: Free Huey Rallies at the Oakland Courthouse, Chinatown Forums, McCarran Act lobbies, MASC Boycott, Third World Liberation Front Strike, development of Asian Studies, and liaison with and development of other AAPA's throughout the state.

"AAPA is only a transition for developing our own social identity, a multiplication of efforts. In fact, AAPA itself is not the important link but the ideas generated into action from it—that we Asian Americans are no longer going to kowtow to white America in order to gain an ounce of respect; that we must begin to build our own society alongside our black, brown and red brothers as well as those whites willing to effect fundamental social, economic, political changes; that we have the right for determining our own lives and asserting our yellow identity as a positive force in a new life based on human relationships and cooperation."

Source: Asian American Political Alliance. "AAPA Perspectives." Vol. 1, No. 6, October, 1969, 3. *Stand Up: An Archive Collection of the Bay Area Asian American Movement, 1968–1974*, edited and compiled by Asian Community Center Archive Group. Berkeley: Eastwind Books of Berkeley, 2009. http://aam1968.blogspot.com/2008/01/aapa-perspectives-october-1969.html.

6. FLYER FOR THE YELLOW SYMPOSIUM AT UC BERKELEY, "ASIAN EXPERIENCE /YELLOW IDENTITY" (1969)

Bring this, your invitation, to the 1st Asian Experience in America, Sat. Jan. 11, 1969, 9:00am–4:30pm Pauley Ballroom, ASUC Building UC Berkeley.

"If the Asian American is to live in a very complex American society and an even more complex world, and if he is to be able to assert his own humanity in these life spheres, he must know his own cultural history as an Asian American." 1968 An Asian American Student

"theasianexperienceinamerica/identifiedyellowqueriesqueuesfriends"

"the asian flu in america, blackheads all; gardeners, cooks, laundrymen and toshiro mifune; the golden race, america the beautiful, glittering ghettoes, second class citizens with visiting rights; chinatown, manilatown, little tokyo relocated concentrated, beautification, hallelujah christian colonies; submissive females, passive males, mellow yellows, that strong silent type; run run shaw, made in japan, p.r. 95 %; japanophiles, sinophiles, you likee chop suey, chop chop, me no savee; white paper, brown paper, yellow paper, black paper, red paper, if I were god I'd make everybody white; third world liberation front, all men are brothers, love is a many splendored thing, black eyed blondes; we all live in a yellow submarine, anti-queue law, call me yellow, no vietnamese ever called me a nigger, let's call a spade a spade, a jap a jap; buddhaheads transcendental meditation, Jesus is a'comin so get yourself ready for a hard day's night; reparations for the opium wars, christianity the whole world over, the asians get what they deserve, they breed like rabbits anyways; that fat jap, that skinny chink, chinatown my chinatown, my little houseboy, sayonnara suzie wong; Free University for Chinatown Kids, Unincorporated"

Source: Asian Students of Chinese Students Club and Nisei Students Club, University of California, Berkeley. "Asian Experience/Yellow Identity." *Stand Up: An Archive Collection of the Bay Area Asian American Movement, 1968–1974*, edited and compiled by Asian Community Center Archive Group. Berkeley: Eastwind Books of Berkeley, 2009. 1968. http://aam1968.blogspot.com/2008/01/yellow-symposium-1969-flyer.html.

Indochina Migration and Refugee Assistance Act
(1975)

On April 29, 1975, after approximately 13 years of military engagement, nearly 60,000 American casualties, and mounting public protest, the United States ended its involvement in the Vietnam War. United States Marine and Air Force helicopters began a massive airlift of Americans and South Vietnamese out of Saigon. The fall of South Vietnam to Ho Chi Minh's North Vietnamese communists precipitated a new wave of Asian immigration to the United States.

The first wave of Vietnamese refugees, airlifted out of Saigon, differed substantially from subsequent waves of refugees from the rest of Vietnam and Laos and Cambodia. They tended to be more educated and wealthy and spoke more English; almost half were Christian. A good portion of these refugees were former South Vietnamese military or government workers, and they arrived mostly in family groups. In contrast, the second and third waves of refugees tended to be less educated and poorer. A significant percentage were ethnic Chinese, and many had become separated from or had lost family members on their journey to the United States. They were called "boat people" because they escaped their war-torn countries on leaky sea vessels, braving storms and pirates to flee to Thailand and the Philippines. They languished in refugee camps for years before arriving in the United States during the late 1970s and early 1980s.

The Indochina Migration and Refugee Assistance Act of 1975 set the terms for the initial migration from Cambodia and Vietnam, granting these refugees special migration and parole status. The act was amended in 1976 to include refugees from Laos, and again in 1977 to extend the period of assistance provided to refugees. The Refugee Act of 1980 created a comprehensive refugee migration system, establishing the Office of Refugee Resettlement to administer refugee programs and services. Resettlement plans intentionally dispersed refugees across the country to prevent ethnic community formation and to integrate them into American society more quickly. However, within a few years, considerable secondary migration to California and Texas created thriving communities of Southeast Asian Americans in those states.

PUBLIC LAW 94–23—MAY 23, 1975

AN ACT

To enable the United States to render assistance to, or in behalf of, certain migrants and refugees.

Be it enacted by the Senate and House of Representatives of the United States of America in Congress assembled, That this Act may be cited as "The Indochina Migration and Refugee Assistance Act 1975".

SEC. 2 (a) Subject to the provision of subsection (b) there are hereby authorized to be appropriated in addition to amounts otherwise available for such purposes, $455,000,000 for the performance of functions set forth in the Migration and Refugee Assistance Act of 1962 (76 Stat. 121), as amended, with respect to aliens who have fled from Cambodia or Vietnam. . . .

SEC. 3. In carrying out functions utilizing the funds made available under this Act, the term "refugee" as defined in section 2 (b) (3) of the Migration and Refugee Assistance Act of 1962, as amended, shall be deemed to include aliens who (A) because of persecution or fear of persecution on account of race, religion, or political opinion, fled from Cambodia or Vietnam; (B) cannot return there because of fear of persecution on account of race, religion, or political opinion; and (C) are in urgent need of assistance for the essentials of life.

SEC. 4. . . . (b) Not more than thirty days after the date of enactment of this Act, the President shall transmit to such Committees a report describing fully and completely the status of refugees from Cambodia and South Vietnam. Such report shall set forth, in addition—

1. a plan for the resettlement of those refugees remaining in receiving or staging centers;

2. the number of refugees who have indicated an interest in returning to their homeland or being resettled in a third country, together with (A) a description of the plan for their return or resettlement and the steps taken to carry out such return or resettlement, and (B) any initiatives that have been made with respect to the Office of the High Commissioner for Refugees of the United Nations; and

3. a full and complete description of the steps the President has taken to retrieve and deposit in the Treasury as miscellaneous receipts all amounts previously authorized and appropriated for assistance to South Vietnam and Cambodia but not expended for such purpose, exclusive of the $98,000,000 of Indochina Postwar Reconstruction funds allocated to the Department of State for movement and maintenance of refugees prior to the date of enactment of this Act. . . .

Approved May 23, 1975.

Source: Indochina Migration and Refugee Assistance Act, 1975. 94th Cong., H.R. 6755; Public Law 94–23. U.S. Statutes at Large 89 (1975): 87.

Asian American Alliance, Political Committee, Columbia University (2006)

The Asian American Alliance at Columbia University, founded in 1995, is one of the campus's largest student organizations. Christina Chen, then-chair of the Political Committee, wrote the following mission statement in 2006, laying out various issues of concern to Asian American students. In the second section of the document, Chen invokes the original Asian American Movement of the 1960s to highlight the contemporary campaign to maintain a viable Asian American Studies program at Columbia.

The Asian American Alliance Political Committee seeks to . . .

. . . heighten awareness of issues affecting the Asian Pacific Islander American community in New York City and beyond, issues such as affordable housing, education, LGBTQQI rights, mental health, voting rights/civic participation, labor reform, domestic violence, healthcare, environmental justice, etc . . .

. . . become a catalyst for social change by organizing around such issues and, by the same token, support progressive APA (and non-APA) political candidates who advance such issues by means of legislation and public policy . . .

. . . tackle cultural stereotypes and discrimination and eradicate them by facilitating open and honest dialogue about the causes of such bias in the media, literature, and other societal milieu . . .

. . . build coalitions with like-minded campus organizations and ally with other students of color . . .

. . . research, study and chronicle the history of Asian Americans in the United States, thereupon promoting the awareness of APA history among our fellow students and allies . . .

. . . and lastly, though perhaps most importantly, explore what it means to be Asian American (whether we believe this term to be legitimately applicable to all APA's or otherwise) and what it means to be an "Asian American" in society today.

Asian American Studies Campaign

"Join us. Support the demand for Asian American Studies! Don't let the Man divide us from our Third World brothers and sisters! We have a right to learn about our own history, not just the history of Whites! We are not the Model Minority! We want relevant education that meets the needs of our community!"—November 6, 1968: SF State Ethnic Studies Strikes

Asian American Studies emerged from grass-roots movements that attempted to critically resist the Eurocentric historical narratives dictated by people outside of our communities. Asian American activists advocated for forms of scholarship that could counter the oppressive schema employed by educational institutions before the Third World Strikes of the 60's and 70's. Recognizing the need for community-controlled education and popular pedagogy in our class-rooms, as well as the lack of spaces for Asian American students to confront issues of power, privilege, inequality, and oppression on our cam-pus, the Asian American Alliance Political Committee fights for the resources necessary to maintain a truly sustainable Asian American Studies program at Columbia University.

Source: Chen, Christina, Chair of Columbia University Asian American Alliance Political Committee, 2006–2007. Asian American Alliance Political Committee mis-sion statement. August, 2006. http://www.columbia.edu/cu/aaa/pc.html. Used with permission of Columbia University's Asian American Alliance.

SAALT (South Asian Americans Leading Together), "Making the Case: Why Build a South Asian Identity"

(2006)

People from the South Asian diaspora to the United States come from all over the world: India, Pakistan, Bangladesh, Nepal, Tibet, Bhutan, Sri Lanka, and the Maldives; they also come from the Caribbean, Africa, Asia, and Europe, where their forebears immigrated generations ago. South Asians in the United States number approximately 2.7 million and are very diverse in terms of language, religion, and socioeconomic and residency status. In 2000, a group of first- and second-generation South Asians formed SAALT (South Asian American Leaders of Tomorrow; later changed to South Asian Americans Leading Together) to address the needs of their communities. In subsequent years, SAALT has created a documentary about anti-Asian hate crimes, *released reports on the post–9/11 backlash against South Asians, argued for immigration reform, and published materials on the South Asian community in New York. SAALT's document "Making the Case," published in the early days of the organization, lays out their rationale for a broad South Asian identity: finding a common history in the United States and advocating for an engaged and unified voice in American politics.*

WHY USE THE TERM "SOUTH ASIAN" TO DESCRIBE SUCH A DIVERSE COMMUNITY?

The use of the term "South Asian" is fairly recent. Progressive activists in the 1980s began using the world to reflect their belief that people from the same geographical area should ignore their historical divisions for the sake of building a unified political identity in the United States. During the 1990s, the term became increasingly used, especially by activists, and artistic organizers who sought to bring together individuals tracing their roots to South Asia.

SAALT's work is rooted in the development of coalitions that bring together groups and individuals from all parts of South Asia and the diaspora. Our common experiences as immigrants and people of color in American provide the foundation for a South Asian political identity. The South Asian community empowers itself by working together to address issues that affect us all.

While we come from diverse backgrounds, South Asians in America have many common problems that require immediate attention and broader, community-wide responses. These issues include hate crimes, racial profiling, immigration policies, education inequity, and poverty. Moreover, in the post-9/11 world, many of these issues have been greatly exacerbated to the point where Indians, Pakistanis, Bangladeshis and other South Asians are seen as a collective "other." By coming together to respond to stereotyping, discrimination, and other matters, we establish a more visible and powerful presence.

IS IT POSSIBLE TO UNIFY SUCH A COMPLEX AND DIVERSE COMMUNITY?

While it is a daunting task, there remain clear reasons for South Asians to unite and to project our influence on America through active civic and political engagement. There have been precedents in America of such unity. China, Japan, and Korea all have very long, distinctive, and intertwining histories that have created animosity towards one another. Yet in the 1960s, Chinese, Japanese and Korean Americans began to build coalitions for the purpose of political power. As a result, Asian American Studies classes emerged at universities

in California. Groups organizing Asian Americans around legal rights, unionization, domestic violence, and other issues took on a visible role in the American fabric. Such unity was based on the understanding that Asian Americans, through shared experiences in America dealing with immigration, access to benefits, and discrimination, would have greater power to influence and change policy—from university curricula to immigration law—if they worked together.

Similarly, South Asians have a myriad of issues around which we can organize and unite. The post September 11th backlash, which included hate violence and immigration policies, had a significant impact on South Asians. Hundreds of immigrants—mainly from Pakistan—were detained in the aftermath of September 11th; many have either chosen to seek asylum in Canada or return to Pakistan, or have been deported.

WHAT IF I PERSONALLY AM NOT AFFECTED BY THE ISSUES YOU MENTIONED?

There are many reasons why these issues affect ALL of us, instead of only the individual person or ethnic or religious group to which we belong. Racism is not logical. It does not discriminate in terms of educational attainment, place of residence, or income level. Marginalization and discrimination can affect any member of our community.

While certain issues may personally affect particular members of the South Asian community more so than others, this also means that those who are not affected are generally more able to create change. For example, citizens may be less affected by certain immigration measures that hurt noncitizens. However, this also means that citizens have a certain degree of power that noncitizens do not have to challenge discriminatory laws and regulations, and petition for change without the fear of losing their rights or livelihoods.

By articulating our common experiences in America, South Asians can identify issues and points of interest around which we can work together.

SOUTH ASIANS ARE FREQUENTLY SINGLED OUT AS A "MODEL MINORITY." WHAT ARE THE PROS AND CONS OF THIS REPRESENTATION?

While many South Asians fall within the higher than average socioeconomic bracket of this country and tend to be educated, it would be an oversimplification to believe that all South Asians are the same. The average incomes and education levels often hide significant problems of many South Asians, and obscure the fact that South Asians are prone to marginalization and discriminatory treatment in America. For example, according to the Asian American Federation, New York City's Pakistani Americans experience greater poverty, earn less, speak less English and live in larger households than city residents. With the per capita income of these New Yorkers ($11,992) being almost half the citywide average, and fourth of the Pakistani population living in poverty, the assumption of South Asians being a very wealthy population proves to be incorrect.

WHY SHOULD SOUTH ASIANS BE MORE ENGAGED IN THE COMMUNITY AROUND US?

Active participation and engagement in the community around us are vital civic acts that will improve and empower the lives of South Asians in the United States. Civic engagement involves taking an active role towards the betterment of one's community. It can be defined as one's capacity to

- work with others to bring about common goals;
- see oneself as a stakeholder in public life; and
- believe that individuals have a responsibility to contribute to the range of communities in which they interact.

By actively being civically engaged—whether it is in the political process, in the academic context, or in the South Asian community itself—we join ourselves with a larger collective voice to bring about equality and justice for all.

Source: South Asian Americans Leading Together (SAALT), "Making the Case: Why Build a South Asian Identity." http://www.saalt.org/attachments/1/Making%20 the%20Case.pdf.

Belinda Dronkers-Laureta, "Asian Family Values"
(2008)

Invoking the history of Asian American activism and struggles for equality, Filipina American Belinda Dronkers-Laureta cofounded Asian and Pacific Islander (API) Family Pride to address the specific needs and concerns of Asian American families. Many gay Asian Americans face additional challenges when coming out: cultural and community stigmas frequently characterize homosexuality as a "white disease." For the same reason, their family members often believe they *need to keep their loved one's identity a secret. Often, shame prevents many gay APIs from attending the mainstream gay community's already-established support groups. API Family Pride reaches out to Asian American families in culturally sensitive ways by employing translators; relying on more individualized settings, such as one-on-one sessions with parents; and making connections with other ethnic organizations.*

In her "Beyond Borders" post from Asian Week, *Dronkers-Laureta, on behalf of API Family Pride, describes the isolation felt by many homosexual Asian Pacific Americans and their families and how her organization seeks to overcome that isolation.*

Belinda cofounded an organization (Asian & Pacific Islander-Family Pride) dedicated to end the isolation of APA/API families with lesbian, gay, bisexual, or transgender children. In her workshops, PowerPoint presentations, and dinner speeches Belinda cites the central importance of family in the lives of APA/API individuals. We read the research that supports the claims she makes in her workshops and it is beyond question, family is a principal value in Asian culture and APA/APIs derive much of their identity from being members of their family.

Our experience is also that when a child "comes out" to parents, often the parents reject that child. Rejection takes several forms; for example, parents withdraw financial support, banish the child from family gatherings, or even deny access to the home. But now there is a contradiction, does not rejection of a child violate the paramount importance of family? We have not satisfactorily worked out the answer, but are developing several threads.

Thread one is that family is the basic unit of analysis for Asian cultures and the central focus of an APA/API's life; there is no smaller unit, there are no individuals. The behavior of an individual family member reflects on the entire family. The family unit is part of a larger social network that imposes norms developed over a long time. Our experience is that when a child tells parents that he or she is lesbian, gay, bisexual, or transgender, the reaction more often than not is shame. A sexual orientation other than the accepted norm is not acceptable. In fact, many Asian languages have no word for alternative sexual orientations and in some [Asian countries] it [homosexuality] is illegal.

Thread two is that harmony is another highly praised Asian value. In fact, the clinical psychologist Sam Chan writes that for Asians harmony is the keynote to existence. A lesbian, gay, bisexual, or transgender child violates a social norm that reflects on the family and disturbs social harmony. Belinda reports that often parents agonize over what their family will think. Will their friends think them bad parents?

The explanation is, of course, too facile for so complex a phenomenon. The implication for our work, though, is clear. If we want to end the isolation of APA/API families with lesbian, gay, bisexual, or transgender children, then talking to families is not enough. We have to somehow reach the whole community.

Source: Dronkers-Laureta, Belinda. "Asian Family Values." *Asian Week,* April 12, 2008. http://beyondborders .asianweek.com/?p=7. Reprinted with permission.

Hindu American Foundation, "Yoga Beyond Asana: Hindu Thought in Practice"

(2010)

The Hindu American Foundation (HAF), a multiethnic, progressive advocacy group, was formed in 2003. It supports reform efforts in public policy and education, works to highlight and eradicate the persecution of Hindus, and advocates for fair media representations of Hinduism, both in the United States and globally. The HAF releases reports on anti-Hindu hate crimes, has testified in the Supreme Court case on public displays of the Ten Commandments, and won a lawsuit against the California State Board of Education for misrepresenting Hindus and Hinduism in textbook adoption procedures. In addition, the organization's lobbying led to the passage of House Resolution 747 and Senate Resolution 229 in 2007; the United States now recognizes Diwali as a nationally significant holiday.

The HAF published the following position paper on the importance of yoga's Hindu foundation. Like many religious communities in the United States, the HAF is grappling with the tensions that often arise between religious and American identity, especially as religious forms increasingly are adopted—and adapted—by the mainstream. "Yoga Beyond Asana: Hindu Thought in Practice" argues against the despiritualized version of this essential Hindu practice.

> "There is no physical yoga and spiritual yoga. If it is exclusively physical, it won't be yoga. Yoga is dealing with the entirety; it is a union."
> —*Prashant Iyengar, son of B. K. S. Iyengar*

Yoga, from the word "yuj" (Sanskrit, "to yoke" or "to unite"), refers to spiritual practices that are essential to the understanding and practice of Hinduism. Yoga and yogic practices date back more than 5,000 years—the Indus Valley seals depict figures in yoga poses. The term covers a wide array of practices, embodied in eight "limbs," which range from ethical and moral guidelines to meditation on the Ultimate Reality. Yoga is a combination of both physical and spiritual exercises, entails mastery over the body, mind and emotional self, and transcendence of desire. The ultimate goal is *moksha*, the attainment of liberation from worldly suffering and the cycle of birth and rebirth.

With the popularity of Yoga skyrocketing throughout the world, particularly in the West, there arise two main points in need of clarification. First, that which is practiced as "Hatha Yoga"—a form of Raja Yoga—in much of the Western world is but merely a focus on a single limb of Yoga: asana (posture). From Yoga studios that recommend room temperatures to be maintained at 105 degrees to 90-minute Vinyasa flow classes that prescribe one Suryanamaskar (Sun Salutation) sequence after another, this *"asana* heavy" form of Yoga—sometimes complimented with *pranayama* (breathing)—is only a form of exercise to control, tone and stretch muscles. Ignored are both the moral basis of the practice and the ultimate spiritual goal.

Second, there is the concerning trend of disassociating Yoga from its Hindu roots. Both Yoga magazines and studios assiduously present Yoga as an ancient practice independent and disembodied from the Hinduism that gave forth this immense contribution to humanity. With the intense focus on *asana*, magazines and studios have seemingly "gotten away" with this mischaracterization. Yet, even when Yoga is practiced solely in the form of an exercise, it cannot be completely delinked from its Hindu roots. As the legendary Yoga guru B. K. S. Iyengar aptly points out in his famous *Light on Yoga*, "Some *asanas* are also called after Gods of the Hindu pantheon and some recall the Avataras, or incarnations of Divine Power." It is disappointing to know that many of the yogis regularly practicing *Hanumanasana* or *Natarajasana* continue to deny the Hindu roots of their Yoga practice.

In a time where Hindus around the globe face discrimination and hate because of their religious identity, and Hindu belief and practice continues to be widely misunderstood due to exoticized portrayals of it being caricaturized in "caste, cows and curry" fashion, recognition of Yoga as a tremendous contribution of ancient Hindus to the world is imperative. Yoga is inextricable from Hindu traditions, and a better awareness of this fact is reached only if one understands that "Yoga" and "Asana" are not interchangeable terms.

Asana aka Yoga

A perusal of a few of the best-known Yoga texts, such as Swami Svatmarama's *Hatha Yoga Pradipika* or Patanjali's *Yoga Sutras*, will quickly demonstrate that *asana* (posture) is only one component of Yoga.

The *Pradipika* is divided into four main sections, of which 25% of only the first section focuses on *asana*. The *Yoga Sutras* are also divided into four parts, with a total of 196 sutras. The second part, composed of 55 sutras, briefly mentions asana as one of the eight limbs of Raja Yoga.

In his forward to an English translation of *Pradipika*, Iyengar aptly describes, "Hatha yoga . . . [to be] commonly misunderstood and misrepresented as being simply a physical culture, divorced from spiritual goals. . . . *Asanas* are not just physical exercises: they have biochemical, psycho-physiological and psycho-spiritual effects."

In a 2005 interview published in *Namarupa* magazine, Prashant Iyengar, son of B. K. S. Iyengar, clearly espouses a similar view when he said, "We cannot expect that millions are practicing real yoga just because millions of people claim to be doing yoga all over the globe. What has spread all over the world is not yoga. It is not even non-yoga; it is un-yoga." The undue emphasis, particularly in the West, on *asana* as the crux of Yoga dilutes the essence of the spiritual practice and its ultimate goal of *moksha*.

B. K. S. Iyengar again reminds readers of the purpose of *asanas* in his *Light on Yoga,* when he states, "Their [*Asanas*] real importance lies in the way they train and discipline the mind. . . . The yogi conquers the body by the practice of *asanas* and make it a fit vehicle for the spirit. . . . He does not consider it [the body] his property. . . . The yogi realizes that his life and all its activities are part of the divine action in nature."

The Hindu American Foundation (HAF) concludes from its research that Yoga, as an integral part of Hindu philosophy, is not simply physical exercise in the form of various *asanas* and *pranayama*, but is in fact a Hindu way of life. The ubiquitous use of the word "Yoga" to describe what in fact is simply an *asana* exercise is not only misleading, but has lead to and is fueling a problematic delinking of Yoga and Hinduism, as described further in the section below.

This attempt to clarify Yoga as far more complex than just *asanas* is not intended to discount the array of health benefits gained by practicing *asanas* alone. Beyond increasing muscle tone and flexibility, regular practice of *asana* has been associated with lower blood pressure, relief of back pain and arthritis, and boosting of the immune system. Increasingly, many believe *asana* practice to reduce Attention Deficit Disorder (AD/HD) in children, and recent studies have shown it improves general behavior and grades. But the Foundation argues that the full potential of the physiological, intellectual and spiritual benefits of *asana* would be increased manifold if practiced as a component of the holistic practice of Yoga.

REVERSING THE EFFORTS TO DECOUPLE YOGA FROM HINDUISM

Although the Western Yoga community fully acknowledges Yoga's Indian roots, and even requires study of Hindu philosophy and scripture in most of its teacher certification programs, much of it openly disassociates Yoga's Hindu roots. While HAF affirms that one does not have to profess faith in Hinduism in order to practice Yoga or *asana*, it firmly holds that Yoga is an essential part of Hindu philosophy and the two cannot be delinked, despite efforts to do so.

Shyam Ranganathan's analysis gets to the crux of the issue when he writes, "Though some modern atheistic minds and aspiring yogis may disagree, textually there is no getting around the fact that Patanjali uses words, that in the context of Hindu culture, have obvious theological implications." Patanjali describes the goal of Yoga as *chitta-vritti-nirodha* or "the cessation of mental fluctuations", a core concept also expounded in Hinduism's *Bhagavad Gita*: "Thus always absorbing one's self in yoga, the yogi, whose mind is subdued, achieves peace that culminates in the highest state of Nirvana, which rests in me [Lord Krishna/Brahman/Supreme Reality]."

Similarly, Swami Svatmarama's opening line in the *Pradipika* is in honor of the Hindu God Shiva (Siva): "Reverence to Siva the Lord of Yoga, who taught Parvati hatha wisdom as the first step to the pinnacle of raja yoga."

In the same 2005 interview cited previously, Prashant Iyengar expounds upon Yoga with references to both Hindu epics and Hindu philosophy: "*Mahabharat* has so many aspects of yoga like yama (restraint), niyama (observance), sama (calmness). . . . *Ramayana* gives us so many beautiful aspects of bhakti yoga and karma yoga. Essential yoga starts with karma yoga. . . . Without karma-consciousness, there will be no progress in yoga."

The Hindu American Foundation (HAF) reaffirms that Yoga, "an inward journey, where you explore your mind, your awareness, your consciousness, your conscience," is an essential part of Hindu belief and practice. But the science of yoga and the immense benefits its practice affords are for the benefit of all of humanity regardless of personal faith. Hinduism itself is a family of pluralistic doctrines and ways of life that acknowledge the existence of other spiritual and religious traditions. Hinduism, as a non-proselytizing religion, never compels practitioners of yoga to profess allegiance to the faith or convert. Yoga is a means of spiritual attainment for any and all seekers.

Source: http://www.hafsite.org/media/pr/yoga-hindu-origins .Used with permission of the Hindu American Foundation.

Momo Chang, "Who Was Richard Aoki?: Community Reactions to Richard's Hidden Life"

(2012)

When he was four years old, Richard Aoki and his family were interned with other Japanese Americans at the Topaz War Relocation Center in central Utah. There, Aoki's father joined the No-No Boys, Nisei internees who refused to sign the loyalty oath and register for the draft. During internment, Aoki's parents separated, and after the war, Aoki moved with his father to a predominantly black neighborhood in Oakland, California. When he went to college, Aoki joined Bobby Seale's and Huey Newton's fledgling Black Panther Party and became the only Asian American to serve as a Panther Field Marshal. Aoki also helped organize the Third World Liberation Front, the student group whose strike prompted the University of California–Berkeley to establish one of the nation's first ethnic studies programs. Aoki was involved in radical activism for the rest of his life. Until his untimely death in 2009, he was revered as one of the founders of the Asian American movement and as a fearless advocate for racial and economic justice in the United States.

In 2012, investigative reporter Seth Rosenfeld published a story in the San Francisco Chronicle *alleging that Aoki had been an FBI informer while he was supplying guns and providing arms training to the Black Panther Party. According to Rosenfeld, who based his findings on Aoki's FBI file (released in redacted form to the public under the Freedom of Information Act), Aoki worked as a paid informant from 1961 to 1977, likely initially reporting primarily on socialist groups (the heavy redactions in his FBI files make it difficult to give a definitive statement on Aoki's involvement). It is not clear from the files whether Aoki provided information on the Black Panthers. Rosenfeld's story sent shockwaves through the Asian American and activist communities. After the initial round of denials, some of Aoki's colleagues have come to the conclusion that although he was initially an informant, Aoki legitimately became radicalized through his lifelong and deep involvement with many different activist organizations.*

Momo Chang, a freelance journalist based in Oakland, California, wrote a four-part series of articles analyzing Richard Aoki's life and legacy for Hyphen, *a magazine and Web site focusing on Asian American arts, culture, and politics. The multimedia series, a collaborative project run by Chang, Lawrence Guzman, R. J. Lozada, Lisa Wong Macabasco, and Catherine Traywick, includes an interactive timeline of Aoki's life and an extensive collection of audio clips from interviews with Asian American and other civil rights activists reflecting on Aoki's complicated legacy. In section four, Chang explores the ways people responded to Rosenfeld's story, and the reevaluation of Richard Aoki that it prompted.*

The revelation that Richard Aoki was an FBI informant has created a firestorm of responses from former Black Panther Party members, activists of all ages and backgrounds, and Asian American and African American scholars.

After a story by Seth Rosenfeld broke the news in the *San Francisco Chronicle* on August 20, 2012, some attacked Rosenfeld's credibility as a journalist. Many activists and people of color were distrustful of the initial report because of the mainstream media's contentious relationship with those communities, said Jamilah King, an editor at Colorlines, a website devoted to coverage of race, culture and politics. "The reaction to the first report and the length to which people went to discredit Seth Rosenfeld showed how deeply imbedded that distrust is in communities of color of mainstream journalists and of white journalists who are trying to shape or form the story of people who lived through this time."

Some took issue with Rosenfeld's reporting techniques. In a video that accompanied the original article, Rosenfeld interviews Harvey Dong, Aoki's friend and executor of his estate, and then films his reaction as he presents Dong with a stack of Aoki's FBI documents. Audiences see the shock on Dong's face and his response that he had no idea Aoki was an informant. Dong said he thought the interview would be about the 60s and 70s; others felt like it was an unfair "gotcha" moment.

Rosenfeld said that since Dong was Aoki's executor, he wasn't sure what Dong knew, and he felt it was fair to ask him the question.

Diane Fujino, author of Aoki's 2011 biography, *Samurai Among Panthers: Richard Aoki on Race, Resistance and a Paradoxical Life* and chair of the Asian American studies department at University of California at Santa Barbara, publicly critiqued Rosenfeld's evidence, as well as his framing of the Third World Liberation Front, a coalition of students-of-color groups including the Asian American Political Alliance. Fujino says that Rosenfeld "over-relies on the FBI files as if they are accurate" and also that Rosenfeld sets up the Free Speech Movement as the "good," nonviolent 60s, while setting up the later Third World Liberation Front movement as violent, or "bad." Rosenfeld believes that in his book he places the violence in context and is also critical of the violence used against the Third World Liberation Front strikers. "The Third World Strike is presented in the context of gradually increasing violence by both protestors and police as the 60s continues," he told *Hyphen*.

Fujino also questioned the reliability of the FBI reports, some of which she also received through her own FOIA requests. "Could it be true? Or was this a 'snitch-jacketing,' a classic FBI tactic used to cast suspicion on a legitimate activist by spreading rumors and manufacturing evidence?," Fujino wrote in an op-ed shortly after Rosenfeld's *Chronicle* article was published. There is no evidence that the FBI falsified information in order to discredit Aoki. But Fujino argues, "The FBI documents need to be scrutinized. All kinds of motivations go into the FBI documents, people careers, or for money. What people report isn't always accurate."

Rosenfeld said in a recent interview with *Hyphen* that while he expected surprise and skepticism, he was not prepared for the barrage of what he felt were personal attacks on his credibility as a journalist. Since Aoki's death in 2009, Rosenfeld has relentlessly pursued all the FBI records on Aoki and his FBI connection, filing numerous requests and even suing the bureau for access to the files. (The bulk of Rosenfeld's recently released book does not focus on Aoki—in fact, Aoki is only in about 10 pages.)

The resistance by some Asian Americans and activists to believe that Aoki was an informant is understandable given his role as a prominent Asian American activist from the 60s and 70s, some say. "When some people only know about two or three prominent Asian American activists, and one of the three turns out to be an informer, that's a terrible ratio," said Bob Wing, a longtime activist who met Aoki when they were both students at UC Berkeley and active in the Asian American Political Alliance and Third World Liberation Front. (The two other widely known activists, according to Wing, are Yuri Kochiyama and Grace Lee Boggs.) "It can be demoralizing for some people, whether you're Asian American or not."

Aoki also stands as a rare symbol of interracial solidarity between African Americans and Asian Americans, two groups that have struggled with very real interracial tensions. There is something powerful about an Asian American who was not only affiliated with but also had leadership roles within one of the most intriguing and controversial black revolutionary groups in the 60s and 70s. "He deserves all of our respect," said Elbert "Big Man" Howard, one of the first members of the Black Panther Party, to an audience at a community forum. "I miss Richard. I will always remember him."

The Socialist Workers Party has also come to Aoki's defense recently, stating that they give no credibility to FBI sources. "These charges are not solely about destroying the reputation of Richard Aoki," reads a letter signed by Willie Cotton of the SWP in San Francisco. "The 'snitch-jacket' against Aoki is meant to put a chill on groups—those active today and in the future—who seek to politically organize workers, youth, farmers, and others interested in building a mass work-class movement."

Many argue that Aoki's contributions—mentoring and inspiring young activists, helping community college students gain access to higher education, and his political contributions during the 60s and 70s—cannot be taken away and Aoki's role helping forge unity between different racial groups cannot be denied: his work helped "rearticulate the nation's ideological constructions of race," Fujino noted in her biography on Aoki.

But some argue that Aoki's reputation made him an untouchable figure, resistant to critiques. "Was there something about what Aoki represented to us as progressive people of color—especially we who are Asian American leftists—that made many of us refrain from a healthy skepticism of Aoki and indeed, any person whose celebrity rests largely on racial border crossing?" wrote Tamara K. Nopper, a writer and a lecturer in Asian American studies and sociology at the University of Pennsylvania, in The New Inquiry.

Nopper is one of the few who have become more critical of Aoki's legacy since the news of his relationship to the FBI broke. She said that the wave of public reaction—mostly in defense of Aoki—make it difficult to raise tougher questions. "There seems to be this perverse need to protect his legacy," she said. "It's been very difficult to speak out critically of Aoki and to be okay with considering him an informant."

Nopper points out that many other activists, including ones in the black community, have been branded as informants with less evidence, yet it seems no one has spoken out publicly to the same degree as they have for Aoki. "If he agreed to collude with the FBI for so many years," Nopper told Hyphen, "the ethical thing to do is to seriously reconsider Richard Aoki's legacy. You can't be an FBI informant for so long, and never reveal it so as to work towards community accountability, and still be considered a hero to the movement. To me, it raises serious questions about why there is so much need to keep Richard a hero."

King, of Colorlines, warns against glorifying leaders. "When you build someone up to be this mythic creature . . . that is so embodied of all the political values that we hold dear, it doesn't leave room for complexities, it doesn't leave room for contradictions," King said. "You can be a revolutionary person who has complicated motivations for doing things."

In a widely read post on Facebook, Scott Kurashige, a professor of Asian/Pacific Islander American Studies and American Culture at the University of Michigan, was one of the first to question Rosenfeld's assertions (accusing Rosenfeld of failing to provide adequate context about why the Third World Liberation Front students were striking) and one of the first to suggest that if Aoki was an informant, he could have become politicized over the years. (Kurashige was criticized at the time for even entertaining the idea that Aoki could have been an informant.)

Although Kurashige remains skeptical of Rosenfeld's work, he sees value in revealing FBI secrets, and exposing the struggles that idolized movement leaders went through, including their complexities and flaws, as a way to understand their political work and contributions. "[Aoki] was a trusted, loyal comrade of many people for many years, and that's a very important side of him," he said in an interview with *Hyphen*. "And yet there may have been other things going on with him that don't in any way detract from the work that he did but makes us, as students of history and as people who are trying to make history, in need of learning some deeper lessons."

Fujino agrees that this is a "teachable moment," demonstrating that "all history is interpretive." She points out that the incarceration of Japanese Americans during World War II was once framed as necessary for their safety. "Now there's a different frame. It's not like what they did changed, but the interpretation changes. I think we have to be careful about how we interpret facts, and about FBI files in particular." Fujino now acknowledges that Aoki could have been an informant based on the more recent documents released. She and Rosenfeld both say they will continue to follow this story.

It took Rosenfeld three years and a lawsuit to compel the FBI to release several thousand more pages on Aoki; on November 1, the bureau is scheduled to release hundreds more. What information Aoki gave the FBI remains to be seen—and with the release of more documents, more questions than answers may be raised. Many doubt that the new files will provide any definitive answers. "They're not going to release everything," said [M. Wesley] Swearingen, [a former FBI agent and whistle-blower]. "They're going to withhold some stuff that would be embarrassing to the FBI." Rosenfeld believes there are still more records and plans on pursuing them, including the information that has been redacted.

Meanwhile many of Aoki's friends and associates continue to believe that his alliance and friendships with them were real. Aoki's story has taken an even more complex turn, showing that nothing is black and white.

Source: Chang, Momo. "Who Was Richard Aoki?: Community Reactions to Richard's Hidden Life." Part IV, *Hyphen,* November 1, 2012. http://www.hyphenmagazine.com/content/who-was-richard-aoki-part-iv. Used with permission of Momo Chang.

American Samoans

Amy Taxin, "Samoans Abroad Pray for Family Back Home"
(2009)

American Samoa is a group of Polynesian islands in the South Pacific; the islands make up an unincorporated territory of the United States administered by the Department of the Interior. Westerners have had sustained contact with what is now called American Samoa since the mid-19th century. During the 1899 Tripartite Convention, the United States and Germany divided control of the Samoan islands. The U.S. Navy took administrative control over the islands in 1900 and soon dominated their economy. During World War II, naval operations expanded rapidly, transforming the city of Pago Pago. When the Pago Pago naval base was decommissioned in 1951, many Samoans who worked for the U.S. Navy, as servicemen, administrative workers, or the like, began relocating to the mainland. Although the western group of islands gained independence in 1962, calling themselves the Independent State of Samoa, the United States has retained control of the eastern islands.

American Samoans are U.S. nationals. They may travel to and from, and live and work in the United States without obtaining special visas, but they may not vote, and they must apply for American citizenship like any other foreign national. American Samoans have enlisted in the U.S. military in numbers disproportionate to their population, primarily because of the dearth of economic opportunities in their homeland. Today, most of the estimated 130,000 Samoans or part Samoans residing in the United States live in Hawai'i, California, and Washington. In general, Samoans have higher levels of poverty, lower rates of home ownership, lower educational levels, and lower labor force participation than the general population. Samoans living in California tend to have a higher standard of living than Samoans in Hawai'i.

On September 29, 2009, an 8.0 magnitude earthquake struck off the coast of American Samoa. The quake triggered a monster tsunami that devastated the islands, killing more than 100 people. In the immediate aftermath of the disaster, Samoans in Southern California formed the Help Samoa Coalition, sending medical aid, food, and basic necessities to the victims. The article reprinted here describes the efforts of the Help Samoa Coalition and shows how ties between far-flung communities remain strong.

Scores from California's Samoan community—many with traditional white flowers in their hair and clutching woven fans—gathered in church Thursday to pray for family members in tsunami-ravaged Samoa—some still waiting to hear from them.

In the sweltering Samoan Congregational Christian Church in Carson, Calif., roughly 200 people joined in a special twilight service in the aftermath of the devastating earthquake and tsunami that have left at least 160 dead.

Lusi Timai, 44, has been trying to reach her aunts and cousins in American Samoa since the tsunami hit Tuesday but can't get through.

"We just pray . . . we just come here to pray for them," she said, clutching the cell phone she's been using to call.

The urban sprawl south of Los Angeles is a hub for the Samoan community and ground zero for coordination of relief efforts that local community leaders are getting underway.

About 40 percent of the country's 72,000 Samoans live in California, according to data from the 2008 American Community Survey.

In the hours since the tsunami, local community leaders have fielded a stream of calls from Samoans frantically trying to reach their relatives. They also formed a network of clergy, community leaders and non-profits to harness and transport donations of canned food, water, tarps and other necessities to the affected regions.

Outside the church on Thursday, local politicians offered to do what they could to help the communities in American Samoa and Samoa. Inside, the faithful belted out spiritual Christian songs to a band's music and batted themselves with fans to stay cool.

Aitofi Muaina, 62, came to pray for her 94-year-old aunt who holed up on the second floor of her house in American Samoa while the ocean waters rushed in below.

"She's alive. It's all that counts," said Muaina, who traveled from Las Vegas for the service. "It's a miracle."

Source: Taxin, Amy. "Samoans Abroad Pray for Family Back Home." *U-T San Diego*, October 1, 2009. *Help Samoa: Disaster Relief Coalition For American Samoa*, 2009. http://www.help samoa.com/samoans-abroad-pray-for-family-back-home.

Tafea Polamalu, "Diasporic Dream: Letter to Grandfather" (2009) and "Daddy Said"

(2010)

Tafea Polamalu is a Samoan American who grew up in rural southwestern Oregon, hundreds of miles from the nearest Samoan community. Polamalu traces his ancestral ties to the island of Ta'u in the Manu'a archipelago, part of U.S.-controlled American Samoa. Polamalu received his master's in Pacific Islands Studies from the University of Hawai'i at Manoa. He uses poetry,

fiction, and painting to explore and express his relationship to Samoa and his identity and experiences as a Samoan American. In these two poems, Polamalu takes readers on a journey that crosses oceans, identities, and generations, and challenges our assumptions about what it means to be a Samoan, an American, and an immigrant.

DIASPORIC DREAM: LETTER TO GRANDFATHER

I am the final result of your foresight:
The end product of opportunity

I am what they call
"Second-Generation US Samoan:"
That generation who has
Never been to Samoa

I am "First-World"
"Fully-developed"
"Fully-civilized"

I come from no island
I come from "The Mainland"

I was born among them
Raised among them
Melted into them
Fluent in their language and ways

I am "Educated"
"Modernized"

"American"

I am the quintessential neo Samoan:
A walking wealth of Western knowledge

I know my Pledge of Allegiance
I know my presidents
I can name all fifty state capitals

I can solve quadratic equations
Formulate a thesis
Type over 60 words per minute

I can dissect a frog and identify all of the vital organs
I can spot a dangling modifier
I have read the works of countless classic European
writers

I can tell you the difference between
Polynesia, Micronesia, Melanesia
I am well versed on the Lapita Theory

I know all about Samoa:
Population
Climate
Average life expectancy

Margaret Mead

I am the vision
I am progress
I am a masterpiece of assimilation

I have forgotten what is useless
I have learned what matters
The world is at my finger tips

I am the future:
Woven of fear and survival
I am the "fully-evolved" immigrant
The Diasporic dream

I am what eventually becomes of those who left:
Not native like you
But settler like them
But not one of them
Nor one of you

I am lodged perfectly between worlds
In the war zone where razor wire
And minefields connect cultures

I wish I would have known you
I would like to show you this place

But I do not remember you
I do not speak your language
I do not know your ways
I do not know why I am here
I feel gone from you
Lost to you

I know nothing of Samoa

I sometimes think
it is too late

DADDY SAID

Son,
I prunk you hea
pecause tis is ta lan of
opprotunity

In Samoa,
te is nofing
To you heard me Son?
Nofing

Hea in Ameika,
ta worlt is at
yo finka tip
and ta sky is ta limits

You know why I nefa
teach you Samoan Son?
cause Samoan no ket you
anyfing in life

tis is ta white man's worlt
an Enklish is
only fink tat matta

You heard me Son?

Tis is ta white man's worlt
an at ta en of ta tay, we all haf
to walk fru his toor

at ta en of ta tay, we all haf
walk fru his toor
cause he sign ta check Son

look at me,
my whole life i strukle wif
fo try speak ta Enklish

i strukle my ass off Son
so tat you can ket you
pestes echucation

So i make tamn sure
my sons masta Enklish
pecause tis is what pestes

You see what I'm said Son?
Tis is why it pisses me when

te say, 'How come I nefa teachet
you speak Samoan?'

What ta hell te fink I prunk you here fo eh?
tes stupit hets know
nofing apout Samoa

Rememper sumfing Son,
Ameika is ta pestes place in ta worlt
so ket ta echucation

pe ta tocto
pe ta lawya
tis is my tream fo you
tis is why fo i prunk you hea

fo to kif you ta
opprotunity to haf ta
fings i nefa haf

You see what I'm said Son?

Okay, koot talk
alu su'esu'e
ko prush ta teef
an to ta maf homewok

Sources: Polamalu Tafea. "Diasporic Dream: Letter to Grandfather." In *The Space Between: Negotiating Culture, Place, and Identity in the Pacific*, edited by A. Marata Tamaira. Honolulu: Center for Pacific Islands Studies, School of Hawaiian, Asian & Pacific Studies, University of Hawai'i at Manoa, 2009; Polamalu, Tafea. "Daddy Said." In *Mauri Ola: Contemporary Polynesian Poems in English, Whetu Moana II*, edited by Albert Wendt, Reina Whaitiri, and Robert Sullivan. Honolulu: University of Hawaii Press, 2010.

Kanwal Rahman, Interview by Rajika Bhandari
(July 15, 1999)

Bangladesh is nearly surrounded by India, with the Bay of Bengal to the south and a short border with Myanmar (Burma) on the southeast. European traders arrived in the Bengali region in the 16th century. The British East India Company wrested control of the region from the Mughal Nawab of Bengal in 1757, and the British Crown took over the territory after the 1857 Sepoy Mutiny. In 1905, and again in 1946, Bengal was partitioned into Muslim and Hindu territories; the 1946 partition left West Bengal under Indian rule and East Bengal, later renamed East Pakistan, under the rule of Pakistan—a country more than 1,000 miles away to the west. Tensions over political and economic issues grew between the noncontiguous dominions. This culminated in the 1971 civil war, during which East Pakistan, under the Awami League and with aid from India, defeated Pakistan's military. East Bengal/Pakistan then became the independent nation of Bangladesh.

Bengalis began immigrating to the United States in the late 19th century, until exclusion laws cut off Asians. The first wave of Bengalis immigrating after 1965 tended to be upper and middle class, fleeing religious and political persecution in their unstable region. Since the 1971 establishment of Bangladesh, immigrants have primarily been men, who establish themselves in the United States and then send for their families. Immigration increased steadily until 2013, when Bangladesh exceeded the Diversity Immigrant Visa program's quota of 50,000 emigrants in five years.

Kanwal Rahman came to the United States from Bangladesh in August 1991 to study public health policy and administration at the University of North Carolina–Chapel Hill. She had worked as a dental surgeon for the Ministry of Health in Bangladesh. At the time of this 1999 interview, Rahman had been living in North Carolina for eight years, working in public health and insurance research. In the interview, she speaks about the difficulty she had when she first arrived in the United States, her determination to persevere, the ways she has evolved personally since immigrating, her occasional feelings of alienation from mainstream American culture, and her strong desire to live a transnational life. The interviewer, Rajika Bhandari, notes that South Asian "men and women . . . go through very different experiences when they come [to the United States] . . . they evolve very differently." Rahman corroborates this observation in her discussion of gender roles. Although influenced strongly by Bangladeshi traditions, her perspective has also been colored by her commitment to universal ideals of independence and liberation.

RAJIKA BHANDARI: Did you, when you were on your way here, did you ever imagine you would be here—what—eight years now?

KANWAL RAHMAN: I said [to myself] it's maybe, it's my wanderlust, and, if I don't make it, fine, I'll come back. But I never imagined I would stay eight years. . . . My heart still wants to go back to Bangladesh. That's where my home is, and I think, America will always be a home—a second home—but never my first home.

RAJIKA BHANDARI: Could you talk a little bit about your experiences [in America]? And have they largely been positive, or negative, or mixed?

KANWAL RAHMAN: Well, I had a very hard time the first year, too . . . I don't really have a hard time with making friends but I do feel that I still have to explain a lot about myself. . . . I still feel that there are certain things that make me feel I am one of them but I'm still an outsider. . . . I don't know, it isn't anything to do with race or people; I think it's the American—, American-ness. . . . Of course, my expectations of very close-ness is different from the expectations of an American person. . . . It's a more . . .

independent culture and I guess independence is taught from the very childhood, which we [immigrants] are not taught, but thrown into.

RAJIKA BHANDARI: Do you think that that sense of community that you had back in Bangladesh is reflected here in any way? In the life that you live?

KANWAL RAHMAN: I would say there's no resemblance to what the life I left, lived back home. Even the sense of community—. Sure, I was a newly graduated dental surgeon, but I was still living with my parents and I had relations distant and close, dropping in all the time. You're having interactions of community festivals . . . wherever everyone goes regardless of any religion. . . . Here, more or less, it has been isolated because . . . people spend time with their own families and not go out of their way to invite, outsiders for the family . . . reunions during Christmas or Thanksgiving. There the life was more protected. Here the life is totally independent.

RAJIKA BHANDARI: I was wondering if you could talk a little about, a) how you feel you've changed as an individual, and b) how you've changed as a woman?

KANWAL RAHMAN: Well, of course, eight years in a culture without going back home . . . It has changed me a lot . . . It has made me mature . . . In Indian cultures— regardless whether it's Pakistan, Bangladesh, or India—girls, or daughters of relatively upper middle-class families, or upper class families, are sort of encouraged to be . . . "dependent." You are not allowed to drive, because your father forbade you, so you come to United States not being able to drive. You can't go out and do grocery shopping, because you've never done it, so you have to learn that. You have never cooked in your life because somebody had always cooked— whether it's your mother, or whether it was somebody [else]. So, those are the things that you learn very fast. How to be on your own footstep, and also, not to expect the world to do it for you, or give it to you. . . . You end up learning to respond the way they [Americans] expect you to. Not necessarily giving up your identity, but basically, you end up . . . behaving and acting in a way that is more common with Americans, and that's also giving out the image that you're very confident and mature, and responsible. . . . But inside, you can still be insecure, regardless of the fact that you have developed all these other aspects, too. The feeling of insecurity as a single Asian woman in America, for the future, or for anything or, you know, the fact that we don't have a support system—is there.

RAJIKA BHANDARI: Do you feel that the American experience has made a difference to how South Asians from each of the different South Asian countries . . . respond and react to each other?

KANWAL RAHMAN: . . . The way I feel every time I see a South Asian—, doesn't matter if he's from Burma or Sri Lanka and, you know, and I can just tell that he's from South Asia, I feel immediately bonded and I also feel that the other person bonds because they have a common basis of, if not language, a common cultural basis, common food habit basis —those are very strong aspects of a culture, food and other cultural aspects of, living and family life—that I think makes us feel more unified together . . . in America. . . . A lot of friends say, "You're very Americanized"—but I don't perceive how Americanized I am, because I don't feel as American as them. I'm not as American as apple pie, because I wasn't born or raised here, but I feel the bonding immediately with any South Asian person I see, regardless of the background.

RAJIKA BHANDARI: So, are you happy [in the United States]?

KANWAL RAHMAN: [pause] No, I'm not. . . . At this stage of my life, I'm looking, you know, looking for more, in just a career, and a good living. I'm looking for a meaning. Looking for a meaningful career which would give out, rather than take in. Like, you know, like public health, have a family. Those things are becoming more and more crucial as the years are going by. . . . And I guess I would define myself completely complete only when I have a meaningful career and a conducive home life and being able to step back into my country every two years. I think, right now, that is what I would strive as my ideal situation of living.

Source: Excerpted from Interview with Kanwal Rahman by Rajika Bhandari, 15 July 1999 (K-0817), in the Southern Oral History Program Collection (#4007), Southern Historical Collection, Louis Round Wilson Special Collections Library, University of North Carolina at Chapel Hill.

"Bangladesh in the Eyes of the Second Generation of Bangladeshi-Americans"

(2004, 2006)

The largest Bangladeshi community in the United States is located in Queens, New York. This is a relatively new immigrant population. Although Bengalis have been immigrating to the United States since the 19th century, Bangladesh did not exist as an independent nation until 1971. The following pieces were written by two young people, Rimi Dhar and Riman Dhar, and were introduced and edited by Jahed Ahmed. The essays highlight the teenagers' emotional and intellectual connection to Bangladesh history and culture—evidence of their own immigrant experience (both were born in Chittagong, a major city in southwestern Bangladesh)—and the influence of the adult immigrant community, which tends to maintain strong social and political ties to the homeland. In particular, both essays reference the 1952 Language Movement, during which students at the University of Dhaka demonstrated against Pakistan's establishment of Urdu as the country's (then West Bengal) sole official language. The movement remains a touch point for Bangladeshi American identity, even 50 years later.

The pieces were published by Mukto-Mona, an international Web organization that fosters communication and sponsors projects on behalf of events and people in Bangladesh. The organization's secular humanist philosophy represents a deliberate move away from the Bengali region's history of violent sectarian clashes between Muslims and Hindus. Bangladesh itself enshrined secularism (defined as freedom of religion) in its 1972 constitution, although several military regimes have attempted to establish Islam as the national religion (the country is nearly 90 percent Muslim), and the future of Bengali secularism is uncertain. Expatriates feel more freedom to criticize the

rising Islamic fundamentalism in Bangladesh, even if obliquely; this is evident in the essays' celebration of Rationalist Day.

JAHED AHMED, "INTRODUCTION"

It was February, 2004. M-M had decided to celebrate 1st March as a Rationalist Day. I was trying to collect articles from different sources. *How do the second generation of Bangladeshi-Americans— those who have been either born or raised in the USA—view the land of their parents and ancestors?* The question came into my mind. Biswarup Das Gupta, a longtime close friend of mine introduced me with a few young Bangladeshi-American school going students. Admittedly, from what I had seen I was skeptic that the second generations would not give much of a damn to Bangladesh. Just like citizens of their host country USA, most of the second-generation Bangladeshi Americans do not think highly of Bangladesh. At least that's what I thought. I, however, later realized—mine was an overly simplified conclusion. Not all are same, as the saying goes. I spoke to three young Bangladeshi Americans (although they rather identified themselves as Bangladeshi Bangalee): Tanni Baidya, Rimi Dhar and Rimon Dhar. Talking to them was a very pleasant experience for me. Their love, devotion and will to do something for Bangladesh and its people prove—they are a great and honorable exception to most children of their generations. . . .

RIMI DHAR, "*AMAR* BANGLADESH" (2004)

My name is Rimi Dhar. I am a Bangladeshi girl. I was born in Chittagong. I spent first few years of my life in Bangladesh. I came to America when I was 10 years. Today I am a junior student in

Fort Hamilton High School. In those 10 years, I saw many fabulous things that I haven't noticed in America. For instance, people of Bangladesh were so adorable and caring that even a fellow-Bangladeshi stranger looked like very dear to me, as if I knew him/her for long time. In the USA, however, I can't find the same expression or feelings inside people that I meet every day on the streets. Here people are very different than those in Bangladesh. It makes me sad to see that some of my fellow friends of Bangladesh origin in USA don't like to talk much about their motherland. They seem to be simply content with their identity such as "proud to be an American." However, there are certain things going on in Bangladesh that sometimes make me sad too. Sometimes I feel this is not what our ancestors dreamed about our country, neither do I myself. I dream of Bangladesh a peaceful nation where people from all the races live happily together, share feelings with each other, and where we all should stand together to fight those people who are against our culture and society. We should not forget that we are the only nation who fought for our mother language.

I am very proud of myself to be a Bangalee and a Bangladeshi. I want to see inside all the Bangladeshis Bangalees—pride, love and respect for our nation, and the promise to reach the dreams that our ancestors had during 1952 and 1971.

I greet all fellow Bangladeshi and other members of Mukto-Mona on the occasion of Rationalist Day celebration. I wish you all love, reason and peace!

New York
March 1, 2004

RIMON DHAR, "AMAR SONGLA BANGLA" (2006)

Hi! My name is Rimon Dhar. I was born in Chittagong, Bangladesh in 1989. My bad luck is that I didn't get the chance to live in Bangladesh for the rest of my life. I left Bangladesh for USA when I was only 8 years. Leaving so many friends and relatives behind was the hardest thing ever happened to me so far in my life. Now I am in the freshmen year in Fort Hamilton High School. In my school, I feel happy to see many other Bangladeshi students and love to think that we share same culture. But I am shocked about the fact that a few Bangladeshi children don't care much about our Bengali culture. They don't care about Bangladesh. They are rather proud identifying themselves as an American than a Bangladeshi. It shows—they are not patriot. I am not satisfied with their attitudes. Once our ancestors fought for our motherland. They fought for Bangla language. Anyway, I will do my job—to love and work for my country and its people.

People say, Bangladesh has changed a lot over last few years. However, I would love to live with the memory of a Bangladesh which is the sweetest place to live in!

WHAT I DREAM ABOUT BANGLADESH
I have a dream that—
People in Bangladesh will live peacefully.

I have a dream that—
People in Bangladesh will have a happy life.

In next few years, I want to see my Bangladesh as a peaceful, self-sufficient and an educated nation where every citizen will think of the betterment of our country whether we live at home or abroad.

AMAR SONAR BANGLA, AMI TOMAY VALOBASHI

Source: Dhar, Rimi. "Amar Bangladesh." 2004. Dhar, Rimon. "Amar Songla Bangla." 2006. Excerpted from "Bangladesh in the Eyes of the Second Generation of Bangladeshi-Americans," Jahed Ahmed, ed. Mukto-Mona .http://mukto-mona.net/Articles/jahed/2nd_generation_ Bangladeshi_Americans.htm.

Farah Akbar, "A Troubling Cultural Gap"
(2010)

Religion often plays a key part in immigrant identity, facilitating cultural continuity and community cohesiveness in an unfamiliar and unsettling environment. The lines between culture, ethnicity, and religion are blurry, however, and as immigrants and their children begin to adapt to and incorporate aspects of American life, these demarcations begin to be questioned and challenged. For Asian American Muslims, the issue is particularly fraught, as people wrestle with the Americanization of Islam.

Farah Akbar was born in Bangladesh, moved to the United States when she was a child, and grew up in Queens, New York. She is a freelance author who writes about civil rights and immigrant issues and the Muslim American community. Her essay "A Troubling Cultural Gap," written for Salon.com, explores second-generation Asian American Muslims: how they struggle to reconcile widely disparate questions of sexuality, radicalism, liberalism, and popular culture with Islam; how they attempt to mesh their evolving religious, ethnic, and national identities; and how they answer for themselves what it means to be truly Muslim in America.

Ishak Khan, 17, wants to know if it's OK to get a tattoo in his religion. He also wants to know if it's OK to write rap songs and if it's OK to have a Muslim girlfriend.

Like many of his Muslim American contemporaries, Ishak isn't quite sure how to balance his religion with American culture. He does talk to friends about these issues, but he'd really like to speak with an adult who understands both American culture and Islam. But he can't really talk to his parents because they're very traditional, and he's definitely not going to that imam "straight out of Bangladesh" who gives the boring sermons at the Queens, N.Y., mosque he attends once a month.

"I don't think I can connect or talk to him, because he's not from here," says Ishak, who was born here to Bangladeshi parents. "I can't even tell him that I write music, 'cause he's just gonna tell me that it's bad. And if I tell him about getting a tattoo, he's gonna tell me that it will look dirty." And about the girlfriend? "He's gonna say it's haram [forbidden]."

Says the aspiring rapper: "I just want a cool person who I can ask questions to and who can give me a reasonable response."

Ishak's dilemma is one familiar to many Muslim Americans of his generation. Going to a mosque to pray or to receive Islamic education is an integral part of their lives. Though not all young Muslims are mosque-goers, those who do go often look to their local imams for guidance, only to be turned off by the cultural gap that exists between them. This has caught the attention of some Muslim community members, who fear that too many young American Muslims are left feeling alienated and frustrated.

Some Muslims are voicing their opinions and calling for change. They would like imams, who tend to be older, male and "imported," to be able to connect with a generation of Muslims raised in America. They also want mosques, which have the potential to develop leadership and community-building skills among young Muslims, to make youth outreach a priority. Failing to address these issues, they fear, could sever the connection between a generation of American Muslims and their religion.

There may be another fear, too. Abdul Malik Mujahid, an imam and author, has written that young people who feel marginalized or alienated can constitute "a breeding ground for extremism."

A common frustration among young Muslim Americans is that many imams speak to their congregations in languages other than English, often to accommodate immigrants who are more comfortable with their native tongue. (Some imams themselves may be more comfortable speaking in their native tongues as well.) This can leave the younger generation, which often has limited or no knowledge of its parents' mother tongues, uninterested.

Muntasir Sattar, 30, who works with many Muslim youths as a program coordinator at the South Asian Youth Action organization in New York, has seen how this causes the imam's message to go right over the heads of younger congregants—even when it's aimed straight at them.

"A lot of Khutbahs [sermons] on Fridays are about youth, about vices and virtues and the importance of staying on the right path," he says, "but from a youth's perspective, they're like, 'OK, that's great, but you're talking in Arabic, or Urdu or Bengali, and I don't speak that language!'" he says.

Ishak admits that he's dozed off more than once during sermons, usually when they've been delivered in Bengali. "I speak Bengali, but it would be better if it was in English. I'd understand it better," he says. He does remember one time hearing a great sermon in English about how praying to Allah can make life less stressful during trying times. "I had exams and I was so worried. I prayed to Allah that I would pass them and I did," Ishak recalls. He would like sermons to be about issues closer to his life.

Tania Ahmed, a 17-year-old high school senior, agrees that language is an issue. (Tania is not her actual name, which she asked be withheld.) "I don't care where [the imam] comes from, as long as he can communicate," she says. If the imam cannot speak in English, it hurts the youth who are seeking answers about their faith, Tania says. And she feels that some imams are too judgmental. "I know that some of them would react in a certain preachy way if I were to ask them about personal issues," she says. "They might even just shun you," she says. "I wouldn't really go to anyone outside my circle of friends."

But many imams believe it's their job to provide a rigidly Islamic viewpoint on issues and that even stylistic concessions to American culture are out of the question. Ben Yahya Abdel-Ghani, the director of the Flushing Muslim Center in Queens, says that when young people ask him for his advice, he has to answer according to the rules of Islam. Abdel-Ghani, 45, is from Morocco and has been living in the United States since 1997. Should a young person ask about whether it was OK to drink alcohol, his answer would be swift. "All kids know that alcohol is wrong," he says in slightly accented English. "Alcohol is prohibited—so the discussion is almost closed."

Abdel-Ghani admits that youth don't often go to him for advice about personal matters, but, for example, if a young person were to confide to him that he or she might be gay (a situation he says he's never encountered), he would reply that being gay in Islam is not accepted. "Youngsters know that the answer will be that it is wrong," he insists. "They have to find a way to solve the problem. I don't think they will have the urge to say it to someone who is older."

Another issue complicating youth outreach is financial, with many mosques struggling just to pay their rent. Immigrant mosques in New York, for instance, are often run by working-class individuals and limited funds tend to be an issue. Sattar, the SAYA program coordinator, understands this and empathizes with these mosque officials, but he stresses that mosques should try to find room for youth programs even in their tight budgets. "Youth need opportunities to be active in their religious institutions," he says. "They need those roles, those opportunities, to shape the world."

Dr. Mahbubur Rahman, a professor of political science at the City University of New York who teaches a course called Islam and Democracy, agrees. He thinks that this is a way young Muslims can steer clear of fringe Muslim groups that may have extremist agendas or whose teachings are not in line with mainstream Islam. For example, the "Lackawana Six," a group of young Muslim American men from Buffalo, ended up in a militant training camp in Afghanistan. They were apparently recruited by a man named Kamal

Derwish, who preached a radical brand of Islam and who won them over through meetings in his apartment. (Derwish was ultimately killed in a CIA mission in Yemen.)

A symbol of hope for Muslim American reformers can be found in the heart of Manhattan's West Village, the home base of a man who epitomizes the kind of spiritual leadership that so many young American Muslims yearn for.

Khalid Latif, 27, serves as the first-ever Muslim chaplain at the school's Islamic Center, a place that he boasts of running on progressive values rooted in authentic Islamic sources. Latif graduated from New York University with degrees in political science and Middle Eastern studies and attended the Hartford Theological Seminary briefly, then became the executive director of the Islamic Center at 24. He is also the youngest chaplain ever hired by the New York Police Department, brought in to cater to the spiritual needs of Muslim officers and civilian employees.

Latif says he understands why some young people don't feel comfortable going to religious places. Born and raised in New Jersey, he doesn't have fond memories of the local mosque he attended as a teenager. Back then, he had long hair and no beard, a violation of Muslim tradition, and congregants would accuse him of attending services just to mingle with the girls. "People weren't very nice to me," he recalls.

Membership at NYU's Islamic Center has increased significantly since he took over. He is well-liked and popular among students. One Pakistani-American student named Raza, after finishing his afternoon prayers, wrote "I love the I.C." on a whiteboard near the center's entrance. Raza credits Latif for uniting Sunni Muslims and Shia Muslims in prayer, something the student, who is of the Shia sect, had never experienced before. "It was really special," he says. "It was an incredible feeling."

Students come to Latif to seek his advice about any and all issues, including some that are traditionally deemed "haram," or forbidden, in Islam. They appreciate his easygoing attitude and feel comfortable enough to talk to him about sexuality,

depression, mental-health issues, domestic violence, relationships and even experiences of rape.

So is Latif a rare breed of imam? "I'm not like Nemo, alone in this ocean of loneliness," he says. As the Muslim community begins to respond to the needs of its diverse members, he believes, more imams who espouse progressive values that are in line with Islamic teachings will emerge. "As needs have changed, as dynamics have changed, I think it's just a logical trend to a people who are well versed in how this society functions that they are going to be stepping into roles as community activists and leaders and specifically, at times, even imams," Latif says.

Sitting on the floor of the large prayer room located in the basement of a white church that serves as the Islamic Center, he says: "What it means to be an imam is contingent upon a community's needs at the time." He is wearing blue jeans, a blue button-down shirt, has a trimmed beard and is wearing a black skullcap called a "kufi." "In some Muslim countries and in immigrant mosques, the idea isn't that the imam will be a community leader," he adds. "He's expected to just lead the prayers."

Latif isn't sure if it matters whether an imam was raised in the U.S., or if he's young or old. "It's hard to create an archetype on what an individual needs to be like that can deal with the diversity of some 8 million Muslims [in the U.S.]," he says. "Different people have their own preferences."

If a student confides to Latif that he or she might be gay, he won't claim that homosexuality is permissible in Islam. "But, like, it doesn't change the fact that we have kids or adults who are homosexuals," he says. "An outright denial of its existence causes us to have more issues than solutions."

After listening to a student talk about his or her background, he encourages the student to understand what his or her "life choice" means. "Some people will be nice to you, some people will treat you like garbage," Latif might say.

"With any issue, it's about, 'Where do we go from here?'" he says. "In Islamic tradition, you see numerous instances with men and women going to the prophet Mohammed, peace be upon him, about their sins. The relationship with the Prophet was such that you could speak with him and he wouldn't be judgmental. He would respond in a way that made the most sense for the person coming to him with the issue."

Being a young and progressive imam has its challenges, too. "Especially in religious communities, when somebody comes in and does it differently, you kind of have to legitimize yourself," says Latif. "You have to prove to people that they can take you seriously. Because you're dealing with religion. And if you're wrong, Muslims perceive that wrong means hell."

At first, he says, people thought that NYU's Islamic center was too liberal. But now he claims that those same people simply see the center as "accepting."

Young Muslims in America are clearly hungry for some spiritual guidance from the right people, and they're asking for some specific things. For one, they say, imams should be raised or should at least understand what it's like growing up in America. They also shouldn't be quite so judgmental. And being on the younger end, though not required, is desirable. They should also be able to speak English and be reasonably current with American culture and technology. Ishak, the 17-year-old aspiring rapper, says he's met another imam, a young, American man, who showed him some Islamic prayers on YouTube that he liked a lot. "I don't think my imam [from the Queens mosque] even knows what YouTube is," he notes.

Tania once heard Latif speak at a conference and she absolutely loved what he had to say. Latif spoke about peer pressure and about the challenges of being a Muslim teenager in America. Still, she doubts that she'd ever confide in any imam about her personal life. "Except," she says shyly, "maybe for Khalid Latif."

Source: Akbar, Farah. "A Troubling Cultural Gap." May 16, 2010. This article first appeared in Salon.com at http://www.Salon.com. An online version remains in the Salon archives. Reprinted with permission.

Reihan Salam, "About Me"

(2012)

Reihan Salam is a conservative political commentator and columnist; he writes for The National Review *and* Reuters. *His parents moved from Bangladesh in 1976, during the first wave of Bangladeshi immigration to the United States. Salam was born and raised in New York City, home to the nation's largest Bangladeshi American population. Salam's short biography gives a humorous account of his life as the youngest child of immigrant parents, his haphazard college years, and his career development into a policy analyst.*

Reihan Salam (b. December 29, 1979) is an American non-fiction writer and policy analyst.

Raised by two exceptionally intelligent, cool, and eccentric parents, he was the third of three children, and by all accounts a taciturn shut-in as a small child, primarily interested in LEGO and reruns of *Full House*. He did, however, rock a stylish bowl cut for most of his youth. His heroes as a small boy were his sisters, various superheroes, and his sisters' high school friends, one of whom was notorious for casually carrying around a machete. His middle sister, Anjum, would regularly send him mixtapes from California, with a heavy emphasis on monologues by Jim Carroll and Jello Biafra and music from the Pharcyde and the Beastie Boys. Basically, she played an essential role in informing and shaping his emerging tastes and sensibilities. His oldest sister Rifat sparked his interest in comic books, film, and all things foreign. And though his parents worked near-constantly, they provided the family with a constant stream of magazines, books, and charged conversation about race, culture, politics, and the virtues of a balanced diet.

As a student at Stuyvesant High School, he had a checkered academic record, redeemed in part by a mostly untutored intellectual curiosity. Fortunately, his best friend, now a distinguished economist, shamed him into not actually flunking out by being a pretty amazing example of dedication, creativity, and general dopeness.

He had the good fortune to attend the Telluride Association Summer Program, an experience he credits with "lighting a fire under his ass" and convincing him that the pursuit of academic excellence was not, in fact, "for the birds."

After an intellectually fruitful but socially problematic year at Cornell University, where he'd often spend Friday nights reading biographies of Walter Reuther in the stacks, he transferred to Harvard, where he concentrated in Social Studies. His senior thesis, on the normative implications of pervasive public ignorance, was written hastily and under extreme duress, reflecting what was fast becoming a lifelong pattern. His intellectual development was for the most part self-directed, though he profited immensely from having taken two seminars with the political scientist Samuel P. Huntington, a fellow Stuyvesant alumnus and an unfailingly generous scholar.

Having graduated in 2001, a year that coincided with what in hindsight looks more and more like a minor economic speed bump, he was quite confident that in lieu of finding suitable employment, he'd become a handsome grifter, roaming the countryside in search of easy marks. The trouble, alas, was the handsome part. And so he instead spent a short period of time as a reporter-researcher at *The New Republic*, influenced in part by his admiration for the work of senior editor and pioneering political blogger Andrew Sullivan. This was followed by a similarly brief stint as a research associate at the Council on Foreign Relations.

Shortly after David Brooks had been hired as a columnist at the *New York Times*, he pluckily decided to apply for a position as Brooks's editorial researcher, where he spent the next two years. Having admired Brooks for some years, he was impressed to learn that the newly-minted columnist was exactly as kind, humble, and insightful as he seemed to be from a distance. For a few short months, he served as a junior editor for the *New York Times* op-ed page before leaving (a bit too abruptly) to become a producer for NBC Universal's *The Chris Matthews Show*. Roughly two years on, he served for a time as an associate editor at *The Atlantic* before accepting a fellowship at the New America Foundation. At some point during this stretch, he decided to start shaving his head, not realizing that this would lead some of his detractors to conclude that he was a beardless Barbary Corsair hellbent on seizing treasure on the high seas. He also co-authored a book, which you can indeed purchase for the astonishingly low price of $0.01, with one of his very good friends, Ross Douthat.

He is now a policy advisor at e21and the lead blogger for *National Review Online*'s The Agenda and a contributing editor at *National Review*, where he writes on politics and policy, economics, and culture. He also serves as a CNN contributor and as an interviewer for VBS.tv. Despite his controversial eyebrows, he has appeared on CNN, ABC, PBS, FOX, NBC, MSNBC, BBC, CBC, TVO, AJE, RT, HBO, and a number of other television networks that may or may not exist outside of his imagination. He also appears on the radio, where listeners are less likely to be alarmed by his disconcertingly shiny pate.

He has given talks at PopTech (an unmitigated disaster), Georgetown, the National Constitution Center, Yale, Zócalo Public Square, the National Defense University, Macalester College, the

Personal Democracy Forum, and points beyond. To put it crudely, he'll go anywhere there is delicious free food.

He has a long-standing interest in, among other things, economic geography, the history of ideas, diasporas and migration, comparative politics, political economy, cities, and diets rich in saturated fats and Omega-3. To the surprise of many, he has suddenly started writing a lot of long-form stuff.

Though born in New York, NY, at Bellevue Hospital, he spent his formative years in Brooklyn, first in Borough Park and then in the shadowy borderland between Kensington and Ditmas Park. At present, he lives in the West Village, though he often works from other cities as part of an ongoing effort to stay one step ahead of "The Fuzz."

Source: Salam, Reihan. "About Me." http://reihansalam .com/about/.

Karen Kauv Sun, Interview by Janean Baker

(1993)

Karen Kauv Sun, born and raised in the Cambodian countryside, moved to the capital city of Phnom Penh in 1964 after graduating from high school. While living in Phnom Penh, Sun worked as a nurse, married a professor, and had three children. Then, the Khmer Rouge took power in 1975 and began enacting their sociopolitical engineering programs to transform Cambodia into a communist agrarian society. The Suns were caught up in the anti-intellectual purges and were sent to the reeducation camps, where Sun's husband was killed. In 1979, Sun escaped to Thailand along with her children; the next year, they were sponsored for immigration to the United States by her cousin, under the auspices of the newly passed Refugee Act. A few years later, she met some Mormon missionaries and became a convert.

In the following excerpts from her interview with Brigham Young University's Janean Baker, Sun talks about the similarities and connections she sees between Mormonism, her own life history, and Cambodian culture. She speaks extensively about the practical aspects of being part of the church: specifically, the community and social aspects as well as the help she received in navigating an unfamiliar American culture. However, Sun is equally adamant about her commitment to and love for the Mormon church; she frames the sincerity of her faith as entirely separate from the pragmatic benefits of being a Latter-day Saint.

S: After I lived with my cousin for three months [after arriving in the United States], I got money from the government to help me. I got an apartment by myself. It had two bedrooms. I started to go to school . . . I finished the English class. The lady teacher said, "You are writing good. Everything is good for you in English but speaking. You need to communicate with the people. You need to go to get a job." I was a nurse. They found a job at nursing home for me . . .

God blessed me. I moved to another apartment. I met the missionaries of our church, the Mormon church. It was 1984. This is how I met the missionaries . . . Mr. Brown and Sister Brown . . . talked about teaching me about the gospel and about Book of Mormon. I understood them. They showed a movie. I felt something. I thought, "These two are not like Cambodian family. They like to live together. They like family together." After the movie, I said to Elder and Sister Brown, "Why don't you come to visit me? I want to show my children the movie." She asked me my address and phone number.

She came to my house. She taught me about the gospel. I learned. After that I was baptized. Elder Brown baptized me. It was in 1984. It was in June or July, something like that.

B: Were all three of your children baptized?

S: Yes, all three together. They learned, and then they were baptized, too.

I learned more English. It is the true church. It is the same as my country people. They like the family together. I believed. I learned more and more so I start believing in the church. It is the true church. The Bible is true. It's real. Book of Mormon is very interesting. It is the same way that I escaped.

I worked very hard. I'm so happy. I am very proud of myself. I can remember my husband. I can do my job as a housewife and work. I can take care of three children, go to school, and go to work. I feed my children. I know that God loves me. I'm in good health. I take care of everything. I go to church all the time and teach my children.

After I learned in my Bible and Book of Mormon, I knew it was a good way to send children to church. I am by myself. If they go to church, they learn more about good things. They can help me because I'm a single parent. The Church can help me learn good things . . .

B: Has the culture been an adjustment for you and your children?

S: I was born in Cambodia country. My children grow up here. It's very hard for me. It's very different.

B: In what ways?

S: This country is too free. Over there they are very strict with the kids.

B: In what ways?

S: We train the kid. We can spank a little bit. It is not too much. It is just a little bit to let them know, "Don't do this wrong." They respect the parents more. My generation respects the family more, brother and sister.

We come here. We cannot do anything. We train them how to be good. Sometimes they do not listen to us. We cannot spank them and hit them. I hit the children a little bit, and they say, "I don't want to do anything to get spanked a little bit."

It's hard. When they go to school, they know if a teacher hits them it is child abuse. They call police. We cannot do anything. It's happened with children in this country. It's very hard. . . .

B: How did your relatives respond to your joining the Church? What did your cousin who sponsored you do when he found out you joined the Church?

S: He said, "It's good. Find a church for your children. It is up to you. It's okay. It's freedom. This country is a free country. If you think it's a good way to go, you go." He didn't say anything . . .

B: How do you feel non-member Cambodians feel about the church?

S: Most people that come over here are Buddhist. It's hard to change from Buddhist to Christian until people learn. But some people come from Cambodia. Educated people are being killed. Most people are killed. I heard two million people were killed by hunger and by sickness. Of the rest of the people, some don't know how to greet Cambodian. They never went to school. Those people came over here to United States.

It's hard for them sometimes. They need a translator when a missionary goes to the house. Not too many people have free time to go along every Sunday. There were not too many members when I became a member.

Some Cambodians believe and some do not. Now more people come. They have become members of the Church. They believe strongly that they need to go to church. But some people are uncomfortable by not understanding English.

But now more missionaries know how to speak Cambodian. I heard in the Asian branch now that more people come now. I don't know in the future . . .

B: Do the Cambodians like them or dislike [the Mormon missionaries]?

S: In general, they like them. Sometime they don't like the missionaries knocking on the door and going right away. Sometimes they have privacy, too. It is better if the missionaries have started to know them already. They should call and make a time. They knock on the door and see the house is messy. They cooked and spilled. They don't like that. They want to inspect the carpet and they prepare everything.

One lady came to my house. She's a member of the church, too. She said, "Missionaries always go to my house, but sometime I feel like I don't want to go to the house because my house is messy. It smells. I cooked some Cambodian food. It has a Chinese food smell." It's good if they go to the house and call first.

B: Are there any other things that you think the missionaries could do to improve their missionary work among the Cambodians?

S: If they go to their houses, they invite you to eat their food . . . I know sometimes it is different food.

Some may not like that. They should at least drink the water. Then we are happy. We don't force them to eat, but sometime we feel, "The missionaries don't like my family and Cambodians."

My people are very friendly especially when they were in Cambodia, but now they are mixed up. If missionary do that, maybe they will be happy. The missionaries should be kind, friendly, smiling, and talking. We like people that are friendly. If people don't talk to us, we say that is discrimination or prejudice. They don't want to get close with them and go to church . . .

B: Tell me about your children's dating and social experiences. Have the Church's teachings have helped them? Do you think that being members of the Church has helped your children?

S: Yes, I think it has helped a lot. For me as the mother, the parent, it's hard to teach them. We didn't have dating over there. They come to church and they teach them about dating. I think it helps a lot. I teach them, but I've never been to an American school. It's hard for me to teach them. They know better than me. I teach them the Cambodian ways. It's not right how to grow up in this country.

For me, a parent, it is very hard to be from Cambodian culture to American culture. But I learn a lot from going to church and from going to work. Everywhere I ask what to do when my children grow up to teenager and how to deal with them.

I don't tell my daughter anything. If you go out and bring problems to the home, it's okay. If you go somewhere, call wherever you are. I teach my children, "Just let me know where you are. If you report, I'm happy. You go out, then tell me with whom."

I like to do the middle, not too tight, not too loose, not too easy. I know my children grow up with different culture. I went to the high school. I saw a lot of teenage boyfriends and girlfriends kissing at school. It is hard for me to see. I am thinking about my children. Maybe they do the same thing.

I don't know why in this country they are not a little bit stricter for the teenagers. They're too easy for the kids . . .

B: Overall has the Church influenced your life?

S: I think it's good for me. I learn a lot. It is better than staying home and not know about the war going on. I go to church. Every time something new come up. They tell me about a storm coming up. They told us how to change the time back. That would be something new especially if I didn't speak English. I didn't know about the change of time. I like going to church.

Source: Karen Kauv Sun Oral History Project. Interviewed by Janean Baker, April 1, 1993. LDS Asian American Oral History Project, Charles Redd Center for Western Studies, L. Tom Perry Special Collections, Harold B. Lee Library, Brigham Young University. Used with permission of the Charles Redd Center.

Kong Phok, Interview by Barbara Lau

(2000)

The roots of Cambodian migration to the United States can be traced to America's involvement in the Vietnam War. During the war, the United States conducted secret carpet-bombing campaigns targeting North Vietnamese troops and supplies in Cambodia. The destruction caused by these campaigns created strong anti-American feelings and increased support for the communist Khmer Rouge. When Saigon fell in 1975 and the United States withdrew from Vietnam, the Khmer Rouge quickly defeated Lon Nol's U.S.-supported government. Under Pol Pot, the Khmer Rouge instituted a radical

program intended to create an agrarian socialist state. The vehicle for this societal restructuring was a brutal forced labor program that eliminated political opponents, ethnic minorities, religious communities, the professional and educated classes, and any other groups that posed a threat to Khmer Rouge rule. Over the next five years, 2 million people, one-third of the Cambodian population, were killed, mostly by starvation and disease, in what became known as the "Killing Fields."

In 1979, Vietnam defeated Cambodia and the Khmer Rouge regime fell. In the meantime, thousands of Cambodians had been escaping to refugee camps in neighboring Thailand and applying to the United States and other countries for asylum. Kong Phok was one such refugee. Born in Battambong, Cambodia, in 1976, Phok, his parents, and two of his siblings escaped first to Thai and then to Philippine refugee camps when the Khmer Rouge took power. In 1985, sponsored by an American Lutheran family, they joined Phok's uncle in Greensboro, North Carolina. After his graduation from high school, Phok got a job as a machine operator at Guilford Mills, a textile factory in North Carolina. After a few years, he was promoted to supervisor; however, the mill then closed down operations in Greensboro and moved to Mexico. In the following excerpt from his interview with Barbara Lau, Phok describes how he negotiates his identity as both a Cambodian and an American.

BARBARA LAU: We were talking about how you think about yourself—you think about yourself as Cambodian-American?

KONG PHOK: Yes.

BARBARA LAU: Why that instead of Cambodian? How do you figure that out?

KONG PHOK: Because I spend so many my life—I mean, you can say more of my lifetime in America than Cambodia, but I am always Cambodian, would never change. But I celebrate every holiday like American people do. Actually, I'm doing everything almost exactly the same like American. That's how I consider myself as Cambodian-American, because I spend more of my lifetime [in the U.S.], more than in my own country. But I'm Cambodian.

BARBARA LAU: Do you sometimes feel like there's a struggle there, or you're being pulled in different directions?

KONG PHOK: No, never. I never had that problem.

BARBARA LAU: You just kind of bring it all into the center?

KONG PHOK: Yeah, just I have people ask me all the time, just say, how you feel? You think you're American or Americanized, or whatever. I think I say I'm both. I'm Cambodian and American, I guess. That's how I feel. Maybe it's not like that, but that's how I feel.

BARBARA LAU: What kind of people ask you that question?

KONG PHOK: Friend (sic), workers, people who you know. See some people, they won't admit to themselves, you know. They don't believe themselves like Cambodian or Cambodian-American or Americanized Cambodian or whatever, because that's two different thing. I am Americanized Cambodian, and like I said, I'll respect, I'll cherish, I'll do everything Cambodian, but right now I consider myself as Cambodian-American, because America is like my country too.

BARBARA LAU: What do you think about your son? What will you tell him?

KONG PHOK: I'm not going to tell him. I'm just going to tell him that you [are] both. You're Cambodian, Laos [Phok's wife is Lao American], and I'm not going to teach him what, hey you are Cambodian, you're not Laos or anything. It's up to him. It's not up to him if I keep on telling him, yeah, you're Cambodian or whatever. Like myself, I am Cambodian, Laos and American, you know. I mean, it's not Cambodian only; I'm Laos because my wife is Laos. I have, you can say, two different blood because I'm not really American blood, but I consider myself American. But my kid has, you know, two different bloods, and he is Cambodian, Laos and American. I know this might be hard for him when he grow up.

Source: Excerpt from interview with Kong Phok by Barbara Lau, 19 December 2000 (K-0273), in the Southern Oral History Program Collection (#4007), Southern Historical Collection, Louis Round Wilson Special Collections Library, University of North Carolina at Chapel Hill. Reprinted with permission.

Ran Kong, Interview by Barbara Lau
(2001)

Ran Kong, originally from Cambodia, was 21 years old and a student at Salem College in Winston-Salem, North Carolina, when the United States was attacked on September 11, 2001. A month later, she spoke with Barbara Lau from the American Folklife Center's "September 11, 2001, Documentary Project." Kong recalled being mistaken for an Arab and explained how her family members' reactions to the attacks were conditioned by their memories of wartime Cambodia, their continuing ties to family in the homeland, and their ambiguous position as immigrants in the United States.

BARBARA LAU: Did [the attack] make you think differently at all about your own future?

RAN KONG: Yes, my initial thought was, 'OK, they'd already suspected it was going to be terrorists.' Then the name Osama Bin Laden came up, and 'Arabics,' and my impression was, *You know what? Americans right now probably aren't going to like foreigners. And even though I'm a US citizen, they're not going to know that. They're not going to be able to tell just by looking at me.* And, this was actually confirmed [wry laugh] when I went to work on the following Saturday . . . I went to work [at a local hospital] the next day, and this lady, the first question that she asked me was "Are you Arabic?" She was on a ventilator, so I couldn't tell—was she asking me this? So I read her lips again, and was like "What?" and she said, "Are you Arabic?" — she mouthed it again—and I said, "No. I'm not Arabic." And she said, "Well, what are you?" And I said, "I'm Cambodian." And she said again, "Is that Arabic?" . . . I

told her "Cambodia's in Southeast Asia; it's Asia, but it's not the Middle East, and it's not really anywhere near where Osama Bin Laden is from . . . " And so from a *patient*, who was on a ventilator, who couldn't get up and do anything to me, I felt really uncomfortable. But then I stepped out of the hospital after work, and I just thought, "If it had been a guy, on the street, that had approached me and asked me that, what was I to do?" You know, would he have believed me? And so, I just can't imagine being in New York City, and looking like . . . me. Or anybody with brown skin and black hair. Of Asian descent.

BARBARA LAU: Do you think your reaction to it was similar to your family's or was yours different?

RAN KONG: I think it's different, simply because my parents actually lived through a war; they lived through all the atrocities. So for them, immediately: 'There's going to be a war. You know, war is really bad. We remember what war is like. The hunger, the fear—feeling unsafe all the time.' For me, I think I have more belief in the American government; I have a working knowledge of how America might handle things. Just being able to keep up with the news, and being able to understand what's going—but for my parents, who are not going to understand everything that's broadcast on the station—they just see the American people's reactions. For them, their immediate fear is: 'They're not going to like us. They're not going to want us here anymore. What's going to happen to us, what's going to happen to my family? I'm not a US citizen. You know, my kids are [citizens] — what's going to happen with that?'

BARBARA LAU: ...What do you think people in the Cambodian community did as a result of this?

RAN KONG: I think their first thought was 'OK... what happens in a war time, well: there's no food. There's no money.' I don't know how many people actually went out to the banks and withdrew money. But for my parents, their first thought was 'Well, how much cash do we have at home right now? And we need to go to the store, let's go ahead and buy some stuff.' We went to our store, bought like 15 more bags of rice, to keep at home... And I think that to a certain extent that other families are doing the same thing. The Cambodian store, the only Cambodian store in Greensboro, by Tuesday night: no more bags of rice. The owner herself was like, "Wait, we were supposed to keep some for our family. We don't even have some for our own family! It's all gone." And I just thought that was really funny.

BARBARA LAU: Do you think that your family or other families in this community are afraid that the war's going to come to Greensboro, that things could happen here?

RAN KONG: I think so... People in Cambodia heard about this, and... are afraid, because, we are their backbones, here, and if we're gone, then what's going to happen to them?... Yes, maybe you can take care of your family here, but what's going to happen with your family over in Cambodia? What if we can never fly again, to go visit

them; what if we never ever get to see our native country again?

BARBARA LAU: What do you think about the choices that have been made about how to respond to what happened last September 11th?

RAN KONG: ... It wasn't until recently that Bush gave the go-ahead to start bombing Afghanistan, and just seeing the situation, the country— from a refugee standpoint: just seeing the images of the Afghani people living in the refugee camps, and dying in the refugee camps, that that really—it really bothers me... I personally disagree with just bombing a country, even though you say, "Oh, you know, in the end it's going to help the Afghani people to have the Taliban taken out, and have all the terrorists rid of." But... we're doing what the terrorists did, by bombing these people. We're killing innocent civilians, too... Maybe the world needs to stop, and... just look, look at your foreign policy, look at how you treat the other countries, look at how other countries treat smaller nations... I know that America—Nixon—bombed Cambodia too, during the Vietnam War, and we were a neutral country; we weren't really directly involved with the Vietnam War, yet we were bombed also. And so just taking—stepping back and maybe re-examine everything instead of just reacting out of anger...

Source: Excerpted from Interview with Ran Kong, conducted by Barbara Lau, Greensboro, North Carolina, October 14, 2001, September 11, 2001, Documentary Project Collection (AFC 2001/015), Archive of Folk Culture, American Folklife Center, Library of Congress. http://hdl.loc.gov/loc.afc/afc2001015.sr320a01. Reprinted with permission from Ran Kong.

Leendavy Koung, "You Cannot Lose Your Spirit"
(2001)

Defying traditional Cambodian mores, which stipulate that only men can become professional musicians, Leendavy Koung's father taught her to play Khmer musical instruments when she was a child. After the Vietnam War reached Cambodia in 1969, the Koung family fled their country to escape Pol Pot, Cambodia's brutal dictator. They carried their father's handcrafted instruments through the jungles to Thailand and brought them with them to the United States, where they settled in Philadelphia.

Today, Koung is a teacher in her immigrant Philadelphia community, working to preserve Cambodian musical and dance forms in the United States. In 2001, Koung spoke with Debora Kodish from the Philadelphia Folklore Project, a 20-year-old independent public folklife agency. In her interview, Koung talks about how arts and culture give immigrants a strong sense of identity and about the importance of the younger generation taking responsibility for cultural preservation.

Back then, when I was a child, music never interested me. I always wanted to learn to dance. When you are dancing you get to interact with other children, wear nice clothes, be out there on stage, and look beautiful. Dancing was more fun and exciting than being a musician.

Playing music, you had to sit still, and you didn't get to dress up nice! And, especially, I didn't like it because my dad would wake me up at four or five o'clock in the morning, when everybody else was still having good dreams. There I was, out there early in the morning, trying to hit the instruments and trying to find all the sounds. Sometimes I practiced in tears, but I had to do it because he wanted me to. He forced me to learn! In fact, none of my brothers and sisters wanted to learn music either, but the thing was, we had the gift. We were talented at it, and we could learn so much. . . .

In Cambodian music, I did not learn by reading notes. Everything is in your head. You have to remember the sounds. You have to remember where the sounds are at. That's how I was taught. When I was learning to play the *khim* [a Cambodian hammered dulcimer], my father would tell me where to hit with the hammers. So pretty much you have to recognize where all the sounds are at. From learning the *khim*, I kind of got the sounds in my head, so then I could pick up any instrument. Now, I can learn any instrument on my own, any song or music, as long as I can hear the music. The basic learning is in my head already. I have the sounds. All I need to do is to use that sound and turn it to music. That's how I learned and that's how I still learn.

So when I was little, I went along and tried to learn. And it came in my head that the way to make my dad stop teaching me was to learn everything, so he would have nothing left to teach. That way, I thought I could get some free time! If he taught me one thing, the next day I'd learn three different things! He would teach me one instrument. I'd catch up—learning two or three other instruments, sometimes on my own. He would teach me one, two or three songs—I would learn five or 10 songs over the next week or month or so. I caught up so fast that now I know almost more instruments, songs and music than he does, which is weird.

One thing that has always motivated me to learn, even when I didn't love music, was that I always have wanted to challenge myself. Always. If I see an instrument, I try to see if I can play it. And I find I can do it! I don't always play music because I love it—I do it because I want to know. I want to find out what it is, and how I can learn it, and if I have the ability to learn it.

It was only later on in my life that I came to recognize the importance, the value, of music. Now, I really, really, appreciate my dad so much for teaching me all that he did. Now, I am so happy that he forced me to learn all that music and all those instruments. Because now I understand that it is very important. Especially when you come from a country like Cambodia, where not a lot of artists survived the killing fields.

I have come to realize that in our culture, music is the most important thing of all. Everything we do—weddings, funerals—everything has to have music. The sad thing about it is that now we have to dance to taped music instead of live music. It makes it more difficult for the dancers to learn, because they have to follow the tape. And sometime we have to cut out some of the hand gestures that a dance is supposed to have, and dancers have to fit themselves into the amount of time on the taped music that we got from wherever! You don't feel like you are doing a full performance. It's following something that's not real. That's the sad thing about it nowadays, for us, is doing any performance here.

As a teacher, I want the children of this generation to recognize their arts and culture. A lot of the Cambodian parents who went through the war and who came to live here don't have great communication with their children. If Cambodian children are going to wait to learn about their culture and their history from their parents, forget it! It's not going to happen. For one thing, the parents are working hard making enough money to support the family. There are so many expenses here. In their country, there were no taxes. And we could grow vegetables around the house to support the family. Here, everything is money. So it's hard to blame the parents if they don't have enough time to teach their children anything about who they are. The children in this generation learn about who they are from the influence of outsiders. And sometimes they pick up bad things. Sometimes what they pick up is not really who they are, so sometimes they are lost.

Some of them feel that it is degrading to be called Cambodian. They'd rather be called American. I want to really help these children recognize who they are, where they come from, why their arts and culture are so important, and why they need to see that and appreciate it, for themselves. From arts and culture, you learn a moral standard. You also learn how to identify yourself, and you get a little background about where you come from. It helps you so you don't get lost too much. These things give you an identity. If you don't know your arts and culture, who are you? How are you going to explain to other people who you are? When people ask you, what are you? If you say, "I'm Cambodian," then what is Cambodian? If you can't tell them that, then you are empty behind your own face. If you can't tell people about who you are, how are they going to appreciate you? First, you got to appreciate yourself. And you learn to appreciate yourself through your arts and culture, through your tradition. And that's how I look at it.

Whenever I teach, I am teaching them something for the long run. When I teach dance, it's not just for a one-time performance, or something that will be used once in a while. I am also teaching students to learn about the outfit of our traditional costume. (And how long it takes to make the costume, first of all!) So they need to appreciate that. And from there, the songs for dance speak in a different language, at a level that they don't understand. So I talk to them about it. And the history of the dance—Why? How did this dance start? Who created it? And that will bring us back to the history of where dance comes from, and that will give credit to our ancestors and all those older generations that came before. And dance also has a moral standard with it. Because every movement in the dance shows how a Cambodian woman is supposed to be—going far back. The slow movement is all coming from a very respectful way, the way we walk, we talk—all of this goes to the movement of our dance. The song also speaks in a language of royalty . . . In the dance, and in our language, there are certain words you can speak in referring to other people. In American English, there's only "you" and "me"—so it's very general and it's all at the same level. But in our language we have many different words. You speak one way to those who are older, another way to those who are younger. These are the things that students have to understand.

Teaching Cambodian arts and culture does not mean that I don't want Cambodian children to learn about American culture. It's not that. You're going to be here for so many years, you're going to learn about American culture, and you need to learn about it. You live here. No matter what. So you have to get along. But at the same time, you have to learn about yourself, too, so you won't be lost. Right now, we depend on the older generation to help us plan New Year celebrations, to marry us, and to do whatever it is that needs to be done for us culturally. But someday we are going to be the ones to carry on those traditions. And if we lose the knowledge, it is worse than losing your country. You lose yourself. You lose your spirit. Who is going to know what is Cambodian any more? If we lose our identity, we lose everything, and Cambodia will be completely history.

I came back to teach arts and culture for the younger generation who know nothing about these things. I did it because I cannot depend on their parents to teach them and to keep the arts alive. I didn't see other people teaching, or caring much about it. So I had to make a decision, somehow, for me, for my community, and for my children. And I don't regret what my decision has been. I love what I am doing.

I was taught so much, and have accomplished so much. I survived the war and overcame so many tragedies in my country, and the war, and here. For all this, I feel that I should do my best to return the favor to my country, my homeland, and my father. I must return the favor given to me by trying to continue to carry on our arts and culture.

[S]ee how important it is to keep the spirit alive. We lost our country. And I know that anybody can lose their country over anything. But one thing you have to remember is that you cannot lose your spirit. And as long as you have your spirit, your country will still be around you. Now, I understand the value and importance of arts and culture. That's what really motivates me to continue to do this.

I was away from it, but arts and culture never did leave my mind. My soul was gone, but my spirit was still here. That's what got me to come back. That's who I am. It doesn't matter how far you try to get away—you can never get away because you are already attached to it. I think I was put in a position to explode! I was put in a position to help carry on these things, whether I like it or not. I had a choice either to fix my personal relationships or to fix my arts and culture, and I had to choose between that. And it's not easy, you know. Especially, it's at a point where—are you willing to give up your family? Or are you willing to give up everything else that you have that was given to you to give to others or to share with others?

Source: Koung, Leendavy. "You Cannot Lose Your Spirit." Recorded and edited by Debora Kodish. *Works in Progress*, Philadelphia Folklore Project, Volume 14: 1/2, Summer, 2001, 26–29. http://www.folkloreproject.org/folkarts/resources/pubs/wip/summer01.pdf. Used with permission of the Philadelphia Folklore Project.

Vatey Seng, *The Price We Paid*

(2005)

Vatey Seng was 15 years old in 1975, when the Khmer Rouge took power in Cambodia. As educated, light-skinned Chinese Cambodians,

Seng's family faced intense persecution from the nationalistic communist regime. The next year, they were imprisoned in a reeducation camp. They worked as slaves for the Khmer Rouge until 1979, when they were liberated by Vietnamese troops. After fleeing to refugee camps in Thailand and the Philippines, Seng, her mother, and her siblings eventually immigrated to the United States. They left behind many other family members, including her father, who had disappeared or was killed during the years of turmoil.

Three decades after fleeing the devastation of her homeland and her family, Vatey Seng wrote her memoir, The Price We Paid: A Life Experience in the Khmer Rouge Regime, Cambodia. *The following excerpts highlight the trauma of the refugee immigrant experience for her family and how powerfully the memory of Cambodia affects Seng's personal and political identity in the United States.*

Refugee Camps

In July 1979, my family decided to flee to the Cambodian-Thai border to be with Uncle Sok. We wished we could go back to our house in Phnom Penh City, but Mae [Seng's mother] said she would not look back without Pa. In addition, she didn't trust the new government backed by the Vietnamese. We couldn't afford to take any more risk. We had to get out of this country as soon as we could, and this was a good opportunity.

Many people traveled on the road and most of them headed our direction. Traveling by foot and carrying heavy belongings, it took us two days to reach Srok Svay Sisophon, Battambang province [in northwest Cambodia], which was about 35 miles away. This district was the meeting point of all traders and salesmen. Some salesmen delivered goods from Thailand and sold here, and some salesmen bought goods and sold in Battambang city. Since Mony [Seng's older brother] had been to the refugee camp before, he knew where to meet other people that were headed our way. My family waited with a big crowd of a hundred people until dark, to avoid the Vietnamese patrol. Our escape would be led by a group of men who knew the way well. They didn't charge us anything because they had to go to refugee camps, too, to do their trading

business. They did not allow anyone with babies to travel with the group. There were a couple reasons why babies and small children could put the group in jeopardy during an escape. If they cried, robbers could spot us and robbed us. They said there were two to three groups of thieves that waited for travelers at about mid-point. Besides, we had to walk across the thick forest and mine fields. They told us to meet them at a certain place before sunset. . . .

[The Sengs settled in at Nong Mak-moon refugee camp, located in the disputed borderlands between Cambodia and Thailand. In April, 1980, Seng got married; she soon became pregnant.]

In July 1980, the Old Camp was attacked heavily. One night, Mony got information from one of Uncle Sok's secret agents that thousands of the Vietnamese troops were marching toward our camp. They planned the attack after midnight. Mony immediately went to get Sothan [Seng's oldest brother] from his workplace, but Sothan didn't believe that information because his office was the headquarters which was supposed to receive all secret information first. Mony returned home and told us to pack our belongings. Only the children could sleep that night. We hoped the information would be false.

A few minutes after midnight, we could hear gunfire from surroundings of the camp. This sounded like popping corn but much louder. Refugees got trapped in the middle of the battle zone between Vietnamese troops and Thai soldiers. Everywhere was gunfire and bombardment. Normally, refugees could escape to the Thai village, but this time, Thai soldiers fired at refugees and prevented us from entering their land. Hundreds of refugees got killed and there were many casualties. We could see blood everywhere.

Since Sothan usually stayed at his workplace, he was separated from my family at that time.

My family and our neighbors moved from one hut to another in order to stay away from the battlefield. Few hours later, one of the bombs dropped right nearby the place we were hiding. A piece of shrapnel grazed the left side of Mony's abdomen. Chhora [Seng's younger sister] was also got hit on her right cheek. They were bleeding a lot. Mae and Mony's wife cried out in fear. Mony and Chhora put pieces of cloth on top of their wound to minimize bleeding.

Since this place was not safe anymore, Mony said we had to get out the camp as soon as we could because it seemed like both troops attempting to kill all refugees. So, other survivors and my family crawled through disgusting sewage filled with worms, and walking passed dead bodies. We hid behind any small hills or barriers and headed towards the thick forest away from the camp. All the way, we prayed to God to protect us from bombs and gunshots . . . [Seng and her family fled from one camp to the next, eventually ending up at Thailand's Keo I Dang Camp.]

A Road to the Third Country

I gave birth to twin boys on February 5, 1981. It was the greatest event in my life. They were so precious little babies. The older weighted 5.28 pounds, and the younger weighted 4.18 pounds. Mae and my husband were with me during the labor. I was thankful to two young French doctors and Cambodian nurses who took good care of me and helped me through my first experience of my life in delivering babies. Moreover, a young French Catholic nun named Denise du Bois came to visit me and other young moms and taught us how to take care babies. She provided me baby clothing, baby supplies, and some money. She even named my twins: Jean and Jacque.

Sister Denise and another sister . . . came to this refugee camp to help children and new moms by providing supplement food and clothing. They made many trips every day to visit those families without the feeling of weariness.

To honor Sister Denise, I named my twins by combining French and Cambodian names. I named the older Jean Kavey. Kavey means a poet or a writer. I named the younger Jacque Vithey. Vithey means a road that leads people to the right direction, like a leader. Unfortunately, the immigration worker wrote their names wrong. Jean Kavey became Jankavey, and Jacque Vithey became

Jakvithey. I didn't request to make any changes because it could delay my case up to a year or two.

Fifteen days later, our family was accepted to migrate to the United States of America based on the political status because my dad was in former military. Normally, my husband used to check the listing whether our names were on it or not. With despair, he didn't go to check on that day until someone came to tell us with joy. It was the greatest news to my family. Finally, our hope in having better and safer lives in the third country came true . . . !

Before we immigrated to the United States, all refugees were transported to the camp in Chun Borei province, in Thailand. We were screened for any contagious diseases before we departed to a camp in the Philippines.

We arrived at the refugee camp in Morong, Bataan, in the Philippines, in May 1981. The camp was a beautiful site near waterfall and near the beaches. We stayed in wooden buildings which were organized into section. Fresh vegetables and seafood fish were adequate and provided every day. Besides, Filipinos could come in to trade food for clothing or jewelry. Refugees were allowed to travel outside the camp if they had money.

This camp was also known as the processing zone. All refugees, young and old, were required to go to school to learn the English language for three months, and then they had to attend a class for learning American culture for a week. If anyone missed the last class, that person would not be allowed for departure.

With twin babies, it didn't stop me from studying and doing my homework assignments. I did well in my English language class. Chhora and Sotheavy [Seng's sister] would bring Jean and Jacque to my class and let me breastfeed them, and my Filipina teacher Mrs. Guevara was happy to hold one while I breastfed another. My classmates and my teacher were proud of me because I consistently scored the third among youngsters, Cambodian English teachers and interpreters who took the same class.

In the culture class, we were taught that American people didn't like the smell of most

Asian food. So, we had to be careful not to cook food that had stinky smell like pickled fish. We learned that most American women were independent and could stay single in the late 30s whereas women in our culture liked to get married in early age. We also learned that American liked to keep things personal. Being aware that our culture was so different from American culture. It made us have fear of what we could confront when we came to live in America. . . .

America, America

[Seng's family, nine people in all, landed at the San Francisco Airport on February 19, 1982. They relocated to Illinois, sponsored by a Catholic church in Peoria.]

When the first Cambodian worker came, he brought us lots of clothes and shoes. His name was Chhun. He told us that the supplies were donated by members of his church. He also told us that our sponsor was Catholic Church and that they were paying for all our expenses. We were so grateful and wished to meet them, but our worker said we didn't have to.

Chhun was in charge of taking us to see the doctor, enroll in school, and bring us food—plenty of food. He demanded that we finished one chicken a day, which made us feel so fortunate because we didn't have this much food before. It was almost overwhelming for us to finish a chicken a day. To us, one chicken could be enough for a week. To add to our happiness, Chhun got us all kinds of Asian food, especially rice, and we were so happy about it. We were not used to American food, in both quantity and quality. . . .

[In 1985, the family moved to California, joining the extended family, including Sothan and Mony who finally had arrived from Cambodia.]

I gave birth to a baby girl on September 1, 1989. When I was in delivery room before giving birth, Wendy Tokuda, a television reporter, came to conduct an interview concerning healthcare of Alameda County that faced budget crisis. I was so excited to see her in person although I was in pain.

After I delivered the baby, the nurse asked what the baby's name was.

I already chose her name Amanda; somehow, I changed my mind at the last minute.

"Wendy. Wendy Seng."

I hoped my daughter would grow up to be a reporter like Wendy Tokuda. This career was one of my dreams. However, I would give freedom to my daughter in deciding what she wants to be.

She was a cute little baby. The most unique thing about Wendy was that she always smiled every time she woke up. Most babies would cry so often. She grows up to be a happy and funny girl with self-confidence. She is like the sunshine brightens my life and helps to ease my pain. . . .

My whole extended family lives in California now. We enjoy being together at Mae's house on most weekends. Although we all got married and have children of our own, we still feel as close as when we were young. Sometimes, we talk about our past in the Khmer Rouge regime. We make fun of each other: Sothan was so skinny that he couldn't walk straight. Chhora looked like a beggar and she always ran away to avoid work and ate all kinds of wild vegetables and even small fish heads thrown away at the communal kitchen. Sotheavy looked cute in her worn-out clothes with many patches and a big pocket in front of the shirt so that she could put her rice ration. Although she was skinny, her cheeks were pink and plumy. Tevy [Seng's youngest sister] was chubby while other children were so skinny due to lack of food.

Actually, during those horrible years, we endured all the difficulties, pains, starvation, and deadly diseases. The bond of affection between parents and children, brothers and sisters, kept us strong. We stood by one another in order to survive. The most painful part of this experience was that we lost our pa, whom we admire and love very much. How we wish he had made it through those days and be with us now. Twenty years later, pain still exists in our hearts. It's like a wound that cannot be healed.

Although I live freely and have a good life in the United States, I always think about other

Cambodians who struggle every day back home, just to put food on the table. I remember what Pa told me, "You're lucky because you didn't have to suffer through World War II as I did." Contrarily, my generation was the worst and most destructive in the history of Cambodia. Whenever leaders of political parties fight each other for their own power, we the people are the ones who suffer, sacrifice, and die for them. Those powerful leaders do not care about their people—it is all about their personal interests. Cambodia is a poor country. Its size is approximately the state of Nevada. Today, because of corruption and poor leadership its economy is probably even worse than it was during the old regime before the Khmer Rouge regime. We the people want to live peacefully. We demand liberty and justice for all, and we need leaders who enhance the country towards prosperity. We need leaders who believe in a country for the people and by the people.

It is painful to have these memories in the deep recesses of my mind, and I learn to forgive and have no feelings of hatred or retaliation toward those who have hurt me. I just wish that my story could help the new generation understand what happened in the past and stop attempting to put people through the terror again.

Source: Excerpted from Seng, Vatey. *The Price We Paid: A Life Experience in the Khmer Rouge Regime, Cambodia.* New York: iUniverse, 2005, 227–252.

Pete Pin, "The Cambodian Diaspora"
(2012)

Pete Pin was born in a Thai refugee camp just over the border from Cambodia. Khao-I-Dang, established in 1979, housed more than 100,000 refugees escaping Cambodia's Killing Fields, erected under the regime of Pol Pot. Pin immigrated to the United States when he was a child; he grew up in California, in Stockton's Cambodian community. He is now a photojournalist; his work has appeared in Time Magazine, The New York Times, *and* Forbes. *Pin began taking photographs of Cambodian Americans in 2010, uncovering stories long suppressed by the traumatized survivors of Pol Pot's holocaust. The following Kickstarter biography outlines his proposed project on the Cambodian diaspora: he seeks to strengthen intergenerational ties by documenting his community's history and showing pictorially how the horror of the Killing Fields continues to reverberate 40 years later and thousands of miles distant.*

I will photograph in Cambodian communities across the U.S. Northeast, generating intergenerational dialogue around unspoken memories.

Between 1975–1979, 1.7 million Cambodians—a third of the country's population— perished during the Killing Fields, one of the most horrific state-sponsored genocides of the twentieth century. In the years since, over 150,000 Cambodians displaced in refugee camps along the Thai-Cambodian border resettled in the United States.

My immediate family is among the survivors.

BACKGROUND

In the fall of 2010, I set up a makeshift portrait studio in my grandmother's garage in Stockton, California. Right before I took her photo, she recounted to me the heartbreaking details of my family's experience during Cambodia's Killing Fields for the first time in her life. As she spoke, I was overcome with a sense of history and a connection to a past that had for so long been withheld from me.

The encounter sprung a need to learn more. I began talking with Cambodian-Americans across the country in an attempt to piece together our collective story—of trauma, displacement, and resilence—and to understand how this has affected the lives of Cambodian-Americans across generations. I discovered that the generational divide I experienced in my family was common amongst survivors and their children. In photographing these communities, I recognized the power such images have in generating discussion about this shared, yet often unvoiced legacy.

Last year, with support from the Magnum Foundation, I spent five months photographing in the Bronx, New York. The experience was personally transformative and strengthened my desire to continue documenting in Cambodian communities across the country.

THE PROJECT

With your support, I will build on the process I began years ago. I will first photograph in Philadelphia, where I spent considerable time as an organizer for a grassroots Cambodian American organization, the One Love Movement, founded and led by young Cambodian Americans like myself. From Philadelphia, I will travel to Lowell, Massachusetts, one of the largest Cambodian communities outside of Cambodia itself. I will photograph community members and create informal exhibitions to generate intergenerational discussion among community members. Your support will enable me to work on this project for nearly four months uninterrupted, covering my living, travel, and equipment expenses.

The time to act is now. As survivors gradually pass away, their children—many of whom, like myself, were born in refugee camps and raised in the US—harbor questions about their identity and family history. There is a need to make these untold stories heard. Like the generation after the Holocaust, Cambodians of my generation are uniquely capable of writing this narrative. It is this story that I seek to honor, preserve, and share with the world.

Thank you for your support.

Source: Pin, Pete. "The Cambodian Diaspora." http://www.kickstarter.com/projects/181740424/the-cambodian-diaspora. Reprinted with permission.

The Golden Hills' News, "The Chinese Exodus"
(1854)

Kim Shan Jit San Luke, *or* The Golden Hills' News, *was North America's first Chinese-language newspaper.* The Golden Hills' News *was established in 1854 by American Methodist missionaries in San Francisco. This venture was closely connected with the denomination's overseas mission efforts; these missions had taken off in the wake of the Opium Wars and the 1842 Treaty of Nanking, which forced China open to Western nations—and their churches. The first Methodist missionaries arrived in Foochow, China, in 1847.*

 The Golden Hills' News *covered a wide variety of topics, from shipping information to local news to updates on the political situation in China—in particular, the Taiping Rebellion, which by then had reached Guangdong, the home province of most Chinese immigrants to the United States. Although it ran only for a few months,* The Golden Hills' News *served as a model for future ethnic press publications in the United States. Most of the newspaper was lithographed in Chinese characters, but the May 27, 1854, edition included the following publisher's column written in English. The publishers called for Americans to embrace the Chinese immigrants for reasons of commercial and economic self-interest and from principles of common humanity.*

The people of San Francisco are a great people—great in the rapidity of their growth, great in the aspect of enterprise and determination, which their cities, villages and Institutions present, and in the original characteristics of their inhabitants. They are great by origin—they are sui generis—they are a comminglement based on Liberty, which fuses all into oneness. They are great by their love of freedom. They hold no seven by nine creed, which, like that of some of the Press, would cry privilege for themselves and despotism for others. They are great in the "Constitution," which declares, that all men are free and equal. The people and eschutchon [sic] of California are things to rejoice over—they are DEMOCRACY.

 But the California picture is unique—their tout ensemble is the history of Civilization. The "Eastern States" have their Irish exodus, their German exodus, and hordes and Saxons, Danes,

Celts, Gauls and Scandinavians, but we have all these, and the most wonderful of all a CHINESE EXODUS! The great wonder of the century is the astonishing flight of the hitherto immobile Chinamen across the Pacific ocean, to seek refuge and liberty in the bosom of the "Golden Hills." It actually tickles the fancy to even think of Chinamen quitting the celestial empire—the paradise of earth—the garden of green Byson [?]—the Flowery Land, beyond which was supposed to lay outer darkness, and to come and mingle in the search for yellow gold, instead of remaining at home to fight and struggle for the "yellow robes of office."

Yes, John Chinaman disregarding the threats of the bastinade, and the tortures said to await his return to the "Flowery abode," for having forsaken the habits of his forefathers, joins the tide of Progress, and the Rubicon once passed, where shall his exodus end? The days of Chinese exclusion, small feet, and stand-still-ism, are ending—Chinese are no longer rare avis in terres—to see them is no longer to see "the Elephant." They are fast assisting to colonize California and various islands in Polynesia.

Statistics show, that the principle emigration of the Chinese is from the Canton river, and the rising port of Shanghai. The revered Charles Taylor and M.P. Yates, both Missionaries at Shanghai, say that the latter port is thrown open, without restriction to the Foreigner, that Americans wander unmolested 40 miles into the interior, and that the Natives instead of calling Americans "outside barbarians," look up to them with profound respect. "No Chinaman sneers at you in the streets; there is no hindrance whatever to your study of their character and habits; they will always look at you with an expression of goodwill," says Bayard Taylor. Is it too much to ask of a Christian population "to do unto them," at least, what it seems "they do to us," in their own land? Is it too much to ask of this Cosmopolitan state, in the veins of whose population flows the blood of a thousand tribes, to give freedom of growth and fair play to the Mongol element? Is it too much to ask of a Commercial People to give a generous and liberal encouragement to any means, that assist the Chinese to a knowledge of our laws and habits, and a sympathy with our interests? Surely not. Therefore Merchants, Manufacturers, Miners and Agriculturalists, come forward as friends, not scorners of the Chinese, so that they may mingle in the march of the world, and help to open for America an endless vista of future commerce.

Published by Howard & Hudson.

Source: "The Chinese Exodus." *The Golden Hills' News,* 1854. California Historical Society, Newspaper Collection. http://content.cdlib.org/ark:/13030/hb3j49n625/. Courtesy of the California Historical Society.

Kwang Chang Ling, "Letters of Kwang Chang Ling: The Chinese Side of the Chinese Question"

(1878)

Anti-Chinese sentiment grew steadily on the West Coast throughout the 19th century. The Foreign Miners' Tax, enacted in 1850 and reinstated in 1852, was aimed particularly at the Chinese, and laws were passed prohibiting Chinese from testifying against whites in court. In 1878, the United States was on the eve of passing the Chinese Exclusion Act, the nation's most restrictive piece of immigration legislation. Xenophobia, fueled by economic fears and racial prejudice, was rampant, especially in California, and racist speeches and newspaper articles circulated widely. Some people spoke out against the propaganda, however, challenging mainstream assumptions and claims about China and Chinese immigrants. In a series of letters written for The San Francisco Argonaut, *a literary journal published in the late 19th century, Kwang Chang Ling argued that the Chinese were integral to California's economy. The following excerpt exposes the double standards in the United States' dealings with China and immigrant Chinese laborers and the self-serving hypocrisy underpinning American denigration of Chinese morality.*

WHY SHOULD THE CHINESE GO?

A Pertinent Inquiry from a Mandarin High in Authority

Letter I.

PALACE HOTEL, August 2, 1878

TO THE ARGONAUT: — You will doubtless gather from the superscription and general appearance of this letter that I am what Europeans, in the abundance of their vanity, would be very likely to regard as an anomaly—an educated Chinaman. It a word, I speak and write your language, as I believe, correctly. And it is because of this slight accomplishment that my general unworthiness has been overlooked by my countrymen residing in California, and I have been selected by them to communicate to the public the Chinese side of the Chinese question. The ARGONAUT has been especially preferred as the medium for the promulgation of these views on account of its reputed fairness to all.

The cry is here that the Chinese must go. I say that they should not go; that they can not go; will not go. More than this, that, were it conceivable that they went, your State would be ruined; in a word, that the Chinese population of the Pacific Coast have become indispensable to its continued prosperity, and that you cannot afford to part with them upon any consideration.

If this be true—and I believe I can demonstrate it even to your satisfaction—the truth is an important one. It concerns every element of the future social life of California; it lies at the basis of your industries; it is bound to subvert that demagogism by which politics, as you call it, have been degraded to a level scarcely higher than incendiarism, pillage and murder. . . .

Clothed in this dignity of discourse, I enter the lists without fear. I am upon your soil; I am surrounded at the best by unsympathetic spectators; my only buckler is the truth; my only weapon your language, the peculiarities of which can never be wholly mastered by a foreigner. Far from complaining of any disadvantage in these respects, I am free to own that no soil is freer, no assemblage more noble, no regulations more just than those which claim the proud title of American.

And now let the heralds be heard and my grievance stated. Hear, oh, ye just and valiant men, ye beauteous and compassionate women, the plaint of Kwan Chang Ling, a *literate* of the first class, a warrior and noble, a leader of the Chinese and a representative by authority. . . .

Letter II.

Palace Hotel, August 2, 1878,

Under these articles [from the 1868 Burlingame Treaty, establishing friendly relations between the United States and China] a numerous body of your citizens have established themselves in China, possessed themselves of the coasting trade, and many other branches of navigation and traffic, and thus deprived thousands of Chinamen of employment. The complaints of these poor people are not conveyed to you; because our government has too much respect for its treaty obligations to permit you to be annoyed with any expression of regret concerning the working of its compacts with you. On the other hand, while the profits of which the Chinese coast and river junk trade have been deprived, by American steamers, go to swell the dividends of your navigation companies and afford employment to your maritime classes, your shipbuilders, and your machinists, your newspapers are filled and your halls of legislation resound, with outcries against Chinese labor in America.

Thus it appears that the United States maintains precisely the same position in respect to China as the other European nations do. You all desire to possess advantages in China which, at the same time, you would deny to Chinamen in America. You have bombarded our ports and forced us into an unwilling commerce with you, which now you desire shall be entirely one-sided. Your reason for this unfairness is not a sordid one. You are clear-headed enough to perceive that the benefit to commercial intercourse cannot be unilateral. But you fancy that the advantages of social intercourse may be monopolized by one party. You will not permit us to shut ourselves up. You demand every privilege for Americans in China, but you would deny the same privileges to Chinamen in America, because, in your opinion, the presence of the Chinese amongst you is a menace to your civilization. You shrink from contact with us, not because you regard us as mentally or bodily inferior, for neither fact nor argument will support you here—but rather because our religious code appears to be different from yours, and because we are deemed to be more abstemious in food, clothing and shelter.

If our religious forms, our daily bill of fare, and our demands for wages were the same as yours, it would be difficult to see what grievances, either real or fanciful, you would have to complain about. Since you profess in your political constitution, your pulpit declamations, and, more than all, in your manner of living, that you are not bigoted, and care nothing for religious forms, the menace to your civilization appears to resolve itself into a fear of losing your accustomed roast beef, white shirt-collars, and carpeted houses. It is a menace to the sensual indulgences to which you have been accustomed for the last three centuries—that is to say, since the opening of sea trade to the Orient. . . .

Let me in this place, however, endeavor to correct one great misapprehension in respect to the Chinaman. You are continually objecting to his morality. Your travelers say he is depraved; your missioners call him ungodly; your commissioners call him uncleanly; and your *sans culottes* call him everything that is vile. Yet your housewives permit him to wait upon them at table; they admit him to their bed-chambers; they confide to him their garments and jewels; and even trust their lives to him, by awarding him supreme control over their kitchens and the preparation of their food. There is a glaring contradiction here.

The plain truth is, that what you have regarded as evidences of immorality and depravity are simply evidences of indigence and misery. China is in a feudal condition. Her nobles are enormously rich and powerful; her peasants are extremely poor and wretched. The unpleasant things which your travelers and missionaries have observed in China, are not common to Chinamen. They have never been observed in connection with rich Chinamen. They are peculiar only to poverty. They belong to the miserable—to the miserable of all countries. . . .

The nobles are the richest in the world; the peasants are the poorest. What little of the latter's habits and surroundings has provided repulsive to Occidental eyes, is the result, not of inferior morality, but of inferior wealth. The European peasant was in the same condition three centuries ago, and in some countries—for example, Russia, Eastern Germany, Roumania [sic], Ireland, and parts of Italy and Portugal—he is very nearly in a similar condition today. Yet you not only tolerate him in America, you share with him your political privileges; you admit him to social communion; he is your brother; while the poor Chinaman you would drive away with blows and contumely. What if it should appear that, after all, there was nothing defensible beneath your hatred of Chinamen but ignorance and religious bigotry? Where would then stand the bases of your vaunted civilization?

Source: Ling, Kwang Chang. "Letters of Kwang Chang Ling. The Chinese Side of the Chinese Question, by a Chinese Literate of the First Class, Communicated to the San Francisco Argonaut, on the dates of August 7th, 10th, 17th, and September 7th, 1878," 2, 7, 8. California Historical Society, 325.251.Sa5a. http://www.oac.cdlib .org/ark:/13030/hb3m3n99bq/?brand=oac4. Courtesy of the California Historical Society.

Woman's Union Mission of San Francisco
(1881)

Middle-class American evangelicals became increasingly interested and invested in foreign missions in the years after the end of the Civil War. Women in particular became very involved, supporting missionaries abroad, forming domestic mission societies, and, in some cases, going out into the field themselves. San Francisco's Chinatown provided a closer-to-home mission opportunity, and evangelicals sought to bring Christianity and Western social mores to the Chinese immigrants and their children.

The interdenominational Woman's Union Mission of San Francisco established a school in Chinatown. The organization's 1880 Annual Report includes a series of anecdotes about the interactions between Chinese people and the American teacher Marian Bokee, a copy of the mission's constitution, a short history of the mission, and a list of members and supporters. The following excerpts reveal the contours of Chinatown tourism-voyeurism, complete with obligatory visits to opium dens and reinforced notions of Western cultural superiority. They also demonstrate the ways in which 19th-century Progressive organizations encouraged the assimilation process among immigrants.

THE MARRIAGE CERTIFICATE

Chinese women are beginning to understand something of the dignity and rights of wifehood. They prize beyond expression the certificate of marriage, and both husband and wife secure one at the same time. Each keeps the valuable document, so that neither can run away without being overtaken with justice. As an illustration of this Mrs. Bokee says:

"As Jung Gow, our baby, did not come to school for several days I went after him, and while waiting for him, a woman in the building that calls the little fellow her 'heart's child,' motioned me to sit down and talk with her. She was busily engaged finishing off pants for a clothing store. On a low stool at her feet was Jung Gow's baby sister. The woman pointed to the child and said: 'Seen Sang, me love the children. Their mother not muchee sabee. Their father dead long time. You love children, me sabee. You wash Jung Gow's face, you love he. Me love he. Me work alle time, give money to husband. Seen Sang, you shuttee door— no man see, I likee show you;' and darting under the bed she brought forth a box, which she unlocked, and took out a certificate of marriage. Had she been displaying diamond solitaires she could not have manifested deeper pride, as she added: 'Seen Sang, you my dear sister; you kind to Chinese woman. Some time I have trouble, I come to Seen Sang, you help me? You take care me. I be kind to you—me heap smart.' I promised the poor woman that I would do all I could for her, should she ever need me, and she grasped my hand in grateful recognition. . . . "

CHRISTIAN AND HEATHEN CHINESE HOMES

I accompanied several ladies through the Chinese quarters recently. I first took them to the heathen homes in the narrow alleys, and showed them the opium-smoking and other vices allied to these homes. We then went to the Christian homes with their little suggestions of refinement and cultivation. The contrast was striking. The visit made a deep impression upon the party, some of whom were not especially interested in the Chinese.

A recent visit from the Census taker revealed the fact that nearly all the Chinese children in San Francisco are American born. We ought to at least teach these children to abandon the cruel and inhuman practice of mutilating the feet of their children, should they ever become parents. In speaking to one of my own Chinese mothers on this subject I asked: 'Why do you make your little ones suffer so?' She replied: 'When I go back to China, my girl have big feet, no rich many marry her—she marry only poor man. I no likee she marry poor man.' I concluded that folly was not confined to the women of any particular nation. . . .

CONSTITUTION

PREAMBLE—In view of the deplorable condition of heathen women and children of the Chinese race in San Francisco, a Woman's Society has been organized with the following Constitution, under which women of every Christian denomination may work together effectually by distinct, voluntary effort for the saving of these perishing ones.

ARTICLE 1. This Society shall be called "WOMAN'S UNION MISSION TO CHINESE WOMEN AND CHILDREN."

ART. 2. The object of this Society shall be the evangelization of Chinese women and children. For this purpose a Missionary shall be employed at a certain salary, to visit the houses of the Chinese, to hold a daily school for the instruction of children in the elementary branches of secular knowledge, and in Bible truths. . . .

TO OUR FRIENDS

Eleven years ago a few ladies of San Francisco, irrespective of religious creed or denomination, formed a society called "THE WOMAN'S UNION MISSION TO CHINESE WOMEN AND CHILDREN." A competent teacher was employed, and a school for Chinese boys and girls has been kept in successful operation till the present time.

In addition to the school for children, the original design, as the name indicates, was to found an asylum for the Chinese women who might be anxious to escape from their life of servitude and shame; but church societies having subsequently taken up that distinctive work, this Woman's Union Mission has confined its efforts to the school, together with such missionary service as their teacher, and others appointed to cooperate with her, may be able to do, in visiting from house to house amongst the Chinese women.

The school is held in the Globe Hotel, on the corner of Jackson and Dupont streets, and is one of the points in "Chinatown" to which strangers are shown, and which they can remember as one of the most interesting features of this cosmopolitan city. Several hundred Chinese children, of both sexes, have been pupils in this school—the average attendance being about twenty-five—and there are always on the list, children of marked ability and great promise.

There are many reasons why this school should be continued and liberally supported:

First—We believe that work among the young, of whatever name or nationality, carries along with it the largest promise and the surest guarantee of success. The saving hope of the world rests in the children.

Second—This school affords the only means for secular and religious instruction which those gathered into it would likely be able to receive.

Third—The children born in this country will become American citizens, and some provision should be afforded for their education; or, should they return to China, what they learn in this school will fit them for becoming teachers of good things amongst their people at home.

Fourth—Chinese are not allowed to attend our public schools, and but for the benevolent efforts of philanthropies and Christians, no provision would be made for their education. . . .

Source: The Annual Report of the Women's Union Mission of San Francisco to Chinese Women and Children. San Francisco: George Spaudling & Co., Steam Boat and Job Printers, 1881, pp. 7–8, 11, 28, 29–30. xF870.C5.C51 v.3:13, The Bancroft Library, University of California, Berkeley. http://sunsite.berkeley.edu/cgi-bin/flipomatic/cic/brk5198.

Transcript of the Chinese Exclusion Act
(1882)

Beginning in the 1850s, in the wake of the Opium Wars, Chinese began immigrating to the United States to work in the mines, on the railroads, on the farms, and in the forests of the West Coast. As more and more Chinese came looking for work, anti-Chinese sentiment began to rise, particularly among the white working class, who viewed the Chinese as competition for jobs. However, anti-Chinese sentiment was not merely a by-product of labor competition. Because of pervasive cultural stereotypes, many white Americans saw the Chinese as culturally backward, dirty, unsanitary, diseased, sexually deviant, and addicted to opium. By the 1880s, white hostility toward the Chinese became so great on the West Coast that Congress passed the first of three Chinese Exclusion Laws in 1882. The act banned Chinese laborers for 10 years. The federal government renewed the act for another 10 years in 1892 and then renewed it indefinitely in 1902. This act is the only immigration law in American history that targeted a specific ethnic group. The following excerpts from the Chinese Exclusion Act lays out the prohibition on Chinese laborers and miners, establishes protected clauses for certain classes of Chinese immigrants, and lists the penalties for shipmasters who bring in illegal immigrants.

AN ACT TO EXECUTE CERTAIN TREATY STIPULATIONS RELATING TO CHINESE

Whereas in the opinion of the Government of the United States the coming of Chinese laborers to this country endangers the good order of certain localities within the territory thereof: Therefore, *Be it enacted by the Senate and House of Representatives of the United States of America in Congress assembled,* That from and after the expiration of ninety days next after the passage of this act, and until the expiration of ten years next after the passage of this act, the coming of Chinese laborers to the United States be, and the same is hereby, suspended; and during such suspension it shall not be lawful for any Chinese laborer to come, or having so come after the expiration of said ninety days to remain within the United States.

SEC. 2. That the master of any vessel who shall knowingly bring within the United States on such vessel, and land or permit to be landed, any Chinese laborer, from any foreign port or place, shall be deemed guilty of a misdemeanor, and on conviction thereof shall be punished by a fine of not more than five hundred dollars for each and every such Chinese laborer so brought, and maybe also imprisoned for a term not exceeding one year.

SEC. 3. That the two foregoing sections shall not apply to Chinese laborers who were in the United States on the seventeenth day of November, eighteen hundred and eighty, or who shall have come into the same before the expiration of ninety days next after the passage of this act, and who shall produce to such master before going on board such vessel, and shall produce to the collector of the port in the United States at which such vessel shall arrive. . . .

SEC. 6. That in order to the faithful execution of articles one and two of the treaty in this act before mentioned, every Chinese person other than a laborer who may be entitled by said treaty and this act to come within the United States, and who shall be about to come to the United States, shall be identified as so entitled by the Chinese Government in each case, such identity to be evidenced by a certificate issued under the authority of said government, which certificate shall be in the English language or (if not in the English language) accompanied by a translation into English, stating such right to come, and which certificate shall state the name, title or official rank, if any, the age, height, and all physical peculiarities, former and present occupation or profession, and place of residence in China of the person to whom the certificate is issued and that such person is entitled, conformably to the treaty in this act mentioned to come within the United States. . . .

SEC. 7. That any person who shall knowingly and falsely alter or substitute any name for the name written in such certificate or forge any such certificate, or knowingly utter any forged or fraudulent certificate, or falsely personate any person named in any such certificate, shall be deemed guilty of a misdemeanor; and upon conviction thereof shall be fined in a sum not exceeding one thousand dollars, and imprisoned in a penitentiary for a term of not more than five years. . . .

SEC. 11. That any person who shall knowingly bring into or cause to be brought into the United States by land, or who shall knowingly aid or abet the same, or aid or abet the landing in the United States from any vessel of any Chinese person not lawfully entitled to enter the United States, shall be deemed guilty of a misdemeanor, and shall, on conviction thereof, be fined in a sum not exceeding one thousand dollars, and imprisoned for a term not exceeding one year.

SEC. 12. That no Chinese person shall be permitted to enter the United States by land without producing to the proper officer of customs the certificate in this act required of Chinese persons seeking to land from a vessel. And any Chinese person found unlawfully within the United States

shall be caused to be removed therefrom to the country from whence he came, by direction of the President of the United States, and at the cost of the United States, after being brought before some justice, judge, or commissioner of a court of the United States and found to be one not lawfully entitled to be or remain in the United States.

SEC. 13. That this act shall not apply to diplomatic and other officers of the Chinese Government traveling upon the business of that government, whose credentials shall be taken as equivalent to the certificate in this act mentioned, and shall exempt them and their body and household servants from the provisions of this act as to other Chinese persons.

SEC. 14. That hereafter no State court or court of the United States shall admit Chinese to citizenship; and all laws in conflict with this act are hereby repealed.

SEC. 15. That the words "Chinese laborers", wherever used in this act shall be construed to mean both skilled and unskilled laborers and Chinese employed in mining.

Approved, May 6, 1882.

Source: An Act to Execute Certain Treaty Stipulations Relating to the Chinese, May 6, 1882; Enrolled Acts and Resolutions of Congress, 1789–1996; General Records of the United States Government; Record Group 11; National Archives. From ourdocuments.org, a website maintained by the National Archives and Records Administration. http://www.ourdocuments.gov/doc.php?flash=false&doc=47&page=transcript.

Tape v. Hurley

(1885)

Mary McGladery was raised in an orphanage in Shanghai. She moved to the United States with some missionaries when she was 11 years old, and, in 1875, she married Joseph Tape, another

Chinese American immigrant. The Tapes had four children, all born in the United States. In 1884, the Tapes tried to enroll 8-year-old Mamie in Spring Valley School in San Francisco. When the principal, Jennie Hurley, denied her entry, Mamie's parents sued, citing the 1880 revised California Political Code that stipulated that every school must be open to all children residing in the district. Both the Superior Court and the California Supreme Court ruled in favor of the Tapes.

After the Tapes's victory, however, the San Francisco School Board lobbied the California State Legislature for a special provision in the political code establishing separate schools for "Chinese or Mongolian children." Despite her mother's impassioned protests, Mamie Tape, along with her brother Frank, was one of the first children to attend San Francisco's newly opened segregated Chinese Primary School, only one month after they had won their court case. Following is the California Supreme Court summary of the case and its ruling instructing the San Francisco public schools to admit Mamie Tape.

MAMIE TAPE, an Infant, by her Guardian ad Litem,

JOSEPH TAPE, Respondent, *v.* JENNIE M. A. HURLEY et al., Appellants

SUPREME COURT OF CALIFORNIA

March 1885

SHARPSTEIN, J.—The main question in this case is whether a child "between six and twenty-one years of age, of Chinese parentage, but who was born and has always lived in the city and county of San Francisco," is entitled to admission in the public school of the district in which she resides.

The language of the code is as follows:

> "Every school, unless otherwise provided by law, must be open for the admission of all children between six and twenty-one years of age residing in the district; and the board of trustees, or city board of education, have power to admit adults and children not residing in the district, whenever good reasons exist therefor. Trustees shall have the power to exclude children of filthy or vicious

habits, or children suffering from contagious or infectious diseases." (Political Code, § 1667.)

That is the latest legislative expression on the subject, and was passed as late as 1880. Prior to that time the first clause of the section read, "Every school, unless otherwise provided by special statute, must be open for the admission of all *white* children between five and twenty-one years of age, residing in the district."

As amended, the clause is broad enough to include all children who are not precluded from entering a public school by some provision of law; and we are not aware of any law which forbids the entrance of children of any race or nationality. The legislature not only declares who shall be admitted, but also who may be excluded, and it does not authorize the exclusion of any one on the ground upon which alone the exclusion of the respondent here is sought to be justified. The vicious, the filthy, and those having contagious or infectious diseases, may be excluded, without regard to their race, color or nationality.

This law must be construed as any other would be construed. "Where a law is plain and unambiguous, whether it be expressed in general or limited terms, *the legislature should be intended to mean what they have plainly expressed*, and consequently, no room is left for construction." (*Fisher* v. *Blight*, 2 Cranch, 358, 399.) "When the law is clear and explicit, and its provisions are susceptible of but one interpretation, its consequences, if evil, can only be avoided by a change of the law itself, to be effected by legislative and not judicial action." (*Bosley* v. *Mattingly*, 14 B. Mon. 73.) This rule is never controverted or doubted, although perhaps sometimes lost sight of. In this case, if effect be given to the intention of the legislature, as indicated by the clear and unambiguous language used by them, respondent here has the same right to enter a public school that any other child has. It is not alleged that she is vicious, or filthy, or that she has a contagious or infectious disease. As the legislature has not denied to the children of any race or nationality the right to enter our public schools, the question whether it might have done so does not arise in this case.

We think the superintendent of schools was improperly joined as a defendant in this action, and that the court properly dismissed the action as to the board of education. In *Ward* v. *Flood*, 48 Cal. 36, the action was against the teacher alone. That it was properly brought, seems to have been conceded.

The board of education has power "to make, establish, and enforce all necessary and proper rules and regulations *not contrary to law*," and none other. (Stats. 1871–2, p. 846.) Teachers cannot justify a violation of law, on the ground that a resolution of the board of education required them to do so.

The judgment must be modified, so as to make the writ run against the defendant Hurley alone.

In other respects it is affirmed.

THORNTON, J., MYRICK, J., McKEE, J., McKINSTRY, J., ROSS, J., and MORRISON, C. J., concurred

California Supreme Court Case Summary

PUBLIC SCHOOLS—CHINESE CHILDREN ENTITLED TO ADMISSION.—Children between six and twenty-one years of age, of Chinese parentage, who were born and have always lived in the city and county of San Francisco, are entitled to admission into the public school of the district in which they reside. And teachers are not justified in excluding them, notwithstanding a resolution of the Board of Education purports to command them so to do.

ID.—PROCEEDING TO COMPEL ADMISSION—DEFENDANT.—The teacher of a public school is the only necessary defendant in a proceeding to compel the admission thereto of a child unlawfully excluded.

APPEAL from a judgment of the Superior Court–of the city–and county of San Francisco.

The respondent, through her guardian *ad litem*, applied to the appellant Hurley, the principal of one of the public schools of the city and county of San Francisco, for admission therein. The respondent is a Chinese child, and because of this fact Miss Hurley, acting in obedience to a resolution of the board of education of the city and county of San Francisco, refused to admit her as a pupil into the school. A writ of mandate was then sued out against Miss Hurley, A. J. Moulder, superintendent of public instruction, and the members of the board of education, individually. The Superior Court dismissed the writ as to the members of the board of education, and ordered it to issue against Miss Hurley and A. J. Moulder. From such judgment the appeal was taken. The further facts are sufficiently stated in the opinion of the court.

H. G. Platt, for Appellants.

William F. Gibson, and *Sheldon G. Kellogg*, for Respondent.

End California Supreme Court Case Summary

Source: *Tape v. Hurley*. 66 Cal. 473 (1885).

Yick Wo v. Hopkins
(1886)

Initially, Chinese immigrants arriving in California in the 1850s were welcomed, albeit with reservations, by Americans. But within a few years, racial and economic antagonism, legally sanctioned and physically enforced, had come to define the immigrants' way of life. Local and state legislatures passed laws and taxes singling out the Chinese: the 1852 foreign miners' tax levied a *monthly fee on aliens "who did not desire to become a citizen" (applicable only to Asians, who were prohibited from naturalizing). The California Supreme Court ruled in 1854 that Chinese and Chinese Americans could not testify against white citizens. Newspapers up and down the West Coast ran articles denigrating the Chinese. And between 1850 and 1990, more than 200 Chinese miners were lynched, and thousands more were driven out of their homes, neighborhoods, and towns.*

Chinese Americans did not passively submit to this treatment. They filed various lawsuits against cities for negligent protection against mobs and for discriminatory treatment. Yick Wo sued the city of San Francisco after he was jailed for refusing to pay a $10 fee. In 1880, San Francisco had passed an ordinance requiring a permit for laundries housed in wooden buildings. By this time, nearly two-thirds of the laundries in San Francisco were run by Chinese Americans—and not one of them was granted a permit. In contrast, all but one of the white laundry owners received a permit. Yick Wo, who had owned and operated his laundry for years and who had never received any fire safety violations, protested, brought his case all the way to the U.S. Supreme Court, and won. In 1886, the Supreme Court unanimously ruled that the selective application of an ostensibly race-neutral law violates the U.S. Constitution's Fourteenth Amendment.

Yick Wo v. Hopkins was not invoked to halt Jim Crow laws and, in fact, was effectively bypassed in the 1896 Plessy v. Ferguson decision, which established the legality of the "separate but equal" theory. However, in the civil rights era and beyond, Yick Wo served as a precedent to uphold the rights of minorities to equal protection under the law. In the following excerpts from Yick Wo v. Hopkins, Supreme Court justice Stanley Matthews provides the salient details of the case and argues that noncitizens are protected by the Fourteenth Amendment and that the Constitution prohibits the discriminatory application of laws.

APPEAL FROM THE CIRCUIT COURT OF THE UNITED STATES FOR THE DISTRICT OF CALIFORNIA

Syllabus

In a suit brought to this court from a State court which involves the constitutionality of ordinances made by a municipal corporation in the State, this court will, when necessary, put its own independent construction upon the ordinances.

A municipal ordinance to regulate the carrying on of public laundries within the limits of the municipality violates the provisions of the Constitution of the United States if it confers upon the municipal authorities arbitrary power, at their own will, and without regard to discretion in the legal sense of the term, to give or withhold consent as to persons or places, without regard to the competency of the persons applying, or the propriety of the place selected, for the carrying on of the business.

An administration of a municipal ordinance for the carrying on of a lawful business within the corporate limits violates the provisions of the Constitution of the United States if it makes arbitrary and unjust discriminations, founded on differences of race between persons otherwise in similar circumstances.

The guarantees of protection contained in the Fourteenth Amendment to the Constitution extend to all persons within the territorial jurisdiction of the United States, without regard to differences of race, of color, or of nationality.

Those subjects of the Emperor of China who have the right to temporarily or permanently reside within the United States, are entitled to enjoy the protection guaranteed by the Constitution and afforded by the laws.

These two cases were argued as one, and depended upon precisely the same state of facts; the first coming here upon a writ of error to the Supreme Court of the State of California, the second on appeal from the Circuit Court of the United States for that district. The plaintiff in error, Yick Wo, on August 4, 1885, petitioned the Supreme

Court of California for a writ of habeas corpus, alleging that he was illegally deprived of his personal liberty by the defendant as sheriff of the city and county of San Francisco. . . .

The following facts were also admitted on the record: that petitioner is a native of China and came to California in 1861, and is still a subject of the Emperor of China; that he has been engaged in the laundry business in the same premises and building for twenty-two years last past; that he had a license from the board of fire wardens, dated March 3, 1884, from which it appeared "that the above described premises have been inspected by the board of fire wardens, and upon such inspection said board found all proper arrangements for carrying on the business; that the stoves, washing and drying apparatus, and the appliances for heating smoothing irons are in good condition, and that their use is not dangerous to the surrounding property from fire, and that all proper precautions have been taken to comply with the provisions of order No. 1617, defining 'the fire limits of the city and county of San Francisco and making regulations concerning the erection and use of buildings in said city and county,' and of order No. 1670, 'prohibiting the kindling, maintenance, and use of open fires in houses;' that he had a certificate from the health officer that the same premises had been inspected by him, and that he found that they were properly and sufficiently drained, and that all proper arrangements for carrying on the business of a laundry, without injury to the sanitary condition of the neighborhood, had been complied with; that the city license of the petitioner was in force and expired October 1st, 1885, and that the petitioner applied to the board of supervisors, June 1st, 1885, for consent of said board to maintain and carry on his laundry, but that said board, on July 1st, 1885, refused said consent."

It is also admitted to be true, as alleged in the petition, that, on February 24, 1880, "there were about 320 laundries in the city and county of San Francisco, of which about 240 were owned and conducted by subjects of China, and of the whole number, viz., 320, about 310 were constructed of wood, the same material that constitutes nine-tenths of the houses in the city of San Francisco. The capital thus invested by the subjects of China was not less than two hundred thousand dollars, and they paid annually for rent, license, taxes, gas, and water about one hundred and eighty thousand dollars."

It was alleged in the petition, that "your petitioner and more than one hundred and fifty of his countrymen have been arrested upon the charge of carrying on business without having such special consent, while those who are not subjects of China, and who are conducting eighty odd laundries under similar conditions, are left unmolested and free to enjoy the enhanced trade and profits arising from this hurtful and unfair discrimination. The business of your petitioner, and of those of his countrymen similarly situated, is greatly impaired, and in many cases practically ruined, by this system of oppression to one kind of men and favoritism to all others. . . ."

It was also admitted "that petitioner and 200 of his countrymen similarly situated petitioned the board of supervisors for permission to continue their business in the various houses which they had been occupying and using for laundries for more than twenty years, and such petitions were denied, and all the petitions of those who were not Chinese, with one exception of Mrs. Mary Meagles, were granted. . . ."

Mr. JUSTICE MATTHEWS delivered the opinion of the court.

. . . The rights of the petitioners, as affected by the proceedings of which they complain, are not less because they are aliens and subjects of the Emperor of China. By the third article of the treaty between this Government and that of China, concluded November 17, 1880, 22 Stat. 827, it is stipulated: "If Chinese laborers, or Chinese of any other class, now either permanently or temporarily residing in the territory of the United States, meet with ill treatment at the hands of any other persons, the Government of the United States will exert all its powers to devise measures for their protection, and to secure to them the same rights, privileges, immunities and exemptions as may be enjoyed by the citizens or subjects of the most favored nation, and to which they are entitled by treaty."

The Fourteenth Amendment to the Constitution is not confined to the protection of citizens. It says: "Nor shall any State deprive any person of life, liberty, or property without due process of law; nor deny to any person within its jurisdiction the equal protection of the laws."

These provisions are universal in their application to all persons within the territorial jurisdiction, without regard to any differences of race, of color, or of nationality, and the equal protection of the laws is a pledge of the protection of equal laws. It is accordingly enacted by § 1977 of the Revised Statutes, that "all persons within the jurisdiction of the United States shall have the same right in every State and Territory to make and enforce contracts, to sue, be parties, give evidence, and to the full and equal benefit of all laws and proceedings for the security of persons and property as is enjoyed by white citizens and shall be subject to like punishment, pains, penalties, taxes, licenses, and exactions of every kind, and to no other."

The questions we have to consider and decide in these cases, therefore, are to be treated as invoking the rights of every citizen of the United States equally with those of the strangers and aliens who now invoke the jurisdiction of the court. . . .

Though the law itself be fair on its face and impartial in appearance, yet, if it is applied and administered by public authority with an evil eye and an unequal hand, so as practically to make unjust and illegal discriminations between persons in similar circumstances, material to their rights, the denial of equal justice is still within the prohibition of the Constitution. . . .

The present cases, as shown by the facts disclosed in the record, are within this class. It appears that both petitioners have complied with every requisite deemed by the law or by the public officers charged with its administration necessary for the protection of neighboring property from fire or as a precaution against injury to the public health. No reason whatever, except the will of the supervisors, is assigned why they should not be permitted to carry on, in the accustomed manner, their harmless and useful occupation, on which they depend for a livelihood. And while this consent of the supervisors is withheld from them and from two hundred others who have also petitioned, all of whom happen to be Chinese subjects, eighty others, not Chinese subjects, are permitted to carry on the same business under similar conditions. The fact of this discrimination is admitted. No reason for it is shown, and the conclusion cannot be resisted that no reason for it exists except hostility to the race and nationality to which the petitioners belong, and which, in the eye of the law, is not justified. The discrimination is, therefore, illegal, and the public administration which enforces it is a denial of the equal protection of the laws and a violation of the Fourteenth Amendment of the Constitution. The imprisonment of the petitioners is, therefore, illegal, and they must be discharged. To this end,

The judgment of the Supreme Court of California in the case of Yick Wo, and that of the Circuit Court of the United States for the District of California in the case of Wo Lee, are severally reversed, and the cases remanded, each to the proper court, with directions to discharge the petitioners from custody and imprisonment.

Source: Yick Wo v. Hopkins, 118 U.S. 356, 6 S. Ct. 1064, 30 L.Ed. 220, 1886.

"An Address from the Workingmen of San Francisco to Their Brothers throughout the Pacific Coast"

(1888)

The 1868 Burlingame Treaty established friendly relations between the United States and China and called for immigrants in each country to be treated fairly and equally. In 1880, the treaty was amended, and Chinese immigration to the United States was temporarily suspended; two years later, the Chinese Exclusion Act prohibited all skilled and unskilled Chinese laborers and miners from immigrating to the United States. The Chinese Exclusion Act was renewed many times over the following decades, in large part because of pressure from labor organizations.

The "Address from the Workingmen of San Francisco" was published by the California Workingman's Party in 1888. This labor organization, founded in the 1870s, consistently used racist rhetoric against Chinese immigrant laborers, whom they viewed as their primary competition, especially for jobs on the railroad. The address is a long political advertisement extolling the glorious history of the exclusion movement and calling for Californians to vote against Benjamin Harrison in the upcoming presidential election. The address seeks to frame exclusion in terms of class: according to the pamphlet, working-class men have had their wages cut and have lost jobs because of the influx of cheap Chinese labor. However, classic yellow peril rhetoric permeates the text, inciting racial fears and the propagation of stereotypes about Chinese culture and Chinese Americans.

FELLOW-CITIZENS OF THE PRODUCING AND WORKING CLASSES OF THE STATE OF CALIFORNIA: –

We have met here in San Francisco to-night to raise our voice to you in warning of a great danger that seems to us imminent, and threatens our almost utter destruction as a prosperous community; and we beg each and every citizen of the State, without distinction of political party, depending on their own labor for the support of themselves and families, to hear us and to take time to examine with the utmost care the reasons and the facts we will give for believing a great danger to be now confronting us.

No consideration of a partisan character should weigh with us for a moment when our *all* is at stake. That *all* means the opportunity to work at some honest avocation which will insure us a respectable living and the support of our families in the reasonable comforts of life. The danger is, that while we have been sleeping in fancied security, believing that the tide of Mongolian immigration to our State has been checked and was in fair way to be entirely stopped, our opponents, the pro-China wealthy men of the land, have been wide-awake and have succeeded in reviving the importation of this servile slave-labor to almost its former proportions. So that, now, hundreds and thousands of Mongolians are every week flocking into our State. Let us go back, say, ten years in the history of our struggle against this heathen invasion which so plainly threatened the destruction of the white population of this coast.

The first outcry against them came from the mining districts of the State. The people of the large cities and agricultural districts were at first slow to follow in the demand made by the miners that the Mongolians must be driven back to their own country. Soon, however, as they spread over the entire State, the blight they brought wherever they located was recognized by all, even by those who gave them employment. The white laborers all over the State were not wanted except at starving rates of wages. The large cities soon became crowded with white men seeking employment.

Storekeepers in the country towns found that they sold no goods, for the white men had gone and the Chinese lived on rice, and made or imported their own clothes. All sorts of employment soon became monopolized by the Mongolian cheap workers; they began to farm extensively in the raising of all kinds of vegetables, always underselling the white farmer. A general stagnation of all sorts of business was manifestly the situation all over the State, our boys and our girls had no employment, and were becoming a scandal instead of a blessing to their parents; the values of real estate began to shrink. All this was so, and yet no one seemed to understand the cause. Then suddenly there came that never-to-be-forgotten cry from the San Francisco sand-lots, "The Chinese must go!" . . .

Now, what is our position to-day on this whole question? Are we through with the fight? No sensible or sane man will say we are. To-day we have two hundred thousand Chinese in the State, which is more than we had the day the miners first demanded their expulsion. Of these over forty thousand of both sexes live in San Francisco. We have a worse Chinatown now than we had then, with all the same filth, nastiness and other unspeakable horrors, dragging down to leprosy, shame and death, thousands of our white youths, who have been made idle vagabonds by the presence of the Chinese and the impossibility of finding work to make an honest living all this is much worse than it was eight years ago. To-day every avenue to labor, of every sort, is crowded with Chinese slave labor worse than it was eight years ago. The boot, shoe and cigar industries are almost entirely in their hands. In the manufacture of men's overalls and women's and children's underwear they run over three thousand sewing machines night and day. They monopolize nearly all the farming done to supply the market with all sorts of vegetables. This state of things brings about a terrible competition between our own people, who must live, if they live at all, in accord with American civilization, and the labor of a people, who live like what in fact they are, degraded serfs under masters who hold them in slavery. We should all understand that this state of things cannot be much longer endured. . . .

We will conclude, fellow-citizens, by urging and imploring of you to calmly consider what we have said in this address. Merchants, mechanics, professional men, farmers, real-estate owners, dealers in real estate, bankers, dealers in money, as well as wage-workers, are all deeply interested. We ask you all to look back to the years 1878 and 1879, and ask yourselves if you want a possible return to that dark and gloomy time. We ask you to remember that the first dawn of returning prosperity appeared just as soon as all political parties became united in vigorous action against the influx of Chinese slave labor, and that that dawn broadened into sunshine brighter and brighter as our efforts at Washington seemed to grow hopeful and more hopefully that every succeeding session of Congress would result in the ultimate fruition of our struggle to drive the Chinese plague forever from our State.

Then came the vast immigration to California from the Eastern States, and with it prosperity beyond our most sanguine hopes, making us almost dizzy with the view it disclosed to our excited imagination of the future glory and grandeur of our State.

But now, fellow-citizens, observe that a check in our onward career of prosperity has undoubtedly appeared at this time—not much, so far—but enough to warn us of what it may come to, if we do not arouse ourselves from apathy and look the fact square in the face; that the Mongolian invasion has again commenced, and that if the people of California go back on their record on that all-important question on the 6th of November next, by casting the electoral vote of the State for a man with Harrison's record, the return of the dark days of the past seems inevitable. This must be the conclusion that every thinking man will come to on a calm reflection over the past history of our State.

We have shown you, fellow-citizens, beyond a question of doubt, that this cry about "free trade" is not sincere, but a lying fraud put forth by an unscrupulous partisan press in an effort to deceive the masses of the people. We ask you now, will the vile trick succeed?

Fellow-citizens: This question you will answer on the 6th day of next November. On that momentous day answer it as your patriotism and love of country will dictate to you. Answer it with your eyes on the fireside homes of your wives and your children, threatened with destruction by the Mongolian hordes. Your country is our country. Your prosperity is our prosperity. Your destruction will be our destruction; and in all we have said, you must believe us as only seeking for our united and common welfare.

Source: "An Address from the Workingmen of San Francisco to Their Brothers throughout the Pacific Coast," 1888, 2–3, 4, 24. California Historical Society, 325.251.Sa5a. http://content.cdlib.org/ark:/13030/hb7199n8g9/?&brand=oac. Courtesy of the California Historical Society.

Angel Island Poem, by One from Ziangshan
(undated, ca. 1910–1940)

In 1882, under pressure from xenophobic labor organizations, including the Knights of Labor, and racist political groups, such as the Supreme Order of Caucasians, the United States passed the Chinese Exclusion Act. Along with prohibiting Chinese laborers from entering the United States, the Exclusion Act, and its subsequent renewals also made it difficult for Chinese immigrants residing legally in the United States to leave and reenter the country. However, the 1906 San Francisco fire destroyed the City Hall and all the government documents it housed—including birth certificates. Chinese immigrants seized the opportunity to claim that they were born in the United States and thus were American citizens. Prospective immigrants claimed fictitious family ties to resident Chinese American citizens, thus bypassing the strictures of the Exclusion Act.

The Immigration Station on Angel Island in San Francisco Bay processed hundreds of thousands of immigrants from its opening in 1910 until it burned down in 1940. Upon disembarking at Angel Island, men and women were separated, subjected to medical examinations, and detained in barrack housing. Chinese immigrants often waited for months before appearing before the Bureau of Immigration's Board of Special Inquiry for interrogations. Some of the detainees carved poems into the wooden walls of the Immigration Station, mimicking classical Chinese poetry forms in their colloquial Cantonese. They wrote of their experiences and emotions on Angel Island, often bitterly castigating the United States for not extending to the Chinese its promise of freedom and opportunity. The following poem was written by an anonymous man from Ziangshan (Zhongshan), a city in Guangdong Province in southern China, where most early 20th-century Chinese immigrants originated.

There are tens of thousands of poems composed on these walls.
They are all cries of complaint and sadness.
The day I am rid of this prison and attain success,
I must remember that this chapter once existed.
In my daily needs, I must be frugal.
Needless extravagance leads youth to ruin.
All my compatriots should please be mindful.
Once you have some small gains, return home early.
By One From Ziangshan

Source: Lai, Him Mark, Genny Lim, and Judy Yung. *Island: Poetry and History of Chinese Immigrants on Angel Island, 1910–1940.* Seattle: University of Washington Press, 1991, 66. Reprinted with permission from the University of Washington Press.

Case of Huey Jing and Huey Fong
(1913)

Many Chinese circumvented the Chinese Exclusion Acts by posing as "paper sons." The spotty birth and immigration records in China and the United States allowed people to falsely claim American citizenship or legal residency. Documented Chinese residents in the United States would journey back to China to visit their wives and family. When these men returned to America, they would claim to have fathered as many children as was plausible given the duration of their time away. For example, someone who was in China for two years could claim he had two children. Every fictitious child represented one immigration slot that could be used by a relative, a friend of the family, a neighbor, or even a stranger. These people became known as paper sons.

Immigration officials were well aware that the Chinese were claiming invented familial relationships. To counter what they saw as outright fraud, officials carefully scrutinized prospective Chinese immigrants, conducting incredibly meticulous and detailed interviews with them and their alleged fathers once they landed in America. Such was the case of Huey Jing and Huey Fong.

On February 4, 1913, the Hueys arrived in San Francisco aboard the S.S. Mongolia. *The two men claimed they were the sons of Huey Wah, a native citizen of the United States, and they were interviewed to determine the validity of their relationship. Huey Wah's citizenship had already been established through an interview conducted with immigration officials in 1898. Although Huey Wah's U.S. citizenship was confirmed, Inspector J. B. Warner recommended that Huey Jing and Huey Fong be denied entry, basing his decision on what he saw as a number of serious discrepancies in their testimonies. The commissioner at Angel Island ruled against the brothers on March 3,*

1913. One day later, Huey Fong filed an appeal to contest his denial through his attorneys Oliver Stidger and Henry Kennah (from the San Francisco law firm Stidger, Stidger, and Kennah, which often acted on behalf of Chinese immigrants, the Chinese consulate, and the Chinese Six Companies). However, his attorneys withdrew their client's appeal and requested that the two men be placed on a steamer to China the next day.

The following excerpts from the case file include the original interviews of Huey Fong and Huey Wah. The interviewer asks very detailed questions about everything from their alleged neighbors to the layout of their village to their family history in an attempt to find dissimilarities between their two accounts that will prove they are lying about their relationship.

STATEMENT OF APPLICANT HUEY FONG

United States Immigration Service Chinese Division

Angel Island Station, San Francisco, California February 14, 1913
#12505/2–11, Huey Jing, and: Inspector J.B. Warner
#12505/4–2, Huey Fong, sons:
of Native, ex ss "Mongolia": Stenographer S.W. Buchanan
2/14/13:
Interpreter Ed. L. Park

Statement of applicant—Huey Fong, _____ Sworn.

Applicant speaks See Yip dialect; Interpreter Park originally speaks Sam Yup dialect and is qualified in See Yip dialect.

Q   What are your names?

A   Huey Fong; no other names; not married.

Q   How old are you?

A   19 . . .

Q   Where were you born?

A   Huey Oak village, S.N. Dist.

Q   How large is that village?

A   About 20 houses.

Q   How is this village arranged?

A   10 houses to each row (2 rows).

Q   Where is your house located?

A   5th row second house.

Q   Who lives in the first house 5th row?

A   Huey You Jung; married; wife has natural feet; no children.

Q   Are they living or dead?

A   Yes, living there when I left China: always lived there; he is about 60 years old.

Q   Who lives in the first house 6th row?

A   Huey You; married; wife has natural feet; one boy
     Huey Lin Woon; 12 or 13 years old; no girl.

Q   Who lives in the second house 6th row?

A   Huey Jung Chung; married; wife has natural feet; one boy Huey Fook; about 11 or 12 years old; no girl . . .

Q   Who lives in the 2nd house 4th row?

A   Huey Sick Poy; married; wife has natural feet; one girl about 3 years old, I don't know her name. No boys . . .

Q   Where is the school located?

A   7th row, first house.

Q   Do you know anybody in your village by the name of Huey Mon Nam?

A   Yes, he lives 3rd row, first house.

Q   Is that man married?

A   Yes; wife has natural feet; one boy Huey Bo, about 10 years old.

Q   How is your village supplied with water?

A   Well opposite the first row.

Q   Any wall around your village?

A   No.

Q   What is the nearest market?

A   Look Bo market one li away to the east.

Q   Name some of the nearby villages?

A   Jock Mee to the east.

Q   Has that village any other name?

A   No other name. To the West is a Lew Village, I don't know the name.

Q   Where is the nearest ancestral hall in your village?

A   I don't know any.

Q   Where do your family worship?

A   I don't know.

Q   Is there any temple near there?

A   May be there is a temple there I do not know.

Q   Why don't you know if you came from that village?

A   Temple must be far away—I do not know about it.

Q   Do you live in that village?

A   Yes.

Q   How is it that you do not know anything about the surroundings?

A   I have never seen one.

Q   Did you ever hear anyone talk of a temple?

A   I never heard of it . . .

Q   What is your father's name?

A   Huey Wah alias Huey Sing.

Q   How old is your father?

A   41.

Q   41, that is right is it?

A   Yes.

Q   When did you last see your father?

A   Last year.

Q   Where did you see him?

A   Home.

Q   What was he doing while in China?

A   Doing nothing—stayed at home.

Q   Stayed at home all the time?

A   Stayed at home a little over a year.

Q   Did he have any business interests in China?

A   No.

Q   You never heard of his having any business interests in China?

A   No.

Q   You are positive of that?

A   Yes, I am.

Q   Did your father remain at home during his entire stay in China on his last trip; that is most of the time?

A   Yes.

Q   Was he gone from 10 to 15 to 20 days a month?

A   Never away so long.

Q   He was never away 15–20– or 25 days at a time during his last visit home?

A   No.

Q   When did you see your father in China before his last trip?

A   KS 31.

Q   How long did he remain at home?

A   Until KS 34.

Q   Did he have any business interests in China during that stay to your knowledge?

A   No.

Q   Was he at home most of the time?

A Yes . . .

Q What is your paternal grandfather's name?

A Huey Yee Wah; that is the only name I know for him.

Q Living or dead?

A Dead; I never saw him.

Q What is your paternal grandmother's name?

A Yip Shee.

Q Did you ever see her?

A She is dead.

Q Did your paternal grandfather have more than one wife?

A One only.

Q And her name is Yip Shee?

A Yes.

Q Has your father any brothers or sisters?

A No.

Q What is your mother's name, age and what kind of feet?

A Lew Shee; natural feet; 36 years old.

Q Native of what village?

A Hong How village; 5 lis away.

Q What is her father's name?

A Lew Hee; I don't know his other name; he is dead; I never saw him.

Q What is your maternal grandmother's name?

A Dead; I don't know her name; never saw her.

Q Has your mother any brothers or sisters?

A One brother, Lew Lip Gip; I never saw him; he is married and has one boy; I have seen the boy; he has been to my village; his name is Lew Fook, 12 or 13 years old.

Q How many brothers and sisters have you?

A Four brothers and one sister.

Q Names, ages, and dates of birth if you know.

A Huey Jung, 17 years; applicant
Huey Heung; 16; in China in the home village.
Huey Sin; 9 years old; at home.
Huey Toy; 6 years old.
Huey Ngook; 7 years old; sister . . .

Q Where did he sleep when your father was home?

A Home.

Q When your father was home did he ever take you and your brother Huey Jing anywhere?

A No.

Q Where did you have your photograph taken?

A Hong Kong.

Q When?

A When I left home to come to the United States.

Q Did you send your picture to the United States to your father?

A No.

Q Who attached it to the paper?

A My father wrote to the man who looked after my papers in Hong Kong and he pasted it on.

Q Who was that man?

A A man in the firm of Quong Lung Company, Hong Kong . . .

Q Is there anybody now in the United States who has seen you in China?

A Dong Leong Gow.

Q When and under what circumstances?

A He came to visit us the latter part of KS 32.

Q Did he come from the United States?

A Yes, came to visit my father while my father was home.

Q Did he visit the house more than once?

A Twice.

Q Was your father home both times?

A Yes.

Q Anyone else?

A Gee Soon.

Q When, where, and under what circumstances did he see you and your brothers in China?

A ST 1–6th or 7th month he brought a letter and $10 Mex. to my mother from my father.

Q Did he ever visit your village again?

A Yes.

Q What was the occasion of his second visit?

A He came to see if there was a letter to bring back to my father from my mother but he didn't get any, we didn't give him any letter.

Q He saw all the family members at that time?

A Yes he saw us all.
(Identifies all photographs)

Q Have you anything further to state?

A No.

(Interpreter Louis Fon called and he asked the applicant if he had understood the interpreter in the case and he answered in the affirmative.)

Signed Chinese Characters,
2/20/13—SWB

ALLEGED FATHER RE-CALLED

Q What are your names?

A Huey Wah and Huey Sing.

Q Will you kindly remember that you are under oath and that you have sworn to tell the truth concerning your alleged sons?

A Yes.

Q   I will ask you to identify certain photographs? (Showing photograph No. 6 Doric May 17, 1898, Huey Way?[)]

A   Myself.
(Showing No. 3 Mongolia November 22, 1908?[)]

A   That is myself.

Q   You stated that you had made three trips to China, is that correct?

A   Yes.

Q   Will you state what your occupation was from KS 30 to KS 34?

A   I didn't do anything.

Q   No occupation at all?

A   Just visiting.

Q   You had no business interests in China at all?

A   No.

Q   Have you any business interests in China now?

A   Yes.

Q   Where?

A   Gong Moon city.

Q   When did you acquire that interest in Gong Moon city?

A   KS 34 before I returned to the United States.

Q   Do you still retain that interest?

A   Yes.

Q   Did you take an active part in the conduct of that business in ST 2 and 3?

A   No active part.

Q   How much time did you spend in Gong Moon city in that store?

A   10 or 20 days each month.

Q   All the time you were in China on this last trip?

A   Yes.

Q   Were you absent from your village from 10 to 20 days a month each month during your stay at home during ST 2 and 2?

A   Yes.

Q   Your family, of course, knew that you had business interests in Gong Moon?

A   My boys would not know but my wife would.

Q   Why wouldn't your boys know?

A   I would not tell them.

Q   Why not?

A   They attended school—I would not want to tell them about it.

Q   What time was it last year that you took your boys to Hong Kong?

A   About the 4th or 5th month of last year.

Q   How long did you stay?

A   A few days.

Q   Where did you stop?

A   Quong Lung Company.

Q   Did Huey Fong and Huey Jing both have their photographs taken at that time?

A   I came out with them to the city but I did not take them to the photograph gallery; somebody from Quong Lung Company did.

Q   Did you bring the photograph back to the United States with you?

A   No . . .

Q   When you were in China did you worship?

A   Gee Lip Sing temple.

Q   How far distant?

A   2 or 3 lis.

Q   Did you take your family to worship there?

A   No.

Q   Did your family ever go there to worship?

A   No, I do not think they have ever been there.

Q   How does it happen that you went there and did not take your children?

A   I just went there—I did not have to take my boys.

Q   Have you anything further to state?

A   No.

(Interpreter Robert Lym called and he asked the alleged father if he had understood the interpreter in the case and he answered in the affirmative.)

Signed Chinese Characters.

2/21/13—SWB

REPORT BY INSPECTOR J.B. WARNER IN REGARDS TO HUEY CASE

Department of Commerce and Labor Immigration Service

Nos.
12505/4–2
12505/2–11

OFFICE OF THE COMMISSIONER

ANGEL ISLAND STATION

VIA FERRY POST OFFICE

SAN FRANCISCO, CAL.
February 24, 1913
Inspector in Charge,
Chinese Division,
Angel Island Station,

San Francisco, California.

In re Huey Jing and Huey Fong, Sons of native, ex ss "Mongolia"

2/4/13:

In my report on form 2020, I stated that I did not believe that the relationship existed between these applicants and their alleged father nor did I believe that they are brothers. In the first place, there is absolutely no resemblance between either of the applicants nor between the applicants and their alleged father. Again, the alleged father experienced considerable difficulty identifying the photographs of the applicants and finally did identify them correctly, and then identified the photograph of the identifying witness as his oldest son. This witness, however, did not testify and the alleged father did not know his whereabouts.

Huey Wah alias Huey Sing, states that he is 38 years of age; both of the alleged sons gave his age as 41.

He has made three trips to China, first returning May 17, 1898; second return November 22, 1908.; and third return September 30, 1912. Applicant Huey Jing states that he never saw his father from KS 24 until ST 2: that he, the applicant, was present in his village in his 9th, 10th, and 11th years, and that he is positive that he did not see his father in KS 31, 32, 33, or 34.

The alleged father states that his father died in KS 30 before he returned to China. Both of these applicants state that he died before they were born.

The alleged father states that his mother's name was Lew Shee; and that his father never had but the one wife. Applicants state that their paternal grandmother's name was Yip Shee.

The alleged father states that he took both of these applicants on a visit to Hong Kong; the applicants both say that he never took them to Hong Kong at any time.

The alleged father further states that he was not at home for from six to ten days a month during his last visit in China as he was interested in a store in Gong Moon city, Sun Wooey District, which is about 4 or 5 lis distant and is an entirely different district from his home. The applicants both say that the only time their alleged father was away from home was to walk to the market in the morning returning the same day in the evening.

These to my mind, are the most important discrepancies, but there are other discrepancies concerning the inhabitants of the home village, but I think those enumerated are enough to show the fraudulent nature of these cases[.]

I recommend that both these applicants be denied landing.

J.B. Warner
Immigrant Inspector

Source: Statement of Applicant, Huey Fong, February 14, 1913; J. B. Warner, Immigrant Inspector in Charge, Chinese Division, Angel Island Station, February 24, 1913; Statement of Huey Wah, February 26, 1913; 12505/4–2 [HUEY Fong]; Box 666; Immigration Arrival Investigation Case Files, 1884–1944 (ARC 296445); Records of the Immigration and Naturalization Service, Record Group 85; National Archives and Records Administration-Pacific Region (San Francisco).

Portland Tong Peace Agreement

(1917)

Early 20th-century Chinese immigrants to the United States encountered an intimidating environment characterized by discriminatory laws and ordinances, economic antagonism, constant threats of racial violence, and government attitudes ranging from indifference to outright hostility. In response, the Chinese retreated into ethnic enclaves. Organizations and structures imported from their homeland provided financial and physical support as well as cultural continuity. Tongs were one such organization. Originally 18th-century secret societies that occasionally engaged in violent political insubordination, tongs resurfaced as mutual protection societies in 19th-century Chinese immigrant communities. However, many tongs also took over organized crime in Chinatowns, trafficking in Chinese women; controlling international drug, gambling, and prostitution rings; and exploiting business owners with protection rackets. Inter-tong feuds over territory and profits often turned violent, and several tong wars occurred across the United States between the 1860s and the 1920s. The following document records a peace agreement between several tongs in Portland, Oregon.

It is hereby covenanted and agreed between the Hip Sing Tong and SUEY Sing Tong on the part of said societies, its officers and each and all of the members thereof and of all persons associated and allied with them, and the Bing Kung-Bow Leong and Hip Sing Tongs on the part of said societies, its officers and each and all the members thereof and of all persons associated and allied with them, that they will maintain peace and order among their members and all persons mentioned in this agreement within the County of Multnomah, State of Oregon, for a period of thirty (30) days from the day of execution of these present, and it is further hereby covenanted and agreed that they will prevent each and all, of their said officers and members of said societies and associated persons from entering into any quarrells [sic], disorders or unlawful acts with any of the members of the said societies or its officers or said persons associated or allied with them, and that they will not give aid, assistance, contenance [sic] or shelter to any of their members or others who shall violate any of the covenants herein contained or any other persons who shall within said period come into the County of Multnomah, State of Oregon, for any unlawful or disorderly purpose.

And we further hereby agree that we will make every effort to bring about permanent peace between the respective parties hereto and adjust all differences between us at the earliest possible date.

And we further hereby agree that in case either of the parties hereto shall violate any of the covenants or agreements herein contained we will forthwith furnish to the proper officers of the law, the information and evidence necessary to obtain redress for said wrongs in the courts of law.

IN WITNESS WHEREOF the said societies have caused these presents to be executed this 31st day of March, 1917, by the Secretaries of the said societies and have authorized the official seal of said societies to be attached to this compact.

WITNESS
By H.R. Albee
By HIP SING TONG, Secretary

Source: "Portland Tong Peace Agreement," 1917. Mss 190, Oregon Historical Society Research Library. http:// kaga.wsulibs.wsu.edu/cdm-imls_2/document.php? CISOROOT=/wsuvan1&CISOPTR=1260&REC=5 . Courtesy Oregon Historical Society.

Yee Wee Thing Betrayal Letter
(1920)

In 1907, Yee Guey, a Chinese American man living in San Francisco, signed an affidavit saying that he was a U.S. citizen and that he wanted to bring his Chinese son, Yee Wee Thing, to the United States. A year before, the San Francisco earthquake and fire had destroyed all the birth certificates, immigration files, and naturalization forms stored in the records office. It was impossible to tell who among the Chinese Americans had been born in the United States and thus could legally bring in children born in China and who were immigrants, ineligible for citizenship and unable to sponsor relatives. Yee Wee Thing's actual relationship to Yee Guey is uncertain. However, in 1916, nearly 10 years after his alleged father filed his affidavit, and after one day of interrogation at Angel Island, he was deemed a legitimate son and allowed to go to the mainland.

Yee Wee Thing soon moved from California to Globe, Arizona, where he worked at the Sang Tai restaurant owned by Dea Gin Foo of San Francisco. While in Arizona, Yee became entangled in a dispute between rival factions of the Dea family. One member accused Yee of being the child of the cook at the Sang Tai restaurant and actually sent a letter to the immigration office accusing the restaurant owner, Dea Gin Foo, of running a smuggling operation that brought Yee into the country under false pretenses. The immigration officer was not impressed with the story or the accusation, and he allowed Yee to stay in the United States. On September 23, 1923, Yee was granted a certificate of return, allowing him to go back to China for a visit. He returned two years later and claimed that he had married a woman and fathered a son in the interim. In 1938, Yee Bing Quai arrived in Boston claiming to be Yee Wee Thing's son.

The following is the letter written by Dea Goon Foo, the rival family member, accusing Yee of entering the United States illegally. Dea's letter illustrates the complexity of exclusion-era Chinese immigration. Although U.S. laws created the context of institutionalized racism, the Chinese themselves took advantage of the unpredictable situation to make a living, settle rivalries, and create a space in the United States for themselves and their loosely defined family members.

833 Grant Ave.,
San Francisco, Cal.
March 2nd, 1920
To the Tucson Immigration Office.

Gentlemen: —

Am sending you this letter today for no other reason than to inform you that one Dea Gin Foo, a resident of Globe, has been assisting people to gain illegal entrance into the United States. There is now in Globe, in the Sang Tai restaurant, working as waiter named See Hoo Kay. He came to the United States on a paper which he bought, and admitted as a son of native. His real name is See Hoo and is not Yee. He is a grandson of Dea Gin Foo's wife's people. I can testify to that fact; I can testify to the place where he belongs, his village, and whose son he is. If you have authority to deport him back to China, I am willing to serve as witness. If you need me to testify you will furnished me my railroad transportation then I will surely come, and give testimony before court.

You arrest and bring See Hoo Kay to Tucson then I will testify, but not in Globe. With kind regards.

(Signed) Dea Goon Foo (In English)

On envelope:
Sent by Wee Po.

I hereby certify that the above is a correct translation of the letter written in Chinese attached herewith.

Lee Park Liu
Chinese Intpr

Source: 24212/2–4 [YEE Wee Thing]; Box 2101; Immigration Arrival Investigation Case Files, 1884–1944 (ARC 296445); Records of the Immigration and Naturalization Service, Record Group 85; National Archives and Records Administration-Pacific Region, San Francisco.

Mary Young Chan, Marriage Certificate and Court Summons (1921)

In 1921, Mary Young Chan initiated divorce proceedings against Jack Chan, her husband of two years. Both native Californians, the Chans married in Oakland and lived in Alameda County. The records from the court proceedings include her 1919 marriage license and certificate, Mary Chan's court deposition, and the Superior Court of Alameda's summons to Jack Chan. The documents, although filtered through the attorney's interpretation, paint a descriptive—and harrowing—picture of Mary Chan's life with her husband.

The Superior Court of the State of California, in and for the County of Alameda.

Mary Young Chan, Plaintiff, vs. Jack Chan, Defendant.

Plaintiff complains and alleges:

I.

That said plaintiff and said defendant intermarried at Oakland, County of Alameda, State of California, on November 25th, 1919, and then and there became husband and wife, and ever since have been and now are husband and wife.

II.

That said plaintiff now is, and for more than one year preceding the commencement of this action has been, a bona fide resident of the State of California and of the County of Alameda.

III.

That said plaintiff is now pregnant with and is carrying, an unborn child, to which she expects to give birth within the next two or three weeks.

IV.

That said plaintiff and said defendant separated on or about June 9th, 1920, and that six (6) months and fifteen (15) days have elapsed between the date of said marriage and the date of said separation.

V.

That ever since said marriage, said defendant, disregarding his marital duties, has by his acts and conduct treated said plaintiff in a cruel and inhuman manner, and has wrongfully, cruelly, wilfully [sic] and inhumanly inflicted upon said plaintiff, and still does wrongfully, cruelly, willfully and inhumanly inflict upon said plaintiff great mental anguish and physical suffering more particularly as follows:

(a) That said defendant is of a jealous, morose, and morbid disposition, and has frequently and continuously, on occasions too numerous to mention, the exact dates of which said plaintiff is not now informed, unjustly and without provocation or cause, wrongfully accused said plaintiff of improper familiarity with men other than said defendant, and has accused her of adulterous intercourse with said men.

(b) That said defendant repeatedly, and on occasions too numerous to specify, the exact dates of which the said plaintiff is not now informed, unjustly and without provocation or cause, denied the paternity of the said child, and openly stated that said child was conceived as a result of intercourse with various white men.

(c) That said defendant has refused to pay the necessary medical and hospital bills required in connection with the birth of said child, and has refused to support it after its birth, and has told said plaintiff that after the birth of said child, she should place it in a public park and there abandon it.

(d) That during the entire married life of the parties hereto, said defendant has frequently and continuously and repeatedly gambled, and lost his earnings, and thereby been unable to contribute to the support of said plaintiff in a proper manner, and has stayed out nights and stayed away from home several days at a time, all without the leave, knowledge or consent of said plaintiff.

(e) That said defendant has frequently, and on occasions to numerous to specify, the exact dates of which said plaintiff has not now informed, sworn, cursed, reviled and applied opprobrious epithets to said plaintiff, such as "whore" and other lewd and lascivious terms, and implied a want of chastity on the part of said plaintiff.

(f) That frequently during the entire married life of said parties, said defendant, on occasions to numerous to specific and the exact dates of which plaintiff does not now recall, has violently and brutally beaten, struck, mistreated and maltreated said plaintiff, and has violently struck her in the face and upon her body with great force and violence, and bruised and lacerated her body; that in this connection, said plaintiff particularly alleges that on or about February 20th, 1920, without cause or provocation, said defendant, with great force and violence, and in a fit of unwarranted rage and anger, repeatedly struck her with his fist about her body, and that on February 5th, 1920, said defendant grabbed her by the hair, without cause or provocation, and pulled her and pushed her to the floor with great force and violence, thereby causing great physical pain to be suffered by said plaintiff.

(g) That in the latter part of February, 1920, said defendant told her to go away from the home of the parties hereto, and to go to the man that she wished, thereby implying a want of chastity on the part of said plaintiff; that in fear of the threats of said defendant, and forced thereby, said plaintiff did leave the home of the parties hereto, and did stay over night in a hotel in San Francisco.

(h) That said defendant, on occasions too numerous to mention, and the exact dates whereof said plaintiff is not now informed, did frequent and consort with women of lewd and lascivious nature, and in this connection said plaintiff particularly alleges that during the week given up to the celebration of the Chinese New Years, in the month of February, 1920, said defendant did remain away from the home of the parties hereto, and did spend his time gambling, drinking, carousing and consorting with and cohabiting with fast women.

(i) That frequently during their entire married life, said defendant would, at the home of the parties hereto, without any cause or provocation given to him by said plaintiff, fly into a violent rage and curse and swear at said plaintiff in loud and boisterous tones, and upbraid said plaintiff for imaginary wrong doings on her part, and would break the furniture and electric fixtures and threaten the life of said plaintiff.

VI.

That there is community property now in the possession of said plaintiff consisting of certain household furniture of a probable value of Two Hundred and Fifty ($250.00) Dollars.

VII.

That said plaintiff is a fit and proper person to have the care, custody and control of the said minor child; that said defendant is not a fit and proper person to have the care, custody and control of the said minor child.

WHEREFORE said plaintiff prays that she be granted a decree of divorce dissolving the bonds of matrimony heretofore existing between the parties hereto, granting to her said community property in her own right, and awarding to her the care, custody and control of the said minor child, and such other relief as may seem meet and proper in the premises.

Leon E. Gray [signature], Attorney for Plaintiff, State of California, County of Alameda

MARY YOUNG CHAN, being first duly sworn, deposes and says: that she is the plaintiff in the above entitled action; that she has read the foregoing Complaint and knows the contents thereof, and that the same is true of her own knowledge, except as to the matters which are therein stated upon her information or belief, and as to those matters she believes it to be true.

Mary Young Chan [signature]

Subscribed and sworn to before me this 2nd day of December, 1920. Helen G. Christiansen [signature], Notary Public in and for the County of Alameda, State of California.

Source: Marriage Certificate and Court Summons: From Papers relating to Chinese in California. 1920, 1–5. BANC MSS C-R 153: fol. 4, The Bancroft Library, University of California, Berkeley. http://sunsite.berkeley.edu/cgi-bin/flipomatic/cic/brk4703.

Carol Green Wilson, *Chinatown Quest*
(1931)

Donaldina Cameron was born in New Zealand in 1869, the daughter of a Scottish emigrant, who subsequently moved his family to California's San Joaquin Valley when she was two years old. Cameron's mother died a few years later, and the family moved yet again, first to a suburb of San Jose, then to Oakland, and finally to a ranch in the San Gabriel Valley, where Cameron spent the rest of her childhood. After finishing teacher's college, Cameron went to work at Margaret Culbertson's Occidental Missions Home for Girls in San Francisco. The Missions Home cared for female Chinese trafficking victims, brought to the United States to serve as house slaves or prostitutes. White San Francisco authorities turned a blind eye to the slave trade, protecting brothels from police raids and regularly accepting bribes from the Chinese tong members who brought the women into the country illegally. Culbertson, and then Cameron, conducted clandestine raids on the brothels, rescuing thousands of women who they then boarded, educated, trained, and—most importantly— evangelized at the Missions Home (later renamed Cameron House).

In 1931, Carol Green Wilson published Chinatown Quest, *a biography of Donaldina Cameron. The following excerpts chronicle some*

of the daring rescues conducted by the Missions Home and highlight the plight of the Chinese women—made worse by the collusion of American judges, lawyers, and policemen in the trafficking business. Chinatown Quest also presents a highly romanticized view of Cameron and rehashes many of the anti-Chinese stereotypes so prevalent in early 20th-century popular literature. Even the most progressive reformers of the day, including Cameron herself, believed the Chinatown sex trade was a result of inherent Chinese immorality, rather than originating in restrictive U.S. immigration laws that created an extreme gender imbalance in the Chinese American community. The excerpts also reveal Cameron's fundamental assumption that rehabilitation meant conversion to Christianity and the adoption of Western cultural forms.

"Now to get home, fast. Forget the speed laws."

The young immigration official glanced at the tightly pursed lips of the white-haired woman beside him; but he lost no time in obeying. He stepped his engine up to sixty as they sped into the blackness of the night. In the back seat of the closely curtained sedan a sobbing little Chinese girl was still shrieking, "Fahn Quai! Fahn Quai! ["White Devil"]" as she shrank away from the outstretched hand of the strange foreigner in the front seat. The calm interpreter beside her spoke in soothing native tongue: "But she is not Fahn Quai. She is Lo Mo ["old mother"]. She has come to protect you."

The young official could not turn his head as the road stretched out before him, but he could use his ears. This was the first raid he had taken part in with Miss Donaldina Cameron. Until now he had understood little of her eventful career in Chinatown: but as the whirring motor sped them from Stockton to San Francisco he had opportunity to understand why there was such a ring of authority in the quick-spoken command that had started their dash through valley and foothills to the securely bolted doors of the red brick dwelling on steep Sacramento Street where this gallant Scotch

gentlewoman harbors her family of Chinese "daughters . . ."

It was a Chinatown that has long since passed into fanciful tradition that Donaldina Cameron came to live and work in on that gray, foggy morning in 1895—welcomed unexpectedly by Eleanor Olney, who sprang up to greet her from the carved teakwood chair in Miss Culbertson's anteroom. "Just for one year," her adoring family had reluctantly consented. In her early twenties, unsophisticated and untrained, she came, overflowing with something unexpressed within that poured out freely and fully to meet the need which greeted her on every hand.

"From the first," she says in reminiscence, "I loved Miss Culbertson. I loved the Chinese. I never remember feeling anything foreign about them. Never will I forget the laughing face of Ah Ying, the first Chinese girl I came to know, as she tapped so gently on my door to announce 'Lunch is ready.'"

Miss Culbertson's niece, Anna, was staying with her at the time, while she attended an art school. Her appearance, at the end of that first afternoon, with an armful of white roses to welcome the new assistant so near her own age is another bright memory of Donaldina's introduction to 920 Sacramento Street.

But it was not entirely a world of sunshine and family love where this girl from southern California had suddenly come to stay. Very soon after her arrival Miss Culbertson called her to the office.

"Are you sure you will not be afraid in this work?"

"Oh, no!" she answered quickly.

"It isn't too late to change your mind—there are dangers, you know."

Immediately her Scotch blood was aroused.
"Why?"

Without raising her voice Miss Culbertson explained that on that very morning the girl who was cleaning the halls had found a strange-looking stick. Police were called and after a hasty investigation declared there was enough explosive in that "stick" to blow up a whole city block. This was unusual, for the Chinese seldom went this far with their bitter threats against the Home. But the latest slave girl rescued by Miss Culbertson had represented such a high purchase price that the owner had attempted to wreak direct vengeance.

Miss Culbertson turned quietly to her new helper.

"Now, are you going to stay?"

"Are you?" just as calmly returned Donaldina Cameron.

"Of course."

"Then I shall stay too."

Thus began a relationship between two women of finely tuned sensibilities which made it possible for the ideals of the older one to live on, transmitted through the devotion of the younger to hundreds of girls, who, though of another race, are one in spirit. Reared in the gentle refinement of a western New York home, Miss Margaret Culbertson had come to California as governess for the small boys of a brother of that well-known pioneer and empire builder, D.O. Mills. Because of their common cultural interests a friendship had sprung up between her and Mrs. P.D. Browne, that motherly friend of the Camerons.

Mrs. Browne had been early identified with a group of women who had sensed a unique need in old San Francisco. Hordes of Chinese, lured across the Pacific by that same glitter that had started covered wagons across the plains in '49, had poured into California to supply the labor needed for the development of mining camps and other industries of this pioneer land. By 1876, of the 148,000 Chinese in America, 60,000 were in California, one-half of these crowded into nine teeming, colorful blocks in San Francisco. In the year 1882, 40,000 Chinese immigrants came in. Bitter opposition began to arise. These thrifty Chinese, with their rice bowls and low standards of living, were considered a menace to white labor. Every reader of Bret Harte and Joaquin Miller is familiar with "the heathen Chinee" of those days, with his long, braided queue, and his stealthy, slippered feet, his reeking opium-den, as well as with "John," the ever-faithful servant appearing with his bowl of

pungent China lilies blossoming for Chinese New Year or with the silk-coated gentleman merchants of old Dupont Street.

But perhaps not so many know the stories of the little slave girls kept behind barred doors of the labyrinthine dwellings of back alleys in old San Francisco's Chinatown. Easily forgotten bits of humanity they were, smuggled in like the opium their owners craved, bought and sold with the shining gold that gleams through all the history of these early days.

Ordinary domestic slaves sold for from $100 to $500; the pretty creatures bartered to the keepers of houses of ill-fame brought much larger sums. In the unequal population of these colonies of Chinese workmen, the lives of these children of the dark were pitiful beyond description. . . .

From her window, barred and guarded as were all of the outlooks of this quiet citadel on the edge of Chinatown of the 'nineties,' Donaldina looked up "China Street," as Sacramento Street was known in those days, to Nob Hill, home of aristocrats, where the Hopkinses, Stanfords, Floods, and Huntingtons ruled the salons which their newly won wealth had ingrafted upon picturesque, pioneering San Francisco. Young and beautiful, with family ties that would have gained her entrée anywhere, Donaldina could easily have had her place in the functions that nightly blazed from this hilltop. The path, however, that led her into the heart of the city's night life followed another direction. Down the steep walk to Stockton and Dupont streets below, this young girl followed her courageous leader into dens that frightened the most adventurous of tourists. Here she beheld sights she had never dreamed existed.

"I'll need your help tonight," Miss Culbertson had said, as she glanced up from a tightly folded scrap of paper which had been slipped into her hands a few days after Donaldina's arrival. With three officers as guards they made their way to Spofford Alley, then one of the worst of the narrow by-passes of Chinatown. The door indicated in the note was heavily barred. No amount of pounding would bring an answer. Out came axes and sledge hammers. A shattered window, its iron gratings pried off by the powerful police, was opened, and in crept the rescue party.

They found an anxious girl nervously awaiting release. With true feminine regard for her possessions she begged the officers to help her get her jewelry and watch held in the safe-keeping of her mistress.

"Not here—I get," readily responded that individual, starting out of the house. An officer stepped to her side to insure her return. What she wanted, and accomplished, was to notify the master of the house in a gambling den a few basements away. "Native son of the Golden West," he was, educated in California public schools, and ready with his subtle answer.

"Let her prove she have property, then I give"; adding, "Madam, you know what these women are—how they tell lies, tell things not true."

"Yes," said Miss Culbertson, drawing herself up with stern dignity to stab this schemer with her piercing brown eyes. "We know these women are what you men make them. You compel them to lead these wretched lives while you live off their earnings."

"Madam, you shut up. You talk too much." He turned on his slippered heel.

No amount of persuasion could produce the missing jewelry; but the rescued slave girl went off to gain, through her redirected life, treasures which neither rust nor thieves could touch. . . .

An older slave girl who had made her own escape was safely installed as a member of the Nine-Twenty family. But her owner, who lived in Palo Alto, a new town sprung up in the shadow of the recently established Leland Stanford Junior University, soon discovered where his property was hidden. One cold March day he appeared at the Sacramento Street Home accompanied by a burly constable holding in his hand a warrant for the arrest of Kum Quai on the charge of stealing jewelry. He showed Miss Cameron a "picture" of the girl he wanted, but unaccustomed as she then was to all the subtle tricks, new with each case, she said quite frankly:

"You have made a mistake. We have no such girl here."

"Let us see for ourselves," demanded the constable, producing his search warrant.

The brass gong was rung, lessons were stopped, sewing was dropped to the floor, and brooms were stood in corners, as the excited family quickly gathered in the large chapel room. This was always the custom when a search was to be made; but usually the guardians knew which girl was wanted and she was carefully hidden between a double folding-door or under rice sacks back of the basement gas meter.

This time, however, no one knew. Miss Cameron was quite sure the searchers were on the wrong track. With horror, then, she saw Kum Quai's face pale at the sight of her leering owner, and she was quite helpless to prevent the course of the law as the constable served the warrant on the terror-stricken girl. She pleaded with him with all her usual force; but he was there to do his duty and earn his fee. No silly woman could stop him. Miss Cameron dismissed the other weeping girls and reluctantly turned the key that opened the heavy bolted front door. The biting wind from the Bay swept up the narrow street, sending added shivers over the thinly clad little girl clinging to Lo Mo's hand.

"Come along, we must be off," demanded the impatient officer jerking her from her protector's arm. For one instant Miss Cameron stood hesitant. Then a voice spoke in her heart: "Go with her—she is yours." And, hatless and coatless, she ran after the retreating trio, followed by Yuen Qui, the interpreter, supplying needed outer wraps. All the way to Palo Alto she sought to calm the despairing girl, who shrank trembling from the rough constable and the triumphant Chinese owner.

Even when the cell doors of the shack they called a jail were locked on her charge, Lo Mo stayed beside her. Two boxes were all the bed provided, but sleep was not to come that night. About midnight voices were heard talking excitedly in the corridor. The jailer appeared to open the cell. Kum Quai's "friends" had arrived with bail. Lo Mo knew this trick well enough. Miss Culbertson had told her too many tales of girls thus bailed out who had completely dropped from sight, or who had been found months later in conditions unspeakably worse than those of their former servitude. She barricaded the door with a piece of scantling, but the bailiff took out his ax. When he had succeeded in battering a hole big enough for his arm, he reached through, knocked down the barricade, and grabbed the girl from Lo Mo.

The exulting Chinamen lifted their pretty into a waiting buggy. Lo Mo climbed in too. But rough hands pulled her out and threw her into the tarweed beside the road. Scarcely sensing whether she was hurt or not, the undaunted Lo Mo fled to the heart of the village for help. The only friend she could rouse was Dr. Hall, a druggist on a corner near the Circle. He introduced her to the proprietor of Larkin's Hotel, who gave her a blanket and allowed her to rest on a sofa in the lobby for the few remaining hours of the night. Dr. Hall then telephoned the San Jose sheriff to send a searching party after the fleeing Chinese.

In the meantime the Palo Alto justice of the peace, returning from a ride on the county road, had met the escaping trio. They asked as a special favor that he hold the trial then and there; and so in an improvised road-side court, and two-thirty in the morning, the frightened girl, waiving jury and counsel, pleaded guilty to the charge against her. One of her escorts acted as interpreter, while the other paid the five-dollar fine imposed by the judge, and off they galloped.

Source: Wilson, Carol Green. *Chinatown Quest.* Stanford, CA: Board of Trustees of the Leland Stanford Junior University Press, 1931, 1–2, 10–12, 16–17, 26–28.

Charles Shepherd, "The Story of Lee, Wong and Ah Jing" (ca. 1933)

Charles Shepherd, originally from England, had been a Baptist missionary in China before he moved to San Francisco's Chinatown in 1919. There, he met Donaldina Cameron, superintendant of the Presbyterian Church's Occidental Mission Home for Girls. The Mission Home served as a refuge for Chinese women and girls who had been smuggled into the United States and sold into sex slavery. Cameron told Shepherd about the plight of orphaned and homeless Chinese American boys, whose mothers had been rescued from prostitution by Cameron's organization.

In 1923, Shepherd founded the Chung Mei Home for Chinese Boys in Berkeley, California. In 1934, he moved the Home to El Cerrito, just north of Berkeley. The home closed in 1954; by then, more than 800 boys had lived there. Chinese American memories of the Chung Mei Home are very mixed. Some, including many former residents, remember it fondly. Others see it as a site of ostensibly benign and yet coercive assimilation, run by people who disdained Chinese culture and viewed their U.S.-born charges as not quite American. The following excerpt from Shepherd's booklet tells the stories of two of the children, Ah Jing and Wong Kwai, who lived in the Chung Mei Home. Shepherd's words reveal his complicated perspective on the boys' Chinese American culture and community and their future as upstanding Christian citizens.

THE STORY OF AH JING

This little fellow was the unhappy victim of inhuman treatment on the part of the woman with whom he lived, and by whom he had been purchased from his real parents on account of the extreme poverty of the latter. In spite of his diminutive stature Ah Jing had considerable spirit which rebelled against this cruel treatment and caused him to run away. For several nights he slept in parks and doorways and in the day time begged his food wherever he could until the police found him and brought him to the Home. His body was terribly scarred and bruised from the beatings he had received. Tearfully he told his story. "This woman is not my real mother," he said. "I would rather go back to China and be a 'cowherd' than stay with her." But there is no way to send Ah Jing back to China, and so, because of the unfitness of this woman to care for him, he stays in Chung Mei Home, and there has become one of the most happy and sunshiny members of the family—always willing to do whatever task is assigned him, and ever ready with a cheery word. He is strikingly intelligent, and is doing excellent work at school.

An Averted Kidnaping [sic]

The story of Wong Kwai is one that is difficult to believe by Americans who are not familiar with the workings of certain groups of Orientals. The phone rang in the office, and the writer, picking up the receiver, placed it to his ear. Over the wires there came the agitated voice of Ah Leen, a young Chinese girl in her teens. "My step-mother has just passed away," ran the story. "She is a widow, and since her husband's death has fallen into the clutches of a group of evil men. These men want to take possession of my little half-brother, Wong Kwai, who is just six years old; but I know that they are planning to take him away from here and I shall never see him again, for my step-mother whispered this to me before she died, and begged me to save Wong Kwai. I know what kind of men they are. They will raise him and train him to do the things that they do. Won't you come and get him and take him into the Home?"

"Where is your little brother now?" asked the writer. "I will come and get him right away."

"You do not need to come now," said the quiet voice over the wire. "According to Chinese custom they must permit him to attend his mother's funeral. They are planning to be at the graveside, and to take him away as soon as the ceremony is over. Please come then, for I shall be unable to do anything alone."

They were there, these men, four of them, and they stood dark of countenance and menacing at the back of the little group that gathered about the grave of this woman. One of them had previously argued with the half-sister that they were able to give the boy better care than she; but she had said nothing, for she knew that other plans were being made for him. Thus, when the ceremony was completed and one of these men stepped forward to take possession of Wong Kwai, Ah Leen grasped one of his little hands and American friend grasped the other. They brushed aside the would-be abductors, and stepping quickly into a waiting car drove away. Wong Kwai was taken to the Juvenile Court and there made a ward of San Francisco County. A few hours later he was joyfully received by the family at Chung Mei.

What Chung Mei Does for These Boys

Numerous boys who have gotten off on the wrong foot, so to speak, have been taken into Chung Mei, helped to find themselves and taught to stand on their own feet and walk straight. To such boys Chung Mei Home means a new start in life, an opportunity to forget the past and begin all over again, a chance to make good. Associated with a group of virile, happy, peppy boys, he comes to see boy life at its best. He learns that there are older men and women who are really his friends and are willing to go out of their way to help make a man of himself. He comes into a healthy stimulating school atmosphere where teachers are kind and sympathetic, where the Oriental boy is never oppressed with the feeling of inferiority. He gets abundance of fresh air, exercise, play and hard work. He finds himself an integral part of an institution that keeps ever to the front of its purpose, namely, THE PROMOTION OF HABITS OF REVERENCE, OBEDIENCE, DISCIPLINE, COURTESY, SELF-RESPECT AND ALL THAT TENDS TOWARD TRUE CHRISTIAN MANLINESS. He lives in an atmosphere which is good but not goody-goody, religious but not abnormally pious. The Christian religion is not rammed down his throat, but ever exemplified before him in an endeavor to make it attractive and winning.

Source: Shepherd, Charles. *The Story of Lee, Wong and Ah Jing*. San Francisco: San Francisco Bay Cities Baptist Union, ca. 1933, 2–4. The Bancroft Library.http://www.oac.cdlib.org/ark:/13030/hb409n99qs/?brand=oac4.

Ruth Chinn, Interview by Stafford Lewis

(1938)

Ruth Chinn was born in Seattle in the early 20th century, but attended Ling Nan University in Canton, China. In 1938, she was interviewed by Stafford Lewis, from the Federal Writers' Project, a Works Progress Administration program from the New Deal. In her interview, Chinn talks about Chinese American boys sent to Canton for their college education. Her description of the cultural conflicts between the American students and their Chinese professors reveals the levels of Americanization among the second generation, even in the ethnic enclaves of Chinatown. It also gives a picture of the upper-class Chinese American community, composed primarily of merchants and diplomats; they enjoyed privileges not granted to the majority laborer class, including the ability to move relatively freely between the United States and China.

It was summer in Canton, China, and very hot. So the American Born Chinese boys from Seattle changed to white linen suits and tropical clothing such as is worn in India and other hot countries. They had been sent to Ling Nan University to complete their education in the Chinese language and history. These boys were from wealthy or well to do families, their ages ranging from 14 to 10 years. Chinese boys from all over the world go to this University.

Professor Wong especially, didn't like the Seattle boys because they were mischievous and played practical jokes. Besides their manners were bad, they were frank and outspoken, they ate too much and spent money they should have saved, for extra meals and picture shows.

The true Chinese boys Professor Wong held up as an example were quiet and mild. They sat down thankfully to their meals in the mess hall that was poorly made up of loose boards and bamboo thatching, and were willing to leave the table half-filled and hungry, without protest. The Seattle boys thought the food was stale and scantily portioned out. So after eating in the mess hall they would use their money to take a launch across the water to Canton. They would go to a hotel and get a good meal, of fresh and plentiful food.

Wing was the leader of a little group of three Seattle boys, and Wing liked to correct Professor Wong whenever his American-gained knowledge gave him a chance, making Professor Wong very angry and leading him to use his position of Professor in charge of Wing's dormitory to teach Wing and the other Seattle boys good manners and the value of money through strict discipline.

So Wing was no longer allowed to play his guitar with American harmony and sing American songs after 10 o'clock at night, when all lights had to [be] out and silence was compulsory. Professor Wing thought Chinese music that cannot be harmonized, much more seemly than the discordant noises Wing and his companions took such delight in. Then, to correct the boys of extravagance, he forced the Seattle boys to put all their money in the treasury—and whenever they asked for their own money, they would only receive a dollar.

This wasn't enough; it cost 20 [cents] to cross the water to Canton in a launch, 20 [cents] cents for a show and at least 60 [cents] for a meal. After 6 in the evening, the boys would have to hire a sampan to get back to the University and this cost much more than the motor launch, 60 or 80 cents.

The boys said, we pay for our education and should be able to lead our own lives, as we do in America. We must all work together to force Professor Wong to break away from his severe rules.

Then the Seattle boys would slip out of the dormitory and play their guitars and sing American songs under the Professor's window as he was trying to sleep. But this only made Wong more strict. He gave Wing and his friends much extra work on studies the boys thought were very dry, tying them down even more.

In desperation, while the Professor was out of the dormitory, the boys took all his white linen out of the closet and spilled ink all over it. Then they put the suits back with a note saying.

"Try and find out who did this."

Professor Wong went to bed without noticing his clothing—but the next morning none of his clothing was fit to wear.

Of course, Wong knew who had spoiled his clothing as the resentment of the Seattle boys against his rules was not hidden from him. And only the American Chinese boys would have the courage necessary to attempt such a destructive trick.

Professor Wong called Wing and his two best friends in his office and gave them the choice of either buying a complete new outfit of clothing for him or being expelled. The boys decided to be expelled as they were all anxious to return to Seattle where there was good food and they could lead their own lives.

Source: Ruth Chinn interview by Stafford Lewis 1938. Library of Congress, Manuscript Division, WPA Federal Writers' Project Collection.

Wing Luke, Speech before Seattle's Chinese American Community (August 17, 1960)

Wing Luke was the first Asian American elected official in the Pacific Northwest. Luke was born in a small town near Canton, China, on February 25, 1925. His family moved to Seattle in 1930 when Luke was only six years old. The eldest of six children, Luke excelled in school but, like others, joined the U.S. Army when World War II began. He served in Guam, Korea, New Guinea, New Britain, and the Philippines, where he received a Bronze Star. After leaving the army, he finished his schooling and became a lawyer. In 1952, he was appointed Washington State assistant attorney general for civil rights. He was elected to the Seattle City Council in 1962. Luke gave this speech to a group of Chinese Americans who were interested in creating a political action group. Although no group was formed, the speech shows the increasing political power of Asian Americans in Washington State. Luke's speech also gives a glimpse into Asian American cultural identity during the civil rights movement.

REMARKS

It would appear to any reasonably observant person of Chinese extraction that there is a growing number of Chinese-Americans in this community who have little or no economic, social, or cultural ties with "Chinatown", Chong Wah, Chinese Baptist Church, family and fraternal associations and the rest of the institutions and cultural matrix usually nebulously classified as the "Chinese community".

In former years language barriers, racial discrimination and the concentration of housing in and around the Chinatown area created a close-knit community for whom the older institutions and customs formed an essential haven of refuge for a minority who felt like aliens in the general social environment. Changes, accelerated by the general social and economic upheavals of World War II, have since acted to loosen these ties. Among the many reasons for the feeling of lack of community are the following:

1. greatly decreased racial prejudice against Orientals since the end of World War II;
2. aided by improved economic standards, so that Chinese Americans are moving out of the older districts and purchasing homes in more far-flung areas of the city;
3. a general advance in the level of education, an increasing number of white-collar business and professional men;
4. the coming of maturity of 3rd and 4th generation Chinese-Americans, many of whom have had little or no cultural experience with the older cultural matrix.

All of the above movements act to create greater gaps in communication between the older and the younger generation, and between members of the same generation. The general acceptance by the general community results in lessening vitality for the older institutions that were formerly relevant because they were meaningful and havens of refugee in an alien society.

As Chinese-Americans, we should of course remember that we are Americans first. There should be no question that as citizens of this country that we owe her our allegiance. The greater acceptance of Chinese-Americans is a salutary development. However, preserving the ties and institutions that are part of our cultural heritage is not inconsistent with integration and one's duty as a good American citizen. In fact, the essential vitality of the American life is that it is constantly enriched by heterogeneous cultures. This fact is recognized in the freedoms protected under the Bill of Rights.

Reasons that argue for a continuing community are these:

1. The disappearance of our rich cultural heritage would be a tragic loss
2. For the foreseeable future, racial and cultural identity as groups will still be present;
3. As immigration laws are relaxed in the future, other Chinese will migrate to this country and there needs to exist institutions that will help them bridge the social and educational gaps in becoming naturalized citizens.
4. Greater acceptance by the general community has partially resulted from the cohesiveness of the Chinese community that has resulted in social stability, low incidence of delinquency and crime and a cultural identity that commanded respect, although admittedly begrudgingly in the past.

The Japanese-Americans in this community furnish a good standard to measure ourselves by. They have managed to greatly improve their economic and social status in recent years, yet have managed to maintain their cultural ties and institutions. Several groups in particular are especially vital and far outstrip comparable Chinese groups in most areas of achievement. The Japanese-American Citizens League is an active and influential social and political force; the Japan Society has made tremendous public relations advances for their people; the Japanese Buddhist Church, and the several other Japanese-American Churches boast a far greater percentage of participation and support than does the one Chinese-Baptist Church.

One needs to only look at the daily papers to note the great prestige that has resulted from such projects as the tea-house gift to Seattle, the Kobe-Seattle sister city project. . . .

Source: Luke, Wing. "Speech before Seattle's Chinese American Community." August 17, 1960. A History Bursting with Telling: Asian Americans in Washington State: A Curriculum Project for the History of the Pacific Northwest in Washington State Schools, Matthew Klingle, developer. Courtesy Wing Luke Museum of the Asian Pacific American Experience.

John Dong, Interview by Elizabeth Calciano
(1967)

John Dong (born Dong Hong Goon) was the last Chinese cook at Cowell Ranch in Santa Cruz, California, in the early 1900s. Dong's father was born in San Francisco but traveled to China several times to find a wife and start a family. Dong was born in Canton, China. When he was in grade school, he joined his father, who was then the Cowell Ranch cook, in California; he later took over his father's position. Henry Cowell had opened the cattle ranch to supplement his lime kiln and logging empire; by the time Dong arrived, however, cement was replacing lime, and the ranch was going into decline.

In his interview with Elizabeth Calciano from the University of California at Santa Cruz Regional History Project, Dong, then aged 58 years, primarily described his daily life as the ranch cook, talking about the logistics of preparing meals with no electricity and on a woodstove. This particular excerpt, however, illustrates the transnational aspects of 19th- and 20th-century Chinese immigration. With very few Chinese women in the United States and strict laws prohibiting interracial marriage, many Chinese American "bachelors" had wives and families thousands of miles away, in China.

Calciano: Even though [your father] was born in San Francisco, did he feel China was his homeland?

Dong: Oh yes. He do. He do. He like China very much. You know, when he was young, grandpa took him back.

Calciano: Do you know how your grandfather happened to come over to this country?

Dong: No I don't. I never even see my grandfather.

Calciano: So your father worked for Cowell from 1912 or 1915 until 1928?

Dong: Yes. Till 1928. Then he take me back to China again.

Calciano: Was there anything that made your father decide to go back in 1928 rather than earlier or later?

Dong: Well, I think he feel he wants to retire. He was almost sixty, you know. So finally he think China was more better than the United States, I think.

Calciano: I see you've got Chinese newspapers here. I gather you talk and read it as your native language.

Dong: Oh yes. I'm a pretty good Chinese reader. I didn't go to school too much in the United States, so I don't understand too much, but I went long enough to learn some things.

Calciano: When you go back to China, do you feel right at home?

Dong: Yes. After I stay in China three or four years, I almost lose everything before I come back to the United States.

Calciano: Oh. You have to learn the English language again?

Dong: Yes, yes.

Calciano: Oh dear. When you were the cook for the Cowell's, you lived right in the cookhouse, didn't you?

Dong: Well, that's the only place to stay. You board in a little room next to the kitchen.

Calciano: Were you married at this time?

Dong: Yes.

Calciano: You were married, but you had to live up there?

Dong: Yes. But my wife is not here though. I didn't bring my wife over.

Calciano: Oh, she was still in China?

Dong: Yes, she was still in China. She just came over about three years ago.

Calciano: Oh my goodness.

Dong: Well, one thing, I hate to take her over here because my mother is still living, see. So we had to have a nurse with her. My mother just passed away about a couple of years ago.

Calciano: So you made several trips back and forth to China?

Dong: Yes. A couple or three times.

Calciano: Were both your sons born in China, too?

Dong: Yes. My boys were born in China.

Calciano: I was wondering, since your wife and fam-
            ily just came over from China three years
            ago, how did they avoid getting caught in
            Red China?

Dong: No, it was not that reason they stayed. My
            mother was still in China so it was all or nothing.

Source: Excerpt from "John Dong, The Cowell Ranch Cookhouse." Interview conducted by Elizabeth Spedding Calciano, 1967. Reprinted with permission from the Regional History Project of the University Library at the University of California, Santa Cruz. http://library.ucsc .edu/reg-hist/.

Esther Don Tang, "Memories of Mother and Father" (1995) and "Thoughts on the Chinese Community Today"

(2005)

In the early 1900s, the Chinese population of Tucson, Arizona, consisted primarily of single men, most of whom had worked on the railroads. After they were forced out of that market by racist labor groups and laws, many Chinese moved into vegetable farming, serving the multiethnic Mexican and American communities in Tucson. As Chinatown grew, businesses were established and organizations and associations were formed, creating a vibrant community. In 1906, Don Wah, a Chinese American born in San Francisco and working in a restaurant in Tucson, journeyed to Hong Kong to get married. His wife, Fok Yut Ngan, was originally from Fujian province in southwest China. Don brought her back to Tucson where they lived for the rest of their lives, raising their 10 children and running a chain of grocery stores. Their third child, Esther Don Tang, born in 1917, grew up a few blocks from Tucson's Chinatown. Her early memories highlight the role Chinatown played in cultural preservation for the immigrants. In 1995, Tang gave an interview describing some of the struggles her parents had faced as they tried to make a life in the United States. Ten years later, she reflected on the changes, both positive and negative, that she had seen in Tucson's Chinese American community.

"MEMORIES OF MOTHER AND FATHER" (1995)

My father came from California, uncomfortable with the political climate and prejudices there. He worked as a cook for the Southern Pacific railroads as they laid the tracks across the southern part of Arizona.

In 1906, he went to China to marry my mother from Fukein [sic; Fukien, or Fujian]. She used to recount stories of her life. Her father, who was a wealthy gold smith and manufacturer of gun powder and fire crackers, had 8 wives. He housed them in separate houses and there was a common kitchen and patio. The complex had a ten foot wall with double gates to keep bandits out. Beyond the wall there was an orchard.

Mother's parents felt that their baby daughter from the first family was going to the Gold Mountain. Little did they know she had to learn to cook and worked in the bakery and store my father owned. At 3 in the morning she would carry me, papoose style, to the store and wrap bread. Dad would deliver his bread to stores in a horse and buggy. On his first delivery his horse spooked and the buggy turned over, spilling the bread all over Simpson and Convent streets. The neighbors scrambled into the street for free loaves.

Customers would buy their groceries and my mother would mark the amounts they owed in a *cartera* (notebook) and return the cartera to the customer. On pay day, everyone would return to the store to pay their bill and receive *pelon*, a gift of fruit or candy. That was really trust!

My father was always proud that he made the deciding vote as to where the Drachman Elementary School should be located. He was at the barbershop getting his queue cut off when some men pulled him from the barber chair to come and break the tie vote.

My mother put $2,000 earnest money on a house in the Belmont subdivision on Country Club Road. The salesman did not tell her that originally the subdivision had been restricted to keep Orientals from living there. On revisiting the house, "No Chinks Wanted" was scribbled on the wall.

My mother and father gave the house up, and lost $1,000 of earnest money, which was a great deal of money in those days. Subsequently they bought two lots from Abe Chanin, a writer for the *Arizona Daily Star*, and built a beautiful house in that neighborhood (Water and Vine Streets).

"THOUGHTS ON THE CHINESE COMMUNITY TODAY" (2005)

I see a great change in the school situation today. My son and daughters, my nieces and nephews by and large participate in all school functions. They date students not of Chinese origin, and have married out of their race. This was not always the case. In the 1940's, my parents put a down payment on a house in the Belmont subdivision. The next day there was obscene writing, letting us know that Chinese were not wanted there. Today, the Chinese live all over Tucson. My own family is something like a United Nations: our son has a Polish wife, and our daughters married an Irishman and a Portuguese.

I believe that our Chinese youth have equal, if not better opportunities than other ethnic groups. This has come about through a tradition that emphasizes excellence in education, performance,

and positive attitude. Chinese parents continually plan financially for their children's education.

In celebrations, the Chinese community comes together. Otherwise, families carry out their own work and activities integrated into the general community workplace and community organizations.

There is still a Ying On Benevolent Society which cares and houses the eldest members of the community. The extended family still is very important. Relatives coming from the homeland are usually given jobs by their family or relatives, or recommended to friends. With the mobility of society and job opportunities elsewhere, families do separate, but the strong ties continue to exist, and visits are frequent. Concern for family members do not diminish with distance.

I believe the future of the Chinese in Tucson is as good as any other group. In fact, they are probably better off in Tucson than many places since they have all the advantages any other citizen has. The Chinese population will continue to grow with newcomers from Taiwan and the mainland. The approximate number today is 3,000 individuals representing 500 families. However that does not count the students and trainees who come to Tucson.

Of course Tucson has changed from a small pueblo of a few thousand. Then everybody knew everyone. Doors were never locked. The air was clean, we swam in irrigation ditches, the traffic was not congested, water was not a problem, crime occurred infrequently (well, except when Dillinger came to town!).

Now I walk down the street and strangers wonder when I arrived by slow boat. We can't stop growth and progress, but we need planning and solutions to water pollution, air quality, education, crime and access to medical assistance, especially for the elderly. I'll always love Tucson, no matter what. My hopes for Tucson are the solutions for these problems. Hopefully our governments will resolve them with commitment to the community's future—and not through political pressure or greed.

My parents taught us early that the community is an extension of our home. We never stop caring and helping our family, no matter how much they go astray. And so it is, as long as I can walk and talk I will give my time and energy to public service—to preserve and to insure the possible best for my family and all of Tucson."

Source: Tang, Esther Don. "Memories of Mother and Father." 1995. "Thoughts on the Chinese Community Today." 2005. *The Promise of Gold Mountain: Tucson's Chinese Heritage, 1995.* http://parentseyes.arizona.edu/promise/donwah.html. Used with permission of David Tang and the Web site The Promise of Gold Mountain: Tucson's Chinese Heritage.

Fred Pang, "Asian-Pacific Americans: Microcosm of Greater National Mix" (1997)

Asian Americans have served in the U.S. military for more than a century. There are records of "Manilamen" fighting with Andrew Jackson in the War of 1812. Chinese American men joined both the Union and Confederate armies during the Civil War. In 1901, President William McKinley signed an executive order allowing Filipinos to join the U.S. Navy; and even after Philippine independence in 1946, a series of treaties ensured that Filipinos could continue to be recruited by the Navy. During World War II, Chinese Americans and Filipino Americans enlisted in large numbers, motivated in large part by anger at Japanese atrocities in China and the Philippines. Maggie Gee and Hazel Ying Lee flew with the Women Airforce Service Pilots, the first and only Chinese American women in the organization. Korean Americans were considered enemy aliens because Japan was currently occupying Korea; nevertheless, roughly 100 Koreans managed to enlist in the U.S. Army. Japanese Americans, despite the indignity of internment, volunteered for service in large numbers; they served in the segregated 100th Battalion and 442nd Regiment and provided translation services in the Military Intelligence Service. Due to the historic naval presence in Pago Pago, American Samoans have a disproportionate presence in the American military. Immigrant and American-born Asian and Pacific American women and men have fought in every war over the past century.

Fred Pang grew up in Honolulu, Hawai'i. He joined the Air Force, where he served for 27 years. He was appointed assistant secretary of defense for force management policy in 1994. In 1997, Pang spoke at the Asian-Pacific American Heritage Month Commemoration. In the following excerpt, Pang talks about notable Asian Americans in the military.

The United States, it has often been noted, is a nation composed almost entirely of descendants of immigrants. We call ourselves Americans, but at the same time, we are proud of our roots—proud of where our parents, our grandparents and our great grandparents came from. We honor our heritage in many public and private ways—parades and festivals from St. Patrick's Day to the Chinese New Year; family recipes from sauerkraut to kimchee; and gatherings from the Knights of Columbus to grandma's Tuesday night mah-jongg circle. And even though our association with the old country fades a bit as the generations progress, I daresay there aren't many of us here that do not keep some of the old traditions of our ethnic backgrounds.

And in many respects, the many nationalities which are collectively called "Asian Americans" are a microcosm segment of our greater national mix. Of course, like African Americans, we look a little different from the Pilgrims, so our ethnicity is necessarily more present in our lives than, say, Irish or Greek Americans. But even that will become less and less important as the color of America changes in the next century—when, collectively, what are now called minorities approach becoming a majority of the population.

How diverse are we as Americans? Well, quite frankly, I don't know of any ethnic group in the world that is not represented in our country. The fact is that there is no other country as diverse as we are.

About 3 1/2 percent of that diverse population—almost 9 million people—trace their roots to Asia and the Pacific Islands. And according to the "National Population Projection," the Census Bureau expects Asian-Pacific Americans to be the fastest growing segment of our population. They predict that by the turn of the century, the Asian-Pacific-American population will expand to over 12 million, double its current size by the year 2010, triple by the year 2020 and increase to more than five times its current size, to 41 million, by the year 2050.

So if we are one piece of America's polyglot puzzle, we are certainly becoming a bigger piece. And our diversity within that diversity continues to grow. It may seem like a mouthful to say Asian-Pacific-American Heritage Month, but try saying Chinese-Japanese-Korean-Filipino-Vietnamese-Thai-Cambodian-Laotian-Hmong-Indian-Pakistani-Bangladeshi-Afghan-Polynesian-Melanesian-American Heritage Month. Now that is a very big mouthful, and those were just examples—I didn't even include all of us.

Is there harmony in our diversity? I think that the answer to that question for us, as Americans, is a qualified "yes." It has been over 130 years since we really had it out among ourselves, which is quite exceptional by world standards. And since then, our society has only gotten more complex and more diverse. Of course, it would be wrong to say we don't have problems that arise from our diversity,

and at times these problems can get ugly. But in general, the principles of law and order and tolerance and freedom have won out in the end. We do not see the kind of extreme ethnic violence that has occurred, tragically, in the formerly communist parts of Europe or in Central Africa, for instance.

As a nation, our harmony in diversity is not an absolute, but it is something that we work toward and are getting better at achieving. I think that is because we share one thing in common. Whether our ancestors endured hardship to escape from the tyranny and poverty of a distant land or from the tyranny and poverty of slavery, they became American citizens to seek a better life for themselves and their families. This common goal ties us together in a relatively harmonious community that is unique in the world.

For Asian Americans, the story began in the mid-1800s, when Asian immigrant laborers were hired for the gold mines and railroad construction in the West and to work sugar and pineapple plantations in Hawai'i. Despite discriminatory laws, which restricted immigration and imposed economic inequities, our forefathers and mothers overcame the fear of a "yellow peril." They tenaciously fought for the rights to which they were entitled and proved to other Americans their loyalty as citizens of this nation.

We who have inherited the fruits of their labors, who have more easily joined into American society must be mindful and appreciative of the struggle that has brought us as a group to where we are today.

As part of this event, I would like to highlight the public service of Asian Americans, and I think it is fitting to start with the highest service any citizen can offer to his or her country—service in wartime. We should honor again the bravery of the famed 100th Battalion of the 442nd Regimental Combat Team, composed almost entirely of Japanese Americans, which became the most decorated unit in our country's military history.

These brave soldiers, who answered the call of their country in war, rose from the ashes of suspicion and fear—many from behind barbed wire in the internment camps — to fight with extraordinary valor in seven major campaigns during World War II. In less than two years, the soldiers of the 442nd received among other awards and citations a . . . Medal of Honor; 52 Distinguished Service Crosses; one Distinguished Service Medal; 560 Silver Stars plus 28 oak leaf clusters; 22 Legions of Merit; 15 Soldiers Medals; 4,000 Bronze Stars with 1,200 oak leaf clusters; 9,486 Purple Hearts for wounds sustained in battle; seven presidential unit citations; two meritorious unit service plaques; 36 Army commendations; 87 division commendations; 18 decorations from allied nations; and a special plaque of appreciation from their fellow soldiers in the "lost" Texas battalion, which the 442nd shed blood to liberate.

As President Truman pinned the final presidential unit citation on the colors of the 442nd, he remarked: "I can't tell you how much I appreciate the privilege of being able to show you just how much the United States thinks of what you have done—you fought not only the enemy but you fought prejudice—and you won. . . . "

While war is ugly and tragic, there is no question that many individuals display outstanding courage and valor in battle. The most supreme acts of heroism are recognized by award of the Congressional Medal of Honor. As part of the commemoration of Asian-Pacific-[American] Heritage Month, we in the Department of Defense pay special tribute to those of Asian-Pacific heritage who received the Medal of Honor. I'd like to read that honored list to you and ask you to join with me in paying humble recognition to their deeds:

In World War I:

- Pvt. Jose B. Nisperos, 34th Company, Philippine Scouts; and
- Fireman Second Class Telesforo Trinidad, U.S. Navy, USS San Diego.

In World War II:

- Pfc. Sadao S. Munemori, U.S. Army, Company A, 100th Infantry Battalion, 442 Regimental Combat Team; and

- Sgt. Jose Calugas, U.S. Army, Battery B, 88th Field Artillery, Philippine Scouts.

In Korea:

- Cpl. Hiroshi H. Miyamura, U.S. Army, Company H, 7th Infantry Regiment, 3rd Infantry Division;
- Pfc. Herbert K. Pililaau, U.S. Army, Company C, 23rd Infantry Regiment, 2nd Infantry Division; and,
- Sgt. Leroy A. Mendonca, U.S. Army, Company B, 7th Infantry Regiment, 3rd Infantry Division.

In Vietnam:

- Sgt. 1st Class Rodney J.T. Yano, U.S. Army Air Cavalry Troop, 11th Armored Cavalry Regiment; and,
- Cpl. Terry T. Kawamura, U.S. Army, 173rd Engineers Company, 173rd Airborne Brigade.

These individuals, through their gallantry, have secured a special place in our history and in our Asian-Pacific-American Heritage. . . .

The Asian-American contribution to public and private life is dynamic and growing. We are bound together by a common desire to improve our country. And it is a cause in which we must enlist our fellow citizens, especially the generation just now starting their careers.

This next generation will come of age as the expansion of the Asian-American population hits the national consciousness. The much-heralded Pacific century will be upon us, and American interdependence with the established and emerging economies of Asia will deepen. So this new generation of Asian Americans must be prepared to do their part to help lead this nation down the path of tolerance—to help the country capitalize on the strengths inherent in diversity. . . .

As a young man growing up in Hawai'i, I remember working as a summer employee in a pineapple cannery. During a break, I overheard a couple of regulars talking about their hopes and aspirations for their children. In the course of their conversation, they talked about how it would be if they never left the "old country" to seek a better life.

It was clear to me that their future and those of their children would have been much bleaker. As they concluded their conversation, I heard one of them say, "We lucky we come to America." So I want to conclude my talk today by echoing the simple conclusion of that conversation 45 years ago: Whatever our prefix—African, European,

Hispanic, native or Asian—we are all lucky to be Americans.

God bless those who have gone before us, and God bless this wonderful country.

Source: Pang, Fred. "Asian-Pacific Americans: Microcosm of Greater National Mix." Prepared Remarks of Fred Pang, assistant secretary of defense for force management policy, Asian-Pacific American Heritage Month Commemoration, Asian/Pacific-American Council of Georgia, Atla, Saturday, May 17, 1997. Defense Issues: vol. 12, no. 28. http://www.defense.gov/speeches/speech.aspx?speechid=726.

Sifu Cheung Shu Pui, "Chinatown without Lion Dancers Would Be a Community Filled with Regret"

(2001)

Kung fu, strongly influenced by Buddhism and Taoism, has developed over thousands of years into many different schools and styles. The relationship between student and "sifu," meaning "master," is of utmost importance. "Sifu" is a term of respect; it takes on a more intimate, familial meaning when used by a student for his or her teacher. Sifu Cheung Shu Pui was trained in Hung Gar Kung Fu, a style originating in a 17th-century Shaolin temple in southern China. Cheung, born and raised in Hong Kong, entered the school as a young adult. In the early 1970s, he immigrated to the United States to teach traditional Chinese martial arts. In 1977, Cheung opened his own academy in Upper Darby, a Philadelphia suburb, where he teaches Chinese language, calligraphy, painting, chess, and kung fu.

In the following excerpts, Cheung tells his immigration story and explains why traditional folk arts play vital roles in preserving cultural identity in the Chinese American community. Even more important to Cheung, the arts are essential components of a holistic program meant

to develop moral character. He traces his emphasis on the morality of kung fu back to his own Sifu, drawing out the personal and spiritual connections between Hong Kong and the United States.

When I was young, life was very hard and difficult. My father worked in the Kaitek International Airport in Hong Kong as a fire department officer. I had five brothers and two younger sisters. In those days, the government had some dormitories for the workers inside Kaitek Airport, and we lived there in the government housing.

I studied at Chung Saan Middle School. The students were all very poor. At that time, my family didn't have any money. I studied and completed elementary school and graduated from Form One (which is the equivalent of about seventh grade in the United States) and after that, I didn't have formal schooling. I went out to work and started working at Kingwah Hotel where I opened doors and carried suitcases and things like that. I was about sixteen years old. . . .

[Cheung began attending a kung fu school in Hong Kong Island when he was eighteen years old. Initially, he was taught by the older brothers at the school.]

After I had studied for four years, my Sifu started a National Martial Arts Special Class to teach the more attentive and obedient students. That class consisted of a few of my older brothers, a few of my younger brothers, and myself. Sifu began to teach us especially. There were 11 or 12 of us who were the heart of the school. We had to help the master, listen to what he said, follow him and study him, and we couldn't really oppose anything.

At that time, there were a lot of people who came to study for a short time, and then left. They didn't have the patience to stick it out and learn everything. To learn kung fu, you definitely need patience. That's the first requirement. And after patience you need to have time for yourself. After you determine you have the time, you need to practice hard—you can't fear difficulty or pain. Those are the important characteristics for studying kung fu. . . .

After the special class started, Sifu taught kung fu directly to me. And at that time, I took a lot of time to study *tit da,* Chinese herbal medicine that deals with bruises, sprains and contusions. Sifu gave me some recipes for herbal medicine. The prescriptions are complicated and consist of a lengthy list of ingredients. He gave the recipes to me and taught me how to cook the medicine. My Sifu didn't really teach. He told me to go stand aside and observe how to cook and wrap the medicine. He made us follow him and watch him. We lived together and slept at the school, so we could study everything with him all the time. At that time, we talked a lot about how to make the herbal medicine, how to prepare and organize the ingredients, and how to examine patients and take care of their wounds through performing surgery. I also helped my Sifu clean up the kung fu school. . . .

Every Sifu has his own kung fu values. Twenty or 30 years ago, very few of them had values. The vast majority of Sifus were not moral; a lot of them were corrupt, they were criminals. Many of the Sifus were really bad people. They really did know kung fu. But at the time the government was really messed up, and there was the KMT and the Communist party and the society was so chaotic. So lots of the Sifus just used kung fu for crime. . . .

Right at that time, this other Sifu came from Hawai'i to Hong Kong and was looking for a few Sifus to come to America to teach kung fu. At that time in America, Bruce Lee was just becoming popular, and all these Americans wanted to learn kung fu. So this Sifu decided he would find partners in different cities who wanted to try and start a school. He came to Hong Kong and found my Sifu and asked him whether or not he had any students who would like to go to the United States to teach kung fu. My Sifu asked all the older brothers, but no one really wanted to go. They had careers that paid more than teaching kung fu. So they didn't want to leave their wives and children to go to America and teach kung fu. But it was right at that time that I didn't get the promotion, and so I thought I would go to Philadelphia for just one year.

After I came to America, it was so pitiful. I was alone and I didn't have any friends. I didn't speak English. I was extremely lonely. It was also winter, so it felt even more depressing. At that time, every place had a holiday vacation, and it was Sunday, and everywhere was closed. It wasn't anything like Hong Kong, where everything is so lively. So I would sit at home and wouldn't know what I should do. I couldn't drive and I didn't know how to go anywhere. It was really depressing.

After a year, I started to have a little disagreement with that boss because he kept telling me that I had to teach people how to fight. These American guys liked free fighting. Sparring. But I wanted to teach kung fu—fist forms, two-man forms and weapon forms. And I wanted to teach Westerners the heart—the real authentic Chinese kung fu. I didn't come here to teach Americans how to fight. So I told the boss, "You invited me here to teach kung fu. I cannot teach people to fight." So the boss was really unhappy. . . .

And then there was another problem—the biggest problem. He was supposed to pay me 600 dollars every month. I told him to help me and send this 600 directly to my mom. One year later, I found out he hadn't sent her the money. Not even for one month. He cheated me. He was so hard-hearted. He had cheated me, and I didn't know. He personally went to the bank and told me he was sending the money. I believed him because he was my boss. But I found out, and then we fought even more.

After a year, my contract was done. And our relationship kept getting worse and worse. So he telephoned the immigration department, and the INS came and locked me up. They locked me up and took me to the headquarters on Race Street, and I was in jail for a night. At that time I was so depressed, I cried. The next day, I had to go to court. But I had a few students—Corney, Bob and Rick—these guys immediately went to try and help me to get immigration papers. The judge saw that I had so many students willing to help me. He gave me three months to find a job, and if I could find a job, he said I could apply for a green card. We thought Chinatown probably would like to offer me a job, so we all cooperated and supported each other and went down to Chinatown and asked the associations if there might be a possibility that they might hire me to teach kung fu.

Originally I wanted to teach at the CBA (Chinese Benevolent Association). But the CBA said they didn't have funding and couldn't hire me. They said, "Why don't you go to the On Leong Association. Maybe they'll hire you." So On Leong Association hired me to teach the children of their members. I started teaching there and taught there for about three years— 1975 through 1977. During that time, almost all my students were Chinese. There were three, four, or five kids who were Americans. They were all the senior students. They followed me to On Leong Association and studied with all the other students there. By 1977, September, I started my own school in Upper Darby. . . .

When I started teaching, Chinatown was small and there weren't many people there. There were only six or seven restaurants, and there were three or four grocery stores. At that time, when I taught students, I had to speak English 100 percent of the time. There were some language difficulties. After a while, the language difficulties lessened because my relationship with my students was a little more open. We played together and went out to eat together. We'd go out and see movies. We'd go to New York Chinatown and watch Chinese movies about Hung Hei Kuen and Fong Sai Yuk. I wasn't so stubborn or strict. . . .

My school is very racially mixed. There are black, white, Latino and Asian students. They all get along. I try and teach some of the deeper things about Chinese culture to my students, but it is very hard. Some things about culture cannot be taught in a class, they have to be lived. So they can only understand some of the surface things, not the really deep things. And in the old days, the schools were supported by the community, and students didn't learn just for their individual enjoyment. They learned because the tradition is important for the community. But in the US, everything is about time and money. I have had to run my school like a business, and students come to learn more for themselves than for the connection they might have to Chinatown.

I have always had trouble maintaining Chinese students at the school. The lives of Chinese immigrants in Chinatown are very hard. They work 16 or 18 hours a day in low wage jobs. They have no time for their children. The children too have a hard life. Many of them have to work inside the house and outside as well as go to school. I have always wanted to have more Chinese students, but the pressures of paying my rent and keeping up the school mean I have had to charge tuition, and even when I charge very low tuition they have difficulty paying. Through my classes at Asian Americans United, through the Folklore Project, I now have a small group of Chinese students to carry on the traditions in Chinatown. . . .

People who live in Chinatown or who own businesses in Chinatown are all from China, Taiwan or Hong Kong. After a while, they gradually forget their traditions. Even if they don't forget, there's no way they can celebrate every single holiday. But dragon dance, lion dance and kung fu are traditional Chinese folk arts. If there are none of these folk arts, people will feel disappointed or even unlucky. If the people from China never saw this kind of folk art in Chinatown, they would feel disappointment and carry regrets that such necessary folk arts are not continued here. There would be a sense of loss—the most meaningful folk art form disappears and is not passed on.

Chinatown without the lion dancers or dragon dancers would be a community filled with people with regrets. People have sacrificed so much to come here. People have lost so much—their culture, their language. Without the dances, it would be the final loss. Everything would be gone. Secondly, if they have children, the children won't know anything. They will completely forget everything. What is Chinese kung fu? What is a dragon dance or a lion dance? They've never seen it before. And for the adults, even if they saw it before in their childhood, they may not have a clear memory of what these traditional arts look like.

Source: Sifu Cheung Shu Pui. "Chinatown without Lion Dancers Would Be a Community Filled with Regret." *Works in Progress: Magazine of the Philadelphia Folklore Project,* vol. 14: 1/2, Summer 2001, 18–23, 32. Recorded, translated and edited by Deborah Wei. http://www.folkloreproject.org/folkarts/resources/pubs/wip/summer01.pdf. Used with the permission of the Philadelphia Folklore Project.

Ted Tsukiyama, "Eulogy for Hung Wai Ching"
(2002)

After Pearl Harbor was bombed in 1941, the Japanese American community faced racism and discrimination from other Asian American groups as well as from mainstream America. Historical antipathies brought over from the homeland ran strong. Chinese Americans, whose memories of Japanese atrocities in Nanjing remained raw, joined the U.S. Army in the thousands, hoping to help the United States and to defend China against further Japanese aggression. People wore buttons saying "I'm Chinese" (i.e., "I'm not Japanese"); and in attempt to signify the depths of their feeling, some families destroyed any of their belongings made in Japan. Korean American immigrants angrily protested their enemy alien status, which was doubly insulting because it resulted from Japan's 30-year-long brutal colonization of Korea. The Korean American National Association instructed its members to buy war bonds, volunteer, and wear badges identifying themselves as Korean; and some Korean nationalists even agitated for Japanese American internment, arguing that they were engaged in secret anti-American intelligence operations. Although other Asian American groups had experienced decades of legal, political, and cultural prejudice in the United States, a combination of fear and anger meant there was little sense of pan-ethnic solidarity with the Japanese Americans during World War II.

However, particularly in Hawai'i, certain Asian American people did stand up for the Japanese Americans, protesting the treatment they were receiving and working to reintegrate them into society. Hung Wai Ching was one such man. Born in Honolulu in 1905, Ching was the son of immigrants from Guangdong, China. He graduated from the University of Hawai'i and attended Yale Divinity School; he moved back to Hawai'i and was working for the YMCA when the war broke out. Ching deeply disapproved of the way Japanese Americans were being treated. He organized the Nisei Reserve Officers' Training Corps members—who had been dismissed because of their classification as "enemy aliens"—into what became known as the Varsity Victory Volunteers. In lieu of military training, the Varsity Victory Volunteers performed manual labor at Schofield Barracks. And for the duration of the war, Ching traveled the country advocating on behalf of Japanese American soldiers.

Ted Tsukiyama was a Varsity Victory Volunteer, a veteran of the 442nd Regiment, and a member of the Military Intelligence Service. In his 2002 eulogy for Ching, Tsukiyama remembers his friend's tireless efforts to fight war hysteria, racism, and discrimination, both during and after the war.

Most of the 442nd boys don't know or remember this, but in early April 1943 when the *U.S.S. Lurline* pulled away from Pier 10 in Honolulu Harbor with 2,452 volunteers for the future 442nd Regimental Combat Team, one of the few persons permitted on the pier to see us off was Hung Wai Ching. When the *Lurline* pulled into San Francisco six days later, there was Hung Wai Ching again on the pier to welcome our arrival. After an arduous rail trip across the country, when our troop train pulled into the railroad station at Camp Shelby, there to greet us again was Hung Wai Ching! Just who was this person "Hung Wai Ching," and what is his connection to the 442nd?

Hung Wai Ching was born in 1905 in Honolulu, one of six children born of Chinese immigrant parents. At an early age his father was killed in an accident, leaving his mother to bring up her six children under circumstances of extreme financial hardship, forcing Hung Wai to sell papers and do odd jobs to help his way through school. He lived in the predominantly immigrant neighborhood around the Nuuanu YMCA where he grew up in fellowship and tolerance with peers of Japanese and other races.

He attended Royal School and graduated in 1924 with the famous "McKinley Class of '24"

which included Hiram Fong, Chian Ho, Masaji Marumoto and Elsie Ting to whom he was married for 60 years. He graduated from the University of Hawai'i (UH) in 1928 with a degree in civil engineering, earned a Bachelor of Divinity degree from Union Theological Seminary, and graduated from Yale Divinity School in 1932 with a Master of Divinity degree. Through 1928 through 1938 he worked at the Nuuanu YMCA as a Boy's Secretary, and served as Secretary of the Atherton YMCA from 1938 through 1941.

In December 1940, one year before the Pearl Harbor attack, Hung Wai was invited to attend a meeting with the FBI, Army and Navy Intelligence and community leaders present to form the Council on Interracial Unity to prepare the people of Hawai'i against the shock of imminent war and to preserve the harmonious race relations among Hawai'i's multi-racial population. Many years later he found out his name had been suggested by Charles R. Hemenway, who was his mentor during his University days. When the Japanese bombs fell on Pearl Harbor on December 7, 1941, the Military Governor appointed a Morale Division comprised of Charles Loomis, Shigeo Yoshida and Hung Wai Ching to put into effect the plans prepared by the Council of Interracial Unity. The Morale Division served a key role as a bridge between the Military Government and the civilian community, in particular with the Emergency Service Committee comprised of leaders of the local Japanese American community.

Hung Wai Ching reported to Col. Kendall J. Fielder of Army Intelligence charged with the internal security of Hawai'i and also reported to the FBI Chief Agent Robert L. Shivers. There were any number of Japanese in Hawai'i, who, unbeknownst to them, were either not detained or were released from internment because of Hung Wai's intervention on their behalf. In the first few weeks of the war, the Military Governor assigned Col. Fielder a quota of Japanese to be picked up each day, but upon consultation with Hung Wai, Fielder refused to make indiscriminate quota arrests, even at the risk of court martial and his military career.

Through his Morale Division job Hung Wai met some very high and influential people, including President Roosevelt and Mrs. Roosevelt, but he never used these contacts to benefit himself. During a 1943 visit to the White House, Hung Wai used the occasion to brief the President on the wartime situation in Hawai'i, how well Sen. Emmons and the FBI were handling the "Japanese situation" and assuring him that there was no necessity for a mass evacuation of Japanese from Hawai'i.

But while Japan continued to wage its fierce [war] in the Pacific, all persons of Japanese ancestry in Hawai'i remained "on the spot" and their loyalty to America suspect. Hung Wai had no question about the loyalty of Japanese he had known all his life, but he knew that the general American public would never be convinced of the loyalty of Japanese Americans until they could shed their 4-C (enemy alien) status, get back into military service, and to fight and even die for their country. The greatest contribution made by Hung Wai Ching were his outspoken affirmation of the loyalty of Japanese-Americans and the direct part he played in the long struggle of Japanese-Americans to regain that opportunity to bear arms and to prove their ultimate loyalty to America.

In January 1942, when all soldiers of Japanese ancestry were discharged from the Hawai'i Territorial Guard, comprised of UH ROTC students, Hung Wai Ching met, counseled and persuaded these confused, bitter and disillusioned Nisei dischargees to offer themselves to the Military Governor for war time service as a non-combat labor battalion. The petition of 170 Nisei volunteers was accepted by the Military Governor who assigned this group to the 34 Combat Engineers at Schofield Barracks as a labor and construction corps, popularly to become known as the "Varsity Victory Volunteers." As "Father of the VVVs" Hung Wai showed off the VVVs at every opportunity to military, intelligence and governmental officials. In late December 1942, Hung Wai was asked to escort Assistant Secretary of War John J. McCloy around military installations on Oahu and made certain that McCloy witnessed the VVV volunteers at work in the field. Was it mere coincidence that only a few weeks later in January 1942, the War Department announced its decision to form a volunteer all Nisei combat team. This is exactly what the VVV had been working for, so its members disbanded so that they could volunteer for the newly conceived 442nd.

Hung Wai then adopted the 442nd in place of the disbanded VVV and thereafter dedicated himself to seeing that the Nisei got every fair opportunity to prove their loyalty. With the Military Governor's blessing, the Emergency Service Committee sponsored Hung Wai's assignment to monitor the Hawai'i volunteers' movement to Camp Shelby and flew him up to the mainland. While the *Lurline* sailed to San Francisco, Hung Wai met with the infamous General DeWitt to urge the latter that "These are American soldiers, not prisoners of war" and not to insult and humiliate the Nisei by placing armed guards along the embarkation route. He also asked DeWitt to grant the boys an overnight pass to San Francisco Chinatown for a chop suey dinner. DeWitt thought this man was crazy! During the week the boys entrained overland to Camp Shelby, Hung Wai flew to Washington D.C. to persuade Secretary McCloy to change the training site of the 442nd outside of the South, but to no avail, but he was authorized to go to Camp Shelby to observe the initial organization of the 442nd.

Prior to the arrival of the 442nd volunteers the town of Hattiesburg, Mississippi was in an uproar over the news that "a Jap regiment would be trained at Shelby," generating "Japs Not Wanted" editorials and "Go home Japs" signs in town. Hung Wai met with the editor of *The Hattiesburg American* and the Hattiesburg chief of police to explain that "these boys were all Americans and that they had all volunteered to serve their country." Thereafter, the "Go home Japs" editorials and signs disappeared. Hung Wai convinced the brass that the 442nd should have its own USO, which should be located in the "white side of town" and "not across the tracks." Hung Wai raised hell about the Southern Baptist minister as regimental chaplain and insisted that the boys should have "their own kind." Soon thereafter, Hiro

Higuchi and Chicken Yamada showed up at Shelby as the new chaplains for the 442nd.

When Hung Wai returned to Hawai'i, he went everywhere speaking to families, plantation camps, civic and business organizations about the Hawai'i volunteers and the progress of their training at Camp Shelby. His constant message was: when the boys come back home, treat them like full American citizens, save their jobs for them, let them finish school, and to "give them a square chance." And after the war was over and the boys came home, Hung Wai worked ceaselessly and tirelessly for their orderly rehabilitation and return to civilian life. Through the Veterans Memorial Scholarship Fund which he headed, many returning veterans got scholarship aid to complete their education and vocational training to supplement the inadequate finding from the G.I. bill. He was responsible for placing Nisei war veterans into jobs with the Big Five and other previously inaccessible and unavailable employment opportunities in Hawai'i.

No one ever asked or requested Hung Wai Ching to render all this support and assistance to the Nisei, nor was he ever adequately compensated for the same, for which he never asked. He did not have to speak up nor stand up to defend and affirm the loyalty of the Japanese in Hawai'i, when most others chose to remain silent, but he did so willingly and courageously, in the face of peer criticism, racial animosity and wartime anxiety directed against the local Japanese.

The history of wartime Hawai'i relating to the story of the fair, calm and reasoned treatment of the Japanese in Hawai'i, how the tragedy of mass evacuation and internment was avoided in Hawai'i, and how Americans of Japanese ancestry were restored the right to bear arms to fight for their country and given the opportunity to prove their loyalty to America, cannot be written or told without mentioning the service and contributions of Hung Wai Ching in that historical process. And this is exactly why Hung Wai Ching was one of the very first to be elected and accepted as an Honorary Member of the 442nd Veterans Club.

Source: Tsukiyama, Ted. "Eulogy for Hung Wai Ching." 2002. Used with permission of Ted Tsukiyama.

Maggie Gee, Interview by Leah McGarrigle, Robin Li, and Kathryn Stine (2003)

In 1944, three years after the United States entered World War II, Maggie Gee joined the Women Airforce Service Pilots (WASPs)—one of only two Chinese American women who qualified. Gee was the granddaughter of immigrants from Guangzhou, China; they moved to Monterey, California, in the mid-19th century to escape the depredations of the Taipeng Rebellion. Gee's mother, born in Monterey, lost her citizenship when she married her Hong Kong–born husband. According to the 1922 Cable Act, a woman marrying an alien ineligible for

citizenship—which, in effect, applied only to Asians—forfeited her own citizenship as well. Wanting to raise their children outside of Chinatown, Gee's parents moved the family to Berkeley, where she was born in 1923. Her father died soon after the 1929 stock market crash, leaving her mother to raise six children on her own.

When World War II began, Gee's mother took a job as a burner in the Richmond shipyards. Gee followed in her mother's footsteps, leaving the University of California–Berkeley to train as a draftsman in the engineering department at Mare Island Naval Shipyard, north of San Francisco. She worked at Mare Island for a year, earning enough money along the way to pay for flying lessons. Once she completed 50 hours of flight time, Gee applied for the WASP program. The WASPs were civilian pilots who ferried military planes to different airbases across the United States and flew bombers on mock dogfights to train (male) pilots heading overseas. Although they were flying under military command, the WASPs were classified as civilians and were offered no military benefits. Out of 25,000 applicants, only 1,900 were accepted. Two were Native American and two were Chinese American (including Gee); the rest were white. A children's book based on her life was published in 2009, Marissa Moss's Sky High: The True Story of Maggie Gee *(Tricycle Press).*

Leah McGarrigle, Robin Li, and Kathryn Stine, from UC Berkeley's "Rosie the Riveter World War II American Homefront Oral History Project," interviewed Maggie Gee on several different occasions in April and May 2003. Gee talked about the Chinese American communities in Monterey and San Francisco, her diverse neighborhood in Berkeley, the impact of World War II on Chinese Americans, her year flying with the Women Airforce Service Pilots, and how her political philosophy was shaped by her experiences with discrimination. In the following excerpts, Gee reflects on Chinese Americans' responses to Pearl Harbor and on their conflicted relationships with their Japanese American neighbors. She then talks about her time as a WASP.

APRIL 29, 2003

Li: How did Pearl Harbor affect Chinese Americans in particular, in terms of their treatment?

Gee: America's always had a love affair with China. Why it's had, there are various reasons, but I always felt that particularly the missionaries who went to China, because there's no religion in China, really, they converted all these Chinese to be Christians. But I don't know whether that's the real reason but I think that had a lot to do with it. I think that the Chinese here became more proud of themselves, because they were Chinese and it was the Japanese that were our enemies. You let people know that you were Chinese. I wish I had whatever I wore at that particular time; I don't know if they're around, saying "I'm Chinese." I don't see whether you had Chinese American. I don't think there was that expression, Chinese American. Just Chinese. I mean, they must have been around, a dime a dozen, like little Mao red books that you probably can't find anymore. So we wore them. We were proud.

Stine: Did you wear those throughout the war?

Gee: Oh, I didn't wear them throughout the war, but around here if you went over to San Francisco on the Bridge you wore them, but it was obvious after a while because all of the Japanese were moved out, then.

Stine: I remember being very struck last time—we didn't get it on tape, but you had talked about how in your house you had thrown and broken things made in Japan. I wonder if you could talk about that a little bit.

Gee: Yes. I mean, it's so ridiculous, though. There were a lot of things in this country that were made in Japan. Not a lot of things, but a lot of china-type things. One thing I remember about Japanese goods, they were poor quality. They do such fine quality things, but whatever they imported here, a lot of it was children's toys and little dishes and things. The workmanship, in fact, I will show you something I have that is Japanese that is a plate that is just beautiful handwork, but the quality of porcelain or whatever they used was just so poor. So the idea of taking everything and breaking it that was Japanese was ridiculous, though. There was just a lot of junk that we had, bottom line. We had no money; these were the very ordinary, just common things that you would buy, dishes. That's the one thing I remember, dishes.

Li: Was everyone doing this in their homes? Was there an announcement on the radio?

Gee: How did people start doing this? I'm sure a lot of it, among the Chinese, was just word-of-mouth. Just break all these things; throw 'em away, and I think people did. There was so much—do you know how the dislikes are? Here, I'm speaking among my Japanese friends, part-Japanese friends. [laughs] There was really so much dislike of the Japanese, from the Chinese. Not the people you knew, because I lived in a town where there were as many Japanese as Chinese, and we all went to school together. We were friends. I guess you didn't think of them as being Japanese, though. Japan was the invasion of China and Manchuria, them coming in. The military was so cruel to the Chinese. You didn't see it in the newspaper necessarily in this country, but since everyone had relatives in China that they felt it very personally. So one of the worst things you could do, that I could remember, [was] my sister dating a young Japanese schoolmate. I remember someone said, it's better that she dates a black man than this Japanese young person. But it was really frowned down upon. It's interesting; it's really stuck in my mind in a sense, though. There are so many marriages now between people of Chinese ancestry and Japanese ancestry, and I think oh, that couldn't have happened with my generation. There aren't that many in my generation. I can't think of anyone. . . .

MAY 20, 2003

[After being accepted into the Women's Airforce Service Pilots, Gee went to Sweetwater, Texas, for flight training. She then flew around to different airbases in the Southeast.]

Gee: . . . The Air Transport Command, when I graduated was no longer taking women, but the first group of women that did graduate, they went into the Air Transport Command. The idea of the organization was they picked up the planes at the factory, and the factories really were on the West Coast, and they flew 'em to the East Coast, all kinds of planes. All of the military planes, whether they were checked out on them, or not. So everyone had great adventures, great, great adventures. Then after you get the plane to the destination, then you got to find your way back to the base. Some of them partly by bus, hopping rides and trains and things. There were no commercial planes or anything like that to take you home. So that was part

of the adventure of those days. For me, I was stationed at Nellis Airbase Field [in Nevada]. I did a bit of cross-country while in training, which was really nice. So I did get to see some of the Southeast, which I had never seen before, Atlanta, Georgia; Stuttgart, Arkansas, Greenville, Mississippi; all those places. So many of our airbases were in the South. It was nice. I had not seen that part of the world, and it's different. These small towns are very different than they are out here, at that time. I had no problems in these towns. If I were black, it would have been a different story. We had no black women in the WASPs. There were qualified black women, except Jacqueline Cochran told the women that she could not take them, because it was hard enough just being a woman in the service, but if you're black in the South, they'd have to have separate quarters for them. It just couldn't be done. It really was unfortunate, but in a sense, in those days it had to be that way. There were black women who were pilots at that time, with commercial licenses. Well, I think there were three. Not very many, though, but there were some. Some of them had applied. Two had applied, I think, and she turned them down. . . .

McGarrigle: Did you see segregation in the parts of the South where you were?

Gee: In the little town that I was in, there were Mexicans, I think, but not too many. It was such a small town. It's a larger town now, because they found oil there after the war, but in that particular town it wasn't obvious. It's interesting; I'm sure that if you've been to the South, the Caucasians in the South are really very, very nice and warm people. They're inclined to be very kind, more so than in big cities. They spend a little time with you, as long as you're not black, I'm sure. So that's the one thing I remembered about the South. I didn't have any trouble. My brother, when he was traveling through the South, since he's dark like I am, a little darker, so he had to stay at all the black places. The black Y, because you look a little bit like you're a Mexican, and I guess the Mexicans weren't able to stay in public places where the Caucasians were. There aren't very many Asians, but I think that's where they put them.

McGarrigle: You and I have talked in the past about the difference for minority men, how being a minority male was different at the time we're talking about, then being a minority woman.

Gee: I even think that during World War II that was true. I just gave the example of my brother. I have found that it was much easier as a woman to mix with all groups. I guess that much is true today, too. You see with the African-American women, they can move ahead, where it's difficult for the male African- American. It was that way at that time with the Asians, too. So the reason why, I really don't know, but women aren't a threat to society as much as a male is, an economic threat or a sexual threat, I guess in a way. That's the feeling of a lot of white Americans. . . .

McGarrigle: And you lost women in your group, also. [Thirty-eight women were killed flying with the WASPs.]

Gee: Yes. They were lost in various kinds of accidents. There was another Chinese woman who was quite well known—she's getting to be better known now, who was killed. Her name was Hazel Ying Lee. She was very early in the service. She was killed in an accident. She came in for a landing and someone landed on top of her. They were in Fargo, North Dakota and there was a big storm there, so lots and lots of planes were at this particular airport. They were trying to get them out very quickly, and there was just a lot of confusion. So women were killed different ways. Some were killed during the training, and some were lost. Some of them ran into other planes. There were thirty-eight that were killed. . . .

McGarrigle: Did the women who you were flying with want to fly the same missions as the men, or were they relieved not to have the same status?

Gee: This is 1940, though. You have to remember we were so lucky that we were able to fly that we didn't even feel that we wanted to do the same things that men did. Just to have the ability to fly . . . We all felt we were very fortunate because we could do what we were doing.

Source: Rosie the Riveter World War II American Homefront Oral History Project: An Oral History with Maggie Gee conducted by Leah McGarrigle, Robin Li, and Kathryn Stine, 2003, 52–54, 68, 74–75, 80–81, 88–89, 91, 93. Regional Oral History Office. The Bancroft Library, University of California, Berkeley, 2007.

Eddie Fung, "Chinatown Kid, Texas Cowboy, Prisoner of War"
(2007)

Eddie Fung grew up in San Francisco's Chinatown, chafing against what he saw as his parents' strict traditionalism, and yearning for adventure. Although he was born in the United States and was an American citizen, Fung's childhood in Chinatown, during the 1920s and 1930s, was lived in the shadow of Chinese exclusion. Many in the Chinese American community—including members of Fung's own family—were in the United States illegally, having immigrated as paper sons; this situation created an even more unsettled and fearful atmosphere in Chinatown's impoverished and crowded tenements. Moreover, for Eddie Fung, the benefits of the Chinese American community's strong sense of ethnic solidarity and family loyalty was counteracted by his ever-present awareness of insularity, boundary, and proscription.

At the end of the Depression, Fung ran away from home to become a cowboy in Texas; he joined the Texas National Guard two years later. He became one of the 15,000 Chinese Americans to serve in the U.S. Army during World War II— and the only Chinese American soldier to become a Japanese prisoner of war in Burma. He spent many months in captivity, building the Burma-Siam railroad. In the following excerpts from his biography, cowritten with his wife, Asian American Studies professor Judy Yung, Fung describes his family background, which was made complicated by the strictures of the Chinese Exclusion Act, and the way he came to terms with his Chinese American ethnic identity.

I had two older adopted brothers who were born in China, and four other sisters and a younger brother who were born at home like me. My father, being a progressive man, chose to use a lady doctor instead of a midwife. The reason we had two adopted brothers was because after my parents got married in China and before Pop came over to America, it was thought that Mom was barren. So since he was going to find his fortune in the West, he decided to adopt two sons to keep her company in China. But when he finally got her over here in 1914, one year later, my older sister Mary was born! How did Pop get his wife and two sons over here when he was illegal? He had a brother in San Francisco who had a wife and three sons in China. As a merchant, he could have brought them to America, but he never intended to do so. Instead, he sold the papers to my father. Mom came over legally as my uncle's wife, and my oldest adopted brother, Al, came as my uncle's ten-year-old son, Ho Li Quong. Somehow, Pop knew the Chinese consul general, and in 1939 the consul fixed it so that Mom and Uncle were divorced, and Mom and Pop got married. As to my second adopted brother, Francis, or Pee Wee as we called him, Pop was able to buy immigration papers for him to come in 1920 as Hom Sin Kay, the nine-year-old son of a native-born citizen. Both Al and Pee Wee retained their paper names because it would get too complicated. The consul general could do only so much.

This would create all kinds of problems for us later, like when I went overseas in November of

1941 and my mother said, "You stop in Honolulu and find out how Pee Wee is doing." At the time he was a seaman on the Matson lines. We had one day in Honolulu, so I went to the Seamans Union. I was in uniform, and I said, "I want to find out if my brother is in port." "What's your brother's name?" I said, "Hom Sin Kay." He said, "What ship is he on?" I said, "*Lurline*." And he said, "*Lurline* is not in." So he said, "Who are you?" I said, "I'm his brother." So I pulled out my dog tag. He said, "You're Fun, Edward. How can he be your brother when his surname is Hom?" I said, "I don't know, but he's always been my brother." This "paper son" business—I just never thought anything of it because it was so common in Chinatown. . . .

My father died in September [of 1940]. . . . I remember that the funeral was very old-fashioned and quite a departure from Pop's progressive ways, because we had a Chinese procession with official mourners. There was a Chinese marching band with the horns that play that strange wailing sound, and each family member was dressed in a white hemp cloak and a white pointed cap. We were each escorted, and my escort was my oldest sister Mary's husband, Tye. He had to lend me a suit jacket because all I had were ranch clothes. We marched along Stockton Street to the Chinese United Methodist Church at the corner of Washington and Stockton. Then we went upstairs to the second floor of the church, which was full with people—both relatives and business acquaintances of my father's—and Reverend T.T. Taam gave a long eulogy in English and Chinese about what an upstanding citizen my father had been, always trying to help other people. I thought it was quite a conglomeration of customs, because there was also the blanket ceremony, in which the children of the deceased lay blankets made of cotton cloth over their parent's body to provide warmth and comfort in the next life. As the first natural-born son, I covered my father's body with the first blanket. I didn't realize it then, but I took precedence over my older adopted brothers and sisters. In other words, I was now the head of the family. From there, we went to the Chinese cemetery for the internment, followed by a funeral meal at the Universal Café in Chinatown. My mother told us afterwards that instead of wearing the mourning armbands for three years, we would do it for one year, and that would be adequate. She said, "We're living in modern time, and one year is sufficient to show that we are in mourning." . . .

On a personal level, it was Dr. Hekking [the prison camp doctor in Burma] who helped me come to terms with my ethnic identity as a Chinese American. I remember when I first arrived in the jungle, Captain Fitzsimmons called me in one day and said, "Eddie, I can change your service record so it reads that you're half Chinese." And I said, "Why would we do that, Captain?" He said, "They [the Japanese] may not be as rough on a half Chinese." I told Captain Fitzsimmons, "My father would turn over in his grave if I did that. Let's just take our chances and leave it the way it is." That was when I realized that I was Chinese culturally and philosophically. There was nothing I could do to change that. I wasn't extra proud of it; I wasn't ashamed of it; I just knew that was the reality of it—I am Chinese, period.

Dr. Hekking reinforced this when he gave me a copy of Lin Yutang's *Importance of Living* to read. I think from our past conversations, he could sense my ambivalence about being Chinese. I told him I had left home twice, and he probably wondered, "What are you running from? After all, at sixteen years old, you haven't even gotten your education yet." Since he was born in Indonesia and had dealt with a lot of natives, he probably could see how the natives had suffered under the Dutch restrictions that were imposed on them. Maybe that was what he saw as the analogy to the restricted life I had experienced in San Francisco Chinatown, and the explanation as to why I felt almost ashamed of being Chinese. I think he gave me Lin Yutang's book because he wanted me to learn about China's rich culture and history.

Source: Excerpted from Yung, Judy, ed. *The Adventures of Eddie Fung: Chinatown Kid, Texas Cowboy, Prisoner of War.* Seattle: University of Washington Press, 2007, 4, 73, 155–156.

Eddy Zheng, "Autobiography @ 33"
(2007)

Eddy Zheng immigrated to California from China in 1982, when he was 12 years old. Speaking little English and alienated from his new Oakland community, Zheng allied himself with a few other Chinese immigrant youths and began sinking into crime. At 16, he was convicted of armed robbery and kidnapping; sentenced as an adult, he was incarcerated in San Quentin prison. There, he learned English, earned his GED, and began a decades-long attempt to rehabilitate himself and work on behalf of other Asian American prisoners and at-risk youth. Although he was released on parole in 2005, changes in federal law mandated that noncitizens be deported for aggravated felonies, and Zheng is presently in limbo. Zheng wrote the following poem during his time in San Quentin. CCCMS stands for Correctional Clinical Case Management System; PC stands for Protective Custody of prisoners.

> I am 33 years old and breathin'
> it's a good year to die
> to myself
> I never felt such extreme peace
> despite being mired in constant ear-deafening screams
> from the caged occupants—triple CMS, PCs, gang validated,
> drop-outs, parole violators, lifers,
> drug casualties, three strikers,

human beings
in San Quentin's 150 year old solitary confinement
I don't want to start things over

@ 33
I am very proud of being who I am
I wrote a letter to a stranger who said
"You deserve to lose at least your youth,
not returning to society until well into middle
age . . . "
after reading an article about me in the San Francisco
Weekly

I told him
"A hundred years from now when we no longer exist
on this earth of humankind the seriousness of my crime
will not be changed or lessened. I can never pay my debt
to the victims because I cannot turn back the hands of
time . . . I will not judge you."

whenever I think about my crime I feel ashamed
I've lost my youth and more
I've learned that the more I suffer the stronger I
become
I am blessed with great friends
I talk better than I write

because the police can't hear my conversation
the prison officials labeled me a trouble maker
I dared to challenge the administration
for its civil rights violation
I fought for Ethnic Studies in the prison college
program
I've been a slave for 16 years under the 13th
Amendment
I know separation and disappointment intimately
I memorized the United Front Points of Unity
I love my family and friends
my shero Yuri Kochiyama and a young sister named
Monica
who is pretty wanted to come visit me
somehow I have more female friends than male
friends
I never made love to a woman
sometimes I feel like 16
but my body disagrees
some people called me a square
because I don't drink, smoke, or do drugs
I am a procrastinator but I get things done
I've never been back to my motherland
I started to learn Spanish
escribió una poema en español

at times I can be very selfish and vice versa
I've never been to a prom, concert, opera, sporting
event
or my parents' house
I don't remember the last time I cried
I've sweat with the Native Americans, attended mass
with the Catholics, went to service with the Protestants,
sat and chanted with the Buddhists
my mind is my church
I am spoiled
in 2001 a young lady I love stopped loving me
it felt worse than losing my freedom
I was denied parole for the ninth time
I assured Mom that I will be home one day
after she pleaded me to answer her question
truthfully
"Are you ever going to get out of prison?"
the Prison Industrial Complex and its masters
attempted to
control my mind

it didn't work
they don't know I've been introduced to Che, Yuri
Kochiyama, Paulo Freire, Howard Zinn, Frederick
Douglass, Assata Shakur, bell hooks, Maurice Cornforth,
Malcolm X, George Jackson, Mumia, Buddha,
and many others . . .
I had about a hundred books in my cell
I was internalizing my politics
In 2000 I organized the first poetry slam in San
Quentin
I earned my associate of art degree
something that I never thought possible
I've self-published a zine
I was the poster boy for San Quentin
sometime in the '90s my grandparents died
without knowing that I was in prison

@ 30
I kissed Dad on the cheek and told him that I love
him for the first time
I've written my first poem
I called myself a poet to motivate me to write
because I knew poets would set us free
in 1988 I was granted parole
then it was taken away
the governor's political career superseded my life
some time in the 90s
I participated in most of the self-help programs
In 1996 I really learned how to read and write
I read my first history book "A People's History of
the United States"

my social conscious mind was awakened
in 1992 I passed my GED in Solano Prison
I learned how to take care of my body from '89 to '93
in 1987 I turned 18 and went to the Pen from youth
authority
    the youngest prisoner in San Quentin's
    Maximum Security Prison
    I was lucky people thought I knew kung fu

@ 16
I violated an innocent family of four and scarred
them for life
    money superseded human suffering
    I was charged as an adult and sentenced to life
    with a possibility
    no hablo ingles

I wish I could start things over
I was completely lost

@ 12
I left Communist China to Capitalist America
no hablo ingles
I was spoiled
in 1976 I went to demonstrations against the Gang of
Four
    life was a blur from 1 to 6
    on 5/29/69
    I inhaled my first breath

Source: Zheng, Eddy. "Autobiography @ 33." Originally
published in *Other: an Asian & Pacific Islander Prisoners'
Anthology,* a project of the Asian Prisoner Support
Committee, 2007, 37–41.

Joy Wong, "The Whole Picture"

(2008)

*Asian American Christianity is a strong and
growing force in the United States today. Many of
the congregations are immigrant churches,
offering services in two or more languages and
providing a space for cultural maintenance and
ethnic community solidarity as well as for
spiritual teaching and development. The place of
women in Asian American churches thus is
affected both by diverse theological beliefs and by
different cultural expectations about gender.*

*In 2004, in response to these pressures and
opportunities, a group of evangelical women
formed a support group called the Asian
American Women for Leadership (AAWOL). Over
the years, AAWOL has evolved into an
organization providing mentorship, training, and
a safe space for conversations about the place of
women in the Asian American evangelical
community. Joy Wong, MDiv, has worked with
several Chinese and Taiwanese immigrant
churches in Southern California and works as a
hospital chaplain in Los Angeles. In "The Whole*

*Picture," originally published on AAWOL's blog,
Wong talks about the importance of recognizing
and honoring all aspects of identity—cultural,
ethnic, family, and religious—rather than
privileging one over the rest.*

As a hospital chaplain intern, I visit a diverse variety of patients. One particular patient who stood
out in my mind was an 89-year-old Asian man who
had suffered a stroke. When I first visited him, he
seemed non-responsive. His eyes were open but
fixed upon the corner of the room, not on the television or upon me. There was no indication that
he knew I was in the room; he didn't acknowledge
my presence. His patient chart noted that he was a
Christian originally from Taiwan.

On my second visit, I decided to sing some
Taiwanese songs to him. As before, his eyes were
open but were not making any eye contact. I first
sang a Taiwanese worship song, but that did not
draw much of a response. I then sang a Mandarin
worship song, which also did not evoke anything

out of the ordinary. Finally, I sang an old, familiar Taiwanese folk song. As soon I began singing the folk song, the patient began making noises with his mouth as his eyes welled with tears. I was startled, but happy that I had made some sort of connection with him.

This experience caused me to reflect on the significance of our identity. This patient was moved not by a Christian song, but rather a folk song, probably one that had been sung and heard many times throughout his life. Each of us has a cultural identity, whether it is a specific culture, a mix of two or three cultures, or some combination of various traditions of our childhood and upbringing. When we encounter something that speaks to that cultural identity, it moves us. I believe it is because it evokes emotions from our longing for familiarity, belonging, and our home.

God is our ultimate Parent and ultimate home and our identity as Christians is important, but our earthly, cultural identity is also God's intention. I believe our cultural identities need to be discovered and fully embraced in order to delve deeply into our knowledge of God. After all, our understanding of God must be grasped as who God made us to be, including our ethnicity, background, and upbringing. For Asian American evangelical women, the lens through which we see God will become ever clearer as we learn to love and embrace the entirety of who God made us to be.

Source: Wong, Joy. "The Whole Picture." Asian American Women on Leadership, 2008. http://aawolblog.blogspot .com/2008/08/whole-picture.html. Reprinted with permission from Joy Wong.

Beverly Chen, "The Strength of Sisters"
(2008)

Experts have pointed to many factors leading to depression and mental illness among Asian Americans. Underemployment in the United States can lead to depression over the loss of economic and social status. Refugees often suffer post-traumatic stress disorder, which can persist decades after arrival in the United States. Conflicts over gender roles, cultural expectations, and assimilation can stress family relationships. Experiencing prejudice, discrimination, and racism is stressful, particularly for second- and third-generation Asian Americans; identifying strongly with mainstream culture, they find it difficult to reconcile the dislocation between their self-image and their treatment by other Americans. Compounding these factors are cultural stigmas about mental illness. Many Asian Americans tend to not talk about psychological

problems or even recognize them as existing, focusing instead on physical symptoms. Moreover, language barriers and lack of insurance make it difficult for people to access services (according to the surgeon general's report, rates of uninsurance among Asian Americans and Pacific Islanders are 25 percent higher than the national average).

Beverly Chen, the assistant dean of student emotional health at Harvey Mudd College, talks about her own experience growing up in an immigrant household, the specific challenges faced by Asian American families struggling with mental health challenges, and the often-accompanying tragedy of domestic violence. She sees her involvement with Asian American Women on Leadership as a way to bring these issues into the open.

I met many challenges as the oldest child of immigrant parents. One of the major challenges was being forced to take on parental responsibilities for my younger sister because my parents were busily working long hours at their restaurant. Their business had placed tremendous emotional toll on their marriage and on their relationship with their children. My sister and I had to take care of ourselves without much guidance or supervision. While I became the caretaker and peacemaker in the family, my sister voiced her frustration and anger with the family by acting out in various ways in high school. In many ways, her behavior served as a wake-up call for the whole family. It forced us to be honest and real with one another. It gave us permission to examine the various underlying unmet needs, frustrations and emotional isolation we had all experienced for many years.

These challenges were the impetus for my desire to pursue psychology in college and eventually a career in mental health. In college, I was deeply impacted by a course on Asian American families. At the time, the course felt very much like God's gift of personal therapy. It opened my eyes to the many hidden shame and struggles common to many Asian American families. It was such a relief to know that I was not alone in my identity and family struggles! I became aware of the array of mental health issues that exist in the church when my professor shared her research on the secret presence of domestic violence in many Korean American Churches. I felt my heart break over the things I experienced and heard. At the same time, I also felt convicted in my desire to see God's healing go forth in my family and other Asian American families in the church. I am grateful that throughout my college, graduate school and professional journey, I have seen the awesome transformative power of God to heal and restore individual lives and family relationships.

I got involved in AAWOL because I believe that there is still a lot of shame and stigma towards mental health in Asian American churches and families. AAWOL creates a place for me to give voice and to empower other Asian American women in the church to obtain the support and healing they need. It has been exciting to have the professional network to serve alongside other AAWOL sisters in our respective spheres of influence, but more importantly, I have appreciated the personal friendships and mentoring that I have been able to cultivate with my sisters in AAWOL. The times that I've spent with them—whether formally at a retreat or informally over a meal—have strengthened and renewed our soul. Through our personal stories and prayers, we have been able to connect on a deeper level and I have felt energized to serve and lead in greater capacity. . . .

Source: Chen, Beverly. "The Strength of Sisters." 2008. Asian American Women on Leadership (blog). http://aawolblog.blogspot.com/2008/08/strength-of-sisters_19.html. Reprinted with permission.

Kathy Wang, "Racism: An Amateur's Perspective"
(2009)

Ever since they began settling in the United States, Asian Americans have faced the problem of "racial lumping." Mainstream Americans, unable to differentiate between Asian ethnic groups and their distinct histories and cultures, labeled everyone

"Orientals," attributed the perceived vices of one ethnic group to all of the rest, and indiscriminately lobbed ethnic-specific slurs at Asian Americans of all ethnicities. Today, the model minority myth functions as an ostensibly more benign form of

racial lumping. However, one of the effects of assuming that all Asian Americans are hard-working, are successful, and do not need any government assistance is that struggling people and communities are erased from public consciousness, and their needs and concerns are not heard.

One historical response to this racial lumping was ethnic disidentification, a self-conscious distancing of one group from another to avoid being associated with their stereotypes and affected by their exclusion. This happened in Hawai'i, as successive waves of Asian immigrant groups tried to prove themselves to be different, higher quality, and more desirable than the others in a futile attempt to stave off exclusion. A second response to racial lumping was the deliberate creation of a pan-ethnic Asian American identity during the 1960s, which invoked the experience of exclusion and discrimination common to all Asian American ethnic groups.

Kathy Wang was born in Beijing, China, and immigrated to the United States with her family when she was five years old. She studied psychology as an undergraduate at the University of California—Berkeley. Wang wrote "Racism: An Amateur's Perspective," for Hardboiled, *Berkeley's Asian American issues newsmagazine. In her essay, she discusses the insidious effects of racial and ethnic stereotypes, assumptions, and biases, and demonstrates how racial lumping still occurs today.*

I used to be flattered to get attention when people asked me how to say things in Chinese . . . or Japanese . . . or Korean. It meant that they thought I was an expert on something, right? They wanted to learn something from me! However, since coming to Berkeley, I have realized that being asked how to say something in an "Asian language" is not always a compliment. In certain instances, such a request is an ignorant assumption about my ethnicity, my culture, my background, and my knowledge. Bet you didn't think a simple question could contain so many important implications, huh?

While I was walking on Sproul last Thursday, a pamphleteer tried to pass me a flyer. Unfortunately for me, his propaganda was accompanied by a "Ni Hao."

What the heck.

It gets worse. "Arigato" followed. First of all, fool, I can speak English. Second, good job for somehow guessing that I was born in Beijing, but I'm going to wager that you didn't figure that out by my mannerisms, my way of speaking, or the content of my words. No, because you didn't stop for one second to let me get a word out of my mouth.

FOB: Fresh Off the Boat. Sorry to break it to you, but the preferred means of transportation overseas nowadays is an airplane.

Is this term a point of Asian pride? Or is it a derogatory label that perpetuates the "Asians as outsiders" view? Until I was asked to consider this issue, I had never given the acronym "FOB" much thought.

It's common for Asian Americans to refer to themselves as "fobby-looking." This descriptor basically means that they are sporting hairstyles or clothing or accessories that are more commonly seen on Asian idols than on teenage kids from California. But what about those students who do come from Asian countries? Hey, I'm one of them. Isn't it okay for us to use that term? I mean, we're legit, right?

After quite a bit of pondering, I can honestly say that I have no idea what my stance is on the word "FOB." I guess it's a matter of interpretation. On the one hand, you can argue that reinforcing the idea that someone is "Fresh Off the Boat" means that we're also reinforcing the belief that he or she can never assimilate into American society. On the other hand, why shouldn't we of Asian descent and heritage reclaim a word that has been used to segregate and exoticize us? Pick your poison.

Let's consider the fraternal twin of fobbiness—being whitewashed. I've never been accused of being too "Americanized," but I'm pretty sure that it's always been on the back of people's minds.

Although I was born in Beijing, I moved to the States when I was five and haven't really looked back since. I can probably rattle off *People Magazine*'s top five Hollywood scandals faster than I can name ONE Chinese celebrity. I've eaten more fries in my lifetime than pot stickers.

Here's the question that we've all been waiting for: Does being assimilated into one culture mean that one has to give up another culture? I don't know. I'd like to say no. But recently, I've been noticing how much longer it takes for me to find the right words when speaking in Mandarin with my parents. Those Chinese characters that used to be roll right off of the pages into my brain have acquired a more unnatural tone. In my mind, it's not about choosing sides. Life is about balance. Sure, I might fall in my great balancing act, but I'm trying . . . okay?

Work with me here.

Angry Asian Man, the moniker for the writer of a blog that goes by the same name, concludes certain news items with the exclamation: "That's racist!" I can't do that. I'm not angry enough. I get it though, I really do. Racism still exists. It sucks majorly to be defined by the color of your skin and sometimes (if they care enough to look past the yellow), your physical features. The problem is, it happens too often and too subtly for a stray eye or comment to faze me anymore. Numbed by the avalanche of little, ignorant comments that threaten to bury me, I have begun to adopt a stoic stance towards cultural assumptions or ethnic biases expressed through looks, words, and actions.

And hey, here's a question for those of you who've ever cracked an Asian joke involving the phrase "me love you long time": What makes you think that you have the right to sexualize me based on the color of my hair or alienate me because my eyes aren't the same shape as yours?

In their Def Poetry Jam performance, the lovely ladies of Yellow Rage conclude: "Don't talk to me anymore, don't fuck with me anymore, because I am done talking to you."

But is blocking out the problem really the cure? No.

We can bash racists all we want, but dialogue is necessary if we want to bring about change. Okay, I know that sounds idealistic and unfeasible. But hey, I'm not asking for some kind of world summit on racist here. I don't expect everyone to agree with me on an issue of this gravity. But let's talk it out. If we don't try to promote education about the pervasive problem of racism, we're screwed.

Recently, in my Asian American Studies class, we were posed the question: Does racism still exist?

That's a difficult question to answer. I am already overwhelmed by the deluge of criticism and disagreement that I can see looming in the minds of the readers.

My initial reaction is to say "yes." Maybe it's not overt, as some people may argue. No, it's more insidious. It's in the way that a school administrator treats me, giving me the benefit of the doubt because I am a good little Asian girl. It's in the way that strangers approach me, hesitating to speak English because they are afraid that I will open my mouth and blare out unrefined Chinglish back at them despite the fact that I have no Chinese accent. And that's even worse. Because people whom I don't know, and whom I will probably never get to know, assume that there is something that inherently makes me the unapproachable "other."

Racism is not skin deep anymore. It has penetrated us to the core.

So listen up. Look around. Stop assuming. We're all unique. Really, we are. And I'm sure you'd love me, or at least understand me, if you gave me a chance. Talk to me.

Source: Wang, Kathy. "Racism: An Amateur's Perspective." *Hardboiled* 12, no 4 (March 2009). http://hardboiled.berkeley.edu/issues/124/124-4-racism.html. Used with permission of the author and *Hardboiled,* the Asian American issues newsmagazine at UC Berkeley.

Frances Kai-Hwa Wang, "From a Whisper to a Rallying Cry" (2009)

On June 19, 1982, Vincent Chin, a Chinese American engineer, was brutally beaten to death by two Detroit autoworkers. Chin, a Chinese American, had been adopted from China and grew up in Detroit. On the night he was murdered, Chin was celebrating his bachelor party at the Fancy Pants strip club. In the club, Chin and his friends got into an altercation with another group of men. Witnesses stated that Ronald Ebens, a Chrysler plant supervisor, and his stepson Michael Nitz, an unemployed autoworker, called Chin a "Chink" and a "Jap" and told him, "It's because of you little motherfuckers that we're out of work." After they were all thrown out of the club, Ebens and Nitz caught up with Chin in front of a restaurant and bludgeoned his head with a baseball bat. Chin fell into a coma and died four days later. Ebens and Nitz were convicted of manslaughter and sentenced to three years' probation and fined $3,000 each.

Vincent Chin's murder occurred during the recession of the 1980s. American automakers were laying off large numbers of employees, and, especially in Michigan, Japan had become the scapegoat for the nation's economic woes. Nitz's and Ebens's light sentence outraged the Chinese American community in Detroit, who saw it as evidence of widespread xenophobia and racism, an endemic devaluing of Asian life. They began to mobilize, and soon, other Asian Americans joined the struggle. In 1983, American Citizens for Justice was formed, a national civil rights organization campaigning for a federal trial for Nitz and Ebens. Chin's death sparked the creation of a pan–Asian American movement and community.

In this excerpt from her remarks at the State Bar of Michigan's 34th Michigan Legal Milestone conference in June 2009, Frances Kai-Hwa Wang, the executive director of American Citizens for Justice, talks about how the media's coverage of the Vincent Chin case helped bring about a new Asian American civil rights movement.

One of my favorite stories surrounding the Vincent Chin case is how it went from a local story about a barroom brawl to a national one about civil rights in America . . . at a car rental place. Helen Zia was a founding member of American Citizens for Justice and one of the lead activists, and her car was in the shop, so she had to rent a car. As she stood in line at the rental car agency, she noticed that the tall African American woman in front of her had both the *Detroit News* and *The Detroit Free Press* open to articles about the case, and she noticed that the woman was also holding a small notebook embossed with the words, "*New York Times*." So she leaned over and asked, "Are you interested in this case? I have some press packets right here, if you'd like." It turns out that when reporters are on vacation, if they can find some story to write about while they are there, they can get part of their expenses reimbursed. So this *New York Times* reporter, Judith Cummins, was in Detroit visiting family and looking for a story to do while she was here. I believe that this story caught her eye, in part, because she was African American and had some understanding that race and racism sometimes play into these things. And so from the beginning, this case has been about people recognizing across ethnicity and across race that this could have been any one of us, this could have been me, that the danger of racial stereotypes is that real people and real lives are reduced to caricature.

I have been asked to speak about the role of the media regarding the Vincent Chin case and the birth of the Asian American civil rights movement, and so I will talk about the role of the media at the time of the case, what has happened since that time, and what the future holds for American Citizens for Justice and civil rights.

When Judge Kaufman sentenced Vincent Chin's killers, Ronald Ebens and Michael Nitz, to a $3000 fine and three years probation, Asian Americans came together at the Golden Star Restaurant, and in the stunned silence that followed the lawyers' conclusion that legally there was nothing more to do, counterpointed by the sobs of Mrs. Chin, Vincent's mother, Journalist Helen Zia's voice broke the silence, "But we have to say something. We can't not say anything."

Before this moment, there were many Asian Americans who thought that if they just worked hard, laid low, and taught their children good English, that they would be able to quietly assimilate into the American dream. This case taught them that they cannot make such assumptions. And thanks in part to the leadership of American Citizens for Justice, Asian Americans woke up to the importance of being involved, speaking up, being visible, forming coalitions and building networks. There were protest rallies and remembrance vigils across the country—including Detroit, San Francisco, Los Angeles, Chicago—that brought together Asian Americans of all ethnicities. And these protests were well-covered by the media because they seemed so incongruous—the Model Minority waving protest banners?

In *Asian American Dreams,* Helen Zia talks about how the Chinese American scientists and engineers from Ford, GM, and Chrysler planning the protest in Detroit joked that this would be "the most precisely planned demonstration in history." The signs were all uniform, and the words were all in straight lines, and they had it choreographed down to 20-second intervals what people would chant and how they would turn.

This was the first time that Asian Americans spontaneously mobilized around a unified cause. It taught Asian Americans how to organize, network, build coalitions, fundraise. It created new organizations to watchdog and monitor civil rights issues for Asian Americans. This was the birth of the Asian American civil rights movement.

Key to this awareness and mobilization was education and media coverage—education of the Asian American community about their rights in America, education of the general public about what Asian Americans are really like, education of the legal community about whether or not Asian Americans are even covered by civil rights laws, education of elected officials about the impact of racially suggestive campaigns directed against Asian imports. Without this national mobilization, and national and international media attention, there never would have been a federal hate crime trial, and we would have been left with only Mrs. Chin's words:

"What kind of law is this? What kind of justice? This happened because my son is Chinese. If two Chinese killed a white person, they must go to jail, maybe for their whole lives & Some thing is wrong with this country."

Since then, the history of the Vincent Chin case has become a staple in Asian American Studies, Ethnic Studies, American Cultures, and law courses around the country. The Academy Award winning documentary film by Christine Choy and Renee Tajima-Pena, *Who Killed Vincent Chin?* has been shown to generations of college students. There have been remembrance events—vigils, dinners, conferences, poetry slams—organized around the country on the 10th, 20th, and 25th year anniversaries of Vincent Chin's death. Now there is a new documentary film produced by Asian Pacific Americans for Progress, *Vincent Who?* about how too many college students—who at this point are all born after 1982—do not know about this case or its importance, even as they take being Asian American and being a part of Asian American clubs and communities for granted. . . .

And so for the future, American Citizens for Justice will continue to educate the Asian American community about hate crimes, fair treatment, and civil rights; continue to educate the public, the legal community, and elected officials about Asian American civil rights issues; continue to build coalitions with other Asian American and civil rights groups; continue to do Court Watches and monitoring of cases that may have civil rights implications; continue to advocate and speak out against racially motivated injustice everywhere.

From a Whisper to A Rallying Cry, indeed.

Source: Wang, Frances Kai-Hwa. "From a Whisper to a Rallying Cry—The Role of the Media in the Vincent Chin Case and in the Birth of the Asian American Civil Rights Movement." June 19, 2009. http://www.multiculturaltool box.com/American_Citizens_for_Justice/MediaChin .html. Reprinted with permission.

Adam Cheung, "Encounter with Crazy Ming"
(2010)

Boston's Chinatown was established in the early 1870s, after the transcontinental railroad was completed and Chinese laborers came to the East Coast to work in manufacturing plants. Like most 19th-century American Chinatowns, the community in Boston began as a bachelor society. Over the generations, especially after 1965, when Asian immigration restrictions were lifted, the population of Boston's Chinatown grew; however, its physical boundaries were continually contested and limited by urban expansion and major transportation projects in Boston proper.

Adam Cheung grew up in Boston and is a martial artist in Chinatown, specializing in White Crane Kung Fu. His essay "Encounter with Crazy Ming" paints an evocative picture of the culture and characters of Chinatown's Kung Fu community. According to Cheung, "Chinatown used to be a very small and tight community where everyone knew each other, so the man I am telling a story about in this article might be known to many of the old timers. His nickname was Crazy Ming or 'Ngau Ming'."

I think I was in College when I met him. Jing, Sifu's son, told me Ngau Ming would be stopping in with his son so I should try to be at the school when he came so that we could do some forms for him. He was an old friend of the school and had brought us down to Worcester to do Lion Dance (he owned a restaurant there). Before we used to have people with sticks to barricade some space for the Lion Head to move. Apparently in Worcester, Ngau Ming had done this job himself by swinging a Gwan Do (Polearm Sword made famous by General Gwan) around hard. Needless to say people moved and obviously Ngau Ming had his nickname for a reason.

Upon going into one of the restaurants, the head waiter in the front had said, "Oh that's okay. We don't need a Lion Dance." Ngau Ming replied in angry tone dabbled with expletives about the man's mother, her reproductive organs, their age and smell, that he should get the owner out to the front right now, and did he know who he was talking too, etc.

In Chinatown Ngau Ming had quite a name for loving to fight. He would hang out at the bars, get drunk and get into fights with Americans, and then befriend them afterward. When I met him I realized more clearly why it was easy for him to get into a fight. He had a crazy stare that just looked off and made you nervous even if you were his friend. Whether he was born like that or became like that over a lifetime or a combination of both is unknown to me. He had met Sifu in China. And at that time I think he was already in "Collecting" business. He did the same sort of occupation in Hong Kong and probably in the States too. He saw a great deal of violence and talked with one of the other Chinese Workers associated with our school about just how disgusting those fights can look in real life, when hands are being hacked off etc. In other words he was a Gong Wu/Jiaghu person if there ever was one. And he also practiced various forms of Kung Fu.

In China he had actually questioned Sifu's skill. Sifu demonstrated a technique which passed/parried his attack and pushed him flying out the door. He came running back in and bowed down saying "Sifu!"

But for some strange reason I do not understand, when he came to the school with his son, he seemed to praise Jing's (the son) Kung Fu over the father, our Sifu, Woo Ching. All of us know that Woo Ching's power, fighting, skill, Gung Lik, and many other aspects of the art far exceeded Jing, especially when Woo Ching Sifu was in his prime. But Ngau Ming kept talking about Jing's sword form. When I performed a form, he said, "That's alright, but it's not as intelligent as Jing's Kung Fu. I only want my son to learn from Jing." I should back up and say that by this time he had already written a large check to our Sifu.

Now all these events I describe didn't happen one after another, but rather all jumbled up, mixed together, repeated again in a very bipolar schizophrenic like fashion.

"Son bow down to Jing and let's take a picture of it!"

"Take a picture in the Lion Head!"

"Son show them that Karate form that Lo Fahn taught you. They don't have Kung Fu where we are so he has to do Karate. But you can't use that form if you're really fighting!"

"See son block this punch." He threw a punch at his son and his son passed it and avoided. "See that's not what they taught you that's the hand techniques I showed you."

The techniques in the Karate form were a lot like Fukienese White Crane and were more straight in and a hand to hand philosophy of fighting. His son was very courteous and good at his form. I have heard that he has since grown very tall and done well in some fighting tournaments.

Then at some point he started praising my Kung Fu, saying that I was strong and young and should keep practicing, while touching my stomach. I stepped back he stepped forward. I sort of thought he was going to punch me in the ribs as hard as he could. Not to be mean, but just out of excitement, like "Wow you do Kung Fu!" Punch.

I said, "Hey what do you want to do first." I wasn't sure if he wanted to try hands or what, but I got the feeling he was going to start punching. I was getting a little on edge because he had already challenged my skill and now it looked like he was going to physically challenge me. At the same time, he had just donated a large sum of money to the school. Awkward situation, you had to be there. His wife told him to stop scaring people.

Suddenly the conversation shifted to story telling, "You know Master X?" (Master X is a Sifu who was quite well known in Chinatown for being a good fighter, and people say able to punch while holding 100 pound bags of rice. His name is not really Master X, but I will refer to him as Master X in this story unless he reads this story and tells me I can use his name.)

"Master X and me are sworn brothers. (geet bai hing dai) I was able to hit him like this!" and he demonstrated his Kung Fu (now at a distance from me.) A second ago I thought that if I went hard to hard with him at close range I would 90% win because he was old and short and skinnier than me. After seeing him demonstrate, if I had to fight him, I would definitely stay outside and be cautious.

His hands were so fast. The technique was to touch the attacking punch and then follow it in with a counter punch. Now many people practice this, but his hands were very fast. Real Kung Fu Fast. As in not just technique, and youthful quick hands, but the counter strike had gung. Even when I demonstrate this technique to others and they say "Wow that is fast." I have to explain that his hands were much faster.

Now if people ask me, do you think Ngau Ming could beat Master X in a fight, I would say I don't know, and maybe not. Ngau Ming often tied or even lost his bar fights. He also didn't always look where he was punching and hunched his head over much the same way boxers do, which can leave the back of the head open or leave you open to a tackle which would result in two people rolling on the ground.

But if you ask me, "Do you think Ngau Ming really was able to hit Master X?" I would reply yes, because of the speed of the hands, and the technique's philosophy. Especially if it was unexpected. Apparently Master X's reply was, "You are the first person able to hit me." And none of the students wanted to play hands with Ngau Ming. Again, he was also sworn brothers with Master X, which would explain the dynamic of the situation.

If I had played hands with Ngau Ming before seeing him demonstrate, I could easily have been knocked down, out, or dead, especially if the counter strike attacked the neck. He learned the techniques in China from Tong Bak (Grandfather Tong?) who other of our members have also talked to recently when they went back to China to visit family. That Kung Fu is supposed to be Hung Gar, but is recognized as the practitioners as completely different than any other Hung Gar, and is claimed to be by the practitioners to be more original than other Hung Gar. To us, the stances and philosophy is similar to Bak Mei or some Hung Gar Bak Mei mix. But who are we to judge since that is not the system we practice. (We practice White Crane. Both the Shaolin and Tibetan Branch. Sifu also absorbed the best of the Kung Fu of the surrounding Villages, and Masters he defeated in Guangzhou while hiding out there.)

As Ngau Ming left he continued to touch my stomach pushing on it with his fist even as we saw him off to his car. "Keep up! Keep Practice! More Power! Very Powerful." He kept telling me in English, despite the fact that we had been conversing in Chinese.

Meeting him was definitely an eye opener in many ways and a good experience. His was the true face of many of the average Kung Fu practitioners in China of that generation. They learned Kung Fu for fighting, but also were so excited by the joy of doing the moves that besides life or death fights, they might not be able to restrain themselves from challenging friends. I think if he was younger, he definitely would have started hitting me. Not that he would have meant anything bad by it, but simply because seeing how my Kung Fu was in the form, we would want to try and crack its code, or solve the puzzle playing out the Kung Fu in real time fist to face.

The reason why he so respected Jing's Sword form, was because he saw no counter to those moves. They were too fast and smooth. Also, I think his real fights, the gang related ones, involved the long knives they used to hack away at each other and seeing that must have left a deep impression in his mind, as he spoke of regret of having been a part of that stuff now that he had dealt with those memories in old age.

I have heard since that he passed away in his sleep. Considering his life, which had much violence, drugs, and gambling in his youth, I would say he had a good and peaceful end, being survived by a strong son, and a good wife who was a good businesswoman as well.

I don't know where his son is now, but we would love to have him at our school if he would still want to learn with us.

Source: Cheung, Adam. "Encounter with Crazy Ming." March 13, 2010. Used with permission of author and bostonchinagateway.com. Reprinted with permission from Adam Cheung, Kung Fu and Chi Gung Instructor at Woo Ching Crane Chi Gung Institute.

Alice Shi Kembel, "My Mother's Purse"
(2010)

Taiwan, also known as the Republic of China (ROC), is an island off the southeast coast of mainland China. In the aftermath of the 1949 communist revolution, the proto-democratic government-in-exile Kuomintang took control of Taiwan, wresting power from the ethnic Taiwanese. The ROC and the mainland Communist People's Republic of China (PRC) warred intermittently over the next three decades, fighting for physical control of the island of Taiwan and for political legitimacy in the eyes of the world community. Motivated primarily by Cold War fears, the United States recognized the Taiwanese ROC as the legitimate government of China until 1971. However, as the Cold War waned, relations with the PRC warmed, and today, fewer than 25 countries officially recognize Taiwan as an independent nation. Moreover, the PRC has effectively blocked it from joining the United Nations.

Taiwanese immigration to the United States was slow before 1950. During first-wave immigration, plantation labor recruiters tended to skip the small island in favor of much more highly populated mainland China. After 1949, however, the PRC banned almost all emigration to the United States, so the bulk of Chinese immigrants came from Taiwan. Many of these emigrants were middle class and educated, especially from the 1960s on when Taiwan's rapid industrialization transformed it—along with Singapore, Hong Kong, and South Korea—into one of the "Four Asian Tigers." Included among them were thousands of young people who moved to the United States to study abroad; many then sent home for their spouses, and fewer than 5 percent moved back to Taiwan after completing their education. The Taiwanese immigrants established new ethnic communities in the United States. Instead of moving to urban Chinatowns like previous waves of immigrants, they formed Taiwanese suburban communities in places like Monterey Park in Southern California, and Flushing in New York City. By 2008, there were more than 340,000 native Taiwanese in the United States, both aliens and naturalized citizens.

Alice Shi Kembel is a second-generation Taiwanese American living in Northern California. Her father immigrated to the United States in 1970, attending graduate school in New York. Her mother joined him in 1971, and they had their first daughter in 1972 and their second (Kembel) in 1975. After graduation, the Shis remained in the United States; today, they live in Southern California. Kembel's essay, "My Mother's Purse," is a humorous reflection on her parents' lives as Americanizing Taiwanese immigrants and the ways in which their experiences have influenced her own habits and attitudes.

I was raised in a frugal family. My parents immigrated to the United States from Taiwan in their early twenties to attend graduate school in New York. Graduate students, in general, are already poor, but add to that the international travel, learning a new language, and my sister being born within eighteen months of their arrival, and they faced definite financial struggle. They both came from humble beginnings in the city of Jiayi: my father, one of seven children, grew up helping his family make peanut oil in their home to sell to families in the neighborhood. My mother, as a child, helped her father sell large bags of rice off the backs of their rickety bikes, falling often as she strained to pedal forward because the heavy bags weighed more than she did. The story goes that my parents arrived in the United States with only two hundred dollars and the promise of a better life. With the help of some kind families who loved helping international students, they were able to weather the transition, and always had a place to go to celebrate holidays that meant nothing to them. They were also savvy and sharp in their financial decisions, and that, combined with their extreme frugality, elevated them quickly to the upper middle class in the time span that it took for me to be born and develop long term memory. I have no recollection of being poor, just of pretending to live like we were.

When I was growing up, we never bought things full price. Our meals were determined by specials at the grocery store, our outfits consisted of end of season clothing from the sale racks or clearance items from K-mart or Ross. My parents would drive an extra twenty miles to buy gas for a few cents cheaper per gallon than the gas station around the corner from our house. The drawers in our kitchen were stuffed with packets of ketchup and hot sauce, plastic utensils, tiny cups of creamer, and sugar pouches pilfered from dining establishments that allowed their customers to help themselves. Our olive green napkin holder with a daisy painted on it, purchased at a garage sale, held thin, rough napkins that you could find only in the metal dispensers smudged with fingerprints at fast food restaurants. When my father returned home from business trips, he would unpack rolls of toilet paper and tiny bottles of shampoo, conditioner, and body lotion taken from the hotel bathroom rather than gifts for his daughters and wife. I don't remember ever owning a book until I was in middle school, as we made weekly Wednesday trips to the library, our arms laden with musty-smelling books to return. My parents even re-used dental floss, rinsing off the waxy green strands and carefully draping them in styrofoam cups on the bathroom counter, ready for use the next day. And while most families I knew spent their Sunday mornings having brunch or attending church, we spent ours sitting at the kitchen table, flipping through the ads and coupons that came with the Sunday paper. My mom was always armed with a pair of scissors, and my sister and I fought over who got to look at the Target ad first, as though there was some sort of victory in having first

access to the thin pages of smiling faces and brightly colored products.

My mother always carried an enormous black purse. I didn't understand why, since it seemed only to contain her wallet bursting with coupons, her sunglasses, and her car keys, and she was forever rummaging around in the depths trying to find one of those three things. It made more sense one day when we went out to dinner at Souplantation, my mother clutching a "buy one get one free" coupon in her hand. My sister and I were thrilled—not only did we get to eat out, but it was American food! We grabbed our trays and slid them along the counter, our eyes barely able to peer over the edge to see the delicacies that awaited us in unlimited quantities. Spotlights mounted to the ceiling illuminated the rows of salads, pastas, muffins, and soups. With the help of our parents, we loaded our plates and made our way to a table. There, we gorged ourselves on food that had never crossed our kitchen table at home. We all went back for seconds, of course, to get our money's worth. My parents even went back for thirds, returning with their plates heaped with as much food as they had on their first run through the line. My sister and I stared at their plates, impressed. I was already bursting, but was determined to have a soft serve vanilla ice cream cone for dessert. I couldn't imagine, however, eating another entire plate of food. My dad dove in, wolfing down his food with singular focus, while my mom took a only a few bites and said, "Oh, I'm so full! I just can't finish the rest!" She watched my father eat for a few more minutes, and then, to my horror, pulled out some plastic bags from the produce section of the grocery store and began surreptitiously stuffing food into the bags. I noticed that she had a disproportionate number of foods on her plate that traveled well: rolls, slices of congealed pizza, blueberry muffins, carrot sticks, cherry tomatoes. Seeing our dismayed expressions, she said, "They're going to throw it away anyway. I don't want it to be waste!" She finished loading the bags, tied them off efficiently, and stowed them in her purse.

Despite the embarrassment that my parents' thrifty habits often caused me, I seem to have inherited some of them. It is difficult for me to buy any clothing unless it's on sale, and at restaurants, I always look at prices first, before I can even consider ordering any of the dishes. I still love shopping at garage sales, and I always buy generic brands when I have the option. Being married to my husband, however, has opened my eyes to a new way of thinking. George grew up in a family in which finances were tight—they always had enough to eat, but never had leftovers. He and his three brothers have reacted to their financially strapped childhood differently. George and his twin brother, once they landed real jobs with healthy salaries after graduate school, loved to spring for indulgences—the latest technological gadget, expensive dinners with fine wine, clothes at full price. As George's wife, I have benefited from his splurges, but I struggle with his flippant attitude towards saving and his ability to justify any purchase, big or small. In contrast, George's youngest brother is even more stingy than my parents. He was nicknamed "Bank" because he always had extra money in his savings account and was willing to lend it out to family members, with interest. When he first graduated from college and was living on his own, he lost nearly twenty-five pounds off his already lean frame. When I first saw his emaciated body, I worried that he had somehow developed an eating disorder, but it turned out that he was losing weight because he was eating ramen for almost every meal. It was the cheapest thing he could find at Safeway that tasted good, and for nineteen cents a pouch, who wouldn't?

Now, after ten years of marriage, George and I have struck a balance. He falls on the carefree spending side of things, and I often feel like the party pooper having to say, "We shouldn't go out for sushi tonight; it's not in our budget," but thanks to the other, we are both a little more thoughtful in our approach. He is sometimes willing to order one less glass of wine at dinner to save money, and I am sometimes willing to spend a little more on something I really love rather than buy things

merely because they are an amazing deal. I am still very driven, however, by freebies. When I get coupons in the mail for a free pair of underwear at Victoria's Secret, or a free travel size lotion from Bath and Body Works, I take a special trip to the mall to get my freebie, even if it means lugging all three of my boys there with me, something I usually avoid. On the way into the mall, we stop at See's Candies and buy one chocolate after receiving four samples. Then I foil the marketing tactics of the retailers by marching into the store, picking out my free item, presenting my coupon, and leaving without having spent a single cent. On the way out, we stop by the cupcake store and get free cupcakes by whispering the secret phrase posted on Facebook that day. "Neapolitan," I whisper. "Neapolitan," says my six year old. "Neepowitan," says my four year old. "Knee un," says my two year old. And off we go with our four free vanilla cupcakes with strawberry frosting, dipped in chocolate ganache. As a reward for tolerating a trip to the mall, the boys each get half a cupcake. I treat myself to the remaining half, then save the other two cupcakes for George and me to eat later, after the boys have gone to bed. I once left the mall with a pair of underwear, a trio of mascaras, a travel size shower gel, four cupcakes, and one chocolate (with four samples already consumed), only having paid for the single chocolate.

Perhaps I have retained some of my parents' penny-pinching behavior because I witnessed how this approach to life benefited them greatly. They lived out the American dream, turning their two hundred dollars into significant wealth in a relatively short period of time. I also eventually discovered that they were willing to spend money on things they deemed worthwhile. They invested in violin lessons for us starting from the age of four. They never bought used cars once they could afford new ones, and they favored Japanese and German vehicles. They bought a lavender-colored house in a good school district when I was six years old, and kept their previous home as a rental property, later purchasing several other investment properties. They took us on vacation every summer, ranging from road trips to national parks when we were young to a bus tour in Europe when we were in high school. They paid for our education, putting both of us through Stanford, my sister through medical school, and me through graduate school. They travel several times a year to exotic international destinations. They have been incredibly generous to our family, helping us buy our first house, giving us money for every birthday, Christmas, and anniversary, and buying gifts for the boys constantly. Despite their financial success, however, my parents still rely on some of their old habits. On our most recent trip to visit them, as the boys scarfed down some Costco chicken nuggets purchased especially for them with a $3.00 off coupon, my father, his eyes magnified behind thick glasses, blinking slowly like an owl, said, "Tomorrow we need to go to McDonald's or Jack in the Box to get some more ketchup."

Source: Kembel, Alice Shi. "My Mother's Purse." 2010. Reprinted with permission.

Interview with Ching-Yu Hu
(2013)

Although Asians and Asian Americans make up half of Silicon Valley's technical workforce, they make up less than 10 percent of the executive teams and boards of directors of Bay area companies—and this number falls to under 1 percent for Asian American women. Researchers have cited subtle biases that hold back Asian Americans, including the perception that they are not assertive or collaborative enough for high-level positions. Moreover, people who do not conform to this passive stereotype are more likely to be unpopular, and thus less successful in the office.

Some Asian American women are fighting these obstacles, carving out a place for themselves in the Valley. Ching-Yu Hu is one of the four founders—and the only female and minority—of Skybox Imaging, an aerospace/information start-up company in Mountain View, California. The daughter of Taiwanese immigrants, Hu was born and raised in Silicon Valley; she met her business partners in a Stanford engineering class, and they founded Skybox in 2009. In this 2013 interview, Hu describes her family life growing up, her evolving career path, and the challenges and advantages of being an Asian American woman in Silicon Valley.

Emily Moberg Robinson: What was your life like growing up as a first generation Asian American kid?

Ching-Yu Hu: I was born at Stanford Hospital and grew up in Saratoga in Silicon Valley. All around me, kids were publishing books in junior year, winning Seimens Technology competitions, performing at Carnegie Hall. I was fortunate to grow up in an environment where I was surrounded by kids who felt empowered to do something great with their lives.

EMR: Were you interested in space as a teenager?

CYH: I wasn't remotely interested in space. I didn't even watch Star Trek (I still don't)! I did, however, love data. Growing up, I thought I was going to be a quant on Wall Street, writing models to optimize investment portfolios. I studied financial optimization theory in undergrad with my statistics and operations research degrees at UC Berkeley, and for my Master's at Stanford as well.

EMR: So how did you end up founding an aerospace startup?

CYH: I was studying Management Science & Engineering at Stanford, and I took this graduate entrepreneurship class where they teach you the basics of how to start a VC-backed technology startup. Dan Berkenstock, John Fenwick, and Julian Mann were sitting in the back and throwing out really cheeky comments, and I knew I wanted to work with them because they were clearly the smartest people in the room. At the end of the class, I literally ran to the back of the room and said, "Hi, I'm Ching-Yu, I'm going to be part of your team." And they were like, "Who are you?"

In that class, Dan, John, Julian and I wrote the first business plan for Skybox, and that's how I became the fourth founder. The class was a great 'dating period' for the four of us; we got to know how we worked together. I am incredibly fortunate that they let me be a part of their team—and ultimately part of a phenomenon that has the potential to change the world.

To this day, I have no idea why I was so bold to approach them.

When I graduated, I had a job lined up in a major investment bank in NY. I had to decide whether to go to NY and have a very predictable and respectable career trajectory, or join three brilliant friends to try and see if we could build a startup that involves launching (many) satellites in space. My thought process at the time was that I had nothing to lose—I had no mortgage, no kids, no commitments. The only risk was not to take the risk at all. Worst case scenario, it would be a great story to tell.

From there, we moved into John Fenwick's living room for several months with no pay while we were fundraising for Series A. Since then, we've raised $91M, assembled a team of 100 from the intersection of Silicon Valley and aerospace, and have completed the design, manufacture, and testing of our first two satellites.

EMR: Can you give a brief description of what the company does?

CYH: Skybox Imaging is a VC-backed startup born in the Silicon Valley. Our vision is to provide unprecedented insight into daily global activity by combining the power of the web data platform and a constellation of microsatellites. We were founded on the premise that the ability to drastically increase the availability, timeliness, and accessibility of satellite imagery would have the potential to change the way that consumers, businesses, and governments make decisions, and the way people view the world.

EMR: What is your job? How has your position evolved as the company's grown?

CYH: I have assumed a broad spectrum of roles as we've taken Skybox from a graded business plan into an actual business. At various points, I was managing HR, business ops, finance, customer development, sales, fundraising, and most recently, marketing. I've enjoyed it all. I would have paid tuition for my experience at Skybox.

EMR: How many women, Asian Americans, and Asian American women do you know in Silicon Valley? Are there any mentorship programs?

CYH: Many and growing! Many of my Asian American girlfriends are smart, chic, up-and-coming working women, and are making significant impacts in their organizations. One of my girlfriends, Angie Chang, is the founder of Women 2.0 (women2.com). Organizations like this have really elevated the conversation around women, entrepreneurship, and technology.

EMR: Any ideas on things that can be done to make Asian American women successful here?

CYH: Creating a startup has been an incredible experience for me, and I always wonder how we can encourage more Asian American women to take on greater leadership positions and start game-changing companies. Working in a startup is remarkably gender-neutralizing. On a small team, everyone has a huge responsibility and is largely judged on the quality of the results. I think we can help level the gender playing field by having more females make the playing field.

I've been pleased to see greater spotlight put on successful women in the Valley—the Marissa Mayers and Sheryl Sandbergs of the world. I would love to see more spotlights on successful Asian American women.

EMR: Does being an Asian American woman give you a unique perspective on the aerospace industry, the Silicon Valley/start-up culture?

CYH: My trajectory from Stanford to a space startup in a male-dominated entrepreneurial environment and the even more male-dominated aerospace industry has been one of the most profound learning experiences of my life.

I think the combination of me being 1) Under 30, 2) a woman, 3) Asian, 4) someone with no prior aerospace or startup experience has given quite a different perspective than my peers in my industry. I am not tied down to traditional industry thinking and I can work through various challenges in different ways.

As with everything else in my life, I have never quite fit the mold. Sometimes it's just easier to create your own mold.

EMR: Does it pose any challenges?

CYH: I was in a business meeting in Asia a few months ago. The facilitator assumed that I was the translator, and I was expected to sit outside of the discussion table. He was genuinely shocked when the actual translator told him otherwise. I think the person had never seen a woman from an aerospace company before; he probably was expecting a white, middle-aged male. As awkward as it was, I don't think he'll make the same mistake again if he sees another woman come into a business meeting.

EMR: Let's end on a high note. Any advantages to being an Asian American woman in this male-dominated field?

CYH: I think being an AA woman working in a global business and having these brushes against conventional molds has made me a better entrepreneur.

Source: Hu, Ching-Yu. Interview by Emily Moberg Robinson. September 7, 2013. Edited by Emily Moberg Robinson. Used with permission of Ching-Yu Hu.

Excerpt from Angeles Monrayo, *Tomorrow's Memories: A Diary, 1924–1928* (1924)

Early Filipino immigration peaked in the second and third decades of the 20th century. Before 1910, few Filipinos came to Hawai'i or the mainland. However, the 1908 Gentleman's Agreement Act severely restricted Japanese and Korean laborers from entering the United States, thereby limiting the supply of labor for West Coast agricultural fields and Hawaiian sugar cane plantations. With few options left, American employers began recruiting workers from the Philippines. The Hawaiian Sugar Planters Association (HSPA) began recruiting Filipino labor in earnest during the first decade of the 20th century, and by the late 1920s, Filipinos had replaced the Chinese as the second-largest group of workers on the plantations. In addition, their status as U.S. nationals allowed Filipinos to migrate freely among any U.S. territories, making them more desirable to employers.

Plantation owners exploited their Asian immigrant workers, instituting a paternalistic labor system that included heavy fines for drinking, insubordination, and damaging equipment. Owners also created a stratified labor force, paying different wages to workers of different ethnic backgrounds. This practice created tensions among workers and discouraged them from striking together. Despite this, workers soon began organizing for better pay and benefits. Typically, strikes were ethnic specific; although there were occasional multiethnic/multiracial strikes; a true multiethnic labor movement did not form in Hawai'i until after World War II.

The following excerpts are from Tomorrow's Memories, *a compilation of Angeles Monrayo's diary entries from 1924 to 1927. Monrayo left the Philippines with her family when she was only three months old, arriving in Hawai'i in 1912 with 5,000 other Filipinos, most of them men. In 1924, Filipino plantation workers began a slow-growing strike that eventually involved about 60 percent of Filipino plantation workers. Their leader was Pablo Manlapit, the leader of the high wages movement. (Manlapit had come to Hawai'i in 1910, one of the earliest HSPA recruits.) Plantation owners evicted their workers from their plantation homes in an attempt to break the strike. Like other Filipino workers, the Monrayo family relocated to the Middle Street strike camp in Honolulu.*

Monroyo's parents separated when she was six years old, and she, her father, and her brother eventually left for San Francisco in 1927. These excerpts, written when she was only 12 years old, illustrate the contours of Filipino community life during the 1924 plantation strikes. Life was difficult, but as one of only a handful of girls and women, Monrayo and the other young girls found ways to help their families survive.

Waipahu, Oahu, T.H.

March 3, 1924

Dear Diary:

Mary and her folks had moved to Honolulu. I feel so lonely now without her. The reason why they went to Honolulu, because it's been heard that all Filipinos must strike for higher pay. Mr. Pablo Manlapit is the leader of this strike. Mr Manlapit says that all Filipinos must strike or else there will be many hurt. So I think that's why they left and moved to Honolulu to stay. Oh, why did this strike has to come up for. Now no one to pal with, now, I have to sleep all by myself from now on, go to school alone and I'll have to go to shows alone. Gee, I don't think I'll have any more fun, now that Mary is gone. I have other friends but they're not as close to me like Mary is. Speaking of the strike, I wonder, if Tatay (father) will go to Honolulu too. Gee, Tatay is making good here tho' he is steadily putting money in the bank. Anyway, I'll let you know if we do go to Honolulu. Oh Diary, before I forget, Father bought a new car. An Oakland Touring car. Boy, it's nice to have, I mean, own a car. A friend of our will drive it for us. And my brother will learn from him. Faustino will drive the car—I'm scared of him somehow. I do not like him.

Strike Camp, Middle St., Honolulu, T.H.

May 10, 1924

Dear Diary:

We have just arrive here today, here, at the Strike Camp. There are so many Filipinos here, married couples and unmarried men. They're from all parts of Oahu. There are five other young girls here too. I become friends with two of them already. Their first names are Esperanza and Victoria. They are both very nice girls. They showed me the place around here, as soon as we settled, I mean, found our sleeping quarters. You see, we all live in one big house, and so all we did was put curtains around our bed, and that will have to serve as our room, for how long, we don't know. I guess we have to stay here until this strike is over. And Manlapit is going to feed the whole crowd. We're suppose to go down to his office every other day to get our ration of food. Gosh, I hope this strike won't last long. You see, Diary, Mr. Manlapit wanted the plantation to give the laborers $2.00 a day and eight hours work. I certainly hope Manlapit wins, 'cause then it will be for our own good. Will tell you some more later on as the girls are draggin me. I told them I want to finish this.

Strike Camp, Middle St., Honolulu, T.H.

May 11, 1924

Dear Diary:

Another day had gone by. Do you know, as soon as we finished breakfast, I went over to Esperanza's sleeping quarters and she was just finishing breakfast. I asked her if she has anything to do today. She said "No." And I asked her to show me the place again. We looked into everything. The bath room, the toilet, the kitchen and do you know there are so many mango trees close by. Boy! Wait until the mangoe season is in full blossom, by that I mean when they get ripe, and that's not far-off—it is next month, and Ill surely do some climbing again. I haven't climb trees for so long, it seems. Oh well, it won't be long now. I told Esperanza about it, and she says, "That's good, 'cause that means we don't have to ask any boys to get the mangoes for us. We can get them ourselves." And Esperanza introduced me to the other 3 girls—Sofia, Marcella, and Trinidad. I don't know which of this girls is the oldest, but I do know I am the youngest of them all. Triny is sort of snobbish—'cause she's better looking—but she has such mannish walk. But just so they are nice to me I'll be nice to them. And Diary, the men here play basketball and volleyball. And there are 3 woman here that "cooks" and sells" "Maruya," you know, fried bananas and other good things to eat. Oh, I just love "Maruya." I bought four today and gave 2 to Esperanza. Somehow Esperanza kind of fill Mary's place; but I don't think I'll ever forget Mary. I do hope I'll see her soon. Well, Diary, that's all for now. If something new happens here I'll let you know.

Strike Camp, Middle St., Honolulu, T.H.

May 13, 1924

Dear Diary:

Say, there'll be something going on here on every Saturdays and Sundays from now on. You know what? Well, I'll tell you. It's this; there's going to be dances here every Saturdays and Sundays. Gee, won't that be fun. You see, Diary, I'm so crazy about dancing. And another thing, we are going to charge the men 10 cents for 3 minutes dance. Gosh, that's not bad is it? You know, Diary, someone thought of this idea, and it is for our own good, 'cause you see, we are very far from "show-houses." This dancing business is for our benefit so that the place here won't be as dull every Saturday and Sunday. And I know we girls are going to have lots of fun when that day comes around. Gee, I hope all the girls will be in it. I'm sure Esperanza and Victoria and Sophia will join in—including myself.

Strike Camp, Middle St., Honolulu, T.H.

May 20, 1924

Dear Diary:

Sorry, I couldn't tell you anything last night when the dance was over because I was so tired and sleepy, but I was happy, 'cause I made $7.20. I counted it before I went to sleep and I gave it to Father this morning. I kept just a dollar for myself to spend on something I'd like to eat. Gee, I didn't think I would make that much, but I did. And tonight there's going to dancing again. Hope I'll make just as much as I did last night. Oh, there were only four girls that dance last night. The other two didn't join in 'cause they say nice girls don't dance at all. Marcela didn't say that but Trinidad did. Gee, I wish one of these days she'd be really jealous about us making some money and she won't, so that she will really join us. That way we'll make her eat her words without us forcing her to. 'Cause she says too, that it's bad for us girls to dance, 'cause dancing will lead us to something else later on. She's just evil-minded, that's all. Gosh, we just dance. I don't see any harm in it, do you? These dancing isn't anything like they have in dancehalls. The dancing we have here is just-clean-good-fun, for all of us here. Oh well, if that's the way she feels about it, well, that's up to her, eh Diary?

Strike Camp, Middle St., Honolulu, T.H.

May 22, 1924

Dear Diary:

I've got to tell you this. Do you know Esperanza and I took in washing today from the men here in the camp, 'cause after all, we just play and play and so it so happened that one of our friends here brought this thing up about us washing his clothes 'cause he doesn't have any wife, he says, and, the laundry shops are so far-away; besides he says he's getting tired of washing his own clothes, and he say he'll pay us like he would pay the laundry-man. And so he says why don't you wash some of the boys clothes here, you'll make some extra money besides dancing on Saturdays and Sundays? And I says, "Gee, that is a very good idea."

And he says "sure" and he says too, that I can wash clothes and iron them pretty good for a young girl like I am. And so I thank him so much for telling me about washing clothes, and to show he was in earnest, he gave me 4 shirts and 4 pair of underclothes. He says as soon as you wash them and iron, bring them to me and I'll pay you. Well, Diary, I put his clothes all bundled-up, and put his name on it and I ran out to find Esperanza 'cause I want her in it too. You know, her and I wash and iron and whatever we make, we'll divide it equally. I found her, she was talking to Victoria, and so I called her and says, "Let's go walking," and she came to me as soon as her legs could carry her. Then when we were far from everyone I told her of the good news. Gee, she was so happy as I was. So, we turned and walk towards the camp and asked a few more of our friends, all men, if they have any dirty clothes that they would like to be washed. At first they thought we were just joking but when they saw how earnest we were, they all say, "Sure, we have," but they say, "Be sure and return them nice and clean or else we won't pay you a cent," and I caught them winking at each other. Anyway, they know I can wash them, 'cause they always see the clothes I wash every Monday. Boy, they certainly gave us a great bundle. Anyway, we finished them in three hrs. We hung them late this afternoon about 2:30 but I think they'll dry before evening comes, 'cause the sun is shining so hot. Tomorrow we will iron again—'cause yesterday we iron our clothes, you know. Maybe it will take us about half day in iron all the clothes we washed today, but we don't care, 'cause we know we'll be paid well for our hard work. Gosh, I'm glad I could really wash, and Esperanza is too, 'cause she doesn't have much money. You know the money she earned last Saturday and Sunday, her father took nearly all of it. And so this money we earned washing, well, her father wont' have to know about it. And that way she can keep every cent she'll get. About my father, well, he let me keep the money I earned, only I don't want to. One dollar out every dance-money I earned, is all I want. After all, he saves them and it helps to buy food too. So I don't worry about my father, he is so good to us. Esperanza and I are tired, but we don't care. After we finished washing I took her to the store and we had ice cream and vanilla snaps and we walked home slowly and we told stories all the way home. We laughed so much. It was fun, Diary.

Source: Monrayo, Angeles. *Tomorrow's Memories: A Diary, 1924–1928.* Honolulu: University of Hawai'i Press, 2003, pp. 15–21. Reprinted with permission.

Antonio E. Velasco, "Filipino Student Suffers from Pang of Race Prejudice" (1928)

During the 1910s and 1920s, Filipino emigrants journeyed to the United States for many reasons. Some were looking for well-paying jobs, which were difficult to find in their increasingly impoverished homeland. Others were seeking academic opportunities; the United States had established American-style primary schools when it colonized the Philippines, and so it seemed logical for Filipinos to journey to the United States for higher education. These included Victor Velasco, who, along with a handful of other Filipino immigrants, attended the Normal School near Seattle, Washington (the Normal School later became Western Washington University). Velasco was the editor-in-chief and publisher of the Filipino Forum, *a biweekly Seattle newspaper that ran from 1928 to 1969. Calling itself the "Independent Organ of Filipinos in the Pacific Northwest," the* Forum *covered a range of issues, including Philippine independence, the struggle of Filipinos in the United States, and labor unionism. In this excerpt from a November 30, 1928, article, Velasco describes an incident of racial discrimination at his school dance, when some of the white female students did not want to dance with the Filipinos.*

Among the biggest activities sponsored by the Freshman Class this quarter here in the Normal-by-the-mountain-and-by-the-sea, was the traditionally known, "Freshman Dance of the Nation," which was held on Nov. 10 at 8:30 p.m. in the big gym of the school.

A contribution of twenty-five cents was collected from every member. Those contributions have no doubt given something toward the success of the dance. I am proud to say that all the Filipino members had given their share heartily, although they knew that they didn't have any chance to enjoy the dance.

We were three among five Filipino members who bravely attended the dance. We did so with the idea of showing in particular our spirit in the activity of the Freshman Class of which we are members, and in general our spirit in any activity of the school. I, for one, admired the beautiful decorations of the hall, and appreciated the kind greetings of some friends. But nothing left on me a more lasting impression than Mrs. Fisher's attention to us Filipinos. She was the only lady in the hall who showed us that she was a woman. She was very kind indeed; a woman who possessed the spirit of sportsmanship.

We the Filipinos never aimed to dance with the charming white beauties in the hall, but Mrs. Fisher, wife of the president of the Normal School, inspired us to do so. We were feeling something in our hearts that made us so bashful. Somehow we tried to show that we know how to attend such gathering. By chance, one of us danced with one of the girls. Then after an hour or so, another companion of mine was inspired to approach a classmate of his to ask for a dance. I was near by when my companion said, "May I have the pleasure to dance with you Miss R . . . . . ? And Miss R. responded in quite harsh words, "no, thank you." Oh, what a pang I suffered although I was not the one addressed to. If only I had the divine power to disappear, I would have done so that very moment. If Mrs. Fisher had only witnessed the event, I would have told her that she put us in shame. For she had told us previously that the ladies were generous to welcome everyone. She encouraged us to dance. But that moment we found out that an attitude of race prejudice was being entertained by some of the girls. It was really a strange thing to me to know that such a discrimination prevail in this school. Some white friends consider themselves to be the best educated, most cultured, and above all they consider that all races other than theirs are inferior. . . .

Source: Filipino Forum. November 30, 1928. University of Washington, Suzallo Library, Microforms and Newspaper Collection, A4137. Seattle Civil Rights and Labor History Project.

Mariano Guiang, Interview by Carolina Koslosky
(1976)

Mariano Guiang was born in the Philippines in 1904, in Ilocos Norte, the northwestern province on Luzon Island. He immigrated to Seattle, Washington, when he was 20 years old, joining

his uncle, who had moved there in 1918. Several years later, Guiang began a boxing career that took him all over the United States and the Canadian Pacific Northwest. In 1976, Carolina

Koslosky, from the Washington State Oral History Project, interviewed Guiang. In the following excerpt, Guiang talks about his experiences as a boxer and the ways he maintained ties with his family in the Philippines.

"I came here by steamship, *President McKinley*. At that time, we landed on what they call Pier 91 now. It was just two piers in there. At that time there was no plane for coming from the Philippines. I was 19.

Coming to America

"[I came from] Norte, Ilocas Norte. I was raised—my mother died while I was 7 years old—we were lucky enough to be raised by our aunt. And when I went with my father to Manila, you know, when I went back from vacation, my aunt told me, 'All your friends are gone to America now, I think you better be going.' I didn't want it, I didn't want it. They finally convince me but they doubt if I wanted to come, see, because, you know, I refuse at first. Then my sister came with me to Manila and see [that] I really came. I didn't, in my mind, I was not willing to come. But they finally convinced me to come.

"I had my uncle [in Seattle], you know, Pedro Guiang, he got his doctorate of education I think in here, in the University of Washington. He was here then. He came here in 1918. I arrived at his apartment, see. But he was staying with somebody else, you know, so I went to a hotel in Chinatown, Panama Hotel.

"It was hard, the Depression was on at that time. I was lucky enough I arrived on June and July, I went to Alaska, see, for two months. And then when we came back we . . . I didn't have no work again, so I . . . went to Franklin High School. But I didn't stay very long again because it was very hard. You couldn't even find a schoolboy's work at that time, see. So I quit again and finally I drifted to going to boxing shows, you know.

Boxing through Washington

"Every Friday they had boxing shows by 9th and Olive at that time. That's what they called the Austin and Bishop Gymnasium at that time. So I go there every Friday, they had a show. In fact, I was going while I was going to Franklin High School. Just to watch.

"But it was a funny thing that came up, you know, one guy named Ray Woods was beating everybody in his size, you know. One night I went over there and they asked me if I could fight. 'Sure, I could fight.' And they put me over him. And at that time I was not in very good shape, see, but I was strong because I was an athlete, I was a track man in Franklin High School. It's hard to believe. So, they put the gloves on, and said 'Are you going to fight?' I was not never scared or anything. I was never nervous, even the doctor, 'How come your heart never even, you know, vary in its beat?' Why should I? It's just a game to me, a sport, I should say. We fought over there but he got the decision. But that's how I got started.

"We boxed around Seattle, Everett, Mount Vernon, Yakima, and Wenatchee and Klamathe Falls, Oregon and so on. [I started] somewhere around 1927, '26, '27, yeah, I think it was '26. My name at that time was Young Marino. [The crowds] like Filipinos at that time because they were so many good Filipino fighters. They like me, they, in fact, I fought several good fights, but not money-wise, you know, I fought many men in Wenatchee. In fact, in 1931 I fought the champion of Eastern Canada and Toronto, Canadian, Territory of Alaska at that time. Bantam and Feather Weight. I fought mostly feather-weight. Sometimes, I even fought 129 pounders and I use to weigh 114 to 15. But I had to fight sometimes to live at that time. It was very hard, but what we can get, we could get something to eat and wash our clothes.

"They were quite a few [Filipino boxers], there's Clarence Corpuz, he was one of them. Johnny, Johnny, I forgot his name, he's a cook now . . . but there were quite a few Filipino boys before, but none of them took it . . . really serious like I did. I tried to learn because I didn't want to get beat.

"It's the opportunity that got me into [teaching] boxing, you know, when I got with the Navy, back in Bremerton—in Bremerton I didn't have nothing to do then. But when they transfer you to Pier 91, that is the time when I really taught boxing. That was Korean War, 1949, when I started teaching boxing. As a boxer, I quit in 1933.

Father Fighter

"I promise that when my son is born, that when I could go no place, I quit boxing then. I fought the same night he was born . . . So, well since I was a champion of Alaska, they book me to fight in Ketchikan, Alaska. But since my son was born, I wanted them to send me some money, you know, advance some money, so I could leave them. They said, you come over here, we'll fix you. I said, No you're not going to fix me. So I give the ticket and accommodation to another Filipino boy that use to fight. They were surprise, you know, they had a band that meet him, they were surprised that was not me.

"When my son was eight years old, we was living over there in Greenwood and they had, they started a Greenwood Boys Club over there at that time . . . I think it was during the war, Japan war. So Dick Francisco was looking for me because my son said, 'My father was a fighter.' So he came to the house. 'Well, I like to help but I'm working, you know how it is at Bremerton. I started so early dark and I arrive here dark, I can't help you.' 'Well, I just wondered because your son is a natural fighter.' But after the war, just until 1944 . . . they transfer me to Pier 91 and that time, I met a colored boy and he ask me to train him. Freddy Brown. I know these kids because they were running around with my son then. 'Well, you come to the house with your mother and we'll talk.'

"So I trained him and he became good. And at that time they started, that was 1950, yeah, during the Korean War then. They have that KING's RING in television. Then I had so many boys that was winning all the time. I used to train, you know, we train them at the Professional Gymnasium, see over there by Fourth and Wall Street, that use to be a big K-Mart at one time.

"I exercise every morning. Me and my wife, I make my wife exercise too. It's doing her good. To tell the truth, my wife is my sister-in-law.

"She was the wife of my youngest brother that got killed during the Japanese war. But he was a member of the U.S. armed forces then. So, she was receiving pension when I married her. But when I married her it stopped. But when I first went over there [Mr. Guiang returned to the Philippines in '67, '71, and '74] I never think that we are going to . . . When my first wife died, I saw her over there then, well, 'How do you like to come to the states?' I said. Well she refuse at first but then . . . of course she got a sister you know, Mrs. Domingo Aurelia. That's her sister. So, she said 'I'll come see my sister.' Well, she came and she finally consented that she was going to marry me. It was alright, she's very nice, we get along fine. Well, I consider myself lucky . . . I'm fair with people, see.

So, that's my life here in America.

Source: Excerpt from Guiang, Mariano. Interview with Carolina Koslosky. September 24, 1976. Washington State Oral History Project. Washington State Archives, Olympia, Washington. Edited by Stacy Carlson, May 2000. http://www.historylink.org/index.cfm?DisplayPage=output.cfm&file_id=2428. Reprinted with permission.

Apolonia Dangzalan, Interview by Meri Knaster

(1977)

Apolonia Dangzalan emigrated from the Philippines to Hawai'i in 1924 and sailed to San Francisco two years later. After a few years, she divorced her husband and moved to Watsonville, California, where she opened a restaurant, a pool hall, and a boarding house. Dangzalan then became one of the only female labor contractors in California, coordinating seasonal jobs for Filipino agriculture workers on Watsonville farms. Dangzalan faced many challenges in California:

she was an Asian immigrant living in a period of intense xenophobia, she was an entrepreneur looking for opportunities during the Depression, and she was a single woman in a primarily bachelor Filipino community. However, throughout her long life, Dangzalan remained an active and successful businesswoman; she was still working in her grocery and liquor store at the time of her 1977 interview with Meri Knaster. In this excerpt, the 81-year-old Dangzalan describes her many business ventures, her social life in Watsonville, and her firm belief that she would have achieved success wherever she lived, regardless of the strictures of gender and ethnicity.

KNASTER: when you came to Watsonville and you started the business with the boarding houses . . .

DANGZALAN: Me and Frank did it. [Frank Barba was Dangzalan's nephew; she sponsored him to come to the United States from the Philippines.]

KNASTER: . . . were there other Filipino women in the community?

ANGZALAN: No, in 1927, not yet Filipino women in that time.

KNASTER: Were you the only one?

DANGZALAN: No, but I don't going around to see them, just meet them at the social, that's all.

KNASTER: Social. What is the social?

DANGZALAN: Well, we got the Filipino club here in Watsonville . . .

KNASTER: Oh, so when you first came, in 1927, were there some women here?

DANGZALAN: Yes.

KNASTER: Did you have friends?

DANGZALAN: I got some in Salinas and Watsonville, but I don't get them right away because I don't have too much time to go and look around. I take care of the kitchen, watch the cook.

KNASTER: Did you live in the boarding house?

DANGZALAN: Yes. I lived in the kitchen. My cook, Frank, and me stayed in the house, because I got three bedrooms, and kitchen and dining room, for eating the boys.

KNASTER: was it considered unusual that a woman was in business at the time?

DANGZALAN: I don't remember.

KNASTER: well, when you were dealing with people were they surprised? Did they not want to deal with a woman in business?

DANGZALAN: Well, some of the American people got surprised. Usually first time see the woman working like this. Especially when I am in camp, separate from Frank. Frank is in another place working under the company. Frank lived in Aromas, the place he now staying. There is the place he stay running the boarding house, too. I am to the Salinas Road to run my business, a boarding house . . .

KNASTER: So when you said you had the labor camp you also said you had a business you went to at night. Where was the business?

DANGZALAN: Main Street.

KNASTER: The same liquor store that you have now?

DANGZALAN: No. That is the first one I make in the building, Monterey Club. A Mexican runs it now.

KNASTER: And you have the liquor store.

DANGZALAN: Yes.

KNASTER: What was it before, a restaurant?

DANGZALAN: Restaurant, gambling. I run gambling too. I make that Monterey Club. I buy the dry cleaning business next door to the Monterey Club. I open a pool hall in 1936.

KNASTER: Were there women, too?

DANGZALAN: No Filipino women. Mexican women. American woman working under my beer parlor. And barber shop, Filipino, too.

KNASTER: Was there music in the restaurant?

DANGZALAN: Yes. I got some dancing, too. Then after that I buy license for nightclub. I run that, too. Soon after that I put a grocery to the place now I am. After that I reopen for nightclub . . .

KNASTER: Do you think that if you had stayed in the Philippines that you would

DANGZALAN: have been able to do as much—houses and business and everything.

DANGZALAN: Yes.

KNASTER: The fact that you are a woman would not have prevented you?

DANGZALAN: Not at all.

Source: Excerpt from "Apolonia Dangzalan, Filipina Businesswoman, Watsonville, California." Interview with Meri Knaster. Reprinted with permission from the Regional History Project of the University Library at the University of California, Santa Cruz. http://library.ucsc.edu/reg-hist/dangzalan.

Frank Barba, Interview by Meri Knaster
(1977)

Frank Barba was born in 1898, the year the United States took control of the Philippines after the Spanish-American War. After attending American-influenced schools in the Philippines, Barba immigrated to the United States in 1924. He eventually joined his aunt, Apolonia Dangzalan, in California, where he took over a Filipino labor camp that she had been managing. Barba worked in the agricultural industry for the rest of his career, primarily as a labor contractor.

This interview, conducted by Meri Knaster in 1977, when Barba was 78 years old, illustrates the effects of American colonization on the Filipino school system and describes the ethnic community created by Filipino laborers in central California.

KNASTER: What [*sic*] were you born?

BARBA: In San Nicolas, Ilocos Norte, in the northern part of the Philippines. I attended school there until seventh grade. Then I went to the capital of the province, to high school. We've got Filipino teachers and an American principal. During my third year [of high school] I was sick and we moved to Manoag, Pangasinan. I went to Lincoln High School. Then I moved back to my hometown, and went to high school [until] my graduation in 1924 . . .

KNASTER: What, in all of the years that you were going to school, did they teach you about the United States?

BARBA: Yes, we had the history of the United States.

KNASTER: Well, how did you picture the United States to be?

BARBA: Oh, we picture it as very rich. We would like to go. It's very exciting. A rich country and a beautiful country. I would like to see and maybe make a better living . . .

[Barba's aunt and uncle sponsored him to move to Hawai'i, where he worked on a sugar cane plantation for a month. He then moved to the mainland, staying with some relatives in San Francisco for six months before moving to Watsonville.]

KNASTER: Who were these relatives?

BARBA: Oh, my cousin and second cousin. They've been down here in the United States for a long, long time.

KNASTER: Do you remember when they migrated here?

BARBA: No, I don't.

KNASTER: Where they from the same town?

BARBA: Yes.

KNASTER: What were they doing in San Francisco?

BARBA: Well they were working . . . waitresses or busboy, dishwasher or cook.

KNASTER: Had they come here as single people, or as a family?

BARBA: Single people.

KNASTER: Were they only men, or were there women too?

BARBA: No, mostly men.

KNASTER: Most of the time it seems that Filipino people came to the United States as single people, and mostly men, rather than families.

BARBA: Right. Mostly men. Then after a while the man maybe go back and bring his wife.

When I liked the place, I wrote to my aunt in Hawai'i. So they came over and joined me here. They stayed for a while in San Francisco, but they didn't work. I stayed in San Francisco for a while. I went and visited them once in a while in Stockton. They were working on Sherman Island in asparagus . . .

One day when I went to visit them, my friend who was insurance agent was talking to me. He was a neighbor of mine where I was born. He said, "Why don't you come here and look for a job? They are looking for a night clerk. So I got the job in Stockton in a hotel, renting rooms. I worked there for more than a year. Then my aunt and my uncle moved to Watsonville.

KNASTER: Do you know why they came to Watsonville?

BARBA: They figure that there's lot's [sic] of work in agriculture . . . lettuce and what-not. When they came here they rented a couple of big houses in town. Keeping of boys. There's a lot of boys wanting to work.

KNASTER: Filipino boys?

BARBA: Yeah, all Filipinos then. They had a camp, and about fifty-five boys, sending boys to work for everybody who needs some help. There was this one big company from Salinas. He has a camp at the foot of Warner Hill in Watsonville. [The company] told them if they want to move in, you stay in the camp and keep boys and board boys. One day when I came down from Stockton to visit them, they said, "You'd better come back here and keep this camp and we move to another."

Source: Excerpt from "Frank Barba: Filipino Labor Contractor: Watsonville, CA, 1927-1977." Interview with Meri Knaster. Reprinted with permission from the Regional History Project of the University Library at the University of California, Santa Cruz. http://library.ucsc.edu/reg-hist/barba.

Rufino F. Cacabelos, *Autobiography*
(1992)

Rufino F. Cacabelos immigrated to Seattle from the Philippines in 1929. He worked in the Alaskan canneries, as a houseboy, and as a migrant worker for a Japanese farmer. He graduated from the University of Washington with an English degree in 1939; he began graduate school, but World War II interrupted his studies. He was drafted into the all-Filipino 1st Infantry Regiment. Cacabelos never completed his graduate studies, but he found a fulfilling career as a distribution clerk in the U.S. Postal Service. He married and settled in Seattle, where he and his wife raised their only child, James. Throughout his life, Cacabelos was active in many

Seattle-area Filipino American organizations, including the Filipino Columbians, Columbianas, the Northern League, and the Narvacanian Club. In these two excerpts from his autobiography, Cacabelos recounts his first experience in an American school and his stint working for a Japanese farmer during the Depression.

Jason Lee Junior High School

I will always remember September 4, 1929, when I met an American High School principal for the first time. Mrs. Ross took me to the Principal's office herself. The school was 5 blocks from the Rosses. We walked. She enrolled me in the 8th grade, talked to the clerk and Principal and left. The principal kept looking at my report card which I brought with me from Vigan. I cannot figure out what he thought of it as he gave it back to me, anyway, I was enrolled. A lady clerk gave me a schedule and told me to go to room 108 my homeroom, she explained. I entered the room with boys and girls who were all taller than I was although I was seven years older than the oldest of them. Since it was the homeroom and being the first day of school that fall, seat assignments took over an hour. Mrs. Jessica Reed, our homeroom teacher must have taken psychology in college. She was very systematic. She made us stand up against the wall according to height. This way, the short ones were placed in the front seats, while the taller ones in the back rows regardless of sex. With this method, I occupied the 9th seat from the left, since she alphabetized each row from left to right. I was in the middle of the front row in front of her desk. She was very strict, but she liked me because I was the quietest pupil in the room.

During the first weeks of school, I had difficulty talking with my classmates because of my poor accent and enunciation. Gradually many of my classmates understood me well enough and a few became close to me. My teachers too were kind and generous because I believed that they graded me better than I deserved. So, I adjusted myself easily at school even easier than at washing the piled dishes of the day at the Rosses.

On school days Mrs. Ross rose early and prepared breakfast. Carolyn had to go to school, the doctor to his office and I to my classes. While Mrs. Ross was in the kitchen, I kept busy in the dining room, squeeze orange juice for Carolyn (7) and Bud (William Jr. - 3), set the plates, silverware, glasses for juice and milk, cups for coffee, napkins, and place the morning paper by the Doctor's plate. Then I tidied the living room cushions, dusted a few of the furniture pieces and cleaned the cigarette ashtrays. Ate my breakfast and got ready for school. Coming home at four, I washed the morning and noon dishes waiting in the kitchen. Then helped Mrs. Ross peel potatoes for cooking. Mrs. Ross did all the cooking. I served dinner the

way she taught me. After the family had eaten, I had mine, wash the dishes and then hit the books.

During Saturdays, I washed the Oldsmobile, helped Mrs. Ross with the laundry, mop the kitchen floor. I mowed the lawn, wash the big living room window on both sides and also Toby (brown family dog) besides washing the dishes. After that I was free for the day. I just had to wash the dishes when I came home at night. On Sundays, I rode with them and they dropped me at church while they attended Presbyterian services. As a rule I had Sunday off unless the Rosses entertained. I went to Mr. Bolong's house and visit where I would meet Narciso now and then, or go to a show with one or two friends. Then I walked home and studied for the Monday's assignment.

This went on for years since I entered Jason Lee Jr. High, then to Stadium High. I graduated from Jason Lee as an honor roll student, 9th grade on January 30, 1931. Immediately I enrolled at Stadium High School for the 1st semester in 1931. In Stadium High, I also got in the honor roll list in my first semester. That was the end of my honor roll laurels until Senior High. Dr. Ross and family went to Yakima for a better position where his specialty was in demand. The family, especially Mrs. Ross wanted me to go with them, so I accepted with joy. With Buddy and Carolyn, I learned English faster than I had expected. I read all the children books Mrs. Ross brought home from the Yakima Public Library. It was then 1932 and I was a junior at Yakima High. I graduated with honors from Yakima High School in June 1933. The family bought me a new suit for my graduation present. After graduation, I said farewell to the Ross family that had showed me kindness and a degree of affection. I always had pleasant thoughts when I remember the Ross family. Indeed, I lovingly treasured their good wishes for my well being.

The Depression

After graduation, I came to Seattle looking for a chance to go to Alaska, there was no luck. I went to work at Auburn in a Japanese farm. Once again I came in contact with mother soil, the giver and source of life. Japanese workers are superior in the fields, It was no contest for one to keep pace with any of them. I just plodded along from early morning until sunset. The Japanese farmer raised strawberries, tomatoes, lettuce, cabbage, carrots, asparagus, radishes and onions. All of good quality for market. All summer long, we start work by 6 am after breakfast. Stop an hour for lunch and resumed work until 8 pm. A 14 hour back-breaking farm laborer. It was in such times that I regretted leaving Apo Ramon. I kept saying to myself, "If I stayed, I would be in the U. of Santo Tomas by now." In a 14 hour day's work, I was paid an amazing 90 cents plus my board and lodging. The good thing about working for a Japanese family is soaking in a very large hot tub. At first, I felt scalded and did not particularly enjoy the soaking. In my third night in the water, I experienced the most pleasant feeling of the 30 minutes soaking. From then on until the end of summer, I looked forward for the intoxicating experience where my tiredness evaporated and a great feeling settled my entire body. The Japanese discovered a pleasant secret of living. I give credit to them. In 85 days I had earned 76.50 plus a bonus of ten dollars for being a diligent worker. A few of the other workers had a 12 dollar bonus. Years later, when Mr. Ted Yamari, a shrewd Japanese cannery contractor included me in his 80 man crew as a can reformer, I was to enjoy once more the ecstasy of that glorious hot tub soaking. That was 1938 in Port Arthur cannery.

I worked for the Japanese farmer from July 10, 1933 until Friday September 15th. When the University of Washington opened in the fall, I did not earn enough for a quarter's tuition because my ninety cents a day that I earned in the farm was spent in bus rides to Seattle or Tacoma on Sundays to visit acquaintances. I ended up at Mr. Mariano Bolong's house. There I met Leo de Leon from Cagayan who would someday have a daughter to become first lady in waiting in the Seattle Seafair.

Franklin Delano Roosevelt became President in 1933 and the NRA, CCC and many other agencies were created to put men back to work. I went to apply to the Civilian Conservation Corps, the WPA, etc. But the race prejudice was still strong against minorities. On top of that, I was told that I was not big enough to be hired. So that fall, many of us students were penniless. We steeraged with Pinoys who were lucky to have restaurant jobs such as busboys, dishwashers, cook helpers and elevator boys. They had rooms of their own, so we steeraged with their permission. When they went to work, we joyfully used their beds.

Tacoma had a red light district wherein the Chinese operated gambling. Pinoys frequented these places both the penniless and those who worked. The place was at least warm and so in winter we spent hours there inhaling their opium smoke. They often gave us dry biscuits to go with the hot tea which was accessible to everybody.

Source: Cacabelos, Rufino. *Autobiography.* 1992. http://cacabelos.us/home.html. Accessed November 2009. Reprinted with permission.

Excerpt from Evangeline Canonizado Buell, *Twenty-Five Chickens and a Pig for a Bride: Growing Up in a Filipino Immigrant Family*

(2006)

On February 15, 1898, the U.S. battleship Maine *exploded and sank in Havana harbor. Despite Spain's attempts to withdraw from* Cuba, the incident quickly devolved into armed conflict. Fifty years of Manifest Destiny rhetoric and expansionist policies fueled

American desire for its "splendid little war" with Spain. Spain's defeat resulted in Cuban independence, but it did not have the same effect in the Philippines: the United States paid Spain $20 million for the Philippine islands that December.

The Filipinos did not go quietly into the night, however. Under the leadership of Emilio Aguinaldo, the Filipinos waged a war of independence. The United States labeled it an insurrection and in 1902, after three years of fighting, officially proclaimed the rebellion over. The Philippine Organic Act of July 1902 established a Philippine Commission and a civilian government in the Philippines. American proclamations notwithstanding, elements of Filipino resistance groups continued to fight the U.S. military and the Philippine Constabulary for another decade. This was the Philippine American War.

African American regiments that had originally fought Native Americans in the American Southwest were sent to the islands to fight Filipinos. The soldiers in these all-black regiments were known as buffalo soldiers; the nickname is commonly believed to have come from the Cheyenne Indians, a reference either to the black soldiers' curly hair or to their fierceness. Although some buffalo soldiers hoped that their service in the Philippines would improve their lot back home, others found they shared a common experience with their enemies, namely racism and discrimination at the hands of white Americans. A few actually threw in their lot with the Filipinos, switching sides and fighting against the United States. Others remained stationed in the Philippines after the fighting ended, voluntarily integrating with the local populace.

In this excerpt from her memoirs, Oakland, California, native and Filipina activist and writer Evangeline Canonizado Buell tells the story of her grandfather, a buffalo soldier who stayed in the Philippines after the war and eventually returned to America with his Filipina bride.

Grandpa Stokes was among 6,000 African-American soldiers who were sent to the Philippines in 1898 to fight in the Spanish-American War. Upon arriving in the Philippines, he became part of the Ninth Cavalry of the U.S. Army. My grandfather became sergeant in that unit consisting of African-American members, who were called "Buffalo Soldiers."

Grandpa Stokes could not escape racism even in a foreign land. He and the members of his division were put in the forefront of the battles and used as shields for the Caucasian soldiers. In order to survive, they used their cunning, toughness, and defiance.

The Spanish-American War ended in 1898, and Spain ceded its Philippine colony to the U.S. as part of the Treaty of Paris. About one hundred Buffalo Soldiers, including Grandpa Stokes, remained in the Philippines to fight in the ensuing battle between the American colonizers and the Filipino fighters for independence that became known as the Philippine-American War. During this conflict, the Buffalo Soldiers had benefited from the solidarity of Filipinos, who refused to shoot African American soldiers because they felt an affinity with them. The Caucasian soldiers had referred to both groups as "savages." This War, which lasted for three years, resulted in hundreds of thousands of Filipino casualties and successfully solidified American control of the Philippines. Like many of the surviving Buffalo Soldiers, Grandpa Stokes chose to remain on the island archipelago.

In 1902 Grandpa Stokes married Maria Bunag, the daughter of Gregoria Rodriguez, a native of Penaranda, Nueva Ecija. They had three daughters, who were born at Fort Stotsenberg (later known as Clark Air Base), located in the province of Pampanga.

Despite the prejudice that he still experienced in the U.S. Army, it seemed that Grandpa Stokes had finally fulfilled his dream to find a better life outside the United States. He loved the Philippines, its people, culture, and customs. Grandpa learned to speak Chinese and Spanish, and local dialects like

Ilocano, Kapampangan, Tagalog, and Visayan. He communicated with Filipinos in their own dialect and enjoyed the local food, including the strong-smelling *bagoong*, a salty paste of fermented fish or shrimp. At home, he ate peasant-style, using his fingers to dip the grilled fish in *bagoong*, scoop it up with rice, and thumb it into his mouth with relish. He washed the dinner down with a glass of *tuba*, a potent local wine made of palm sap, and ended the meal with a satisfied sigh and a compliment to his wife, "*Ay, masarap ang pagkain,*" "Oh, the food is delicious."

After my grandmother Maria died in 1917, Grandpa Stokes had to send his three daughters to stay with his late wife's relatives because he could not care for them while fulfilling his Army duties. Ten-year-old Felicia and five-year-old Theodora went to live with their Uncle Nicolas in Cabanatuan, Nueva Ecija, and eight-year-old Dominga stayed with her grandmother, Gregoria, in Penaranda. While Dominga found love and nurturing in her new home, Felicia and Theodora did not fare as well. Their uncle and other relatives treated them like servants because they were half black and did not look like their cousins with straight hair and fairer skin. Older male cousins repeatedly raped and beat the two girls, who endured physical, emotional, and sexual abuse for five years, until their father rescued them from this horrifying experience.

In 1923 Grandpa Stoakes met Roberta Dungca, a beautiful and vivacious 16-year old from Angeles, Pampanga, where his army base was located. She was thirty years younger than my grandfather, who was then in his late forties, and was only a few months older than his eldest child Felicia. Grandpa was deeply in love with Roberta and wanted to marry her and bring her back to the States. She was the first woman he had considered marrying since the death of his wife Maria, but he was wracked with doubts as to whether she would reciprocate his feelings or whether her parents would approve. Though Roberta was also unsure about Grandpa because of their age difference, she thoroughly enjoyed his company, appreciated that he spoke her Kapampangan dialect, and thought that he looked handsome in his uniform . . .

Grandpa Stokes, desperate to make Roberta his wife, decided to take matters into his own hands . . . Grandpa found the perfect opportunity to implement his plan. Fully aware that Filipinos forbade kissing during courtship and only marriage could save the family's honor if such a custom were violated, he grabbed Roberta, put his arms around her, and kissed her in front of her shocked parents. Her angry father blurted out the words that her daughter's suitor had been secretly wanting to hear, "You have to marry her immediately!"

While still reluctant to wed a much older man, Roberta knew that she could not break an honored tradition. Her parents also had misgivings about their daughter marrying Grandpa, but they had to save face and allowed the wedding to take place. Their biggest fear was that they would lose Roberta forever once she and Grandpa left the country. In 1928, Grandpa Stokes and Roberta sailed for the United States, and her parents' worst nightmare would be fulfilled. Their daughter would never have a chance to visit the Philippines and see her family again.

Grandma Roberta cried for days in her mother's arms before their departure and everyday on the ship bound for San Francisco. Once in the States, Grandpa helped his wife, who was illiterate, to write letters to her family and read their letters to her. He fulfilled his promise to make her happy and provide a stable home for her, but it took Grandma Roberta a long time to forgive him for kissing her in front of her parents. "We always had a chaperone whenever we went out together, and he never touched me, but he was worried that someone else might come along," she told me. "I learned to love your Grandpa only after we arrived here. It broke my heart to leave the country. I'm still very lonesome for my parents."

Like Grandpa Stokes, many of the African-American soldiers who had remained in the Philippines after the Spanish-American War eventually returned to the U.S. with their Filipino wives in the late 1920s and early 1930s. Among them were Grandpa's friends like Messieurs Brown, Hawkins, James, Jones, McQuinney, Nicholas, and Pitts who also settled in the Bay Area. The men taught their wives to play poker and they spent many evenings partying and playing cards together. Over the years, they often visited our home until they passed away, one after another. As a sign of deference for our elders, we children called the men "Grandpa" and their Filipino wives "Manang," a term of respect for an older sister or female relative.

The grandpas loved reminiscing about the Philippines and held the children's attention with stories about their adventures. One evening, while Grandma Roberta was still preparing dinner, one grandpa said, "Oh, how your Grandpa Stoked loved to make homemade gin . . . " Another raved about the culinary talent of my late grandmother Maria . . .

Grandpa Stokes and Grandma Roberta lived in West Oakland, together with my father Stanley and my mother Felicia. Grandpa had retired from the Army, and my father was in the Navy, stationed on Yerba Buena Island between Oakland and San Francisco. There were very few Filipinos and African Americans in West Oakland in the 1930s, and these minority groups had difficulty finding housing because of racial discrimination. Therefore, extended families tended to stay together to survive, especially during the Depression. After countless rejections from landlords, Grandpa and Grandma were able to rent the upper flat in an old Victorian home from a Portuguese family they had met through friends.

Although Grandpa and Grandma did not have children of their own, they had a household full of kids. They had adopted my cousin Rosario right after she was born in 1932 because she was abandoned by her mother, my Auntie Theodora. Because we were the same age, we were raised as sisters and dressed alike as twins. Grandpa would sit us on his lap and sing to us in Tagalog and Spanish, bouncing us up and down to the rhythm of the songs. He also taught us how to count in

Chinese. When my sister Rosita was born in 1934, the whole family, especially Grandpa, was thrilled to have another addition to the brood. While Grandpa took care of amusing the children, Grandma handled the task of nourishing the growing family.

Grandpa taught Grandma how to cook American, including Southern soul food from his native Tennessee and other cuisines, helping us to develop a multi-cultural palate. Fried chicken that had been soaked in buttermilk, mashed potatoes, cream gravy, sausage bread dressing, spaghetti, and lemon and sweet potato pies. Grandma learned to bake biscuits, but she always served rice, no matter what else was on the menu. Even now, my sister Rosita must have rice with every meal.

Grandpa died in February 1936, when I was just four years old. I was left with few but very fond memories of him. Two years later, Grandma married Manuel Unabia. Since Filipinos were barred from buying real estate property, one of Grandpa's friends helped Grandma and Uncle Manuel by placing his name on the deed for the house that the couple bought for $5,000. He said that before Grandpa Stokes died, he had asked him to take care of Roberta and the grandchildren in case anything happened to him. "Berta, Sergeant Stokes was like a brother to me, and I'm glad I can help you in this way. May you be happy and secure in this house," the helpful grandpa stated. When it finally became legal for Filipinos to buy homes, he turned over the deed to Grandma, who changed the title in her name . . .

Buffalo Soldier Ernest Stokes is buried in the Presidio in San Francisco, where in 1898 he trained as a soldier before sailing for his assignment to fight in the Spanish-American War in the Philippines. His brave journey to find a better life had begun and ended on a windy hill that now looks down on a monument honoring the Tennessee volunteers, who fought in foreign wars.

Source: Buell, Evangeline Canonizado. *Twenty-Five Chickens and a Pig for a Bride: Growing Up in a Filipino Immigrant Family.* San Francisco: T'Boli, 2006, 17–22. Reprinted with permission from the author.

Robert Bernardo, "Strangers Among Us" (2006)
and Interview with Eliyahu Enriquez
(2009)

Forced to leave Spain during the 16th-century Inquisition, many Jews and Jewish converts (called conversos *or* Marranos*) fled to the Philippines, a Spanish colony where the Inquisition was not as strong. A small and covert Jewish community grew in the Philippines, and once the United States took over in 1898, Jews were allowed to practice their religion openly. In the 1930s, Filipino Jews opened their doors to their European brethren who were escaping the Germans during the buildup to World War II.*

Filipino American Robert Bernardo is an activist, attorney, and former cochair of the Gay Asian Pacific Alliance (GAPA). He converted to Judaism when he was an adult, after discovering his Sephardic Jewish ancestry through his Spanish grandmother. In 2006, Bernardo gave the following drash *(sermon) for the Rosh Hashanah service at Congregation Sha'ar Zahav. "Strangers Among Us" is an exposition on the many meanings of "stranger," illustrated with examples from Bernardo's own life and experiences as a gay Jewish Filipino man.*

That same year, Bernardo served as grand marshal for the San Francisco Gay Pride Parade. Three years later, in an interview with Eliyahu Enriquez (author of the Bahay Shalom blog), Bernardo remembered his experience: "I was extremely proud to wear my Filipino Barong Tagalog shirt. It was lavender with traditional white embroidery. I also wore a Hawaiian lei that was given to me by founding GAPA member and former parade grand marshal, Hoover Lee. To represent my Jewish side, I wore a rainbow-colored yarmulke on my head. It felt truly liberating to show the different components that make me who I am." In the following excerpt from his interview, Bernardo talks about the ties between Spain, the Philippines, and Judaism; the

place of homosexuals in Israel; and his own multifaceted identity.

"Strangers among Us" (2006)

In 1974, when my family lived in San Francisco's Richmond District, I remember spending warm, summer afternoons walking along Ocean Beach with my father. Together, we would collect seashells and then head off to Playland, the nearby amusement park (at the time) near 48th Avenue. I remember one day as we were heading back to our apartment, a group of teenagers heading toward us with white flowers in their hair. They wore bright tie-die shirts, multi-colored beads, and sandals. As they walked, they laughed, giggled, smoked . . . cigarettes and sang songs. I was thrilled to see these young people because they all looked so happy. I looked up and smiled at one of them, as he kindly offered me a piece of candy. As I was about to reach out, my father said, "Wag ka tatanggap sa hindi mo kilala!" Don't take things from strangers. He smiled at the man, yanked me toward him, and we continued back to the apartment. My family had only been in the United States for four years.

That was my earliest experience with "strangers." Several years later, my notions were reinforced in Mrs. Roy's second grade class at Brown Elementary in Daly City. I remember a police officer coming into my class to talk about child safety issues. Officer Bob (yes, his name was Officer Bob) began to explain about never talking to strangers or taking things from strangers—in lessons that came to be known as stranger danger.

Understandably, there is a human tendency to fear strangers. Some bio-sociologists believe that we are programmed with a built-in mechanism to protect us from harmful situations. They say that our intuitive senses help keep us safe—and often times, help keep us alive. How many times have we looked down a dark street at night and seen suspicious people coming toward us, and we felt the urge to cross the street or walk a little faster?

What does Judaism teach us about "ger," or the "stranger?"

Parashat Mishpatim states, "You shall not wrong a stranger or oppress him, for you were strangers in the land of Egypt (Exodus 22:20)." One of the great teachings of Judaism is "hachnasat orchim," welcoming the stranger. The Torah provides over 30 guidelines about our behavior towards the stranger. That's even more than other mitzvot such as loving G-d, keeping the Sabbath, and refraining from eating forbidden foods. The treatment of strangers is one of those rare topics that is listed not only among the 248 commanded acts but also among the 365 prohibited acts.

The Torah also tells us that Abraham would sometimes seek out strangers and offer them a meal. In Parashat Vayera, while being visited by G-d, Abraham sees three strangers passing by his tent in the wilderness. He tells the Almighty that the travelers need his assistance, and so he puts G-d on hold, while he offers the strangers proper hospitality.

We derive an important lesson from this action, and the Talmud supports it: "Welcoming a guest can take priority over welcoming the Shechinah." Furthermore, Rabbi Yochanan teaches us that, "One is permitted to move heavy bundles on Shabbat in order to make room for guests."

Where else can we find similar teachings?

In Hebrew, Sodom means *Burnt* and Gomorrah means *A Ruined Heap*. Respectively, these names were given to the two cities after they were destroyed by G-d for their sinfulness. And while many religious fundamentalists use this well-known story to justify their homophobia, some Torah scholars believe that the truly wicked act was the fact that when strangers (in the form of angels) came to visit Abraham's nephew, Lot—these angels were not treated with respect and hospitality by the people of Sodom. As you may recall, the Sodomites demanded access to the strangers, and Lot denied them access. And as the story goes, the Sodomites were struck with blindness,

allowing Lot and his family, who were then instructed to leave the city, to escape, while Sodom and Gomorrah were destroyed with fire by G-d.

Lot's need to protect the strangers came even before the protection of his own family. What Lot did was act as his culture expected him to. This was the norm. Hospitality, in these times, meant that if a person asked for assistance, you were completely obliged to help and protect your visitor—even if that meant losing your property, family or life.

So, the real Sodom and Gomorrah lesson here is not, "G-d will be displeased if you're LGBTQQI", rather "G-d will reject you if you don't stand up for those among you who are strangers, those who are different—those who may need your help."

The prophets remind us that, "G-d wants you to love those who are outsiders, and protect those who are defenseless."

In order to fully understand the reasoning behind these teachings, we must remember that our people were a nomadic people who traveled and wandered in an often hostile environment. Weather conditions and suspicious neighbors made hospitality a matter of survival. Being welcomed in a stranger's home or tent could mean the difference between life and death.

Jews have a history filled with kindness to strangers. During Shabbat dinner, aren't we commanded to welcome strangers to join us for a meal?

And we must also remind ourselves that many times in our history, we were strangers ourselves. One such example is the Kaifeng Jews of China. During the so-called "Holy War Crusades" of the 1090s, many Jews living in small towns along the Eastern coast of the Mediterranean and throughout Persia saw their homes burglarized and their synagogues burned down. They were threatened: either convert to Christianity or die.

So, a handful of Jews headed east, down the Silk Road to China because they had heard that the Chinese people had a reputation for kindness and hospitality. It is believed that the original group of settlers included about 70 Jewish families, totaling approximately 500 people. By 1163 C.E., a great synagogue was built, where it remained standing for over 700 years. During the Ming Dynasty, which lasted until about 1644, the Kaifeng Jewry reached its peak with a population of about 5000. Clearly, their survival depended upon the kindness of Chinese strangers.

One only has to remember the events of September 11th to realize that the kindness of strangers can often determine who lives and who dies. Many average and ordinary people became heroes in the days that followed. After the devastating Hurricane Katrina in New Orleans, there were families around the country who opened their homes to complete strangers. Shortly after the hurricane, I remember hearing about Web postings by kind-hearted individuals who invited strangers to live with them, asking for nothing in return.

As we reflect upon the past year and as we take inventory of each moment, let's ask ourselves—what have we done to help the stranger? How have we helped another human being survive in this world?

If we examine the survival of modern Jews, don't many of us depend upon the kindness of strangers? The hostile desert environment that early Jews faced has been replaced with other hostilities: perhaps its discrimination in the workplace, or unfair housing, or perhaps unequal marriage laws.

And who exactly are the strangers of today? Who were the strangers 10 years ago? A hundred years ago?

As many of you know, Congregation Sha'ar Zahav was formed to welcome a new "type" of stranger in 1977. Lesbian and gay Jews found a home here. Since then, this congregation has continued a tradition of welcoming strangers from all walks of life. We were once considered "progressive" to acknowledge bisexual and transgender people. Today, it's a common thing at Sha'ar Zahav. Even the term sexual minority has evolved with the growing understanding of intersex, two-spirit, and genderqueer people.

In the mid-1990s, many Sha'ar Zahav members marched in support of immigrants' rights when the Governor supported a state proposition that would deny access to healthcare to the undocumented—many of whom were children. More recently, CSZ members stood in solidarity with other religious communities like the San Francisco Organizing Project (SFOP) to support access to universal healthcare.

I considered myself a stranger in that place that my parents called the Richmond District. Aren't we all strangers at some time or another? Aren't we all guests at one time?

I am reminded of a December night three years ago when I first stepped into this sanctuary. I very much felt like a stranger—not only because I am Filipino, but also because I was in the process of converting to Judaism.

Early rabbinic interpreters believe that the word, "ger" did not only mean stranger. They tell us that the word also can be interpreted as "convert." G-d so loves the stranger that Abraham's circumcision was postponed until Abraham was ninety years old so that future Jewish converts would know that one can be a Jew at any age.

So, when I walked into this sanctuary for the first time, I really had no idea how I would be received. I wondered if I would meet other Filipinos, other Asian/Pacific Islanders, and other people of color.

I did, of course. In fact, I met a wide variety of people at Sha'ar Zahav—different people with unique philosophies, political beliefs, and traditions, but who still have much in common. One of those common values is "tikkun olam," repairing the world.

Tikkun olam is central to Reform Judaism—and to the Zohar, the most important book in kabbalah. It's the obligation to repair the world in the kingdom of G-d. It's what we pray every time we say the Aleinu. And don't we repair the world by welcoming strangers? We do this by taking in the widow for example, or the orphan, or the homeless—and caring for them.

As we take inventory of our actions during the past year, let us also reflect upon all of the times when we welcomed and cared for a stranger. As we embrace the New Year, let us also remember to embrace the stranger. How exactly can we do this? How can you embrace the stranger?

Some of the ways in which you can do this is by getting involved in activities and organizations that may seem "foreign" to you. For some, it may mean volunteering at the Transgender Law Center to challenge your gender paradigms and to gain a broader perspective on issues concerning transgender equality. For others, it may mean supporting the National Network for Immigrant and Refugee

Rights in order to gain insight into the challenges of being an immigrant. It may mean taking a stroll at today's Folsom Street Faire to expand your understanding about the leather community.

One group that I support is LGBT seniors, so I attend monthly meetings with the San Francisco "Prime Timers" and the "Lavender Seniors of the East Bay." There are many groups out there that need our help.

Earlier, I spoke of the Kaifeng Jews. I encourage you to visit the Jewish library this Fall because there will be an entire program on Asian Jews and Jews living in Asia. One of our members, Rose Katz was instrumental in bringing the Kaifeng photo exhibit to the San Francisco Jewish library for all of us to enjoy and learn. So, let's take this time to educate ourselves for the new year.

Together, let us continue our Jewish tradition of welcoming the gay man, the lesbian, the bisexual, the transgender, the gender queer, the straight person, the two-spirit, the single parent, the intersex, the child, the widow, the orphan, the poor, the oppressed, and everyone in between.

May your new year be sweet, and may it be filled with the kindness and sweetness of strangers.

INTERVIEW WITH ELIYAHU ENRIQUEZ (2009)

BAHAY SHALOM: There are approximately 30,000-60,000 Ha'Filipinim (Taglit/Tagalog-Hebrew for "The Philippines" or "The Filipinos") currently living and working in Eretz Yisra'el, a majority concentrated in Tel Aviv's Shuk Tahana Merkazit, otherwise known as "The Little Manila of Israel"; the city is also considered "The Gay Capital of the Middle East" (*Out Magazine*). Since some Jews consider living in Israel a mitzvah, do you see yourself making aliyah [immigrating to Israel] one day?

ROBERT BERNARDO: Yes, I do hope to visit our Holy Land someday, but not anytime soon because right now, I do have a genuine fear of terrorist activity due to the general instability in the region. I also realized that this fear is probably unfounded because so many Jews visit Israel without problems— including my own synagogue. Our Rabbi takes a group to Israel at least once a year, and one of these days, I will do it. But not right now.

BAHAY SHALOM: Tropical Goshen: Manuel Quezon—President of The Philippine Commonwealth, 1935–1941—assisted in harboring/resettling 1,200 Jewish refugees, escaping Nazi persecution, in the South-Eastern stronghold of Mindanao and posthumously honored with the title of "Righteous Among The Nations," as well as commemorative Israeli citizenship. Nevertheless, patriotic and hardworking Ha'Filipinim with children born in Israel currently struggle for benefits that come with official state recognition. If given the opportunity for advocacy, what steps would you take to advance the cause of Israeli Ha'Filipinim?

ROBERT BERNARDO: Although I have neither lived in the Philippines nor in Israel, I still feel that I can make a difference by continually educating people about Filipino Jews—whether they are similar to my situation or not. I feel that Filipino Jews need to be respected and accepted within the larger Jewish family. There is plenty of room for Jews of all colors and nationalities.

BAHAY SHALOM: Since 1993, homosexuals have been allowed to openly serve in the Israeli Defense Forces, including special units (unlike the "Don't Ask Don't Tell" policy of the U.S. Armed Forces). Were Ha'Filipinim

OFWs, as well as Filipino Jews, encouraged to serve in the I.D.F., how would this concrete act of solidarity transform societal perceptions of Filipinos in Israel and bring about lasting reforms?

ROBERT BERNARDO: I feel that this act of inclusion would make a global statement that would boldly say: "We accept Filipino Jews because you are part of the Jewish family." Also, if Filipino Jews wish to risk their lives for the safety and security of Israel, that should be respected, honored and encouraged.

BAHAY SHALOM: On *LiveJournal*, you blogged about the discovery of Spanish Jewish roots on your Grandmother's side of the family. Ako rin [me, too]! To embrace dormant Jewish roots, dating back to the Inquisition, would understandably be a challenge for fundamentally-reared Filipinos. How extensive do you think this Hudyo-Matrix phenomenon of Sephardic/Ladino ancestry is within the Filipino diaspora? What would its significance be?

ROBERT BERNARDO: I strongly believe that Filipino Sephardic ancestry is much more common than we have come to believe. The only challenge is that there is little research in this area because the Philippines is such a mega-Christian country. If studies were conducted, I feel that the significance of the findings would completely alter what the next generation of Filipinos believe . . .

BAHAY SHALOM: Your Rosh Ha'Shanah 5767 message, "Strangers Among Us" compliments the spirit of The Pilipino, whose kindness to strangers is also chronicled in Frank Ephraim's WWII biography, *Escape to Manila: From Nazi Tyranny to Japanese Terror*. Diplomatic relations between Israel and The Philippines remain strong and dynamic, yet the two Democratic nations also share the burden of extremism and terrorism from within their respective borders. Could you describe how hospitality can be both a blessing and a curse, from a Filipino-Jewish perspective? As an openly Gay Jewish man of color, how has anti-Semitism manifested itself in your life? Because of these existential risks, would you discourage Filipinos from converting to Judaism?

ROBERT BERNARDO: Hospitality is always a blessing, regardless of how horribly we are treated sometimes. Whether we like it or not, we Jews have an obligation to both educate non-Jews as well as protect ourselves from slander and violence. I find that I have to educate people nearly every day, and although I feel tired and frustrated in having to teach people, I still believe that it is my job because as we decrease the ignorance around us, this allows the seeds of tolerance and acceptance to grow.

BAHAY SHALOM: *Tiebreaker*: The decisive vote in the United Nations on November 29, 1947 reviving Israel as a sovereign nation was cast by The Philippines (and was the only Asian nation to support Jewish Nationhood). What kind of impact would greater Filipino-Jewish identification—Pilipinong-Hudyo Pride, if you will—make in promoting peace and tolerance?

ROBERT BERNARDO: Again, it's about education and teaching Filipinos around the world that their duty is not over . . . Our duty did not end with the tie-breaking vote. We have a daily obligation to help Jews around the world and to teach our children about Jewish history and Israeli history.

BAHAY SHALOM: Rob Schneider, arguably the most high-profile Filipino Jew in entertainment, quipped: "My mother's side had the better food, my father's side had the better jokes" to describe his Filipina Ima and Jewish Abba. Other notable Filipino Jews include Dean Devlin, Producer of Independence Day, Godzilla, and The Patriot; Nicole Scherzinger, lead vocalist of the Pussycat Dolls; Michael Schwartz aka Mix Master Mike, American Turntablist and contributing member of the Beastie Boys; Actress, Phoebe Cates (wife of Academy-Award winner, Kevin Kline); and Author, Geronimo Tagatac. We should all go out for merienda and Kosher Kamayan, diba? What makes Filipino Jewry unique from other burgeoning cultural kehilot [congregations], such as Beta Israel, The Kaifeng Jews, and B'nei Menashe? To my knowledge, a Filipino Jew has not yet been ordained as a Rabbi. Do you think Sefer Ha'Torah should be translated into Taglit-Tagalog? Is there a need to establish an authentic, Filipino-Jewish community identity?

ROBERT BERNARDO: I feel that we are unique because Filipino culture is so heavily influenced by American culture. Just look at our pop idols. That's one of the reasons that most of the people you listed are pop stars (actors/singers/etc.) No, I do not believe the Torah should be translated. I believe Filipinos (and others who wish to learn Torah) should learn Hebrew. Also, I do not feel that an "authentic Fil-Jew community" identity needs to be established because by being Filipino and Jewish—one already exists. It exists in every shul across the country. I feel that to "create" a community means that you take

something away from what already exists. I feel at home in my local community at Congregation Sha'ar Zahav. We have Filipinos at the shul, and that's MY community.

BAHAY SHALOM: Gay and Lesbian Jews seeking Rabbinical ordination in Yeshivot are on the rise. And with Jewish Queer Cinema such as *Bent, Trembling Before G-d*, and Yossi & Jagger garnering accolades, significant strides have been made through a Jewish lens in combating homophobia, while maintaining halakhot relevant to the GLBTIQA community. You are active in a Gay-affirming synagogue in San Francisco, namely Congregation Sha'ar Zaav. How do you see the GLBTIQA Jewish community serving as a "Beacon to the Nations"?

ROBERT BERNARDO: I feel that Jews are natural ambassadors of peace in the world because our religion teaches us to embrace the stranger. Also, Judaism generally accepts homosexuality—unlike a lot of Christian religions which condemn it.

BAHAY SHALOM: *Paper Dolls* is an award-winning documentary which follows the lives of transgender migrant workers from The Philippines who work as health care providers for elderly Orthodox Jewish-Israeli men. Furthermore, *JDate* has a flurry of Filipino men seeking Jewish men, myself included =) Can you explain the significance of this mystical magnetism?

ROBERT BERNARDO: Hmmm... I can't really explain this phenomenon because although there are many attractive gay, Jewish men, my partner is not Jewish. So, I can't say that I feel this "mystical magnetism." LOL! My only explanation is that it's like preferring strawberry ice cream over vanilla ice cream. It's a matter of taste and not something that can be explained . . .

BAHAY SHALOM: If you were the Grand Marshal of the Jerusalem Gay Pride Parade, how would you envision such a landmark event?

ROBERT BERNARDO: Wow, I couldn't even imagine what that would be like! However, if it were to happen—I would try to include Filipinos, Jews and Gays in my contingent in the same way I did it in San Francisco when I was elected. I believe that I can be a BRIDGE to cultures, sexualities and religions. As a BRIDGE, the goal is always to bring people together . . .

BAHAY SHALOM: Just as the Hebrews struggled with overcoming a slave mentality after being physically emancipated from Mitzrayim and Pharaoh, as well as spiritual liberation of the giving of the Torah at the foot of Mount Sinai on Shavu'ot, to a certain extent the Wandering Filipino (estimates of Overseas Filipinos correspond to the population of Diasporic Jews) still struggles with an island mentality. With Pesakh and Shavu'ot approaching, how will you commemorate Liberation?

ROBERT BERNARDO: During Pesach, I commemorated liberation by being the "Out, Gay, Filipino Jew" that I am . . . Being public about my sexuality and religion are the ways in which I feel liberated and how I feel I can help liberate others.

Sources: Bernardo, Robert. "Strangers Among Us." Congregation Sha'ar Zahav, Rosh Ha'shanah 5767. September 24, 2006. http://www.shaarzahav.org/sites/default/files/HHD2006-Drash-RH2-Bernardo.pdf. Used with permission of the author; Bernardo, Robert. Interview by Eliyahu Enriquez. May 2009. http://www.bahayyosef.com/2009/05/face-to-face-with-robert bernardo.html. Used with permission of Eliyahu Enriquez and Robert Bernardo.

Catherine Ceniza Choy, "How to Stand Up and Dive" (2007)

For more than a century, most people have thought of race in the United States in terms of black and white. This conception is gradually being eroded, in part by the growing Asian American population. Catherine Ceniza Choy, a second-generation Filipina American and an ethnic studies professor at the University of California–Berkeley challenges the black-white racial paradigm in the following essay. "How to Stand Up and Dive" reflects on the importance of providing Asian American children with Asian American role models. Using her own daughter's experience as an example, Choy shows the power of enabling children to see the reality of a diverse America—one in which they can see their own faces reflected.

My six-year-old daughter Maya bobs up and down in the pool water smiling all the while. Her slender body makes the water gurgle and ripple just so. Thick strands of sopping wet hair stick to her face, partly covering an eye here, curling along the roundness of her nose there. She does not seem to mind. I enjoy watching her like this as if I can feel her joy of being in the water. Tired clichés of parenthood fill my mind. Yes, nothing can prepare you for being a parent. They indeed grow up so fast. Yes, learn to understand the power of now. While these statements hold truths, I find myself continually reflecting on the past in the present. As I smile and wave at her from the bleachers, I remember the way she made ripples in my womb. How her kicks made small half spheres that popped up from my then pregnant belly. Now her body makes waves in the water of Martin Luther King Pool, a public pool run by the city of Berkeley. How ironic, I chuckle uncomfortably to myself recalling a moment in February, Black History month.

I am standing next to Maya, who is perched on a step stool so that she can watch herself brush her teeth in the bathroom mirror. She swishes water in her mouth and spits it out, leaving a trace of toothpaste foam on her lips. "Mommy, are we black or white?" Although I am physically and mentally exhausted, thoughts unfurl quickly. I have spent much of my career challenging the dual nature of U.S. race relations. I live in the Bay Area where the significant presence of Asian Americans complicates this binary. I teach on a campus where Asian Americans comprise the largest group of people of color. And yet here stands my daughter, toothpaste foam dribbling down her chin, thinking of the world around her in terms of black and white. The academic language I have become accustomed to—racialization, Orientalism, panethnicity—does not translate well in this situation. I tell her, "We are neither. I am a second generation Filipino American. Daddy is a third generation Korean and Chinese American. You are a third generation Filipino American and a fourth generation Korean and Chinese American." I know my response does not have the catchiness of "black" or "white" and sure enough Maya responds, "But Martin Luther King said we were black or white." Later when Maya is in her pajamas and lying in bed, I tell her that Martin Luther King believed in the equality of people of all colors. He stood up for the belief that we are and can be many things. I tell her that she is a talented artist, an amazing reader, an impressive dancer, and now a budding swimmer. I look into her eyes and whisper these truths: "You are a wonderful big sister. You are my most perfect daughter." I say to her as well as to myself this plea: "Please do not forget this."

Maya is in a level one-plus swimming class. She is learning how to float on her belly and her back using what her instructors refer to as "starfish"

moves, arms and legs spread out from her sides. "Watch me do the starfish, Mama," Maya would later say during a family swim day, proudly demonstrating her new swimming maneuvers. At the conclusion of the two-week intensive course, she will receive a progress sheet that lists 17 skills needed to pass level one-plus. None of the skills refer to starfish. Skill number three is the "back float with recovery (unsupported)" and skill number four is "front float with recovery (unsupported)."

The word "dive" also does not appear on the list of skills. But on one of the final days, the instructors tell the children to climb out of the shallow part of the pool and line up at its edge. They must take turns jumping feet first into the pool. When it is Maya's turn, I see some hesitation in her body. Instead of jumping up and over the edge, her body tenses, she crouches down and jumps in (well, scoots in, would probably be more accurate) barely making a splash. I do not think much of her hesitation until the following day when she and her classmates are instructed to climb out of the shallow end of the pool and walk over in a line to the deeper end. With two instructors in the water, they are supposed to take turns jumping in. I find myself nervous for Maya. I read fear in the way her body stiffens, the way her eyes cast downward. No joy here.

It is Maya's turn to plunge in the deep water. The instructors' voices are muffled, but I hear sounds of encouragement. Maya's toes curl against the rim of the pool's edge. She heeds the instructors' words, but fear jolts her shoulders back each time she leans forward preparing for her jump. I hear other parents coo as they watch her. "She's so small. She's so cute." But my body tenses too. When she first jumps in, her body is so stiff, that she lands almost face flat into the water making a huge splash, the water slapping against her hard. And yet Maya pulls her body up out of the water only to jump back in. Again and again. Her body continues to hesitate with each time. But she continues to stand up and dive.

A blowing whistle signals the end of class. I rush over to her and drape a towel over her shoulders. I tell her with the biggest smile I can muster, "I am so proud of you. You were terrific." I say this over and over as her body shivers and shakes from the coolness of the air as well as her struggle to fight back the tears. For the time being, she is not proud. She does not feel terrific. Later, she receives her progress report stating matter of factly that she has passed level one-plus and can move on to level two.

I know when something is wrong even though Maya laughs, tells stories, and plays games like nothing is wrong. I go along with the typically playful behavior until her eyebrows crinkle and tears well up and I know we will have to confront what's bothering her. And this time it is not difficult for me to predict that Maya is unhappy about moving on to level two. Because in level two you begin to learn strokes that move you from one end of the shallow pool to the other. You are almost in constant motion. You do not play water games like "Mr. Fox" and "Marco Polo." And with these certainties, comes uncertainty. How will you do in level two, where some of the kids are "big" kids who are in second and maybe even third grade? The tears stream down her cheeks and some mucous bubbles at the tip of her nose. "Please," she pleads, "I don't want to be in level two." She continues while choking back her tears, so that her voice sounds like gasps of air, "I don't want to go swimming anymore." "Not swim anymore?" I respond in disbelief. "You are so talented in the water," I tell her. "You look so natural as you bob and float and kick." I realize that I am raising my voice at her. And that does not help matters.

We do not continue to speak about this while Maya brushes her teeth and changes into her pajamas. But when she lies down on her bed, I tell her that swimming is much more than a level one or level two class. "First," I explain, "it's great exercise for the body." "You mean, swimming is a sport?!" Maya asks incredulously. I nod my head. I tell her how I did not learn how to swim until I was in college at the very relatively old age of twenty. By that time, I had had the opportunity to visit some amazing parts of the world: Belize in Central America and Kenya in East Africa. During both those journeys, my inability to swim impacted what

I could experience. In Belize, I jumped off a boat with a friend thinking I would be able to tread or float in the water. But upon breaking the surface of the water, panic spread over me and I spent the rest of the afternoon desperately climbing back into the boat and nursing the bruises forming along the backs of my arms. At the coast of Kenya, I was hanging out with two friends on a beach when they decided to explore an empty boat anchored close to the shore. The water was calm, but I told them to go ahead and they swam on without me. "So second," I continue, "swimming is more than something that's good for you. It can enrich your life. When I finally learned to swim a lap in college, when I was twenty years old, mind you, I can still remember how good it felt, how good I felt when my hand touched the pool's edge. I had done something I was unable to do before, something I thought many times before I would never be able to do."

Maya is having trouble falling asleep from the stress of the impending level two class. So I reach for one more story to tell. "Once upon a time," I begin, "there was a girl who was born in San Francisco. Her name was Victoria Manalo. Victoria's daddy was from the Philippines. Her mommy was from England. Victoria did not learn to swim until she was about nine or ten. She was much, much older than you. Can you imagine? She was afraid of the water, which meant that she missed out on playing games in the water like 'Mr. Fox.' Can you imagine that? But when Victoria was much, much older, when she was a teenager, she was interested in learning how to dive. But in the 1920s and 1930s, people in California were not kind to Filipinos even though Filipinos did very difficult farm labor that other people did not want to do. A swimming and diving coach in San Francisco separated Victoria from the other swimmers and divers because she was part Filipino. And then he insisted that Victoria use her mother's English last name, Taylor, instead of her father's Filipino last name, Manalo. Victoria faced many challenges. But she faced her fears about being in the water and learned to love to dive in it. She faced people who did not like her because she was Filipino, but she continued to love herself and treasure both her Daddy's and Mommy's backgrounds. And, can you imagine, Victoria Manalo went on to win two gold medals in diving at the Olympic Games, a competition that includes swimmers and divers from all over the world. All over the world! In 1948, Victoria became the first woman ever in Olympic history to win two gold medals in two individual diving events. It's good to know who Martin Luther King was and what he stood for. It's also important to know who Victoria Manalo is and what she accomplished. Do not be afraid, little one. Just enjoy being in the water, moving across it, smiling as you bob in it."

The next morning as we walk over to the pool, I doubt that anything I said the previous night mattered. Maya whimpered and whined through breakfast and during our walk she does little different. When we arrive at that part of the pool where we must separate—I must go to the bleachers and she to the shallow pool's edge, I think about saying, "Remember the story I told you about Victoria," but I do not. I know that these stories do indeed matter, but I think that they must be told again and again in order for the worlds of the listeners to reshape, bend, look different. I tell myself, it takes time for these narratives to seep into the bones of our being. But then, as I watch Maya enter the pool, I think that perhaps it may not take

as long as one might think. "Stand up and jump in," her instructor calls out to her. So Maya stands straight and plunges in, feet first, body straight. No hesitation. No fear. From the bleachers I can see that she is looking up at her instructor waiting for what comes next. And she is smiling.

Dedication Paragraph:

The narratives we construct and impart in academic teaching and research do matter in the "real world." They are integral to the continued success of social justice movements. Author, activist, teacher, and mentor Helen Toribio, who passed away in the fall of 2004, exemplified these truths throughout her life. And she continues to do so in her legacy. I feel privileged to have received a little bit of Helen's mentorship. I will always admire her scholarship and her commitment to Filipino American students and studies more broadly. Throughout her life, Helen encouraged students to bridge their education with social justice issues. The new "Helen Toribio Legacy Fund" donates an internship grant to enable an organization to hire a young adult to work on progressive community issues.

Source: Choy, Catherine Ceniza. "How to Stand Up and Dive." Originally published in *Cheers to Muses: Contemporary Works by Asian American Women.* San Francisco: Asian American Women Artists Association, 2007, 48–51. Used with permission of author.

Gem P. Daus, "Discovering Carlos Bulosan"
(2010)

Carlos Bulosan was a Filipino American novelist and poet whose semiautobiographical book, America Is in the Heart, *remains a seminal work on the early Filipino immigrant experience. Bulosan was born in the Pangasinan Province on November 2, 1911, fifteen years into the American imperial experiment in the Philippines. After taking control in 1898, the United States*

instituted a colonial system based on the idea of "benevolent assimilation." Americans did not see themselves as imperialists according to the European pattern. Instead, they preferred to see their colonial project as a kinder, gentler, paternalistic attempt to remake Filipinos into their own image. The prevailing belief among white Americans was that Filipinos were primitive

savages who needed to be civilized. As one
American judge put it, Filipinos were "little
brown men . . . only a decade removed from the
bolo and breechcloth." They instituted American
forms of governance as well as American social,
political, and economic principles and
regulations. And they established American-style
schools, with instruction in English, staffed by
idealistic teachers who taught Filipino children,
including Carlos Bulosan, that the United States
was the land of freedom and equality—with no
mention of the country's racism and inequality.

Bulosan's family leveraged their farm to pay
for his older brothers' passages to the United
States. Bulosan followed—arriving in the United
States in the 1930s, during the height of the Great
Depression—and received a crash course in
American racism. Bulosan suffered dreadful
conditions as a laborer and endured constant
humiliations and discrimination because of his
race. He became a labor activist, and like other
radicals, he later was blacklisted during the
1950s. Bulosan's writings became a way for him
to fight the injustices that he and his fellow
Filipinos suffered in the United States. In the
following article, Filipino American writer,
activist, and teacher Gem P. Daus writes about
his debt to Bulosan, who believed being American
was really a matter of the heart.

I became an American on February 19, 1975. But I think I was meant to be an American from birth. I was born in an American-engineered city (Baguio) in a former American colony (the Philippines). Yes, there were Filipinos in Baguio before the Americans. But when the Americans found this haven, on top of a mountain, a mile above sea level and a respite from the heat, they decided to build an "R and R" (rest and relaxation) station. Daniel H. Burnham, a famous architect and urban planner from Chicago, Illinois, came to Baguio in 1905 and laid out the plan for the city. The central park is named after him.

When I was born, on April 25, 1966, my father was fighting in an American war in Vietnam as a member of the U.S. Navy. (Well, actually, he was below deck cooking. Of course, "ya gotta eat," and every job is important, but most Filipinos "fought" in the job that American prejudice allowed at the time.) It's because he was away that I was born in Baguio and not our home town of Binalonan, Pangasinan, which is at the foot of the mountain leading to Baguio. While he was in Vietnam, my mother lived in dependent housing in Baguio. Good thing too because that meant she was close to proper maternity care: I was born breached at Notre Dame de Lourdes Hospital which is part of Saint Louis University. I don't think Binalonan would have had the facilities.

We immigrated to the U.S. on October 27, 1968 as part of the new surge of immigrants in the civil rights era. But it wasn't the immigration reform of 1965 that let us in, but rather the 1947 Military Bases Agreement, which allowed my father to serve, emigrate, and bring my mom and me over. We left on my grandmother's birthday. My mom was pregnant but I don't know if she knew that then. We settled in Long Beach, California where my sister was born. After two years, we moved to Pensacola, Florida. After another two years, my dad was transferred to Norfolk, Virginia. Contrary to what a lot of military families experience, families stationed in Norfolk tended to stay there. Every two years my dad alternated between ship duty and shore duty. Sometimes he was away for six months "in the Med" (Mediterranean). But we never had to move to another base, and I rarely lost friends to a father's reassignment. Except for kindergarten, I attended Norfolk Public Schools until I graduated from high school.

So in February 1975, I took a note to my third grade teacher excusing me from school the next day. I was going to be naturalized. She shook my hand after reading the note. All I remember from that day was waving a little American flag and saying the pledge of allegiance in a courtroom. I probably knew I was becoming a citizen, but I don't think I really knew what that meant. I was wearing a polka-dot shirt according to the picture on my naturalization certificate. I don't remember taking a test. Because I was a minor and in school, I guess they figured I'd be learning everything I needed to know.

I grew up with lots of Filipinos around. In fact, I grew up thinking all Filipinos were in the Navy. I couldn't imagine any other way of leaving the Philippines. But I didn't know anything about the Philippines, nor was I encouraged to. My parents had left it behind, and were more than content to do so (later, I found out this was partly due to family drama). But the upshot is that I became an English-only American kid who had no need of any other identity, just like the naturalization officials expected.

But America does not let us escape the burden of race for long. You either deal with it or deny it. But there's no ignoring it. I tried. I am American, I told myself. I'm even more American than white people because I had to earn it (yeah I got to take a shortcut but I did well in school; and never mind that I used white as the standard for comparison). My birthplace and race were incidental. America was in my heart and American was my identity.

I still believe that, but now I also believe that my birthplace and race are integral to my American identity. Of the various experiences that helped me realize that, my first trip back to the Philippines was the most transformative. In February 1995—28 years after leaving, 20 years after becoming an American citizen—my father, mother and I became "balikbayans". Homecomers. Returnees. It was stamped on our passports. All the sights and sounds and emotions I felt on that two-week trip are a story for another day. But I came back with new lenses from which to view the world. And in my search for new meaning, I found "America is in the Heart" by Carlos Bulosan. That seminal work of the Filipino American experience was not my family's experience, but it hurt to read, so it must be my story. I really connected when I read the passage where he described helping build the road to Binalonan. Wait! I was just there! That's my hometown! We're from the same place?! This pioneer who so eloquently described what it meant to be American while getting beat up for being brown . . . he was literally my kababayan. My townmate. It's kind of a goofy connection. Accidental. Coincidental. Or maybe it's fate. Whatever, it woke me up to a new self-image that embraced my heritage but also affirmed that I was meant to be an American.

Source: Daus, Gem P. "Discovering Carlos Bulosan." *Our Own Voices.* April 2010. http://www.oovrag.com/essays/essay2010a-5.shtml. Reprinted with permission.

Robert Francis Flor, "Alaskero Memories"
(2010)

Robert Francis Flor is a Seattle native and the son of an immigrant Filipino. He is a published poet and coproduces the Pagdiriwang Festival's Words Expressed event, hosting readings by Filipino American writers, poets, and dramatists. In his poem series "Alaskero Memories," Flor recalls his early years spent working in the Alaska canneries. The Alaskeros were migrant Filipino American laborers who worked in the canneries during the summer and on the West Coast farms during the fall. In 1933, the Alaskeros organized the Cannery Workers and Farm Labors' Local Union, the first Filipino American labor union in the United States. By the time Flor began working, in the 1960s, the union was well established, fighting the unequal treatment Filipino American workers received in the canneries. "Alaskero Memories" provides an evocative look at the everyday life of these cannery workers.

Alaska Union—Seattle 1960s

In April and May, warm weather carries a wave of Filipinos north from Stockton, Delano and Watsonville fields. Sun companions them. They inhabit Chinatown hotels. Gamble underground dens. Shoot nine ball. Loiter 2nd, outside Local 37. Wait. Wish. Hope. Hope for assignments as sorters, butchers, slimers, fillers, or the catch 'n can. Hope to once again for Alaska towns . . . Falls Pass, Naknek, Bristol Bay, Chignik or Karluk. Hope for a salmon cannery with Kings, Reds, Humpies, Dogs and Silvers, their migrant brothers and sisters.

A compadre reunion, names float air . . . passed lips . . . Abaya, Torres, Navarro, Madayag. No longer young, some no longer able. Dreams deferred. Dreams suppressed. Unseen money changes hands under the table to pass the heath check. A way of life. A receding journey.

Alaska Series No. 1

Boeing Field—1963

A summer evening, my folks drive us to Boeing Field.
Linda and I silently sit the back seat.
My first time to the canneries. Mahogany men cram the airport.
Their hard, brown Pinoy faces rim the waiting area.
"Young boys" like me cluster in close uncertainty.
I squeeze her picture tight against my chest.
In my duffle, the Four Tops and Righteous Brothers.
We hug goodbyes before I board for Cold Bay.
A final kiss. I cross the tarmac.
Fly north.

Alaska Series No. 2

Becoming Alaskero

We depart Boeing Field, wedged among
Manong migrants blown north to can salmon . . .
their summer hiatus from asparagus fields
and almond orchards. Our Reeve Aleutian circles
Cold Bay's fog-laced clutch of corrugated huts,
nestled on grizzled ground and shrub-terrain.
We descend into our frigid cloud breaths.
Huddle in warm pool hall. Like netted fish,
we wait a tender bound for King Cove.

Alaska Series No. 3

Bunkhouse

Cookie welcomes us to his mess hall.
A stocky Filipino, he wears an apron over t-shirt.
"Hot muck-a-lucka-sigh!" he laughs.
Coffee and lunch served, rooms assigned,
we climb to upper floor. Rummy and pai gow tables
full with seasoned Alaskeros great us.
We unpack. Sweep. Carve our beings
into plywood walls.
"Bob loves Linda. 1963"

Alaska Series No. 4

5:30 a.m. King Cove

Mr. Acena, our foreman, wears Vaquero Stetson and Mackinaw.

Traipses hallway. Calls to each room —

"Get up boys! Get up! Time to go!"

Breakfast. Cookie prepares eggs, ham and hot *"mucka-lucka-sigh,"*

- colorful coffee word.

Mr. Acena orders, *"Young boys, you go slime!*

We don rubber suits, waddle to stations. Three butchers straddle an Iron Chink, separating salmon heads and tails. Slimers gauntlet tables, gutting the remains.

"Blood money!" Hard work!"

Alaska Series No. 5

The Fishhouse

Willie, head butcher, jerks the pneumatic lever for the overhead bin. Fish rush the counter like holiday shoppers. He whirls and twirls sockeyes, silvers and humpies . . . draws tails; spins bodies. Organizes them for processing. Musters them to line and guillotine.

Down chained conveyer, fish carcass rotates through a drum of knives. Circle, twist and turn . . . pirouette blades. Guts and fins shear. Flung upon a table, the final entrails cut away.

I admire Willie for the long hours he works 'til the cutting's complete.

One day he says: "Now, you try."

Alaska Series No. 6

Manong Ralph Agbalog

He enters our room. Perfumed and pomaded hair.
Sports a cardigan sweater. Seats himself on my bunk.
Eyes Linda's picture. *"You marry?"*
In conversation, I learn he'd killed a man
over a gambling debt. *"Punched him in the jaw.*
Dropped him on a curb.
Hit his head. Manslaughter."
He tries to teach me pai gow which I don't get.
"Better, you don't understand."

Alaska Series No. 7

Retorts

Steam soars 'round the catch 'n can.
Hot ovens brim with salmon.
Kings, Pinks an' Sockeye cookin'.
Soon to grace the country's pans.
Charlie Woods stokes the retorts.
Loves "Bird." Carried two. 38 Police Specials.
"I'll never leave here. Wanted
in the lower forty eight."

Alaska Series No. 8

Packing and Shipping

Few fish today. Mr. Acena sends us to the warehouse. We toil the day to dusk. We pallet 50 pound salmon cartons. Backs break. Moling drives his blue Clark forklift. Careens like a carabao through rows of crated canyons. Chomping cigar, he stacks loads three high . . . longshore for distant tables.

Alaska Steamships anchor. We handpack cargo holes. Little time for sleep.

America must be fed.

Alaska Series No. 9

Letter from Linda (1965)

The Blue Goose swoons over the town bringing mail. Descends on King Cove's rocky shore, delivering word from home. We collect in the bunkhouse, like hungry chicks in a nest, our hands stretch for sustenance. I gather my letters. Recline on my bed. Linda writes:

"My high school boyfriend's returned. I'm getting married. You weren't ready. Don't write. Mom reads my mail. Take care of yourself."

I slip on my waders. Wobble from the bunkhouse to the bank. Manongs clench bait-cans and metal rods, fishing the shallow lagoon. Lure octopus from submerged rocks.

I select a rod and wander into the water.

Alaska Series No. 10

Weekends

Saturdays, Aleut fishermen return. Our canning work complete, we shower and have dinner. Later, a movie or dance at the bunkhouse. Jimmy plays his sax. Freddie strums a washtub bass. The girls come to mingle and flirt.

Sundays, we climb the bluff north from town to fire our guns. I pack a .22 rifle and kill a gull. Kenny carries a .32 Barretta. By accident, he shoots himself. They send him home. I sell my gun.

We play ping-pong or shoot hoops in a warehouse where we hung a rim. Sometimes, we stroll King Cove's boardwalk to its sweet shop for shakes. Native girls hang out there.

Alaska Series No. 11

LAIGO'S "EAST IS WEST" TRITYCH *(IN MEMORY OF VAL LAIGO.)*

Mahogany artist of mahogany men fashions homage to Filipinos
  who crossed the ocean of dreams. Articulated with Alaskeros,
  sakadas, waiters, asparagus and hop pickers, nurses, pensionados,
  barbers and boxers. Accented with gambling dens, cockfights,
  dime-dances, brothels and bunkhouses. Affixed with in-laws and outlaws of

Spanish cross and Moorish moon.
Hearts in search of America,
Pinoys arrived with tamaraw and carabao memories.
Silent servants apprenticed in this new Eden.
Melting into the melting pot yet clinging to an adobo
past,
    they came . . .

Your east-west star celebrates their memory and
yours.

Alaska Series No. 12

Source: Flor, Robert Francis. "Alaskero Memories." 2010.
Used with permission of the author.

Eliyahu Enriquez, "Inquisitory Karma" and "Mahogany Mantle" (2010)

Eliyahu Enriquez is a Jewish Filipino author, poet, and playwright in New York City. His multimedia work, interspersed with Tagalog and Hebrew, examines the intersection of sexual identity and ethnic and religious diaspora. "Inquisitory Karma" is a short piece reflecting on the interplay between his Jewish and Filipino identity. Written for the 2010 Be'chol Lashon Media Awards competition, featuring portrayals of ethnic and racial diversity within Judaism, "Mahogany Mantle" expands on the themes laid out in "Inquisitory Karma."

"INQUISITORY KARMA"

Inspired by Alex Epstein

In May, I turned 34. 6 weeks and 6 days of the Omer. My sister, Mercy flipped through Sephora, while her drowsy husband wrestled with Esau's Angel. There were no fireworks. No intoxication. That night, a Chamelion painted your plans, neon. And for the first time since my last cruci-fiction, we dreamed in Tagalog.

"MAHOGANY MANTLE"

"Tell me about your experience/upbringing as a Filipino Jew and the challenges you have confronted as a Jew of Color*?"*
    — Akira Ohiso, Zinc Plate Press

Ima {Taglit-Tagalog for "Mother"} Virginia was the primary nurse for New Square's Rebbitzen during the 1980s. I distinctly recall her endearing smile and waving from her bedside. The curious neighborhood Orthodox Jewish children reminded me of the provincial squalor kids in Quezon City, Philippines. I'm not sure who threw stones at me anymore.

Ima worked the night shift for many years. I think I've inherited her alertness, in that respect. I take intermittent naps, throughout the day. I suppose I can wake up on time for mid-day prayers more often, actually.

Ima was really quite beautiful in her innocence and long, ebony bangs—upon immigrating Stateside. We don't talk much these days. A silent, bitter recognition. And her hair has had the appearance of a Sheitel [a Jewish woman who wears a wig] since (she's a cancer survivor).

Each year, she plants Ampalaya in her exotic garden [bitter melon, often used in the Philippines for medicinal purposes].

Then there's David Levi, an old soulful teen crashing in a Monsey basement, below a renovated Yeshiva-residence. One morning, a spattering of shocked students stand at attention, upon my fashionably-late, but desperate disruption, beside the bimah [platform from where the Torah is read]. The Rabbi puts his index finger to the lips, completes a prayer in whispers, while I catch my breath, then escorts me to where

David was couch-surfing. From the top of the stairs, pre-pubescent kids peek in on our drowsy conversation, cajoling David to "daven with us." Unwavering, they shut the door, continue to shift their wooden chairs, back and forth, the shadowy ceiling screeching above us. He was cursing up a storm, really sore at the general state of things. We decide to sneak out and go on a simkha ride [joyride] to Brooklyn, chain-smoking Reds along West Side Highway (eventually ending up at an Egyptian Hookah bar on the Lower East Side) . . . Finally come home, the following foggy morning, where he proceeds to take the wheel of my ghetto vehicle, embodying Neo-Speedracer: papawheeling over suburban curbs, skidding DNA knots around the pristine block, all the while ignoring my pleas, *ling*ol, and wrecking the breakpad in the process.

David told me he only dons a yarmulkewhen traveling through Monsey, as a sign of respect, honor; otherwise, he's just like any anonymous rebellious punk—Hasidic Hitchhiker—getting their kicks along this pearl-studded journey of ours known as Mabuhai [Tagalog for "live" or "thrive"].

I think that's why Eliyahu Ha'Navi ascended to Shamayim [Hebrew for "sky"] in a fiery chariot so *hastily*:

He needed a new kippah.

We're still rebuilding Bahay Yosef, where identifying as Filipin@ and Jewish is a work-in-progress, much like an impending marriage: Loneliness—a memory album of loved ones our only companion—until a Bamboo Ketubah exchange at the altar between Yesha-Efrayim.

And I miss giving complementary Poi shows to off-duty IDF soldiers in Tel Aviv (aka The Little Manila of Israel), very, very much.

In the meantime, I cherish the company of Heavenly Birds—from Eagles to Pigeons to Sparrows to Ravens to Duchifat to Doves to Twitter-Anghélim.

I worked as a Mental Health Worker in Westchester, New York (home to Professor Xavier's Shul for Gifted Youngsters)—where I'd have a hasty smoke during lunch breaks. Remember the time, when the concentration camps were finally liberated? When the prisoners of hope were given cigarettes by the army companies: and ravaged them, they were so famished? One day, I realized I had no matches left in my book. Since Filipinim are known to scavenge for manna in wilderness shantytowns, I naturally bowed my head, my pearl vision cast to the ground, scanning the periphery about me, dejected. Like Aba. Suddenly, I notice a bird land on the stairs leading up to the entrance of the youth ward. I squint, as it pecked away, knocking on the concrete slab—weeds and tiny sticks and leaves, rustling. Instinctively, the bird soars, when I notice a single, unlit match buried among the end with thorns.

Source: Enriquez, Eliyahu. "Inquisitory Karma" and "Mahogany Mantle." 2010. http://www.bahayyosef .com/2010/05/babaylan-names.html and http://www .bahayyosef.com/2010/01/honey-brown-patches.html. Used with permission of the author.

Cynthia Vasallo, "Most American"
(2010)

The United States colonized the Philippines in 1898, Americanizing its educational and political systems, undermining its economy, and paving the way for thousands of Filipinos to immigrate to the United States. Most early Filipino immigrants came to the United States as agricultural laborers—and by joining the U.S. Navy, which recruited thousands of stewards and mess boys from its many bases in the Philippines. Filipinos were classified as "nationals" and were the only non-Americans allowed to join the U.S. military. In 1934, Congress passed the Tydings-McDuffie Act, reclassifying Filipinos as aliens and cutting off most Filipino immigration. However, the act exempted members of the U.S. Navy from this restriction, and, in 1947, the year after the Philippines gained independence, the Military Bases Agreement allowed the Navy to continue to recruit and hire Filipinos. The Navy thus became the major vehicle for Filipino immigration to the United States, creating transnational Navy families along the way.

Cynthia Vasallo is a first-generation Filipina American, born in Manila and living in California. Several generations of men in her family have served in the Philippine Army (controlled by the United States after 1898) and the U.S. Navy. Her grandfather was a survivor of the Bataan Death March, and her father received his U.S. citizenship in the 1950s after enlisting in the Navy; he later served in Vietnam. Vasallo's short story, "Most American," is a semiautobiographical piece describing the Americanization process for an immigrant family, highlighting the unique—and profoundly disruptive—role of the military in the Filipino American community.

Kuya and I used to love playing this game called *Most American*. We invented it when we first came to the US—my brother was almost nine that year and I was six. Because we were the only players, we made up all the rules as we went along. The only prize was bragging rights and enthusiastic applause from our parents.

One of my earliest memories of the game was of Kuya walking around the house with his thumbs and forefingers pressed up against his eyelids in order to open them wider—as if he could reshape them by force. After a while, he convinced me it was working, and maybe to humor him, my parents had agreed. I couldn't really see any difference but because I believed everything they told me, he easily won that round.

Not too long after this, we begged Nani and Tati to shop at Sears, for clothes. If we couldn't exactly *look* like our classmates, at least we could dress the part. That's when Kuya started to wear blue jeans and t-shirts; I wore plaid jumpers over frilly blouses with chunky black Mary-Janes. It didn't matter that the old faldas and pantalones we brought with us from Manila resembled the new ones we had on. *Those* clothes came from *there*, *these* were from *here*—that's what mattered. Nani and Tati said because we both looked equally American in our new outfits, that round of the game ended in a tie.

Then for my birthday a couple of years later, they let me join the Brownies. I never let on that I didn't really like the tan colored vest—it was always stiff and scratchy. But I wore the uniform anyway. Not only because I threw such a huge tantrum in order to have it (something I would never have been able to get away with back home, under the quick eyes and sharp tongue of my lola), but mainly because of the merit badges. Those badges, like the one for safety, and another for good citizenship, were something I could put my hand on during the Pledge of Allegiance and be proud of. I still have a Polaroid that my parents took of me in that outfit, one of many they sent to the relatives back home. In the blank space beneath it, Nani wrote a caption that reads: *8 year-old María. New Brownie. Pic in front of apartment. Calif, USA*. For a couple of months that year, I was Most American. Until Kuya, just dying to have a uniform of his own, joined the Boy Scouts. Then we were tied once again.

As time passed, we found other ways to claim our victories. Like the year I started dating white boys. *Too American*, my parents had said frowning and shaking their heads. With that, I thought Kuya might concede. But then on his twenty-first birthday he enlisted in the Navy and that put a huge win in his column. My parents were so thrilled they pretty much left me alone—so in a way, I guess I won, too.

Now it's a half-dozen years later and we've stopped playing altogether. Our tongues have been so tightly wrapped by blue, red, and white, they've become clumsy, tripping and tumbling over Tagalog. We no longer call each other by our old names. Kuya is now big brother, I am Mary, and Nani and Tati are Mom and Dad. My parents have become sentimental. They've carefully put away our old clothes—even our Brownie and Boy Scout uniforms—saving them as hand-me-downs for grandkids that they hope will someday come along.

Today I'm clothed head-to-toe in black. Instead of my brother's favorite Levis and t-shirt he is shrouded in dress-blues, a suit as dark as midnight with six gold buttons marching in formation down the front, a medal for each year of his service. It's the uniform he was wearing when Mom and Dad used their new video camera to shoot footage of his academy graduation, the one he wore when he pledged his allegiance. It's the suit my parents have chosen for this occasion.

Mom and Dad are seated on either side of me, front and center in the midst of a tearful but silent crowd. We watch as members of my brother's division fold a flag into a perfect tri-corner before one of them salutes, then hands the bulky packet to my mother. Her shaky outstretched arms don't quite know what to do with it; she hugs it tightly to her breast before finally passing it to my father. He underestimates the weight of it and I catch it before it falls, claiming my brother's final prize.

Source: Vasallo, Cynthia. "Most American." 2010. Used with permission of author.

Blue Scholars, "Yuri Kochiyama"
(2011)

Yuri Nakahara Kochiyama, born in 1921, was interned with her family in Jerome, Arkansas, during World War II. This experience marked the beginning of her transformation from a largely apolitical young person to a leftist activist. In 1960, she and her husband, a 442nd Regiment veteran, moved to Harlem, where they joined the civil rights movement spearheaded by their African American neighbors. Kochiyama grew increasingly radical, working closely with

Malcolm X and his Organization of Afro-American Unity; she was with Malcolm X when he was assassinated at the Audubon Ballroom. Kochiyama has remained an activist her whole life, protesting on behalf of Puerto Rican political prisoners, fighting for reparations for the Japanese American internees, and speaking out for prisoners' rights.

Geo Quibuyen, a Filipino American rapper, journalist, and photographer, is the Town Hall artist-in-residence in Seattle, Washington. Along with Alexei Saba Mohajerjasbi, Quibuyen formed Blue Scholars in 2002; the hip-hop duo performs music engaging with the themes of racism and social justice, immigration politics, community identity and activism, and Filipino culture and history. Blue Scholars' song "Yuri Kochiyama" reflects their deep admiration for this influential woman and highlights the multiethnic, intergenerational, and cross-genre aspects of Asian American activism.

[Verse 1: Geo]
Oh, yeah!
I got that third world militant, still think it's relevant
Even if them kids copped the shirts and stopped wea-rin 'em
Humbled in the presence of the veterans
And not the ones who picked up their guns
But who picked up their brethren and sister and
History in the making I was witnessin'
Listenin', seein' this old Japanese lady with a sticker on her walker, said "Free Mumia" and
This was before the Trustafarians were sayin' it
Taking it for granted that we talk about the 60's and
Never get to talk to anybody who done live this shit and still exist
Or better yet, shit, she still resist, speaking to a myriad of young, dumb and ignorant kids
I was one of 'em
Stuck around lingering
Said that "It's a privilege to meet you in person" and
She took my hand, said "It's good to meet you too"
And when I'm out of school asked me what I'm gonna do
I had to think about it, but truth is I knew
That it was something for the youth and shit
Truly I'd probably be a teacher if the music didn't make enough
To make me wanna gamble on its sustenance
And that's why I'm writing this, to tell ya'll
From a scholar

[Hook]

When I grow up I wanna be just like Yuri Kochiyama
Holla, swear to my kasamas
When I grow up I wanna be just like Yuri Kochiyama
And if she ever hear this it's an honor

Cause when I grow up I wanna be just like Yuri Kochiyama
Imma, serve the people proper
When I grow up I wanna be like Yuri Kochiyama
When I grow up I wanna be like Yuri Kochiyama
When I grow up I wanna be like Yuri Kochiyama

[Verse 2: Geo]
I see the picture up in Life magazine
You were sittin' front seat for Malcolm's last speech
Saw the first man with the shotgun (Boom)
Two more came to get the job done
Now who would've thought that it'd be you holding him?
I wonder what you felt when his eyes were going dim
And if he never died, would we know that he exists?
Or would he have been the leader that we always seem to miss?
Now there's no taking back whatever happens in our midst
You remind me that it's more than just a martyr and a myth
You could've said it quits many times ever since and you find
There will always be a reason for the fist
The last one to hold him could've been somebody else
You'd still be remembered for the people that you helped
They said to keep trying but never losing hope
Revolutionaries die, but the revolution don't
And it won't and I put that
On my momma

[Hook]

Cause when I grow up I wanna be just like Yuri Kochiyama
Holla, swear to my kasamas
When I grow up I wanna be just like Yuri Kochiyama
And if she ever hear this it's an honor
Cause when I grow up I wanna be just like Yuri Kochiyama
Imma, serve the people proper
When I grow up I wanna be like Yuri Kochiyama
When I grow up I wanna be like Yuri Kochiyama
When I grow up I wanna be like Yuri Kochiyama

Source: Quibuyen, Geo, and Alexei Saba Mohajerjasbi. "Yuri Kochiyama." 2011. Used with permission of Blue Scholars.

Hartley Ochavillo, "Leaving Guam"
(2009)

American imperialism has a long history. Colonial expansion characterized the founding of the nation and continued apace once the Constitution was ratified: after subjugating the native peoples and forcibly acquiring huge swaths of Mexican territory, Americans moved through the Pacific islands. The United States took possession of Guam, eastern Samoa, and the Philippines after defeating Spain in the War of 1898. Although the Philippine islands were colonized for their economic potential, eastern Samoa and Guam were taken for their strategic and maritime value. Because the Philippines and Guam were U.S. territories and there was a large military presence in both colonies, many Filipinos found their way to Guam, even after Philippine independence in 1934.

In this short oral history, Hartley Ochavillo speaks about why he left Guam and headed for the United States. His maternal grandparents emigrated from the Philippines years before, when his grandfather was offered a job driving vehicles for the U.S. Air Force. His father's family moved to Guam in 1986. At the time, Ochavillo's father was attending Manila University, where he participated in the many college protests against President Marcos. He and his family, fearing they would be jailed, fled the Philippines. Ochavillo's parents met and married in Guam, and he was born and raised on the island. His family still resides in Guam, but Ochavillo left in 2007 to pursue his educational dreams. Today, he continues to live and study in the San Francisco Bay Area.*

Guam is a beautiful place. The beaches, the landscape, the tropical weather, the coconut trees swaying slightly in the wind, mango trees in people's backyards, and flowers and butterflies all scatter the landscape of the little island I grew up in. It is a beautiful island, and the people there are some of the kindest people you will ever meet. Nobody knows hospitality like the people of Guam. And oh the people, in terms of ethnicity and what people looked like, you often couldn't tell what people were. Filipinos, Chamorros, Chuukese, Paloans, Yappese, Chinese, Koreans, Japanese, White, Black, Mexican, the island was diverse and welcomed all walks of life. The island I grew up in was a place where prejudice was not quite as apparent, and outright racism was very difficult to find. The idea that we were all "che'lu" (family) was pervasive. Most people just wanted to get by life and have a good time. Life was slow paced, relaxed, and lazy. Life was quiet, but occasionally (frequently) the silence was disrupted by a party. Good food, good music, good people, good times, why would anyone leave?

Well for one, the tourism based economy has been in a downturn for years, which leaves the island and the government with little to no resources to spend on infrastructure and things like roads, schools, and hospitals. To make matters worse, there are still many corrupt politicians in Gov Guam that take the money the government makes and uses it for their own personal purposes. What results then is a school system that struggles to keep its schools open and pay its teachers, a hospital that cannot staff the Emergency Room from midnight to 4 A.M., and the privatization of many of the services the government once provided. Couple that with the lack of job opportunities for most people, and you find quite a few reasons to leave. That, and the psych department down in UOG wasn't quite doing it for me. I wanted to see where breakthroughs and new things were happening. I felt like I wasn't going to get that in an insular community. So here I am, living in the Bay and loving it.

Source: Hartley Ochavillo. Oral History, interview by Sang Chi. November 14, 2009. Reprinted with permission.

Mike Blas, "Hafa Adai"

(2013)

The Guam Society of America serves members from around the country, although its membership comes primarily from the Washington, DC area. The civic organization, established in 1952, promotes Chamarro (i.e., originating in Guam, Saipan, or the Mariana Islands) culture and language, grants scholarships to college-age members, and holds an annual Cherry Blossom Princess contest. In the following message, President Mike Blas lays out the mission and yearly activities of the Guam Society. His piece focuses on the more mundane aspects of running an organization, like budgeting and membership drives; these prosaic tasks undergird the Guam Society's mission to preserve cultural heritage, attract and retain young people, and create a sense of community among first- and second-generation Guamanian Americans.

Hafa Adai Guam Society Members, Family and Friends!

Happy New Year and may 2013 bring you prosperity and happiness. It has been a challenging and rewarding past two years as President of the Guam Society of America. I'm thankful for all of the support that you have provided me and my fellow officers during the 2011 and 2012 Guam Society Administration.

So many improvements, "firsts," and milestones have occurred during the past two years, that I thought it would be best to summarize and highlight these accomplishments, as they would not have been possible without you and your support.

In terms of general operations and management of our organization, we rebranded the Guam Society by introducing a new logo along with the new look and feel of our website. Our by-laws were updated in May of 2011 after almost 8 years—resulting in a more streamlined process for membership, communication, and the leverage of social media and other more modern forms of communication. Inventories were accomplished, streamlined committee reports and processes were put in place. Use of teleconference capabilities to support meetings as well as online and smartphone payment processes helped to expedite payment processing and financial accountability.

Membership—Under membership, we updated the membership procedures and redefined the membership period to run from Jan 1st to Dec 31st of each year—thereby making accountability of memberships more simplified. We upgraded membership databases and synchronized the membership payments and database updates for a more efficient and accurate membership listing. We held Membership Appreciation Night and provided no cost raffles at meetings and events for our members; along with significant membership discounts for our paid events. Membership email listings were generated to give members more in depth reports about Society-related events and reports, including meeting minutes, email notifications and invitations for special events. We achieved milestone membership numbers in 2011 (411 members) and 2012 (414 members)—the first in the 60 year history of the Guam Society.

Financial Accountability—Current Treasurer Reports and balances were available at each Executive Board and General Membership Meeting. Internal Reviews were accomplished and results disseminated to members. Documentation of reimbursements and payment of recurring expenses in advance/on time were accomplished each year. Events were targeted for break-even or profit generation. Annual budgets were submitted and approved by the general membership at the beginning of each administrative year. Use of Square and PayPal accounts helped to provide immediate financial updates, deposits and assisted in accountability of all incoming funds.

Cherry Blossom—Selection process for the Guam Society Cherry Blossom Princess was revamped with candidates given criteria and essay requirements to meet for eligibility. Selection of the Cherry Blossom Princess was done six months in advance of the Cherry Blossom Festival. We welcomed Guam Community College President

and CEO, Dr Mary Okada and Congresswoman Madeleine Z. Bordallo as guest speakers for the 2011 and 2012 Cherry Blossom Princess Coronation Balls. Congratulations again to 2011 Guam Society Princess Christina "Paige" Ruff and 2012 Guam Society Princess Mariana Cruz—you both did an awesome job in representing the Guam Society during the annual Cherry Blossom Festival events and activities. We fielded a Guam Society Softball Team for the National Conference of State Societies' Softball Tournament and World Series—earning the distinction of being the most cordial and fun group during the World Series.

Scholarship Program—continued to meet the objectives of helping Guam Society member students achieve their education goals both here in the continental United States and on our beautiful island of Guam. During 2011 and 2012, we awarded $9,500 in educational scholarships.

Congressional Activities/Events—We continued our partnership in sponsoring and hosting the annual Congressional Reception on Capitol Hill—bringing recognition of our island of Guam and the Society's relationship in supporting the Guam Congressional Office with events promoting Guam, its people and our culture.

Roberto LG Lizama Memorial Golf Classic—continues to be the life's blood of support for our operations as an organization. Additionally, proceeds from the tournament also provide the funds for our Scholarship Program. Both 2011 and 2012 annual tournaments were highly successful and in 2012 we realized our goal of having enough golfers/participants to use two courses for our annual tournament.

Picnics/Gatherings—Our annual Memorial Day and Guam Liberation Picnics continue to draw a huge number of participants. 2011 brought a record number of attendees to both our Memorial Day and Liberation Picnics. We also were honored by the Guam Visitor's Bureau as part of their Hafa Adai Pledge Program Member during our 2011 Liberation Picnic.

Santa Marian Kamalen Patronage—we had significant increases in attendance of the nightly novenas and for the mass on the December 8th (Feast of the Immaculate Conception) at the National Basilica of the Shrine of the Immacuate Conception in Washington, D.C. This support is only fitting for our island Patroness, Santa Marian Kamalen.

60th Anniversary Events and Activities—Kutturan Chamoru Foundation held its first Dance/Cultural workshop for the Guam Society in 2012; publication of the 60th Anniversary Booklet reflecting on the accomplishments of the Guam Society during the past 60 years; receipt of recognition letter by Vice-President Joe Biden on the celebration of our 60th Anniversary during the 2012 Chamorro Night; and recognition by the Honorable Madeleine Z. Bordallo of our efforts as the oldest Chamorro Club/Organization in the United States.

Most importantly, the Guam Society has provided a positive and fun experience for all of its members, families and friends!

I would like to thank our officers from the 2011 and 2012 Administration—Vice-President Charlotte Harris, Treasurer Maria Pangelinan, and Secretary Aylene Mafnas and all of the committee chairperson who stepped up to support their respective committee activities during the past two years. You've made it a pleasure to be a part of this organization and have made me proud to have served with you in doing our best for the Guam Society and its members.

To the incoming 2013 and 2014 Guam Society Officers and Committee Chairpersons—thank you for taking the challenge and the responsibilities for the next two years in leading and supporting this great organization. I welcome Vice President Ray Duenas, Treasurer Aylene Mafnas and Secretary Pete Camit in their new roles as the Society's leaders, but most importantly, I welcome all of our returning members, any first time members, and all of our families and friends within the Washington, D.C. Metro area to the next two years of a vibrant and dynamic Guam Society that will continue to promote, preserve and practice our island culture as Chamorros and Americans!

I hope that you will come out to our annual events and I challenge you become more active as members in this great organization of ours!

Si Yu'os Ma'ase,

Mike Blas

President, Guam Society of America

Source: Blas, Mike. "Hafa Adai." 2013. http://guamsociety .org/2013/01/202/. Reprinted with permission.

Ke Ali'i Bernice Pauahi Paki Bishop, "Will and Codicils"

(1883)

Ali'i (Chief) Bernice Pauahi Bishop was the last royal descendent of King Kamehameha I, who united the Kingdom of Hawai'i in 1810. Bishop grew up in a land increasingly taken over by Anglo-American businessmen and agriculture magnates. Over Bishop's lifetime, the native Hawaiian population declined by more than 50 percent, and three-fourths of their privately held land was transferred to haole *(white) ownership. Planters imported successive waves of laborers from all over Asia to work on the sugar cane and pineapple plantations, and white Americans inexorably seized economic and political control of the Kingdom of Hawai'i.*

Bishop, concerned for her remnant people, deeded a large portion of her extensive estate to establish a school for native Hawaiian children. In the 13th article of her will, excerpted here, she specified that all admitted students be of native Hawaiian ancestry and that all teachers be of the Protestant religion. In 1887, four years after her death, the Kamehameha Schools for boys and girls were founded according to the terms of Bernice Pauahi Bishop's will.

Know all Men by these Presents, That I, Bernice Pauahi Bishop, the wife of Charles R. Bishop, of Honolulu, Island of Oahu, Hawaiian Islands, being of sound mind and memory, but conscious of the uncertainty of life, do make, publish and declare this my last Will and Testament in manner following, hereby revoking all former wills by me made . . .

Thirteenth. I give, devise and bequeath all of the rest, residue and remainder of my estate real and personal, wherever situated unto the trustees below named, their heirs and assigns forever, to hold upon the following trusts, namely: to erect and maintain in the Hawaiian Islands two schools, each for boarding and day scholars, one for boys and one for girls, to be known as, and called the Kamehameha Schools.

I direct my executive trustees to expend such amount as they may deem best, not to exceed however one-half of the fund which may come into their hands, in the purchase of suitable premises, the erection of school buildings, and in furnishing the same with the necessary and appropriate fixtures furniture and apparatus.

I direct my trustees to invest the remainder of my estate in such manner as they may think best, and to expend the annual income in the maintenance of said schools; meaning thereby the salaries of teachers, the repairing buildings and other incidental expenses; and to devote a portion of each year's income to the support and education of orphans, and others in indigent circumstances, giving the preference to Hawaiians of pure or part aboriginal blood; the proportion in which said annual income is to be divided among the various objects above mentioned to be determined solely by my said trustees they to have full discretion.

I desire my trustees to provide first and chiefly a good education in the common English branches, and also instruction in morals and in such useful knowledge as may tend to make good and industrious men and women; and I desire instruction in the higher branches to be subsidiary to the foregoing objects.

For the purposes aforesaid I grant unto my said trustees full power to lease or sell any portion of my real estate, and to reinvest the proceeds and the balance of my estate in real estate, or in such other manner as to my said trustees may seem best.

I also give unto my said trustees full power to make all such rules and regulations as they may deem necessary for the government of said schools and to regulate the admission of pupils, and the same to alter, amend and publish upon a vote of a majority of said trustees.

I also direct that my said trustees shall annually make a full and complete report of all receipts and expenditures, and of the condition of said schools to the Chief Justice of the Supreme Court, or other highest judicial officer in this country; and shall also file before him annually an inventory of the property in their hands and how invested, and to publish the same in some Newspaper published in said Honolulu; I also direct my said trustees to keep said school buildings insured in good Companies, and in case of loss to expend the amounts recovered in replacing or repairing said buildings.

I also direct that the teachers of said schools shall forever be persons of the Protestant religion, but I do not intend that the choice should be restricted to persons of any particular sect of Protestants . . .

In witness whereof I, said Bernice Pauahi Bishop, have hereunto set my hand and seal this thirty-first day of October A. D. Eighteen hundred and eighty-three.

BERNICE P. BISHOP (SEAL)

The foregoing instrument, written on eleven pages, was signed, sealed, published and declared by said Bernice Pauahi Bishop, as and for her last will and testament in our presence, who at her request, in her presence, and in the presence of each other, have hereunto set our names as witnesses thereto, this 31st day of October A. D. 1883.

F. W. MACFARLANE

FRANCIS M. HATCH

Source: Excerpt from Probate No. 2425, Bernice Pauahi Bishop, from Probate Records of the First District Court [Series 007], Judiciary of Hawai'i. Hawai'i State Archives.

Lili'uokalani, *Hawai'i's Story by Hawai'i's Queen*
(1898)

Lydia Kamaka'eha Kaola Mali'i Lili'uokalani was the last monarch of the Kingdom of Hawai'i. Lili'uokalani succeeded her brother, David Kalakaua, in 1891. She was deposed two *years later by a cabal of American and European businessmen and plantation owners who were supported by the U.S. Navy. They formed the Republic of Hawai'i, with Sanford*

Dole as president, and advocated strongly for U.S. annexation of the islands. In 1895, after an unsuccessful coup attempt, Lili'uokalani abdicated the throne and was placed under house arrest. And although President Grover Cleveland believed Lili'uokalani to be the lawful ruler of Hawai'i and refused to cede to the annexationists, his successor, William McKinley, through a congressional joint resolution, made Hawai'i into an American territory in 1898.

Ostensibly her autobiography, Hawai'i's Story by Hawai'i's Queen *is Lili'uokalani's impassioned defense of the sovereign rights of the Kingdom of Hawai'i. In this excerpt, she argues that the 1893 Treaty of Annexation purportedly ceding Hawaiian sovereignty to the United States was illegal and unconstitutional, and she petitions the U.S. Senate to deny its ratification.*

My Official Protest to the Treaty

"I, LILIUOKALANI of Hawai'i, by the will of God named heir apparent on the tenth day of April, A. D. 1877, and by the grace of God Queen of the Hawaiian Islands on the seventeenth day of January, A. D. 1893 [sic], do hereby protest against the ratification of a certain treaty, which, so I am informed, has been signed at Washington by Messrs. Hatch, Thurston, and Kinney, purporting to cede those Islands to the territory and dominion of the United States. I declare such a treaty to be an act of wrong toward the native and part-native people of Hawai'i, an invasion of the rights of the ruling chiefs, in violation of international rights both toward my people and toward friendly nations with whom they have made treaties, the perpetuation of the fraud whereby the constitutional government was overthrown and, finally, an act of gross injustice to me.

"Because the official protests made by me on the seventeenth day of January, 1893, to the so-called Provisional Government was signed by me, and received by said government with the assurance that the case was referred to the United States of America for arbitration.

Yielded to Avoid Bloodshed.

"Because that protest and my communications to the United States Government immediately thereafter expressly declare that I yielded my authority to the forces of the United States in order to avoid bloodshed, and because I recognized the futility of a conflict with so formidable a power.

"Because the President of the United States, the Secretary of State, and an envoy commissioned by them reported in official documents that my government was unlawfully coerced by the forces, diplomatic and naval, of the United States; that I was at the date of their investigations the constitutional ruler of my people.

"Because such decision of the recognized magistrates of the United States was officially communicated to me and to Sanford B. Dole, and said Dole's resignation requested by Albert S. Willis, the recognized agent and minister of the Government of the United States.

"Because neither the above-named commission nor the government which sends it has ever received any such authority from the registered voters of Hawai'i, but derives its assumed powers from the so-called committee of public safety, organized on or about the seventeenth day of January, 1893, said committee being composed largely of persons claiming American citizenship, and not one single Hawaiian was a member thereof, or in any way participated in the demonstration leading to its existence.

"Because my people, about forty thousand in number, have in no way been consulted by those, three thousand in number, who claim the right to destroy the independence of Hawai'i. My people constitute four-fifths of the legally qualified voters of Hawai'i, and excluding those imported for the demands of labor, about the same proportion of the inhabitants.

Civic and Hereditary Rights.

"Because said treaty ignores, not only the civic rights of my people, but, further, the hereditary property of their chiefs. Of the 4,000,000 acres composing the territory said treaty offers to annex,

1,000,000 or 915,000 acres has in no way been heretofore recognized as other than the private property of the constitutional monarch, subject to a control in no way differing from other items of a private estate.

"Because it is proposed by said treaty to confiscate said property, technically called the crown lands, those legally entitled thereto, either now or in succession, receiving no consideration whatever for estates, their title to which has been always undisputed, and which is legitimately in my name at this date.

"Because said treaty ignores, not only all professions of perpetual amity and good faith made by the United States in former treaties with the sovereigns representing the Hawaiian people, but all treaties made by those sovereigns with other and friendly powers, and it is thereby in violation of international law.

"Because, by treating with the parties claiming at this time the right to cede said territory of Hawai'i, the Government of the United States receives such territory from the hands of those whom its own magistrates (legally elected by the people of the United States, and in office in 1893) pronounced fraudulently in power and unconstitutionally ruling Hawai'i.

Appeals to President and Senate.

"Therefore I, Liliuokalani of Hawai'i, do hereby call upon the President of that nation, to whom alone I yielded my property and my authority, to withdraw said treaty (ceding said Islands) from further consideration. I ask the honorable Senate of the United States to decline to ratify said treaty, and I implore the people of this great and good nation, from whom my ancestors learned the Christian religion, to sustain their representatives in such acts of justice and equity as may be in accord with the principles of their fathers, and to the Almighty Ruler of the universe, to him who judgeth righteously, I commit my cause.

"Done at Washington, District of Columbia, United States of America, this seventeenth day of June, in the year eighteen hundred and ninety-seven.

"LILIUOKALANI.

JOSEPH HELELUHE, WOKEKI HELELUHE, JULIAS A. PALMER, Witnesses to Signature

Source: Liliuokalani. *Hawai'i's Story by Hawai'i's Queen by Liliuokalani, Queen of Hawai'i (1838–1917).* Boston: Lee and Shepard, 1898, 354–358. http://digital.library .upenn.edu/women/liliuokalani/Hawai'i/Hawai'i.html#LV.

U.S. Public Law 103-150, the "Apology Resolution"
(1993)

In 1993, one hundred years after the United States overthrew the Kingdom of Hawai'i, President William Clinton signed U.S. Public Law 103-150. Otherwise known as the "Apology Resolution," the document acknowledges the sovereignty and independence of the Kingdom of Hawai'i before 1893 and the collusion of the Church of Christ, Anglo-Hawaiian planters, and

William McKinley's administration in deposing Queen Lili'uokalani and stealing Native Hawaiian lands. The following excerpt of the resolution outlines some of the historical context leading up to annexation, offers a formal apology, and calls for reconciliation. However, by delineating "Native Hawaiians" as "descendent[s] of the aboriginal people" who inhabited the Kingdom of Hawai'i "prior to 1778," the Apology Resolution avoids acknowledging the claims of today's Hawai'i sovereignty movement, which seeks redress at an international level rather than in a subnational or racial context.

To acknowledge the 100th anniversary of the January 17, 1893 overthrow Nov. 23, 1993 of the Kingdom of Hawai'i, and to offer an apology to Native Hawaiians on (S.J. Res. 19) behalf of the United States for the overthrow of the Kingdom of Hawai'i.

Whereas, prior to the arrival of the first Europeans in 1778, the Native Hawaiian people lived in a highly organized, self-sufficient, subsistent social system based on communal land tenure with a sophisticated language, culture, and religion;

Whereas, a unified monarchical government of the Hawaiian Islands was established in 1810 under Kamehameha I, the first King of Hawai'i;

Whereas, from 1826 until 1893, the United States recognized the independence of the Kingdom of Hawai'i, extended full and complete diplomatic recognition to the Hawaiian Government, and entered into treaties and conventions with the Hawaiian monarchs to govern commerce and navigation in 1826, 1842, 1849, 1875, and 1887;

Whereas, the Congregational Church (now known as the United Church of Christ), through its American Board of Commissioners for Foreign Missions, sponsored and sent more than 100 missionaries to the Kingdom of Hawai'i between 1820 and 1850;

Whereas, on January 14, 1893, John L. Stevens (hereafter referred to in this Resolution as the "United States Minister"), the United States Minister assigned to the sovereign and independent Kingdom of Hawai'i conspired with a small group of non-Hawaiian residents of the Kingdom of Hawai'i, including citizens of the United States, to overthrow the indigenous and lawful Government of Hawai'i;

Whereas, in pursuance of the conspiracy to overthrow the Government of Hawai'i, the United States Minister and the naval representatives of the United States caused armed naval forces of the United States to invade the sovereign Hawaiian nation on January 16, 1893, and to position themselves near the Hawaiian Government buildings and the Iolani Palace to intimidate Queen Liliuokalani and her Government;

Whereas, on the afternoon of January 17, 1893, a Committee of Safety that represented the American and European sugar planters, descendants of missionaries, and financiers deposed the Hawaiian monarchy and proclaimed the establishment of a Provisional Government;

Whereas, the United States Minister thereupon extended diplomatic recognition to the Provisional Government that was formed by the conspirators without the consent of the Native Hawaiian people or the lawful Government of Hawai'i and in violation of treaties between the two nations and of international law;

Whereas, soon thereafter, when informed of the risk of bloodshed with resistance, Queen Liliuokalani issued the following statement yielding her authority to the United States Government rather than to the Provisional Government:

"I Liliuokalani, by the Grace of God and under the Constitution of the Hawaiian Kingdom, Queen, do hereby solemnly protest against any and all acts done against myself and the Constitutional Government of the Hawaiian Kingdom by certain persons claiming to have established a Provisional Government of and for this Kingdom.

"That I yield to the superior force of the United States of America whose Minister Plenipotentiary, His Excellency John L. Stevens, has caused United States troops to be landed a Honolulu and declared that he would support the Provisional Government.

"Now to avoid any collision of armed forces, and perhaps the loss of life, I do this under protest and impelled by said force yield my authority until such time as the Government of the United States shall, upon facts being presented to it, undo the action of its representatives and reinstate me in the authority which I claim as the Constitutional Sovereign of the Hawaiian Islands.".

"Done at Honolulu this 17th day of January, A.D. 1893."

Whereas, without the active support and intervention by the United States diplomatic and military representatives, the insurrection against the Government of Queen Liliuokalani would have failed for lack of popular support and insufficient arms;

Whereas, on February 1, 1893, the United States Minister raised the American flag and proclaimed Hawai'i to be a protectorate of the United States;

Whereas, the report of a Presidentially established investigation conducted by former Congressman James Blount into the events surrounding the insurrection and overthrow of January 17, 1893, concluded that the United States diplomatic and military representatives had abused their authority and were responsible for the change in government;

Whereas, as a result of this investigation, the United States Minister to Hawai'i was recalled from his diplomatic post and the military commander of the United States armed forces stationed in Hawai'i was disciplined and forced to resign his commission;

Whereas, in a message to Congress on December 18, 1893, President Grover Cleveland reported fully and accurately on the illegal acts of the conspirators, described such acts as an "act of war, committed with the participation of a diplomatic representative of the United States and without authority of Congress", and acknowledged that by such acts the government of a peaceful and friendly people was overthrown;

Whereas, President Cleveland further concluded that a "substantial wrong has thus been done which a due regard for our national character as well as the rights of the injured people requires we should endeavor to repair" and called for the restoration of the Hawaiian monarchy;

Whereas, the Provisional Government protested President Cleveland's call for the restoration of the monarchy and continued to hold state power and pursue annexation to the United States;

Whereas, the Provisional Government successfully lobbied the Committee on Foreign Relations of the Senate (hereafter referred to in this Resolution as the "Committee") to conduct a new investigation into the events surrounding the overthrow of the monarchy;

Whereas, the Committee and its chairman, Senator John Morgan, conducted hearings in Washington, D.C., from December 27, 1893, through February 26, 1894, in which members of the Provisional Government justified and condoned the actions of the United States Minister and recommended annexation of Hawai'i;

Whereas, although the Provisional Government was able to obscure the role of the United States in the illegal overthrow of the Hawaiian monarchy, it was unable to rally the support from two-thirds of the Senate needed to ratify a treaty of annexation;

Whereas, on July 4, 1894, the Provisional Government declared itself to be the Republic of Hawai'i;

Whereas, on January 24, 1895, while imprisoned in Iolani Palace, Queen Liliuokalani was forced by representatives of the Republic of Hawai'i to officially abdicate her throne;

Whereas, in the 1896 United States Presidential election, William McKinley replaced Grover Cleveland;

Whereas, on July 7, 1898, as a consequence of the Spanish-American War, President McKinley signed the Newlands Joint Resolution that provided for the annexation of Hawai'i;

Whereas, through the Newlands Resolution, the self-declared Republic of Hawai'i ceded sovereignty over the Hawaiian Islands to the United States;

Whereas, the Republic of Hawai'i also ceded 1,800,000 acres of crown, government and public lands of the Kingdom of Hawai'i, without the consent of or compensation to the Native Hawaiian people of Hawai'i or their sovereign government;

Whereas, the Congress, through the Newlands Resolution, ratified the cession, annexed Hawai'i as part of the United States, and vested title to the lands in Hawai'i in the United States;

Whereas, the Newlands Resolution also specified that treaties existing between Hawai'i and foreign nations were to immediately cease and be replaced by United States treaties with such nations;

Whereas, the Newlands Resolution effected the transaction between the Republic of Hawai'i and the United States Government;

Whereas, the indigenous Hawaiian people never directly relinquished their claims to their inherent sovereignty as a people or over their national lands to the United States, either through their monarchy or through a plebiscite or referendum;

Whereas, on April 30, 1900, President McKinley signed the Organic Act that provided a government for the territory of Hawai'i and defined the political structure and powers of the newly established Territorial Government and its relationship to the United States;

Whereas, on August 21, 1959, Hawai'i became the 50th State of the United States;

Whereas, the health and well-being of the Native Hawaiian people is intrinsically tied to their deep feelings and attachment to the land;

Whereas, the long-range economic and social changes in Hawai'i over the nineteenth and early twentieth centuries have been devastating to the population and to the health and well-being of the Hawaiian people;

Whereas, the Native Hawaiian people are determined to preserve, develop and transmit to future generations their ancestral territory, and their cultural identity in accordance with their own spiritual and traditional beliefs, customs, practices, language, and social institutions;

Whereas, in order to promote racial harmony and cultural understanding, the Legislature of the State of Hawai'i has determined that the year 1993, should serve Hawai'i as a year of special reflection on the rights and dignities of the Native Hawaiians in the Hawaiian and the American societies;

Whereas, the Eighteenth General Synod of the United Church of Christ in recognition of the denomination's historical complicity in the illegal overthrow of the Kingdom of Hawai'i in 1893 directed the Office of the President of the United Church of Christ to offer a public apology to the Native Hawaiian people and to initiate the process of reconciliation between the United Church of Christ and the Native Hawaiians; and

Whereas, it is proper and timely for the Congress on the occasion of the impending one hundredth anniversary of the event, to acknowledge the historic significance of the illegal overthrow of the Kingdom of Hawai'i, to express its deep regret to the Native Hawaiian people, and to support the reconciliation efforts of the State of Hawai'i and the United Church of Christ with Native Hawaiians;

Now, therefore, be it *Resolved by the Senate and House of Representatives of the United States of America in Congress assembled,*

SECTION 1. ACKNOWLEDGMENT AND APOLOGY.

The Congress —

(1) on the occasion of the 100th anniversary of the illegal overthrow of the Kingdom of Hawai'i on January 17, 1893, acknowledges the historical significance of this event which resulted in the suppression of the inherent sovereignty of the Native Hawaiian people;

(2) recognizes and commends efforts of reconciliation initiated by the State of Hawai'i and the United Church of Christ with Native Hawaiians;

(3) apologizes to Native Hawaiians on behalf of the people of the United States for the overthrow of the Kingdom of Hawai'i on January 17, 1893 with the participation of agents and citizens of the United States, and the deprivation of the rights of Native Hawaiians to self-determination;

(4) expresses its commitment to acknowledge the ramifications of the overthrow of the Kingdom of Hawai'i, in order to provide a proper foundation for reconciliation between the United States and the Native Hawaiian people; and

(5) urges the President of the United States to also acknowledge the ramifications of the overthrow

of the Kingdom of Hawai'i and to support reconciliation efforts between the United States and the Native Hawaiian people.

SEC. 2. DEFINITIONS.

As used in this Joint Resolution, the term "Native Hawaiians" means any individual who is a descendent of the aboriginal people who, prior to 1778, occupied and exercised sovereignty in the area that now constitutes the State of Hawai'i.

SEC. 3. DISCLAIMER.

Nothing in this Joint Resolution is intended to serve as a settlement of any claims against the United States.

Approved November 23, 1993
NOV. 23, 1993
103d Congress
Joint Resolution

Source: U.S. Public Law 103-150. 103rd Cong., 1st Sess. *Congressional Record* vol. 139, 1993.

Hawaiian Constitutional Convention
(2008)

Ever since the United States took over the Kingdom of Hawai'i in 1898, Native Hawaiians have fought for sovereignty over their national and ancestral lands. Different groups hold very different opinions on how sovereignty should be achieved, what a sovereign land or territory looks like, and how the U.S. government should be involved in the process and outcome. In 2008, after years of activism around the sovereignty movement, a group called the Nation of Hawai'i called for a constitutional convention. They opposed the Akaka Bill, which calls for a federal policy of self-governance toward Native Hawaiians, on the grounds that Native Hawaiians are not indigenous to the United States, and that the bill does not adequately address the United States' historical violation of international laws and conventions in its treatment of the Kingdom of Hawai'i. In this resolution, the Nation of Hawai'i calls for a constitutional convention for Hawaiians, both native and "national," to have the full measure of self-determination.

Whereas, the fear of losing grants and entitlements for not supporting government programs or legislation, is the biggest threat and obstacle facing the native Hawaiian people (Kanaka Maoli) to freely determine the government of their choosing.

Whereas, the native Hawaiian people, will need a substantial period of time in which they can engage freely, and without fear of threat or intimidation, in the processes of educating themselves. They need the freedom to publicly debate amongst themselves, the various options of self-governance available to them. It is imperative that they also have meaningful access to the mainstream news media in Hawai'i.

Whereas, the Hawaiian Constitutional Convention will automatically protect and preserve the *Sovereignty* of the native Hawaiian people over their National and Ancestral Lands.

Let it be known to All peoples, governments, financial institutions, multinational corporations, and affiliated entities, throughout the World, that the native Hawaiian people proclaim their right of self-determination, in accordance with Article 1 (2) of the United Nations Charter as well as the recent Hawai'i State Supreme Court Injunction, on January 31, 2008.

Be It Resolved That We, the undersigned native Hawaiian and nonnative Hawaiian people, Hereby Declare the Hawaiian Constitutional Convention in Session, on this, 27th day of May, 2008 @ 8:PM.

Source: Nation of Hawaii. "Hawaiian Constitutional Convention." 2009. http://Hawaiianconstitutionalconvention.com/. Used with permission.

Waiola Church, "History" and "Culture"
(2008)

In many ways, the reign of King Kamehameha the Great marked the apogee of Hawaiian cultural and political identity. Kamehameha united the seven Hawaiian islands under his rule, establishing the Kingdom of Hawai'i in 1810. He upheld traditional Hawaiian religious practices, serving as priest of the god of war; and although he used Western arms and ships in his battles with the island chiefs, and often interacted with and entertained foreign businessmen, Kamehameha limited the power and presence of Westerners in Hawaiian affairs. However, the growing influence of white America in Hawai'i could not be held back. Soon after Kamehameha's death in 1819, Keopuolani, one of his most influential wives, began dismantling the kapu system, undermining traditional Native Hawaiian religion. (Kapu were religious taboos meant to preserve purity; many of them circumscribed the actions of women.) Christian missionaries arrived at the same time, and the American colonization of Hawai'i—which would take economic, religious, cultural, and political forms—commenced.

The Waiola Church, located in Lahaina, on Maui, was established during this turbulent period of Hawaiian history. Dedicated in 1823, it is one of the earliest examples of Hawaiian Christianity and, as such, sits at the crossroads of Hawaiian history. The following two short essays, published by Waiola Church, highlight the 19th-century tension between the Native Hawaiians' desire to embrace Christianity and their determination to preserve their own culture and autonomy in the face of Western encroachment—a tension still felt today.

"History"

Waiola Church is rich with history. The church has played an extremely important role in Lahaina, as well as the rest of the state and the many developments over the years. It has lasted through many hard times, and still stands as an example of our cherished Native Hawaiian culture, always persisting and persevering. There are 3 aspects of the church we plan to cover on this webpage. Those are, Physical, Spiritual, and Cultural. And now we begin our journey through time:

Physical

Waiola Church was first dedicated in 1823, as Waine'e Church. Just three years later in 1826, the first church was blown down by wind and replaced by stone and wood. In 1832, the second church building was dedicated, and stood for a proud 26 years. In 1858, a whirlwind ravaged the roof and church steeple, but was repaired without too much trouble. The church stood safely for another 36 years, until it was destroyed by fire in 1894. A new church building was built, a gift from Henry P. Baldwin, and that lasted another 50 years until it was partially destroyed by fire again. It was restored and re-dedicated only to be completely destroyed by a Kaua'ula wind three years later. The Church finally changed its name from Waine'e Church, to Waiola Church in 1954, and has been safely and well taken care of for the last 54 years. The materials changed over time from grass, to coral, then to stone and wood, and then to the stronger materials such as brick.

Also built were other establishments somewhat connected to the church and its congregation such as the Lahuiokalani church established in 1850 in Honokowai, known as current day Kaanapali Congregational Church. Also built was Honokohua Church, Established by D.T. Flemings on what is now Flemings beach. Honokohua Church serves as a preschool for Kapalua children. Although there are only crumbling rock walls left where it once stood, another branch of the Church was built in 1850 by Native Hawaiians, and was constructed of local materials. Lastly there was the branch out in Kahakuloa where John Kukahiko was a priest at for over 60 years. The priesthood at the church has changed 16 times since the original establishing of the church, and some reputable and well-known priests and preachers include the current Kahu Kekapa Lee, who is a renowned storyteller, singer and song composer, back to father W. Dwight Baldwin who preached from 1837 to 1868.

Spiritual

Waiola Church was where Christianity basically began for the Island of Maui. The Christian religion really caught on when High Chiefess Keopuolani became interested and impressed with the Missionaries and the message they brought. Keopuolani had a great say in literally the whole territory of Hawaii, and was considered to be the highest-ranking Ali'i in Hawaii, higher than her husband, Kamehameha the Great. Keopuolani was a very influential, controversial, and important person in Hawaiian history. Kamehameha and Keopuolani had twelve kids together, two growing up to become Kamehameha II and III. Keopuolani was spoken of "with admiration on account of her amiable temper and mild behavior", said William Richards, a missionary who befriended the Hawaiian Monarchs. Keopuolani thought that the Kapu system of laws weren't very good for the people and later, after Kamehameha the Great died in 1819, banished the Kapu system. Unfortunately she fell ill and died on September 16, 1823, but not without being the first baptized Christian in Hawaii. She was granted her request to be buried in a royal tomb, and still lays in the Waiola Cemetery, as she has for the past century and a half.

Cultural

Waiola Church has extremely strong cultural ties to the people and land of Hawaii. Waiola Church served royalty for years as Lahaina was the capital of the territory, and is on some of the most rich land in the state. The many church leaders and congregates participate in many cultural practices such as hula, taro planting, and speaking and teaching tradition and the Native Hawaiian language. Waiola Church is one of the most important church sites in the state of Hawaii, and hopefully it will remain that way for years to come. . . .

Waiola Church is one of the few still standing buildings and monuments of the Hawaiian royalty long ago, and the great changes that Hawaii and its people went through in the 19th century. We are glad to hold this significance and cherish it and plan to perpetuate the culture and religion here at the church.

"Culture"

Waiola Church is one of the few churches in the state that can claim true cultural ties to the indigenous people of the land, and the unique and special environment offered here on the island of Maui.

During the past 2 centuries, the Native Hawaiian culture has gone through a rollercoaster ride of changes, both positive and negative, emotional and physical. Here is a general history of the Hawaiian Islands and how the Native Hawaiian Culture has devolved and resurged back to what it is today, and how people can continue the traditions and cultural practices:

Over 200 years ago, King Kamehameha the Great ruled over the islands of Hawaii. He was born in 1758, and in 1779, met Captain James Cook in Kealakekua Bay on the big island. Little did he know, the future consequences of accepting and allowing Cook to join and establish port on the island for the next few years. The Hawaiians back then originally mistook Cook as the god Lonoikamakahiki, because he fit the description perfectly, white sails that look like clouds, arriving during the *makahiki* (festival) season, among many other details. He spent his time after Cook's arrival amassing an army that could overpower anything, and took them from island to island, conquering each islands ali'i and their warriors. By 1813 he had conquered all islands in the Hawaiian chain but Kaua'i and Ni'ihau. Kamehameha became ill because of a few diseases contracted by Hawaiians from those on Cook's ship, but fought back and got healthy again. Sadly, that wasn't the case for most of the other *maka'ainana* (commoners).

Over the next few years, things changed drastically for the Hawaiian community. Disease was taking over towns at a time, and for the Hawaiians, who were indigenous people, there were no immunities towards the new diseases, as well as no cure. Kamehameha grew ill and old, and died in 1819. Although the chiefly line and ali'i lived on and kept the islands in order for about a hundred years more, this was the breaking point in terms of the race, population, and soon to be tradition.

The first missionaries to Hawaii, after a trip of 164 days and 18,000 miles on their ship the Thaddeus, arrived the year after Kamehameha passed away, in 1820. Hiram Bingham and Asa Thurston were the two ministers that arrived with a few others on the ship. They could not have come at a worse time for the Hawaiians. The 'Ai Kapu, or religious laws Hawaiians held, had just been broken and overturned by Ka'ahumanu, Keopuolani, and Hewahewa, leading women in the monarchy at the time. The Hawaiian religious and governmental system was full of chaos and desperately in need of some help and direction. It was an opportune time for them, and the Hawaiians, who were left unsure of what to do about their religion, listened and converted to Christians, as the missionaries spread their message to all of the Hawaiians. With them, they brought to the Hawaiians a single 'god' which the Hawaiians had never seen or thought of before, set up a governmental system of laws to get the people back in order and to take the place of the Kapu that had been broken, religious holidays, a daily and monthly calendar, and the concept of time. Many of these things had never been experienced previously by the Hawaiians so they were intrigued and interested in what the missionaries had to offer. The Hawaiians believed that they were headed in the right direction, and they were, evident in today's society, Christianity is the largest religion in Hawaii, but with the new religion and gods, came some guidelines that the missionaries believed should be followed.

These guidelines the missionaries brought ranged from putting a stop to inter-family marriage, which had been occurring for a long time within Hawaiian families to keep the chiefly bloodline, to making the women and men dress up according to European and American standards, instead of malo's and other traditional wear. One of the most detrimental actions the missionaries took towards the tradition was that they banned hula and talking Hawaiian in the schools that they erected in the mid 1800's for Hawaiian students. With this came the decline of the language, and cultural practices, at least for another 50 years or so.

Within the time span between Kamehameha's death and the early 1900's, the Hawaiian population, as stated above, declined from almost a million down to 40,000. From 1910 to approximately 1950, the population began to grow back to a more current figure of 140,562 100% native blooded Hawaiians, and 401,162 Native Hawaiians of many nationalities around the world. The worst negative non-Hawaiian influence on the culture was the illegal Hawaiian Monarchy Overthrow on Jan 17, 1893. It was masterminded by Lorrin A. Thurston, a 'leader' of a few annexationist groups, under PRO-Hawaiian names. The overthrow was not only brought on by the fact that he believed that Hawaii would be in better hands if annexed to the United States, but because of greed and money. This overthrow set off so many more alarms and problems for the Hawaiian society. The haole government, known as the 'Provisional Government' believed that power should be taken away from the King at that time, Kalakaua, and managed to sign into government, a new constitution, taking power away from him, and giving land, power, and the control of many resources and money to them. When Queen Lili'uokalani took over the throne while Kalakaua was gone on his trip around the world, she attempted to reinstate the power of the government back into Hawaiian hands. The provisional government did not like where she was going, and during the overthrow, imprisoned her within her house for apparently committing an act of 'treason'. This swiped the rug from under the Hawaiians feet once and for all.

Over the next 60 to 70 years, things slowly got better for the Hawaiians. As more haole (foreigners) arrived in Hawaii, and began to colonize and take over, the Hawaiians dipped away into an almost unknown culture. Hawaiians were ashamed to speak their native language, even if they were fluent. They were teased, ridiculed, and punished for speaking, and doing Hawaiian things during the school day.

In the last 40 years or so, there have been many efforts to regain the culture and pride the Hawaiians once had. And to finally see something positive in the direction of Hawaiian culture and tradition resurgence for many was relieving. The 1978 Hawaii State Constitutional Convention was held on O'ahu, an exact 200 years after when Captain Cook arrived, and at the convention, the Hawaii State Government pledged and committed itself to preserve, study, and educate others on the Hawaiian culture, history, and language. This constitution called for at least two credits of Hawaiian language and culture courses to be required for every graduate, and also spawned the trust organization otherwise known as OHA, the Office of Hawaiian Affairs. OHA was established to "To malama (protect) Hawaii's people and environmental resources and OHA's assets, toward ensuring the perpetuation of the culture, the enhancement of lifestyle and the protection of entitlements of Native Hawaiians, while enabling the building of a strong and healthy Hawaiian people and nation, recognized nationally and internationally."

The resurgence of culture and pride within the Native People and the general population and followers here at church enlightens us towards learning new things, and being more aware of those around us and their cultures and traditions.

Source: Waiola Church. "History." 2008. http://www.waiolachurch.org/History.htm. "Culture." 2008. http://www.waiolachurch.org/Culture.htm.

M. J. Halelaukoa Garvin, "How Do You See Yourself?" (2009)

Native Hawaiians have struggled with health issues, impoverishment, and the loss of cultural identity since the colonization of their islands began in 1778. Anglo missionaries often imposed their cultural norms while spreading Protestantism, and they condemned Hawaiian clothing, dance, and religious practices as primitive and superstitious. Businessmen and planters from the mainland overturned the traditional Hawaiian system of land stewardship; by introducing Western-style land ownership, haoles (whites) also managed to take possession of three-quarters of the privately held Hawaiian land by 1890. The legacy of colonization can be seen today in the high incidence of chronic disease, substance abuse, and poverty among the Native Hawaiian population.

M. J. Halelaukoa Garvin works with numerous Native Hawaiian groups, including Malama Hawai'i and the Hokule'a Worldwide Voyage. In her short essay, Garvin reflects on and shows how institutionalized racism and stereotypes have conditioned Native Hawaiian self-perception, and she expresses her hope that today's Hawaiian community will reject these images and embrace its true identity.

Recently, having lunch with friends, I was struck by how much Native Hawaiian self-image has changed over the years.

There was nothing particularly unusual about this lunch—a typical get-together of the cronies gathering for a highly anticipated talk story session. However, on this occasion we were lucky to be joined by one of our hui's, Grandpa Joe.

A distinguished gentleman in his eighties, Grandpa Joe is one of those wonderful people you want at all of your parties. A raconteur at heart, his lifetime of experiences and wry wit combined to have us all rolling with laughter. Drawing us in as confidants, he would lean forward conspiratorially. His shock of white hair edging ever nearer and his eyes dancing, he wove amazing tales of the "old days."

During the course of the lunch, the conversation turned toward us. "What do you do?" he asked. A physicist, a lawyer, a writer, a professor and a flack (yes, I'm the underachiever of the bunch) were the answers.

"Wow, a group of smart Hawaiians," he said completely devoid of irony.

"Grandpa!" his namesake mo'opuna squawked. But, Grandpa Joe was nonplused. He had no idea why his grandson was upset.

Grandpa Joe wasn't being racist though; he was simply reiterating what he'd heard for a lifetime. Graduating from Kamehameha Schools nearly 70 years ago, his was a world in which native opportunities were few. What we now consider commonplace—a group of college educated Native Hawaiian professionals from ordinary backgrounds—was unheard of in his day.

But more interesting to me, he did not see the very incongruity of his thinking. Here was a man—a Hawaiian man—who without the benefit of higher education used his intellect and will to forge a highly successful international career. There is absolutely no question that Grandpa Joe is an extremely "smart Hawaiian." Yet, he was unable to place his own life example above the stereotypes embedded within him decades before. He continues to carry the century old bias that Hawaiians are somehow inadequate.

A generation later, my father followed along the same path of self-deprecation. A recurring conversation in our house went something like this.

Dad:	"Hawaiians are lazy."
Child:	"Dad, aren't we Hawaiians?"
Dad:	"Yes."
Child:	"Is anyone in our family lazy?"
Dad:	"No."
Child:	"So what Hawaiians are you talking about?"
Dad:	Silence

Coming from a household of incurable workaholics, I never understood how my father could make such an outrageous statement. However, in speaking with Grandpa Joe, I began to better understand my own history. My father, like Grandpa, could not reconcile the gulf between his own experiences and the prejudices of long ago.

Yet—even though they could not see it within themselves—both of these smart, hardworking men are part of changing how Native Hawaiians are perceived. Amazing examples like theirs are the lens through which my friends and I view ourselves and our people.

Now, it is incumbent upon us to ensure that others of our generation, as well as the next, deliver on the potential we so clearly see.

Source: Garvin, M. J. Halelaukoa. "How Do You See Yourself?" January 16, 2009. Man'o Ulu Wale: Random Musings (blog). http://ainaaloha.wordpress.com/2009/01/16/how-do-you-see-yourself/. Reprinted with permission from M. J. Garvin.

Native Hawaiian Federal Recognition Act, S. 381

(2010)

Daniel Kahikina Akaka is the first U.S. senator of Native Hawaiian descent. Born in Honolulu in 1924, Akaka served in the U.S. Army Corps of Engineers during World War II; he became a congressman in 1976 and was elected senator in 1990. In 2001, Akaka introduced the Native Hawaiian Federal Recognition Act, S. 381, which calls for the extension of federal self-governance and self-determination for Native Hawaiians. A revised version of the Akaka Bill was passed by the House of Representatives in February 2010.

The bill is controversial among more radical sovereignty groups in Hawai'i, who believe it will create a governing entity that implicitly legitimizes the 1898 overthrow of the Kingdom of Hawai'i. Akaka nevertheless believes this act will forward the process of reconciliation between the United States and native Hawaiians. The following two excerpts from the Native Hawaiian Federal Recognition Act discuss the importance of the ceded lands (more than one million acres set aside for Native Hawaiians in 1959, as part of the conditions for statehood) in maintaining Hawaiian culture, reference the 1993 Apology Resolution (when the U.S. government took responsibility for the overthrow of the Kingdom of Hawai'i), and call for a reorganization of the Native Hawaiian government and its recognition by the U.S. government.

SECTION 1. FINDINGS.

Congress makes the following findings:

(9) Throughout the years, Native Hawaiians have repeatedly sought access to the Ceded Lands Trust and its resources and revenues in order to establish and maintain native settlements and distinct native communities throughout the State.

(10) The Hawaiian Home Lands and the Ceded Lands provide an important foundation for the ability of the Native Hawaiian community to maintain the practice of Native Hawaiian culture, language, and traditions, and for the survival of the Native Hawaiian people . . .

(13) The Apology Resolution acknowledges that the overthrow of the Kingdom of Hawai'i occurred with the active participation of agents and citizens of the United States and further acknowledges that the Native Hawaiian people never directly relinquished their claims to their inherent sovereignty as a people over their national lands to the United States, either through their monarchy or through a plebiscite or referendum.

(14) The Apology Resolution expresses the commitment of Congress and the President to acknowledge the ramifications of the overthrow of the Kingdom of Hawai'i and to support reconciliation efforts between the United States and Native Hawaiians; and to have Congress and the President, through the President's designated officials, consult with Native Hawaiians on the reconciliation process as called for under the Apology Resolution.

(15) Despite the overthrow of the Hawaiian government, Native Hawaiians have continued to maintain their separate identity as a distinct native community through the formation of cultural, social, and political institutions, and to give expression to their rights as native people to self-determination and self-governance as evidenced through their participation in the Office of Hawaiian Affairs.

(16) Native Hawaiians also maintain a distinct Native Hawaiian community through the provision of governmental services to Native Hawaiians, including the provision of health care services, educational programs, employment and training programs, children's services, conservation programs, fish and wildlife protection, agricultural programs, native language immersion programs and native language immersion schools from kindergarten through high school, as well as college and master's degree programs in native language immersion instruction, and traditional justice programs, and by continuing their efforts to enhance Native Hawaiian self-determination and local control.

(17) Native Hawaiians are actively engaged in Native Hawaiian cultural practices, traditional agricultural methods, fishing and subsistence practices, maintenance of cultural use areas and sacred sites, protection of burial sites, and the exercise of their traditional rights to gather medicinal plants and herbs, and food sources.

(18) The Native Hawaiian people wish to preserve, develop, and transmit to future Native Hawaiian generations their ancestral lands and Native Hawaiian political and cultural identity in accordance with their traditions, beliefs, customs and practices, language, and social and political institutions, and to achieve greater self-determination over their own affairs.

(19) This Act provides for a process within the framework of Federal law for the Native Hawaiian people to exercise their inherent rights as a distinct aboriginal, indigenous, native community to reorganize a Native Hawaiian government for the purpose of giving expression to their rights as native people to self-determination and self-governance.

(22) The United States continually has recognized and reaffirmed that—

A. Native Hawaiians have a cultural, historic, and land-based link to the aboriginal, native people who exercised sovereignty over the Hawaiian Islands;
B. Native Hawaiians have never relinquished their claims to sovereignty or their sovereign lands;
C. the United States extends services to Native Hawaiians because of their unique status as the aboriginal, native people of a once sovereign nation with whom the United States has a political and legal relationship; and
D. the special trust relationship of American Indians, Alaska Natives, and Native Hawaiians to the United States arises out of their status as aboriginal, indigenous, native people of the United States. . . .

SEC. 3. UNITED STATES POLICY AND PURPOSE.

(b) Purpose- It is the intent of Congress that the purpose of this Act is to provide a process for the reorganization of a Native Hawaiian government and for the recognition by the United States of the Native Hawaiian government for purposes of continuing a government-to-government relationship.

Source: Native Hawaiian Government Reorganization Act, S. 381, 111th Congress, 1st Session, 2009.

Anonymous, "Migyul Youth" Questions and Answers (2005)

"Migyul Youth" is the youth section of Migyul *magazine, a journal founded by activists in the Himalayan American community in New York City. After the Dalai Lama's visit to New York in 2003, community leaders decided to create a magazine that could be a voice for Bhutanese, Tibetan, Sherpa, and Yolmo Americans. This excerpt comes from interviews with two Tibetan American young people in New York. Tenzin Yeshi was a high school senior and Tenzin Lhundup was a second-year student at Stony Brook University at the time of their interviews. Yeshi and Lhundup reflect on their Tibetan American identities, the Tibetan culture, and generational relations within the community. Their responses provide a rare glimpse into a very understudied community that in many ways sees itself as a society in exile.*

Since *Migyul Youth* has just come out, we the editors decided to keep it very general with this interview. And since this is our first interview, we thought it would make sense to start off with views from our youth. There is definitely a disparity of thought between generations—not just between parents and children but also between Migyul and Youth and most of all amongst the youth themselves. The interview thus reflects.

We would like to add that we tried our level best in trying to involve all youths of the Himalayan community but there was a lack of participation. For the time being, here are [two] of our participants. We hope their opinions will get your thinking juices going a little more and we cross our fingers and hope that more of the Himalayan Youth will join us in expressing their ideas in the near future.

- Tenzin Yeshi is a high school senior from New York.
- Tenzin Lhundup is a second-year student at Stony Brook University . . .

[Migyul Youth]:	*Define culture in your terms of understanding.*
[Tenzin Yeshi]:	I define culture as a customary belief and social forms, which has a variety of traits that reflects racial, religious and social groups.
[Tenzin Lhundup]:	I believe culture is something that defines us—the way we dress, eat,

live, think and react with other people from different societies. It is also something that is passed on from one generation to another.

MY: *How do you feel about our culture in exile today?*

TY: Basically, culture had changed a lot in these 50 years after our country was invaded by the Chinese. As compared to early cultures and the modern culture of the Tibetans, it had changed in both ways, negatively as well as positively. From the positive aspect, we (Tibetans) have learned the strategy of developing our ethnic culture and put in a new version, to make it more entertaining and aesthetic, so that new coming generations will find an interest in our culture, in which the culture remains to flow through to the following generations. There is a huge advantage for us to retain the threads of our culture within our society and the nation. We can be proud of being Tibetan and having a unique culture; also we can significantly prove the world that "Tibet was an independent nation" invaded by Chinese. Unfortunately we had also lost our abundance of regional culture in these years. Obviously, most cultures were destroyed by Chinese, after invasion of our country. I believe that it is not that our people are ignorant and unwilling, but owing to desperate situations and harsh livelihood in Tibetan's settlement at the periods of time culture has taken a back seat. Since from the repression and the losing of our country, and being a refugee in these years, Tibetans had advanced greatly in many fields, like finance, education, politics and religion . . . From that view, I feel that Tibetan culture that is lost or became invisible for a moment, is being revived, even further developed. I believe that Tibetan culture will be develop to a level as earlier when it was unique and rich.

TL: In exile, I think we are not preserving our culture enough which I believe is due to a lack of communication between our elders and younger generation. Our youth are very eager to cope with present advancement in our culture with very little effort. There are more youths at a party compared to other age groups in any Tibetan function.

MY: *What do you feel of the importance to maintain and preserve our culture?*

TY: Culture plays an important role in representing one's diverse nation; for an individual, it represents nationality and that part of a particular nation he/she belongs to. Without culture is without identity, culture defines nationally, identity and ethnic backgrounds. It gives you a voice and defines who you are and what is your right. Speaking through my experience, being a Tibetan, our strong inheritance culture defines my identity, who I am and what my ethnicity and nationally is. Chinese government had already separate propaganda that Tibet is a part of China. In this abstract situation of defending our nation, our unique culture has helped to differentiate and prove that Tibet was a separate independent nation. It is very important to show to the world and let them know that we are totally different from Chinese.

TL: It is important to maintain what our culture is consisted of because, our culture will show the differences between us and the Chinese. If we constantly, try to cope with other cultures then one day, we will have a mixed culture which is clearly shown in the way we speak. I have noticed that people over here in USA constantly speak Tibetan mixing the English words (there must be a reason behind this).

MY: *What about the importance in finding a medium between what "our" culture was, is and what "we" aspire it to be?*

TY: Sorry Migyul Youth, I don't know how to answer this Q . . . or maybe I don't like this Q . . .

TL: What do we mean by a "medium", is it that we are trying to make a new kind of Tibetan culture which is composed of both previous and the cultures which we get by living here in USA or in other countries. I think, we should preserve and keep our old culture which is passed down by our elders.

MY: *How do you feel about the elder generation? And their opinion towards the younger generation? Whether if they are in tune with younger generation?*

TY: I believe that elderly generations are representing an ideal for the younger generation. I absolutely appreciate and respect those elder generation for showing us the right path. I can't comment on how the previous generations view the younger generation. But for the moment through my experiences with the elderly, especially my parents; I think they hope for us to sustain our culture and traditions and want us be concerned for our country. I think many elderly are in tune with the younger people but it depends on the individual. Those elderly generations, who are educated and conscious about modernity, are more likely to adjust with the younger generation. For elderly generation that are orthodox and unaware in academic fields, are less likely to link with younger generation. I think it is based on modern education.

TL: I think, our elder generation have to take the responsibility to teach and pass our culture to their children. They also have to understand the present necessities of our youth like not judging us by the way we dress or behave (these things can change) and have to find a way to pass our culture on us (youth). Every household should try to preserve our culture starting with speaking clear Tibetan, eating Tibetan food and respecting each other.

MY: *Do you feel a need to prove yourself to the elder generation?*

TY: I think that, it is not always necessary always that the elderly show the way first but younger generations can teach lessons to the elderly. Some people are better in one field than others.

TL: I think there is no need to prove anything to anybody but our Tibetan youth have to listen to what our elder generation.

MY: *Is there a need for a magazine, like the* Migyul Youth?

TY: I think we need "Migyul Youth" magazine, I totally agree with it. It is really a good idea of having our own magazine. For me, a magazine symbolizes an inspiration and expression of one's opinions and ideas. To participate in a magazine, gain education in variety of fields, writing, journalism, communication, dealing with the people and etc.. We definitely need a magazine; it's not only to teach ourselves to write in the magazine but it also encourages and invites other readers to participate in our magazine, which will expand our group. So let us start! fellow people . . .

TL: I think it is really a good idea to create a Migyul Youth where we can express our thoughts about our current situation and to listen to what other youths think about our culture and about Tibet.

Source: "Questions and Answers." *Migyul: The Himalayan Community Magazine* no. 5 (Spring 2005). Reprinted with permission.

Sonam G. Sherpa, "My Identity" and "As American as Apple Pie. What's in a Name?"

(2005)

The Sherpa are a Nepalese ethnic group, primarily subscribing to Nyingma Buddhism, a sect with roots in pre-Buddhist, shamanic traditions. Living in the Himalayas, the Sherpa have become famous for their mountaineering skills, and they guide climbers from all over the world up Mount Everest. Sonam Sherpa is originally from the Solukhumbu district in northern Nepal. He was sent to a boarding school in the capital city of Kathmandu when he was seven years old and spent a few years there before transferring to a school in Kalimpong, in West Bengal, India. Concerned about his lack of religious education, Sonam's father then sent him to study at the Central Institute of Tibetan Higher Studies in Varanasi, India. In search of a new life, Sonam eventually moved to California in the 1980s. He now resides in New York, working as a senior treasury analyst for a commuter railroad company. He is also a community activist and leader who has helped form several Himalayan American organizations in the New York/New Jersey region, including the Regional Tibetan Youth Congress of NY/NJ, the Tibetan dance group Cholsum, the Sherpa Kyidug, and the United Sherpa Association. In the following two magazine articles for Migyul, *Sonam discusses what it means to be a Sherpa and why it is important for him to retain his identity as a Sherpa living in the United States.*

"MY IDENTITY"

On a trip to Dharamsala, India, in the summer of 1991, the wife of my cousin gave birth to a baby boy. On this happy occasion, I went to see her at the Delek hospital. Barely a day old, the bundle of joy, the baby lay beside the exhausted mother. Fruits and cookies or biscuits as they called them in India, brought in by visitors were scattered all around the private room. After exchanging pleasantries, and commenting on how beautiful the little boy she had just given birth to was, she remarked, "Sherpa babies look like monkeys!!!"

Not only was I taken aback but, was quite furious to hear such blatant mockery of my people. There were a few questions which came to mind. Did she know that I was a Sherpa too? Just because I spoke Tibetan, did she think I was not a Sherpa? Did she know that many of her husband's relatives were Sherpas? Was it because of a few Sherpas that she had dealt with, she somehow had a negative perception of them and that had made her comment in that manner? Did it even matter to her what ethnic group I preferred to be?

I was a Tibetan for her, and she must have figured, it was ok to make such comments amongst Tibetans.

Her husband, my cousin, was born in Dharamsala. His father is a first cousin of my father and both their grand parents had immigrated from Gyarong, Tibet, to Nepal, gradually becoming Sherpas. My father and most of his relatives still living in Nepal are as pure Sherpas as they come. But my uncle, who had moved to Dharamsala many years ago and settled there with his family, had become 'Tibetan'. Making everyone born to his family and other relatives that moved to India, Tibetans as well. Well, I wouldn't be a bit surprised if their perception were contrary to mine.

From an early age, I joined Tibetan schools and spoke Tibetan but I had never met any relatives of mine who could speak Tibetan. I was in quite a shock when the first time someone related to me spoke in Tibetan but did not speak Nepali at all or spoke very little of it. My cousins in India grew up as Tibetans, without ties to their relatives in Nepal.

This has always made me wonder that no matter how much I try to blend as a Tibetan, to some Tibetans I'll always be a Nepali, which I am.

This aside, on another occasion, at a get-together of Sherpa friends and families, speaking in Tibetan to a Tibetan friend (who's married to a Sherpa lady), a Sherpa friend jumped on me and made a crude remark, "Why are you guys speaking in 'Bhotey Bhasa' (Tibetan language), speak Nepali". This was the same person who on many occasions had labeled me a Tibetan in his attempt to exclude me from attending Sherpa functions. "Sonam is a Bhotey (Tibetan)", was what I overheard him saying to people at a party.

My answer to him at this gathering was that the Nepali language wasn't even our own language and that if he felt that speaking in "our language" was so important why did the fact that not everyone there spoke in our Sherpa language as [sic] totally unnoticed by him. Others present quickly resolved the hostilities and we continued to speak in a plethora of languages.

It is not easy for someone like me born as national in one country and growing up in the midst of another to always be defensive (although, I feel I am totally capable of distinguishing my own identity, it is oftentimes, others that make judgements about it).

Being born in Nepal to a Sherpa father and a Tibetan mother, I grew up as a Nepali. As the majority of Nepal's population is of Hindu religion and of a different race, they occasionally called us 'Bhotey' as in Tibetan, to which we would defend ourselves as not being one. Sherpa culture and religion is similar to that of the Tibetan's but by birth and national origin we are Nepalese.

I started life in a boarding school in Kathmandu early. With my sister and I being the only Mongoloid students, we were often teased for being different, as children usually are. The rest of the school population was Nepalese of the Hindu faith, as in the Dravidian race. We were called Bhotey, an innocuous term for people from Tibet, but used derogatorily. My sister and I certainly didn't come from Tibet. That was also a time when

many Tibetans started moving to the Boudh Nath area, where a huge stupa stands. It is a holy place for people of Buddhist faith. This was also a neighborhood in the outskirts of Kathmandu, where local alcohol was sold openly. Although prohibited by the local law, officers looked the other way. One day a fight broke out between two Tibetans, who were intoxicated, that resulted in the death of one.

News spread like fire in the Kathmandu valley. Some of the consequences were ugly as children started calling me a 'murderer', which brought out the worst in me and having to fight those who accused me of such.

Just because a Tibetan murdered another Tibetan, my sister and I were teased as Tibetan murderers also. That brought out some kind of negative feelings in me for Tibetans, so much so that, I would play the part of 'brave Chinese soldiers' as depicted in the propaganda comic books and magazines sold in Nepal very cheaply. These were the publications that were heavily subsidized by the government of People's Republic of China and sold in Nepal for a few rupees. As children played in the playgrounds, I would be one of the ruthless Chinese Red Armies, capturing and torturing Japanese (as in the imperial war) and Tibetans.

Playing a "brave Chinese army personnel" was a phase that I went through in my boyhood age. No matter how hard I pretended to be a non-Tibetan, walking the streets of Kathmandu always invited catcalls from other boys or bullies in the street to call me, 'Hey Bhotey' which then was similar to calling the African Americans the "N" word.

When I was attending the Central Institute of Higher Tibetan Studies in India, my nationality and being different was something that worked to my advantage. On a Losar day, on being woken up by a teacher to go to a monastery for early prayer ceremony and receiving the traditional share of 'Khapseys', I was able to fool him. Losar is a day to have fun. At that period of my life, nothing was more fun than to sleep late. So, being too lazy to get up early and justify my own crooked way of celebrating Losar by sleeping, when my teacher tried to wake me up, I told him that I was a Sherpa and that we didn't celebrate Losar. He gasped and whispered, "Oh", and left me alone to wake other students up.

From an early age, it seemed like others are always trying to make decisions for me as to what I am. Nepalese call me Tibetan, Tibetans call me Nepali and some call us "monkeys".

Why can't everyone just accept me for who I am? I am just a human being with just one identity, as in the name I was given in my birth?

"As American as Apple Pie. What's in a Name?"

When my daughter was in the first grade, I volunteered as a parent-chaperone to go along with her class for a trip to the Bronx Zoo. When the children arrived at the zoo, they were whisked away into a classroom, where an instructor told them all about the animals they were going to see that day. She spoke at great length about the animals, reptiles for that day, and then she began to ask questions. The children's names were all displayed on large index cards hung around their necks, and whoever raised their hand, the instructor would point to and say, "David, do you know the answer?"

There were many questions asked—and I knew for certain that my daughter knew answers to a few of them, as we had discussed some of them in preparation for the class trip. My daughter, even at that young age, was quite an outgoing person and talkative to an extent. To my amazement, she didn't raise her hand even once to questions that I was certain she knew the answers to.

When the information session was over and we got ready to go view the reptiles, I held her hand and asked her if she didn't know any of the answers. She said she did. "Then why didn't you raise your hand to answer?" I asked her. To which, she answered, "Daddy, they can't say my name right."

When my son, who is five years younger than my daughter, was old enough to play with other kids in the park, we spent many hours there. He's the type who would lead other children, some even older than him, to his kind of games. Coming down the slides or on monkey bars, he's the one, usually, leading the pack. On one of these outings, while he seemed to be quite careless, I shouted his name and told him to be careful. Upon hearing his name, he came running to me. Then to my ear, he whispered, "Daddy, my name is MICHAEL. They (his friends in the park) can't say my name right."

As easy as it is for others to pronounce my name, many of my colleagues had asked me if they could call me "Sam". But, knowing Sam would be a short form of Samuel for males and Samantha for females, in general, I declined their request. Just as it falls upon my shoulders to remember my colleagues' names, it is their responsibility to remember mine, if they feel it is worthwhile.

My colleagues have also suggested naming my children "American" names. So, I asked what names would be American. To which they suggested names that were derived from Christian and Jewish faiths. Personally, I have a great deal of respect for all faiths of the world, but to call those names American was a bit too much. I made them aware that the names they suggested were of different religious persuasions than my own and they were most definitely not "American". As America is the land of immigrants, my children's names are "as American as apple pie," I politely reminded them.

On separate occasions, both my children have said to me, "I hate my name". They say people make fun of their names. As a concerned father, I tried to explain them that children are just children. They make fun of any name. I asked them if some of their friends with more common names are also made fun of. Surely, they gave me examples of how other children were made fun of also. After we agreed that children can, when they want, make something up to ridicule any name, not just theirs, I proposed to change their names legally to their desire, if they so wished. I told them that my wife and I gave them their names when they were born based on our cultural background. Now that they are old enough to understand what their special names represent, and they can pick alternate names for themselves, if they desired, and if it would make them happy, I for one was ready to fulfill their wish.

And to my wonderment and pride, they have both declined to change their names. They like their names, they said, as they are unique.

The practice of naming names is different in various part of the world. Some name names that are related to their religion. Some are regional. Some names mean something. Some names are chosen at random.

Most of us from the Himalayan region request a name for our children from a high Lama after the birth of our children. Back home, we would bring the newborns to a Lama and request him to name the child. Lamas are also invited to our own homes for the child's christening.

In today's modern world, many of us simply make a telephone call to the Lama. After giving him the necessary details, such as gender, date and time of birth, the Lama speaks the name over the phone and the child is named as such. This telephone call could be made weeks or months after a child is born.

Since many of us are now in western countries, where a name is required for newborns at the hospital as soon as they are delivered, we require their names for them before they are even born. In such circumstances, to play safe, we ask the Lama for two names—a male and a female name. Of course, if one is certain of the gender of the child with the advent of sonogram and other modern technologies, you ask for just one name.

And many of us name our children on our own. When people ask me who named my children, I jokingly tell them, "Pala Rimpoche". My daughter is named after both my wife's and my own mother's—coincidentally, they shared the same name. My son is named after the Indian guru who brought Buddhism to Tibet. My mother said she had prayed to the guru for us to have a male child. So when her prayers came true, we said why not name our son after him?

So, the names my children have are very special to me. Likewise, any name you name your children has a special meaning. Be it a name you name on your own, from a high Lama, or His Holiness the Dalai Lama. These names signify our background, our religion, our culture, and our tradition that defines each and every one of us. Just because we are in the midst of people who aren't familiar with these names, it does not mean that we should abandon our culture of naming our own in our own tradition.

Here's a quiz: Do you know these names and can you pronounce them correctly? George Stephanopoulos, host of "This Week" on Sundays on ABC TV and a former aide to the president Bill Clinton. Michael William Krzyzewski, often referred to as "Coach K", the Basketball Coach at Duke University. Zbigniew Brezinski, former National Security Advisor to the then U.S. President Jimmy Carter, Kweisi Mfume, the former President and Chief Executive Officer of the National Association for the Advancement of Colored People (NAACP). Or how about General John M. Shalikashveli, former Chairman of the Joint Chiefs of Staff.

If the American people can say the above names, they sure will learn to say ours, if only we reach to the positions where everyone is compelled to know our names. Although very important in relation to one's background, names are not that important in comparison to the qualities that the name-bearer possesses. In William Shakespeare's "Romeo and Juliet," the Bard asked, "What's in a name? That which we call a rose by any other name would smell as sweet."

Sources: Sherpa, Sonam G. "My Identity." *Migyul: The Himalayan Community Magazine*, no. 5, Spring 2005, and "As American as Apple Pie. What's in a Name?" *Migyul: The Himalayan Community Magazine*, no. 6, Summer 2005. Reprinted with permission.

Roshani Adhikary, "Nepali Grrl Blues"
(2005)

Roshani Adhikary was born in the United States to Nepali parents. A graduate of Eastern Michigan University, Adhikary enjoys teaching English and traveling. Her essay "Nepali Grrl Blues" was originally published in Viewpoints, *the newsletter of the Association of Nepalese in Midwest America. Written from the viewpoint of a Nepali American, Adhikary's essay touches on themes relevant to immigrant and Asian American communities, as well as to American families. Adhikary shows how the various perspectives held by people in the same family are conditioned by immigration experiences, generational differences, Americanization and assimilation, and political sensibilities. She also alludes to unconsciously held racial and gender stereotypes that can surface unexpectedly in normal conversation. In 2006, Adhikary began exploring her identity through hip-hop, recording her first album,* Sol Joints, *in Nepali. Hip-hop is still a part of her daily life, and she continues to feel a connection to both the United States and Nepal.*

I listen to hip hop. Matter of fact, I breathe hip hop. I live it. To me hip hop is a lifestyle. It involves critical thinking, creative solutions, art and entrepreneurship. Most of you might be wondering, "Is she talking about the same rap-music we loathe?" This is where things get slightly complicated. You see, I hate rap. I hate the channel Black Entertainment Television (B.E.T) and furthermore I cannot stand main-stream rap entertainers like 50 Cent or even, dare I say it, Eminem. I only listen to the "good" stuff. Black Star. Dead Prez. Common. Hi-Tek. Talib Kweli. Lauryn Hill. Mos Def. The Coup. Even if some of these artists have not come out with anything new or chart-blazing, I am willing to dig out their old joints and place my Walkman (as the vibrations of hip hop can only be felt fully thru a live performance or headphones) on full blast. I guess you could say I am a hip hop puritan.

Hip hop music has a culture that correlates directly with one's sense of style. This is similar to most genres in music. If you're a reggae-head you probably believe in some of the principles of Rastafari, which would lead to much of your wardrobe being red, yellow and green. If you like punk you probably wear Converse's Chuck-Taylors or Doc Martins or something along those lines. While these are sweeping generalizations and there are always exceptions, my point is that people who gravitate towards a certain form of music usually do so because they have like-minds. This is often reflected externally in fashion-trends.

I often wear a head-wrap and an over-sized baseball cap which reads, "Got Melanin?" This does not sit well with my Nepali-born parents. My dad throws his hands in the air—almost on beat—and my mom looks at me funny. Recently I suppose her silence bothered her too much; she blurted out, "Roshani, do you think you're an African American?" I couldn't help but scoff at her blatant hypocrisy. During my high school years when I really had no sense of self she was the very wombyn who paid $106 for me to get my hair highlighted *blonde*! Peculiar that she never asked did I think I was European-American then. Quite the contrary, she smiled with glee as she said I looked, "so pretty."

At our house the Mahabharata takes place on a daily basis. Of course this day was no exception. As soon as my mom asked me if I thought I was Black I responded with the question, "Why would you think that?"

"You know, you wear that topi-cap and you wear that scarf around your head: these are not parts of our culture," she stated feeling triumphant that her points were valid.

I looked at her up and down. Studying her sweater, jeans and socks. Ann Taylor. Gap. Ralph Lauren. "Hmm. I didn't know denim was a part of Nepali culture," I signaled my eyes towards her jeans. "Furthermore, this *scarf* around my head is from Nepal!"

She shook her head and murmured, "Buck-buck, buck-buck, esko khaali buck-buck whooncha." ["Yap, yap, yap, all you do is yap."] After this debate of ours I dropped the baseball cap, but stuck with my dupata-turned-head-wrap. Our house has had peace for a few months since, but of course, like all good things those fleeting moments of harmony passed.

I'm currently writing a play about the South Asian American experience. Two weeks back I went on my first business trip to the east coast in hopes of interviewing South Asians living in Jersey City so I could interview them about the hate-crime group that terrorized Hindus in the late 1980s. Known as the Dot-Busters this group harassed and even killed some South Asian Americans. Their targets were people they called Dot-Heads: people who looked like they would wear the Tika, or red-dot. After speaking with countless organizers and activists from that era, I felt inspired. I decided to start wearing a Tika in homage to the victims of the Dot Busters.

My mom cringed at the sight of my latest fashion choice. "Chya! Ke gurrya tyo? Keena Tika lugga? Kusto Pakhe justo dehkya chow!" ["Tsk! What're you doing? Why are you wearing that thing on your forehead? You look like a total hick!"]

I gasped, "I thought you wanted me to be more in tune with my culture?" So she frowned her face, unaware of what she could possibly say this time.

"We're only supposed to wear that once we've been married," She said.

I reminded her that both my sister and I had a ceremony in which we were married to the sun once we came of age. [Adhikary is referring to a traditional Nepali ritual for girls once they begin menstruating.] Didn't that count for anything?

In the end we agreed to disagree by sighing and shaking our heads in unison as we always do. I put my headphones back on and was comforted by Rakim's lyrics. "It ain't where you from, it's where you at."

Source: Adhikary, Roshani. "Nepali Grrl Blues." *Viewpoints,* Association of Nepalese in Midwest America, New Year 2005. http://www.anmausa.org/viewpoints.aspx. Used with permission of the Association of Nepalese in Midwest America.

Tenzin Shakya, "Living as 'Other' in the U.S.A." (2008)

In recent years in the United States, there has been a growing awareness of the dispute between Tibet and China. The issue is mired in a complex, centuries-old conflict between the two nations. China claims that Tibet has been under its governance and control for more than 700 years and says that it is not and has never been an independent state. The Tibetan government in exile claims that China invaded Tibet in 1949 and forced the Seventeen Points Agreement on the Dalai Lama (which he later repudiated). In any case, years of guerilla warfare waged by the Khampa rebels and brutal repression enacted by the Chinese People's Liberation Army culminated in the 1959 Tibetan Rebellion (or Uprising), when the Dalai Lama escaped to Dharamsala, India. In the aftermath of the rebellion and the Chinese Cultural Revolution, thousands of monasteries, viewed as hotbeds of revolution, were leveled, and hundreds of thousands of Tibetans were killed. Tibetan refugees moved to other parts of the Himalayas and to India, and in the late 1950s and early 1960s, a small number began immigrating to the United States. Community growth accelerated after the United States' Immigration Act of 1990 increased the visa quota for Tibetans.

In this article written for the Diablo Valley College newspaper, Tenzin Shakya explains how this long-standing political dispute has affected her own immigrant experience. Born in Nepal and of Tibetan ancestry, Shakya immigrated to the United States at an early age and now lives in the San Francisco Bay area. Like other Tibetans, she struggles to retain her cultural heritage and national identity in the face of extreme circumstances.

I am a Tibetan, born in Nepal and raised in India until age 8, when I came to the United States.

Mine is a typical journey for this second generation of Tibetan "refugees," who fight against being extinct in the modern world.

Our parents fled from their homeland to become refugees in neighboring countries to save their families' lives and provide better education for their children.

We try our best to preserve our ancestral culture and beliefs by telling anyone who will listen, about the situation in Tibet.

Located in the central Himalayas, Tibet is also known to many as "Shangrila" meaning "utopian peace." I have never been there myself but it is a priority after finishing my studies.

Growing up in America was difficult but surely not impossible. I spoke four languages—Tibetan, Nepali, Hindi and English—and managed to blend in with the rest in elementary and middle school, never really questioning who I was.

But that changed my first year of high school.

I was filling out a form online, when I noticed there was no selection for "Tibetan" under "ethnicity"

Clicking on the word "Asian," I was led to a list of everything from "Indian" to "Chinese" and even "Taiwanese."

I hit the box for "other" and typed in "Tibetan," thinking how America is one of the top countries in the world, and yet there is no room on a form to acknowledge my identity.

Since then, I have felt the need to specify my ethnicity as Tibetan. Sir Francis Bacon (1561–1626) once said, "Knowledge is power." And I believe knowledge is gained through education.

China claims Tibet to be a part of China. Yet Tibetans are forced to be minorities in their own land and lack many economic and educational resources needed to survive.

The Chinese government repeatedly states its invasion benefited Tibet by bringing it into the modern world. How is it possible then that the educational index for Tibet ranks last against China's other 31 provinces? And why must the youth of Tibet learn to speak Chinese in order to go to school? Many of them fail to do so and drop out after the fifth grade.

Due to this lack of educational opportunities, young Tibetans escape every year across the treacherous Himalayas to join the Tibetan exile community in India. And from there, they try to further their education by coming to the west. Thus, the cycle of my story starts all over again.

The Tibetan Association of Northern California estimates the population of Tibetans here is at about 3,500.

But we were invisible until the controversy surrounding the decision to hold the 2008 Olympic Games in China. Now, just about everyone knows of the "Free Tibet" movement.

When people ask me why Tibet should be free, I answer by saying, "Because everyone has the right to basic freedom."

I am pro Tibetan independence, but more along the lines of "Tibetan freedom." I also favor "Chinese freedom" and "African freedom." It is a matter of focusing on the basic principles of human rights.

People deserve the right to make choices for themselves regarding their lives—to speak when they have ideas to share and to practice the religion in which they believe.

The way to participate in a "modern" civilized society is by making dialogues a necessity. Government's primary role should be to protect the rights of its citizens, not restrict them.

Source: Shakya, Tenzin. "Living as 'Other' in the U.S.A." *The Inquirer: Diablo Valley College Student Voice,* Opinion Section, September 25, 2008. Reprinted with permission.

Shilpa Lama, "One Nepalese Woman's Journey to America" (2009)

Shilpa Lama is a Nepalese immigrant living in the United States. The following oral history records the experiences of Lama's cousin, Reema, who immigrated to the United States in the 1990s. Lama conducted the interview and wrote this oral history as part of a project for her Asian American history class at City College of San Francisco during the spring semester of 2009.

Reema is my mother's sister's daughter and they both come from a very poor family. Unlike my mom who was pretty well-off after she got married to my father, Reema's mother was still facing financial and family problems after her marriage. Reema lived in a joint family with her uncles, aunts, their kids, grandparents and so on. I still remember when I used to go there to visit them, there was only one bathroom and basically it was just a toilet. You had to take a bucket of water to the toilet because there was no source of water and for shower, everybody used to go a place called "dhungedhara" which was an open shower taking public place. Ladies would have to wake up 5 in the morning to take showers just so that no man would see them.

Reema came to America because she married a white American man. Uncle Ryan was an acquaintance of my uncle whom he met in New York. Uncle Ryan had come to Nepal to help build an organization. My mother and father let him stay at our house during his stay in Nepal and he met Reema because she used to baby-sit me. Uncle Ryan developed affection for Reema when he noticed her modest and simple nature. At first, Reema rejected Uncle Ryan's proposal because she thought their culture had a vast difference. After many months, Reema contacted Uncle Ryan and decided to meet him. They met and got married 2 months after that. Reema did not marry Uncle

Ryan because she loved him, she married him for financial reasons, she married him so that she could come to America and send money to her poor family in Nepal.

When Reema and Ryan first came to Nevada, they rented a small studio. Reema got a job as a bathroom cleaner at an old home shelter. Life was much better with good food, showers every day, privacy, and good clothes but inside her heart she was lonely, sad and depressed.

When she went to Wisconsin to visit her mother and father-in-law, she was treated with love and respect. However, when she went to stores and shops she would get stares and glances from white people. This was Reema's first experience with prejudice. A Nepalese living in Wisconsin, Reema came to know discrimination well. At work, she experienced unequal treatment between her and a white female employee. People would not bother talking to her if she did not understand what they were saying the first time.

She decided to do something about her situation and enrolled in college to improve her English skills and empower herself. After Reema and Uncle Ryan moved to San Jose, California, Reema sponsored her mother and father to come to the United States. Both of them are now permanent residents of United States. During these years, Reema also opened a successful day care center with the help of her mother. She has found taking care of children and guiding them her passion. Now, Reema has a very good life. Her husband has a great job and she has two great daughters who mean the world to her.

Even though Reema still sees herself as a true Nepalese inside, she has created a bicultural household. She prays every day and she has got pictures of several Hindu gods at her house. She makes Nepalese food every day which her husband and daughters love to eat. Reema has taught her daughters about Nepalese culture and they love knowing their mother's culture. Her daughters who look so white with their blonde and brown hair and white skin actually sing Nepalese songs and have learned the Nepalese language very well. Her family celebrates "Dasain," the major Nepalese holiday, just as they celebrate Christmas and Thanksgiving every year. She gives equal priorities to both Nepalese and American culture and guides her daughters to do so as well.

For Reema, coming to United States was an extremely difficult decision. She sacrificed the life she knew for the sake of her family. Even with the many hardships she faced in Nepal and America, she feels it was worth it. She has two wonderful daughters and a caring, loving husband. I asked her if she would like to go back to Nepal permanently, but she says that California is her home now. She discovered herself here in the United States. She says that Nepal will always be her cherished homeland, but America made her into a whole person and she wants to continue her blissful life here.

Source: Lama, Shilpa. "One Nepalese Woman's Journey to America." Oral history conducted for City College of San Francisco Asian American Studies 20 class. April 2009.

Bhuchung K. Tsering, "Enter the Tibetan Americans"

(2009)

Political instability and war have pushed many recent immigrant groups out of their native countries, which inevitably colors how they see themselves in the United States. This is especially true for Tibetan immigrants, who escaped Chinese colonization in the 1950s and 1960s and have maintained a decades-long exile identity, both politically and culturally, in different countries around the world. Bhuchung Tsering was born in Tibet. After the 1959 Tibetan Rebellion, he and his family fled to India, where he joined the Tibetan government in exile. He now lives in Washington, DC, and works for the International Campaign for Tibet. Tsering's article, "Enter the Tibetan Americans," asks questions about the largely invisible space his community occupies in the United States and in Asian America, and wonders what it takes to propel the voice, concerns, and presence of a new immigrant population into the national conversation.

TIBETAN AMERICANS ESTABLISH A PRESENCE IN THE UNITED STATES.

One of the challenges to the small Tibetan American community in the United States is having to adapt to our new hyphenated identity. The feeling of Tibetanness is so strong among the Tibetan Americans that in many cases even though several decades may have passed since they have immigrated to this country many continue to regard themselves only as being "Tibetan."

In the following write-up, a version of which appeared in the newsletter of the London-based Tibet Foundation in February 2001, I talk about the relevance of the hyphenated identity.

Bhuchung K. Tsering
Tibet Foundation Newsletter
February 2001

Everyone agrees that the Tibetan issue enjoys a high profile in the United States.

However, I was given a reality check when I recently did a random survey on the status of Tibetans as a community here in the multicultural United States.

Today, there are over 7,000 Tibetans residing in the United States. My main reason was to see if I could understand the sort of situation Tibetan Americans would face and how such issues could be dealt with.

My survey of the status of Tibetan Americans was rudimentary. I went to a bookstore close to my office in downtown Washington, D.C. There was a full section on ethnic studies out of which half a shelf were books on Asian Americans. Books ranged from such titles as *The Accidental Asian* (it is an interesting book by a Chinese American who worked in the White House at one time) to Asian Americans, which is a compilation of anecdotes of Asian immigrants from Vietnam, Hong Kong, Korea, Philippines, China, Taiwan and even Hawaii. Then there were investigative studies of how organized mafias smuggle illegal Chinese into the United States. But nowhere in any of the books was a reference to Tibetan Americans. Also, Asian American issues regularly come up in the public forum, be it the Asian American domination in Silicon Valley or the motel industry. But there, too, no reference to Tibetan Americans. Why is it that a high-profile community like the Tibetans does not find a place in the discussions on Asian Americans although no one, including the Chinese, disputes that Tibetans are Asians? We need to look at history for answer.

Tibet arrived in the United States a long time back, but Tibetan Americans have just begun to make their mark here. That, in short, is the answer to this contradictory situation. The other factor has to do with the history of Asian Americans itself. Let me touch on these two issues and see how the newest immigration group in the United States is faring.

The earliest technical Tibetan immigration to the United States took place only in the late 1950s. From then until the 1990s, it was just a trickle of Tibetans, even by our own small population standards, that resettled here. It was only after the congressionally mandated 1,000 Tibetans immigrated here in the first half of the 1990s that Tibetans began to make a formal presence. These 1,000 Tibetans and their families resettled in over 17 states across the United States and planted the seed for a pan-American presence of Tibetans.

Over the years, these and the other Tibetans who immigrated to the U.S. prior to 1990 gradually began to acquire American citizenship yet there has not been a concrete realization of or the desire to understand the implications of this. Except for the fact that the Blue American passport gave them protection and made it much easier to get visas to visit India or Nepal or even Tibet, Tibetans did not seem to comprehend the deeper implication of being Tibetan Americans. In very few of the states did Tibetans participate in Asian American activities or join organizations dedicated to such a community.

Tibetan Americans have hardly tried to play a role in the American political process even though such a development would have a positive effect to the Tibetan freedom struggle. By asserting their Tibetan identity, for example, they could change from being an active supplicant for the support of American Members of Congress to the issue of Tibet, to demanding support from them, as constituents.

Equally important it is essential for the social survival of the Tibetans that Tibetan Americans need to find their place in the multicultural United States. Right now, the Tibetan community is compact and has the infrastructure in place for transferring knowledge about Tibetanness from parent to children. But as the young Tibetans grow up they will face the same dilemma that all other immigrants have faced: Is it essential to grow up as Tibetan Americans or as Americans? Many people in other communities have chosen the latter path, completely immersing themselves into the American melting pot. Thus you have third or fourth generation Asian Americans who do not know anything about their culture, least of all being conversant in the language of their ethnic identity. That, however, is a choice these people have made and it has no implications beyond the personal internal struggle their children will have to undergo as they grow up. With Tibetan

Americans they have an additional responsible in the sense of continuation of the Tibetan identity. No Tibetan immigrant can afford to choose becoming merely an American. Everyone have to be Tibetan Americans, at the least, for the survival of our community.

As with other immigrant communities, Tibetan Americans will face the biggest challenge during the period of their first generation. That is because most Tibetans will be so involved in trying to realize the American Dream as to sacrifice other matters like the proper upbringing of their children. Parents will be working two or even three shifts, seven days a week to earn enough money to buy that car or the house or to send money to parents and relatives in the Indian subcontinent. In the process, their children will be left to fend for themselves, becoming monolingual (opting to speak in English only) and distancing themselves from anything Tibetan. This is a challenge that Tibetan Americans need to overcome and to get their priority right.

If we think of the challenges the Asian Americans had to face, Tibetan Americans have had the going very smooth in terms of their resettlement here. A study of the history of Asian Americans reveals the very many physical and mental sufferings they had to undergo. Chinese, Japanese and Koreans, Indians, etc. had to suffer greatly to be accepted by the American community, the extreme case being the internment of most of the Japanese Americans during the Second World War because their loyalty was a suspect. Racism was something all these communities had to suffer from. For example, despite fulfilling all conditions Chinese weren't allowed to be American citizens until 1943, Filipinos and Indians until 1946 and Japanese and Koreans until 1952.

However, these communities slowly found a place for themselves in the United States, both physically and mentally. Today, the United States has become comparatively tolerant of other communities. Mentally, too, Asian Americans have found a balance between their ancestral cultural heritage and the acquired American identity. A Korean American put it succinctly, "I think I am fortunate to be Asian American. Not only do we have a whole realm of Western culture, but we also have this whole world of Asian culture that is part of us," she said. Is there a lesson from this for the Tibetan Americans?

The coming years will tell us how successful the Tibetan Americans are.

Source: Tsering, Bhuchung. "Enter the Tibetan Americans." January 3, 2009. Tibetreport (blog). http://tibetreport.word press.com/2009/01/03/enter-the-tibetan-americans/.

Prem and Kumari Tamang, Interview by Emily Moberg Robinson (2010)

The Nepalese Civil War, which took place between 1996 and 2006, ushered in an era of great instability in the country. The Maoist Communist Party of Nepal fought with the Parliamentarians and the monarchy; thousands of people were killed, and more than 100,000 were displaced during the conflict. The tourism industry, for decades one of the largest sources of

nonagricultural employment in Nepal, was decimated, and many Nepalese left the country to escape the deprivations of war and to find jobs.

Until the civil war, very few Nepalese immigrated to the United States. However, this changed quickly after 1996, even though it was difficult for Nepalese, especially those with little education and job skills, to get visas and passports.

Now that the small but growing Nepali American community is large enough, it is beginning to differentiate along indigenous ethnic lines.

Prem Tamang worked for a trekking company in Kathmandu, where he met and befriended successive groups of American tourists. A dozen of them sponsored his first visit to the United States, a six-month cross-country trip in 1995. Three years later, fleeing persecution at the hands of local Maoists who were targeting his family, Tamang was granted political asylum in the United States. He brought his wife, Kumari, and their two sons, Milan and Suran, to the United States in 2003. Emily Moberg Robinson interviewed Prem and Kumari Tamang in their home in San Mateo, California, on February 28, 2010. Jessica Ratcliff Kumar, a mutual friend, assisted with the interview. In the following excerpts, the Tamangs talk about their upbringing in Nepal, their immigration stories, and their lives in the United States. Both of them stress the value and necessity of doggedness and hard work in the pursuit of the American dream: owning their own house and providing a college education for their boys.

Emily Moberg Robinson: So tell me about your childhood; where did you grow up; what was it like?

Prem Tamang: I grow up in a little town in my country—my country is name Nepal—I'm from Nepal. And I was grow up in a little home town called Tekanpur. District they called Kavre district. . . . And the home town is Tekanpur.

Like back in two hundred years before how was in America. There was no electric, no TV, no car, no telephone. . . .

When I was ten years old, there wasn't any school close by my home. There wasn't any school. There was one school which was one hour to go up, one hour to come down. Two hours daily walking. . . .

EMR: So you walked an hour to school and an hour back?

PT: Yeah. Then after the first grade . . . second grade . . . one of my relative—their son was going to another school, which is three, four hours away from my home . . .

My father, his cousin was there . . . like a teenager, eighteen years or something like that . . . and I was thirteen years old. I went to there, studied a little bit . . . and then when he graduate from high school, he's gone, right? And I used to live with him and he's gone and I don't have any guardian or friend, right? I have to live there myself from my home town. And it's kind of feel lonely. And other hand was . . . my parents have nine children; I was the oldest boy . . . I see badly they need help from me. Work. And then after that . . . my dad's cousin is gone, after high school graduate, and I feel kind of lonely; and other hand, I see my mom and dad need help; other hand, they don't have money to rent a house there for me an apartment. I see all these problem financial—money—so badly. I see that. And it make me change my life you know. If I study with those struggle, all—I see my future making money is way—I don't know when. But if I run now, I can make some money and my parents can have it. And I decided to run away from home.

Dad doesn't like that. I didn't give any note for dad, but mom knows. I run from home. I still remember that day, when I was just thirteen years old, you know. I was running from home, and I get some construction job which is five rupees a day. Seven AM to six PM.

Jessica Kumar: Where was the construction job?

PT: It's northeast from Kathmandu.

Kumari Tamang: Very far away.

EMR: So you ran away—

PT: A place called Barabise—the road was going toward Khasa

Lhasa. Tibet. China. So there between Nepal and Tibet there was little border that they would take through road—they called Arniko Rajmarg highway road. . . .

I was there eighteen month. Within eighteen month . . . I make two hundred–fifty sixty rupee. . . . I send that money. Then, first time my dad's like, "Oooh, ok, I got some money from my son." I send money with person. Whoever going home.

KT: That's the culture. To send money.

PT: That was the beginning. That happened.

KT: The Nepal way.

PT: After that . . . my dad—still wants me to go to school, and I said no. I will quit this school, I don't go. Let me challenge my life—I did that, Bahini ["little sister"] . . .

Later on, I went to Kathmandu. By the time I was almost seventeen. And I found job—all kind of job in Kathmandu—and I never back away from any kind of job. ANY kind of job. Restaurant worker, construction, everything, right? Something like road builder, house building, painting, carpenter, all kind of things . . .

Finally, when I come seventeen, eighteen, later . . . people are telling me about mountain climbing. I have a big interest to go there. How to get in there. And I must keep asking with someone whoever goes, from the hometown, they said your age is not enough. You may get hurt. You're young. And I have to wait . . .

Finally, finally I got job there. First year I was temporary porter. Second year, finally after those all kind of struggle—"OK, we need people like Prem as a porter. He work fast, he carry the heavy load, and so, and he can speaks some English, why don't we give him chance to cook in kitchen, serve food for the member . . ." I got chance there, and day by day my English was getting better and better . . .

My first trekking start was in 1984, '85, '86. From '86 for me I was becoming more speaking English and '88 I was permanent assistant guide. '89 assistant guide, '90 we got married with this pumpkin girl . . . [lots of laughing]

KT: I don't like you that much! [laughing] I never! I didn't want to marry him! Yeah, I was getting mad all the time when I see him. . . . I was little, like 15 years old!

PT: Yeah, she was 15 years old when we get married. Her parents— her mom did that, mostly.

KT: What they call orange marriage. [lots of laughing] Arranged marriage!

PT: '94, Milan [Prem and Kumari's oldest son] was get born. Milan born '94. '95, finally, I become America, with all the friends [that Prem met while working as a trekking guide] . . .

I always ask them, "How is America. What should I do to go America. I want to go America." So many says, "Difficult. You cannot go there. Number one. You don't know the place. Number two. So difficult. Your English not enough, you don't have any relative there. And number three, four, whatever, hard to get paperwork that you want to be there. But if you want to go, we'll help you. Who knows something about the paperwork?"

[Prem's American friends raised over ten thousand dollars to bring him to the United States for a six-month visit in 1995.]

PT: And after six month, my experience living in America, visiting

America, I went back to Nepal, and then my mind: living in America, think America—and how to bring my bride, life, for future and my two boys . . . And situation also getting worse in Nepal; the political situation was worse, and job cutting, tourism is gone because of situation . . . And I come '98 again back to America, and I'm still here. Never went back.

[Prem was able to get his work visa in 2001; by 2003, he had brought Kumari and their two young sons over to the United States.]

EMR: What sorts of things do you do to remember Nepal, and to try to keep Nepali culture alive for your children while in the United States? Is that difficult?

PT: I love my hometown, I love my culture. But my hometown, my culture—the situation did not give me—to live there. Meaning is, it's too small for me. I just like wild pig, I just run, because that [Nepal] is too small for me. I still love culture, people, my family, my parents are still there, my brother, sister there, mom, dad there still. And here, they have special days, now—back in '95 there wasn't a lot of Nepali, but now there are lots of Nepalis here, so, these days they have Nepali gathering committee, one. Next, they is separated here, then. They have a Tamang group, there is a Tamang society here. Brahman society here. Newar society, Guru society here. They have their own community here, they're just sitting down, just starting . . .

KT: I like to live here, Bahini, it's so nice.

EMR: Do you miss anything?

PT: I miss my family, and the place I play, I go—I miss it, of course. But day by day as long as—now, I feel more like I live here, love here. Life you can take anywhere, anywhere you want to be. So now I think if I go there, it's hard for me. I cannot take a hot shower every day . . . So if I go to Nepal—don't have hot shower, don't have even cold water, right, I freeze—because my body change, system change. Anything could be so hard for me now. Anything would be hard. Maybe the food might not going to digest that I used to . . . because my body change now . . .

My boys need to know [about how hard Prem and Kumari have worked]. Every day we have a Monday special dinner. One we can have all together. Otherwise I will be here all at my work. When I come they don't sleep. When I woke they go to school.

Couple years ago I told Bahini, Jessica, "A couple years ago some friend said, 'How is your family, how big are your boys are?' I said, 'One is this big [holds hands apart horizontally] and one is this bigger . . . ' When I measure from this side—because when I come they laying down sleeping. One this bigger, and the other one, this bigger, and they growing day by day this way. Because when I come at night, eleven o'clock, they are sleeping right? And when I woke up, they gone. To school. So I never see them this way [holds hands apart vertically]. This is the view that I get from my home—I see them like this all the time. Sleeping. Before I check them I don't go myself bed. Even twelve o'clock. I want to look. I saw them one time. Even sleeping. They grow this way. 2004, '5, '6, '7 I see them like this. "

[Prem shows a picture of his family's house in Nepal; he sent money from the United States to build it.]

Later on—right here—that's the
new house, changing new life. You
see that . . . This is the front side of
the house. These are all my nieces
and nephews, yes. See, compared
to the old house—a change! This
is the first town in the hometown I
built . . . First house in that whole
town. Fancy nice great house.

EMR: So they have the American dream,
too—they have it in Nepal.

Source: Tamang, Prem, and Tamang, Kumari. Interview by
Emily Moberg Robinson. February 28, 2010. San Mateo, CA.
Transcribed, edited, and excerpted by Emily Moberg
Robinson. Used with permission of Prem Tamang and
Kumari Tamang.

Pang Xiong Sirirathasuk Sikoun, Interview by Sally Peterson
(2006)

Pang Xiong Siriathasuk Sikoun was born in the mountains of Laos, in the northern province of Zieng Khouang, near Vietnam and China. During her childhood, Xiong learned many forms of Hmong folk art, including traditional storytelling and singing techniques, musical instruments, and sewing and appliqué. In the late 1950s, Pathet Lao communists took over Xiong's village. She and her family fled south to Thailand. There, several of her brothers, along with many other Hmong mountain people, were trained by the U.S. Central Intelligence Agency and the Thai military to fight the North Vietnamese–backed Pathet Lao in a secret war. Five of her brothers were killed in the war. After the 1973 cease-fire, the Americans pulled out of Laos, abandoning many Hmong soldiers and leaving many more civilians in refugee camps.

In 1979, Xiong and her family resettled in Philadelphia along with thousands of other Southeast Asian refugees. There, she formed a Hmong dance troupe and began selling flower cloth, elaborate needlework pieces depicting scenes from Hmong life and experiences, known as paj ntaub. Paj ntaub was made primarily in refugee camps; Xiong brought this art form with her to the United States and successfully introduced it to an American audience.

In her 2006 interview with the Philadelphia Folklore Project's Sally Peterson, Pang Xiong spoke a short prose poem about triumphing over adversity, and what it means to make it in the United States.

We came to this country very sad, and we try to win something.

You cannot win the war. You cannot win the gun. You cannot win the life.

You say, what do I win?

I do not win my brother's life, he died . . . they killed him. They threw him in the Mekong River. He died. We do not win their life, I cannot bring them back.

I [can] not win my five brothers' lives.

But I win because my brothers' children are here.

My mother, my father came here, even though they died, but they win, because they already come here.

We win when we can get a house.

We win, we can get a new car.

We win, we can get a new home, we can be an American citizen.

We try to be strong here. We try to be an example people.

We win. My name is in books, articles, so I win that. People know my name, know Pang Xiong.

I win a lot. My children got bachelor's, master's degrees. That means I win.

Many people win in this country the same way with me. Same way.

But they don't know the meaning. But my meaning's in my head.

Source: Peterson, Sally. "We Try to Be Strong: Pang Xiong Sirirathasuk Sikoun." In *Works in Progress, The magazine of the Philadelphia Folklore Project* Winter 2006, 4–7, 21–22, 24. http://www.folkloreproject.org/folkarts/resources/pubs/wip/2006Winter/Sikoun.pdf. Reprinted with permission.

Chao Xiong, "Waiting, 'Not Knowing If They Are Even Alive'" (2007) and Sheng Xiong, "Address to the United States National Press Club" (2009)

Between 1953 and 1975, the communist Pathet Lao Party and the Royal Lao government fought a civil war over the control of Laos. The United States involved itself once the Vietnam War was under way. Central Intelligence Agency (CIA) agents covertly supplied money, arms, and military training to ethnic Hmong Laotians. The Hmong formed a special guerilla unit, led by Hmong general Vang Pao, that rescued American pilots and blocked the Viet Cong's supply lines on the Ho Chi Minh Trail as it passed through Laos. Thousands of Hmong soldiers were wounded and killed while fighting for the United States in what was known as America's secret war. However, when the Pathet Lao overthrew the Royal Lao government in 1975, the United States abandoned the Hmong, standing aside as the Pathet Lao exacted retribution. Thousands were sent to reeducation camps as political prisoners; thousands escaped to the mountains, where they continued to engage in guerilla warfare against the communists; and thousands more became refugees, seeking asylum in Thailand and the United States.

The first wave of Hmong refugees arrived in the United States in 1976, most of them men who had fought with Vang Pao's secret army. In 1980,

with the passage of the Refugee Act, their family members were allowed to enter. These immigrants formed the core of the growing Hmong American community. Most were overwhelmingly anticommunist and remained invested in the struggles of the Hmong left behind in Laos. General Vang Pao himself migrated to the United States in 1975 after escaping Laos with his CIA case officer. In 2007, the American government accused him of terrorist activity and plotting to overthrow the Pathet Lao government. Although the charges were dropped in 2009, the case had far-reaching ramifications. Hmong Americans were dismayed to see their popular and influential leader arrested and put on trial by the government he had aided with so much sacrifice during the war. And in Laos, the Pathet Lao, who had been attacking the scattered Hmong in their mountain hideouts for years, grew even more suspicious of Hmong Americans and their perceived material support to the embattled rebels.

Consequently, Hmong Americans traveling to Laos are increasingly subject to detention by the government. Chao Xiong's article, from the Minneapolis Star Tribune, *newspaper tells the story of Hakit Yang, Cong Shi Neng Yang, and*

Trillion Yunhaison, three St. Paul men who were arrested while on a trip to Laos on suspicion of being associated with Vang Pao. Following the article is Sheng Xiong's address to the U.S. National Press Club, where she describes in more detail what happened to her husband and his friends. She asks the U.S. embassy to act on their behalf. As of 2013, the three men have not been released, and the Laotian government denies their existence.

CHAO XIONG, "WAITING, 'NOT KNOWING IF THEY ARE EVEN ALIVE'" (2007)

Wives, children and a mother — about 20 relatives in all — lingered at the airport on Sunday on the slim chance that they would see three St. Paul men thought to be imprisoned in Laos.

Sheng Xiong clutched a bouquet of purple and orange flowers at the Minneapolis-St. Paul International Airport on Sunday afternoon — her ninth wedding anniversary—patiently waiting for her husband to return home from a trip to his native Laos.

The slight Xiong watched for an hour and a half as the waves of travelers passing through the international arrivals gate dwindled to a trickle, hoping Hakit Yang would disembark from Northwest Airlines Flight 20 from Tokyo, greet their two children at the baggage claim and head home for a large family gathering.

But in her heart, she knew: Her husband and his two traveling companions, Cong Shi Neng Yang and Trillion Yunhaison, were probably still being held in a Lao jail since their reported arrest Aug. 25. They were all scheduled to arrive on the flight that landed at 11:50 a.m.

"I guess they're not coming," Xiong said. "I was expecting this."

About 20 of the men's relatives showed up at the airport on the slim chance that they'd arrive. No one has heard from them since Aug. 25, when Yunhaison called to say they had been arrested.

Relatives and children carried signs reading, "Daddy, we miss you" and "We love you" and a large poster board pleading with the Lao government to release Hakit Yang, 29, Cong Shi Neng Yang, 31, and Yunhaison, 41. The St. Paul residents left for Laos on July 10 to visit relatives and look into possible business ventures, including opening a guest house, farm and herbal and acupuncture clinic, their family members said.

Xiong, her two children, her older sister and her niece were the last holdouts at the airport, turning away only after the sliding glass doors had grown quiet and the baggage claim nearly empty.

Earlier in the day, Xiong spoke to the media, serving also as a spokeswoman for the other men's wife and mother, who speak little English. "We're hoping to see them," she said before tearing up. "It's been really hard. That's the worst part: not knowing if they are even alive."

Family members said Lao officials have not responded to repeated requests from State Department authorities for confirmation of the arrests. Xiong said she hoped Lao officials would somehow see the men's relatives waiting at the airport and relent.

Philip Smith, executive director of the Center for Public Policy Analysis, which works on human rights issues in Laos, has said that the men were approached by military and security forces and accused of serving as spies for Gen. Vang Pao.

The general led a CIA-backed guerrilla army during the Vietnam War that fought Lao Communists, an alliance that many say has led to persecution of the minority Hmong in Laos. Vang, who has ties to the Twin Cities, was indicted this year by federal authorities on charges of plotting to overthrow the Lao government.

The men's family members said they have no ties to the general and didn't think their safety was at risk because of the case against him. They traveled in Laos on a recent occasion without problems, Xiong said.

Ulond Yang, Xiong and Hakit Yang's 8-year-old son, could barely speak when asked about his father, scrunching up his face as tears welled in his eyes. Ulond and the couple's daughter, Journie Yang, 5, have stopped asking about their father's whereabouts and whether they can call him.

Yunhaison's younger children still ask about him. His 17-year-old son, Feng Yang, said he's always ready with an answer: "He'll be coming home." Although hopeful, Feng Yang said he wasn't expecting a miracle Sunday.

"I'm just here to show support," he said. "If this could happen once, it might not just be my dad. It could be somebody else" next time.

In 2003, the Rev. Naw-Karl Mua of St. Paul was arrested and imprisoned in Laos along with two European journalists who hired him as an interpreter. They were released more than a month later, a fact that Xiong holds onto as hope for her husband's safe return.

Yunhaison and his wife, Neng Lee, have six children ages 22 to 9. Lee said her husband recently earned a degree in China in herbal medicine and acupuncture.

"I'm heartbroken," Lee said through tears. "I'm just one person. I can't take care of all of my kids."

Cong Shi Neng Yang's 5-year-old son, Dennis Yang, ran in circles about the group's legs, unaware that his father had apparently been jailed overseas. Cong Shi Neng Yang's mother, Sao Xiong, stood bewildered at the thought of raising her two grandchildren without her son, a single father.

"They just know he's gone," Sao Xiong said. "I want him to come home."

SHENG XIONG, "ADDRESS TO THE UNITED STATES NATIONAL PRESS CLUB" (2009)

I am Sheng Xiong, the wife of Hakit Yang, one of the missing people in Laos.

First of all I would like to thank Kay Danes, Philip Smith, and other speakers and supporters that I have not mentioned.

Today is a very important and special day for me. Without the supporters and help I've received from so many of you, I wouldn't be standing here in front of you all today. I may not be able to represent all families who have lost a love one from imprisonment in a foreign country, but I hope that as I share some of my thoughts and feelings, I will gain a step closer to the answers that I'd been seeking for.

I am here today on the behalf of the families of the missing men in Laos, who were arrested and detained from Lao Authority on August 25th, 2007. These men are Hakit Yang, Congshineng Yang, and Trillion Yunhansion. On July 10, 2007 the men departed the United States for Laos to pursue business investment opportunities. The men were staying at the #5 Guest House in Phousavan, Laos when they were arrested by secret police forces. They were detained in Phonthong Prison and later transferred to an unknown destination. As of today, the families of Congshineng, Trillion and I have not heard from them, since Trillion's phone call indicating that they had been arrested for an unknown cause. These men were last seen on August 29th, 2007 when they were being transported to an unknown location. We have not received any information to what has happened to them since their arrest.

The U.S. Embassy contacted the Lao government who denied having any record of the men entering their country and any U.S. Citizens being detained or arrest. Later, the Lao government changed their previous denials and admitted that the men did indeed entered Laos, but allegedly claimed that they had departed Laos via the Lao-Thai Friendship Bridge on August 29, 2007. Despite repeated requests from the US Embassy no departure cards have ever been produced as evidence for their departure.

It has been over a year not knowing where Hakit may be and I wonder everyday and night if he is okay and or somewhere waiting to be saved to reunite with his family. Not for a second do I not think about him. Everyday and night, I wish and pray for the safety of Hakit's return. I have many supporters who speak positive thoughts and encouragement but at the end of the day, I'm alone with my children who are still so young to understand the situation of their father. It is hard to face my children sometimes knowing that their father may not be able to hold them tight in his arms again. It is difficult to think and wonder when I am not sure if their father will be able to be by their sides growing up, and to see them go through their milestones whether small or large.

Each day I wake up hoping that I will hear the good news that my husband, Hakit was found and that every thing will be okay and he will soon be home. It's hard to concentrate on the things that I usually do daily. I am so frustrated and often times I don't know what to do anymore. However, I am trying to be strong and focus for the sake of Hakit, my children, and myself. It's not easy being a mother and a father to two small children at this time but I have to struggle through it and I have no choice. Sometimes I say to myself, it's my fate and I will have to live with it. Some things happen for a reason but to accept the imprisonment and then disappearance of my husband is too much.

I have tried to connect with other families who are currently in the same situation, to support each other emotionally. I'm continually seeking help from the US Embassy, the State Department, and other departments, but there has been no accomplishment pertaining the arrest or disappearance. I respectfully ask the US Embassy and the State Department to continue their further investigation. I just want truthful answers.

Sources: Xiong, Chao. "Waiting, 'Not knowing if they are even alive.'" *Star Tribune,* September 9, 2007. http://www.startribune.com/local/11589131.html. Used with permission of the *Star Tribune*; Xiong, Sheng. "Address to the United States National Press Club." April 2009. http://et-ee.facebook.com/topic.php?uid=56985849716&topic=12052. Used with permission of the author.

Critical Hmong Studies Collective, "Persistent Invisibility: Hmong Americans Are Silenced"

(2008)

During the Vietnam War, the United States waged a secret war in the mountains of Laos. Hmong guerilla soldiers, trained by CIA agents, fought the communists on behalf of the United States, attacking and blocking the Viet Cong's supply lines on the Ho Chi Minh Trail and rescuing downed American pilots. After the war, however, the United States withdrew from Southeast Asia and largely abandoned the Hmong. When the communist Pathet Lao Party took power in Laos and began to exact retribution on those who had supported the Americans, thousands of Hmong fled to refugee camps in Thailand, where they lived in squalor for decades. Some of those Hmong who remained in Laos were sent to harsh reeducation camps; others escaped to the mountains, where they established guerilla camps and periodically launched attacks against the Pathet Lao government. A third group of Hmong,

primarily soldiers and their families, escaped to the United States in the 1970s and 1980s.

However, and despite the great sacrifices made by the Hmong, the United States did not even acknowledge the existence of the secret war until 1997. Moreover, it was not until the early 2000s, when conditions in the Thai refugee camps grew steadily worse and when it became impossible to ignore the danger the Hmong faced from the communist Lao government, that the United States opened its doors to tens of thousands of refugees seeking asylum.

Today, there are more than 200,000 Hmongs in the United States, most of whom live in California, Minnesota, and Wisconsin. Their history remains largely unknown to mainstream Americans, and many Hmong Americans fear that they have been defined by vituperative rhetoric about refugees receiving government aid and sensational media reports about maladjusted and violent Hmong soldiers.

In 2007, a University of Wisconsin law professor made some comments about Hmong men and women during a class lecture, setting off a heated debate among Hmong students and the academic community at large. The students claimed the professor's comments reinforced the broader societal representation of Hmong Americans as primitive, militaristic, and violent. The murder of Cha Vang by a white hunter earlier that year had exacerbated fears that racialized images of the Hmong people and culture could result in hate crimes. (Vang's killer had told authorities that the Hmong "kill everything.") The professor first responded with an apology and, then, months later, claimed that his remarks had been misinterpreted.

The Critical Hmong Studies Collective, a multidisciplinary network of graduate students and faculty, issued the following editorial in response to the lecture. "Persistent Invisibility" provides historical and cultural context for the protests, explains why silencing Hmong Americans is particularly damaging, and raises thought-provoking questions about the place of recent immigrant groups in the American consciousness.

In February of last year, a University of Wisconsin at Madison law professor unwittingly ignited a firestorm when he used Hmong Americans as an example in a lecture on legal formalism.

The exact language and context of his statements are disputed, but no one debates that he depicted Hmong men as warriors and killers and referred to a high level of gang activity among young, second generation Hmong men, among other comments.

Hmong law students in the class protested his portrayal and demanded an apology. Students met with deans and the professor, filed a legal complaint with the university and set up a website. A few weeks later, the Chronicle of Higher Education Newsblog reported [the professor] to be in full

apology mode. Suddenly, however, dialogue came to a halt.

[The professor] sent a letter to his Dean for public release denying some of the comments and asserting that context was "critical." The students were increasingly dismissed as being oversensitive and accused of identity politics and ungrounded accusations of racism.

The controversy rekindled in December when [the professor] gave an invitation-only talk at the Madison rotary club. Virtually all press coverage of the event championed [his] courage in exercising academic freedom to pursue controversial issues. [He] criticized his Hmong detractors for a kind of over-eager political correctness: "We are all harmed if professors avoid controversial material in deference to some accepted or imposed correctness or an apprehension that a topic may offend sensitivities."

But political correctness does not apply here in its usual sense; Hmong identities are not sufficiently gelled in the American mainstream for political correctness to be meaningful. Hmong Americans, with only some 30 years in the United States, have not had a civil rights era, a history of campus activism or entries in school textbooks. What is "correct" to say and not say about Hmong hasn't been established.

Instead, there's been a persistent invisibility. Hmong lived as ethnic minority farmers in the northern highlands of Vietnam, Laos, Thailand and Burma for several generations, having emigrated from China. In the late 1970s, fleeing from Laos became a political necessity, as the regime's reprisals were directed specifically at us.

Why was the Laotian government so vindictive? Hmong had been recruited by and [gave] military service to the CIA in the so-called Secret War in Laos. On the frontlines, we were armed and trained by Americans in an effort to battle the North Vietnamese on terrain that was officially neutral.

The secrecy of that effort has meant the enduring invisibility of Hmong veterans. But the situation turned much more serious when the 2001 Patriot Act placed us on the list of immigrant groups to be denied entry or naturalization because we had formerly acted as or materially supported guerillas. Only in January did Congress exempt Hmong from this list, recognizing the injustice of denying us refuge after making us political refugees.

Hmong indignation at the incident in Madison is less about [the individual] than the forces that make experts' voices heard while Hmong are silenced. [The professor] sometimes denied his comments while simultaneously defending their accuracy: "Sometimes you do harm to people's sensitivity by speaking the truth." That [the professor] believed he was sympathetic toward the Hmong, that he presented stereotypes not as slurs but as "truths," is what's alarming.

Before dismissing Hmong reactions as oversensitive, we need to remember the larger experience of hate speech and acts in Wisconsin, where a white man was recently convicted of brutally murdering a Hmong man. He told the sheriff immediately afterwards that he did it because, among other reasons, "Hmong men kill everything that moves."

This is the kind of social context that confronts Hmong Madisonians outside the classroom. What we want to illuminate here is why such statements become even more of a problem when they are validated by the authority of academia.

Source: Critical Hmong Studies Collective. "Persistent Invisibility: Hmong Americans Are Silenced." September 13, 2008. Edited by Louisa Schein, 2010. A version of this piece can be found at http://www.asianweek.com/2008/09/13/persistent-invisibility-hmong-americans-are-silenced/. Used with permission of Chia Vang and the Critical Hmong Studies Collective.

Katie Ka Vang, "Uncle's Visit"

(2008)

Katie Ka Vang is a Hmong American writer, actress, playwright, and performance artist. She works primarily in the Twin Cities area, where many Southeast Asian refugee immigrants settled after the Vietnam War. Along with performing, she works to support Hmong and Asian American artists. Vang originally published the following poem in her poetry chapbook Never Said.

"Uncle's Visit" captures the unspoken but lasting tension and loss of innocence in an immigrant refugee family.

My uncle once came to visit
us.
When he came, we the kids,
the younger ones, who didn't
know any better would jump
up with excitement and say

txiv ntxawm koj lug lawm
los!!!!
We would give him hugs as
though he had survived some
kind of war, freed a million
generations, broke free from
his grave.
Our hearts would praise his
arrival and we'd hop around
him, rejoicing him, as though
he was a king—and he waited
for his feast.

My sisters and my mother
prepared a meal.
They deep fried chicken
and pork.
They made beef jerky.
They made qaab ci.
There were two kinds of rice,

mov txhua and mov nplaum
ntsaav
and one bowl of zaub ntsuab.
which I never ate, that was
something only my parents
ate.
I remember it was a meal
involving mostly oil,

because after uncle ate the
meal, we didn't have any
napkins (at least that's been
my excuse for him to get
through my childhood),
or maybe we did, but he
didn't want to use it, he
had royal hands.

And so he walked over to the
closet,
with his oily hands, from the
qaab ci, and the deep fried
meat

And there in the closet were
Winter coats, my sisters' silk
shirt, the one they both
shared, my mom's double

shift, my brother's soccer
potential, my dad's working
hands, my brother and his
video games, my other sister
and her daughter, my
halloween costume, my
mother's handkerchiefs the
ones she used to hide her
beautiful strands, my father's
ties, the ones he only wore to
church and my memory

his Hands, gathered all these
things together, as though he
was rinsing cilantro squeezing
them into bundles but there
were
too many, that his Godly
hands couldn't hold.
So some of them, most of
them slipped away, but the
things that got caught, were
wiped on.

Uncle's prints were oiled
onto these things

my memory one of them—
stained.
I now wonder,
why my parents didn't say
"damn, that's fucked up?" Or
"what the fuck are you doing?"
of course they didn't know
these words, still don't. They
still struggle to speak english.
But I know they feel them.
And 3 decades later
I feel them.

Translations provided by Katie Ka Vang:

xiv ntxawm koj lug lawm los—uncle you're back
qaab ci—baked chicken
mov txhua—plain rice
mov nplaum ntshsaav—sticky rice the color of blood
zaub ntsuab—green vegetables

Source: Vang, Katie. "Uncle's Visit." *Bakka Magazine.* http://
www.bakkamagazine.com/site/articles/3_poems_by_katie_
vang/. Used with permission of author and *Bakka Magazine.*

Noukou Thao, "Dowry"
(2009)

Noukou Thao was born in Laos; as Vietnam War refugees, she and her family resettled in Selma, Alabama, in 1976. Growing up in a small Hmong American community, she developed a love and affection for her Hmong heritage, the South, and literature. Thao now lives in Minnesota with her husband and two daughters. She is a cofounder of the Center of Hmong Arts and Talent, the first organization dedicated to cultivating Hmong arts. "Dowry" was written between 2004 and 2009, the years in which she transitioned from living the life of a single Hmong woman to living the life of a married Hmong woman. The five-stanza poem is from her poetry collection Lineage, which traces the spiritual journey of a Hmong woman. It draws from the stories of Hmong women she has been exposed to all her life.

"DOWRY"

the money, goods, or estate that a woman brings to her husband in marriage

I

Mother spent years
Cross stitching the aida fabric
The longest and most
Complex piece of my wedding dress.

Her sisters sat next to her under the sun's
Nurturing hands, pressing them against her
Arms and back, scarring her with the
Burn of floral impressions.

The sewing ritual hurried her
daughter to find her daughter's
true clan.

But Mother I cannot live this way
Passing from one clan to another . . .
As though I am a vassal for our family history

When I go into marriage,
The story of my father's clan and my husband's
Clan will be discussed
Bad relations will be fined
Along with negotiation of other fees

My brideprice
The fee for my mother's milk
If I am the younger of sisters
A fee to compensate them for going first into marriage

All accounted for, in this
Meticulous bargaining
For all its labor, its tears
Its complexity
A fundamental human contract

Capabilities and infractions upon laws created
By man to be followed by man
But I am a woman, I cannot wear my Hmong skirt
for these reasons
If I must wear my Hmong wedding dress
I will wear it for my own reasons.

This is why I wear it.

II

I keep the pleated skirt mother spent
Nearly four years laboring over
Inside a cheap suitcase
Along with the rest of my dowry

Each time I take a business trip somewhere
I unpack it
And push it inside a holding place
The dusty closet where I keep my daughter's Easter dresses
Where we keep the vacuum cleaner.

When I return, I re-suitcase it.

Sometimes I want to bury this tradition
Folksy sentimentality

That my mother has shed so many tears to explain
To me, how she wanted a paj ntaub skirt growing up
Like her sisters, but her mother could not
Afford dresses for all her daughters.

How she got married
Without a dress of her own so she lived
The duration of my life when I still lived with her,
Gathering threads
To craft into my wedding gown.

Seems all her life, all she did
Was to collect things for my dowry.

The life of a Hmong mother

Today I carry my dowry with me
To each new house I move to
Each new person I become
I carry my colorful sashes

My skirt of two hundred paj ntaub pleats
My paj ntaub panel money belts and purses
My purple turban
The striped wrap-around the turban

These stitches my mother gave me

This is how it happened, the night I got married,
How I got hold of my dowry.

She started, started to sew
Like this.

III

Sacrifice a cow,
Two pigs, twenty chickens
Mix my blood with the animals,
Put a hen's egg beside my
daughter's head

in the moonlight
she stirs, sees the egg.

It has been there
for centuries.

This Hmong dress was a gift from you
A body wrapped in spirit
Creeping in my closet,
Rolled into bones, its color

folding in a body until I unfolded it

You said
Bring it back to me
so I can sew it back into
the pleats, the spine.

The newness of the
thread can be yours. It is yours.
Your bloodline.

This is your lineage.

IV

The pig's blood surrounds me
The room is filled with so many people
Relative voices and words of happiness.

Now you will go away

To become someone else.

Don't go too long, come back and visit.
Now you will go and be their person.
Don't go too long, come back and visit.

Is four hundred dollars enough
To compensate my mother for her milk?
They dragged the pig into the kitchen —
What is the brideprice?

What are her parents giving her to take
With her into marriage?
What does she see?
What do her relatives give her?

They give me a dusty garden filled
With flowers that have lain down
Under my foot for at least a thousand years
I am carried by their collected fragrance

A smell of death and rot
That at once becomes the color
Purple and fuchsia all at once

Streaming into me, my nose,
My throat, my heart, my art—streaming
Into me, giving me life,

Resuscitating a dusty garden
Into a field of poppies.

This is my amazing village.

V

When I left my dowry is what you gave me
Four Hmong skirts
Two money belts
Three turbans
Wrapped from five yards
Of hemp died purple
At the end, a splash of cream.
Untangled by a relative aunt
Into my wedding dress.

All this material rolled into tubes
Of craft that Hmong women sewed
With their hands, tending to this material

Hands pressing the folds
Stretching out, until they have fully dressed me,
And I have become,
Like them,

A Hmong woman.

Source: Thao, Noukou. "Dowry." 2009. Used with permission of the author.

Sheng Yang and Sami Scripter, *Cooking from the Heart* (2009)

Sheng Yang was born in Laos. After the communist takeover in 1975, five-year-old Yang and her family fled to Thailand, along with thousands of other Laotians who had supported the United States during the Vietnam War. Four years later, the Yang family moved to the United States, eventually settling in Portland, Oregon, near Sami Scripter's home. The two families grew close, sharing American and Hmong cultural traditions and teaching each other how to cook. In 2009, after years of collaboration, Yang and Scripter published Cooking from the Heart: The Hmong Kitchen in America, *a collection of Hmong recipes interspersed with commentary on Hmong practices and traditions. The following recipe for* Nqaij Qaib Hau Xyaw Tshuaj *(Soup for New Mothers) shows the practical ways in which Hmong in the United States preserve their rich heritage.*

Chickens figure prominently in the Hmong way of life. According to the anthropologist Dr. Dia Cha, they are considered one of the "Eight most important spirits in the Hmong cultural tradition" (*Yim tus tswv dab nyob hauv Hmoob kev cai dab qhuas*). Chickens play a role in many traditional Hmong practices. They help heal the sick, divine providence, and guarantee good fortune. A Hmong shaman may employ a chicken's spirit to assist in dealings with the other world. Chickens have an important part in birth, soul-calling, naming, marriage and death rituals. Ask any Hmong person, old or young, what their favorite Hmong food is and the answer often is, "boiled chicken."

Hmong farmers take pride in raising vigorous, beautiful chickens for their own dinner tables. Hmong professionals who are busy with nine-to-five jobs often treat their families by cooking such a chicken that has been purchased at a Hmong grocery store. These chickens have been hand-raised and butchered quietly and quickly using an age-old technique. Although the meat is tender, it is very lean, and flavorful. The difference between a Hmong-raised chicken and one purchased at a mainstream grocery store is tremendous. . . .

Fresh Chicken with Hmong Herbs (Soup for New Mothers)

Nqaij Qaib Hau Xyaw Tshuaj

If Hmong people have a signature dish, this is it. This very simple soup incorporates a fresh whole chicken cooked gently in a lemongrass-flavored broth. The addition of Hmong herbs—some of which do not have common English names—makes it unique. The herbs help new mothers stay warm and gain strength after the strain of giving birth. Women who eat this soup after bearing a child also maintain strong bones in old age. Hmong custom dictates that, for one month after a baby is born, a mother's diet consists of only this chicken soup, freshly cooked rice, and the warm water drained from the second soaking of rice (*kua ntxhai*), or clear, warm water. Hmong Americans often add vegetables to keep their diet well balanced. This soup is also eaten at regular meals by the entire family.

Which herbs are used in the soup depend upon a family's customs and what is available. Some of the herbs in the following recipe are not available in any store in America. They are lovingly grown in backyard plots and on the patios and windowsills of most Hmong homes. Many of these plants originated from seeds and starts carefully brought to the United States from Laos in the handbags and pockets of Hmong women striving to preserve their healthful cooking traditions. In Hmong booths at farmers' markets, bouquets of the herbs are sometimes available in season. The herb bundles are called *Tshuaj Rau Qaib* (pronounced "chua chao kai"). This soup will not taste the same if mass-produced and processed chicken pieces are used.

Ingredients

1   whole fresh chicken (the kind purchased from a Hmong market or home farm)
10 cups water
1   stalk lemongrass, tough outer leaves and root removed
1   tablespoon salt (or to taste)
1/2 teaspoon black pepper

Hmong Herbs

Each cook cites favorite herbs, often including *hmab ntsha ntsuab* (slippery vegetable), *koj liab* (angelica, sometimes called duck-feet herb), *ntiv* (sweet fern), *pawj qaib* (sweet flag), *tseej ntug* (common dayflower), and *ncaug txhav* and *tshab xyoob* (for which no English translations were available).

Preparation

Clean and chop the chicken into about 16 pieces. Refrigerate the giblets in the refrigerator for other uses. Pick or buy herbs shortly before using, and wash them carefully. Several sprigs of each herb is the customary amount. In a medium-sized pot, bring the water to a boil. Add the lemongrass, salt and pepper. Bring the water back to a boil and add the chicken pieces. Boil 15 minutes (do not overcook the chicken). Add the herbs and cook a few more minutes. Remove the lemongrass and serve with rice.

Using Food to Heal

The Hmong prepare another kind of soup, called medicinal chicken (*qaib tsaws tshuaj*), to help heal injuries. They make it with a very small breed of chicken cooked in water along with strictly medicinal herbs (*tshuaj ntsub*). Most elderly Hmong know which herbs treat what illness, and they grow many of them in their backyard gardens. Depending upon the ailment, additional herbs, pods, tree barks, and roots are purchased from Hmong herbalists. Only a few of these plants have common English names. Because healing herbs taste bitter, and because medicinal chicken contains no salt and pepper, this food definitely tastes like medicine!

Food remedies, such as medicinal chicken and medicinal eggs, are used to help heal wounds or ease problems such as indigestion and coughs, but they are not utilized to treat diseases such as cancer or heart problems. Most modern Hmong people supplement Western medicine with herbal food remedies.

A personal experience of Sami and Sheng demonstrates this Hmong practice. When "Little Sami," (Sheng's youngest sister, named in honor of Sami Scripter) suffered at age twenty-four a broken leg and pelvis in a sledding accident, doctors used metal rods and pins to set the bones and hold her leg and pelvis together. Afterward, the medical staff were unsure how well — or even if — she would be able to walk again. When she was finally released from the hospital, Little Sami's family and friends worked together to provide the support she needed. "Big" Sami (this book's co-author) came to help around Little Sami's home and to care for her two young children during the day while Little Sami's husband was at work.

Each morning during the first week that Little Sami was home from the hospital, her father, Gnia Kao, delivered a pot with a cooked medicinal chicken for her breakfast. He also applied a traditional herbal ointment to her many incisions. Gnia Kao instructed his daughter to eat every bit of the chicken, beginning with the chicken's left leg (corresponding to Little Sami's leg most damaged in the accident). The two Samis decided that this must have something to do with restoring the wholeness of her body. But, as is always the case with Hmong healing, the logic and healing properties behind the

prescription were not explained. They also laughingly agreed that it was a good thing that Little Sami did not have a broken skull!

Some people scoff at such remedies, but the home-health professionals who visited were astounded at Little Sami's rapid rate of healing and progress. By the end of the third week after her accident, Little Sami was hopping around, only partly supported by her crutches, fixing everyone's dinner and baking her famous chocolate chip cookies. She was even able to dance with her husband at a nephew's wedding reception.

Making medicinal food is a gift of love and skill. To prepare the dish, Little Sami's father had to drive for miles to a farm that raised the right kind of chickens. Her mother knew exactly how to cook the chicken and which herbs to include.

Source: Scripter, Sami, and Yang, Sheng. *Cooking from the Heart: The Hmong Kitchen in America.* Minneapolis: University of Minnesota Press, 2009, 93–97. Reprinted with permission from the University of Minnesota Press.

May Lee-Yang and Katie Ka Vang, Interview by *Bakka Magazine* (2009)

May Lee-Yang and Katie Ka Vang are Hmong American authors and performance artists. Yang has written and presented several plays, including "Sia[b]," a reflection on different aspects of Hmong American life and on finding home and community. Sia is Hmong for "life," and Siab means "liver" (although it often is mistranslated as "heart"). In May 2009, Yang and Vang performed "Sia[b]" together in Minneapolis. Bakka Magazine interviewed them later that year. In the following excerpt, the two women talk about how their work affects their communities and about what it means to be an activist.

What led to this latest collaboration?

Katie Ka Vang: I guess the first collaboration, or the first act produced by Mu and I was brought in as an actor to read the script. May and I created an energy for the piece and it worked—and now we're trying to expand on that energy.

May Lee-Yang: About two years ago, I was writing what would later become Sia(b). I had an opportunity to hire an actress to perform my work out loud so I could see how it flowed. By chance, my director Robert Karimi and I decided to ask Katie to come to the table because we'd heard about her.

It was a lucky coincidence that Katie and I clicked and though I'm credited as playwright for the show, Katie has played a big part in helping to put the work together. The process of creating this play involved not just writing but also improv work that we did together.

What are some the directions you're trying to take Hmong American performance art?

MLY: For one thing, I'm trying to move beyond the refugee mentality. What I mean by that is that, when people come to a Hmong play, they expect an exposition on who the Hmong people are, how they came to the United States, etc. I want to take us to the next level and talk about real Hmong people who live and breathe beyond just being refugees. Having said this, I should mention that, if you come see the show, you'll notice that, despite what I just said, the "refugee mentality" still finds its way into my show.

KKV: It's quite challenging because I gravitate towards non-traditional processes and I'd like to expose Hmong audiences to non-traditional processes but there is a big pocket of our community that hasn't even seen a traditional plays yet, so I'm still working on finding balance between the two—in many ways, I think Sia(b) does a great job of that . . .

How do you feel your vision as a community activist intersects with your vision as an artist, if at all?

KKV: Lately, I've been hearing the term "activists" alot. And there are all types of perceptions of what "activists" look like and what they're supposed to do . . . (like lead a group or something and throw up fists in solidarity for the revolution) but I'm a bit cynical these days, because so many of those who claim to be "activists" actually lead a very different life, or are completely oblivious to the injustices they put on folks around them (folks they work with) because they are so caught up in being recognized as an activists they don't stop to question whether or not it's benefitting a community or just them . . . and when they create work specifically towards their activism, I question the genuineness of their work. I'd rather not call myself an activists, I prefer to just create work and let those around me decide for themselves. Recently a friend told me something her grandmother said "If you're wearing perfume, you don't have to announce it to everyone, they can smell it for themselves". Sorry for such a long answer, this issue has been in my head for a while now.

MLY: Lately, I've been hesitant to call myself a community activist. When I think of those folks, I think of people who rally in the streets and do grassroots community organizing. But I would also be selling myself short if I didn't acknowledge that my work—whether intentional or not—is a form of community activism. I have to remind myself that the act of someone who has previously not had a voice speaking their stories is powerful.

When I start to create a work, I don't think of how it is a form of activism, but they are. The title of my "Sia(b)" is an example. Some people might say, "Why not choose a title that's more accessible?" My question is, "Accessible to whom?" Of course, the answer is "Non-Hmong people." Why can't I name my show something from a language that is a part of me despite that most people don't know what it means? The activist part of me is always like, "Do what you want to do. Don't compromise."

As a result, even my director, who is an Iranian-Guatemalan by birth, can say my full-length Hmong name (which is way more complex than May Lee-Yang), and can understand enough Hmong to know when I'm talking smack . . .

Can you talk about what challenges have arisen in embarking down the path of an artist?

KKV: There are many challenges—the first one that sticks out in my head right away is the money. You want to do great work, but great work requires time; rarely will you find a gig where you're being paid adequate money for your time and creative energy; but then for me, it encourages me to seek out my own funding. There is also a heavy admin side to this—its like running your own business.

MLY: One of the biggest challenges has been just plain economics. I've always known I wanted to be an artist. About three years ago, I quit my full-time job to live out my dreams. While I now have a flexible schedule and have accomplished a lot more work than I did while working full-time, I still have to think about things like access to health insurance and a steady income. The great thing, however, is that I have a supportive spouse and family. No one has said to me, "May, grow up. Get a job." Instead, most people have said, "What project are you working on next?"

Aside from subject matter, are you trying to do something different now than you did in your previous works, or do you feel you are trying to extend those performances?

KKV: Well since we're here on behalf of "Sia(b)" I'll first speak specifically in relation to "Sia(b)"—I'm trying to dive deeper into these characters— there is a consistency in the content of the script, but the characters have a different journey; there are also a few new characters that invite you into different parts of May's life. It has been a frustratingly useful journey in being a part of this piece because it's really challenging me as an actor and creator in how I handle and portray these characters and situations that are always grabbing for power.

In my personal work I'm trying to find time to work on my own stuff. I have a few projects in the works and hoping to have a few showings by end of year.

MLY: I've been trying to write a memoir (or several ones) for years now and oddly enough, instead of a book, you get a play out of me. But the rules of theater are trickier than books, I think. With theater, there's some wiggle room for playing around whereas, in a book, I'd probably stick to all the rules of keeping it real. I think that I'm also growing as an artist. One of the reasons why Katie was originally cast in my show was that, despite having done acting and performance work, I was apprehensive about being in a show about my own life. Now, having worked through this show, I've already done one solo show through the Naked Stages program at Intermedia Arts and am writing a new one called "The Sex Lady," which is about how we talk about sex in a culture that supposedly doesn't talk about sex. Two years ago, the idea of doing a solo show didn't even click in my head . . .

Where in your work are you trying to push yourself, challenge yourself, risk something?

KKV: I feel like my work comes from a very expository process . . . and I think it comes naturally, even more so when you have a mentor like Laurie Carlos.

MLY: Whether I am conscious of it or not, I am always pushing myself. Because certain pieces of my work needed to exist as a theater piece, I opened myself up to the possibility. It might have been more comfortable for me to not be on stage, but I'm pushing myself to tell my own stories. I've also realized that if I have the nerve to put the audience on the spot, to make themselves vulnerable, I have to do the same. But I think the way in which I have risked the most artistically has just been being honest. I once worked with a sixteen-year-old girl. She shared a poem with me and I thought, "That was great. That was wonderful." This was because she was so raw and honest in her piece I couldn't help but gravitate towards it. Since then, I've told myself, I can't keep hiding behind walls. If I want to create something great, I need to risk something too.

When did you fall in love with the arts?

KKV: I think I'd always loved the arts. I think I liked performing in general— but when I was growing up the only type of performances I was exposed to was music and singing, through church. So growing up, I did a lot of singing at church, I used to sing for this contemporary Christian rock band called Forgiven. And later I discovered theater, so here I am.

MLY: I was twelve. I was stuck at home with nothing to do. From there, I began reading books. I averaged seven per week. I began watching tons of movies and fantasized about directing them. Since then, I knew that I would be involved in some medium of storytelling.

Source: Excerpt from "From Stage to Sia[b]: An Interview with May Lee Kang and Katie Ka Vang." *Bakka Magazine* 23, no. 26 (June 2009). http://www.bakkamagazine.com/site/articles/siab2009/. Used with permission of May Lee Kang, Katie Ka Vang, and *Bakka Magazine.*

Bee Vang and Louisa Schein, "A Conversation on Race and Acting" (2010)

Gran Torino, *Clint Eastwood's 2008 film about the relationship between an immigrant Hmong family and their white Korean War veteran neighbor, received critical acclaim in the mainstream media for its portrayal of Asian Americans. However, there was a significant criticism within the Asian American community of the male Hmong characters and of the white savior trope permeating the film. Scholars argued that the ostensibly benign—even positive—*Gran Torino *actually traffics in infantilizing and alienating stereotypes, made even more dangerous by the 2005 murder trial of a Hmong hunter and subsequent tension between mainstream and Hmong American communities.*

In his 2010 interview with Louisa Schein, lead actor Bee Vang reflects on the film's underlying messages, and his attempts to redeem the emasculated Thao.

LS: *Talk about yourself and your interests growing up. Especially your exposure to film and acting.*

BV: I was born in Fresno, but moved to the Twin Cities as a baby. I remember getting interested in movies at an early age. But my love for film, when I began to appreciate films on a different level, really started at age 9. My family loved to watch Asian movies that had been dubbed in Hmong. We didn't pay any attention to American movies. We watched Japanese, Hong Kong, Chinese, Thai, Bollywood. It wasn't until much later that I heard of anyone like Brad Pitt or George Clooney . . .

LS: *Do you remember being conscious of race in those early years?*

BV: No, not when I was younger, but it might have had something to do with the fact that I grew up watching predominantly Asian films. Living in America, though, it was inevitable that I would start watching some movies made in the West. From my early teens, I remember Kubrick's *Clockwork Orange*, Peter Jackson's *Heavenly Creature*, *Rambo* and other war movies. I found the war movies ridiculous: too much action.

Then when I saw *Heaven and Earth*—the Oliver Stone movie based on a Vietnamese woman's memoir of the war—I felt so critical of it as a white man's story about a white savior. I never wanted the Vietnamese woman to give in to Tommy Lee Jones—I was always for her independence. And when she spoke broken English with him, it made me more angry because it emphasized her lack of power. I always preferred films about Asians in the original language with subtitles . . .

LS: *Did you identify the movie with your own history at all?*

BV: Not really. It just seemed like another war movie. The author hadn't intended to make a movie—she was writing a memoir. The process of turning it into a movie felt like turning it into lies. I objected to the way the cinematography—sweeping shots of landscapes—made the actual war seem more beautiful and diminished that it was a horrible and terrifying experience for her.

I remember thinking, though, that if it hadn't been for the war in Vietnam, there wouldn't have been all those war movies and Asians would never have had as much of a presence in Hollywood. Ironically, the war created acting opportunities for us—even if the roles were undeveloped and we stood for the enemy most of the time.

LS: *How did Americans' chronic confusion of Southeast Asian refugees with Asian enemies play for you personally?*

BV: Well it always made me think that we, as Asians, had to be saved, but also saved from each other. The only way that we could be saved was through Western intervention. Of course, my response at an early age was that we were backwards, cruel and had to be whitened. I kind of took that on, but at the same time, it was a ridiculous idea to me!

LS: *So what went through your head when you started to hear about* Gran Torino?

BV: I never thought I would try out. I heard about the story and the "sides"—the excerpts from the script that were used for auditions—and I was just really repulsed by what I read. I tried to make sense of the characters and their lines. But there were things I couldn't figure out about the relations between Walt and the Hmong characters. For instance, at some point Thao tells Walt "You know you can call me these racist names as much as you want because you know what? I'll take it." I didn't understand why a character like Thao would say that? Why wouldn't he object to being insulted? What does "taking it" even mean? What

was intended by the screenwriter or was this just careless writing?

LS: *The story, as we know, takes place in Detroit and centers on a white man who is probably dying and doesn't have much time left. His Asian neighbors are a backdrop to his search for redemption from acts in the Korean war—*

BV: Of course, those Asians are nothing but FOBs or youth on the streets killing each other . . .

LS: *Right. So Walt has to teach them the "right" way to behave, and to save the good ones from the bad. In the process, he valiantly takes the fall. Talk about your impressions of the plot, the script itself.*

BV: The thing is, the story can't take place without those Hmong characters, especially mine. But in the end, it's Walt that gets glorified. We fade out in favor of his heroism. I felt negated by the script and by extension in my assuming the role. It's almost like a non-role. Strange for a lead . . .

LS: *What about the script's portrayal of Thao's masculinity?*

BV: Well first off, the girlfriend part is totally crazy. . . . Walt and the gangsters and the grandma—all of them have nothing but insults about Thao's manliness—or lack thereof. He doesn't cut it in any way and he's not super-hot. So why is it that the gorgeous girl decides to pick him over all the other guys?

LS: *It sends an incoherent message, doesn't it?*

BV: That the dumb, passive, quiet, loner guy can still get the best girl. It pained me that Thao let his masculinity suffer so badly over the course of the story.

LS: *The only manhood he gains is bestowed by Walt, and that's pretty dubious even up to the end . . . And how did you feel about the character descriptions?*

BV: The Thao character was described as an "Asian Johnny Depp." "A slight, slender Hmong boy with long hair and eyelashes." OK, but I didn't understand the function of those looks in the story. Also I was annoyed at the comparing of Asian men to a white standard of beauty. I mean [chuckles] who's to say we're not even better than Johnny's looks?

LS: *How did you interpret this in terms of your own look?*

BV: I have no idea what look they cast me for. I know I don't look like Johnny Depp. And on set they didn't do anything about my looks, just told me to come as I was . . . it's still a mystery to me.

LS: *So you were uneasy about the lines and character descriptions. Why did you audition and ultimately take the part?*

BV: Friends kept pushing me to try out. I didn't take it seriously. Didn't think I'd get the part. But when I was called back for another round of auditioning, I realized I wanted to be part of the hype, because this would become a great cultural event of our time, especially for Hmong. Most importantly, my intentions were, as I continued to audition and do my best, to try to improve on the script and the ways Hmong were portrayed. I wanted to create a character that people could love. I decided to commit to developing the role of Thao, making him more complex and credible. I imagined a guy who would chafe at his subordination more. So even when he had to obey, he did it with more attitude.

LS: *Did you feel you succeeded in creating this character?*

BV: I added a lot of intonation and gestures to try to give Thao some dignity. For instance, when my sister is offering me to work for Walt, I raised my voice to a shout to indicate I hated the idea of slaving for Walt. That outburst wasn't in the script. But most of the script was not very open to interpretation and it was premised on his not having any dignity. He needs to be clueless and have no self-respect in order for the white elder man to achieve his savior role. He has to hang his head and absorb abuse. So it makes me wonder how a character like Thao could bring any change to Walt.

LS: *Were you able to draw on parts of yourself or your experience for this role?*

BV: Well that was the idea, from what I could tell. The production process didn't include rehearsals or coaching. Eastwood didn't want us to consult with him. He just wanted us to be ourselves. The plan was for us to be so-called "natural actors," just stepping out of our lives and into the frames. This way the production could move efficiently. So we didn't get the scripts until a week before the shooting started and had no prep time to use the method acting process of getting into the psychology of the character.

LS: *How did you feel about the result?*

BV: That's a difficult one. I know I gave it my all, but at the same time, it doesn't look like stellar acting to me. I just wished that perhaps the physical acting aspect would at least be recognizable. Also, it's funny, when I watch the final product of *Gran Torino*, I often have the impression that the takes they chose for each scene were my weakest. I'm not sure what that's about.

LS: *Say more about the role itself.*

BV: But then I think that maybe it's not about the quality of my acting. It's the fact of the character being unsympathetic because of his weakness. It's an odd thing, as a first time actor, to have to step into a role that's disparaged by the script and humiliated by the other characters. Playing him well is like making a deal with the devil. To the extent that I did a good job, I reinforced that image of effeminate Asian guys who are wimps, geeks and can't advocate for themselves.

LS: *Does Thao become a man in your opinion? Does he get stronger?*

BV: I worked on that. It wasn't easy because the scenes were shot completely out of sequence so it was hard to get a sense of the continuity and the progression. I tried to show Thao's change through the physicality of my performances. I hung my head less and less. In the barbershop scene, I made my voice get a bit raspier and more like Eastwood's as they tried to "man me up." I threw in some sassy gestures. By the time I was getting the job at the construction site, I added more of a swagger to my walk. Things like that.

LS: *Did you feel like you were playing Hmong in* Gran Torino? *At what points in the story, if any, did you feel you drew on your Hmong identity to play the role?*

BV: I know there were a lot of Hmong references and scenes in the film, but I didn't feel it in my character. What I felt was being called on to perform the pan-Asian stereotype of the submissive, kow-towing geek with no girlfriend. Plus there's no real reason for us to be Hmong in the script. We could be any minority. And not only that, but Walt is always confusing us with Koreans and other Asians. Even with the enemies he fought in Korea. So Hmong culture, Hmong identity didn't end up seeming so relevant.

LS: *How do you feel about what audiences reflect back to you regarding the film?*

BV: Y'know a middle-aged white guy was telling me the thing he loved most about *Gran Torino* was the interactions between Walt and the Hmong people—that the film "rings true" to him in some kind of way. A lot of people say this. Well—"rings true" for who? Maybe to people who live in a world where whites are the only heroes. Or to those who take the film as a documentary about Hmong culture. Even other Asians do this a lot. And then they tell me how much they learned about my culture. Meanwhile, what a lot of us Hmong feel is that the film is distorting and untrue. I guess watching *Gran Torino* is really subjective. People get all sorts of different things out of it.

LS: *What's next for you?*

BV: I have a lot of ideas. I'm going to study filmmaking and pursue my acting. And I'm also going to study Chinese and see where it all takes me.

Whatever I do, I want to keep social justice work in the mix.

Source: Vang, Bee, and Schein, Louisa. "*Gran Torino*'s Hmong Lead Bee Vang on Race and Acting." 2010. Reprinted with permission.

Mary Bamford, *Angel Island: The Ellis Island of the West* (1917)

Recent scholarship suggests that post–Civil War American Baptists increasingly attempted to redefine citizenship in terms of religion instead of race as a means of limiting the power of millions of newly emancipated African American slaves and a growing influx of Gold Rush Chinese. And although many subscribed to commonly held white supremacist beliefs about the inferiority of Chinese culture and morality, American Baptists still championed progressive attempts to curb racist and exclusionary legislation in the United States. This mind-set permeated their domestic missionary efforts within Asian immigrant communities for the next 50 years.

In 1917, Mary Bamford, a member of the Women's American Baptist Home Missionary Society, wrote a book describing Angel Island and its inmates. In the following excerpt from her foreword to Bamford's book, the Baptist Home Missionary Society's Lillian M. Soares reveals the ways in which religion and civil society were inextricably bound together in early 20th-century America. The next excerpt contains Bamford's description of the Angel Island Immigration

Station and references the paper sons. The final selection describes some of the South Asian immigrants waiting to be processed at Angel Island. Like most early 20th-century Americans, Bamford mistakenly calls these men "Hindus," even though most South Asian immigrants were actually Sikhs. The young men Bamford described were likely among the last Indians to be able to move to the United States. In 1917, the same year Angel Island *was published, Congress created the Asiatic Barred Zone Act, effectively cutting off Indian immigration. Not until the 1946 Luce-Celler Act were Indians again allowed to immigrate to the United States and become naturalized citizens.*

Foreword

We are all familiar with Ellis Island on the Atlantic coast, but many do not know of the existence of Angel Island on the Pacific where the incoming orientals are received.

It was a note of the early Christian that he was "given to hospitality." The spirit of the Master teaches us to share with others. Why should not this attitude characterize our national relations with the incomers who cross the seas to sojourn in our land?

Unrestricted and unregulated immigration would not be wise either on our eastern or western coasts. We need the most careful consideration of the character of our future citizenship. But when we have decided who may be admitted to our land, let us receive all who come with a true Christian courtesy. It is not wholly a matter of legislation and officialism. The observant writer of this little story indicates clearly the significance of what should be done to give our new guests a kindly welcome. The Golden Gate and Angel Island should be worthy of their beautiful names. Here is an important task for the Christian women of our Home Mission Societies.

We can always be sure that every bad influence will meet the stranger. All the tribe that seeks to exploit the new-arrival confused in his unfamiliar surroundings, will be alert, and in spite of all the care which the government can exercise, the immigrant will not seldom be cheated and misled. Strangely enough the Christian forces may give no heed to him. Too busy about our own affairs we may not realize that these are folk coming from old Asia, whence our Savior came, who are getting their first impression of a Christian land. They are sure to see our evil side; we must not fail to let them see our purity, faith, patriotism and Christian love.

Foreign missions come over to us at Angel Island. Those folk from the east will learn our tongue. They will also share our faith if we give them a chance. How touching to read the story of their gratitude for a copy of the gospel! How our hearts thrill when we read of the Chinese Boys' Band and the stirring notes of "America" which they played so well!

"Sweet land of liberty." America has ever been a Promised Land. There ought not to be one soul in all our broad country who does not show the loyalty that makes a nation strong. Patriotism is only at its best when it is Christian.

It is our Home Missionary task to help the strangers within our gates to become Christian patriots.

Lillian M. Soares
May, 1917

Angel Island

Angel Island is a much better place to keep immigrants than the old detention-sheds in San Francisco were, as opportunities for coaching witnesses in fraudulent cases are now prevented by island isolation. Angel Island was first opened as an Immigrant Station in October, 1909. The next report of the Commissioner General of Immigration stated that Angel Island Station had been built largely because the Chinese and their friends and attorneys had persistently complained that the conditions under which the Chinese were detained in San Francisco were unsafe and unsanitary. But when these complainants discovered that the United States Government would have a great advantage in preventing the coaching of applicants and witnesses by occupying the Station at Angel Island, there arose violent protests, which, however, did not prevent the Government from carrying out its plan.

Angel Island is seven miles in circumference, and has an altitude of nine hundred feet. On the south side of the island, the buildings and the khaki-colored tents that we see, do not mark the Immigration Station portion of the island, but comprise what is sometimes called the "Casual Camp," where soldiers from the Philippines are lodged. On the west of the island, out of sight of our boat, is Fort McDowell, the military station. On the north side of the island, is the quarantine station.

The Buildings.—Our boat passes a little further and turns by a wooded bluff. We swing alongside a wharf. Connected with the wharf by a broad wooden walk, is the main building of the eighteen buildings on this section of the island devoted to the United States Immigration Service. Ten acres of the island are fenced in for this purpose. We pass up the walk to the Administration Building and at the door we show our pass to the old door-keeper. While we wait here for our guide, we notice that this large room in which we stand is railed off into sections.

The Japanese.—The Japanese girls with the Japanese young men in one section are "picture-brides," with their prospective bridegrooms and friends. Of the "picture-brides" I shall treat more fully in a later chapter.

Our guide leads us from the main room of the Administration Building into a long curving passageway, made secure by wire netting on the side opening outdoors, and we are ushered into the large dining-room for immigrants. Long, clean rows of tables stretch parallel to one another across the width of the room. . . .

The Indians.—Our guide takes us to the other side of the building to show us the Hindus. Here they come! Fine-looking, stalwart fellows, with white turbans swathing their heads, they come up the long stairway and confront us. Other Indians are in the further room. How different this type of men from the Chinese or Japanese whom we have been seeing! Some authorities hold that the Hindu and the American both belong to the Aryan race, and that whether we like it or not, these Hindus are bone of our bone. Our speech bewrayeth [sic] us, according to the philologists. One looks back through the ages, and sees the time when the Aryan forefathers of these Hindus, and our own forefathers parted in central Asia, the Hindu forefathers going south, and in a subsequent emigration, our forefathers going west. The Hindu is not a Mongolian, but our long-lost brother, and the Californian is not usually any more glad to see him coming than the respectable brother was to see the prodigal son in the parable. I recall seeing a small group of Indians beside the entrance to the Pacific Mail Steamship Company's pier in San Francisco, before the sailing of a steamer, and hearing a white man adjure the harmless group, who were not obstructing anything that I could see, "You move on! You fellows can't stand their talking!"

Those Indians were not devoid of human instinct when treated kindly, for when I gave a copy of the Gospel of John, written in the strange oval and horizontal Punjabi characters, to the Hindu of the group, he drew a nickel from his pocket as if to pay me, and on my refusal he uttered an "Ah-h!" of protest. Another time, after I had given a group of four Indians some Gospels in Punjabi, one of them who wore a red turban came after me and held out his sallow hand in which was a little change, as if he would have paid me. When I refused the money, he thanked me.

The kindly hearted American who pleasantly says, "Salaam," in greeting an Indian, hears "Salaam," in return. A missionary from India, while visiting the camps of Indians in northern California, was gladly received when it was discovered he could speak Hindustani. Once on his way to an Indian camp, this same missionary saw a workman in a field and called to him in his own tongue. The man came running, and was full of joy at being spoken to in his native language. His employer called him, but he enthusiastically shouted back, "I can't work now! My brother has come! My brother has come!"

A San Francisco employe [sic] of the American Bible Society told me of a friend who had carried gospels to an outgoing steamer, and an Indian was so glad to receive a gospel in his native tongue that he kissed the book. A colporteur is said to have found five Indian laborers at prayer one evening in their hut. Not a word of English could any of them speak, but they were reading from a Bible that a missionary had given to one of them in India, and which he had bought with him to America.

Source: Bamford, Mary. *Angel Island: The Ellis Island of the West.* Chicago: Woman's American Baptist Home Mission Society, 1917, 5–6, 12, 20–22. The California Historical Society, PAM 1277. http://content.cdlib.org/ark:/13030/hb7t1nb2dc/?&brand=oac. Used with permission of the California Historical Society.

United States Supreme Court, *U.S. v. Bhagat Sing Thind*, 261 U.S. 204 (1923)

In 1790, the U.S. Congress passed a law restricting naturalization rights to "free white persons." Originally, the Naturalization Act was meant to prevent African American slaves from becoming citizens. However, almost immediately after Chinese laborers began to arrive in California, the restrictions were expanded to apply to successive groups of Asians as well. Although laws denying East Asian immigrants citizenship were reaffirmed in 1870 (against the Chinese) and 1907 (against the Japanese), South Asian immigrants occupied a gray area, especially because anthropologists in the early 20th century had classified them as Caucasians. However, many white Americans saw no commonalities between their own white skin and European culture and the dark-skinned peoples from India. And in 1923, the U.S. Supreme Court eliminated any doubt over Indian citizenship rights in the case of U.S. v. Bhagat Singh Thind.

Bhagat Sing Thind was born in 1892 in the Punjab, a region of northern India. He immigrated to the United States in 1913 and enlisted in the U.S. Army in the last few months of World War I. After being honorably discharged, Thind sought and was granted American citizenship on December 9, 1918, in Washington State. Four days later, a judge rescinded Thind's citizenship on the grounds that he was not a "free white man," as required in the 1790 Immigration and Nationality Act. Eleven months later in Oregon, Thind's citizenship was reinstated on the grounds that he was a "high caste Hindu" from the Caucasus region. (Thind was a Sikh; however, at that point, "Hindu" or "Hindoo" was the term used for all Indians, regardless of their actual religious beliefs.) The Immigration and Naturalization Service appealed the second ruling. On February 19, 1923, the Supreme Court concluded that Thind—and all Indians—were not Caucasian, and

that the "common man's" racial definition of "Caucasian," meaning "white," would be the standard used to determine legal racial status, which in turn determined citizenship rights (following the Naturalization Act of 1790). Thind, along with 50 other Indian Americans, retroactively lost their citizenship. This also meant that in more than a dozen states they were now subject to the restrictive Alien Land Laws that prevented "aliens ineligible for citizenship" from owning land.

Thind regained his citizenship for the third time in 1936, after Congress decided that veterans of World War I, even those from the Asian Barred Zone, could become naturalized citizens. For the rest of his life, he wrote and lectured on spirituality and metaphysical theology.

Argued January 11, 12, 1923
Decided February 19, 1923
261 U.S. 204
CERTIFICATE FROM THE CIRCUIT COURT OF APPEALS FOR THE NINTH CIRCUIT

Syllabus

1. A high caste Hindu, of full Indian blood, born at Amrit Sar, Punjab, India, is not a "white person" within the meaning of Rev.Stats., § 2169, relating to the naturalization of aliens.

2. "Free white persons," as used in that section, are words of common speech, to be interpreted in accordance with the understanding of the common man, synonymous with the word "Caucasian" only as that word is popularly understood. *Ozawa v. United States.*

3. The action of Congress in excluding from admission to this country all natives of Asia within designated limits, including all of India, is evidence of a like attitude toward naturalization of Asians within those limits.

Questions certified by the circuit court of appeals, arising upon an appeal to that court from a decree of the district court dismissing, on motion, a bill brought by the United States to cancel a certificate of naturalization.

MR. JUSTICE SUTHERLAND delivered the opinion of the Court.

. . . .The appellee was granted a certificate of citizenship by the District Court of the United States for the District of Oregon, over the objection of the Naturalization Examiner for the United States. A bill in equity was then filed by the United States seeking a cancellation of the certificate on the ground that the appellee was not a white person, and therefore not lawfully entitled to naturalization. The district court, on motion, dismissed the bill, and an appeal was taken to the circuit court of appeals. No question is made in respect of the individual qualifications of the appellee. The sole question is whether he falls within the class designated by Congress as eligible.

Section 2169, Revised Statutes, provides that the provisions of the Naturalization Act "shall apply to aliens being free white persons and to aliens of African nativity and to persons of African descent."

If the applicant is a white person within the meaning of this section, he is entitled to naturalization; otherwise not. In *Ozawa v. United States,* we had occasion to consider the application of these words to the case of a cultivated Japanese, and were constrained to hold that he was not within their meaning. As there pointed out, the provision is not that any particular class of persons shall be excluded, but it is, in effect, that only white persons shall be included within the privilege of the statute.

"The intention was to confer the privilege of citizenship upon that class of persons whom the fathers knew as white, and to deny it to all who could not be so classified. It is not enough to say that the framers did not have in mind the brown or yellow races of Asia. It is necessary to go farther and be able to say that, had these particular races been suggested, the language of the act would have been so varied as to include them within its privileges . . . "

In the endeavor to ascertain the meaning of the statute, we must not fail to keep in mind that it does not employ the word "Caucasian," but the words "white persons," and these are words of common speech, and not of scientific origin. The word "Caucasian" not only was not employed in the law, but was probably wholly unfamiliar to the original framers of the statute in 1790. When we employ it, we do so as an aid to the ascertainment of the legislative intent, and not as an invariable substitute for the statutory words. Indeed, as used in the science of ethnology, the connotation of the word is by no means clear, and the use of it in its scientific sense as an equivalent for the words of the statute, other considerations aside, would simply mean the substitution of one perplexity for another. But, in this country, during the last half century especially, the word, by common usage, has acquired a popular meaning, not clearly defined to be sure, but sufficiently so to enable us to say that its popular, as distinguished from its scientific, application is of appreciably narrower scope. It is in the popular sense of the word, therefore, that we employ it as an aid to the construction of the statute, for it would be obviously illogical to convert words of common speech used in a statute into words of scientific terminology when neither the latter nor the science for whose purposes they were coined was within the contemplation of the framers of the statute or of the people for whom it was framed. **The words of the statute are to be interpreted in accordance with the understanding of the common man from whose vocabulary they were taken.**

They imply, as we have said, a racial test; but the term "race" is one which, for the practical purposes of the statute, must be applied to a group of living persons now possessing in common the requisite characteristics, not to groups of persons who are supposed to be or really are descended from some remote common ancestor, but who, whether they both resemble him to a greater or less extent, have at any rate ceased altogether to resemble one another. **It may be true that the blond Scandinavian and the brown Hindu have a common ancestor in the dim reaches of antiquity, but the average man knows perfectly well that there are unmistakable and profound differences between them today, and it is not impossible, if that common ancestor could be materialized in the flesh, we should discover that he was himself sufficiently differentiated from both of his descendants to preclude his racial classification with either.** . . .

The eligibility of this applicant for citizenship is based on the sole fact that he is of high-caste Hindu stock, born in Punjab, one of the extreme northwestern districts of India, and classified by certain scientific authorities as of the Caucasian or Aryan race. The Aryan theory, as a racial basis, seems to be discredited by most, if not all, modern writers on the subject of ethnology . . .

The term "Aryan" has to do with linguistic, and not at all with physical, characteristics, and it would seem reasonably clear that mere resemblance in language, indicating a common linguistic root buried in remotely ancient soil, is altogether inadequate to prove common racial origin. There is, and can be, no assurance that the so-called Aryan language was not spoken by a variety of races living in proximity to one another. Our own history has witnessed the adoption of the English tongue by millions of negroes, whose descendants can never be classified racially with the descendants of white persons, notwithstanding both may speak a common root language.

The word "Caucasian" is in scarcely better repute. It is, at best, a conventional term, with an altogether fortuitous origin, which, under scientific manipulation, has come to include far more than the unscientific mind suspects. According to Keane, for example (*The World's Peoples* 24, 28, 307 *et seq.*), it includes not only the Hindu, but some of the Polynesians (that is, the Maori, Tahitians, Samoans, Hawaiians, and others), the Hamites of Africa, upon the ground of the Caucasic

cast of their features, though in color they range from brown to black. We venture to think that the average well informed white American would learn with some degree of astonishment that the race to which he belongs is made up of such heterogeneous elements . . .

It does not seem necessary to pursue the matter of scientific classification further. We are unable to agree with the district court, or with other lower federal courts, in the conclusion that a native Hindu is eligible for naturalization under § 2169. The words of familiar speech, which were used by the original framers of the law, were intended to include only the type of man whom they knew as white. The immigration of that day was almost exclusively from the British Isles and Northwestern Europe, whence they and their forebears had come. When they extended the privilege of American citizenship to "any alien being a free white person," it was these immigrants—bone of their bone and flesh of their flesh—and their kind whom they must have had affirmatively in mind. The succeeding years brought immigrants from Eastern, Southern and Middle Europe, among them the Slavs and the dark-eyed, swarthy people of Alpine and Mediterranean stock, and these were received as unquestionably akin to those already here and readily amalgamated with them. It was the descendants of these, and other immigrants of like origin, who constituted the white population of the country when § 2169, reenacting the naturalization test of 1790, was adopted, and, there is no reason to doubt, with like intent and meaning.

What, if any, people of primarily Asiatic stock come within the words of the section we do not deem it necessary now to decide. There is much in the origin and historic development of the statute to suggest that no Asiatic whatever was included. . . . It is a matter of familiar observation and knowledge that the physical group characteristics of the Hindus render them readily distinguishable from the various groups of persons in this country commonly recognized as white. The children of English, French, German, Italian, Scandinavian, and other European parentage quickly merge into the mass of our population and lose the distinctive hallmarks of their European origin. On the other hand, it cannot be doubted that the children born in this country of Hindu parents would retain indefinitely the clear evidence of their ancestry. It is very far from our thought to suggest the slightest question of racial superiority or inferiority. What we suggest is merely racial difference, and it is of such character and extent that the great body of our people instinctively recognize it and reject the thought of assimilation.

It is not without significance in this connection that Congress, by the Act of February 5, 1917, 39 Stat. 874, c. 29, § 3, has now excluded from admission into this country all natives of Asia within designated limits of latitude and longitude, including the whole of India. This not only constitutes conclusive evidence of the congressional attitude of opposition to Asiatic immigration generally, but is persuasive of a similar attitude toward Asiatic naturalization as well, since it is not likely that Congress would be willing to accept as citizens a class of persons whom it rejects as immigrants.

It follows that a negative answer must be given to the first question, which disposes of the case and renders an answer to the second question unnecessary, and it will be so certified.

Source: United States v. Bhagat Singh Thind, 261 U.S. 204, 1923.

Mary T. Mathew, Interview by Rashmi Varna
(1999)

In immigrant families, generational differences between parents and children are often exacerbated by the cultural expectations of both parties. Tension over the level of Americanization is frequently expressed in conflicts over gender roles and social strictures. Mary Mathew, an immigrant from Kerala in southern India, moved to North Carolina in 1970. In this excerpt from her 1999 interview with Rashmi Varna, she speaks about how she and her daughters navigate between American and Indian cultural expectations, particularly with respect to dating.

MARY T. MATHEW: Both our children are, temperamentally, very sweet and easy to get along with. And, raising both of them in their childhood was delightful. And as they grow up, and during their early growing years . . . mentally, both of us were still firmly rooted in the cultural expectations of typical Indian parents . . . It was unthinkable to us that girls would wear shorts. It was unthinkable to us that our children would think of dating, boys, and . . . It was unthinkable to us that our children would want to . . . go out on dates and return . . . after nightfall. So, all of these are . . . expectations I should say, that we had so firmly implanted in us, that we could not get reconciled to how our girls were changing before our eyes. So, when our older daughter who was the guinea pig in our, child-rearing, went through these stages, . . . we, had encounters when we would try to explain our respective positions and so on. So, I would say that it took us time and a few years to realize that our children were not extensions of our personalities, even though they were Indian in terms of having Indian parents, they had grown up here and so these children who were, in the real sense of the term, Americans and we could not package them into a predetermined cultural entity.

RASHMI VARMA: Did they have questions for you, as to what, you know, their identities were? Did you ever see any confusion in them? Or do you think that it was easy for them to just see themselves as Americans? Did they come ever with experiences from school, you know, where someone had asked them about their identity and that had led to some confusion?

MARY T. MATHEW: It took us a few years for these issues to get resolved, and then, then we had a few tough years when the girls felt that we were unreasonably strict with them, and that we didn't understand what their, needs were, in these social areas, and so on.

RASHMI VARMA: What about cultural areas? Do you think that they were ever confused about their identity? Did other kids perceive them as different? Did they ever have questions about that, as to why they were different?

MARY T. MATHEW: They didn't. They didn't have problems in that area. One reason could be that their friends loved coming to our house and having dinner with us, so they found their cultural background to be a social advantage. [Laughter] Well, and all our spicy food and so on were popular among their friends. Neither of them would wear a sari or, things like that, at that time. Even though now they would.

RASHMI VARMA: They would now?

MARY T. MATHEW: Yes.

RASHMI VARMA: What has made the difference that now they would?

MARY T. MATHEW: Because when you're in your early and mid teens, you think to be different, is to be, socially inept, and now, now that they're more confident of their, themselves as persons, they see it as a way to look more attractive. [Laughter] They see it as exotic, what once they would have seen as different, you know, in a bad way. So, on the one hand as parents, we realized what our mistakes were, and we began to come out of pre-established cultural behavioral expectations. And, [unclear] we started allowing them to date young men, who of course, always, making sure when we could, that these were young men of good character and, you know, carefully counseling them about the dangers of, not sticking within one's moral boundaries and so on. So, I would say that both girls have benefited from our relaxing that stern grip, on their social life and, they have both been very responsible and, we are proud of the choices they have made.

Source: Excerpted from Interview with Mary T. Mathew by Rashmi Varna, April 25,1999 (K-0815), in the Southern Oral History Program Collection (#4007), Southern Historical Collection, Louis Round Wilson Special Collections Library, University of North Carolina at Chapel Hill. http://docsouth.unc.edu/sohp/K-0815/excerpts/excerpt_8773.html.

Anita Chawla, Interview by Peggy Bulger
(2001)

Anita Chawla was born in the United States to Punjabi parents and grew up in Atlanta, Georgia. She is now a physician in the Washington, DC, area. Chawla heard about Al Qaeda's assault on the World Trade Center and the Pentagon while she was stalled on a local expressway waiting for a car repair. Because she lived in a very liberal and politically active community, seeing anti-Muslim signs in her community was particularly distressing for Chawla, who remembered childhood experiences with racial profiling and antagonism during the Iran hostage crisis. In her interview with Peggy Bulger, given two weeks after 9/11, Chawla discussed how the attacks changed her life as a minority person living in the United States. Like many other South Asian Americans, Chawla experienced a heightened sense of racial identity almost overnight, as Americans came to identify brown skin with the enemy.

CHAWLA: I'm Anita Chawla; I'm originally from—well, my family's from India and I was born and raised in Atlanta, Georgia, and now I live in Takoma Park, MD. I'm 34 years old and I'm a physician.

BULGER: AND, ANITA, I'M ASKING EVERYONE: the horrible events that happened on September 11th impacted all of us. . . . Where were you when these events unfolded?

CHAWLA: Well, I was actually on my way—I was on the Beltway on my way to work and right when I had a flat tire—my tire gave out right as the news was coming about well there's a plane that hit the World Trade Center and I pulled over and I spent the next two hours listening to the radio hearing things unfold and news trickling in and waiting for someone to come change my tires so I was just sitting there in total shock listening to these things happen . . . and the confusion and people not sure what exactly had happened . . . and it was very scary. It was very unbelievable, very surreal. . . .

BULGER: And you being of Indian descent . . . how is your life changed since that time?

CHAWLA: Well, unfortunately, I've become very much more self-conscious and aware of being a minority and I've become much more aware of racism and how much do I blend in. You know my mother lives with us and I've explained to her what has happened and encouraged her not to wear her shalwar and kameez, her Indian clothes, outside when she goes out, just because I'm afraid for her and she doesn't speak the language. So I worry about her being out and I'm concerned about that. And I'm much more aware of even going into stores and public places. I'm much more self-conscious, and I know, I can feel—sometimes I feel people looking at me and I'm not sure why—like I'll catch people's eyes. And that's unfortunate because in the past I never thought anything of it. But now I'm having to—I feel unsafe, and I feel unsafe for my family . . .

It feels very isolating and it feels almost like I'm in prison. And I feel so bad for the Sikhs who of course they wear turbans and there's so much misunderstanding and it's just heartbreaking. It's really heartbreaking. And everybody's just afraid.

BULGER: . . . Are there any other things that you think should be, could be done by our government?

CHAWLA: Well, I think I've heard things coming out about remembering that Islam is not—Muslims are not bad, that Islam is not bad, it's the people that distort it, and the politics and so forth and I think that that's—if we could hear more of that. And I certainly appreciated when Bush went out and has been saying those kinds of remarks and so forth. But I really think that there has to be a lot done at the community level. There has to be a lot more educating, and just teachings of tolerance . . .

[We're] trying not to feel so imprisoned and trying to take some steps to remember our community and remember the people, that we are connected and people do support us. So that's important, that is reassuring.

Source: Interview with Anita Chawla, conducted by Peggy Bulger, Takoma Park, Maryland, September 24, 2001, in the September 11, 2001, Documentary Project Collection (AFC 2001/015), Archive of Folk Culture, American Folklife Center, Library of Congress Reprinted with permission from Anita Chawla. http://hdl.loc.gov/loc.afc/afc2001015.sr082a02.

DJ Rekha, Interview by Demetrius Cheeks
(2007)

DJ Rekha is a South Asian American DJ who specializes in mixing Bhangra, traditional music and dance forms from the Punjab region in India, with electronic house music. DJ Rehka's Basement Bhangra music became hugely popular in the New York City club scene in the early 2000s. Rehka, like other South Asians, is part of a new generation of post-1965 Asian Americans. With the liberalization of U.S. immigration policies in 1965, Asian Indians began coming to the United States in large numbers. Because the new policies created a preference system for highly educated professionals, most of those in this second wave of Indian immigrants were doctors, scientists, engineers, or students in American graduate school programs. Many second-generation South Asian Americans feel pressure to follow in their parents' educational and professional career paths. However, a growing number of Indian Americans, like DJ Rekha, have found success in other avenues. In this interview, DJ Rekha describes how her Indian heritage has influenced her artistic development.

Let's assume that the readership is unfamiliar with both Sangament and Bhangra. Can you briefly describe the enterprise and the cultural phenomenon?

Sangament is the name I've given to my company. It's a combination of the words Sangam and entertainment. "Sangam" itself is a North Indian Hindi word meaning the confluence of rivers; it's where the rivers flow, in essence. Sangament Inc. is the entity through which I do all of my work—as a DJ, as a marketer and as a consultant.

How would you describe or characterize Bhangra?

Bhangra is a music and a dance that originally comes from Punjab: a region—and an ethnicity— divided by India and Pakistan. It's one of the forms of music that's indigenous to that area. It was transported to the UK through the immigration of Punjabi peoples that came to the UK post-World War II. And now, roughly three generations later, the music has taken in its environment and developed and transformed in a unique way.

What was it that drew you into that cultural space?

The cultural space was my household in many respects. I was exposed to the language via my parents. I didn't have much exposure to that music. I grew up on Bollywood, which is a Hindi language-based music that emerged in the Hindi-language film industry. I was initially exposed to the music by my mother; she brought back a tape from England after a visit there. This was around the time that the Bhangra scene really started kicking off in the UK. I heard it and it really blew my mind. At the same time, my cousins and I just got interested in DJ-ing and forming a crew.

How was Bhangra initially received in India and how is it received today?

I think initially, in India and maybe even in Pakistan, Bhangra was perceived as sort of regionally based folk music: very specific to a locale, very jubilant, very lively and very festive. It was and is the music of north Indian weddings. In India, that's how people took it; In the UK, in the same way, it was brought over and it kept going through cultural practices. Especially because of the political context in which it sort of incubated in the UK: you had these communities of color that didn't really assimilate or mix and they really held on to their cultural traditions, so they kept it alive. And in terms of its perception, Bhangra has been like house [music]: it keeps having waves in the UK, of breaking and becoming mainstream. There was actually a hit a few years ago with Punjabi MC. This record that broke in Europe, and then Jay-Z actually rapped on it here [in the States] quite by accident. The whole idea has been that this music is really going to break and go somewhere. And it does a little bit and then it doesn't. But there're still a lot of barriers to entry to South Asian artists in the UK. Even though it's a community that's embedded in that cultural landscape, I think that artists there tend to have a hard time breaking out and doing stuff. Society there is still kind of insular and the industry is kind of shallow. I mean it took dancehall 25 years to break outside of Bob Marley. So we have to see the corporate forces that encourage, discourage, exploit and co-opt these cultural forms.

Let me ask you this: India, China and America seem to be the three nations with large enough, and wealthy enough, populations to sustain their own independent cultural forms—commercially speaking. Why hasn't that seemed to happen with Bhangra in India?

Well, it has. But you have to understand that Bhangra is a very specific kind of music, and in India it's popular now, to some degree. But in India, Bollywood and Hindi-language is more accessible to people; it's not simply that Bhangra isn't popular. Also, preferences and taste preferences are different. So where you have a community and you have a large Diaspora, what works in India—and I know first-hand as a DJ—doesn't fly in the UK and it doesn't work here. People's tastes are different. There was a moment in the early 90s where these Bhangra bands were becoming quite popular in the UK. They went to India and no one was feelin' them. Because India is so diverse culturally: so many languages, the largest middle-class in the world, it's hard to generalize peoples preferences. Only after Punjabi MC's track broke internationally did it break in India, very much in the same way a Madonna track would break in India. It got put on a soundtrack in a Bollywood movie—one of the first Indian movies to have a soundtrack of music that wasn't in the film. Usually the soundtrack of Bollywood films are musicals: you see the movie, you hear the music, you buy the CD. Here [in the States] when we buy a soundtrack, we know that what gets licensed for the soundtrack may not be in the film; it's more about the idea or the thematic connection. That helped break that record in India. In fact, that record broke before Jay-Z touched it. In fact, the reason that Jay-Z even knew about it is that he went to Europe and he said "what the hell is this?! . . . "

Ok. Let's take a few steps back: Earlier you mentioned that you got exposed to Bhangra music through your family back home [in India], and that, in turn, stimulated your interest in DJ-ing. Is it accurate to say then that this enterprise proceeded from that interest in DJ-ing?

Well, I grew up in a business-oriented family. So I have this little entrepreneurial . . . problem. I've always worked for my dad, growing up; he had several businesses. For several years I worked at his store in midtown Manhattan and, you know, that was my business education. So there's something very innate in me about not working for anyone, having a certain kind of hustle going. So there's that side to me. And having done it a lot—having dealt with cash growing up—that was always inherent. I always found a way to maintain some autonomy. So when I started DJing, it was a business. I always took it seriously as a business. It took a while to get it down on paper, and what have you, but the minute money was exchanged, it was a business to me. It started with my cousins and just grew from there. I have a real keen sense and interest in branding and remaining a viable entity. I came to it through Bhangra music and as a DJ, but I see it as a larger thing, a larger idea.

What's your relationship—and the relationship of Bhangra—to the American music industry?

To the American music industry, if anything, I'm just a squirrel trying to get my nut. To music industry at large, I'm not overly interested in a "grand success" model. I believe that slow and steady wins the race. After 9 some-odd years, I just signed a deal with Koch Records. And I'm really happy with it. I like the company. I like the way that they work. I also don't see it as my meal ticket; it's just adding something to my enterprise. Koch tends to align with artists that already have their own following. And I think that the most important thing that a label can do for you is to get your music on the shelf. One of the benefits of actually having a business of my own is understanding the other side of the equation, is knowing that the label is a company: they have X amount of resources and the things that will give them a return—and the people who are nicest to work with—is where the energy is going to go. So make it easy for them, and it will be easier for you. In the case of the Punjabi MC record, that song was licensed in this territory. The licensing label made tons of money on the song, but you couldn't find it in the stores. I say that to illustrate that several strategies exist for monetizing music; it's key to understand the tendencies of the label you're affiliated with.

In closing, what are your hopes for Bhangra? Would you like to see it become a cultural institution in the way of, say, hip-hop?

I don't know. I find a lot of similarities between Bhangra and Dancehall, insofar as they both come from a very specific cultural experience . . . as does hip-hop. Not to discount hip-hop in any way. Arguably, hip-hop references Dancehall in many ways. Many of the hip-hop pioneers were second-generation Jamaican and Caribbean immigrants. But the whole notion or structure of success may be problematic. The music is powerful; it has a certain aesthetic and I think it will always have an audience. I'd like to see it exposed to a wider audience in whatever way possible.

Have you contemplated an exit strategy for yourself? As a DJ? As a businessperson?

It's funny, for many years I said that I would stop Basement Bhangra after 10 years, because 10 years is good for a club night . . . And part of me still wants to, believe me. I am not lying. I'm like: let 'em crave, let 'em want it. Go out when you're on a high note. The party definitely requires a large commitment. People have counseled me to hand it over to someone else to run, but I can't do that. In nine years—and we do eighteen a year—I've only missed two nights. If the party starts to weaken, I'll be the first one to say stop. Everything comes to an end; it all functions on a cycle. If the other facets of the company continue to grow, I'll be more inclined to step back.

Source: Cheeks, Demetrius. "The Outsider." NYU Stern School of Business paper, *Opportunity,* March 6, 2007. Reprinted with permission.

Sweta Srivastava Vikram, "Racist or a Victim?"
(2009)

Sweta Srivastava Vikram is a multigenre writer and the author of two poetry chapbooks, Kaleidoscope: An Asian Journey of Colors *and* Because All Is Not Lost. *She is the coauthor of* Whispering Woes of Ganges & Zambezi. *Born and raised in India, Vikram now lives in New York City. In her essay "Racist or a Victim?" Vikram challenges the notion that only white Americans are racist, casting a critical eye on her own community.*

"You are *gori-chitthi*. What problems you have," said one of my *desi* associates when in one of my idealistic moments, I said, "I can't believe people, even today, judge others based on their skin color!" This person, disdainfully, assumed that my life was problem-free because I was a relatively lighter shade of brown than her. Ironically, she hired cleaners based on their ethnicity.

It took over 200 years for one of the largest democracies in the world to pretend to look beyond color. Over a year ago, the world witnessed history in the making when Barack Hussein Obama became the first African American to be elected as the President of the United States of America. But did Obama truly redeem the world or was his victory a symbolic step? Obama might have won majority of the African American votes on election night, but at one point, wasn't he accused, by his own race, of not being truly black? It seems there are "accepted" and "unaccepted" shades of color within each race.

Anyway, on Wednesday morning, November 5th, 2008, the air in NYC smelt different. There were celebratory clouds hovering over the City and at work. In my exhilarated mood, I screamed, "Congratulations," to my coworkers. One of my black colleagues, one of the kindest and professional person otherwise, said, "Congratulations for

what?" "Because Obama won," I explained. "Oh, okay," she added in a suspicious tone. Just then, two other African American women walked up to the same coworker and said, "Congratulations! We made it!" In response, they got a warm hug. I felt alienated. I wondered if my words offended her. If they did, was it because I am a shade different—brown as opposed to black?

It's amazing how, we, South Asians in the west, complain about racism when a significant number commit acts of bigotry themselves. For instance, even today, some people continue to make trips to India to handpick wives/daughter-in-laws. The key criterion in the screening process is "How fair is she?" The woman could be a witch from Eastwick, but all is forgiven if she is light-skinned.

This pseudo-progressive family I know of went to India a few years ago to find their son the perfect wife—"Fair-skinned." I say pseudo-progressive because on one hand they gave their own children the best education, lifestyle, and exposure possible; on the other, they desired a non-ambitious, extremely fair, convent-educated girl as a trophy daughter-in-law, who they could show off to their socialite friends. On the bride-hunting trip, the family stayed at a luxurious five-star hotel in New Delhi to impress the girls' families, who made the final cut; watched videos of each of the candidates dancing, walking, and talking; and, after days of humiliating, degrading, and rejecting the potential girls, announced their final verdict. The fairest maiden amongst them all was selected as the future daughter-in-law. Mind you, these same Indian-Americans voted for Obama to sound progressive, but ultimately made the commitment of a lifetime based on color.

Across the globe, the situation isn't very different. On seeing my picture on my book's back cover, one of my mother's acquaintance screeched,

"Your daughter is fair. Like a foreigner." In the Indian culture, her words would qualify for the elite-class compliment. But I felt nauseated and appalled because my hard work was ignored; the only point noticed was the color of my skin.

On the same trip, as I read *Bombay Times*, one of the local newspapers in Mumbai, I shuddered with shock. Despite the economic growth and aesthetic modernization of India, certain traditions remain unchanged, like the ritual of rejecting and selecting brides based on the color of their skin. The matrimonial columns read: "Wanted tall, fair, convent-educated, etc." Classified ads on Craigslist have more dignified description for furniture than some of these "Bride-seeking" columns.

Growing up, I remember a cousin aunt, who spent her day rubbing "fairness creams" like Fair & Lovely on her face, hoping her skin would become light. She was considered unsuitable bride material by prospective suitors because her complexion was darker than the benchmark they had in mind. Never mind her astute brain or delicate features or warm personality, her parents had to finally pay dowry so she could settle down.

Bigotry is heinous. But before we accuse another human being of it, shouldn't we ask ourselves a simple question: if there is a bigot in all of us, can we truly expect prejudice to ever die?

Source: Vikram, Sweta Srivastava. "Racist or a Victim?" 2009. Used with permission of the author.

Athena Kashyap, Four Poems
(2009)

In 1947, the Indian Independence Act dissolved the British Empire in India and led to the creation of the sovereign nation of Pakistan. Sectarian tension, coupled with conflicts over what regions of India would join Pakistan, exacerbated instability and created massive suffering. As millions of displaced people crossed over the border to join their religious majority, long-standing, deep divisions between Hindu and Muslim parties erupted into violence. Estimates vary, but likely several hundreds of thousands of people were killed in the ensuing riots and massacres, and thousands more died of deprivation during the displacement. Memory of the Partition remains strong and traumatic for its survivors and their families in Pakistan, India, and abroad.

Athena Kashyap grew up in Bangalore and Bombay in India and has been living in the United States since she was 18. Her parents are children of emigrants from Lahore, now in Pakistan, who settled in Delhi and Bombay.

Kashyap teaches writing at City College of San Francisco. Her poems and essays examine the concept of travel and dislocation: the impact of different and changing locations on personal lives. In the following four poems, Kashyap explores the ways in which history and the homeland remain integral to people's new lives in new lands. In particular, "coming down the mountain" is a reflection on the continuing impact of the Partition on South Asian immigrants in the United States. Lahore, the capital of what is now Pakistani Punjab, saw some of the worst sectarian violence among Muslims, Sikhs, and Hindus.

coming down the mountain

Great-grandfather enters my room in Los Angeles, clutching two clumps of roots still bleeding Himalayan mud. He says he's sorry to come so late at night, but he can't find his way. The family house he built in

Lahore still stands, but neighbors have moved in and his family is gone. At the University, the botany lab he founded no longer bears his name. His students have aged terribly—they look right through him. He has trouble with his eyes, sees just half of everything—his students, the map of India on the wall. Even the city landscape is missing parts—temples, sari shops, certain street names. The last thing he remembers is climbing the mountain, up from the city he once knew and loved. He looks so tired, I want to help him but am myself adrift, barely flickering in this city's sea of lights. Our family's dispersed like seeds, searching for each other and their own selves in clouds of lost mountains. *I see*, says Grandfather with his half-blind eyes, but then he's gone, waving dead roots in my face.

world café

I'm diluted, my skin grown permeable, breathable.
With Abraham in his cafe, conversation oscillates, a dance—
he suggests I try *dolma*s in his thick desert English,
I vacillate, trying to locate the exact geography of my craving.
My body succumbs, my tongue a compass for distant tastes:
crunchy Korean fish eyes, sugar-chili Gujarati vegetables,
Burmese floating soups—murky ponds with flotsams of beef and vegetables, red simmering Kerala crab curries,
the salty sweetness of my lover's dark skin.
So many lives I've lived—I revisit them all and more in these cafes,
truck stops for travelers needing to shake off and drink in selves.

the corner store

The owner of the corner store does not know my name, nor I his.
He does not even nod when I enter, but stands gruff and still.
When I complain about the price—fifty cents for an onion—
he tells me "buy elsewhere." But when he chats with his children,

just come back from school, his voice melts. For a moment,
the sound of soft clapping, clouds and rain takes me back to Mumbai,
the sea-washed sidewalks, bare feet slipping out of rubber slippers.
The J-Church screeches past. I look up, the children are gone.
Only mounds of tins, moldy produce surround us once again.
I pay for my onion and count the change. We are careful
not to let our fingers touch. Mountains of miles trail both of us—
we have to keep them untangled.

America

Throat of vase
filled with pebbles
from afar, and memories
plump and sweet, crossing over
continents, thirsty seas, generations
spilling into this living room, bodies
dissolving into each other, strains of music:
o sathi rey, aee, aee, tere bhi nabhi kya jeena—
Soulja boy grew up in this hoe, watch me crank it—
shifting this idea we had about you and me, these worlds
we've built out of paper—visas, passports, bank accounts,
collapsing at the center of time unfolding, the splendor of being—
no fathers and mothers, grandfathers and grandmothers, great grandmothers,
no one, not even our past selves, no one there to catch up, demand explanations.

Source: Kashyap, Athena. "coming down the mountain," "world café," "the corner store," and "America." 2009. "coming down the mountain" was originally published in *The Fourth River* Issue 6 (2009). "world café," "the corner store," and "America" were originally published in *The Noe Valley Voice* May 2009. "world café," "the corner store," and "America" were published in *Same Difference*, edited by Smita Singh. London: J Publishing Company, 2010. Used with permission of author, *The Fourth River*, and *The Noe Valley Voice*.

Rajiv Srinivasan, "My Battle Within: The Identity Crisis of a Hindu Soldier in the U.S. Army"
(2009)

Rajiv Srinivasan was born in Chennai (formerly known as Madras), on the southeastern coast of India. When he was a child, he and his parents moved to Roanoke, Virginia. He graduated from the U.S. Military Academy at West Point, where he studied Arabic and comparative politics. Srinivasan was commissioned in the U.S. Army, and he served a year long deployment in Khandahar, Afghanistan. Srinivasan wrote "My Battle Within" for the Hindu American Foundation's 2009 NextGen Essay Contest, The Importance of a Hindu-American Identity. In "My Battle Within," Srinivasan explains how he reconciles Hindu principles with his combat mission and how his religion affects his actions as an American.

The barrel of my M4 assault rifle is slender, black, and cold. The rippled plastic grips fit ergonomically to a mission driven hand; one that aggresses to protect a nation and way of life. With each trigger squeeze, a 5.56 caliber bullet breaches the muzzle at 2,900 feet per second with the sole purpose of taking another's life. Despite its lethality, this weapon is only a piece of metal. It is nothing without the mind and heart of the soldier perched behind it. As I don my body armor, grab my weapon, and prepare to lead my platoon of 32 soldiers into Afghanistan, I hesitate. I turn to the portrait of Krishna in my office and demand of him, "What is the worth of this fight? Is it worth our limbs, our lives, or the heartbreak of our parents? What cause is so important as to merit the coming violence?" And so begins my war within: the quest for an identity.

Like most Indian youth in the U.S., I faced the inner conflict between my Indian and American identities. At home, I watched Bollywood movies and prayed to Hindu deities; but at school, I spoke English, played football, and did whatever I could to emulate a typical American childhood. I felt pulled in two directions: one identity abandoning my Indian heritage, the other neglecting my American way of life. Thus, I went through my most formative years without knowing who I was, nor what I stood for.

As high school came to an end, I hastily made the decision to attend the U.S. Military Academy at West Point, but did so in vain. At the time, I was not sure about being an Army officer. I was just looking for a shining star for my résumé. I was looking for a way to pay for college. Perhaps on a deeper level, I was looking for a sense of belonging. I wanted an identity to which everyone in my immediate surroundings could relate and respect.

The U.S. Army is a rare home for an Indian immigrant, but no other endeavor has ever given me the professional and spiritual fulfillment than the experience of military service. The army challenged my most extreme patriotic influences against my peaceful Hindu beliefs. How could I serve patriotically as a U.S. Army Officer, owning the responsibility of waging war against our national enemies, but remain a man of the Hindu faith believing in the peaceful coexistence of all beings? This was a deep philosophical confrontation, but I accepted it with resolve.

Through days of wet, cold, hot, humid, tired, and hungry, I maintained a vegetarian diet. After a long day of military training, I returned to my barracks to indulge myself in the poetry of the Bhagavad Gita. I found solace in Arjuna's struggle as a shamed warrior fighting against his blood. I found strength in Krishna's assertion of conviction and discipline. I found that, though typical Hindus and Soldiers lead vastly different lives, both share a common purpose: to serve a higher calling for good. Thus, there was no need for a struggle between my American and Hindu identities; rather, finding strength in one made me stronger in the other.

My Hindu-American Identity is now a defining part of my life. As Arjuna beckons of his charioteer, "How can I wage war against my family? I would rather surrender, than commit such atrocities," Krishna affirms that it is our duty as Hindus to do what we believe is right, regardless of the opposition. When peaceful attempts to reconcile fail, we must be prepared to defend the values in which we so whole-heartedly believe. It is this reasoning that convinces Arjuna to fight to protect his kingdom. It is this reasoning that Gandhi used when supporting the British Army's aggression against the Nazis in World War II. This reasoning is why I feel so compelled to defend this nation, that has given my family countless gifts, against those who wish to do it unnecessary harm. I do not fight *in spite* of my religion. I fight *inspired* by it.

The importance of the Hindu-American identity extends beyond a vague resolve to fight for what you believe in. Each of us is faced daily with moral challenges in this country, and our reactions to them define our spiritual resolve. This nation is in an ethical crisis; from the poorest of American ghettos through the wealthiest of corporate banks. Hindu-Americans are a dominant source of influence, wealth, and intellect in this nation, so what does it say of our personal constitutions if we tolerate the ethical degradation around us? We have the means to drastically improve the ethical standards in this country. We owe it to ourselves as Hindu-Americans to defend, as Arjuna does his Kingdom, the moral foundations which have made this country a haven for religious and ethnic tolerance. We could collectively sit on the sidelines and criticize our leadership as many Americans do. But if we aspire to follow Krishna's guidance, it is our duty to proactively defend the integrity that upholds our great society. This is the new importance, the calling, of the Hindu-American identity: inspired by our faith, we must actively rebuild our nation's character and preserve it for our posterity. So I ask of each Hindu-American, what have you done to make America stronger for our children?

Krishna's picture sits in my office as a constant reminder of my Hindu-American Identity; a reminder that strength in principle outweighs the comfort of indifference. No matter what challenges lie ahead of me, I will wear my uniform each day with pride knowing I am defending a nation I truly love, and caring for a platoon of soldiers who do the same. It is through the discharge of my duties to God and Country that I have finally found the identity I was looking for all along; that of a fulfilled Hindu-American.

Source: Srinivasan, Rajiv. "My Battle Within: The Identity Crisis of a Hindu Soldier in the US Army." 2009. Originally published by the Hindu American Foundation. http://www.hafsite.org/media/pr/rajiv-srinivasan. Reprinted with permission.

Ainee Fatima, "To My Mother," "Blues from a Black Burqah," and "Graceland Part I"

(2009)

Ainee Fatima is an Indian American poet and a spoken-word artist. She is a two-time winner of Chicago's "Louder Than a Bomb" youth poetry slam, the largest of its kind in the United States. Fatima's poetry explores her experiences growing up Muslim in the United States and the ways immigrant families navigate the often-opposing pressures of Americanization and tradition. In "To My Mother," Fatima compares the family ideal of arranged marriage with her growing desire to choose her own spouse. In "Blues from a Black Burqah," she considers how familial relationships and structures are changing the longer the Fatima family lives in the United States. "Graceland Part I" is a humorous poem in which Fatima sheds her burqah for Elvis Presley's clothes, a metaphor for acceptance of her own multifaceted identity.

TO MY MOTHER

My mother is at the garage deflating the tires of my red Schwinn,
Her finger depresses the nozzle.
Over the hiss, *"Zainab Auntie's 18 year old daughter, Leila ran away from home on her bike.*
Ainee, good Muslim girls don't ride bikes; they stay home."
My ten year old head nods in agreement.
I've been disciplined to agree with everything they say
Because I don't know any better and tradition is always followed.
But why would Leila run away?

For the next eight years,
The red bike lay on its side next to the white garage door,
No one ever rode it again; someone must've thrown it away.
All that remains is the rusted outline of the bike.

October rain falls hard, pressing
Ochre maple leaves on sidewalks.
Wind howls in the ruby Maple
Like the "no" that cyclones my eyes each time they say
"You're ready to get married."
If I am old enough to get married off,
I should be old enough to choose to whom.
A child's soul is more important than tradition being kept.

The wind trips the motion detector of the garage light,
And through the glass, I stare at the rust outline of the bike.
In the window's condensation, I trace away the rims that still stain the cement,

Drawing a stick figure of myself riding away on it.

There is no one home.
I pull the suitcase from my mother's closet.
The traffic light over the intersection of Crawford and Touhy Avenue
Goes from red to green to yellow before I make up my mind to open it.
Inside, all the clothes my mother got for her wedding lie dormant.
Beneath the green, blue, yellow, pink saris and Rajasthani silk,
I remove her red wedding dress.

I want to see if it fits.
If this dress fits me as it hugged my mother's seventeen year old body.
If this idea of an arranged marriage fits.

The traffic light bleeds red down the street,
With my nose soft against the window,
I hear Pachelbel's Canon in D major in my mind.

The lace touches my bare shoulder blades.
Flat folds of red satin,
A casing for a forced love nineteen years ago.
But it's the red of the bike I want touching my skin, not the dress.

Outside, a whoosh of cars pass me in the wake of a life I loathe
I force aged metal hooks tight against my spine,
Fastening me into a future with a stranger.
It doesn't fit; this is not meant for me.
I know I will never love.

My parents' idea of freedom is a ring binding my life to another.
I will never be free to climb onto the Schwinn
And ride through a green light to flee into this October night to join Leila.
The traffic light always remains red in reality.

The autumn rain pops on the window,
The light changes from yellow to red,
Tree limbs sway as the wind howls,
The rusty stain remains.

So much depends
On the memory of a red bike
Glazed by rain,
Beside the white garage.

BLUES FROM A BLACK BURQAH

I.

We moved into our house when I was eight.

My grandfather wanted to ensure the house was blessed, so

He sat at the kitchen table writing prayers on paper rectangles

To place on doorways of the house.

Above door in the green kitchen: *There is no God but Allah.*

On the brown front door: *Thee do we worship, and Thine aid we seek.*

In the doorjam of my room: *Praise to Allah the most Beneficent and Merciful.*

As he wrote this out,

Ink from the word *rahim* bled through the paper,

Tattooing "mercy" onto the table top.

Once the house was blessed

My mother hung a drawing of mine from kindergarten.

It was the same crayon house every kid draws:

A square house, two windows with curtains -

A door, don't forget the knob,

A chimney on the peaked roof with smoke curling out in spite of

the smiley face sun shining in the corner,

3 red tulips against a white picket fence,

Smiling stick figures lined up according to height,

"Home is where the heart is," bubble-lettered along the bottom.

It was a happy home.

II.

In the years following,

Dinners opened with *Bismillahi wa'ala baraka-tillah*

plates passed over my head in a blur,

wooden troughs of basmati rice,

white platters of curries,

silver dishes of tomato chutney, yet

My eyes always fixed on the word *rahim* magnified under my water glass.

an inky fish floating under my glass

Many times they yelled my name because I was lost in the aquarium under my cup

Rahim floated in calligraphy curving spines

Tracing in it with eyes the arc of its tail

I tried to drink mercy from an early age

With every mouthful I drank a bit of it away.

Until it finally faded.

Now there is no mercy for me at the table.

Each night before her bedtime prayers, with tasbih in hand.

My mother walked into our rooms, whispering a string

Of Arabic words I do not know.

As she slides each bead, she leans over our beds

Blowing prayers of protection, praying we wake up each morning.

Hoping, that the gravity of God's words make their way to our souls

So we may forge a path that keeps our faith intact.

Making sure obedience does not falter, for the Prophet once said

"Paradise lies at the feet of your mother."

III.

"Home is where the heart is, Ainee. What happened?!"

She threw the drawing at my feet the day I disobeyed her.

I bit my tongue and resisted to give her an answer.

"I just want to write . . . "

Months following that, Grandfather's prayers were taken down

In result of the wallpaper being torn down.

My mother never bothered to put them back up.

My father never came home for dinner anymore.

Instead of breaking bread, we broke each other's hearts.

Each night before bed, she kisses prayers onto foreheads,

She walks past my bed saying nothing.

Nothing will push her to turn her head towards me.

She doesn't pray for me anymore.

My name is no longer on her tongue.

I was always told to write what I know.

But, I do not know my mother

Nor my father or this home anymore.

GRACELAND: PART I

"I ain't no saint, but I have tried never to do anything that would hurt my family or offend God."

—Elvis Presley

I shift into park, kill the engine, unbuckle my seatbelt.

I've been casing the joint for days.

The Tennessee twilight hangs in pastel orange, blue, purple.
As sweat drips down my temple, the light above the front entrance goes out.
And step out of the minivan into the Memphis evening.
I pop the trunk, grab my guitar case.
(You will breathe in deep through nose now)
The air is clean, close, and sweet.

My black burq'ha conceals me as I climb each music note on the gate and drop in.
I move unnoticed past the stone lions, and
Slide in through the window into the kitchen.
Past guitars, past gold and platinum records, past gun collections that glow beneath lights:
I pass it all—even the velvet rope that secures the second floor from tourists.
No one is here except me, my guitar case,
And the things of the King I came for.
Inside the double padded doors of his bedroom,
A shoulder high statue of Christ greets me.
I slide Jesus some skin and wink at him.
"Gotta date with the King, Issa."

Pleated red velvet lines the bedroom walls.
Smoked mirrors trimmed in black velvet.
I put my guitar case on the bed, next to the '68 come-back leather jacket.

I'll get that on my way out.
I stroll slowly into in his closet:
Hundreds of jumpsuits
I caress them as I pass,
Chinese Dragon, no.
Bengali Tiger, no.
Powder Blue two-piece, maybe.
The 77 Hawai'i gold-studded American Eagle on white, absolutely.
I liberate myself from my *Burqah* and slide on the jumpsuit.
Adjust the belt, fasten the cape . . . the cape
I make my way back into the bedroom, and
The drag co-efficient is Elvis awesome.
In the smoky mirror rimmed in black velvet,
arms stretched eagle wing wide
I'm a Muslim woman who must be covered; I accept that,
But I'm also American, baby: You accept that.

Wise men say
only fools rush in
But I can't help
falling in love with you

Source: Fatima, Ainee. "To My Mother," "Blues from a Black Burqah," and "Graceland: Part I." 2009. Used with permission of author.

Sanjay Patel, Interview by grain edit
(2010)

Sanjay Patel moved to the United States in 1980, along with his Gujarati parents, who ran a motel in Southern California. His first book, The Little Book of Hindu Deities, *includes comic book–style illustrations and short descriptions of Hindu gods. His book* Ramayana: Divine Loophole *is a graphic-design adaptation of the Hindu epic. Patel hopes to create a bridge between Indian immigrants and their Indian American children, retelling the ancient stories in a way that makes sense to young people today. The following is his 2010 interview with grain edit, a design blog.*

Chronicle Books has just released *Ramayana: Divine Loophole* the latest book from Pixar anima-tor and illustrator Sanjay Patel. As one of the core legends of Hindu mythology, *Ramayana* recounts a tale of Rama, a god-turned-prince, and his quest to rescue his wife Sita after she was kidnapped by a demon king. Sanjay is able to breathe new life into this 2,500-year-old epic tale with over 150 pages of lush, detailed illustrations.

In this interview, he gives us a glimpse into the making of the book and some of the challenges he faced along the way.

Let's start off with a little bit about your background. Where are you from originally?

I was born in the UK and lived there till I was five. My parents then immigrated to Southern California, and began running and living in a motel off of route 66. So next time you're in San Bernardino be sure to drop in on my folks at the Lido Motel . . . They've been living and running the motel for thirty fucking years now!

When and how did you become interested in illustration?

As far as I can remember I was drawing. In elementary school my third grade teacher gave me a wonderful collection of hard bound vintage Superman comics. She wrote an inscription inside the book about what a wonderful artist I was and how I apparently had so much talent. She must have had me mixed up with someone else. Because the first thing I did with that book was draw all over the pages adding poop and pee coming out of all the great Superman panels. Eventually I began respecting my comics a lot more. I was really obsessed with a marvel artist named Michael Golden and his series called The NAM. From there I started watching a ton of Robotek and Looney tunes. But it was only until my high school art teacher gave me the famous Nicolaides *The Natural Way To Draw* book, did I finally get what drawing and illustration was all about. I dropped my comics and fell in love with Michelangelo, the Renaissance, and Norman Rockwell. The desire to communicate through a visual language has stayed with me ever since.

What led you to create a book on the Ramayana?

There were a lot of different impulses that led to the decision to tackle the Ramayana. In many ways

The Little Book of Hindu Deities was a success and at the same time really didn't capture the full scope of my talent. As I began to read the *Ramayana* it became very clear that the mythology was loaded with a visually rich world. It was also very clear that no one has tried interpreting the epic story in pictures and illustration with a modern graphic flair. Or at least in a visual language that was in line with my aesthetics and love of mid-century animation.

How much time did you put into researching for the project?

I'm almost embarrassed to say this but I spent close to four years on the project. It took me the better part of a year to read different translations of the story and write my own summarized version. After selling both my manuscript and a full black and white dummy I took a year sabbatical from PIXAR to work on the ridiculously detailed vector illustrations full time. After working day and night for over a year and not leaving my apartment for days at a time I eventually ended up burning out. Luckily I discovered yoga and therapy and was able to finish the project.

How long did it take you to create the illustrations for the book?

Once a pencil sketch was done which took about two days I could jump into Adobe Illustrator and start building vector shapes, which took another three days depending on how complicated the illustration was. If I was lucky I would get things right, but in almost every case I redid things dozens of times.

What were some of the obstacles/challenges that you faced along the way?

The biggest obstacle was of course the scope of the project, *The Ramayana* has dozens of character and locations, mega war scenes and complicated crowd illustrations. But somehow I was able to get things running fairly quickly that is until till

I decided to redo everything top to bottom a few times. I kept fighting to work in a design style that was cute and silly, when *The Ramayana* is anything but that. As a reaction of too much cute I ended up turning the illustration into something much more grown up and stiff. Eventually the design pendulum settled somewhere in between cute and boring. Somewhere that I hope captures the action and drama in a fun modern style that honors this great mythology.

During the day you work at Pixar, how did you find time to work on this massive project?

That's a long story, but what I can say is this. Growing up in a motel in a grimy part of San Bernardino I had very few friends let alone neighbors. I spent most of my time drawing alone. In many ways once I come home from work I want nothing more than to return to that same comfort of pencil and paper and solitude. Not much has changed in that way.

What artists/books served as inspiration for your illustrations?

My office at Pixar is covered in Charley Harper pages. I actually bought two copies of the massive monograph that Ammo Books put out. I took one of the books and had it professionally cut and started using all the pages as wall paper for my office. So of course there is a ton of Harper in my everyday life and in my *Ramayana*. Like many other Cal Arts students I love mid century illustration. My favorites are Saul Steinberg, Provensons, & Sasek. Of course there are tons more artist that I love like Peter Arno, Tezuka, Steig, Boutavant, Lindberg, Wyeth, . . . And of course the great master Mr. Bill Watterson and his Calvin & Hobbes.

In what ways did the initial concepts differ from the finished book?

I wanted the book to be cute and silly like a Richard Scary version of *The Ramayana*. Instead I think I ended up with a weird Charley Harper, animation hybrid. Hopefully the combination works.

Source: Patel, Sanjay. Interview. 2010. http://grainedit.com/2010/02/26/sanjay-patel-interview/. © 2010 by www.grainedit.com.

Nadia Syahmalina, "Kamu Bukan Orang Sini"
(2001)

Historically, only a relatively small number of Indonesians have immigrated to the United States. As part of a national effort to combat communism abroad, U.S. foreign aid programs encouraged students from all over Asia to experience American higher education; so most of the early migrants from Indonesia arrived during the 1950s as exchange students. The political upheaval and violence that followed the ousting of Indonesia's first president, Sukarno, resulted in a new wave of Indonesian immigrants to the United States during the mid- to late 1960s. Most of these new arrivals were Indonesians of Chinese descent. As the turmoil subsided in Indonesia, so did immigration. Today, as in the past, most Indonesians come to the United States for educational or economic reasons, and most reside in Southern California. Indonesia's cultural, ethnic, and religious diversity, coupled with the small number of immigrants, may have attributed to the absence of ethnic community development on the scale of that in other Asian American communities.

Nadia Syahmalina was born in Jakarta, Indonesia, and raised in Morgantown, West Virginia. Her essay "Kamu Bukan Orang Sini" was originally published by InvAsian *in 2001 and was published again the next year by the (currently inactive) Society of Indonesian Americans. Syahamalina lives in the Washington, DC area and is vice-president of the Indonesian Muslim Association of America. "Kamu Bukan Orang Sini" describes the cultural and generational conflicts in immigrant Indonesian families and the difficulty of finding one's place in either country.*

My 17-year-old sister has not set foot in Indonesia since she was four years old. I see her struggling in trying to count the numbers in Indonesian, and I am reminded of myself.

There was a point in my life when I had a hard time pronouncing "satu, dua, tiga, empat" which in English is "one, two, three, four." I still find it hard to even say "selamat pagi" sometimes, but I know that her troubles would far exceed mine because she is just starting out. I know that she would be hassled for having this impairment. People, it seems, find it hard to swallow that this girl who looks like them could be in anyway different.

Their inability to understand is what usually brings out the worse in them. They start with asking questions, and when they find the answers unsatisfactory, they find other ways to satisfy themselves; and this is usually at the expense of the one being questioned. How do I know this? Because I had been the one questioned, the one at the end of gibes and mockeries. The sole reason behind all this is that I was different—internally.

Being different on the inside is more hard to grasp because you can't really see it, and usually people judge you on the exterior. So it was therefore accepted if you were different physically, and it was appalling to some that one who looks so similar outwardly could be so different inwardly.

My parents also had similar opinions all throughout my childhood. They usually never forget to remind me of how different I was from my friends because they were not Indonesian. I was not an "orang sini" whenever I wanted to spend the night or go to a party at friends. I was not an "orang sini" whenever I wanted to date boys. Most of the things that I wanted to do with my friends that were foreign to them were answered with "kamu bukan orang sini, jadi kamu tidak boleh."

As the years went by the invitations to parties and sleepovers slowly decreased, and my friends became afraid of inviting me to anything because I usually wasn't allowed to go. At this, I distanced myself from my friends and became extremely confused. My parents, though, didn't seem to notice the change in my attitude, so they continued with their remarks, unaware of how belittling they were.

They then added that my real friends would be in Indonesia because Indonesians could understand me more. Confused and hurt, I wanted to go to Indonesia and be an "orang sini," be among my "true friends," and just be accepted.

I got the chance to go to Indonesia in the summer of 1997. I was a very eager person when I boarded that plane in Singapore. "In a couple of hours I would be home," I said to myself. I kept checking the on-flight map just to see how close the plane got to Jakarta. As soon as the rice paddies (farm lands) below came to view, this up-till-now-unexplainable feeling came over me.

When I had stepped out of that plane and breathed in the air that was perfumed with the smell of wet grass and rice growing in the fields, I did feel home. I couldn't wait to meet my relatives and old childhood friends again, and especially make new lifelong friendships (just like my parents said). Everything was fine during the first few weeks. Only after a couple of months had passed I noticed something was not right.

I longed for the smell of my house in the States and to gab with the friends who I had distanced myself from, but I shrugged this off as homesickness; and besides, I was "home," right? So I suppressed my longing and tried so hard to adjust to my new surroundings. It was never enough though, because no matter how hard I tried, I could never really fit in. Everything I did got a disapproving look and every word I said got a snicker or a smirk because it was odd to them how an Indonesian spoke or acted like a foreigner. Some even found it insulting.

I couldn't walk around my neighborhood without hearing whispers or catcalls. The cab drivers would look at me funny once I spoke even a "hello." They'd ask my mom or whoever was with me at the time, "Bu, nih anak kok susah amat yah ngomong. Mang dari mana sih?" My relatives were pretty hostile to me too because I disrupted their seemingly quiet life. I could never do anything right, and making friends was even harder than I thought.

Most parents were afraid that I would have a bad influence on their children, since I came from a country that had an enticingly bad culture and reputation. I once heard a rumor that I was the cause behind a friend's present non-diligent behavior. The adopted belief among my neighbors was that I was "an unruly child with no manners."

I then realized how much of an outsider I really was, how I wasn't accepted at all. It hurt, and it hurt a lot. This was supposed to be my "home," the place where I would feel like I belonged, but I didn't feel like I belonged at all. Instead I felt the complete opposite. "What am I supposed to do, aku mo kemana lagi? Ini kan home saya, tapi kenapa aku gak merasa demikian?" I'd say to myself over and over again. I resorted to crying almost every single night because I was so confused.

I wanted to go back to America, but in America I'm not accepted—well that's what my parents said. And I couldn't stay here: I wasn't accepted here also. I felt like I had nowhere to go, since I wasn't accepted in either of the two countries that I had resided in.

After a year and a half in Indonesia of trying so hard to conform and almost succeeding, a twist of fate came and I returned to America. Did this solve my problem? Nope, it only added to it. I was very wary of how people acted towards me and remained very distant, maybe even more so. Someone summed it all up when he said that "I was here, yet wasn't here."

My parents' words replayed itself in my mind almost on an everyday basis. I could not understand what brought them to say those things to me at such an impressionable age. After many arguments and bitter quarrels, though, I finally understood the reasons behind their actions. I realized that this all came about because they were afraid that I would lose my Indonesian heritage, forget who I was and where I came from.

Their apprehension increased by the fact that they were amateurs in this: They had no one to consult with about family matters, especially on how to raise children in a foreign land. So they reared their children the best way they knew how. After this moment of realization, I no longer harbored deep anger for my parents; now it is more like sympathy. They were trying their best after all.

From all this I've concluded that you don't need to be almost mirror images of someone for you to be "kindred spirits" with them. Dissimilarity isn't so bad nor is it a thing for ridicule. You do not generally need to be skilled in the native language to have pride in your country nor do you have to act like everyone else does over there to be proud of where you come from. That should not be what gives you pride. If it is then that is a false sense of pride, because true pride comes from within.

There are many people who talk Indonesian fluently and eat bakmi and somay on a regular basis who aren't proud of being an Indonesian. What makes them better than those Indonesians who were born and/or raised out of Indonesia who do have pride yet speak in broken Indonesian and eat pancakes and pizza almost everyday?

Neither is this whole cultural conflict the fault of the parent who brought the child to a foreign land. This kind of assumption is wrong too. It's not their fault. It is just a risk a family takes when emigrating or immigrating to another country. Cultures will clash, identity crisis will happen. It's just a matter of whether a family handle it or not; and sadly for me, my family couldn't.

In the end, though, I think going through the rough and turbulent times was worth it. My parents realized their mistakes and now embrace a more open attitude towards strange and new things, and a communication line is now open between parent and child. They realize that maybe their children are also an "orang sini" as well as an Indonesian.

And maybe because of my stay in Indonesia, my relatives won't be as hostile and my neighbors will have a more understanding attitude towards my sister when she goes there. Seeing her struggle with the numbers "delapan, sembilan, sepuluh" I sincerely hope so.

Translations from Indonesian:

Selamat pagi: Good morning

Kamu bukan orang sini: You are not someone from here.

Orang sini: Someone here

Kamu bukan orang sini, jadi kamu tidak boleh: You are not someone here therefore you can't.

Bu, nih anak kok susah amat yah ngomong. Mang dari mana sih?: Mam, this child has a lot of difficulty in talking. Where is she from anyway?

Aku mo kemana lagi? Ini kan home saya, tapi kenapa aku gak merasa demikian?: What . . .

where am I supposed to go now? This is my home, but how come it doesn't feel like it?

delapan, sembilan, sepuluh: eight, nine, ten

Source: Syahmalina, Nadia. "Kamu Bukan Orang Sini." 2001. Used with permission of author.

Peter Phwan, "Game of Chance: Chinese Indonesians Play Asylum Roulette in the United States"

(2009)

In May 1998, after decades of institutionalized discrimination and state-ignored violence against ethnic Chinese Indonesians, yet another series of race riots broke out in Jakarta, the capital of Indonesia. The collapse of the Indonesian currency in the Asian economic crisis, exacerbated by government corruption under President Suharto, led to widespread protests in 1998, which then erupted into violence targeting Chinese Indonesians. Although they were only a small percentage of the Indonesian population, Chinese Indonesians controlled a disproportionate amount of the country's wealth. They thus were held up as scapegoats. During the May 1998 riots, more than 1,000 Chinese were killed, more than 100 women were raped, and many shops and homes were looted and burned. As a result, more than 70,000 Chinese Indonesians fled to countries in Asia and the Pacific and to the United States.

Peter Phwan, under the pseudonym Damai Sukmana, wrote the following article for Inside Indonesia, *describing the plight of the Chinese Indonesian refugees and their reception in the United States.*

Ten years after winning his asylum interview, Victor Liem (not his real name) is now a permanent resident of the US and one step away from becoming a US citizen. Despite the improved situation for ethnic Chinese in Indonesia, Liem —who has built and runs his own business in Silicon Valley—and his wife still feel nervous about returning. In the 1990s Liem was a hopeful businessman in Jakarta. He was a London School of Engineering graduate and owned two companies in West Jakarta. On 14 May 1998, driving home along the Kebon Jeruk highway, Liem was confronted by an angry mob attacking motorists with rocks, wooden bats and metal bars. The thugs were checking motorists' identity cards. He saw light skin-coloured men being dragged from their cars and beaten. Liem made the decision to drive at high speed through the makeshift blockage rather than risk being stopped. He finally reached Serpong Gate and was saved by locals who secured the area. His car was severely damaged by rocks. There were serious cuts on his face and hands. He then realised that a long sharp metal bar, which had broken the windscreen, had fallen just next to his stomach.

Liem and his family got the first available flight out of Indonesia. They landed in the United States in June 1998. The whole family applied for political asylum, and their application was approved soon after. Today there are at least 7,000 Chinese Indonesians—former asylum seekers—living in United States.

Fleeing after May 1998

Thousands of Chinese Indonesians left Indonesia after the anti-Chinese violence in Jakarta and other major Indonesian cities in May 1998. Many fled to the US seeking sanctuary either temporarily or with the hope of permanent settlement. Indonesia is currently one of the top 25 countries whose citizens seek asylum in the United States, peaking at 12th ranking in 2004. According to the US Department of Justice, over twenty thousand Indonesian asylum cases have been filed since 1998. In 1998 alone, at least 1,972 Indonesians were granted asylum in the United States; the highest number granted for Indonesians as a result of the relatively fast and non-adversarial process of 'affirmative asylum interviews', in a decade. The majority of these political asylum seekers from Indonesia were of ethnic Chinese descent.

This unusually high number of successful asylum applicants was greatly influenced by considerable and high-profile lobbying on their behalf by Chinese American groups. In the wake of the May riots members of the ethnic Chinese diaspora, particularly those in the United States, were outraged at the targeting of ethnic Chinese Indonesians and lobbied their own governments to condemn the inaction of the Indonesian government to protect them. Those approached by Chinese American groups included high profile politicians such as the present Speaker of the House, Nancy Pelosi, and Gavin Newsom, currently Mayor of San Francisco. Liem and his family were beneficiaries of this effort. But as the political heat around this issue cooled, so too did the relative ease with which asylum applications were granted. Now Chinese Indonesians whose claims are yet to be resolved face a game of asylum roulette.

Asylum Roulette

In the ten years to 2007, 7,359 asylum cases involving Chinese Indonesians were approved and 5,848 cases denied. Chinese Indonesians commonly relate their asylum claims to the history of government-sponsored discrimination, persecution and violence towards the minority. While many may not have experienced personal physical harm, they have feared persecution in the past, and now fear present and possibly future persecution.

A decade after the May riots and despite important changes in law and the lack of anti-Chinese violence in this time, Chinese Indonesians continue to seek asylum overseas because they fear persecution. Many continue to suffer trauma as a consequence of events in the past and maintain a continued sense of vulnerability about their situation in Indonesia, seeing these legal changes as simply cosmetic. Recent arrivals to the United States indicate that they simply do not trust the government to provide them with the protection they will need in a time of potential future crisis and targeting of ethnic Chinese. Although, all hope that these new legal and cultural freedoms will help more ethnic Chinese feel safe at home, and when they don't, asylum should always be an option.

Proving a credible fear of persecution is crucial to winning an asylum case. As the political system in Indonesia and the legal conditions for ethnic Chinese have improved, including the repeal of discriminatory legislation in recent years, proving such a fear has become less straightforward than it was in 1998. Moreover, in recent times applicants have found the asylum seeking process to be considerably more difficult. If their application is denied at the first hurdle by the Asylum office, an applicant's case is then referred to an Immigration Judge. This process is usually called a Defensive Asylum Hearing and applicants must find legal representation. If they lose their case before the Immigration Court they may then appeal at the Board of Immigration Appeal (BIA) and Circuit Courts.

The lives of Chinese Indonesians currently in the US with asylum cases still pending in the Courts remain in limbo. For many years now they have counted the days until the US Circuit Courts issue the final order for them to, in all probability, leave the country. Some are even detained for immigration violations before being deported.

Outcomes depend on how individual judges interpret the case, how convincingly an applicant's story is presented to the court, if they can afford or find pro-bono counsel willing to provide representation, as well as the standard of such representation.

However, an important and relatively recent precedent for these later Chinese Indonesian asylum cases is that of *Sael vs Ashcroft,* decided in October 2004 by the Ninth Circuit Court. This court covers many states, including California, Washington, Oregon, Nevada and Hawaii. It is the largest circuit court in the United States and overall second only in size to the US Supreme Court. The Court ruled that Taty Sael and her husband were eligible for political asylum after finding that the woman faced likely persecution in Indonesia. The US Court of Appeal gave three reasons for finding Taty would be in danger if she were deported. These were the historical pattern of anti-Chinese violence that dates back to 1740, laws still on the books that prohibit Chinese schools and other institutions, and mob attacks and threats against the applicant before she fled with her husband. Her husband's asylum claim was based on her situation.

This marks the first time a US Court has ruled there to be government-sanctioned discrimination against Indonesia's Chinese minority. Despite this precedent however, many Chinese Indonesian asylum seekers still face challenging legal battles in US immigration courts. Those who lose face the reality of returning to Indonesia.

Source: Phwan, Peter. "Game of Chance: Chinese Indonesians Play Asylum Roulette in the United States." *Inside Indonesia* 95 (January–March 2009). http://www.insideindonesia.org/edition-95/game-of-chance. Reprinted with permission.

William Wright, "Indonesian Makes New Life in America"
(2009)

The following article, published in the Cleveland (Tennessee) Daily Banner, *recounts the story of one Indonesian woman's journey to the United States. Unlike most Indonesian Americans, Dianingrum does not live in Southern California and did not come to the United States for education or economic opportunities. She moved from her home in Indonesia to Cleveland, Ohio, in 2006 because she married an American soldier. Her marriage soon ended in divorce, and with no family in the United States, she found herself alone in a country she never expected to call home. Nevertheless, and despite her difficulties adjusting to her new life, Dianingrum decided to remain in the United States. She found strength in her Indonesian cultural heritage, which values diversity, something she has also found true of the United States. Her story highlights some of the difficulties experienced by persons in cross-cultural marriages and is a reminder of the diversity within the immigrant experience.*

Growing up in Indonesia, Wilis Dianingrum never thought she would go live in the United States or be married to an American, but she did.

Three years ago the 33-year-old Cleveland State Community College student moved from her homeland in Southeast Asia and married a U.S. soldier only to become a divorced woman striving to make a new life for herself in a new country.

Dianingrum admits her life has been one struggle after another after losing her full-time job at Rubbermaid and her part-time job at a local restaurant six months ago. To top it off, her father died last year in a motorcycle accident and she was unable to attend his funeral.

With no family in the states and few friends to rely on, she said she took the matter to the highest authority.

"I believe God will help take care of me. He gave me the wisdom to go back to school. Cleveland State accepted me and I received financial aid," said Dianingrum. "I'm trying to survive here."

With the dramatic change in the U.S. economy and a more casual view of divorce in Western civilization, Dianingrum had to learn about life in America the hard way, from reality.

"I never dreamed of living in America," admits Dianingrum. "It was too far away. I never dreamed I would marry an American. Now I am the first in my family to get divorced."

Dianingrum said it seems people give up too quickly on marriage, adding, "In Asia we believe marriage is to be respected. Husbands take care of their wives and wives respect their husbands. There is not a lot of divorce there."

Raised Catholic but attending a Baptist church in Cleveland, Dianingrum said it was a shock to learn her husband wanted a divorce and did not want to work out their differences. It was another painful disappointment to learn she was losing her only means of making a living.

"When I lost both my jobs I was very sad but I went back to school," said Dianingrum. "Maybe the economy will get better soon and I will be able to find a job or get a better one. I cannot give up. I'm trying to be a strong, tough woman."

Although she said it is not easy for her to trust men after what happened in her cross cultural marriage, Dianingrum said she hopes to find lasting love one day but no time soon. When the time comes, however, she said she will be aware of how cultural differences can affect relationships.

"Living together is not part of my culture," said Dianingrum. "Having children out of wedlock is not my culture, but I do not judge others. I realize the culture here is different."

The Republic of Indonesia comprises 17,508 islands. With a population of more than 240 million people, it is the world's fourth most populous country, with the world's largest population of Muslims.

"We have 26 states and every state has a different language," said Dianingrum who speaks two languages. "Our national language is Bahasa."

Indonesia's national slogan, "Bhinneka Tunggal Ika" is translated "unity in diversity" which expresses the diversity that shapes her country. Dianingrum said she noticed a similar unity in diversity developing in Cleveland which she likes.

"I decided to stay here because I like to learn the language and the culture," she said. "I love traveling. I went to Europe for three months as an exchange student. I like the adventure. I like to try new things. Since I don't have any kids I would love to visit every state in the U.S. some day."

Of all the things that make her happy, Dianingrum said she is happiest when people accept her as she is.

"Most educated people are open-minded," she said. "I like living in Cleveland. People try to reach out to others."

Dianingrum said she still likes to eat with her hands although she sometimes uses a spoon. She has never eaten cereal. A favorite dish of Indonesians is a mixture of rice, coconut milk, meat and vegetables. According to Dianingrum, Indonesians also eat less bread than Americans.

"I come from Jakarta, the capital of Indonesia. They don't hunt animals where I live and I've never eaten deer," she said. "Also, we don't drink much beer, wine or liquor in Indonesia. You can get it everywhere here but not there. It's very expensive."

Dianingrum, who is majoring in accounting, said she carries the hope that more people will understand the importance of embracing diversity and avoid stereotyping others as they strive to become more united.

In her own struggle for survival in a land far from home, Dianingrum reflected on the American Dream that is still within her grasp and wondered why some people only see the negative rather than focus on the positive in life.

"I live by myself and I'm doing good," she said. "You can go to school and make a better life for yourself. It's easier when you already know the language. I have to learn a different language, a different culture with different values. It's harder for me but it's the most important thing right now. If I can do it, so can others."

Dianingrum said she is making no plans to return to Indonesia where her mother lives with one of her three brothers. She has a 10 year green card she must carry before she can apply to become a U.S. citizen.

Despite her challenges to make a life in America, Dianingrum said she is positive her life will be a learning experience full of adventure, happiness and love, things that also flourish in America.

Source: Wright, William. "Indonesian Makes New Life in America." *Cleveland Daily Banner* (TN), October 28, 2009. Reprinted with permission from the *Cleveland Daily Banner* of Cleveland, Tennessee.

Joseph Heco, *The Narrative of a Japanese; What He Has Seen and the People He Has Met in the Course of the Last Forty Years*

(1895)

The 1790 Naturalization Act, restricting naturalization to "free white persons" and originally enacted to prevent African slaves from becoming U.S. citizens, was also systematically applied against the Chinese beginning in the 1850s. However, the Japanese did not immigrate in any numbers until 1888, pushed by the upheavals of the Meiji Restoration and pulled by a labor shortage in the United States caused by Chinese exclusion. Initially, the Japanese immigrants were not perceived as economic or social threats; correspondingly, they were not legally defined as "non-white" by the Supreme Court until 1922 (although the attorney general had prohibited Japanese from naturalizing in 1907). Taking advantage of this short-lived loophole, a few hundred Japanese immigrants, including Joseph Heco, managed to become U.S. citizens before the 1952 McCarran-Walter Act abolished racial restrictions for naturalization.

Born Hizoko Hamada in 1837, Heco was a sailor on his stepfather's junk. He was shipwrecked when he was 13 years old, rescued by the USS Auckland, an American ship, and brought to San Francisco with the other survivors in 1850. Over the next decade, Heco lived in California and Maryland, learning English, going to school, meeting various American officials (including presidents Franklin Pierce and James Buchanan), converting to Christianity, and, in 1858, becoming the first naturalized Japanese American citizen. For a brief time, Heco served as an interpreter for Commodore Matthew Perry in Macau and Hong Kong; he then moved back to Japan where he worked for the U.S. Consulate, survived the Meiji rebellions, and built his own business.

Heco wrote a diary chronicling his experiences in Japan and the United States, which James Murdoch edited and published in 1895. The following excerpts describe Heco's experiences working at the Port of San Francisco, his introduction to American culture at the Baltimore house of his employer, and his naturalization. Along with narrating the life of a singular early Japanese immigrant, Heco's work also illustrates the fluidity of American perspectives on race, ethnicity, nationality, and whiteness.

June 15th [1853]. On this day it had been agreed I was to enter the service of the Collector of the Port. So when we reached San Francisco Capt. Pease and I went ashore, Thomas accompanying us as interpreter. After the Collector and the Captain had had some talk they requested Thomas to tell me what my duties would be. These were to wait on the Collector in the office, to fold papers and file letters and go round with the gentleman whenever he wished me to do so. Then, after some good advice, Capt. Pease and Thomas left me alone with the Collector. He indicated by signs that I was to fold the old letters and file them, and I began to do so. I felt as if I had been made a gentleman all in a twinkling, and felt quite proud of myself for having had the luck to jump so quickly from the sort of work I had been compelled to do before.

In the afternoon I was introduced to a large, gray-headed, clean-shaven man in a black suit and swallow-tail coat. And my old gentleman said to me, by holding up his thumb "That's a big man." I fancied he referred to the size of his body, since it really was big in every way. When I was introduced, the man shook hands with me, stretching out a great fist which completely wrapped my little hand out of sight, at the same time saying, "How are you?" He also said something else the only part of which I understood being "Can you speak English?" This personage was no other than the famous Senator Gwinn of California. . . .

[Heco went out east with the Collector, Mr. Sanders]

In the middle of July we sailed for the East *via* San Juan del Sue and arrived at New York on the 5th August 1853, and went to the Metropolitan Hotel. . . .

We left New York next morning at 7 o'clock. On the way to the Depot he told me we were to ride in a carriage drawn by a steam-engine, which could go at the rate of 25, 40, or even 60 miles an hour. This, of course, I set down as another story told by the old gentleman to excite my wonder. However when we got to the Depot I saw a number of beautifully fitted carriages with a steam-engine at their head. We took our seats in one of those, and while we sat there the engine began to snort and puff and the car to move.

It moved slowly at first but presently it sped along so rapidly that what we passed could not be distinctly seen, while the train itself vibrated and undulated like a snake chased in the water.

At 9 p.m. we reached Baltimore, and found the carriage waiting, as Mr. Sanders had said. We drove to the residence of his family. Here I was introduced as a stranger from a strange land, and as perhaps the first Japanese that had ever been in Baltimore. They one and all received me kindly, looking upon me as a sort of curiosity. . . .

[In the summer of 1854] I was sent with Mr. Sanders' children to live at a farm owned by his mother-in-law about 7 miles from the city. Here there were about forty negro slaves, the most healthy and cheerful people I ever saw. Their ways and manners were exceedingly funny; their dances in the evening used to interest me especially.

The day after my arrival the old lady ordered me a glass of milk fresh from the dairy, with sugar and a lump of ice in it. When the house-keeper brought it to me I asked what it was, and she pointed to the cattle in the distance and said cow's milk. So I declined to take it, inasmuch as in my country we had been taught to look upon all four-footed animals as unclean. The housekeeper went and told the old lady that I had refused the milk, and upon this the old lady came to me and said that the milk was good for me and would make me strong and that I must drink it. So I had to obey, as all were standing round watching me. And I drank that milk, and was greatly surprised to discover that it tasted so nice and soothing. And I began to think that there were many more good things in the world than I had dreamt of. From that time onward I have always been very fond of milk. . . .

Nov. 1st, 1854. As our departure for California was near at hand, Mrs. Sanders, who was very ardent in the matter of religion, was anxious that I should be Christianized, or converted to the Christian faith and baptized before I left Baltimore. So I agreed, and one day I went with a lady who was staying in her house to the Cathedral. There we met Father—I forget his name—who ushered us into a closet, a little enclosed box-like place. Here he questioned me on various matters and points. Then he told me to select a name out of those he read from a book and repeated. Several of the names he repeated did not sound nice, and all seemed to be the same. At length he game to, and read out the name of "Joseph." That sounded so pleasant to my ears that I at once said "that name will do for me." After this the Priest and all of us walked up to the front door of the altar and here I was christened and baptized with Holy Water and received the above name of Joseph. . . .

June 7th [1858]. As the day for my departure to my native country drew near at hand, Mr. Sanders thought it best that I should be naturalized before I left Baltimore. So he took me to the U.S. Court where I applied for and obtained a certificate of naturalization signed by the U.S. District Judge Gill and Mr. Spier, Clerk of Court. And thus I became a citizen of the United States of America.

Source: Heco, Joseph. *The Narrative of a Japanese; What He Has Seen and the People He Has Met in the Course of the Last Forty Years*, edited by James Murdoch. Tokyo: Maruzen, 1895, 134–139, 145–147, 158.

George Henry Himes, "An Account of the First Japanese Native in Oregon" (ca. 1904)

Most 19th-century Japanese immigrants came to the United States as laborers, taking advantage of the Meiji government's willingness to allow emigration and the insatiable demand for agricultural workers in Hawai'i and the American West. However, Suzuki Kinzo was an exception. He escaped political persecution in Yokohama, moving to Hakodate where he lived for a year in the household of the American consul and became almost fluent in English. In 1860, he met H. C. Leonard, a shipping merchant from Portland, Oregon, who agreed to bring 20-year-old Kinzo with him to the United States on board the Orbit. *Several decades later, George Himes, an acquaintance of Leonard, wrote the following account of Kinzo's thrilling escape to the United States. He also describes Kinzo's subsequent career, his first job working for Leonard's firm in Portland and then his serendipitous entrée into the Japanese diplomatic corps. Himes's account illustrates the experience of a white-collar Japanese immigrant, which was significantly different from that of a typical laborer in terms of* occupation, opportunities for education and advancement, and consistent close and friendly contact with white Americans.

The "disturbance" now going on between Japan and Russia in the far east recalls to mind the eventful career of the first native of Japan to come to Oregon, so far as known. His name was Suzukie Kinzo, and the story of his arrival in Oregon is in substance as follows: In the year 1861* a Portland merchant with his vessel was in the harbor of Hakodadi [Hakodate], Japan, homeward bound from a voyage to the Amoor [Amur] River, Siberia. An American gentleman—there were but four or five in that port at the time—told this merchant that he knew an intelligent Japanese lad there who was a political refugee from Yokohama, upon whose head a prize was set, and that he wanted to go to America. In reply the merchant said the boy could go with him providing he could be put on board his vessel without arousing suspicion. The other gentleman stated that he would take all responsibility in the matter, notwithstanding it was believed that spies were all about. At length the Portland bound vessel weighed anchor and started on her voyage. When about twenty miles at sea, in the dusk of the evening, a small craft was discovered, and upon this the young Jap was found and at once taken on board. Five or six uneventful weeks passed by when Portland harbor was entered, and the young foreigner, gratified for the saving of his life, went into the employ of the firm of which the merchant was a member, in the capacity of a servant, and remained several years. During this time he was sent to the Portland High School for three years, and his natural ability and studious habits won for him the head of his classes in mathematics and history. He was employed by the company of which his benefactor was a member to light lamps. To his employers he was faithful to the highest degree. His vigilance was untiring and his integrity unquestioned. It came to be known in due time that he belonged to high rank in his native land, but being free from false pride, the consciousness of his rank, only care he gave to every duty he was called on to perform than otherwise. In due time the turning point in his life came. In 1868, his health being somewhat impaired, his employer advised him to take a trip to San Francisco and remain a few months. This he consented to do. While there he accidentally met a number of young Japanese gentlemen who were on their way to Washington, among whom he recognized former acquaintances. They invited him to dine with them one day. In turn he invited them to dine with him, and the best in San Francisco was placed at their disposal. These young men were found to be attaches of Governor Ito, of Yeddo, who sent for Kinzo, and was astonished to find a countryman who had been in the United States eight years and could speak English as fluently as a native American. The Governor invited him to accompany the embassy to Washington, but he refused because he considered his first duty was to serve the gentleman who had saved his life. Not long after Kinzo returned to Portland Governor Ito started back to Japan from Washington. When he arrived in San Francisco, he caused the Japanese Consul there to telegraph to Kinzo, offering him an important position. He showed this dispatch to his employer, who advised him to accept the offer; that now he was in no danger of his life, and that honors awaited him in his own country which he could never hope to gain in the United States. With a saddened heart over leaving his benefactor, yet buoyed up with the bright promise waiting him, he left Portland to San Francisco. Upon arrival there he was at once made secretary and went to London, remaining there some time. Later, he was recalled to Japan, and was selected as one of the embassy to visit the courts of Spain and Portugal. Afterwards he was again sent to London as secretary of the Japanese legation at the Court of St. James, where he resided five years. For the next two years he held an important position in the foreign office at Tokio, Japan's capital, always rendering most efficient service, thus increasing his distinction. Later on he was given the choice of two important positions, one being that of Secretary of the Japanese legation at Washington. His remembrance of the kindness of the American merchant to him in his days of adversity, with the hope that he might meet him face to face some day, caused him to accept the latter place. But a vigorous and active mind had worn down a feeble body and he sickened and died in Tokio [sic] two days before the date of sailing to America, surrounded by powerful friends and every luxury that wealth and worth could win in the battle of life.

Kinzo was known to the writer in the late sixties and is remembered as having a thoughtful face and being a constant student, improving every moment not employed in physical labor in improving his mind. He had been lost sight of, however, and probably would have never been thought of again had it not been that a chance inquiry about the "little Japanese Lamplighter", brought out the story of his strange career from the lips of the aged merchant who first brought him to Oregon.

George H. Himes
Portland, Oregon

*There is a date discrepancy between Himes' account, reproduced above, and H. C. Leonard's recollections, published in *Portland, Oregon, Its History and Builders*, by Joseph Gaston (Chicago: S. J. Clarke Publishing Co., 1911).

Source: Himes, George. "An account of the first Japanese native in Oregon," ca. 1904. George Henry Himes Collection, Mss 1462, Oregon Historical Society Research Library. http://kaga.wsulibs.wsu.edu/cdm-imls_2/document.php?CISOROOT=/wsuvan1&CISOPTR=1391&REC=2. Used with permission of the Oregon Historical Society.

The Gentlemen's Agreement
(1907–1908)

The Gentlemen's Agreement was not a single document but rather a series of informal notes written between 1907 and 1908, through which Japan and the United States negotiated an agreement on Japanese immigration. Japan agreed to bar the emigration of Japanese and Korean contract laborers to the continental United States (Koreans were Japanese colonials at the time, since the Japanese takeover of Korea in 1905). In exchange, the United States allowed Japanese already in the United States to remain in the country and bring over their wives and children. The primarily male Japanese immigrant population took full advantage of this clause, bringing over wives, children, and picture brides in significant numbers until the 1924 National Origins Act closed this loophole. Because of this, the Japanese American community escaped the extreme gender imbalances found in contemporary Chinese and Filipino American communities.

In addition to the immigration stipulations, the United States also agreed not to segregate Japanese children in San Francisco public schools. The turmoil of the 1906 earthquake, mixed with mounting anti-Asian racism in San Francisco, had culminated in the San Francisco School Board's attempt to place all Asian students into a separate Oriental school (Chinese American children had been segregated since

1885). Korean immigrants, who were fewer in number, complied with the school board decision, but Japanese immigrants did not. President Theodore Roosevelt was anxious to pacify Japan, an ascending world power that had recently defeated Russia in the Russo-Japanese War (1904–1905). Roosevelt feared that the Japanese government's anger about the San Francisco School Board's attempted school segregation might set off an international crisis.

Excerpts from two documents relating to the Gentlemen's Agreement are reproduced here. The first excerpt is from the executive order Roosevelt signed to prevent Japanese and Korean laborers with passports from Hawai'i, Mexico, and Canada from reimmigrating to the U.S. mainland. The second excerpt, from the "1908 Report of the Commissioner General of Immigration," describes the general conditions of the Gentlemen's Agreement.

1. PRESIDENT THEODORE ROOSEVELT'S EXECUTIVE ORDER (1907)

Whereas, by the act entitled "An Act to regulate the immigration of aliens into the United States," approved February 20, 1907, whenever the President is satisfied that passports issued by any foreign government to its citizens to go to any country other than the United States or to any insular possession of the United States or to the Canal Zone, are being used for the purpose of enabling the holders to come to the continental territory of the United States to the detriment of labor conditions therein, it is made the duty of the President to refuse to permit such citizens of the country issuing such passports to enter the continental territory of the United States from such country or from such insular possession or from the Canal Zone;

And Whereas, upon sufficient evidence produced before me by the Department of Commerce and Labor, I am satisfied that passports issued by the Government of Japan to citizens of that country or Korea and who are laborers, skilled or unskilled, to go to Mexico, to Canada and to Hawai'i, are being used for the purpose of enabling the holders thereof to come to the continental territory of the United States to the detriment of labor conditions therein;

I hereby order that such citizens of Japan or Korea, to-wit: Japanese or Korean laborers, skilled and unskilled, who have received passports to go to Mexico, Canada or Hawai'i, and come therefrom, be refused permission to enter the continental territory of the United States.

It is further ordered that the Secretary of Commerce and Labor be, and he hereby is, directed to take, thru Bureau of Immigration and Naturalization, such measures and to make and enforce such rules and regulations as may be necessary to carry this order into effect.

Theodore Roosevelt
The White House
March 14, 1907
No. 589

Source: CIS Presidential Executive Orders and Proclamations, EO-589, March 14, 1907. Microfiche, Law Library of Congress, Washington, DC. http://www.novelguide.com/a/discover/dah_09/dah_09_04762.html.

2. COMMISSIONER GENERAL OF IMMIGRATION, REPORT (1908)

In order that the best results might follow from an enforcement of the regulations, an understanding was reached with Japan that the existing policy of discouraging emigration of its subjects of the laboring classes to continental United States should be continued, and should, by co-operation with the governments, be made as effective as possible. This understanding contemplates that the Japanese government shall issue passports to continental United States only to such of its subjects as are non-laborers or are laborers who, in coming to the continent, seek to resume a formerly acquired domicile, to join a parent, wife, or children residing there, or to assume active control of an already possessed interest in a farming enterprise in this country, so that the three classes of laborers entitled to receive passports have come to be designated former residents, parents, wives, or children of residents, and settled agriculturists.

With respect to Hawai'i, the Japanese government of its own volition stated that, experimentally at least, the issuance of passports to members of the laboring classes proceeding thence would be limited to former residents and parents, wives, or children of residents. The said government has also been exercising a careful supervision over the subject of emigration of its laboring class to foreign contiguous territory.

Source: "Report of the Commissioner General of Immigration," 1908. Historic Books and Documents on the Internet, 125. Ethnic Studies at University of Southern California. http://www.usc.edu/libraries/archives/ethnic studies/historicdocs/. Race, Demographics, and History in Monterey County: Local History Resources. http://web .me.com/joelarkin/MontereyDemographicHistory/ Gentlemens_Agreement.html.

Alien Land Law, California
(1913)

As Japanese migrants became increasingly involved and successful in farming, white farmers and anti-Asian advocates began turning their anger toward the new wave of "Orientals" entering the United States. Like the Chinese before them, Japanese immigrants were seen as economic, moral, and societal threats. Anti-coolie clubs, which had formed in opposition to Chinese immigration during the late 19th century, quickly moved against Japanese and Koreans in the early 1900s.

California enacted its first Alien Land Law, also known as the Webb Heney Act, in 1913, although the state assembly had begun discussing such measures as early as 1907. The Alien Land Law prohibited aliens from owning, leasing, possessing, enjoying, or transmitting property for more than three years. However, issei (first-generation Japanese) farmers found their way around the prohibition. Because of the influx of picture brides and their more balanced gender demography, Japanese in the United States were able to have families and American-born children in much larger numbers than other contemporary Asian immigrant groups. To circumvent the Alien Land Laws, some issei put the deeds to their farms and homes in their American-born children's names. Others used a white friend's or business associate's name or bought names from strangers.

In 1920, California amended its Alien Land Law to stop Japanese from using their children's names on their property deeds. The total acreage of farmland owned or leased by Japanese Americans decreased in the immediate aftermath of the land laws, but it stabilized during the mid- to late 1920s. California was not alone in its fear and hatred of Asian Americans. Washington, Arizona, Oregon, Idaho, Kansas, Louisiana, Montana, New Mexico, and Utah all passed similar legislation. California's Alien Land Laws were not declared unconstitutional until 1952, in the Supreme Court case Sei Fujii v. California. The following is the original 1913 California statute.

An act relating to the rights, powers, and disabilities of aliens and of certain companies, associations and corporations with respect to property in this state, providing for escheats in certain cases, prescribing the procedure therein, and repealing all acts or parts of acts inconsistent or in conflict herewith.

[Approved May 19, 1913. In effect August 10, 1913]

The people of the State of California do enact as follows:

SECTION 1. All aliens eligible to citizenship under the laws of the United States may acquire, possess, enjoy, transmit and inherit real property, or any interest therein, in this state, in the same manner and to the same extent as citizens of the United States, except as otherwise provided by the laws of this state.

SECTION 2. All aliens other than those mentioned in this section one of this act may acquire, possess, enjoy and transfer real property, or any interest therein, in this state, in the manner and to the extent and for the purposes prescribed by any treaty now existing between the government of the United States and the nation or country of which such alien is a citizen or subject, and not otherwise, and may in addition thereto lease lands in this state for agricultural purposes for a term not exceeding three years.

SECTION 3. Any company, association or corporation organized under the laws of this or any other state or nation, of which a majority of the members are aliens other than those specified in section one of this act, or in which a majority of the issued capital stock is owned by such aliens, may acquire, possess, enjoy and convey real property, or any interest therein, in this state, in the manner and to the extent and for the purposes prescribed by any treaty now existing between the government of the United States and the nation or country of which such members or stockholders are citizens or subjects, and not otherwise, and may in addition thereto lease lands in this state for agricultural purposes for a term not exceeding three years.

SECTION 4. Whenever it appears to the court in any probate proceeding that by reason of the provisions of this act any heir or devisee can not take real property in this state which, but for said provisions, said heir or devisee would take as such, the court, instead of ordering a distribution of such real property to such heir or devisee, shall order a sale of said real property to be made in the manner provided by law for probate sales of real property, and the proceeds of such sale shall be distributed to such heir or devisee in lieu of such real property.

SECTION 5. Any real property hereafter acquired in fee in violation of the provisions of this act by any alien mentioned in section two of this act, or by any company, association or corporation mentioned in section three of this act, shall escheat to, and become and remain the property of the State of California. The attorney general shall institute proceedings to have the escheat of such real property adjudged and enforced in the manner provided by section 474 of the Political Code and title eight, part three of the Code of Civil Procedure. Upon the entry of the final judgment in such proceedings, the title to such real property shall pass to the State of California. The provisions of this section and of

sections two and three of this act shall not apply to any real property hereafter acquired in the enforcement of in the satisfaction of any lien now existing upon, or interest in such property, so long as such real property so acquired shall remain the property of the alien, company, association or corporation acquiring the same in such manner.

SECTION 6. Any leasehold or other interest in real property less than the fee, hereafter acquired in violation of the provisions of this act by any alien mentioned in section two of this set, or by any company, association or corporation mentioned in section three of this act, shall escheat to the State of California. The attorney general shall institute proceedings to have such escheat adjudged and enforced as provided in section five of this act. In such proceedings the court shall determine and adjudge the value of such leasehold, or other interest in such real property, and enter judgment for the state for the amount thereof together with costs. Thereupon the court shall order a sale of the real property covered by such leasehold, or other interest, in the manner provided by section 1271 of the Code of Civil Procedure. Out of the proceeds arising from such sale, the amount of the judgment rendered for the state shall be paid into the state treasure and the balance shall be deposited with and distributed by the court in accordance with the interest of the parties therein.

SECTION 7. Nothing in this act shall be construed as a limitation upon the power of the state to enact laws with respect to the acquisition, holding or disposal by aliens of real property in the state.

SECTION 8. All acts and parts of acts inconsistent, or in conflict with the provisions of this act, are hereby repealed.

Source: California Session Law 1913, Chapter 113. http://www.jstor.org/pss/2212307.

Ryu Kishima, Deportation Documents
(1936)

Ryu Kishima first arrived in the territory of Hawai'i in 1912 as a picture bride. She married Joshiro Kishima, and for the next two decades, the couple worked for several wealthy families in Hawai'i. Around 1930, both Ryu and Joshiro were employed by Miss Bernice E. L. Hundley in Kapa'a, on the island of Kaua'i. Kishima worked as a house servant, and her husband was a yardman. Kishima was paid $30 a month, and her husband was paid $40. She resided in the servants' quarters at the Hundley home. The couple never had any children.

Over their 22 years in Hawai'i, both Kishima and her husband made several return trips to Japan. Joshiro left for Japan one final time on February 27, 1935; Ryu followed him the next month. When Kishima attempted to come back to the United States on July 2, 1936, she was detained because she had failed to produce a return permit. After her hearing by the Immigration and Naturalization Service (INS), she was ordered to be deported under the stipulations of the 1917 and 1924 Immigration Acts. Kishima was sent back to Japan on the SS Taiyo Maru *on August 25, 1936.*

Included here are a brief submitted by Kishima's attorney, Robert K. Murakami; a handwritten note from Bernice E. L. Hundley, read during Kishima's hearing; and the INS decision.

Office:
Residence:
KING AND SMITH STREETS
2045 COYNE STREET
TELEPHONE 4345
TELEPHONE 93063

ROBERT K. MURAKAMI

Attorney-At-Law
205-207 SUMITOMO BANK BLDG.
HONOLULU, T.H.

July 17, 1936

File No. 4395/352
In the Matter of RYU KISHIMA
Japanese female, married, age 47 years.

BRIEF ON BEHALF OF RYU KISHIMA, APPLICANT

To the Honorable,
The Secretary of Labor,
Washington, D.C.
Sir:—

The applicant, RYU KISHIMA, arrived at the port of Honolulu on M.S. Tatsuta Maru on July 2, 1936, with a Japanese Passport No. 0296668 issued to JOSHIRO KISHIMA and RYU KISHIMA, husband and wife, and Immigration Visa Stamped No. 86 issued at Kobe by the American Consul as a returning immigrant under Section 4 (b) of the Immigration Act of 1924. According to her manifest date, the applicant's last permanent residence was at Kapaa, Kauai, Territory of Hawai'i, where she had resided from 1914 to 1935.

The Board of Special Inquiry, after a hearing, found that the applicant was not entitled to enter the United States under Section 13 (3) of the Act of 1924, on the ground that the applicant was not a non-quota immigrant as specified in the Immigration Visa and the Board also found that she was a person likely to become a public charge under the act of 1917.

The applicant is in good health, not too old or crippled. She had been in the employ of Bernice E.L. Hundley of Kapaa, Kauai, for five or six years prior to her departure from the Territory of Hawai'i in April, 1935. She is returning to her former employer with an assurance of employment and livelihood, as appears from the record at page 4 (letter from her former employer); and so we could assume that the excluding decision of the Board was not really based upon the fact or finding that she might become a public charge.

The only question in this case is whether or not the applicant had established her status as a returning immigrant, returning from a temporary visit abroad to her unrelinquished domicile and residence of twenty years' duration at Kapaa, Kauai, Territory of Hawai'i. In other words, the sole question is: Did the applicant relinquish or surrender her permanent residence at Kapaa, Kauai, Territory of Hawai'i, when she boarded the Taiyo Maru leaving the port of Honolulu for Japan on April 25, 1935?

On this point, the record shows that the applicant followed her husband, JOSHIRO KISHIMA, on a trip to Japan for the purpose of visiting her sick father. She testified that her husband went to Japan ahead of her and that she was called to Japan in a hurry and that she left the Territory of Hawai'i without applying for a return permit for the reason that she had been informed that she had to carry the permit herself and that not having the time to wait for the permit she did not file her application for same prior to her departure. There is nothing inconsistent in her disposing of a few dollars' worth of household effects prior to her departure and her intention to retain her domicile in Hawai'i inasmuch as she had been lodging and boarding with her employer and consequently had very little, if anything of value to dispose of in the line of household goods or effects. Had she been in a home of her own and not in servants' quarters, the fact that she had given away household goods might militate against the idea that she was retaining her comicile at Kapaa, Kauai; but under the circumstances, she really had nothing worthwhile to give away and that the fact that she did dispose of her household effects should not and could not be held to substantiate the finding of the Board that she really and truly intended to leave the Territory of Hawai'i, forsaking it forever.

In her testimony she made it clear to the Board that it was on account of her father's illness that she had to remain in Japan for over a year and that her father had become paralyzed as a result of his illness. True, she also testified to the fact that she helped in her husband's umbrella business, in Japan, for a few months, just prior to her return to the Territory of Hawai'i. But in view of the fact that the applicant is not in affluent circumstances, her helping in the business to augment the family income should not be taken as the controlling factor in determining the question of whether or not the applicant actually relinquished her domicile in the Territory of Hawai'i, either at the time of her departure from Kapaa, Kauai, or while temporarily visiting in Japan. The record shows that she was honest and frank in all her answers and that she revealed all the facts and circumstances in connection with her residence abroad without attempting to hide anything or to mislead the members of the Board. The applicant now makes the explanation that she helped in the umbrella business while in Japan because she had hopes of carrying on that trade after her return to the Territory of Hawai'i in case her services might not be required at the Hundley home, but that she was not asked as to her intentions in this regard at the time of the hearing before the Board.

We respectfully submit that in a case of this kind the only issue involved is one of the intention on the part of the person taking the trip away and that after all overt acts alone do not change a person's residence or domicile but that there must also be the intent to relinquish the old residence or domicile and to acquire a new one. In the instant case, we respectfully submit that even though one might be able to say that the applicant's conduct in helping her husband's business and her living in a rented house with her husband in Japan might be taken as the overt acts but that there is an absence of any intent on her part to give up or relinquish the Territory of Hawai'i as her permanent residence. In fact, it was her express purpose and intention to visit her sick father and to return to the Territory of Hawai'i, which she did.

It is, therefore, respectfully submitted that under all the circumstances in this case, the Board should not have inferred that there was an intention on her part to forsake her Hawaiian domicile form the mere fact of her giving away a few pieces of household goods of inconsequential value and her failure to obtain a Return Permit, which was, we submit, satisfactorily explained by the applicant. In this respect we feel that the Board of Special Inquiry erred and that the appeal in this case should be allowed and the applicant permitted to return to her permanent residence and domicile of twenty consecutive years.

Respectfully submitted,
Signature
Robert K. Murakami,
Attorney for Ryu Kishima, Applicant.

Dated at Honolulu, T.H.,

July 17th, A.D. 1936.

****

FORM 611
HEADING FOR TESTIMONY
U.S. DEPARTMENT OF LABOR
IMIMMIGRATION AND NATURALIZATION
SERVICE

District No. 22
File No. 4395/352
B.S.I. No. 2
Manifest No. List 3, Line 4
(Date) July 3, 1936

IN THE MATTER of
RYU KISHIMA
Japanese female; aged 47
At a meeting of
BOARD OF SPECIAL INQUIRY
held at

PRESENT: Inspectors: F.P. Rivas, Chairman, Geo. L. Coleman, Member, Clerk S.M. Ferguson, Member
Interpreter: Suma T. Tanaka

Arrived via: M.S. Tatsuta Maru Date: July 2, 1936
Held by J.G. Clemson Immigration Inspector
Cause: Proof of Status

Q Have you any letters from Miss Hundley that she was would reemploy you upon your return to Kauai?
A Yes

Applicant presents:
Letter written on the stationary of MISS BERNICE E.L. HUNDLEY, Kapaa, Kauai, Hawai'i, 'undated':
Dear Girl:
We may not be able to pay you much as we already have your folks at work but your home can always be with us as we consider you part of the household. Kameyo + Hide gave us your letters.
(signed) The Hundleys.

CASE FORMALLY DISCUSSED BY THIS BOARD:

STATEMENT BY MEMBER COLEMAN:
While the statements of this applicant in her testimony as to her arrivals and departures vary greatly from those shown by the records of this office, however, from the photograph and other information it is believed that the present applicant is the person she claims to be, and that the discrepancies were due either to nervousness or failing memory.

According to her testimony, the husband, JOSHIRO KISHIMA, departed shortly before the applicant, RYU KISHIMA; and, immediately upon his arrival in Japan opened up an umbrella shop of his own, which he is still operating, and from which he has been supporting his family. The applicant followed her husband to Japan, after disposing of all her household effects. For this trip they secured no Re-entry Permits, although when making the two former trips in 1929 and 1934, Re-entry Permits were obtained.

The applicant definitely stated that she returned first, since her husband had no proof of unrelinquished residence; and that she felt her proof was sufficiently established by the letter she presented from Miss Hundley, while in fact, the letter would indicate that she would very likely become a charge, at least on private charity of Miss Hundley. Miss Hundley apparently was not expecting the return of this applicant as she employed some other person for the position formerly filled by this applicant. This applicant has no children to take care of her in this country, and she arrived here with only $20.

I am of the opinion the testimony discloses that the applicant and her husband relinquished their residence in the United States, and had no intention of returning, and that if this applicant is admitted, her husband will close his shop in Japan and also attempt to return to the United States as a Returning Resident Alien.

I am also of the opinion that if Miss Hundley failed to take care of this 47 year old alien, as indicated in her letter, she would probably become a public charge.

MOTION: (By Chairman):

I move that the applicant, RYU KISHIMA, be denied admission to the United States under the Act of 1924, on the grounds that she is not a non-quota immigrant as specified in the immigration visa presented by her; and, that under the Act of 1917, on the ground that she is likely to become a public charge:

Member Coleman: I second that Motion.
Member Ferguson: I concur.

Source: 4395/352 [Ryu KISHIMA]; Box 2: Appeal Case Files of Japanese and Korean Aliens Denied Entry by Boards of Special Inquiry, complied 1917-1940 (ARC 628461); Records of the Immigration and Naturalization Service, Record Group 85; National Archives and Records Administration-Pacific Region (San Francisco).

Executive Order 9066 (1942) and Evacuation Poster, "Instructions to All Persons of Japanese Ancestry Living in the Following Area"
(1942)

After the Japanese navy attacked Pearl Harbor on December 7, 1941, the United States declared war on the empire of Japan—and Japanese Americans suddenly became targets of extreme suspicion. On the evening of December 7, 1941, Federal Bureau of Investigation agents, local police, and military police detained 736 Japanese aliens. Within four days, authorities had taken a total of 1,370 Japanese aliens into custody. These were people officials believed could most likely be spies or saboteurs: Shinto and Buddhist priests, newspaper reporters, community leaders, Japanese language teachers, fishermen, and others. The government created Enemy Alien Hearing Boards to determine the loyalty of these people.

Military curfews were instituted on the West Coast in early February 1942. Then, several weeks later, on February 19, 1942, President Franklin Roosevelt signed Executive Order 9066. This presidential order authorized the military to exclude "any and all persons" from certain areas in the country, in the name of national security. Executive Order 9066 paved the way for the wholesale evacuation of all people of Japanese ancestry from the West Coast of the United States. Both aliens and citizens of Japanese descent were relocated to 10 permanent internment camps located in remote areas. The camps, run by the War Relocation Authority, held Japanese Americans behind barbed wire and under armed guard for up to four years. The Department of

Justice ran an additional 22 camps that held more than 7,000 Japanese Americans and Japanese from Latin America, who were to be used in prisoner-of-war exchanges. Another 14 U.S. Army facilities were also used to hold Japanese Americans. In all, more than 120,000 Japanese Americans, more than two-thirds of them American citizens, were imprisoned for the duration of the war. Reproduced here are Roosevelt's Executive Order 9066, which paved the way for the internment camps, and an evacuation notice posted in May 1942 in San Francisco.

Executive Order No. 9066 (1942)

The President

Executive Order

Authorizing the Secretary of War to Prescribe Military Areas

Whereas the successful prosecution of the war requires every possible protection against espionage and against sabotage to national-defense material, national-defense premises, and national-defense utilities as defined in Section 4, Act of April 20, 1918, 40 Stat. 533, as amended by the Act of November 30, 1940, 54 Stat. 1220, and the Act of August 21, 1941, 55 Stat. 655 (U.S.C., Title 50, Sec. 104);

Now, therefore, by virtue of the authority vested in me as President of the United States, and Commander in Chief of the Army and Navy, I hereby authorize and direct the Secretary of War, and the Military Commanders whom he may from time to time designate, whenever he or any designated Commander deems such action necessary or desirable, to prescribe military areas in such places and of such extent as he or the appropriate Military Commander may determine, from which any or all persons may be excluded, and with respect to which, the right of any person to enter, remain in, or leave shall be subject to whatever restrictions the Secretary of War or the appropriate Military Commander may impose in his discretion. The Secretary of War is hereby authorized to provide for residents of any such area who are excluded therefrom, such transportation, food, shelter, and other accommodations as may be necessary, in the judgment of the Secretary of War or the said Military Commander, and until other arrangements are made, to accomplish the purpose of this order. The designation of military areas in any region or locality shall supersede designations of prohibited and restricted areas by the Attorney General under the Proclamations of December 7 and 8, 1941, and shall supersede the responsibility and authority of the Attorney General under the said Proclamations in respect of such prohibited and restricted areas.

I hereby further authorize and direct the Secretary of War and the said Military Commanders to take such other steps as he or the appropriate Military Commander may deem advisable to enforce compliance with the restrictions applicable to each Military area hereinabove authorized to be designated, including the use of Federal troops and other Federal Agencies, with authority to accept assistance of state and local agencies.

I hereby further authorize and direct all Executive Departments, independent establishments and other Federal Agencies, to assist the Secretary of War or the said Military Commanders in carrying out this Executive Order, including the furnishing of medical aid, hospitalization, food, clothing, transportation, use of land, shelter, and other supplies, equipment, utilities, facilities, and services.

This order shall not be construed as modifying or limiting in any way the authority heretofore granted under Executive Order No. 8972, dated December 12, 1941, nor shall it be construed as limiting or modifying the duty and responsibility of the Federal Bureau of Investigation, with respect to the investigation of alleged acts of sabotage or the duty and responsibility of the Attorney General and the Department of Justice under the Proclamations of December 7 and 8, 1941, prescribing regulations for the conduct and control of alien enemies, except as such duty and responsibility is superseded by the designation of military areas hereunder.

Franklin D. Roosevelt
The White House,
February 19, 1942.

Source: Executive Order 9066, February 19, 1942. General Records of the United States Government, Record Group 11, National Archives, National Archives and Records Administration. http://www.ourdocuments.gov/doc.php?doc=74&page=transcript.

EVACUATION POSTER, "INSTRUCTIONS TO ALL PERSONS OF JAPANESE ANCESTRY LIVING IN THE FOLLOWING AREA" (1942)

Western Defense Command and Fourth Army Wartime Civil Control Administration Presidio of San Francisco, California
May 3, 1942

Instructions to All Persons of Japanese Ancestry Living in the Following Area:

All of that portion of the County of Alameda, State of California, within the boundary beginning at the point where the southerly limits of the City of Oakland meet San Francisco Bay; thence easterly and following the southerly limits of said city to U.S. Highway No. 50; thence southerly and easterly on said Highway No. 50 to its intersection with California State Highway No. 21; thence southerly on said Highway No. 21 to its intersection, at or near Warm Springs, with California State Highway No. 17; thence southerly on said Highway No. 17 to the Alameda-Santa Clara County line; thence westerly and following said county line to San Francisco Bay; thence northerly, and following the shoreline of San Francisco Bay to the point of Beginning.

Pursuant to the provisions of Civilian Exclusion Order No. 34, this Headquarters, dated May 3, 1942, all persons of Japanese ancestry, both alien and non-alien, will be evacuated from the above area by 12 o'clock noon, P. W. T., Sunday, May 9, 1942.

No Japanese person living in the above area will be permitted to change residence after 12 o'clock noon, P. W. T., Sunday, May 3, 1942, without obtaining special permission from the representative of the Commanding General, Northern California Sector, at the Civil Control Station located at:

920 "C" Street, Hayward, California.

Such permits will only be granted for the purpose of uniting members of a family, or in cases of grave emergency.

The Civil Control Station is equipped to assist the Japanese population affected by this evacuation in the following ways:

1. Give advice and instructions on the evacuation.
2. Provide services with respect to the management, leasing, sale, storage or other disposition of most kinds of property, such as real estate, business and professional equipment, household goods, boats, automobiles and livestock.
3. Provide temporary residence elsewhere for all Japanese in family groups.
4. Transport persons and a limited amount of clothing and equipment to their new residence.

The Following Instructions Must Be Observed:

1. A responsible member of each family, preferably the head of the family, or the person in whose name most of the property is held, and each individual living alone, will report to the Civil Control Station to receive further instructions. This must be done between 8:00 A. M. and 5:00 P. M. on Monday, May 4, 1942, or between 9:00 A. M. and 5:00 P. M. on Tuesday, May 5, 1942.
2. Evacuees must carry with them on departure for the Assembly Center, the following property:
   a. Bedding and linens (no mattress) for each member of the family;
   b. Toilet articles for each member of the family;
   c. Extra clothing for each member of the family;

d. Sufficient knives, forks, spoons, plates, bowls and cups for each member of the family;

e. Essential personal effects for each member of the family.

3. All items carried will be securely packaged, tied and plainly marked with the name of the owner and numbered in accordance with instructions obtained at the Civil Control Station. The size and number of packages is limited to that which can be carried by the individual or family group.

4. No pets of any kind will be permitted.

5. No personal items and no household goods will be shipped to the Assembly Center.

6. The United States Government through its agencies will provide for the storage, at the sole risk of the owner, of the more substantial household items, such as iceboxes, washing machines, pianos and other heavy furniture. Cooking utensils and other small items will be accepted for storage if crated, packed and plainly marked with the name and address of the owner. Only one name and address will be used by a given family.

7. Each family, and individual living alone, will be furnished transportation to the Assembly Center or will be authorized to travel by private automobile in a supervised group. All instructions pertaining to the movement will be obtained at the Civil Control Station.

Go to the Civil Control Station between the hours of 8:00 A. M. and 5:00 P. M., Monday, May 4, 1942, or between the hours of 8:00 A.M. and 5:00 P. M., Tuesday, May 5, 1942, to receive further instructions.

J. L. DEWITT Lieutenant General, U.S. Army Commanding

Source: San Francisco, California. Exclusion Order posted at First and Front Streets directing removal of persons of Japanese ancestry from the first San Francisco section to be affected by the evacuation. April 11, 1942. Record Group 210: Records of the War Relocation Authority, 1941–1989.

442nd Regimental Combat Team, Monthly Report (1944) and Letter of Commendation

(1945)

In the immediate aftermath of Pearl Harbor, the nisei (second-generation Japanese Americans) serving in the Hawai'i National Guard did their utmost to help protect and secure the islands. A mere three days after the attack, these young men were reclassified as enemy aliens (C-4 status). Japanese Americans made up more than 37 percent of the Hawaiian population, and more than half of the Hawai'i National Guard were nisei. Military officials were extremely uncomfortable with this; they openly questioned the loyalty of nisei guard members and proposed replacing them all with whites. However, local officials managed to convince the State Department that the nisei were loyal and patriotic Americans. The War Department eventually formed a special all-Japanese American combat unit, the 100th Infantry Battalion, nicknamed the "One Puka Puka" (puka means "hole" in Hawaiian).

The 100th eventually merged with the famous 442nd Regimental Combat Team (RCT), activated in 1943. This all-nisei battalion (it was not until after World War II that the U.S. military integrated its fighting units) remains one of the most decorated military units in U.S. history. Its members fought in France, Italy, and Germany, and their heroism on the battlefield convinced many white Americans that Japanese Americans could be loyal Americans. That it took such lengths to prove their loyalty was an indication of the rampant racism that Japanese Americans faced during World War II. Reproduced here is the 442nd RCT's July 1944 monthly report and a 1945 letter of commendation from General Francis Oxx praising the 442nd RCT's conduct while waiting to return stateside.

442ND RCT JULY 1944 MONTHLY REPORT

22 June

First contact of 442nd Infantry with enemy troops occurred approximately 1600 21 June. Pfc H. Aramaki and Pfc I. Nakamura, of Cannon Co, while acting as road guides at Sansano, took prisoner three German infantrymen (stragglers) turning them over to 34th Division MP's.

24 June

The Combat Team moved out via truck convoy to new assembly area via GRAVASANNO. CP at new area opened 0930. At the same hour two PW's were taken by 1st Sgt Jamese Dakamoto and S Sgt Yano of Antitank Co, who came upon them resting in a concealed location at the new assembly area. The prisoners offered no resistance. The prisoners were Turko-men, members of an East Asian (Tukestan) organization. Their clothing was worn and dirty but they appeared well nourished, were not wounded and were apparently stragglers.

25 June

On this day the regiment made an approach march of 15 miles to a position immediately behind the front lines and were scheduled to take over on the following day. First elements departed bivouac at GRAVASANNO approximately 0945; last elements closed 1845. Artillery firing overhead. Visit by Major General RYDER with final instructions re the following day's operations. The basic plan was to have 2d and 3d Bns jump off with the 100th Inf Bn in reserve, forward elements to pass thru the 142nd Infantry Regiment and the 517th Parachute Infantry Regiment at 0600 26 June.

26 June

First day of combat. The regiment left assembly area and moved up at 0400. The objective was to push along the road leading through and beyond Survereto and Belvedere. Fighting was continuous throughout the day, losses were suffered, prisoners taken and by night the position of the forward elements was approximately 267985. The towns of Survereto and Belvedere were cleared out and our strength was astride the road immediately south of Sassetta.

Early in the day while on forward reconnaissance, the armored car of General RYDER and the jeep of Colonel PENCE were attacked and captured by the Germans and later recovered by our units.

During the day, the 100th Infantry Bn cleaned out the town of Belvedere, reporting 50 enemy killed. The battalion took 50 prisoners and the following enemy materiel:

1 – tank
8 – jeeps
2 – amphibious jeeps
1 – 105mm gun
1 – CP intact
4 – trucks
2 – motorcycles

Further report on first day's action. COF engaged enemy forces at 1130 26 June. Received direct fire from German 88 mm gun and three M-4 tanks. 2 EM KIA, 10 EM WIA and 12 MIA.

Engagement ceased 1800. Also engaged approximately one company of enemy infantry.

Co E attacked and captured Hill 104 0700. Proceeded to next objective. Attacked and captured Hill 127 1330. Co G relieved 2d Bn, 142d Infantry, gained objective, Hill 101 at 0630. Moved along both sides of Massaro River, met resistance at the junction of Lodama and Massaro at 1230.

27 June

The plan for the 2d day of operations was to follow artillery fire into Sassetta, with the 100th Bn leading and the 3d Bn on its left, with the 2d Bn coming up in reserve. The units were to reorganize North of Sassetta for a further attack.

The regiment cleaned out Sassetta against stiff resistance and pushed on. The regimental CP moved up to approximately 3 miles South of Sassetta at 1145. Antitank Co reported two enemy tanks destroyed South of Sassetta.

On the 28th, the 2d Bn pushed through and beyond the 3d Bn, left of the road between Sassetta and Castegnetta. The 100th continued and took the road junction North of Sassetta at 0910, reached Al Grillo at 1620 and the stream at 275060. The 2d Bn reached its objective, the stream junction 262061 at 2040. Fighting continuous throughout the day.

29 June

A strong motorized reconnaissance patrol was sent out on Divisional order, consisting of two rifle platoons, one machine gun section, one 81mm mortar section. This patrol operated with 34th Division Reconnaissance troops to Casale and Guardistallo. At approximately 0800 the 135th Infantry passed through our lines. At 0950 the 3d Bn was ordered to Monteverdi where they maintained a roadblock supported by Cannon Co. During the day the 100th and 2d Bns moved by foot to vicinity of Bibbona and bivouacked. On the 30th the 100th and 2d Bn were at the assembly area near Bibbona. The 3d Bn was released from its roadblock and closed in to the assembly area at 0050 1 July. The combat patrol returned approximately 0840, reporting slight contact with the enemy and no casualties. During the day the enemy counterattacked the 133d Infantry near Cecina. Enemy artillery fire fell in the assembly area. The regiment was alerted for ½ hour movement, but the counterattack was checked later in the day and the 442nd was not called up.

Source: University of Hawai'i at Manoa Library; JAVC; NARA documents, 442nd; Monthly Reports, July 1944.

COMMENDATION LETTER FROM BRIGADIER GENERAL FRANCIS H. OXX (1945)

Headquarters Peninsular Base Section, United States Army, Office of The Commanding General

15 October 1945

SUBJECT: Commendation

TO: Commanding Officer, 442nd Infantry Regiment, APO 782

1. At the present time, when a large number of the enlisted personnel — and some of the officers — yet remaining in the theater are indulging themselves in complaint and criticism arising out of their impatience at not being returned more rapidly to the States or out of their disappointment at having to remain over here for a few more months of duty, it is especially gratifying to be able to commend your regiment for its continued high morale, exemplary conduct, willing acceptance of all assigned tasks and superior standard of discipline.

2. The 442nd Infantry Regiment attained an enviable record in combat, a record rarely if ever surpassed by any similar unit. Now it is engaged in a far less colorful and interesting, though necessary task in a "rear echelon" organization. From the members of my staff I have heard nothing but praise for the manner in which this task is being executed and for the complete lack of the "griping" and indifference which have, unfortunately, been characteristic of some of out other ex-combat units.

3. I commend you and all the members of your command for the splendid manner in which you have performed your duties since your assignment to the Peninsular Base Section. I am confident that you will continue to adhere to the same high standards throughout your service.

FRANCIS H. OXX

Brigadier General, U.S. Army, Commanding

Source: University of Hawai'i at Manoa Library; JAVC; NARA documents, 442nd; Letters; Commendation from General Oxx, October 15, 1945.

Hayao Chuman, Letters and Affidavit
(1946–1967)

Hayao Chuman was born in the United States in 1913. When he was an infant, his parents sent him to Japan to live with relatives, where he stayed until he was 18 years old. When he moved back to the United States, he finished high school and opened a horticulture shop. When World War II broke out, Chuman was sent first to the Rohwer War Relocation Center, and then to Tule Lake. He, along with his wife Toshiko, was one of roughly 5,000 Japanese Americans who renounced their U.S. citizenship. This was made possible by Public Law 405, passed in 1944, which, for the first time, allowed Americans to give up their citizenship during wartime.

After the war ended, most of these Japanese Americans regretted their decision and began attempting to get their renunciations overturned. They were aided by Wayne Collins, a California attorney. Collins filed a class action suit against the U.S. government, arguing that the stress of the camps and pressure from radical pro-Japan groups (whose activities went unchecked by camp authorities) created untenable conditions for the internees. It took more than 20 years for the suit to be successful, but in 1971, President Richard Nixon signed the repeal of Public Law 405.

The following excerpts from Chuman's depositions and letters to Collins were written between 1946 and 1967, when his renunciation was finally overturned. These excerpts describe the events leading up to Chuman's renunciation

and his subsequent attempts to regain his citizenship. In particular, Chuman's testimony seeks to prove that, despite his renunciation, he is a good and legitimate American.

LETTER FROM CHUMAN TO COLLINS (SEPTEMBER 1946)

. . . 4. Concerning questions asked at Hearings, I wish to supplement my answers and circumstances as follows

A. REUNCIATION OF JAPANESE CITIZEN-SHIP

I returned to the U.S. with my determination to become a law-abiding American citizen in 1931. Upon my arrival in the U.S. I appeared briefly before the consul of Japan at Los Angeles, California, and legally renounced my Japanese citizenship, because I never believed in a person's dual allegiance. I tried my best to assimilate into American society and such in view I contributed annually out of my meager income to Community Chest and American Red Cross Society. I took to the American way of life and learning. Since I started my nursery business my business dealings were centered among American retailers.

B. EXPATRIATION

My best effort to maintain my American Citizen's liberty was abruptly ended as the result of the outbreak of the war, when I was herded into the concentration camp. The deprivation of my citizen's rights was such a shock to me that I thought my future was doomed as far as the United States were concerned, because of the racial reason. This race consciousness prompted me to apply for repatriation and intended to do so until after the cessation of hostilities.

C. MY RECORD SINCE THE EVACUATION

When I was transferred to Tule Lake Center, I taught Japanese language in Kokumin Gakko for 10 months to nisei minors, using the text books approved by the director of the center. My teaching was solely of Japanese language exclusive of ideological or political matters. I never brought out the loyalty question in my classes. . . .

F. RENUNCIATION OF CITIZENSHIP

This decision [to renounce] was born out of my disgust and despair over the disenfranchisement of citizens of Japanese origin on racial ground, despite the fact that I was not a subject of Japan by the vertue [sic] of my renunciation of Japanese citizenship in 1931. . . .

5. RECRUDESCENCE

In the first place, I returned to the United States with no other thought than to live my life in America as a law-abiding loyal citizen of the United States. I was not in any way connected with anti-American movement nor pro-Japanese organization. My business was no other than horticultural enterprise in my best effort to establish myself like an American. My thought never ran beyond my business affair. I know that my duty is to abide by the duty and responsibility vested in me as an American, and I was ready to assume all of that when called for to perform. But when the evacuation started I could not help feel the injustice brought upon nisei of Japanese ancestry. Discontentment and confusion were the natural outcome of the bitter experience. Regardless of the bitterness, only patience, tolerance and contentment were the means with which I had to wait for the

judgment by the will of God, for I was no judge of affairs beyond my understanding. It is true that I have been influenced by the racial intolerance of the American public stimulated by the war hysteria. I misjudged the mentality of an average American and the ideals brought about by the historical foundation of Christian principles. Through this misjudgment I was led to commit myself to the regrettable errors in many matters, during the war. After the cessation of the war, I found the victorious American's attitude toward the vanquished Japan is such that I have come to appreciate the true American spirit borne out of American tradition and Christian ideals. With this realization and understanding, my sense of repentance gushes out ashamed of my past ignorance. Conscientiously I have lost all interest in Japan years ago. My recrudescence reversed my former ideology to the true ideals of the United States. My discontentment, doubt, confusion and despair have vanished like a bad dream. Not only my thought and desire returned to those of prewar conditions, but I confidently believe myself can now be a better American than ever have been. Should I find an opportunity, I shall exercise every effort to prove my worth.

AFFIDAVIT EXPLAINING CHUMAN'S RENUNCIATION (OCTOBER 22, 1954)

When I was in Japan, the people in Japan looked upon me enviously that I could return to the United States. They all knew that the United States was the best country in the world to live in. In effect it is the next best place to heaven while in this world. Therefore during my early childhood, I had a sincere desire to return to my native land when such an opportunity should arise. . . .

[Once in high school in the United States,] I learned to realize how wonderful the democratic government functioned. Everything seem different from the functions of government in Japan, and one was able to exercise a tremendous amount of initiative. I learned that there was a Constitution in this country, and men and women had fought for its principles. That all the persons were considered an equal in the eye of the law, and each and every person were possessed in an inalienable rights. I spent many an evening over the history books, that furnished the struggle that was necessary to keep this country free. I was proud of the fact that I could distinguish myself as an American citizen.

Therefore when the evacuation order was issued by the Western Defense Command without the declaration of martial law, I felt that everything I had learned in the history book was not the truth. I felt on the eve of evacuation that the policy of the government was to assist the white race, and they were not going to apply the rights and privileges to the person of Oriental or Japanese race. I was really discouraged and disillusioned from this fact, and I felt that I was really stabbed in the back.

LETTER TO WARREN FROM CHUMAN (NOVEMBER 2, 1958)

As far as my wife Toshiko is concerned, she is absolutely innocent. Because she lost her own will as soon as she married me. She was educated in Japan that once a women married, she should never separate from her husband and sacrifice herself for family. In fact I am very grateful to her that she is devoting herself to raise healthy and happy family. Our children are all getting outstanding qualities of citizenship in school. Her brother already served in U.S. Army. Our two sons will serve in U.S. military some day. I would like to regain my citizenship so that they will go in service as true American sons without any doubt. . . .

LETTER FROM CHUMAN TO COLLINS (MARCH 8, 1967)

[This letter was written after the courts had repeatedly denied Chuman's case, and Collins had urged him to become a naturalized citizen.]

As far as naturalization concerned, I am not worrying too much because I came along for twenty years without U.S. citizenship even I felt a little handycap [sic] and inconvenient. I am now fifty three years old and I'm not sure if I will live another twenty years. Besides, I do not have any ambition to be a politician, an important leader or a millionaire. I believe when I go to beside God, I do not need any country's passport. Only thing I need, is how I lived in this world. I wish this whole world will be one country and a passport or a tariff will be unnecessary thing some day. Then there be no prejudices between races or wars between countries.

Right now I'm struggling to raise my eight children to be decent and well educated. Three of my children are now going to colleges and next fall another.

I hope someday before too long, I could see you in person and express my deep appreciation.

Sincerely your renunciant.

LETTER FROM COLLINS TO CHUMAN (JUNE 14, 1967)

Enclosed find a certified copy of the conclusive final judgment which cancels your renunciation and which declares you to be and at all time to have been a U.S. citizen and national and as such entitled to all the rights of citizenship.

The judgment cancels your renunciation as at the time it was made and, in consequence, it was a void renunciation from the beginning.

Source: Excerpt from *Series 2: Tule Lake Defense Committee Files, 1940–1972. Individual Case Files. Renunciants, 1944–1969.* Reel 8, 15–16, 36, 57, 62–63. Wayne M. Collins Papers, BANC FILM 2162, The Bancroft Library, University of California, Berkeley.

Territory of Hawai'i Legislature, House Resolution No. 61
(1955)

The 1952 Immigration and Nationality Act, also known as the McCarran-Walter Act, overturned the race-based prohibitions on immigration and naturalization that had been in place since 1790 (although strict immigration quotas for Asians still remained). For the first time, Japanese immigrants, the issei, could become naturalized American citizens. The next year, Houn Tamayose, a Buddhist missionary from Okinawa, obtained his U.S. citizenship. Tamayose had immigrated to Kauai in 1920 and moved to Oahu a few years later. As a community leader, Tamayose sought to bridge the gap between Okinawans and mainland Japanese in Hawai'i, combating the pervasive anti-Okinawa prejudice that many Japanese had brought with them. The following document, a House Resolution passed by the Territory of Hawai'i Legislature (Hawai'i would not become a state until 1959) on March 28, 1955, congratulates Tamayose on his new citizenship.

WHEREAS, the Reverend Houn Tamayose was born on March 28, 1881 in Japan; and

WHEREAS, at an early age the Reverend Houn Tamayose decided to enter the Buddhist priesthood; and

WHEREAS, pursuant to this intent the Reverend Houn Tamayose entered Ohtani University from which institution he graduated in 1907; and

WHEREAS, in the year 1920 after a decade of fruitful service in his native Japan the Reverend Houn Tamayose set sail from Japan and arrived in the Territory of Hawai'i on December 13, 1920; and

WHEREAS, in the thirty-five (35) years following, the Reverend Houn Tamayose has faithfully and conscientiously served his Church, his community, and the United States of America; and

WHEREAS, in recognition of his long and faithful service to his church the Reverend Houn Tamayose was made Bishop of the Hawai'i Higashi Hongwanji Mission in February of 1948; and

WHEREAS, in February of 1952, ill health compelled his resignation from the office of Bishop of the Hawai'i Higashi Hongwanji Mission; and

WHEREAS, after thirty-five (35) productive years in the Territory of Hawai'i the Reverend Houn Tamayose on April 30, 1953 realized his life's ambition by becoming an American citizen; and

WHEREAS, the Reverend Houn Tamayose in becoming an American citizen on the 30th day of April became not only the oldest first generation Japanese subject to become an American citizen, but also the first Buddhist priest to become an American citizen under the provisions of the IMMIGRATION AND NATIONALITY ACT; and

WHEREAS, at the age of 74 years, the Reverend Houn Tamayose in becoming an American citizen exercised his franchise in casting the vote for the first time in the last elections; and

WHEREAS, it has come to the knowledge of the members of this House that the Reverend Houn Tamayose is the father-in-law of the Honorable Toshiharu Yama, Representative from the Island of Kauai and therefore makes the offering of this Resolution doubly pleasing; now, therefore, be it

RESOLVED by the House of Representatives of the Twenty-Eighth Legislature of the Territory of Hawai'i that this House congratulate the Revered Houn Tamayose on this occasion and wish him continued success and happiness in the days ahead; and be it further

RESOLVED that a duly certified copy of this Resolution be forwarded to the Revered Houn Tamayose.

Source: House Resolution 61, *Journal of the House of Representatives of the Twenty-Eighth Legislature, Territory of Hawai'i, Regular Session, Convened Wednesday, February 16, 1955; Adjourned Friday, April 29, 1955.* Honolulu: Fisher Corporation, Ltd., 1958, 953.

Fred Korematsu, Writ of *Coram Nobis*
(1984)

After the attack on Pearl Harbor in 1941, American hysteria over the Japanese threat boiled over, especially on the West Coast, where most Japanese Americans resided. In February 1942, Franklin D. Roosevelt signed Executive Order 9066, which laid the legal groundwork for the eventual incarceration of more than 120,000 Japanese Americans. The military's War Relocation Authority oversaw the 16 temporary detention centers that held Japanese Americans until the 10 permanent WRA camps were completed.

Fred Korematsu was working as a welder in the San Francisco Bay area when the Japanese attacked Pearl Harbor. When the evacuation order came down, Korematsu did not comply and hid out instead. He was eventually arrested by the Federal Bureau of Investigation and convicted as a felon for violating the evacuation order. The San Francisco chapter of the American Civil Liberties Union took up his cause (against the wishes of the national headquarters) and appealed his case to the U.S. Supreme Court. Korematsu challenged the evacuation on the grounds that he was targeted for removal because of his race. The Korematsu case, along with two other internment cases, Hirabayshi v. U.S. *and* Yasui v. U.S., *became major civil rights test cases about whether the state could suspend individual liberties in the name of national security. In 1944, the Supreme Court decided that the government could indeed do so in the case of "military necessity."*

However, in the early 1980s, historian Peter Irons found that the U.S. government had withheld key documents from the court in the original 1944 case. These internal documents reveal that claims of Japanese American espionage were not based on any concrete evidence. In 1982, a group of young sansei and yonsei (third- and fourth-generation Japanese American) lawyers filed a landmark coram nobis *petition to overturn Korematsu's 1944 conviction. Led by Dale Minami, Korematsu's legal team argued that withholding key evidence revealed the government's racism, undermining its original claim that internment was a military necessity. San Francisco District Court judge Marilyn Patel heard the case and agreed with Korematsu's legal team. In 1984, she overturned Korematsu's conviction, saying the government had perpetrated a great wrong. The following are excerpts from the opinion given by Judge Patel and the actual* coram nobis *petition, which included the original government documents that were excluded from the original 1944 trial.*

FRED KOREMATSU PETITIONER V. UNITED STATES OF AMERICA, Respondent. United States District Court, Northern District of California. April 19, 1984.

William T. McGivern, Asst. U.S. Atty., San Francisco, Cal., Victor Stone, Counsel for Special & Appellate Matters, General Litigation & Legal Advice Section, U.S. Dept. of Justice, Washington, D.C., for defendant.

Dale Minami, Minami & Lew, San Francisco, Cal., Peter Irons, Leucadia, Cal., Robert L. Rusky, Hanson, Bridgett, Marcus, Vlahos & Stromberg, Ed Chen, Coblentz, Cahen, McCabe & Breyer, Eric Yamamoto, San Francisco, Cal., for plaintiff.

OPINION

PATEL, District Judge.

Fred Korematsu is a native born citizen of the United States. He is of Japanese ancestry. On September 8,

1942 he was convicted in this court of being in a place from which all persons of Japanese ancestry were excluded pursuant to Civilian Exclusion Order No. 34 issued by Commanding General J.L. DeWitt. His conviction was affirmed.

Korematsu v. United States, 323 U.S. 214, 65 S.Ct. 193, 89 L.Ed. 194 (1944).

Mr. Korematsu now brings this petition for a writ of coram nobis to vacate his conviction on the grounds of governmental misconduct . . .

On March 2, 1942 General DeWitt issued Public Proclamation No. 1 pursuant to Executive Order 9066. The proclamation stated that "the entire Pacific Coast . . . is subject to espionage and acts of sabotage, thereby requiring the adoption of military measures necessary to establish safeguards against such enemy operations."

Thereafter, several other proclamations based upon the same justification were issued placing restrictions and requirements upon certain persons, including all persons of Japanese ancestry. As a result of these proclamations and Exclusion Order No. 34, providing that all persons of Japanese ancestry be excluded from an area specified as Military Area No. 1, petitioner, who lived in Area No. 1, could not leave the zone in which he resided and could not remain in the zone unless he were in an established "Assembly Center." Petitioner remained in the zone and did not go to the Center. He was charged and convicted of knowingly remaining in a proscribed area in violation of § 97a.

It was uncontroverted at the time of conviction that petitioner was loyal to the United States and had no dual allegiance to Japan. He had never left the United States. He was registered for the draft and willing to bear arms for the United States.

In his papers petitioner maintains that evidence was suppressed or destroyed in the proceedings that led to his conviction and its affirmance. He also makes substantial allegations of suppression and distortion of evidence which informed Executive Order No. 9066 and the Public Proclamations issued under it. While the latter may be compelling, it is not for this court to rectify.

However, the court is not powerless to correct its own records where a fraud has been worked upon it or where manifest injustice has been done. . . .

THE PETITION FOR A WRIT OF CORAM NOBIS

A writ of coram nobis is an appropriate remedy by which the court can correct errors in criminal convictions where other remedies are not available . . .

Ordinarily, in cases in which the government agrees that a conviction should be set aside, the government's position is made clear because it confesses error, calling to the court's attention the particular errors upon which the conviction was obtained. A confession of error is generally given great deference. Where that confession of error is made by the official having full authority for prosecution on behalf of the government it is entitled to even greater deference . . .

In this case, the government, joining in on a different procedural footing, is not prepared to confess error. Yet it has not submitted any opposition to the petition, although given ample opportunity to do so. Apparently the government would like this court to set aside the conviction without looking at the record in an effort to put this unfortunate episode in our country's history behind us . . .

Because the government has not acknowledged specific errors, the court will look to the original record and the evidence now before it to determine whether there is support for the petition and whether manifest injustice would be done in letting the conviction stand.

GOVERNMENT MEMORANDA

Petitioner offers another set of documents showing that there was critical contradictory evidence known to the government and knowingly concealed from the courts. These records present another question regarding the propriety of judicial notice. They consist of internal government memoranda and letters. Their authenticity is not disputed. Yet they are not the kind of documents that are the proper subject of judicial notice, and they are offered on the ultimate issue of governmental misconduct . . .

The substance of the statements contained in the documents and the fact the statements were made demonstrate that the government knowingly withheld information from the courts when they were considering the critical question of military necessity in this case. A series of correspondence regarding what information should be included in the government's brief before the Supreme Court culminated in two different versions of a footnote that was to be used to specify the factual data upon which the government relied for its military necessity justification . . .

Brief for the United States, Korematsu v. United States, October Term, 1944, No. 22, at 11.

The final version made no mention of the contradictory reports. The record is replete with protestations of various Justice Department officials that the government had the obligation to advise the courts of the contrary facts and opinions. Petitioner's Exhibits A-FF. In fact, several Department of Justice officials pointed out to their superiors and others the "willful historical inaccuracies and intentional falsehoods" contained in the DeWitt Report. E.g., Exhibit B and Exhibit AA, Appendices A and B hereto.

These omissions are critical. In the original proceedings, before the district court and on appeal, the government argued that the actions taken were within the war-making powers of the Executive and Legislative branches and, even where the actions were directed at a particular class of persons, they were beyond judicial scrutiny so long as they were reasonably related to the security and defense of the nation and the prosecution of the war . . .

There is no question that the Executive and Congress were entitled to reasonably rely upon certain facts and to discount others. The question is not whether they were justified in relying upon some reports and not others, but whether the court

had before it all the facts known by the government. Was the court misled by any omissions or distortions in concluding that the other branches' decisions had a reasonable basis in fact? Omitted from the reports presented to the courts was information possessed by the Federal Communications Commission, the Department of the Navy, and the Justice Department which directly contradicted General DeWitt's statements. Thus, the court had before it a selective record.

Whether a fuller, more accurate record would have prompted a different decision cannot be determined. Nor need it be determined. Where relevant evidence has been withheld, it is ample justification for the government's concurrence that the conviction should be set aside. It is sufficient to satisfy the court's independent inquiry and justify the relief sought by petitioner.

CONCLUSION

. . . At oral argument the government acknowledged the exceptional circumstances involved and the injustice suffered by petitioner and other Japanese-Americans. See also Response at 2-3. Moreover, there is substantial support in the record that the government deliberately omitted relevant information and provided misleading information in papers before the court. The information was critical to the court's determination, although it cannot now be said what result would have obtained had the information been disclosed. Because the information was of the kind peculiarly within the government's knowledge, the court was dependent upon the government to provide a full and accurate account. Failure to do so presents the "compelling circumstance" contemplated by Morgan. The judicial process is seriously impaired when the government's law enforcement officers violate their ethical obligations to the court . . .

Korematsu remains on the pages of our legal and political history. As a legal precedent it is now recognized as having very limited application. As historical precedent it stands as a constant caution that in times of war or declared military necessity our institutions must be vigilant in protecting constitutional guarantees. It stands as a caution that in times of distress the shield of military necessity and national security must not be used to protect governmental actions from close scrutiny and accountability. It stands as a caution that in times of international hostility and antagonisms our institutions, legislative, executive and judicial, must be prepared to exercise their authority to protect all citizens from the petty fears and prejudices that are so easily aroused.

ORDER

In accordance with the foregoing, the petition for a writ of coram nobis is granted and the countermotion of the respondent is denied.
IT IS SO ORDERED.

APPENDIX B

EXHIBIT A

MR HERBERT WECHSLER SEP 11 1944

J. L. BURLING

Assistant Attorney General

SUBJECT: Korematsu v. U.S. War Division

The Solicitor General has gone over the revised page proof of the brief and has made certain additional changes. I desire to invite your attention particularly to the footnote which appears on page 11 of the revised page proof. As set out in the first page proof at page 26, the footnote read:

"The Final Report of General DeWitt (which is dated June 5, 1943, but which was not made public until January 1944) is relied on in this brief for statistics and other details concerning the actual evacuation and the events that took place subsequent thereto. The recital of the circumstances justifying the evacuation as a matter of military necessity, however, is in several respects, particularly with reference to the use of illegal radio transmitters and to shore-to-ship signalling by persons of Japanese ancestry, in conflict with information in the possession of the Department of Justice. In view of the contrariety of the reports on this matter we do not ask the Court to take judicial notice of the recital of those facts contained in the Report."

. . . You will recall that General DeWitt's report makes flat statements concerning radio transmitters and ship-to-shore signalling which are categorically denied by the FBI and by the Federal Communications Commission. There is no doubt that these statements were intentional falsehoods, inasmuch as the Federal Communications Commission reported in detail to General DeWitt on the absence of any illegal radio transmission.

In addition, there are other misstatements of fact which seek to blame this Department with the evacuation by suggesting that we were derelict in our duties. These are somewhat more complicated but they are nevertheless demonstrably false.

In view of the fact that General DeWitt in his official report on the evacuation has sought to justify it by making important misstatements of fact, I think it important that this Department correct the record insofar as possible and certainly we should not ask the Court to take judicial notice of those facts. . . .

In view of all these circumstances, it seems to me that the present bowdlerization of the footnote is unfortunate. There is in fact a contrariety of information and we ought to say so. The statements made by General DeWitt are not only contrary to our views but they are contrary to detailed information in our possession and we ought to say so.

I press the point not only because I would like to see the footnote restored to its earlier form, if possible, but because it is now contemplated that the revised brief be submitted again to the War Department. I assume that the War Department will object to the footnote and I think we should resist any further tampering with it with all our force.

Source: Korematsu v. United States, 323 U.S. 214 (1944) and Asian American Bar Association of the Greater Bay Area, aaba-bay.com, 2009.

Hiroshi Shikuma, Interview by Randall Jarrell
(1986)

At the time of this 1986 interview with Randall Jarrell from the University of California–Santa Cruz, Hiroshi Shikuma was a prominent strawberry grower in Pajaro Valley. He describes his early years working on farms with his issei parents and the thriving Japanese American community in California's Central Valley. In 1913, California enacted the Alien Land Laws, prohibiting "aliens ineligible for citizenship" from owning or buying land. The Alien Land Laws targeted the issei, who were enjoying economic success in California's truck-farming industry— and who were unable to become naturalized U.S. citizens because of the racial restrictions of the 1790 Naturalization Act. Issei farmers, like Shikuma's father, bypassed the Alien Land Laws by purchasing property in their American-born (nisei) children's name. The following excerpt from Shikuma's interview describes life on a Japanese American farm and the ethnic solidarity within the community.

JARRELL: During your growing-up years, what kind of food did you eat? What did your mother prepare?

SHIKUMA: Japanese style rice; rice was our basic food. We also had fish and vegetables, but not too much meat.

JARRELL: Did you always have a family vegetable garden?

SHIKUMA: Yes. They always raised the Japanese vegetables: daikon [radish] and nappa [cabbage] and things like that.

JARRELL: Where did you get the rice?

SHIKUMA: In town.

JARRELL: Where did your mother or you[r] father shop? Later I suppose your mother did the shopping.

SHIKUMA: Well, there were Japanese merchants in town. We could get all the Japanese food from them. And then once a week, these Japanese people [in my time, they were able to have old cars] would come with what amounts to an old panel or pickup. They would come to peddle these Japanese food items.

JARRELL: I see. I never knew that was practiced around here.

SHIKUMA: Fish peddlers would come weekly, too.

JARRELL: Japanese peddlers?

SHIKUMA: There was one Japanese fish peddler, and then there was an Italian peddler that would call on the Japanese . . .

JARRELL: You started school about 1924?

SHIKUMA: 1925 I think. I was born 19th December, very close to 1920.

JARRELL: Oh. I see. Do you recall if there were many Japanese children?

SHIKUMA: Quite a few, quite a few, because the Japanese kind of stayed together, you know. We had to move with the strawberries because, unlike now, we had to seek new soil. At that time, when you grew a crop of strawberries, you never replanted back onto the same soil. So the community would kind of move from one area to another.

JARRELL: What kind of distance would be involved in moving?

SHIKUMA: Well we were pretty close. I can recall as a child that the little group that I was with was within a quarter mile of the next group. Many of us were together. There'd be two or three families all within a quarter mile of us, and we would move kind of like a group. We'd rent or get a piece of ground . . . my dad was unable to rent ground, but a lot of it was rented through his son's name or my brother's name.

JARRELL: Now this had to do with the alien land rights?

SHIKUMA: That's right.

JARRELL: So that your father himself . . .

SHIKUMA: Was unable to lease, rent, or to buy land.

| JARRELL: | So he used whose name then? |
| SHIKUMA: | I think that first there was an older Nisei who was born here who was able to rent or lease a parcel of ground; the whole group would farm it. When my brother became old enough, why then he was able to lease ground. That's when we finally purchased our first |

property in Corralitos. It was under my brother's name.

Source: Excerpt from "Hiroshi Shikuma: Strawberry Growing in the Pajaro Valley." Interview conducted by Randall Jarrell. The Regional History Project of the University Library at the University of California, Santa Cruz. http://library.ucsc.edu/reg-hist/. Reprinted with permission.

Milton Murayama, *Five Years on a Rock*
(1994)

In the early 1900s, many immigrant Japanese laborers in Hawai'i sent back to their homeland for wives. This followed the traditional Japanese practice of arranged marriages, in which a broker would bring pictures of the prospective spouses to the prospective in-laws and negotiate a match. In Hawai'i, the negotiations were conducted via transpacific mail; the men sent (often woefully out-of-date) photographs back to Japan, where they would be selected by a woman's family. She would then travel to Hawai'i, bound by contract to marry the man she selected, regardless of his actual appearance or financial position.

Born in Maui in 1923, Milton Murayama is a Japanese American novelist whose work examines immigrant and ethnic communities in Hawai'i. Murayama's novel Five Years on a Rock *tells the story of a Japanese picture bride, Sawa Ito. Sawa travels to Hawai'i to marry Isao Oyama, a man she has never met, giving her engagement money to her impoverished new family. She intends to stay in Hawai'i for only five years; however, Sawa soon learns that she has entered a life of ceaseless work and constant conflict with her in-laws. In this excerpt, Sawa is entering a sanitarium on Haleakala (one of Maui's volcanoes). Her hard life on the plantations has destroyed her health,*

and she cannot see an end to the mounting debt burdening her family. Murayama's novel presents a compelling description of Maui plantation life, particularly for women, in the early 20th century.

"I'm sorry to be such a burden," I said to Isao. I cuddled Toshio as we rode the Miaki taxi to Wailuku and up Haleakala.

"Don't be silly."

"The debt just keeps growing."

"Don't worry about the debt. Your health is more important."

"I hope the children will be all right."

Isao had to drag Toshio back to the taxi.

I felt so empty afterward. Joji was still a part of my flesh.

The next day I sat outside in the wan sunlight and watched a butterfly wafting from flower to flower. *How much longer does it have to live?* I thought. I kept rubbing the slight cleft at the tip of my nose. People with such clefts died young, the villagers said. Death and sadness were everywhere.

"I feel like I've climbed into Heaven," Teruko, another patient, said in a hushed voice.

"Can you imagine a place like this in Japan?" Mitsue whispered.

We felt like conspirators in the presence of awesome Haleakala. There were a dozen picture brides in the two nontubercular cottages. The other ten cottages housed the consumptives.

"We're so lucky. They're not even permitted to walk in the yard," Teruko said. "Very few consumptives who come up here ever go back down again."

Teruko had four children; Mitsue, five. They'd both worked in the cane fields till they'd literally collapsed. "I'm such a crybaby; I shouldn't *amaeru* so," I said to myself.

There was an autumn chill without the autumn colors. We wore layers of clothes and *haori* jackets or shawls and walked with unhurried grace. The garden felt summery with poincianas, red-skinned avocadoes, poinsettias, geraniums, red ginger, willows, and gardenia. Skylarks hovered overhead, trilling their birdsongs. Rainbows arced to Haleakala, which gave birth to the sun each morning. In the afternoons the fog would creep down the massive slope and shroud the bean-sized cattle, trees, and cacti.

"Rest, don't excite yourselves," Dr. Sherwood kept saying.

Milk was served with every meal. It gave us diarrhea.

"I don't see how you ladies are getting your calcium," Miss Kaya translated for Dr. Sherwood.

They served cheese, which stank of butter and crumbled in our mouths like clay. We had meat once a day—beef stew, meat loaf, hamburger, hot dogs, or pork. There was enough meat in one dish to flavor a dozen vegetable dishes! No wonder the *haole* were so tall!

Isao came up in the Mikami taxi once every two weeks. He and Toshio would visit Joji in Honokawai, then backtrack to Pepelau and come east. Toshio would jump into my arms and refuse to let go. Joji was getting fat on Mrs. Arisumi's milk, Isao assured me.

We sat in the cool afternoon sun. Green pastures swept down from the sanitarium to the patchwork of cane fields in the flatlands. Farther *makai* was the town of Kahului and the blue ocean rising to the horizon. Beyond Kahului were the lush green peaks of the West Maui mountains.

"Pepelau is just beyond those mountains," Isao said.

"*Ah so*. So we're actually two mountains joined by Wailuku."

***

Toshio seemed so desperate on their last visit. He held me so tightly I could scarcely breathe. "What's the matter?" I tilted his face. His ribs and arms felt bony.

"He's lost some weight. Are you feeding him enough?"

"Yes, when I'm home."

"What about Jiro and his wife?"

"I give them $5 a month. That should be plenty."

"I understand she's very haughty and leads him around by the nose."

"She's a Tokyo girl, unlike other brides. And they're both heavy drinkers."

"Won't they get arrested?"

Isao shrugged. "Everybody does it."

"I'd feel better if somebody else looked after Toshio.

"There's nobody else."

The taxi cost $5. Isao was making $25, compared to the $20 on the plantation, but rent, medical care, water, and kerosene were no longer free. He talked of borrowing $500 from Tani Fish Market to buy his own sampan.

"*Soh, ne?*" I said, feeling strangely detached.

Source: Murayama, Milton. *Five Years on a Rock.* Honolulu: University of Hawai'i Press, 1995, 84–86. Used with permission of the author.

Naeko Isagawa Keen, Interview by Daniel Clark
(1995)

Naeko Isagawa Keen was born in 1933 on Tinian, a small island in the Marianas, and she grew up in nearby Rota. These Pacific islands saw some of the fiercest fighting during World War II; the United States used their air base on Tinian as a launching site for the Enola Gay. Isagawa and her family survived the World War II bombing raids by living in Tinian's caves. After the war, the Japanese government relocated the Isagawas to Okinawa. There, Isagawa met her husband, Robert Daniel Keen, who had come to Okinawa as a member of the American occupying forces. After the birth of their first child, the couple moved back to Keen's native Virginia.

Daniel Clark interviewed his grandmother as part of Rocky Gap High School's Appalachian oral history project. In this excerpt, Keen talks about her wartime experiences on Rota and her decision to leave Japan for the United States in the hopes that her biracial children would have more opportunities and face less discrimination.

Daniel: You were in Okinawa when the war took place?

Naeko: No, I was in the Pacific Islands next to Guam.

Daniel: You ran to the cliffs for safety right?

Naeko: We stayed in caves, big caves, a big ole hole and under a rock.

Daniel: Was there a lot of fighting near you?

Naeko: Everyday bombing, sometimes we had school, even though war was going on under the rock, we had to sit down, fix up like a chair, everyday we'd get bombed, you'd get use to it, in behind, bombs would drop, sometimes in front, that's the way we use to live for a long time for three years.

Daniel: What had you been told about the Americans?

Naeko: We didn't say nothing, we didn't know what they were like.

Daniel: You didn't know nothing about them.

Naeko: No, we didn't know nothing about them, this war, they bombed us out and scared us out every time they dropped a bomb and you know, machine guns and shoot it up every which way, scattered bullets every which way, scared us, we just got use to it in everyday life, bullets would fly every which way, we just jumped up, you know, tried to dodge.

Daniel: Where were you, when you saw your first Americans?

Naeko: It was about 1943, I think, everybody was looking for people, we thought we were still fighting, the Americans GI's were coming in big ole GMC Trucks, plumb full with G. I.s there and they were hollering and we thought the war was still going on, we were use to the war, so every day, every day, we'd hear the airplanes coming or machine guns, we'd just humped up hide behind a rock, anything you'd just laid, and if you come out, you were lucky, I guess, we'd dig potatoes, and I guess they seen us sometimes . . .

Daniel: Why did you decide to leave Japan? You and Papa, why did you decide to come?

Naeko: Well, he came . . .

Daniel: Uh hum, and you left with him to go to America, back to his family, Why did you come?

Naeko: Well, we got married, and I had Bobby, at that time, I had Bobby.

Daniel: Was it frightening to leave your home and family.

Naeko: Yes, I did, but you see, you had a child, you have to look to his future, cause I know, what kind of future held have if I stayed in Okinawa, and raised him it was going to be an outsider, you know Okinawa. . . .

Daniel: People would look down on you.

Naeko: Yeah, people would look on you, racist, you know they're not nice to you even though they laugh at you. So I didn't want that to happen to him, I was married, even though I was afraid to come to the United States.

Daniel: What was it like coming to a new land?

Naeko: First, I was real worried because it was a strange place then, I didn't know their kind, I didn't know what it was like. I didn't know how to act, you know, I didn't know nothing about it. A new land and people.

Daniel: Completely different.

Naeko: Yeah, you know, my mother-in-law was real nice and friendly they treated me like one of their own and then I had Bobby, it made it easier . . .

Daniel: To accept you . . .

Naeko: Yeah,

Daniel: How did you get to the U.S., what did you take, did you take a boat?

Naeko: A boat.

Daniel: What was it like on the boat?

Naeko: It took about two weeks to get there, so it was real hard, it was rough waters, and I got sick, I was pregnant about three or four months along with Betty.

Daniel: So when did you come to the U.S.?

Naeko: When, I think it was 1955, I think we came in April or May.

Daniel: How did you feel when you first got off the boat in San Francisco, since it's such a big city? What did that feel like?

Naeko: I was just seem like excited, never seen it before, and different and I was scared to because it was a different country.

Daniel: Where did your husband take to make your first home?

Naeko: Well we stay hotel that night in San Francisco, then we bought a car, and then we drove, I didn't, he did, all the way from San Francisco to Grundy, VA all the way to his, of course, it took us a week.

Daniel: It took you all a week?

Naeko: Uh hum, it took us a week to get to his home.

Daniel: You all stayed in motels and stuff like that?

Naeko: Oh yeah, every night, almost every night, he would drive until he couldn't drive. He'd drive all day long and by evening time, he'd get tired and stopped and sometimes it would be 10:00 or 11:00 p.m. before we'd stop. We stay the night and the morning we'd start again and the baby, Bobby was small, he was only a year old. It was too hard on him too.

Daniel: Did you feel like the people in the States were racist then, were they rude or were they helpful?

Naeko: I thought they were real nice . . .

Daniel: When did you first come to Bland County [a rural community in the mountains of southwest Virginia]?

Naeko: First, we lived where his Daddy and Mommy were in Grundy, on Dismal.

Daniel: You lived on Dismal.

Naeko: Yeah, we lived on Dismal, and he hunted over here and we found a place.

Daniel: How did you feel about coming here?

Naeko: I liked it because you know, it's quiet and peaceful place.

Source: Clark, Daniel. "Interview with Naeko Isagawa Keen." May 18, 1995. http://63.160.254.53/naekokeen .html. Used with permission of the Bland County History Archives, a 17-year oral history and technology project of the students of Rocky Gap High School in Rocky Gap, Virginia.

Alice Ohashi Kuroiwa, "Life and Education of the Older Children of Immigrant Parents (born between 1910–1925)"

(1996)

Thousands of Hawai'i's American-born nisei grew up on the plantations. They lived in plantation housing, working alongside their parents in the sugarcane fields, governed by the *hierarchical economic and racial system overlaying agricultural life in Hawai'i. The Japanese Americans, who soon became the ethnic majority in the islands, held a relatively high status among other ethnic labor groups. This racial pecking order was reinforced by the white elites, who pitted workers of different nationalities against each other to prevent interethnic labor organizing.*

Plantation children often remained unaware of these complex social and political dynamics, however. In her memoir of her early years on Kipu Huleia sugar plantation, Alice Kuroiwa recalls her multiethnic community of Japanese, Filipino, and Korean neighbors. This excerpt illustrates the distinctive plantation culture that developed on the island of Kaua'i: the mix of different religious and cultural traditions, the sharing of different foods, and the common experience of eluding the luna (overseer) that ultimately would unite the different groups of laborers in Hawai'i.

I, Alice Yoshiko, was born Feb. 15, 1922 to Bunjiro and Ima Ohashi, down in Huleia Valley where the mules cry, mynah bird chatted, the doves cooed, and crickets chirped at night and frogs croak at night and during the day. The valley was peaceful and quiet. Father and Mother raised rice for the Ahana family. And for extra money, Grandma raised "hasu" (lotus roots) and she told me she had a little donkey that she called Jimmy. She loaded this hasu on the donkey and she carried me on her back. They call it "opa" and she walked 4 miles up the valley to Seki camp (in Kipu) to sell the hasu to make some extra money. She said it was very hard. After staying in Huleia Valley for 2 ½ years, they thought they would go back to Wm. Hyde Rice's sugar plantation again. So they move to Seki camp. And when they moved up there, they had a son. They called him Fumio and Fumio was kind of sickly boy; he always caught a cold. I don't know what was wrong with him but "yowai", you know, Grandma use to say "yowai", "ittsu domo catch cold" (yowai is weak). I was the healthy one. I was husky and just like a tomboy. My mother always use to say "otemba", that meant tomboy when I was a little child. But, I took care of Charley (Fumio) when he was small and when the other boys would tease him, I was right there to protect him.

There were three reasons why Bunjiro and Ima moved from Huleia Valley to Seki Camp. The first was they wanted to have a son; they had four girls and people said if they moved to a new place, they might have a son. So that was one reason why. The second reason was the plantation was better than raising rice because at a plantation, they had fuel (kerosene), the Rice's gave us wood (fire wood), free housing and medical. Dr. Kuhns was the plantation doctor and Mr. Rice gave us a quart of milk for families who had children. And third, it was so far for Tomiko, the oldest one to walk to go to school. She felt sorry for the little one to walk 4 miles to school everyday. And after that Hayako and Chiyoko, they all had to go to school so they (parents) thought they would move up to the camp (Seki) so the children will all be closer to school (Huleia School). After they moved to Seki camp Fumio was born and of course, Tsugio (Eddie), and Tatsumi (James) and the rest of the children were born there (Eva Yaeko). We had a very good life although we had to work hard. Everybody had their own chores to do each day; it worked out fine.

We always had good friends, Filipino laborers, and I remember a man he was bald headed and he came on a bicycle and he came from Rice camp. His name was Andres. And another man Esteban, who lived two houses below us and mother use to wash their laundry. Mother loved to make bread and she made the beer for father (home brew). We had a garden and my father taught me how to raise vegetables. The most popular flowers in those days were white daisies and Easter lilies. A lot of them grew in the garden. Father grew the vegetables and we used the vegetables he planted. Saturdays, of course, usually people killed pigs. We had the bread and grandma made beer so on Saturday night the Filipinos would come and drink and eat. After they ate, they would sit in the parlor (living room) and I would tell them nursery rhymes. Sundays was very good because the vegetable man came. We loved to eat "natto" (fermented soy beans wrapped in dried cane leaves). It's fermented soy beans which Kajiwara man sold and Mr. Kodama came and sold tofu (bean curd). The tofu, young bamboo shoots and something like chop suey and it tasted so good. We usually ate that on Sundays. Grandma was a very efficient and talented lady. In 1935, we didn't have any electricity but she bought a refrigerator which was run by kerosene (heat). And we put our food in there (ice box) but prior to that, we had an old fashion ice box. A man came, somebody came, to deliver the block of 25# ice and we had some way of preserving the perishable food. . . .

In regards to clothing, we didn't have much choice in the 20's and 30's. The men wore denim pants, khaki pants and ladies wore Indian Head. We had all kinds of colors in Indian Head that was our cotton material and we also wore palaka. We had chambray but my Mom she used to wear a very thin material which looks like chambray, I think. She wore something like a shorty muu muu. You know, she wore apron with pockets. I remember I was going to school one day and a friend of mine was riding the swing. She had a blue bloomers on and Fumio said, "Oh, you have blue pants?" and this girl turned around and said, "Your sister Yoshiko wears rice bag pants". You know we used to wear those rice bag pants. Mother had a way of bleaching the rice bags or flour bags which had No. 1 (rice bags) written on it, which came from Japan and she made the pants with button holes and as we got older and our waist line got bigger, she just moved the button holes so the pants would fit the waist. I remember Mom was always a busy lady. She bought a Singer sewing machine from Akimoto man from Koloa. Why I remember this is because he use to come and collect every month on the easy time payment plan. She use to pay this man every month. He was a young man and he stuttered a little bit but he was a good man. Grandma use to say Akimoto san came, Akimoto san came to collect our money for the sewing machine. Mother did a lot of sewing. She got some patterns from Mrs. Woo (our Korean neighbor) who had a tailor shop in her home and I think Tomiko learned to sew from this lady, Mrs. Woo. Grandma, Mama Ohashi, we later called her Mama Ohashi, she sewed raincoats and riding raincoats

and rain hats, tabis (cloth two toed work shoes) and leggings and everything on this sewing machine. I think the best time was when she was sewing on her sewing machine.

My father passed away in Aug. 1935. I had to quit school in Sept before finishing up 8th grade and work in the sugar cane fields and grandma told me, my mother told me, that someone had to work in the fields. I was 13 years old. No child labor law. I was a child when I started working in the cane fields and got paid 25 cents a day. And didn't know what is a bad weed to cane. I hoed every thing, so Hada man who was the wahine luna, got me a burlap bag. He instructed me to pick up any hono hono grass, put them in the bag and when the bag was filled to empty it at the mo-pali, which I did. When you find a hono hono grass one does not cut it for it will have shoots and sprout. We had about 4 girls doing the same kind of work. . . .

We knew when Eddie Scharsch, the big luna, came, with the smell of his cigar and Hada man would say "be careful", the boss is coming. He rode his horse in the lower part of the field, so we would not see him, but his cigar smell gave him away. Ha! My father passed away on Aug. 1935, so in Sept. I became a steady worker. I remember Hada man (luna) telling me to wear a skirt and dress like the ladies. I never noticed the ladies all had skirts on. Some girls were already working for the plantation. They were 2 or 3 years older than I. We did more of the hoeing of bad weeds. When I became older and my Mom worked in the fields, we took over time work, like cutting seed (pula pula) for extra money. During the day we sometimes cover the pula pula with dirt all day from 7:00 AM to 3:30 PM. We got paid 75 cents a day for ladies and $1.00 for men.

I would get up at 4:00 AM to cook the rice on a wooden stove. I learned responsibility very young. I was to be sure the wood was dry and enough under the stove to use the next day. I was the Kome Bits (rice box). We had a wood shed. The single bachelor Filipino men came on Sundays to help us cut and chop the wood, which Ishida man and lady cut. It was mostly Java plum tree. We like iron wood because it was a hard wood and burned longer. Sometimes in the woodshed we see a scorpion and smash it because they sting and it hurts. One day at work in the field, I felt something crawling on my legs. I lifted my skirt and it was a 3 inch centipede. My girl friend was so excited, she went wham! And the centipede gave me a bite. It was so painful and the other ladies brought ume (pickled plum) and rubbed it on the bite. When I got home I poured vinegar on the bite and it felt better.

In 1937, we sent my mother to Japan. She had never gone back (23 years in Hawai'i). We told her to take some of the tanomoshi and koden money and go visit her parents and family in Japan and she did that. And when she came back from Japan, she brought back 4 or 5 bicycles and one was for me a girl's bicycle, to ride to work. I rode this bicycle and carried mother's raincoat and lunch bag (with lunch pail and bottle of water) to and from work. Sometimes, we would work for 8 hours then we would cut (cane) seed after work. And the boys all pitched in and helped. Charley had the duty of cooking the dinner and Tsugio make the furo and James, well I didn't know what he did. But, he pitched in and helped clean the house. Anyway, after 3:30 PM, the three boys would come to the cane fields and bring Eva along too. They would take the dried leaves off the standing cane stalks and we would cut it in sections about 18 inches long. When we came home, the dinner was already made, the furo was already made hot. We all pitched in. . . .

We had special days. When I was 13 or 14, I was a tomboy and mother wanted to make a lady out of me and she sent me to sewing school. Mrs. Tanji (our Japanese teacher) made us all sit on the floor and sewed (hand stitched) with our hands. Every stitch was hand stitched. Every year we had a "shinen kai" at the Japanese School and we had a contest, red and white competing groups. The girls had races and relay races. And then had a Christmas program at the school or we went to Lihue Christian Church and we had a chorus and we sang. Miss Bessie Weibke was our choir director. Mr. Rice would lend us the plantation truck. We would all get on the truck and go to Lihue. When we were little, we even had a program, a play, at the Lihue Christian Church. Then in August, we had the Bon dance and we all wore our kimono, just like they do today. The Bon dance is a dance festival to honor the spirits of the deceased. And we had that one Buddhist priest from Koloa who came during the Obon season to our house and to me it was very, very strange because I don't know anything about Buddhism. But, anyway, we gave him tea and some goodies like sembei (rice cookies) or something for him to eat. He was Reverend Naito from Koloa Honpa Honwanji (Buddhist temple). Although we were Christians, we respected other religions. In addition, we had many other activities. We had visitors whenever anyone gets sick, but those days they never gave fresh fruits, that was a disgrace. You bring canned goods like canned peaches, canned cherries, and bartlett pears and things like that. They wrap the gift up in red paper and with the words "please get well" in Japanese. When Father got sick, we got cans and cans of fruits by the bed and we ate one can everyday.

Source: Kuroiwa, Alice Ohashi. "Life and Education of the Older Children of Immigrant Parents (born between 1910–1925)." In *Kipu Huleia, The Social History of a Plantation Community,* edited by William Yamanaka, 1998. Used with permission of William Yamanaka.

Brenda Wong Aoki, "Uncle Gunjiro's Girlfriend: The True Story of the First Hapa Baby"

(1998)

Gunjiro Aoki, born in 1883, and Gladys Emery, born in 1888, issued an early challenge to mainstream attitudes toward and prohibitions against miscegenation. After leaving California and traveling through Oregon, both states that banned mixed-race marriage, Aoki and Emery arrived in Washington State and obtained a marriage license in Seattle. The Aokis married on March 27, 1909. In 1998, actress and storyteller Brenda Wong Aoki, the couple's great-niece, published "Uncle Gunjiro's Girlfriend" to celebrate her relatives' courage in the face of extreme racism and discrimination. Aoki's grandfather, Father Peter C. Aoki, founded the Japanese mission in San Francisco and was Gunjiro Aoki's brother.

In our family there has always been a secret shame. It's so bad no one talks about it. Since no one can talk about it we can't find out what we did. But it's there and it permeates all of our lives.

At first I thought it was because we were poor. Everyone knows the Aoki clan started out as dirt poor sharecroppers (but honorable because Grandpa was once an Episcopal priest.) Then I thought maybe it was because we're not pure—I am Japanese, Chinese, Spanish, and Scots. Then I thought, it's the legacy of the Internment. But my family was not interned. We were already in Utah.

So I thought I had better go over and talk with the eldest Aoki, my 106 year old cousin—Sadae. I drove up to Sacramento. I knew I was on the right track because she lives on Green Tree Lane. Aoki means Green Tree. She served me lunch on these exquisite dishes which she said my great-grandmother had brought over from our ancestral home in Japan. After the lunch, Sadae brought out an ancient photo album paging through until she came to a picture of this dashing young man.

"This is your Grand Uncle Gunjiro." Standing next to Uncle Gunjiro was a Hakujin woman in a long white Victorian gown and Sadae said "That's your Aunt Gladys, Uncle Gunjiro's girlfriend." Just then my relatives came home. Someone said, "Humph," and they closed the book. That's when I realized I'd uncovered the secret.

So I went to the library, looked into the archives of the *San Francisco Chronicle, Examiner,* and the *Call.* This is what I found:

March 10, 1909:

Cleric's Daughter Will Marry Samurai

Neither wars nor rumors of wars nor the manifestations of race prejudice interfere with true love, as is proved by the announced engagement of Miss Helen Gladys Emery, daughter of Rev. John A. Emery, archdeacon of the Episcopal diocese of California, and Gunjiro Aoki scion of a noble house of the Japanese Samurai.

Samurai? I thought we were dirt farmers!

March 12, 1909:

Friend of Emery Family Seeks Medical Advice as to Whether Hypnotism Can Explain Girl's Wild Infatuation For Japanese
Hypnotism?

March 16, 1909:

Japanese Barred From Marrying Caucasians

The Sacramento Assembly passed today the Polsley Bill, adding the Japanese to the list of races forbidden to marry Caucasians in the State of California.

Aoki Scorns Bribe to Quit Sweetheart

Shaking $1,000 in the face of Gunjiro Aoki, a representative of the Japanese of San Francisco used every argument he could bring to bear to break up the match. "Not for two million dollars," was Aoki's reply.

I like this guy.

Throw Bricks at Japanese Suitor, Corte Madera Men to Treat Miss Emery's Fiancee to Tar and Feathers

Geez, this is in the days when they lynched Orientals.

Goes to Join Jap Fiancee

Amid hoots and yells, banging of tin cans and an ironical shower of rice and decayed flowers, Mrs. Emery and her daughter left Corte Madera yesterday evening. Every man, woman and child were at the train station to greet them. The women in the crowd were particularly loud in their demonstrations of wrath. One person threw an immense calla lily, striking Miss Gladys full in the face. "My friends" she said "the enemy."

What a woman!

My research revealed that like Joseph and Mary, the couple began a sojourn in search of a marriage license. They left California. In Portland the Deputy District Attorney said, "If she parades the street with her Jap lover I'll jail 'em both." The county clerk added, "If they come to my office looking for a marriage license, I'll throw 'em out." In Tacoma an angry mob of hundreds of people blocked them at the train station. They continued north and were about to be married in international waters off of Victoria when the mayor of Seattle came to their aid. They were married under armed guard at Trinity Church.

Said Uncle Gunjiro after the wedding, "To Christian spirit all things are equal. If you understand about love, you know it is the same in all nationalities. What is the color of love?" The new Mrs. Gladys Aoki replied "I love him. Can't you people understand that I just love him." Mrs.

Emery added "We're all immigrants. What's wrong with marrying another immigrant?"

I wish I could say that everyone lived happily ever after, but there was a horrible backlash. Mr. and Mrs. Emery split up. She went to live with the young couple. Archdeacon Emery submitted his resignation to Grace Cathedral. My grandpa, Father Peter C. Aoki, founder of the Japanese mission in San Francisco circa 1897, was asked to resign by his own congregation. The Episcopal church banished him to Utah where he and my grandma died shortly after, heartbroken, leaving 11 children orphaned. And that is how the Aoki clan became sharecroppers in Utah.

Finally, I found this article in 1933:

San Francisco Chronicle, November 11, 1933

U.S. Judge Restores Citizenship to Wife in East-West Marriage

The federal court here yesterday restored to citizenship Mrs. Helen Gladys Aoki, 45, wife of the late Gunjiro 'Aoki and mother of five children by her Japanese husband. Mrs. Aoki was permitted to change her name to Oakie by federal Judge Kerrigan and thus regain her American citizenship. Despite the storm of disapproval by scores of persons she and Aoki, son of a Japanese General and one of the noble Samurai Families of Japan, were married in Seattle. The romance proved contrary to all expectations, idyllic.

Gladys lost her citizenship over this! That is when I thought, this is the family's secret shame?! I'm proud of these people! I'm proud to be related to these people!! I am going to tell this story and I'm going to pass on to my son what Sadae told me, "No need to lower your head. The Aoki's are an honorable family."

Source: Aoki, Brenda Wong. "Uncle Gunjiro's Girlfriend: The True Story of the First Hapa Baby." *Nikkei Heritage* 10, no. 4 (Fall 1998). Reprinted with permission.

Ryo Imamura, Interview by Stephen Fugita and Erin Kimura
(1999)

Ryo Imamura was born in an internment camp at Gila, Arizona, in 1944. His mother was a nisei from California; his father was a kibei from Hawai'i, sent to Japan when he was four years old to train in a temple. An 18th-generation Buddhist minister (both his father and his grandfather were bishops in Hawai'i), Imamura cofounded the Buddhist Peace Fellowship in 1978, an organization dedicated to compassionate social justice.

Stephen Fugita and Erin Kimura interviewed Imamura on August 3, 1999. In the following three interview segments, Imamura talks about his grandparents' work with the children of Japanese immigrant farm workers in Southern California, the differences between pre- and postwar Buddhist churches, and his grandfathers' efforts on behalf of plantation laborers and the Japanese Buddhist communities in Hawai'i and California.

Segment 3

Ryo Imamura: That's a very exciting story [about Imamura's maternal grandparents' involvement in a children's home in Guadalupe, California]. Lot of course, misfortune and tragedy mixed in with it too. But I think as the people who were present at the time look back—and they're mostly in their, I would say seventies now, they were children back then—they're quite fond of those times. And it really shows the strength of the *Issei* [first-generation Japanese immigrants] and their children, having to struggle and not just overcome, but, but thrive after, after all that. But yeah, my grandparents, my grandfather was there first in California and then I think my grandmother was kind of like a picture bride. It was arranged through, more through religious contacts. But they both—well she was also ordained

as the, I guess, *tokudo* priest, this kind of preliminary ordination so she could perform services. So they did seem to form a nice couple, and with common goals. And they came to California, and my—I hear 'bout him riding horseback to go visit his parishioners—and old, Model T type cars. Of course the *Issei* back then were all farm laborers, just barely getting by. Their children were left by themselves during the week. I guess they worked pretty much six days a week out in the fields. So my grandparents offered to open up the temple as the orphanage, in a way, 'cause they were without parents six days out of the week. And so they had something like fifty kids there of all varying ages. I hear all the stories of how they fed them and lined them up for baths. And my mother and all her, her brother and three sisters were also there. So we, I guess each generation has been raised in kind of a communal setting, where it's just not a nuclear family but many other strangers, all being treated like, like members of the family. So I'm sure that's had an influence on how we see our community now. But there was a terrible plague back then 'course they didn't have all the vaccines. Many of the parents died, so they were truly orphans. And so they any of them stayed a long time with my grandparents. And maybe they got together on Sundays with their parents, but that was all. So they were very much their parents. This went on well into I think the '30s, leading up to when they all had to evacuate 'cause of the war.

Stephen Fugita: What do you think was the ingredient—if you want to call it that—that allowed people to, well, the Japanese community to form this collective, or group, or sort of common community response to this real need of raising the kids? I mean, if you think about it today, I mean it would be extremely difficult to conceive of a bunch of *Sanseis* [third-generation Japanese Americans] getting together and taking care of this need together. Think about it, we'd have to pay, you know, how much, and all that. And people didn't have money and life was hard. What brought them together and how were they able to cope this way?

RI: Well, I think you just stated—part of the main reasons was that life was hard and people didn't have money, and they weren't educated, didn't have any options. And so in times of desperation, this is where certain people step forth. And the *Issei* ministers who came over knew they were coming over to a life of poverty and hardship. So it's really out of almost, you know, dire need that they were coming to help the immigrants who were very displaced and lonely here. And without any community leaders, I think lot of the plantation owners or farm owners were very careful—just like bringing over the black slaves here—to make sure they were not united and didn't have leadership. And they often pitted the Japanese against other ethnic groups—the Mexicans and so on. And so there's just all this turmoil and no support. So here come people like my grandparents who are educated, and have a certain confidence and they have ties to the old country. So when you get a lot of people who are feeling helpless—and here comes a man who's—not only has his heart in the right place, but has the skills to help them. And then with the disease and illnesses and those type of things, it just kind of all came together. And, you know, compared to today where people are educated, and feel quite independent, and all of our leaders are not looked up to, in fact they're often denigrated and made fun of. So it's a whole different environment. I think lot of great miraculous things

happen somehow, some kind of spirit, miraculous resilience in human beings comes forth. Especially if it's inside the, kind of the setting of a religious institution where service and compassion are core messages anyway. Then it's a miracle on the one hand. But, I think if you look at all the conditions, it's understandable why it happened. Even after the war with my parents and the hostels, with people again displaced and nowhere to go. Again, it's not like they sat down and said, "Shall we, or shall we not?" It's like, "Hey, we have to," right?

Segment 4

SF: This is probably getting ahead of ourselves, but you mentioned this coming together. So, how would you contrast the Buddhist church and the ministers, or the priests' role, say in the '20s or '30s compared to, say in a contemporary Japanese American Buddhist temple today?

RI: Ah, yeah, that's a good question. There's been many changes, and of course the—well most of the ministers now who are American born are not from temple families. There might just be maybe two of us out of the whole, whole group. And so this whole kind of conditioning over generations and the allegiances that are built, and all that aren't there. But, I think back when you talk about the '20s and '30s, there weren't a whole lot of options for the *Issei* and the young *Nisei* as far as a social outlet. And when you listen to—I guess they're not around any more—but the old *Issei* ministers, they really, they were identified as leaders, and they felt like leaders, everybody looked up to them, and so they conducted themselves with a great deal of confidence. And they would have people sitting there for hours on Sundays listening to their stories and, not only about experiences here, but back in Japan. And so this whole . . . brought tears to peoples' eyes, just hearing, you know, the familiar themes and stories.

And so it was a very much a bonding experience back then. People always made meals at the temple. They lived right around the temple because, of course all these communities were in areas that no one else wanted to live in back then. And so because of the opposition and the racism and all that, they were pushed to be together and to look to each other for comfort and support. And so it happened very naturally.

Today the needs are quite different, and intermarriage, language barriers now because the, many of the ministers are still coming from Japan. And of course you're talking 'bout fourth and fifth generation Japanese Americans who are Caucasians now. And I think the role of the ministers changed quite a bit. Before the minister—there was no board of directors before, so the minister was identified with the temple. They were synonymous. Today the ministers kind of rotate through. I think the average is six years per stay per temple. And so they're like replaceable cogs in a machine. And the board members stay the same. You find board members who've been on for forty years, right? [Laughs] And so they're the permanent part and they're identified with the temple. And the minister—they always say, "Well who's your minister now?" This is a common question, right. "How long's he been there? Is he on his way out?" And the minister's told, "Just take care of the services, and let the board know if any light bulbs need to be replaced." You know, it gets down to that. The ministers are told to—encouraged to do, I guess Buddhist education. But because there doesn't seem to be a whole lot of interest in the Japanese American lay people in the Buddhist teachings, they're more interested, it seems, in the organizational aspects: having preschool for the little ones, bazaars, basketball leagues, and all that. The minister's role has become quite, I don't want to say minor, but there are temples now who exist without ministers. And I can't say they're completely unhappy. Many of the lay people are highly educated, they can read a lot of the Buddhist literature in English now. So they're, they're used to public speaking also, so they're very likely to go up—they give—they don't call it a sermon in the old sense. At least it's a *dharma* talk you know which is the more commonly used term now. So if you ask the lay people if they'd rather hear professor so and so, or this attorney, whatever, give his views on Buddhism and legal issues or something like that, or, something in perhaps less than perfect English about some unfamiliar complicated Buddhist teaching, often the choice will be, if not stated directly, will be a leaning towards this. Of course we don't have to then pay somebody and make sure they have a home and all that. So I think there's a shortage of ministers, which is in a way corresponding to temples closing down and consolidating. In a way there's—a sadness if you're tied to that kind of tradition. You say, well, there were the glory days before, and there's a decline now. But if you look at the situation, it's perfectly understandable. The writing's on the wall. And I guess I'm not really sad about it in terms of— my interest has always been with the Buddhist teaching tradition, and I see it being adopted in many other ways, not, not only in Asia, but in the West. So that won't disappear, it will just be the forms. I know we have an *obon* [summer festival honoring ancestors] here in Olympia. Before it used to be seen as a Buddhist ceremony, and it is, you know. It's kind of a memorial ceremony for all our departed ancestors. But now it's run by the JACL and I don't know if there are any Buddhists in our local JACL. I think they're either Christian or not religious. And so they made it into a, a just a cultural event without any religious significance. Just like the *ikebana* [flower arranging] display there and the teriyaki chicken. It's all kind of in the same ballpark. And so maybe this is where a lot of the Buddhist temples are headed, more cultural centers. I don't know if it's good or bad. It's served its purpose. This is just a steady transformation that addresses needs. Just as the, the exciting stories of my grandparents, and what they did back then came out of need of their time, at that time. There's a very different need now. So they can't be—we can't maintain the same forms.

Segment 5

RI: I know my, oh my [paternal] grandfather in Hawai'i is a very similar story. The plantation workers, they're all men because the plantation owners didn't want families here. They wanted men just to, to devote themselves to work, and had no concern for their welfare. So you had these little clusters of young single men, and of course they offered them gambling and prostitutes and all these things. But I think many of these men missed the traditions and customs of Japan and realized that the only way they were going to get this was to have Japan send some priests over, because they were dying, too. They died very young in those days, very rough conditions, and there was no one to perform a funeral or memorial service. They had to do a Christian one, which was very strange for them. So my grandfather used to—in Hawai'i—go to all the outer islands. He used to, I always saw him riding this white horse. Very stylish man you know, white suit and on a white horse, a mustache. And they would have all these labor strikes there where the workers, of course, were terribly mistreated. And they would have these major strikes. And the only person they could think of calling at the time who had any respect from the workers, was the bishop. So my father [Ed. Note: Narrator meant to say grandfather] was—became very famous in the city papers and all that for the one who rode in on his white horse, and kinda told them, "Okay, let's work this out. You guys go back

to work and we'll get some better conditions," like that. And so again there was a need—it wouldn't happen today. They wouldn't ask the bishop of BCA to come and mediate a strike, 'cause he would have no influence. But in those days again, the uneducated—feeling helpless with the authorities and policies—asking someone who had the confidence and knowledge to do it, it's most likely the minister or priest. Even in Japan when you go through the countryside, you notice that even today each village has—the biggest building amongst this whole cluster of houses is the *Bukkyokai*, the Buddhist temple. Because the Meiji government, wanting to take away the influence and power of the *Jodo Shin* organization there—who always managed to rally the poor or the downtrodden to speak up for their rights and so on—they forced them to give up those influences and become city halls, so they just recorded births and deaths, and did administrative things for the lay people. So it kind of transferred over here—that same dependence on having the priests in the community who could write letters for them, translations, all these things, right? And all those roles are no longer necessary today. So it's a huge confusion, I think in the ministry even today. Should they be like Christian pastors? Should they be like Zen monks? And the lay people don't know what they want from them either so—very strange.

RI: When you're concerned about a people who are underprivileged and discriminated against, and this is your community, and your heart is awakened, and you'd look to it for your leadership—that the social activism part, I think, comes out. So both of my grandfathers—and I shouldn't discount what my grandmothers did too, you know, they're often not given the headlines, but . . . there was a film that just came out of Hawai'i called *The Six Famous Women of Hawai'i*, and my grandmother was one of them. Just for her kind of feminist ideas. She wore a, as a bishop's wife, usually they wore this real tight little kimono, walked in little steps, following behind her husband. She wore these kind of like a southern belle type of clothes. Then when they had gatherings she would say, "Oh, let's all dance." She would be out there and speak up on public issues and things like that. My grandmother on this side also was very famous for outspokenness about things. And so they formed very good teams. So both are very highly respected and looked up to, both in their times, and even now. And again, I think that times, times produce greatness in people too. Somebody has to come forth and they were very fortunate to be in those positions also. And they stayed for a long time. Nowadays ministers move around every six years.

But my father was—grandfather was bishop for thirty-two years. And built, I think thirty, thirty-eight temples in Hawai'i. I think there's only been one temple built since he died in 1932. So that's why his big statue's still in front of the headquarters and why the gymnasium/auditorium complex is called Imamura Hall, is because of that influence.

And my maternal grandfather, was I think from almost the turn of the century until he died in '47, I believe—that's forty-seven years of, of working every day for the community. I, I remember a story and I forget, I think it's one of my aunts told me that the governor of California—I can't remember his name—back in the, around the First World War times, very cruel towards the Japanese, always trying to pass different ordinances against them, especially hurting the farm workers. And so, my grandfather was a very passionate man. Got so worked up he says, he got tired of writing letters I

guess, getting no response. So I understand he—I don't know if he meant it or not—he got his car, the capitol was Los Angeles then. He says, "I'm driving to Los Angeles," right, "To go see the governor." And everybody's going, "No, no, no, no, no." And so he was going out on the highway—and it's not like I-5, it's those old highways—and he turned the corner too fast, he was in such haste. It was one of those Model Ts with very high center of gravity. So it tipped over into a ditch and fell on top of him. And he was up there, you know, swearing up a storm. "Get this off of me. I gotta go." By the time people saved him, his anger had dissipated, he could just laugh about it. But it's that kind of very humanness and passion, I'm sure, that drove them. And, this is all old talk, this is going back sixty, seventy years now. And so we're only left with the bare outline of things now. Of course we fill in the rest through our own imagination or our own idealism. So what the true details were I can't say. This is before I was born. But this is kind of how I get inspired, by creating these—remembering what I want to, and using my grandparents and my parents as my inspiration for what I do.

Source: Imamura, Ryo. Interview by Stephen Fugita and Erin Kimura. Olympia, Washington, August 3, 1999. Segments 3, 4, 5. Densho, www. densho.org. http://archive. densho.org/Core/ArchiveItem.aspx?i=denshovh-iryo-01-0003, http://archive.densho.org/Core/ArchiveItem. aspx?i=denshovh-iryo-01-0004, http://archive.densho.org/Core/ArchiveItem.aspx?i=denshovh-iryo-01-0005. Used with permission of Densho Digital Archive. The interview videos and transcripts are available on Densho Digital Archive (www.densho.org), a nonprofit organization that documents oral histories of Japanese American internees, both to preserve the historical record, and to explore the issues of democracy, citizenship and civil rights, particularly during war.

Bruce Yamashita, *A Most Unlikely Hero*
(2003)

Captain Bruce Yamashita is a sansei (third-generation) Japanese American from Hawai'i. Following the example of his uncle, a Purple Heart veteran from the World War II 442nd Regiment, Yamashita enlisted in the Marines in 1982. Recently graduated from Georgetown University's law school, Yamashita moved to Quantico, Virginia, and began Officer Candidate School (OCS), hoping to qualify for second lieutenant by the end of the 10-week course. Once he arrived at OCS, however, Yamashita endured racial insults and ethnic slurs from his commanding officers; and a few days before graduation, he was informed that he was being disenrolled because of "unsatisfactory leadership."

Yamashita went back to Hawai'i and began his career as a lawyer. But in 1990, he decided to file a lawsuit against the Marines, claiming that his treatment was part of a pattern of institutionalized racism, and that he had been washed out of OCS because his superiors' racist taunts negatively influenced his peers' evaluations. His case was championed by the Japanese American Citizens League, Hawai'i senator Daniel Inouye, and veterans from the 100th Battalion and the 442nd Regiment. In 1992, the Naval Discharge Review Board agreed to hear Yamashita's case. They found that minorities were being disenrolled from the OCS at a statistically improbable rate and concluded that racism was playing a significant role. Finally, in 1994, the Marine Corps issued an official apology to Yamashita and commissioned him as a captain.

Steve Okino, a journalist, film writer, and producer, wrote and directed the 2003 documentary A Most Unlikely Hero, *chronicling Bruce Yamashita's long fight for justice. The film has been screened at the Smithsonian Institution, the Japanese American National Museum, and other venues in the United States and Japan. The following are some excerpts from the script.*

Prologue

BRUCE YAMASHITA:	I didn't go into the Marine Corps to be a civil rights activist. That was the furthest thing from my mind. I just wanted to be a Marine.
NARRATION:	But as a minority, Bruce Yamashita didn't stand a chance . . .
JAMES DANNEMILLER, President, SMS Research:	The system that he was working in was biased against him from the start to the finish.
DALE MINAMI, civil rights attorney, co-counsel, Korematsu v. United States:	But I'm also proud that somebody like Bruce Yamashita would stand up and fight and take on the United States government.
NARRATION:	His fight for justice took four long years.
FRED PANG, former Assistant Secretary of the Navy:	Bruce persevered, when many others might not have . . .
NARRATION:	And he didn't just serve his country. He changed it . . .

Act 1

NARRATION:	February 1989. Bruce Yamashita entered the 140th Marine Corps Officer Candidate School at Quantico, Virginia. Like the other candidates, he had passed physical and mental exams and background checks. He had been accepted to OCS. Being accepted BY it was a different story.

YAMASHITA (voiceover) . . . We were in the mess hall, I was going down the chow line when I noticed the sergeant came up to me from behind and asked me, "Hey, you speak English?" I thought it was sort of strange, so I turned around and said, " Yes I do sergeant instructor."

And that's when he yelled, "Well we don't want your kind around here, go back to your own country."

NARRATION: The same day, the senior non-commissioned officer came up and spoke to him in broken Japanese . . . and for all nine weeks of OCS, spoke to him only in broken Japanese. Others called him "Kamikaze Man," or "Kawasaki, Yamaha, Yamashita . . . " a litany of Japanese products and his name.

YAMASHITA: During a drill class, Staff Sergeant Brice came up to me and asked me: hey Yamashitee, during WWII was Japan and Russia ever at war? And I told him, I think they were. And he replied, No way, because World War II we whipped your Japanese ass . . .

YAMASHITA: Candidate O'Brien came up to me, I was cleaning my rifle, and he came up to me and asked if he could ask me a personal question. It struck me as kinda strange, but I said sure. And then he said, "Why didn't you just join the Japanese army?" I went on, I was a little shocked, but I did go on and explain to him that I'm an American, and it was just sort of a strange conversation. But at the same time, after all that was going on, for a rural kid from Nebraska, perhaps it was a reasonable question . . .

[After weeks of harassment from both his officers and his fellow candidates, Yamashita was brought before the Ninth Week review board, where he was disenrolled from the OCS.]

YAMASHITA: We were brought here after completing all nine weeks of training. We were brought here for our final battalion review board before Col. Renke right here in this office behind me.

We were called in. Lt. Eshelman recommended that I be disenrolled due to a lack of leadership, and that's when Col. Renke told me you are disenrolled, you are kicked out. I remember getting up, making an about-face, and walking out of the room, and hearing Col. Renke call me one last time. I turned around and he said, "And Yamashita,"—with a chuckle—"I heard you flunked your bar exam too." And I thought it was one last kick in the stomach as I was going down. After nine weeks of humiliation and harassment, this was one last kick they were going to get into me before I left. But I think it did symbolize all that had happened to me for the past nine weeks . . .

Act II

[After returning to Hawai'i and consulting with some of his military friends, Yamashita filed his lawsuit against the Marine Corps. It took two years for the Naval Discharge Review Board, which oversees challenges to Marine Corps discharges, to agree to hear his case.]

YAMASHITA: The morning after the NDRB [Naval Discharge

Review Board] hearing, I got a call from Clayton Ikei [Yamashita's legal counsel] before the sun had even come up, and he told me that we had made the front page of the *Washington Post.*

A few minutes later I got a call from Bill Kaneko [then president of the Honolulu JACL] who said we had made the *New York Times.*

Moments later, I got a call from Good Morning America, and the rest of the day was a blur of media requests.

CHARLES GIBSON: The Marines say you were disenrolled, or washed out in effect, of Officer Candidate School solely on the basis of performance. That's a rather subjective thing. Do you know that's wrong, can you prove that's wrong?

YAMASHITA: Well, the reason I was disenrolled was because of leadership failure, which is subjective, 100 percent subjective. And the very people who were involved in these derogatory racial remarks, harassment over a nine-week period, were the very ones responsible for making these evaluations. Therefore, the Marine Corps needs to recognize that these sort of racial remarks has an effect and taints the evaluation process, the subjective evaluation process.

GIBSON: Colonel, let me ask you first of all. Is there a policy to prohibit the kind of ethnic insults that Bruce talks about?

COL. DAVID VETTER, USMC: Yes in fact those procedures are incorporated in the Standard Operating Procedure as well as the staff training at Officer Candidate School, and any reference to a candidate's ethnicity during the course of the program is now prohibited.

GIBSON: So when the Marines offered him an apology, that was in effect saying we know they were used, they were wrong, we're sorry?

VETTER: Those changes were made subsequent to Mr. Yamashita's allegations.

YAMASHITA: After Good Morning America, I was taken straight to the Newark Airport. I checked in, the man there did my ticket, and he said, "Mr. Yamashita, hang in there," and he kind of winked at me, he said, "Hang in there," and he said, "We're behind you." And then he kind of saluted me as I walked away. It was very supportive.

I walked to the gate and there were these two Black American flight attendants were going off to their flight saw me sitting there and they recognized that I was on Good Morning America speaking about this issue, and they came up to me and they said, "Hang in there. This isn't an issue just about Asian Americans, it's about all minorities."

The flight was delayed, so I went to the cafeteria. There was an elderly Black woman serving food in the cafeteria, and she looked up at me and said, "Hey, you were on Good Morning America today, weren't you?" And I said, "Yes I was." And she just told me one thing. "Yeah, it's bull***, man," and she went back to her job. And I thought it was telling, that someone, a minority, who probably suffered injustices and insults throughout her life, that that was her response. "That's bull***, man." And she went back to work . . .

Act III

YAMASHITA:

My grandparents who had come to this country from Japan in 1892 and worked on the sugar plantations and lived a hard life for a better future for their children. Then of course the history of the 442nd, my parents generation, and for me and my generation to go to Marine Corps Officer Candidate School and to be called Kamikaze Man and "We don't want your kind around here, go back to your own country" and "During World War II we whipped your Japanese ass," for that to be said, again, for me personally it was an insult to my grandfather and my parents and their generation . . .

YAMASHITA:

In November 1992 I was contacted by a General Matthew Cooper from Marine Corps Headquarters who wanted to meet with me to discuss a possible resolution of the case. I went up to Marine Corps Headquarters and met with him, and told him I needed three things:

First, the Marine Corps had to commission me retroactively to the date when I would have graduated from the 140th OCS. It was important, because otherwise the Marine Corps could stonewall and stall and there would be absolutely no incentive for them to resolve future complaints.

Second, the Marine Corps had to admit and acknowledge that indeed there was racial discrimination at the 140th OCS.

And finally, there is something wrong with the Standing Operating Procedures when there's absolutely no language prohibiting the sort of conduct that was directed at me.

CLAYTON IKEI:

In 1993, the Marine Corps had implemented changes in its Standing Operating Procedures to be applied at Officer Candidate School at Quantico. Since then, the Marine Corps has implemented regulations and procedures that are in place at every installation. The other armed services have done likewise.

NARRATION:

Congress also required the military to publish and enforce regulations that prohibit racial and ethnic discrimination. The new requirement cited Bruce Yamashita's case and said it would "ensure that all minorities who volunteer for military service in the future will not face discriminatory conduct in violation of their civil rights and in contravention of the basic principles of our Government which our armed services are pledged to defend . . ."

[Assistant Secretary of the Navy Fred Pang helped broker a resolution with the Marines. Pang concluded that if Yamashita had not been subjected to racial discrimination during OCS, he would have become a second lieutenant upon graduation in 1989. Recognizing what intervening five years would have meant in terms of rank promotion, Pang ordered Yamashita to be commissioned as a Captain in 1994.]

JOAN LUNDEN
[then-co-host of ABC's
Good Morning America]:

Bruce Yamashita joins us again from Washington. And, well, I guess I'll let him give you the good news. Good Morning, Bruce. What's going to be happening?

YAMASHITA: Tomorrow morning at 10 a.m. at the House Armed Services Committee room on Capitol Hill, I'll be commissioned a Captain in the United States Marine Corps.

CAPT PETE KEATING, USMC: Attention to orders. To all who shall see these presence, greetings. Know ye that reposing special trust and confidence in the patriotism, valor, fidelity, and abilities of Bruce I. Yamashita, I do appoint him Captain in the reserve of the Marine Corps.

FRED PANG: It is a vindication of not only soon-to-be Captain Yamashita, it is a vindication of the process of democracy.

(CEREMONY: OATH) Raise your right hand and repeat after me. I, state your full name . . . do solemnly swear . . .

REP. NEIL ABERCROMBIE: This is a situation in the context of character. Character is the key. Character is what Bruce has.

(CEREMONY: OATH) To support and defend . . . the Constitution of the United States . . .

SEN. DANIEL AKAKA: A long-sought victory, not only for Bruce, but for the cause of civil rights in this nation.

(CEREMONY:OATH) I take this obligation freely, without any mental reservation

NORMAN MINETA, Secretary of Transportation: It would have been easier for Bruce Yamashita after being confronted with the discrimination he experienced to remain silent, and to quietly move on to other pursuits. But that would have been a grave mistake. A grave mistake for Bruce, for the Marine Corps, and for the entire United States military.

(CEREMONY: OATH) That I will well and faithfully discharge . . . the duties of the office

REP. PATSY MINK: Often times, those principles of equality and justice are just words because we do not have people in America of the stamina the fortitude, the integrity, and the tenacity like Bruce.

CAPT. KEATING: Honored guests, ladies and gentlemen, at this time, Major Ernie Kimoto, will come forward, USMC Retired, will come forward to pin the bars on Capt. Yamashita.

YAMASHITA (voice over): We did make history in the sense that it was a landmark in the continuation of the struggle. Specifically, those Japanese Americans who had made all those sacrifices. Whether it was on the sugar plantations in Hawai'i or the docks in San Francisco, or the strawberry farms in California, who had sacrificed their lives for the next generation. The whole experience of the internment and World War II and the 442nd who went off to fight for these principles, and many who paid the ultimate sacrifice . . . I think I got emotional because I really felt proud that we were living up to their legacy. It made us, all of us who were involved in this struggle, really a part of a much bigger sense of history. That really makes you feel proud.

CAPT. PETE KEATING: Honored guests, ladies and gentlemen, that concludes the commissioning ceremony. It's my distinct pleasure to introduce for the first time Capt. Bruce I Yamashita.

Source: Excerpts from Okino, Steve. *A Most Unlikely Hero.* Written, directed, produced, and distributed by Steve Okino. American Public Television release version, 2003, 1, 3, 5–7, 14, 17–18. http://www.unlikely hero.org/resources.html. Used with permission of Steve Okino.

LaVerne Sasaki, "Tule Lake Pilgrimage Memorial" and Jeanette Shin, "Transformations"

(2006)

Jōdo Shinshū, or Shin Buddhism, was founded in the 13th century by Shinran, a Japanese monk. As a follower of Pure Land Buddhism, Shinran advocated a less-ritualistic and discipline-based form of Buddhism. Shin Buddhism's central practice is nembutsu: invoking the name of Amida Buddha, the "Buddha of Infinite Light," to proceed on the path to dharma (ultimate reality).

Many of the 19th- and 20th-century Japanese immigrants to the United States mainland were Shin Buddhists. Agricultural laborers came first; they were followed by pastors who came to minister to their countrymen and counter the efforts of American Christian missionaries. Two organizations were established to oversee the priests and build the temples: the Honpa Hongwanji Mission in Hawai'i and the Buddhist Churches of America on the mainland. As time went on, Shin Buddhism in the United States became increasingly Americanized, incorporating many elements of American Christianity, such as children's and women's organizations, temple architecture, and musical forms. Nevertheless, Shin Buddhism remains a very ethnically homogeneous religion in the United States, in large part because of the experience of the Japanese American community during World War II. Jōdo Shinshū priests were targeted by the Federal Bureau of Investigation; even in Hawai'i, where there was no mass internment, priests were one of the few groups of Japanese Americans arrested and sent to camps. After the war, the church's primary focus was on healing its community rather than reaching out to the mainstream; consequently, even today, Shin Buddhism remains almost exclusively Japanese American.

The following articles, both originally published in Wheel of Dharma, *the Buddhist Churches of America's official publication,*

illustrate Shin Buddhist perspectives on two very different experiences: internment at Tule Lake and life as a U.S. Marine. LaVerne Sasaki is a retired Buddhist pastor living in San Bruno, California. When he was a child, Sasaki was interned at Tule Lake, the camp where the "No-No Boys" (interned Japanese Americans who refused to swear a loyalty oath to the United States) and their families were segregated. In his article about his 2006 pilgrimage to Tule Lake, Sasaki reflects on how his journey back to the camp, the service at which he officiated, and his own faith have all enabled him to come to terms with this history. Sasaki concludes his thoughts with the nembutsu, "Namu Amida Butsu," invoking the name of Buddha.

In 2004, Jeanette Shin became the first Buddhist to be commissioned as a chaplain by the U.S. Department of Defense. In her article "Transformations," Shin discusses the tensions and collaborations between ethnic, family, and religious identity. Arguing for the continued relevance of Buddhism in increasingly assimilated Asian American communities, and illustrating her position with examples from her experience in the Marines, Shin asserts that religion transcends ethnicity.

LAVERNE SASAKI, "TULE LAKE PILGRIMAGE MEMORIAL"

I had the privilege of participating in an interfaith memorial service at the site of the Tule Lake Segregation Center of World War II on the July 1–4, 2006 weekend. Because I was among the 18,000 who called it home for a few years (1942–1945), I was invited to speak at the service.

The theme of this year's pilgrimage program was Dignity and Survival in a Divided Community. Tule Lake, in Northern California, was the site selected to incarcerate those who refused to pledge loyalty to the United States government. The theme refers to the fact that for over 50 years, details concerning the no-nos and yes-yeses' have been discussed and debated. However, that is another (very important) story.

The memorial service was held, not at a usual "cemetery site," but on bare unidentifiable ground among sage-brush and tumbleweed. This was once the camp's cemetery site, located off a county road, next to State Highway 139 near the Oregon border. The inter-faith service was co-officiated by Rev. Saburo Masada, a former ministerial colleague of mine from my Stockton Buddhist Church years when he was the pastor of the local Presbyterian church.

The "central altar" was ably constructed by Jimi Yamaichi (Tule Lake committee president and member of San Jose Buddhist Betsuin). It included wooden replicas of Castle Rock (a nostalgic mountain for Tule Lake people), a guard tower and barracks; candles were set in the front. On one side of this table was a portable Buddhist "Omyogo"(Namu Amida Butsu) shrine with incense burner, flower vase and candle, while on the other side was a Christian cross.

During the chanting, I could not help but turn back the clock some 60 years when my late minister father and other BCA ministers had done the same chanting for many of the 331 persons who died there during those camp years. War Relocation Authority records show that only 11 of 331 persons were buried at Linkville Cemetery in near-by Klamath Falls, Oregon. It is also stated that some families cremated their loved ones and kept their remains. Today, there is nothing left at the site to remember and honor those who were actually buried here. In 2005, an archeological survey indicated that the site was excavated sometime in the past decade. The location of the remains of many of the people are therefore unknown. This gave me a great sense of regret and sadness. I am certain that the many who offered incense after the service shared similar feelings.

From my perspective, such public memorial services have deeper meaning and significance than what most of the 260 attendees might have imagined. "Mu en Hoyo" (memorial service for unknown persons) describes the focus of the service. "Mu en Hoyo," a major annual service conducted at the Seattle Buddhist Betsuin, was originally held to remember fishermen lost at sea; it reminds us that true compassion embraces all these unknown persons whose contributions make our lives possible. The more traditional Obon service is another example of this all-embracing ideal of compassion to all living beings. Also, "Eitaikyo" (Perpetual Memorial Service) is conducted by temples in memory of deceased members who may have been forgotten by family and friends with the passage of time.

The service at Tule Lake on the unidentifiable plot of land had similar significance; this time, in solemn remembrance of those who passed away when the Japanese were suddenly uprooted and transported to desolate unknown lands.

As a former Tulean, the oldest of five boys (ages 2–12), with a minister father and his wife, accompanying and serving their many members who had traveled with them from the Sacramento Buddhist Church congregation, I asked myself, "How did they do it?" With their future unknown and for the many hardships endured by my parents, other Senseis, leaders, and all who were incarcerated, I can only express humble admiration and gratitude. The issues with which they had to deal daily must have brought forth great feelings such as helplessness, shame, pain, sorrow, humiliation, anger, fear, betrayal.

Therefore the emotions I experienced cannot be described by inadequate words as "gratitude," "thankfulness" or "appreciation." The Japanese language has more meaningful expressions such as "gokuro sama" (acknowledges the pains and sacrifices to raise me), "sumimasen"(gratitude expressed as self-repentance and inadequacy for not doing more) and "okagesama" (acknowledgment of countless unseen Karma causes).

The Japanese who emigrated from their native country brought with them the spirit of "gaman" (patience, tolerance, or self-restraint) which did help them endure during those difficult, uncertain years.

All these expressions, I believe, is expressed by utterance of the Nembutsu (Namu Amida Butsu) "thank you" for allowing me to live with all of life's ups and downs with peace of mind within the wisdom and compassion of our ageless Dharma.

Our religious/spiritual way allows us to look at the pilgrimage theme of Dignity and Survival from this viewpoint. The history of the Japanese Americans has shown that we have been able to endure with dignity despite this black spot on our nation's history.

From conversations with many who traveled the long five-hour bus ride, I found that each person and family had their own reasons for making the pilgrimage; a karmic push (or pull). They ranged from nostalgia, wish for closure, education, curiosity, fellowship and the wish to honor our common history. Our pilgrimage together gave me a sense of community with all who attended and I feel that this trip certainly fulfilled my wish to honor those who lived, died and survived in Tule Lake.

Namu Amida Butsu.

JEANETTE SHIN, "TRANSFORMATIONS"

I am writing this month's Wheel of Dharma article at the 3rd Marine Air Wing Chaplain's office at the Marine Corps Air Station in San Diego. It is part of my annual two-week training to go to a Marine or naval base and take care of the spiritual needs of the military personnel stationed there, which is part of any military chaplain's responsibility. As I write this, I can hear jets taking off from the flight-line just a few hundred yards away!

Upon arriving, the Chaplain Officer-in-Charge of the Wing, Capt. Donald Lerow, provided me with a list of personnel who listed their affiliation as Buddhist when they reported aboard MCAS Miramar. There were over sixty names! Just in the air wing alone. All enlisted Marines. A quick look at their last names revealed the diversity of possible Buddhist practices: Japanese, Southeast-Asian, Chinese, American-Caucasian, and Hispanic. Nowhere else in the world would this diversity, even within Buddhism, be possible.

Transformations of and within our individual identity occurs throughout our lives.

To become a U.S. Marine, everyone must go through boot camp, either in Parris Island, South Carolina, or in San Diego, California. As you may imagine, it is a tough, three-month course, designed to take away your individual personal identity and replace it with a new one, that of a Marine. A person goes in as a civilian and comes out a Marine. Marines also have a unique culture, emphasizing their history, warrior values and *esprit de corps*, which set them apart from even other branches of the armed forces like the Navy and Army. To acquire this Marine identity and to be part of the culture is understood as a life-transforming process, so complete that it created a saying: "Once A Marine, Always A Marine."

In many religious traditions, including Buddhism and Christianity, there is a spiritual transformation that occurs when one commits and understands. A person who commits to the Christian belief is expected to, and transforms from, a person who does not "know" Christ to a person who does, meaning that person becomes aware of his or her sins and is also aware of the forgiving nature of Christ. That person undergoes a profound transformation. The emphasis on the "Come As You Are . . . And Be Transformed!" message accounts for the success of many of the new "megachurches" phenomenon or the growing "home church" movement; in contrast, Christian churches that do not talk about transformation, the kind people mostly attend only for Christmas or Easter, are in decline. I have learned of this from Christian chaplains.

The Buddha invited people to come as they are, and they too came in order to be transformed, in effect, to awaken to Enlightenment. In Jodo Shinshu, this spiritual transformation experience was identified by Shinran Shonin as the awakening of *shinjin*. To have realized *shinjin* meant that one was the "equal of the Tathagatas [Buddhas]."

Shinran called persons of *shinjin* "excellent persons" and "wondrous persons." But simply attending a Shinshu *dojo* (meeting hall) and later, Shinshu temples, did not guarantee one's attainment of *shinjin*. Shinran Shonin was aware of this; we know from his letters that he was constantly writing about *shinjin*, discussing *shinjin*, and that he was concerned that people should know the experience of *shinjin,* and also know what was not an authentic awakening of *shinjin* (his disciples also felt the same, thus we have the *Tannisho*). Later, Rennyo Shonin also would state that the temples should be where persons could understand Dharma intimately, not just as places to socialize.

Perhaps in contemporary Jodo Shinshu (non) practice, we have neglected this idea that one's ultimate spiritual achievement ought to be this awakening of *shinjin*. This moment of awakening to *shinjin* should be earth-shattering, life-transforming, something that alters us so completely and yet subtly enough that we would find it impossible to say of ourselves, "Yes, I am a person of *shinjin*." It would be presumptuous, much like hearing someone boasting of what a great Marine he or she is, yet only his or her buddies would *really* know if that person was a "good-to-go" Marine! There is no need to boast. We may be able to recognize people of *shinjin*, even if they do not see it in themselves. But how can we know the experience of *shinjin* if we cannot describe it, or inspire others to achieve it?

Because we consider *shinjin* to come directly from Amida Buddha (*tariki*), we do not speak of "working for" the awakening of *shinjin*: it is not something you can necessarily get through lots of ritual work like yoga, or through academic study, or even regular temple attendance! But human beings *need* something to strive for—it is a human instinct to do something, whether it is fulfilling employment, competitive sports, being religious, etc. Like Christian megachurches, Buddhist temples or centers that encourage people to have something to strive for, whether it is an increased understanding of Buddha Dharma, or meditation, or spiritual merits acquired through retreats, are successful and growing. Temples (not just Japanese

Jodo Shinshu ones) that do not emphasize spiritual transformation are simply not growing—they are temples as well as ethnic/cultural centers, which may assist the needs of a newly-arrived immigrant community now (which is important), but the importance of temples and monks or priests will grow increasingly irrelevant and smaller as future, assimilated generations grow up and move on. This will be especially true if English is not spoken, and if Dharma texts are not translated into English. Also, in America, there has always been an innate suspicion about clergy and churches; people are encouraged and inspired to "encounter the divine," or study spirituality on their own initiative, without relying on intercession from clergy, or having to be present in some stone building—American Buddhism is not exempt. Therefore, we find ourselves having to justify even the need for a temple and ministers.

I have heard this statement frequently from young Marines and sailors I have met who have had a Jodo Shinshu background; it runs along the line of, "Oh, that's something my family/parents/ grandparents are. I never go to a temple myself. I grew out of it." I'm sure many of you have heard something similar—can we *really* expect people to simply "come back" one day out of some feeling of ethnic or family loyalty? We talk about the *sansei* and *yonsei* taking over the reins of the temples someday. But if it is *only* ethnicity that makes them come back . . . is it truly for the Buddha's teaching, which does not validate ethnicities? There is no spiritual transformation in simply coming back to a temple only because it has a comforting, family feel to it, as considerable as that may be. Even if they do come back for that reason, there may have been enough changes (different faces, different furniture) to take away that comforting familiarity and they are unhappy. Once again, we need to validate the spiritual reasons for attending a temple.

As human beings, especially those of us who are minorities in America, we do value our ethnic identities, so this article is not stating that our identities are unimportant and must be tossed aside. The history of Jodo Shinshu in America makes that impossible. But the way of thinking that must be focused on in the temple *now* must be the possibility and desirability of a deep, personal, spiritual transformation, ultimately transcending ethnic and cultural lines. We need to emphasize the temple and the *sangha* as a place and a community where this possibility may be thoroughly understood and encouraged; therefore, it is important and necessary to have temples and *sanghas*. We need to emphasize that the focus and work of each temple and each *sangha* is to help ourselves and others to awaken the moment of *shinjin* in each and every individual. In the Marines, we say that the title of "Marine" cannot be given, it has to be earned; since *shinjin* is given to us by Amida Buddha, we do not "earn" *shinjin*, but to "know" *shinjin*, we must learn to be aware of the Buddha's compassion and know gratitude. This is something we can do!

Jodo Shinshu was a very radical understanding of Buddhism in its day: it was inclusive, allowing that all persons were capable of *shinjin*, of being "wondrous persons." We forget that many Buddhist traditions then—and now—simply did not allow for people of certain genders, professions, or social classes to be part of a *sangha*. We must re-awaken that radical spirit once again. We must try new methods in our temples, whether it is meditation, retreats in the manner of other Buddhist traditions, or other activities than what we have been doing so far. If temples are to survive, they must be places where people visit more than once a year for a relative's memorial or for bazaar/odori. Or find another model than the traditional temple: the *howakai* or home-based *sangha*. Undoubtedly, something must be done so that we may re-awaken the spirit that Jodo Shinshu is known for, the possibility of deep spiritual transformation, knowing that we are grasped by Amida Buddha, whether we are hunters and fishermen, warriors, women or scholars.

Sources: Sasaki, LaVerne. "Tule Lake Pilgrimage Memorial." *Wheel of Dharma* 32, no. 12 (December 2006): 2, 5; Shin, Jeanette. "Transformations." *Wheel of Dharma* 32, no. 7 (July 2006): 4, 6. Used with permission of the Buddhist Churches of America.

Fumitaka Matsuoka, "Benediction at the GTU Graduates of Color Ceremony"

(2008)

Christian missionaries have been working in Asia and American Chinatowns for more than a century. However, historically, Asian American Christians have not held equal places in the churches that converted them. In the 19th and early 20th centuries, missionaries were often almost as concerned with ushering their converts into a white, Anglo, Protestant culture as they were with converting them in the first place; Christianity and American-ness were practically undistinguishable. Although some denominations, notably the American Baptists, were ahead of their time in their commitment to integration, a concurrent erasure of Asian—and Asian American—ethnic and cultural history and identity took place. Over the years, however, ethnic Asian American churches began to emerge, and more recently, panethnic congregations are forming. Despite acculturation and Americanization, second-, third- and fourth-generation Asian American Christians often see ethnicity and religion as complementary aspects of personal and group identity.

*The Graduate Theological Union (GTU),
located in Berkeley, California, is an interreligious
partnership of seminaries and graduate schools.
Fumitaka Matsuoka, a professor of Asian
American Christianity at the GTU, researches how
a history of struggle against inequality and
prejudice influences the construction of theology.
Matsuoka gave the following benediction at the
GTU's Graduates of Color Ceremony in 2008. His
benediction reflects a religious sensibility colored
by the awareness and experience of race and
emphasizes the role religion can play in bringing
about economic and social justice.*

You are about to leave this Holy Hill. As you go:
Know how much this world full of wars, racism, and
poverty
    needs your gladness;
Know that there are words of truth and healing that
will never be spoken
    unless you speak them,
    and deeds of compassion, justice, and courage that
will never be done
    unless you do them;
    Do not mistake success for victory,
    or failure for defeat;

Do not be content with whatever the wealth or status
the world may bestow upon you;
    But know at last that you are created, not for happi-
ness, but for joy,
    and that joy is to you alone who, sometimes with
tears in your eyes,
    commit yourself in love to God
    and to your sisters and brothers.
    Most of all, may you be led by God ever deeper into
the knowledge that finally all people,
    regardless of the color of their skin,
    regardless of their economic and social status,
    are indeed one,
    and that there can never really be joy for you
    unless there is joy for all.
    So go from here . . .
    Go in safety, for you cannot go where God is not.
    Go in love, for love alone endures.
    Go with purpose, and God will honor your
dedication.
    Go in peace, for it is the gift to those whose hearts
and minds are in God.
    Amen.

Source: Matsuoka, Fumitaka. "Benediction at GTU
Graduates of Color Ceremony." 2008. http://panainstitute
.org/fumitaka-matsuoka-blesses-gtu-graduates-color-2008.
Used with permission of author.

Yuri Kochiyama, Interview by Amy Goodman
(2008)

*The experience of internment—rounded up and
shipped off to remote, primitive camps, labeled
enemy aliens and threats to the United States,
bombarded by racist rhetoric and subject to
continuing discrimination even after World War
II—affected members of the Japanese American
community in very different ways. Many
attempted to prove to themselves and the country
that they were loyal Americans: they kept their
heads down; worked hard; refused to criticize the
government, even among themselves; and buried*

*their memories of camp for decades after the war
was over. Others protested from the moment
Executive Order 9066 was issued, challenging
internment, the draft, and the loyalty oath, and
continuing to speak out after the camps were
closed. Yuri Kochiyama, a nisei woman living in
San Pedro, California, was one of the latter,
becoming a lifelong radical with a wide-ranging
passion for domestic and international justice.*

*Kochiyama was interned with her family in
Jerome, Arkansas, where she met her husband.*

After the war, the Kochiyamas moved to a predominantly African American community in New York City; there, they joined the Harlem Parents Committee and started participating in civil rights demonstrations in their neighborhood. Kochiyama also became involved in the Black Liberation Movement, working closely with Malcolm X; she was with him when he was assassinated in 1965, and she has continued agitating for social and political justice until her death in 2014. In the following excerpts from her 2008 interview with Democracy Now's *Amy Goodman, Kochiyama talks about how her father was imprisoned right after the attack on Pearl Harbor and about her work with Malcolm X for national civil rights and international human rights.*

AMY GOODMAN: . . . This week marks the sixty-sixth anniversary of President Franklin Delano Roosevelt's signing of the executive order that forced more than 120,000 men, women and children of Japanese descent into internment camps. This included nearly 70,000 American citizens. The US Supreme Court upheld the establishment of the internment camps after civil rights pioneer Fred Korematsu was jailed for refusing to be interned.

Korematsu said years later, "In order for things like this to never happen, we have to protest . . . so don't be afraid to speak up."

We now turn to an interview that we played earlier last year with civil rights activist Yuri Kochiyama. Her father was detained in 1942, hours after Pearl Harbor was attacked. He died soon after. The rest of Yuri Kochiyama's family was eventually sent to an internment camp. She recalled the day federal agents detained her father.

YURI KOCHIYAMA: I lived in San Pedro, California, which is, you know, on the west side of California, and it's where many, many Japanese lived. Well, the Japanese were mostly all living on the West Coast: Washington, Oregon, California and parts of Arizona. And that's the number one war zone. But immediately, the newspaper headlines were "Get the Japs Out!" and people like—who is the guy, that general on the West Coast, the top one, the top general? I can't think of his name. He said, "The only good Jap is a dead Jap." And, anyway, not just the newspaper headlines, but there were signs all over. "Get the Japs out! Get the Japs out!"

. . . [Kochiyama arrived home from church.] And just a few minutes later, three tall white men, I could see through the window. They were right there at the door.

And so I went there to see who they were. And they all, you know, put their— like a wallet out, which had the FBI card. And they said, "Is there a Seichi Nakahara living here?" I said, "Yes, that's my father." They said, "Where is he right now? We need to see him." I said, "Oh, he's sleeping in bed." I said, "He just came home." I don't know if it was that morning or the day before, he came home from ulcer surgery. And they said, "Well, where is he?" And I pointed to one of the bedrooms. And they went in and got—it was done so quickly, it didn't even take a half of a minute, I don't think. And I didn't dare ask a question. They were going out the door immediately. And then, I just called my mother, who was right down the street to say, "Come home quick. The FBI just came and took Pop." . . .

AMY GOODMAN: What was his job, that they went after him?

YURI KOCHIYAMA: Well, he was in the fishing business. That's why it hit all fishermen, because they knew then that the fishermen knew the waters, and if the Japanese ships got close enough, would the Japanese fishermen in America help the Japanese? But, actually, I tell you, the Japanese Americans and even the Isseis, first generation, who could not become Americans, they were so American. And yet, the hysteria about the suspicion of Japanese people was very, very strong. And, anyway, by the end of the day, I think all the Japanese people were calling their friends to say, "Did anyone come to your home and take your father or mother?"

AMY GOODMAN: How long was your father held for?

YURI KOCHIYAMA: Well, he was picked up on December 7th. And, of course, he wasn't getting any better, because they didn't do anything for him while he was in the—first, he was in prison. And my mother kept begging, "Please let him go to a hospital, and then when he gets some treatment, then he could go back to the prison." But we didn't realize that when they did take him to the hospital, he was the only Japanese that was taken there, and all the other prisoners, every single one of the prisoners, were Americans, all white, no black or brown or anyone else . . .

And then they put a sheet around his bed, and it said, "Prisoner of war." And we hadn't—us kids didn't get to go see my father yet, but my mother got permission, and she said when she saw the sheet with the "prisoner of war," and she saw the reaction of all the American prisoners who were just brought in from Wake Island, she didn't think he was going to last. And so, she asked the head of that hospital, could he be given a room by himself and get some medication or something, and then when he was feeling better, could they take him back to the prison, because that hospital, she said, was probably worse than prison, because here were all these Americans who had been injured, you know, in Wake Island or other islands, and at least in the prison, he would be in a—probably in a cell by himself.

AMY GOODMAN: When, ultimately, did he get released? How long was he held?

YURI KOCHIYAMA: He came home. He was home not even twelve hours. He came home, it was around dinner time, 5:30. And they had a nurse come with him. And we put him in his own bedroom. And the nurse was the only one that stayed in that room. And by the next morning, she woke us up and said, "He's gone."

. . . He was only home not even twelve hours, and he was gone. So, we didn't get to talk to him. We don't think he could have talked the way he looked, jumbled or mumbled. We couldn't tell if he could see. We would put our hands in front of him. We didn't know if he could hear. And it was so fast, he was gone. . . .

AMY GOODMAN: Forty-three years ago tomorrow, on February 21, 1965, Malcolm X was shot dead as he spoke at the Audubon Ballroom in Harlem. He had just taken the stage, when shots rang out, riddling his body with bullets. He was thirty-nine years old. We continue now with our interview with Yuri Kochiyama. She was Malcolm X's friend. She was in the Audubon Ballroom the day he was killed. After he was shot, she rushed to the stage, cradled his head in her arms as he lay dying. Yuri Kochiyama talked about that fateful day.

YURI KOCHIYAMA: The date was February 21st. It was a Sunday. Well, prior to that date, I think that whole week there was a lot of rumors going on in Harlem that something might happen to Malcolm. But I think Malcolm showed all along, especially around that time, that there were rumors going on. He was aware, because there were things even in the newspaper, that there was some, I think—I don't know if it was a misunderstanding or just disagreeing about some things that Elijah Muhammad and Malcolm were talking about. They were personal things. But Malcolm was aware that Elijah seemed to be feeling a little— that would be—oh, I'm so sorry that I'm messing this up— but on some very personal issues, there was disagreement between Elijah and Malcolm, and I think there was even talk that was going on, and after the assassination, however, many black people felt it could have been by people who had infiltrated or that the police department and FBI may have actually planted in the Nation of Islam . . .

AMY GOODMAN: Where were you sitting?

YURI KOCHIYAMA: I think about the tenth—equivalent to about the tenth row from the podium and almost right across—well, in the middle, where the two guys got up and said—one of them yelled, "Take your hands out of my pocket!" When everybody started just looking at them, the two guys. They were, like, fighting.

AMY GOODMAN: They had stood up as Malcolm X was speaking, very close to the beginning of his speech.

YURI KOCHIYAMA: Yes, he was just going to speak. And Malcolm just said, "OK, brothers, let's just break it up." But what happened was, it seemed to suck in all his guards closer to what was happening. And then—

AMY GOODMAN: A kind of diversion.

YURI KOCHIYAMA: The diversion, right. Everybody was looking there. When— because we were all watching the two guys in the audience, and everybody was watching, and the guards themselves moved from their post. They're supposed to be protecting Malcolm. Well, Malcolm first said, "OK, now, let's break it up." But because Malcolm had left the podium, he was just a perfect target to be shot. And I don't know if it was two or three men, right in front, went up and started shooting. Well, by that time, the whole place was chaotic. I mean, people were chasing—some of them chasing after those two guys, and people were yelling and screaming and others—because they let women and children in at the very end, the decision. The kids were—could be crying or just running to get near their mother, and mothers were trying to shield the kids. And I guess the two guys who did the—what was the word you said?

AMY GOODMAN: The diversion?

YURI KOCHIYAMA: Diversion. They shot a few times, you know, not to hit anyone, but just, I think, to make the place look even more chaotic there. And Malcolm had told his men, especially the very close Muslims, not to bring any arms, that they didn't want to frighten the women and children. And so, no one was supposed to bring anything, but one Muslim, and I think thank goodness that one did have a gun, and he's the only one that shot one of the people who came to assassinate. If he wasn't there with a gun, I think they would have all fled. And then, anyway, you know the three men who were charged, none of them were even there, and they proved it at the end.

AMY GOODMAN: So when Malcolm was shot and he was laying on the stage, you ran up?

YURI KOCHIYAMA: Yes, because I saw a young brother pass me, and he seemed to know just where to go or how to get up on the stage. And he acted just like—what do you call it? You call it, not a guard. Well, like one of Malcolm's security anyway. And he went up, and I followed him. And he went to the back, and he pulled the curtains to see if there was anyone in the back. And at that time, I mean, Malcolm had fallen straight back, and he was on his back, lying on the floor. And so I just went there and picked up his head and just put it on my lap. People ask, "What did he say?" He didn't say anything. He was just having a difficult time breathing.

AMY GOODMAN: What did you say to him?

YURI KOCHIYAMA: I said, "Please, Malcolm, please, Malcolm, stay alive." But he was hit so many times. Then a lot of people came on stage. They tore his shirt so they could see how many times he was hit. People said it was like about thirteen times. I mean, the most visible is the one here on his chin. He was hit somewhere else in the face, and then he was just peppered all over on his chest . . .

AMY GOODMAN: [Before his death], you would meet with Malcolm regularly. Can you talk about the meetings, the sessions that he had that you would attend?

YURI KOCHIYAMA: Well, they had regular meetings, you know. But it seems like Elijah and Malcolm's problems were getting a little more serious, and I think because

FBI played a role in it, and, of course, they knew which ones of the people in NOI [Nation of Islam] may have had some kind of ill feelings . . .

AMY GOODMAN: You received—Malcolm X wrote you postcards through his trip through Africa and his journey to Mecca.

YURI KOCHIYAMA: Yes.

AMY GOODMAN: What did he write to you in these postcards?

YURI KOCHIYAMA: Well, he sent eleven and from nine countries. There were two countries he went twice. But at the time that he went to Africa, all the major African conferences were happening. Two were even happening in England. And Malcolm went to all of these, and, of course, all the most progressive presidents of African nations were at these conferences. So he got to meet almost all the top ones. I mean, there was Ghana's Nkrumah or Tanzania's [Nyerere]. I can't even think of all of them, but he met about eleven of them, and they were as excited to meet him.

He wanted to learn all about the different countries in Africa. And he—the Africans and he talked about the colonization that took place. Well, it could have happened from even as early as the 1600s, but it was mostly 1700, 1800. And the big day that we've got to remember is, I think, 1885. That was where all those European countries took over African countries . . .

AMY GOODMAN: Well, let me ask you about this. When Malcolm came back, he was also talking about an expanded attitude about human rights, something he had talked about before, as well. Not so much civil rights, but the rights of African Americans to be fully equal was an issue of international human rights.

YURI KOCHIYAMA: Oh, yes. And that's why Malcolm thought that this civil rights thing was really nothing, because African people don't have to wait until some president of another country, even United States, would give civil rights. I mean, Africans already have human rights. And he felt, too, that it was too narrowed down when they would be using words that they were just fighting for civil rights. And I think what was so wonderful is that Malcolm taught his group, American—well, black Americans here, about the history of Africa, where they became colonized, and then he told the people in Africa what was happening here, how blacks were treated, and that many of the African young people didn't even know anything hardly about slavery, because this country never told them anything.

AMY GOODMAN: Yuri Kochiyama, he also came to your house to meet with survivors of the atomic bombing of Hiroshima/Nagasaki: Hibakusha, the survivors.

YURI KOCHIYAMA: Yes, right.

AMY GOODMAN: Can you talk about that?

YURI KOCHIYAMA: Well, we were all so happy, I mean, especially Japanese Americans and even other Asian Americans, that Malcolm would be interested. But Malcolm was interested in every group, and especially when he would hear the kind of harassments and all the negative things that always seemed to be happening to people of color. And he knew about Asian history so well. We couldn't believe it.

AMY GOODMAN: Yuri Kochiyama remembering Malcolm X. Forty-three years ago tomorrow, on February 21, 1965, Malcolm X was assassinated in the Audubon Ballroom in Harlem. He had just taken the stage, when shots rang out, riddling his body with bullets. He was thirty-nine. Yuri Kochiyama ran to the stage. She had been there to listen to him that day, and she cradled his head. Yuri Kochiyama and her family also interned as a result of FDR's executive order after Pearl Harbor bombing with over 100,000 other Japanese and Japanese Americans in this country.

Source: Kochiyama, Yuri. Interview with Amy Goodman. *Democracy Now.* February 20, 2008. http://www.democracy now.org/2008/2/20/civil_rights_activist_yuri_kochiyama_ remembers.

University of California Senate Resolution to Award Honorary Degrees to Japanese American Internees

(2009)

When President Franklin D. Roosevelt signed Executive Order 9066 on February 19, 1942, approximately 120,000 Japanese Americans were forcibly removed from the West Coast of the United States and sent to inland internment camps for the duration of the war. Japanese Americans lost their homes and livelihoods, and the vibrant communities they had worked so hard to establish were destroyed. For Japanese Americans attending colleges and universities on the West Coast, internment indefinitely ended their academic careers. In particular, approximately 700 Japanese American students at four of the state's University of California campuses—Berkeley, Los Angeles, San Francisco, and Davis—were forced to leave school and move to a camp.

In 2009, the University of California and the California State University decided to correct this injustice by granting special honorary degrees to all students who were unable to complete their studies because of the wartime relocation and internment. Not only were former students recognized during graduation services, but posthumous degrees were also awarded. This decision came in the wake of California Assembly Bill 37 (AB 37), authored by Representative Warren Furutani, directing California's postsecondary educational institutions to grant honorary degrees to former internees.

Following is the chaptered text for AB 37 and an excerpt from the 2009 resolution of the University of California's Academic Senate that lays out the argument for granting the honorary degrees.

CALIFORNIA ASSEMBLY BILL 37— CHAPTERED TEXT, OCTOBER 11, 2009

INTRODUCED BY Assembly Member Furutani

(Coauthors: Assembly Members Blumenfield, Brownley, Chesbro, DeLeon, Eng, Hayashi, Jones, Lieu, Ma, Monning, John A. Perez, Portantino, Salas, Torrico, and Yamada)

(Coauthors: Senators Alquist, DeSaulnier, Hancock, Liu, Lowenthal, and Romero)

DECEMBER 1, 2008

An act to add Section 66020 to the Education Code, relating to public postsecondary education.

LEGISLATIVE COUNSEL'S DIGEST

AB 37, Furutani. Public postsecondary education: honorary degrees.

Under existing law, the segments of the public post-secondary education system in the state include the University of California, which is administered by the Regents of the University of California, the California State University, which is administered by the

Trustees of the California State University, and the California Community Colleges, which are administered by the Board of Governors of the California Community Colleges. Existing law authorizes these educational institutions to award various types of degrees.

This bill would require the Trustees of the California State University and the Board of Governors of the California Community Colleges, and would request the Regents of the University of California, to work with their respective colleges and universities to confer an honorary degree upon each person, living or deceased, who was forced to leave his or her postsecondary studies as a result of federal Executive Order 9066 which caused the incarceration of individuals of Japanese ancestry during World War II.

THE PEOPLE OF THE STATE OF CALIFORNIA DO ENACT AS FOLLOWS:

SECTION 1. (a) The Legislature finds and declares all of the following:

(1) On February 19, 1942, President Franklin D. Roosevelt issued Executive Order 9066, which caused the incarceration of approximately 120,000 Americans and resident aliens of Japanese ancestry in camps scattered throughout the United States during World War II.

(2) Executive Order 9066 put the lives of these individuals, who were forcibly relocated from their homes and communities and unjustly detained by the United States government, on hold.

(3) On August 10, 1988, President Ronald Wilson Reagan signed into law the Civil Liberties Act of 1988, declaring that Executive Order 9066 was

not justified by military necessity and hence was caused by racial prejudice, war hysteria, and a failure of political leadership.

(4) The Civil Liberties Act of 1988 apologized on behalf of the people of the United States for the evacuation, relocation, and incarceration of Americans and permanent resident aliens of Japanese ancestry during World War II and provided for the restitution to those individuals of Japanese ancestry who were incarcerated.

(5) The disruption of over 2,500 students' educational pursuits was among the consequences of the country's wartime policy, which removed students enrolled in California's colleges and universities from their studies.

(b) It is the intent of the Legislature that postsecondary educational institutions confer an honorary degree upon each individual whose studies at a postsecondary educational institution were disrupted by Executive Order 9066, and to allow a representative to accept an honorary degree on behalf of individuals who are deceased.

SEC. 2. Section 66020 is added to the Education Code, to read:

66020. (a) The Trustees of the California State University and the Board of Governors of the California Community Colleges shall, and the Regents of the University of California are requested to, work with their respective colleges and universities to confer an honorary degree upon each person, living or deceased, who was forced to leave his or her studies at the public postsecondary educational institution in which that person was enrolled as a result of the issuance of federal Executive Order 9066 on February 19, 1942, which caused the evacuation, relocation, and incarceration of individuals of Japanese ancestry during World War II.

(b) In cases where an honorary degree is conferred upon a person who is deceased, the person's surviving next of kin, or another representative chosen by the person's surviving next of kin, may accept the honorary degree on the deceased person's behalf.

(c) Independent colleges and universities, as defined in subdivision (b) of Section 66010, are urged to comply with the terms of this section.

(d) This section shall be implemented in a cost-effective manner by incorporating, to the extent practicable, any ceremony for the purpose of conferring honorary degrees with a previously scheduled commencement or graduation activity.

Office of the President

TO MEMBERS OF THE COMMITTEE ON EDUCATIONAL POLICY: ACTION ITEM: CONFERRING OF HONORARY DEGREES AND SUSPENSION OF BYLAW 29.1

EXECUTIVE SUMMARY

In September 2008, the Academic Senate and the Vice President for Student Affairs jointly charged a special task force to consider how the University of California might recognize its students whose educations were interrupted by Executive Order 9066. That task force completed its work in March 2009, and has recommended to the administration and the Academic Senate that the University of California award a special honorary degree to students enrolled in the University in 1941–1942 who were unable to complete their degree because of Executive Order 9066. The Academic Senate unanimously adopted the recommendations at the meetings of the Academic Council on April 29, and the Assembly of the Academic Senate on June 17, 2009 . . .

BACKGROUND

In spring 1942, approximately 700 persons of Japanese ancestry who were University of California students at the Berkeley, Los Angeles, San Francisco, and Davis campuses were subject to removal from the West Coast pursuant to

Executive Order 9066. At the time, UC faculty and administrators protested the inclusion of students in the order, arranged for some students to complete the semester's course work while in internment camps, and helped arrange for some students to be enrolled in universities outside of the exclusion area. The Congress has since determined that the internment of Japanese-Americans was wrong, and Congress provided monetary compensation pursuant to the Civil Liberties Act of 1988. The Ninth Circuit Court of Appeals has concluded that had it been presented with complete information by the Federal Government at the time, the United States Supreme Court would not have sustained the validity of the Japanese internment.

In October 1922, the Berkeley campus held a public ceremony to present diplomas to surviving students who graduated in spring 1942, but were not permitted to return to campus to attend their graduation ceremony. Likewise, in 1991–92 UCLA hosted a series of educational events that paid tribute to the campus' Japanese American students from 1942, including awarding a regular (i.e., non-honorary) degree to an alumna who was only a few units short of obtaining her UCLA degree. In spring 2008, public universities in Washington and Oregon granted honorary degrees to individuals and their descendents, in cases of deceased individuals, whose educations at those institutions were disrupted by Executive Order 9066. Since then, UC has received requests to recognize its interned Japanese-American students who were unable to return to UC to complete their degrees . . .

RESOLUTION OF THE ASSEMBLY OF THE ACADEMIC SENATE OF THE UNIVERSITY OF CALIFORNIA . . . ADOPTED BY THE ASSEMBLY OF THE UNIVERSITY OF CALIFORNIA, JUNE 17, 2009

WHEREAS: A large number of Japanese American students enrolled on campuses of the University of California were forced to leave the University under the terms of Presidential Executive Order 9066 and related military orders,

AND WHEREAS: The Congress and the President of the United States declared in the Civil Liberties Act of 1988 that:

The Congress recognizes that, as described by the Commission on Wartime Relocation and Internment of Civilians, a grave injustice was done to both citizens and permanent resident aliens of Japanese ancestry by the evacuation, relocation, and internment of civilians during World War II. As the Commission documents, these actions were carried out without adequate security reasons and without any acts of espionage or sabotage documented by the Commission, and were motivated largely by racial prejudice, wartime hysteria, and a failure of political leadership. The excluded individuals of Japanese ancestry suffered enormous damages, both material and intangible, and there were incalculable losses in education and job training, all of which resulted in significant human suffering for which appropriate compensation has not been made. For these fundamental violations of the basic civil liberties and constitutional rights of these individuals of Japanese ancestry, the Congress apologizes on behalf of the Nation.

AND WHEREAS: Convictions of Gordon Hirabayashi and Fred Korematsu for violating the curfew and exclusion orders proceeding from Executive Order 9066, which were affirmed by the United States Supreme Court (*Hirabayashi v. United States*, 320 U.S. 81 (1943); *Korematsu v. United States*, 323 U.S. 214 (1944)), were set aside on findings by District Courts that were described by the Ninth Circuit Court of Appeal as indicating that, "the reasoning of the Supreme Court would probably have been profoundly and materially affected if the Justice Department had advised it of the suppression of evidence which established the truthfulness of the allegations made by Hirabayashi and Korematsu concerning the real reason for the exclusion order."

AND WHEREAS: But for the exclusion order, in the normal course of events students enrolled in the University of California would have completed the requirements for their academic degrees and would have become members of the University academic community,

AND WHEREAS: University of California Regents Bylaw 29.1 a. requires that honorary degrees may be awarded upon recommendation of the President of the University and approval by a three-fourths vote of the members present.

AND WHEREAS: University of California Regents Bylaw 29.1 c. limits the number of honorary degrees that may be awarded by a campus at a ceremony to three, and to no more than four honorary degrees in any one academic year.

THEREFORE, BE IT RESOLVED BY THE ASSEMBLY OF THE ACADEMIC SENATE OF THE UNIVERSITY OF CALIFORNIA THAT:

The Regulations of the Academic Senate of the University of California are hereby amended as follows:

1. Add to Title II. Curricula, Chapter 1. General Provisions, a new Article 3 to provide as follows:

Chapter 1. General Provisions, a new Article 3 to provide as follows: Article 3. Special Honorary Degree for Students enrolled in Academic Year 1941–1942. 625.

(a) Persons enrolled at a campus of the University of California during the academic year 1941–1942 who were removed or excluded under Executive Order 9066, and who were therefore unable to receive a degree from a University of California campus, are awarded an Honorary Degree of the University of California *Inter Silvas Academi Restituere Iustitiam* (to restore justice among the groves of the academy).

(b) The Chair of the Academic Council shall present to the President a list of those persons determined to meet the requirements enumerated in paragraph (a) of this Regulation . . .

The Honorary Degree of the University of California *Inter Silvas Academi Restituere Iustitiam* awarded pursuant to Senate Regulation 625 shall be represented by a diploma in the following form:

UNIVERSITY OF CALIFORNIA
Honoris Causa
Inter Silvas Academi Restituere Iustitiam

By authority of the Regents and the Academic Senate of the University of California

....

who was enrolled at the .... campus of the University of California in the academic year 1941–1942 and who was excluded from continuing by reason of Executive Order 9066, is awarded this honorary degree.

[seal of the University]

The diploma shall be signed by the Governor of California, the President of the University, the Chair of the Board of Regents and the Chair of the Assembly.

Source: California Assembly Bill 37, Chaptered October 11, 2009. University of California, Agenda/Notice of Meeting (revised), Regular Meeting of the Assembly of the Academic Senate, June 17, 2009. http://www.universityof california.edu/regents/regmeet/jul09/e4.pdf.

Patrick Hayashi, Honorary Degree Ceremony Remarks
(2009)

In 2009, the University of California Academic Senate voted to confer honorary degrees on those Japanese American students who had to leave their studies and go to internment camps during World War II. Patrick Hayashi, the former associate president of the University of California, was born in the Topaz, Utah, internment camp. He spoke at the honorary degree ceremony at the University of California–San Francisco, thanking the university for standing up for its Japanese American students during the war and the nisei for their sacrifice and courage.

What a wonderful, beautiful day.

I have the honor of speaking to the UC community on behalf of the Japanese American community.

I also have the honor of speaking to the Nisei who are being honored today on behalf of their children and grandchildren.

Today, when UC honors these Nisei students, the Japanese American community would like to honor UC.

Today is a wonderful day, but it is not surprising. During our darkest days, UC stood by us. When others treated us harshly, you treated us with kindness. When others persecuted us, you protected us. When others scorned us, you embraced us as family.

Few people know about how UC leaders fought to protect the Constitutional rights, the personal welfare, and, most important, the human dignity of Japanese Americans.

After Pearl Harbor, racial hysteria swept the nation, President Robert Gordon Sproul, Vice President Monroe Deutsch and several other UC leaders helped establish the Committee on American Principles and Fair Play to defend the rights of Japanese Americans.

When it became clear that Japanese Americans on the west coast would soon be put into concentration camps, many UC faculty tried their hardest to place their students in colleges in the mid-west.

Then, when we were imprisoned in temporary assembly centers, like Tanforan, a race track in South San Francisco, UC faculty came to visit. They wrote letters, sent books, passed final exams through the fence. They brought art supplies so that we could start art classes for the children.

At Berkeley, Harvey Itano earned the University Medal as the outstanding graduate of the Class of 1942. President Sproul could have easily given the medal to the next student in line. Instead, at the commencement ceremony, President Sproul said, "Harvey cannot be here today because his country has taken him elsewhere." And he arranged to have the medal presented to Harvey behind barbed wire.

Here at UCSF, Dean of Pharmacy Troy Daniels along with other faculty members displayed uncommon compassion, integrity and courage. Dean Daniels went to the Presidio to speak with the head of the western military command, General John DeWitt. He asked that his eight Nisei students be temporarily exempted from the order to evacuate and be allowed to complete their pharmacy degrees.

He also said that he and his wife would adopt Harry Iwamoto, his first graduate student, if that would allow Harry to stay. But, General DeWitt had publicly stated, "All Japanese, including those born in the United States, are members of an enemy race," He told Dean Daniels that all Nisei students would have to clear out of San Francisco.

But the students and faculty had other ideas.

The students stayed and they studied. The faculty helped them finish their coursework in record time. And then they helped them prepare for their state boards. When the students made their way home after curfew, they had to dodge the soldiers patrolling the city. Dean Daniels arranged for them to take their state boards early.

One of these students, Masao Yamamoto, told me that he was overcome with relief and gratitude when he learned that he had passed because he now had the foundation upon which he could build his life. After the Nisei students passed their exams, Dean Daniels helped them get safe passage out of San Francisco. He personally contacted law enforcement agencies and told them that UCSF students would be traveling to rejoin their families.

How UCSF helped these Nisei students finish their studies is a wonderful, important story.

But, UCSF gave something much more valuable to the Japanese American community. You protected us from the bitterness, rage and despair that could have easily poisoned our hearts. At the worst of times, Dean Daniels and the UCSF faculty allowed us to see the very best in humankind.

Today, UCSF completes the honorable work President Sproul, Dean Daniels and many, many others began 67 years ago. What UC does for our community today is kind and generous, decent and just.

On behalf of the Japanese American community, from the bottom of our hearts, we thank you, we thank you very much.

Kokoro kara, arigato, arigato gozaimasu.

And now, I would like to speak to the Nisei— those who are here today, and those who are with us in spirit. I speak on behalf of your children, grand-children and great-grandchildren.

You never talked much about the camps because you wanted to protect us.

Immediately after Pearl Harbor, community leaders were picked up by the FBI. My mother's cousin was arrested because he taught kendo. A week later, the FBI told his wife where she could claim his body. No word was heard about many others who had been arrested—sometimes for weeks, months and even years.

This was a terrifying time.

You were given just seven days to prepare to go into the camps. You sold your family's possessions for just pennies on the dollar. You desperately tried to find homes for your pets. Many of your parents were already quite old. My grandfather was 75 at the time. So much of the burden fell to you.

You were told that you could only take only what you could carry.

In your hearts, you understood that all you could really carry were your aging parents and your little sisters and brothers.

You carried us with strength and grace and shielded us from pain.

You told us about the good parts of life in the camps—the dances, the baseball games, the festivals, the weddings.

Sometimes, very rarely, you spoke about the hard parts—about the beatings by a few hateful guards, about the suicides, about the arguments over the demands of patriotism and the demands of democracy, bitter arguments that turned friend against friend, brother against brother.

You told us about old Mr. Wakasa who had adopted a stray dog. One day his dog got caught in the barbed wire. When he went to free him, the guard in the watchtower ordered him back away from the fence. But, Mr. Wakasa was deaf and he continued to help his little dog. So, the guard shot and killed him.

When you spoke of the harshness of the camps, you made sure we knew that there was kindness.

My mom and dad told me that when I was born, the Quakers sent a bassinet. Teachers from back home wrote letters and sent books.

At Gila River, 15-year-old Ruth Mix lied about her age, so she could help out in the camp hospital. There, she and other workers smuggled in medical supplies, sanitary napkins, clothing, shoes—anything to help.

You told us about their acts of kindness and courage. But you never talked about your own.

But, now your stories are being told.

One UC grad, Lillian Matsumoto, worked at an orphanage for Japanese American children. When the evacuation order was given, Lillian could have gone to the camp with her family. Instead, she, along with all the other orphanage workers, chose to stay with their orphans. Together, they all went to Manzanar and started the Children's Village, a place where these children who had nobody else could grow up protected and loved.

At Mazanar, California; Topaz, Utah; Heart Mountain, Wyoming; Poston, Arizona; Jerome, Arkansas—at all the camps, you immediately volunteered to teach classes in makeshift schools.

You cared for the sick in hospitals. You buried the dead. You helped deliver the next generation of children.

You never talked about your courage.

In 1943, the government gave you a questionnaire and asked "Are you willing to go into combat and fight for America?"

Some, like my uncle and father, had the courage to say, "No. Hell no! We will not fight until our constitutional rights are restored!" Many of you were sent to Tule Lake, an especially harsh, high security concentration camp.

Others had the courage to say, "Yes. Hell yes!" Many, like Yori Wada, former chair of the UC Regents, joined the MIS and served as scouts, code-breakers and translators in the Pacific. Many others joined the 100th/442nd, the Japanese American Regimental Combat Team, and fought in Europe and became the most decorated regimental combat team in history.

And today, we pay special tribute to those who never returned—to those who fought and fell at Anzio, Salerno, Monte Cassino.

We remember the hundreds of men who were killed or wounded while saving the Texas Lost Battalion. Today, we remember the Nisei broke through the Gothic Line. Two attempts to break through had already failed. The 100th/442nd decided to try. One night, for eight hours, they climbed up a 4,000-foot cliff face to get behind the Germans and break the Gothic Line. They climbed quietly. They could only hear each other breathing.

But every once in a while they felt a gust of wind. And they knew that one of their friends had lost his grip and was falling. The men who fell knew that if they cried out everyone would be slaughtered, so they fell to their deaths silently.

After the war, you came home to start your lives again.

America was characterized then, as now, by violence and prejudice, decency and generosity.

One of the Nisei we are honoring today, Grace Amemiya, pursued her nursing career and served in an Army hospital in Iowa caring for wounded GIs. The hospital director worried about her safety, because former POWs would be returning from the Pacific campaign for treatment at the hospital. The director told Grace that she should never walk alone and that he would provide her with escorts. But, the GIs she cared for, those who could walk, said, "No, we will escort Grace wherever she wishes to go."

With incredible forbearance and fortitude you rebuilt our homes and our communities. Throughout your lives, you guided yourselves by one simple precept, "Kodomo no tame ni." "For the sake of the children." For our sake.

You taught us, by example, the importance of hard work, sacrifice and service. You helped us build our lives upon your lives. Everything we have accomplished all the happiness we have felt was made possible by your sacrifices by your strength and resolve.

For all that you have given us, we thank you from the bottom of our hearts

Kokoro kara. Arigato, Arigato Gozaimasu.

And, most of all, on this wonderful day, we all congratulate you.

Let's have a quick Japanese lesson. In Japanese, congratulations is "Omedeto Gozaimasu"

Now, everyone—on three; One—two—three. OMEDETO GOZAIMASU

Source: Hayashi, Patrick. "Remarks." 2009. http://eo9066 .blogspot.com/2009/12/ucsf-honorary-degree-ceremony- remarks.html. Used with permission of the author.

Wendy Maruyama, Interview by Joyce Lovelace
(2009)

Wendy Maruyama is an artist, furniture craftsperson, educator, and third-generation Japanese American from Southern California. Her work is heavily influenced by Japanese art forms and Japanese American history. She uses a variety of media to explore the effects of Executive Order 9066 and internment on the Japanese American psyche. Inspired in part by the paper crane exhibit at the Hiroshima Peace Memorial and by Dorothea Lange's photographs of internees, Maruyama began the Tag Project in 2009. She and hundreds of volunteers around the United States are hand-writing the names of all 120,000 Japanese American internees on identification tags, replicas of the ones issued in 1942.

In this excerpt from her 2009 interview with American Craft Magazine's *Joyce Lovelace, Murayama talks about how World War II affected her own family. She explains how the Tag Project is enabling her and her collaborators to gain a new perspective on internment and the Japanese American community.*

JL   How did the idea for the Tag Project occur to you?

WM   A couple of years ago my husband and I attended a memorial service in Denver with my aunt and uncle for the 442nd Infantry Regiment. This was a unit that fought in Europe during World War II; it consisted mostly of Japanese-American men who with their families had been consigned to internment camps by Executive Order 9066—the wartime presidential decree that incarcerated West Coast Japanese—but were released to fight in the war. It became the most decorated military unit in U.S. history, with 21 Medal of Honor winners, for instance. Uncle Roy lamented that the numbers attending this event used to be robust but were now dwindling. As I looked at the beautiful glistening marble memorial stone, I realized that I needed to embrace this part of my family history and become more informed about E.O. 9066.

I started looking for images, and the ones that struck me the most were the ones of small children, babies, entire families wearing tags that directed them to their camps. The photos taken by Dorothea Lange were the most compelling.

About 15 years ago I went to Hiroshima and visited the Peace Memorial there. I saw thousands of folded origami cranes strung together and was struck by the delicate nature of the paper, combined with the masses of them which conveyed the urgency and need for advocacy for peace after such a devastating event.

I started replicating tags for internees who came from my hometowns of San Diego and Chula Vista. I was surprised that despite the light, airy structure of these tags, they were also very heavy for their size. I started to imagine the impact of seeing 120,000 tags for all internees. I realized that this was going to be a monumental effort, but at the same time I saw it as a catalyst to bring communities together and make this a collaborative project.

JL   How did the internment touch your family?

WM   My maternal grandparents lived in San Pedro/Terminal Island, in the Los Angeles area, the center for the fishing and cannery industry in Southern California back then. When FDR issued E.O. 9066, Japanese Americans were given very little time to move out of the West Coast areas and had to abandon their jobs, their homes and most of their possessions (they were only allowed to take one bag per person). My mother's father owned a thriving fishing company, which had to be given up. It is said that many non-Japanese became wealthy when they purchased houses and businesses at bottom prices (no one would pay more). My mother's family chose not to go to a camp (the Japanese Americans were given an option: either get out by a certain time or be sent to camps). My grandmother was very fragile mentally and had a nervous breakdown, and my grandfather feared that the camp environment was going to cause even more stress and she would not survive it.

They did not experience internment, but the displacement was still damaging. They lived in a tent and a freight car in Utah as they tried to make their way east. Eventually some friends invited them to relocate to Colorado, where they settled. They were never able to regain their financial security. They first worked on a farm and then ran hotels for a while. In the end, I suppose, the hardships, the discrimination, being uprooted from their homes taught them to persevere. Miraculously, they did not become embittered or angry people.

JL   You've said that growing up, you heard little or no talk of the internment among your older relatives. Why was that, do you think? Do you recall anything about it ever expressed, verbally or otherwise?

WM   The first time I ever heard about this was when I was about nine and we were living in Chula Vista (I was born in Colorado; my parents and I also lived on a farm in Hemet and San Jacinto from the time I was about four to eight, and then we moved to Chula Vista). I was asking my mother about the Holocaust since we were studying world history and I was wondering why the Jews were persecuted in Europe. Somehow that turned into a discussion about racism, and she told me what had happened to their family. I remember being shocked—and sort of angry—because I knew my family was working hard to make ends meet. Both my parents worked during my entire childhood, yet we lived next to people who had fancy houses, cars, swimming pools, etc., and I started to get it in my head that the internment and persecution of Japanese Americans denied us all of that. Of course, being a kid, I didn't understand that such stuff was not really important.

JL   Before taking on this project, had you given the subject much thought?

WM   It's odd, but after that episode I never wanted to think about it. It actually left a bitter taste in my mouth, and at the time I had enough problems overcoming my hearing impairment and dealing with my speech impediment and the fact that we were Japanese American, which made us different from the rest of the kids at school. We had to deal with questions like "Does your dad know karate or judo?" Or "Are you Japanese or Chinese?" Or "Is it true that you people eat raw fish?" I didn't really want to think about the internment. I believe that quite a few other sanseis (third-generation Japanese Americans) like myself felt the same way.

That moment at the memorial service two years ago changed my perspective and made me think about the effect that the internment had on all of us Japanese Americans and how the community became splintered and assimilated into the rest of the American population much more readily than the Chinese Americans, or Korean Americans or any other ethnic group in the U.S.A. There are fewer thriving Japantowns or Little Tokyos. The generations that suffered from the evacuation and the internment are aging; most of them are gone now. I realized I needed to embrace this history somehow. I felt that it would bring me closer to my identity . . .

JL   You've stated that part of your quest was to understand the effects of the internment on the Japanese-American psyche. Have you reached any conclusions about that?

WM   I am still thinking about that and still trying to figure that out. I think there is a certain behavior that has come from that experience. I remember that Mom told us all the time that we needed to be on our best behavior in public because we were Japanese Americans, that we needed to be model citizens. Some behaviors may be cultural, stemming from Japan—to not complain, to do as we are told in school, to not bring attention to ourselves, etc.—but I think the root of it all was that, because of the internment, Japanese Americans had a burning desire to be accepted as "real" Americans and so they tried to raise their families to be as American as possible. Very few sansei learned to speak Japanese, nor were we encouraged to do so. We had to be "perfect." Not being deemed perfect in the eyes of elder Japanese Americans had consequences for some of us. Perhaps that has compelled me to become an artist, so that I could "act out" through my work since I had to practice restraint as a child/teenager/young adult. And then I turned the corner and became more outspoken as time went on. I will probably become an impossibly cantankerous old lady by the time I am 65 . . .

JL   You're well known as a woodworker/furniture maker who has done some highly innovative work, such as incorporating video into your pieces. Is the Tag Project an extension of your interest in exploring different means and media?

WM   The Tag Project just happened on its own, based on my fixation on the Lange photographs. But in general, I am trying to work with whatever materials or processes would provide depth and relevance to what I am making. It may seem that at times I am bouncing all over the place, but I do like to try different things. The repetitive process of working on this project is very close to what I do as a maker: I am '"crafting" this assemblage of tags, working with its texture, to age the paper, etc.

JL As an artist, what has been your approach to making installation art out of the tags, and do you plan to vary this? Visually, what is the effect of the displays?

WM As I am working on these, I am keeping the tags separated by camp. Perhaps there will be 10 separate groups, representing all 10 camps. Ideally, I envision the tags as being a large mass, or I would love the opportunity to see them that way at least once. I envision that some groups will be sent out to their respective camps and interpretive centers. The goal is to convey the sheer numbers of people who were uprooted, and the mass will be dense, visually heavy and imposing . . .

JL Was the project conceived specifically as a collaborative work?

WM Yes it was. I had volunteers in New York, and the best part about working with volunteers is being able to talk to them about it. Many of my non-Japanese-American friends don't really know much about the internment. Some had no Idea that it ever happened. I find this to be disturbing, and it makes me all the more determined to create this project.

On the other hand, a lot of former internees are helping me, and I am learning about their personal experiences in the camps. I am feeling close to my family—I am finally meeting a lot of their friends through this project. The familial camaraderie is being replayed at the various Tag Project events; the spirit is ebullient. Older Japanese Americans are chatting with non-Japanese-Americans and describing their lives in camp. Others are writing name after name after name, and in that process, one begins to envision that period. It is very therapeutic and somewhat meditative . . .

JL What is the larger message of the Tag Project, and how does it resonate for all of us today?

WM The fact that some people still do not know about this, and in some areas of the country it is not even taught in history classes, made it important for me to make this piece as an educational device. Secondly, it gives me an opportunity to teach myself about the internment. Two years ago I don't think I could list all 10 camps. That is shameful, actually.

Thirdly it helps me to come to grips with this, and allows me to gain some understanding of what our families went through. As I am writing thousands of names, I am thinking, how did they deal with this horrible ordeal? What must have been going through their minds as they were taken by train to unknown destinations with the blinds drawn?

Fourthly, as we now have our first African-American president, I am seeing acts of racism and disrespect shown to our president by our own American citizens. It tells me that discrimination and racism are far from eradicated. And as we just passed our eighth anniversary of 9/11, I think again of the prejudice shown against the American Muslim community. It sadly seems never-ending.

Source: Lovelace, Joyce. "The Tag Project: In Search of Cultural Memory." *American Craft Magazine* blog, October 5, 2009. http://www.americancraftmag.org/blog-post.php?id=} 9019. Used with permission of *American Craft Magazine.*

Stuart Hada, "Small Satisfactions"

(2009)

Japanese immigrants brought with them institutions and traditions that helped them survive as an ethnic community in the United States. These have been passed down through successive generations of Japanese Americans. One such custom is the obligation of giving koden, *a monetary gift, to the family of someone recently deceased. The money is meant to be used to pay for the funeral services. A designated family member will keep scrupulous records, writing down names, addresses, and gift amounts. The expectation is that the favor will be reciprocated when someone else dies. Stuart Hada was born in Kaua'i, Hawai'i, and grew up on Kipu Plantation. His essay, "Small Satisfactions," written in 2009, illustrates how the obligation of* koden *has remained a central part of Japanese American culture even today.*

"No forget eh, Stu, bring Ma to the Maenos," Pat told me before he left for Honolulu. Pat is my oldest brother returning to his Makakilo home.

Ma wanted to visit the recently widowed Minnie Maeno to give her *koden*. She wanted to deliver it in person since she missed Mr. Maeno's funeral. She and I sit at her kitchen table. Half her face hangs lazy due to a stroke she suffered in this ninetieth year of her life. She shuffles off to her bedroom back bent from the years carrying hundred pound rice bags as a Yoneji Store clerk.

She returns to the table, slightly scuffed white envelope in hand, scribbled with "With Sympathy, Toshie Hada." She doesn't like the envelope scuffed, her writing shaky. She asks for a new envelope. She writes the same words and slips in a twenty dollar bill. "Only leetle beet," she says and seals the envelope. I sense a great deal of satisfaction on my mother's part. Maybe it's because she is fulfilling an obligation. Maybe it's because the envelope is nice, neat, and crispy, suggestive of the Japanese gift wrapping art form. Clean and simple.

My brother Russ, his wife Bev and I are visiting Kauai for a family reunion. We live on the mainland now, Russ and Bev in Oregon and me, New Jersey. We drive Ma to the Maenos. We arrive to find a number of cars blocking their driveway so we park on the grassy shoulder: the ground uneven enough to make the fifteen yards to the front door a dangerous gauntlet for my mother. Russ takes the envelope and within seconds he's in the garage greeting Minnie Maenos' daughter and son-in-law. Minnie Maeno comes out from behind the screen door.

In the car, Ma insists to get out. "I like go," she says. I sense it's important for her to say something face to face. I help her across the fifteen yards carefully negotiating each clumpy weed. Finally, she takes the envelope from Russ and gives it to Minnie, "Only leetle beet," my mother says. She talks to Minnie for a few minutes. I overhear words that I have heard frequently at Nisei funerals, "Too bad. No can help." It's the fates, she assures Minnie; no one is to blame.

As we drive away, Russ and I explain *koden* to Bev, a native Oregonian. *Koden* was part of the Japanese *giri*, a system of obligations that has bound Japanese communities for centuries. Its strength was enhanced as samurai grew in stature and their obligations to their lord became legendary. For most Japanese folk though, *giri* included obligations to your parents, obligations to your community, and even obligations to your ancestors and deceased family members.

We continue our explanation to Bev. We tell her *koden* is delivered at funerals with dollar amounts ranging from $20 to $50. The small amounts add up to a nice sum that traditionally was enough to tide the family over during loss.

Envelopes are mostly delivered at the funeral to a community *koden* committee who oversee the receipt of the envelopes. The envelopes are opened and names and dollar amounts are recorded in a *koden* register. After the funeral, the money and the registers are presented to the family. From then on, the family uses the register as reference to repay those who gave. On most repayment occasions, old-timers like my mother don't have to refer to the register; they amazingly remember who gave and how much. Still, the register is a back-up. An important one too because as we get older our memory fades; almost in an inverse manner, *koden* repayment grows in importance.

We tell Bev my mother would sometimes refer to the *koden* as *morau*, the Japanese term for borrowing. Upon hearing the passing of say a neighbor, she would mention "I think we wen' *morau* from them when Daddy died." Ma knew that this *koden* was like a loan sometimes repaid years later and, at times, a generation later.

Pat, my oldest brother and first son, will inherit our family's *koden* registers. He will be responsible to discharge our family's *koden* obligations, sometimes to those he may not have met. But as with most things Japanese, he will probably let this lapse. We're Americanized now; it doesn't fit in our world or so it seems.

As we continue to drive, I tell Russ and Bev about my own experience with our family's obligations. On one of my visits several years ago, my mother was 80 years old, then. I had come back from playing tennis. When I got home I told her I had begun to teach tennis to Glenn Katahara, a retired Kauai Community College teacher.

"Oh, 'as good. I know his family. I grew up with his mother in Kealia. She still live there, on the hill. She taught me to cook. I was about 16-years old. Was one of my first jobs, working at the Boyd's home. She wen' teach me a lot." I knew then that Mrs. Katahara was very important in my mother's life since cooking has been a great source of her life's pride.

Thereafter, when I helped Glenn, I felt I was discharging a family obligation. For some reason, I felt a great deal of satisfaction. I felt *samurai*. In my exaggerated sense of *bushido*, I compared my mother and my patience to that of the 47 Ronin. The 47 Ronin patiently let only three years pass before fulfilling their obligation, on the other hand, our family showed more patience by waiting one generation and 65 years.

We pull into my mother's driveway feeling that we have given Bev a good insight into our family. In the spirit of examining rituals, I look closer at my mother's Buddhist altar, her *hotokesan,* in her living room. It is well maintained. The flowers and the rice offerings remain fresh; our deceased relative's pictures are updated and clean. My mother has fulfilled well her obligation to her deceased husband, son and other relatives. Prominent is a picture of my nephew, my mother's first grandson, Randy, who died just two years ago.

"Where he buried?" I ask my mother.

"He scattered at Kalapaki," she says. That made sense since Randy loved fishing. In my mind I pictured Kalapaki Bay; I think of the beauty but before I can think of anything else, my mother continues, "No mo' grave, no feel good, no?"

I knew what she meant. Kalapaki Bay is beautiful and holds many memories of Randy but it also holds many of our family's other memories and those thoughts dilute my recollection of him. Even a plain grave marker would keep my memory of him clearer. Clean and simple. I understood my mother's dissatisfaction.

I return to my home in New Jersey. I think about the *koden, giri*, my mother's *hotokesan*, and the scattering of Randy's ashes. I think about not stopping by to see my old friend, Mike Oride. While at home, my sister Chris encountered him shopping in Big Save, she told him I was home and I would stop by, more so, because his mother died a few months ago.

I missed on that one. I take out a clean white envelope, I write, "With Sympathy, Stu Hada". I slip twenty dollars into the crisp, white envelope and I think, "Only leetle beet." I send it off.

Note: Koden in Kanji: 香奠 means: An obituary gift often given in kind.

Source: Hada, Stuart. "Small Satisfactions." 2009. Used with permission of the author.

Charlene Gima, "Odori Story"
(2009)

Okinawa is the largest in the chain of Ryuku islands, nearly a thousand miles southwest of mainland Japan. Okinawa has its own distinctive history, dialect, and culture, which is strongly influenced by China and Chinese migration. Originally an independent kingdom, Okinawa was formally annexed by Japan's Meiji government in 1872 and became a Japanese prefecture in 1879. Okinawan immigration to Hawai'i began in 1900. Over the next 24 years, approximately 25,000 Okinawans moved to the islands to work as contract laborers on the plantations, escaping successive waves of peasant uprisings, increasing food shortages, and encroaching Japanese political imperialism. Calling themselves Uchinanchu *to distinguish themselves from the mainland Japanese* Naichi, *Okinawans faced discrimination from the Naichi, who looked down on the Okinawans as socially and ethnically inferior. Before Pearl Harbor, the two ethnic groups generally did not mix. This segregation changed after World War II, largely as a result of the solidarity engendered by the* Uchinanchu *and* Naichi*'s identical treatment during the war. Moreover, Okinawan ethnic organizations began to form, and people increasingly viewed Okinawan arts and culture as worthy of preserving and celebrating. Learning and performing Okinawan dance forms, in particular, has become very popular.*

Charlene Gima was born on the windward side of O'ahu but grew up upcountry on Maui. After graduating from the University of Hawai'i at Manoa, she received her MA and PhD from Cornell University. She teaches English at Honolulu Community College and has been studying Okinawan dance and performing arts for seven years. In her short story, "Odori Story," originally published in MANOA *journal's "Voices from Okinawa Online," Gima talks about learning Okinawan* Bon *dances with her friend Melanie and discovering her own roots in the process.*

I blame Melanie for everything that came with odori (dance) and my involvement with Okinawan stuff. It's all her fault. The whole thing started innocently enough with an understandable desire to participate at the Bon dances that happen every summer. I mean participate more fully than the typical routine of "Let's go to the Bon dance, eat lots of chow fun, admire the colorful costumes,

and make a lame attempt at dancing," which I had done all my life. Usually that was enough for us locals, but Mel wanted something more.

First, though, she wanted to attend an O-bon Buddhist service for the dead—typically held for the families of people who had died since the last year's O-bon service.

"But why?" I asked, wrinkling my nose. "It's so boring. Plus, nobody in your family passed away who's a member of a Buddhist church here on Maui." Mel's family was from Argentina, a mixture of Jewish and undecided.

"No, it won't be boring!" Mel said enthusiastically. I thought I glimpsed some Zen fervor in her eyes, but I didn't know enough about the different sects of Buddhism to explain that this wasn't going to be very Zen-like. We ended up attending O-bon service at Mantoku-ji in Paia, where the priest chanted in a resonant monotone and occasionally banged a bowl-shaped bell made of some brassy material. Accompanying him was a choir made up of elderly ladies who sang Buddhist hymns and made zoop-ing noises on mini-xylophones while tinkling bells on long wooden wands. Having never seen xylophones in use in a Buddhist ceremony before, I was mildly intrigued, but Mel was a bit disappointed.

"I hate to admit it, Char, but you're right. That was boring," she said sadly. However, she thoroughly enjoyed the dancing that followed, and was ecstatic at her first taste of andagi, the deep-fried Okinawan doughnut (although I thought this sample was not the best and promised her better ones at the Okinawan O-bon). That had been last summer. Now, it seemed, she was feeling more ambitious.

"Let's join the dancing!" she said, pooh-poohing my weak disclaimer that the only dance I barely knew was Tanko Bushi, the coal-miner's dance. "Aren't there practice sessions?" She knew me well enough to anticipate that I would not enjoy making a fool of myself in front of a large Bon dance crowd that probably contained a few of our students.

"Well, I know Rinzai-Zen holds practices starting in July," I hedged. "They usually go until their O-bon in August."

"Perfect!"

"But you have to understand that these are different dances," I quickly warned her. "They're not the same as the ones at Mantoku-ji or the Wailuku Jodo. This is the Okinawan O-bon, and it's a little . . . different."

"How are they different?" Mel wanted to know.

"Ummm . . . the songs are longer. They're usually performed by live singers and sanshin players. And the dancers sometimes turn around and walk backwards." Those dances had been the worst when I had attempted to dance in the ring as a child. Of course, when you're small and cute, you're forgiven for turning around at the wrong time and bumping into the other dancers. It's different when you're older and have outgrown the cute stage, but this didn't faze Mel, who was still enthusiastic. I had some doubts about whether this activity would satisfy her or leave her bored and disappointed, like the Mantoku-ji service. But deep inside, I was happy to find a friend with whom I could risk looking stupid. Every summer at the Rinzai-Zen O-bon, I would say to my mom, "I should learn those dances," and she would say, "You can always go to the practices, you know." Every summer I would chicken out—but not this year.

It was a typically warm and humid Tuesday evening when I drove into the grassy field that also served as a parking lot in front of the Rinzai-Zen mission. A tall hedge was all that separated the mission from Baldwin Beach Park, the favored hangout of surfers and hippies in the Paia area. I could smell the salt of the ocean, which was no more than fifty yards away, and the iron/zinc smell-taste of seaweed was like a faint trace of blood in my mouth. Ironwood pines on the beach side were a flimsy protection against tidal waves like the one that hit in 1946. After the mission burned down in the 1980s, it was rebuilt to tsunami codes, and now it was a sturdy two-story structure made of cement blocks. A wide stairway led to the upper floor, where the temple hall was located. About twenty feet in front of the building was a small, square concrete stage with lights on slender steel poles at all four corners. The Bon dance ring had been set up around this stage with markers that sketched out a straggling ellipse around forty feet wide.

Mel was sitting on the edge of the stage, and she jumped up to greet me with a relieved smile. She must have felt very out of place as the only blond girl in a bunch of older Okinawan ladies. Up on the verandah of the temple, the sanshin players were plucking and tuning their three-stringed instruments. All the ladies were chatting, some dressed in happi coats, some with gold or silver decorated fans in their hands. A few guys were carrying out the hand-held taiko drums that helped to keep the rhythm going. In contrast, Mel and I looked like what we were: complete beginners with empty hands and nervous smiles.

With a "Yo!" from the lead singer, the introductory music began. Everyone shuffled into a ragged circle, and we followed, trying to guess which of the ladies would be a good person to copy. The three taiko players were closest to the stage, and just outside their circle were the leaders who remembered the dances. Mel and I were in the outermost ring, which had large gaps between groups of four or five dancers.

Then the music began. Afterward, Mel described it as twangy, rhythmic, and set to a musical scale and beat that seemed completely foreign and un-Western to her ears. To me it sounded familiar, half-remembered from childhood years: the music I used to fall asleep to in a living room while my grandparents and their friends played and sang the night away.

There was nothing familiar about the dances, however. They were baffling and immensely frustrating: we were always on the wrong foot, turning at the wrong times, going the wrong way, and putting our hands up when they should be down. The worst part was that as soon as we sort of began to understand the sequence of movements, the dance would end, and as we quickly discovered, the musicians only played each song once. The entire set of fourteen songs took an hour, but it went by in a blur of confusion and left us feeling just as ignorant as we were in the beginning—except that now we knew how much we didn't know. But we were hooked.

And so it went on, every Tuesday and Thursday evening, for the next five weeks. Some dances were simpler than others, like the "Kudaka" that was second in the sequence of songs. Others were fun, like the always-popular dance with the bamboo castanets on our fingers clicking in tandem with our feet. Even the "backwards dances" became easier with time. We acquired accessories: folding fans, castanets that we called "kachi-kachi," red-and-white-striped sticks with red and white fabric flags hanging from the ends. Mel gave names to the dance moves to help us remember better. One move she called "throwing the sun up into the sky" while another was the "thump-thump" dance. We got to know the ladies better, who all seemed to know whose granddaughter I was without my telling them. Still, certain dances remained frustratingly incomprehensible, like the "mystery dance" (which was mysterious because we had no clue what we were doing), or the graceful turn of hand and wrist that Mel called the "serpent swan." So when a flyer arrived in the mail, advertising a class in Okinawan dance to be held at the Maui Okinawan Cultural Center, I thought it was a good idea. "Maybe we can learn more about the dances," I said to Mel, and she agreed. It was August of 2002, a fateful day that would change the direction of our lives forever.

Since Mel had no idea where the Okinawan Cultural Center was, we met up at MCC and I gave her directions to Paukukalo, which lies on the windy side of the island, just past the harbor and off of Beach Road. We pulled into the parking lot a little before 10:30 am and walked up the wide steps to the front porch that was set under a sweeping red-tiled roof. We were a little nervous, but not as much as at that first Bon dance practice. This time we came with our hard-won accessories, and we recognized and said hello to a few of the ladies: Mrs. Isagawa, the mother of my high school classmate; Mrs. Konno, who had shiny lacquered hair and the most graceful hands; and Mrs. Nishihara, whose brown bouffant hairdo made her look positively statuesque among the petite Okinawans.

The inside of the center was a wide, high-ceilinged space, a cool dimness compared to the glare of hot morning sun outside. To one side was the stage with its own mini-roof jutting out, covered with authentic terra-cotta tiles from Okinawa. Along the other walls were glass cabinets containing pictures, scrolls, dolls, kimono, books, musical instruments, and other things. The floor was covered in shiny, polished tiles that reflected the lights far overhead, rippling where the concrete slab underneath had settled unevenly. There was a bustle of voices coming from the kitchen off to our right, and we walked over to the row of white plastic chairs set up in front of the cabinets, perching uneasily on the edge of our seats.

Mrs. Konno called the practice to order and introduced the sensei, a slender, smiling woman with wavy black hair and glasses.

"We so happy because Cheryl Nakasone Sensei come all the way from Honolulu for teach us," Mrs. Konno announced, beaming. "Please, everybody, practice hard!"

We all bowed and mumbled, "Yoroshiku onegai shimasu!" The ritual of greeting was familiar to me from my experiences with aikido, but I slid a quick sideways glance to check on Mel. Her knowledge of Japanese was limited to "neko" (cat) and "an da gi" (which didn't really count as Japanese). But our sensei was stepping forward, introducing herself with a warm smile and speaking in a low, clear voice.

"I've been dancing for forty-five years," she said. (This was clearly impossible since she looked about forty years old at the most, as Mel and I agreed later.) "I strongly believe that everyone should have fun while dancing. You're here to learn, but you're also here to enjoy yourselves, so don't worry if you're not perfect or if you feel awkward. Just follow and eventually you'll learn the dance. Okay, let's start with the basics: walking."

The speech was simultaneously reassuring and terrifying: on the one hand, she clearly wanted us to feel comfortable, but on the other, she just as clearly expected us to screw up. A lot. But how much could we screw up something like walking, which we did every day?

As we soon found out, quite a bit. She started the music, a slow, solemn plucking of sanshin and koto, and demonstrated the women's walk: an ineffably graceful glide with an interesting upward toe-flick when she moved her weight forward. It looked easy, but it wasn't—and this would turn out to be a recurring theme in our future studies with Sensei. When I tried it, my body felt stiff, tense with anxiety, and I wobbled alarmingly from side to side. "Bend your knees," Sensei advised cheerfully, "and if you feel like you're losing your balance, just tap the tips of your fingers against your upper thighs."

Even so, the simple walk across the shiny tile floor and back seemed endless as I shuffled and awkwardly attempted the graceful toe-flick in my borrowed green booties (I had forgotten to bring socks). Sensei told us to drop our shoulders and to lean forward a little at the hips. She also told us to try to emulate a wave's up-and-down motion when our weight moved forward, but this proved impossible for most of us at the moment.

"Okay, what shall we do next? Hamachidori?" Sensei asked. Most of the ladies nodded and smiled in agreement. Mel and I were trying to drift inconspicuously toward the plastic chairs when Sensei caught us. "You'll join us, won't you? Just follow!" Dubious, we joined the tail end of a line of ladies. "What dance is this?" Mel whispered to me. "I don't know," I whispered back, "but I don't think it's a Bon dance."

If we had thought the Bon dances were frustrating, this was exponentially more so: a graceful, wandering dance that seemed to have no discernable sequence of motions. That is, certain motions were repeated, but to no pattern that we could detect. Yet when we watched Sensei dance, it all seemed completely natural and inevitable, each turn of hand leading to the next, her body dipping and rising to some beat we couldn't hear. Mel declared later that it was the most graceful thing she had ever seen, but for me, besides its beauty, the dance seemed to express a deep joy in simply being. It also focused for me the sensation of coming home to a culture and history that I had barely begun to learn. While I had spent my formative adult years soaking up a different kind of knowledge and the challenging learning style of academia, and while

I had happily devoured books about English literature and European languages, I had never given much thought to what made me an Okinawan American. Odori, and Sensei, have given me the opportunity to discover another kind of life.

Of course, just as we had been hooked with the Bon dances, we were completely smitten by Sensei and odori. Rashly, we committed ourselves to practices with the ladies every Sunday afternoon, and a full-day practice when Sensei came over once a month. We even committed ourselves to bringing a dish to the potluck lunch that was held whenever Sensei visited—no small feat for English teachers with stacks of papers to grade, and it wasn't like we were good cooks or anything. What I didn't realize until much later was how completely Mel and I had given our hearts and souls to Sensei and the art of the dance.

I grew to know Hamachidori very well, although I still cannot say I have mastered it completely. I think this is one of the things I love about odori: it is not a subject to master or dominate or perfect, but an art to take to one's heart, to attempt to inhabit and live in. When I study the videotapes of Sensei dancing, or when I copy her moves in practice, I am not trying to become Sensei herself, but to get a little closer to that ephemeral moment when the dancer is the same as the dance, becoming one with the music, the words, the melody, the time, and the space.

Yes, it's all Mel's fault—and I owe her a debt of gratitude that I can never repay for bringing odori into my life. Thanks to her desire to try something new, and her bravery in taking risks, I have found something that I love that resonates with the deepest part of my soul.

This past March, I performed my first solo dance at the Maui Okinawan Association's lunar New Year's party (on Hawai'i time, a month late as usual). The dance, Kajadifu, was the first on the program of entertainment since it is traditionally performed on auspicious occasions and, some believe, to bring good luck for the coming year. I was dressed in borrowed finery: Mrs. Konno's gold-colored hat sat lightly but firmly on my head, hiding my flattened bun of too-long hair; Mrs. Nishihara's silky polyester kimono, a dusty gold color, slithered over my arms, the sleeves a little too long; around my hips was Sensei's stiff brocade obi (sash), pre-tied in a large, elaborate knot and fastened with safety pins. Strapped inside my kimono was a folded towel, meant to give me the bulkier body silhouette for a man's dance. In my right hand was my open dancing fan, gold on one side, silver on the other, with black-lacquered sticks. The crimson curtains opened, and the music began, a slow melody of sanshin, flute, and drum that I had long ago internalized. Behind me, Sensei hovered anxiously. "Okay," she whispered, and I stepped up onto the stage, fan lightly poised in right hand, left holding the edge of my sleeve, knees flexed and body tilted forward a little at the hips. My white tabi-covered feet slid out on the brown parquet floor with the toe flick, and I flowed into the music, that moment of time and space that welcomed me home.

Source: Gima, Charlene. "Odori Story." Voices from Okinawa Online. January 2009. http://manoaokinawaissue .wordpress.com/. Blog created by *Manoa: A Pacific Journal of International Writing.* Used with permission of author.

Midwest Buddhist Temple, Ginza Festival (2010)

During World War II, interned nisei (second-generation, American-born Japanese Americans) were given the option of relocating out of the restricted areas of the West Coast to finish their college education. Approximately 3,600 nisei, aided by the National Japanese American Student Relocation Council, were able to do so; many of them matriculated in Chicago-area schools. After the war was over, even more Japanese Americans resettled in the Midwest, encouraged by the War Relocation Authority, which sought to disperse the population widely over the country. In subsequent years, most former internees decided to move back to the West Coast. The ones who stayed tended to Americanize and assimilate more quickly and thoroughly than their coastal counterparts, a result of geographic separation from family members, living in smaller and more isolated communities with few cultural resources, and concerted attempts to erase any perceived otherness that might negatively affect their standing in their new locales.

However, Chicago retained its thriving Japanese American community: its population grew from less than 500 to more than 11,000 between 1940 and 1950. In 1944, South Side Chicago Japanese Americans established the Midwest Buddhist Temple. Decades later, it still plays an active religious and cultural role in the neighborhood. Every year since 1956, the Midwest Buddhist Temple has thrown the Ginza Festival, celebrating Japanese crafts, food, and music, as well as teaching people about Jodo Shinshu Buddhism. Artists and musicians come from Japan; booths sell snacks, toys, crafts, jewelry, and clothes; and temple priests give dharma talks. The Ginza Festival is a means of community outreach and education, cultural preservation, and the maintenance of ethnic identity. The following documents, published by the Midwest Buddhist Temple, describe the Ginza Festival and its history; also included is a copy of a 2005 letter from Barack Obama, who was then the junior senator from Illinois, congratulating the temple on its 50th Ginza celebration.

THE 55TH ANNUAL GINZA FESTIVAL

In Historic Old Town Chicago

The 55th Annual Ginza Holiday, a large Japanese cultural festival, will be presented by the Midwest Buddhist Temple on August 13th, 14th, and 15th at 435 W. Menomonee Street in Chicago's historic Old Town.

Flown in from Tokyo for this event, four master craftsmen (Waza) will demonstrate their generations-old skills creating their unique crafts. The public will have the opportunity to meet the Waza and purchase their crafts. The Waza create collectible pieces that often fetch many times their purchase price in the after market. Several other exhibits and booths will be filled with Japanese dry goods and snacks, children's toys, kimonos, jewelry, anime and origami folding.

Ho Etsu Taiko is a Japanese drum ensemble based at Chicago's Midwest Buddhist Temple. As we continue to build upon our unique Taiko foundation stemming from both Japanese and American influences, our group aspires to bring a youthful and energizing sound to the stage.

One of our core philosophies focuses on the collective enjoyment of this wonderful cultural art, giving us our name, Ho Etsu or Joy of Dharma. Recent performances include the "Taiko 10" concert series at the 2009 Taiko Conference in Los Angeles as well as the annual installments of JASC Tsukasa Taiko's "Taiko Legacy" at the Museum of Contemporary Art in Chicago and the Chicago Cultural Center.

Our program has produced many talented players who have gone on to further develop their passion for Taiko with groups across the country including Gendo Taiko at Brown University, Cal Taiko at UC Berkeley, St. Louis Osuwa Taiko, and Tsunami Taiko of Seattle. Our membership is open to both seasoned and inexperienced players and interested parties are always welcome to observe our practices. For a preview of Hoetsu Taiko's performance here's a video clip of our performance at the 2009 Taiko Conference in Los Angeles.

In addition to the live performances, an abundance of traditional Japanese cuisine will be offered, including the famous open pit, charcoal grilled chicken teriyaki dinner, udon (Japanese cold noodles), sushi, edamame and grilled corn on the cob. For dessert try the kintoki (Japanese snow cone topped with sweet azuki beans). Premium Japanese beer, Sapporo, will also be available for purchase.

Featured in the festival will be ongoing stage performances with the entertaining taiko drumming by Twin Cities Kogen Taiko Group and the Midwest Buddhist Temple Taiko group, the Midwest Buddhist Temple Minyo Troupe, Fujima Shunojo Classical Dance Troupe, martial arts demonstrations, and the Na Kupuna Ukulele group.

Self defense tactics will be demonstrated by Aikido, Judo and Karate schools, while Kendo (Japanese fencing) will entertain the crowd.

Inside the temple, the exhibit hall will be filled with demonstrations and exhibits of bonsai, ikebana (flower arranging), kaminingyo (paper dolls), calligraphy, brush painting, silk flowers, and Japanese arts and crafts. Many of the products will be offered for sale.

The chapel will be open for guests who are interested in observing the place of worship and learning the basics of Buddhism. During stage intermissions, Reverend Ron Miyamura, Midwest Buddhist Temple minister, will deliver short dharma talks.

Returning this Year

Ginza expands into Saturday evening with Yoko Noge's Japanesque Band. Yoko's music can be described as a combination of Japanese "Minyo" folk music with "Chicago blues." Performed with electric piano, shamisen, horn section, and Yoko's sweet and growly blues vocals, the Japanesque Band will warm the August night at their first appearance at Ginza. Yoko will perform at 8:00 p.m. on Saturday evening.

A benefit donation of $5 for adults, and $4 for students and senior citizens will be collected at the gate. Children under 12 will be admitted free when accompanied by an adult.

The hours are: Friday, August 13, 5:30 pm–9:00 pm; Saturday, August 14, 11:30 am–9:30 pm; Sunday, August 15, 11:30 am–6:00 pm.

For information, call 312-943-7801

History of Ginza Chicago

Ginza Holiday found its beginning in 1956. It was at our former temple within the Old Town Triangle several blocks east of this location. The name Ginza seemed appropriate as it is a district in Tokyo known for entertainment. The event serves two purposes; one as a fund raiser to meet the temple expenses and the other as a way of sharing Japanese traditions with the people of the neighborhood.

The first event proceeded with some apprehension as it intended to draw upon the non-Japanese community. Most members harbored unfavorable experiences in the decade preceding. Uprooted from the West Coast to isolated camps, they made their final trek to Chicago on news of jobs and friendlier surroundings. The dread of non-acceptance ran deep.

The optimists among them proved right as fears were totally unwarranted. The good neighbors of Chicago attended in droves. Teriyaki chicken became an instant success. An old family recipe surely helped. To the consternation of a few, it may have eclipsed some of the cultural events.

The opening of our present temple grounds in 1973 gave us more room to expand and to serve the thousands who passed through our gateway. For many, it's become a yearly must. As coordination passes to the Sansei and Yonsei (third and fourth generation Japanese Americans), maintaining tradition and high quality holds precedence. But the ultimate success of these efforts rests in the knowledge of satisfaction brought to each and every guest.

Fun Ginza Facts from Ginza 2008

In the span of about 18 hours of Ginza last year, we cooked over 3 tons of chicken (more than a Hummer H2 weighs) grilled over 1,600 pounds of glowing charcoal briquets (that's 80 twenty pound bags or about 45 feet tall if stacked in a single column). The results are the best chicken teriyaki in Chicago and the only teriyaki chicken that is charcoal grilled over an open pit. This is what makes our chicken teriyaki the signature dish of Ginza Chicago. And no wimpy portions here, you get a generous serving of half a chicken per dinner.

We cooked over 700 pounds of rice and boiled over a quarter ton of noodles. And talk about eggs, we cook 60 dozen eggs over the 2 1/2 days of Ginza.

Even the little things add up. We go through 10 pounds of garlic and 30 pounds of ginger. There are over 20 pounds of butter melted to drizzle over roasted corn-on-the-cob. We also use over a quarter ton of sugar in various marinades.

The Temple's woman's auxiliary uses 500 sheets of seaweed (nori) in preparing well over 3,600 sushi pieces. There are also 1,200 tofu pouches that have to be stuffed with rice by hand.

The beverages are the easiest part of Ginza, there's little preparation—you just have to serve the customer. Even then there are 10 half barrels of beer that needs to be carried along with well over 2,000 cans of soft drinks. Does anyone know how many cups poured that 10 half barrels of beer represent? Someone also has to make the 90 gallons of lemonade and 40 gallons of iced tea.

And here's an interesting piece of correspondence. Way back when Barack Obama was the junior Senator from Illinois, he sent us a letter of congratulations on the 50th anniversary of Ginza. That was back in 2005.

All in all, even with all the preparation and work that goes into Ginza, we take joy in hosting such a memorable event in the great city of Chicago. After all we've been doing this for 54 years, we must have fun doing it.

* Statistics supplied by Mary Holcomb.

Obama's Letter

Dear Friends,

It is both an honor and a pleasure to have this opportunity to extend my warmest greetings to all those attending the 50th anniversary of the Midwest Buddhist of Chicago's Ginza Holiday.

I am proud of the Midwest Buddhist of Chicago's continuous involvement in Japanese culture. Your work touches the lives of numerous families and individuals throughout our community.

I wish you much continued success and happiness in your endeavors in the many years to come.

Very truly yours,
Barak Obama
United States Senator

Source: Midwest Buddhist Temple. http://www.ginzachi cago.com/, http://www.ginzachicago.com/history-ginza chicago/, and http://www.ginzachicago.com/ginza-fun-facts/. Used with permission of the Midwest Buddhist Temple.

Dean Koyama, "The Fullness of Obon"

(2010)

The Obon festival, originating in Japan and held in July or August each year, is a Buddhist celebration to remember and honor the spirits of deceased relatives and ancestors. Obon is a three-day festival, featuring the Bon dance, bonfires, food, and fireworks; it concludes when people float paper lanterns down the rivers. Japanese immigrants brought Obon to the United States, and it remains a large part of community life, especially in Hawai'i and on the West Coast. Dean Koyama, the pastor at the Mountain View Buddhist Temple in California, traveled to Tottori Prefecture in Japan's Honshu island, where he celebrated Obon and officiated at some of the services. In the following article, Koyama reflects on his experiences in Japan: the similarities and the differences between Japanese and American festivals, and the ways in which the spirit of Obon transcends national bounds. His essay illustrates how religious and ethnic identity often complement each other and how the homeland remains emotionally significant, no matter how many generations removed one may be. Koyama concludes his message with "Namandabu," the shortened form of "Namu amida butsu"—itself a Japanese adaption of the original Sanskrit mantra "buddhānusmṛti," repeating the name of Buddha. "Namandabu" is used in English Shin Buddhist services.

We have just concluded our Obon festivities here at the Mountain View Buddhist Temple. It was marked with wonderful food, wonderful dances, a wonderful crowd and wonderful weather. But one of the most memorable Obons for me was when I was a ministerial student and visited Tottori Prefecture. I received an invitation from a former BCA minister, Rev. Tsuguru Kinugasa (who served at the Los Angeles Betsuin from 1978 to 1980) to visit and participate at the Obon observances of his temple, Gansho-Ji. Gansho-Ji is a famous temple because it is the home temple of the myokonin, Genza.

The Obon dance at Gansho-Ji was so much fun. They played only one song all night and the dance was only a few steps so that even I was able to learn it without any practice. The members would dance for a while, drink a little, go back and dance again. Various people would get up and help sing the song. Sometimes they wouldn't know or would forget the words (because of the *sake*), so they would make them up on the fly. It truly was a festival of joy.

But what was so interesting were the Obon services. Unlike here, where everyone comes to the temple for one service, the minister in Tottori visits each member's home. I was surprised to find out that not only Rev. Kinugasa had to visit the homes, but also his father and mother had to help out. They each had to visit between 15 to 20 homes each day for the next three days. Rev. Kinugasa thought it would be good for me to experience how Obon is observed in Japan by joining him, as he would go from house to house.

At the first home, Sensei announced at the *genkan* (front entrance of the house) in a hearty voice, "*Gansho-Ji desu*! (I'm from Gansho-Temple)." The family came and welcomed us in. We proceeded immediately to the *O-butsudan* (family altar), chanted the sutra and had the family o-shoko (burn incense). Sensei chatted with the family explaining that I was from America and came to Japan to study to become a Buddhist minister. We both politely accepted *mugi-cha* (cold barley tea) and then proceeded to the next house. By the end of the day, I was exhausted and my knees ached tremendously from sitting *seiza* (Japanese style) [seiza position: hands folded on lap and feet tucked under the body] for all the services.

The next day, to my horror, Rev. Kinugasa informed me that he had to take care of a Hatsubon service for a very important member of his temple and asked if I could go on a route all on my own. Fortunately, all the homes were located along one street very close to the temple. I went to the first house and mimicked everything Rev. Kinugasa had done the day before. I approached the entrance with a barely audible, timid voice saying, "*Gansho-Ji desu*." The members of the family came out and warmly welcomed me in. I proceeded to the family *O-butsudan*, chanted the sutra, had the family *oshoko*, drank the tea and chatted **very** briefly before I announced that I had to be on my way just as Rev. Kinugasa had done the first day. Later I discovered that Rev. Kinugasa had made prior arrangements with all the families I was to visit, telling them that an American would be coming to conduct the Obon services for them. They had expected a blond haired, blue-eyed person to come to their house, but instead I showed up. After the first several home services went without a hitch, I slowly gained confidence and fell into a comfortable routine.

At the next house, with my newfound confidence, I announced, "*Gansho-Ji desu!*" I waited

for a few seconds, but I didn't hear a sound. Again I yelled out, "*Gansho-Ji desu*." And still no sound. I didn't know what to do. Just then, Rev. Kinugasa came by to check up on me. I explained to him that no one was home. He told me to go ahead in and conduct the service anyway. To my surprise, I found the front entrance door unlocked. Once again, I announced, "*Gansho-Ji desu*," just in case. I walked into the main room and found the *O-butsudan*. I lit the candle and burned the incense, chanted the sutra. Since no one was there, I got up to leave, but just then I caught site of a tray with a glass of cold tea and a donation envelope to the temple. I was amused that the family knew they wouldn't be here when I came around for the service, yet they still went through all the trouble to prepare for the service anyway. I decided it would be rude to just take the envelope without drinking the *mugi-cha*, so I took a few minutes to enjoy the tea.

A few houses later, again, there was no response. I proceeded to open the front door. Again, it was not locked. I went into the house, found the family altar, lit the candle and incense, and proceeded with the chanting of the sutra. Mid way through, I heard a set of footsteps behind me. After I finished chanting, I turned to greet the person who sat with me for the service. It turned out to be a twelve-year-old boy, who had apparently overslept because his hair was still ruffled and unkempt. He must have missed going out with his family. I invited him to burn incense. After he did so, he proceeded into the kitchen area and brought out a tray. On the tray were again, a glass of tea and the envelope for the donation. He politely set the tray down in front of me and invited me to drink the tea. Imagine, a 12-year-old boy recognizing that since his parents and family were absent, he took on the responsibility of "hosting" the minister and provided the hospitality. I was deeply impressed with him.

In these two circumstances, it may seem strange and perhaps rude that the families were not home when the Buddhist priest made his rounds for the Obon services. There is no way that we would ever leave our homes open and unattended for someone outside of our families to have the opportunity to walk in freely. Later, I found out that it is very common during Obon for the family not to be there when the minister would make his visitation.

Later that evening Rev. Kinugasa and I talked about my experience at the homes where no one was present for the service. I remarked that I could have just gone into the empty, unoccupied house, picked up the donation and left without anyone ever seeing me actually do the service. Flippantly, I asked Rev. Kinuga- sa, "Who would know if I, as the minister, actually chanted the sutra or not?" Rev. Kinugasa's immediate, without-any-hesitation, response was, "You would."

As I reflected upon his words, I realized, that indeed I wasn't the only one in the house. Perhaps physically, the members of the family were absent. But they still took the time to clean the O-butsudan, offer fresh flowers, and even have the *mugi-cha* and donation envelope prepared. And as I reflect, especially about the little 12-year-old boy, who woke up after hearing the chanting begin, came down the stairs and sat in silence, burned incense and offered the tea and envelope to a person who looked Japanese but had a strange accent, I became even more impressed and humbled. He could have taken the easy way out. He could have stayed upstairs and pretended to stay asleep. Here, he had the awareness and kindness to offer me in his very polite manner, his appreciation for my conducting the service. For him to have learned to do this can only be attributed to the upbringing he received from his family and ancestors. It was a tribute to them.

Although there may have been only one small boy in one house and no one in another, while I chanted the sutra for Obon, the houses indeed were never empty.

Namandabu, namandabu

Source: Koyama, Dean. "The Fullness of Obon." *Wheel of Dharma* 36, no. 8 (August 2010): 2, 6. Used with permission of the Buddhist Churches of America.

Han Bong Soon, Immigration Interview
(1940)

Han Bong Soon originally arrived in the Territory of Hawai'i with her husband, Koon Shim Lee, in July 1904. The couple lived in Hawai'i for the next 21 years, where they raised their eight American-born children. However, in 1925, the couple took six of their children and returned to Korea (then called Chosen). The family lived in Korea for the next 15 years, until Koon passed away in 1939. The next year, Han decided to move back to Hawai'i. However, after landing in Honolulu on March 2, 1940, Han was denied reentry as a nonquota alien.

The decision hinged on the immigration officials' claim that Han had had no intention of returning to Hawai'i when she left for Korea in 1925. Han appealed the decision, producing a 1925 petition from the Japanese consul general stating that her family was returning temporarily to Japan. (Japan had effectively colonized Korea beginning in 1905. This meant the United States considered Korea to be Japanese territory and Koreans to be Japanese nationals.) When Han presented an official Japanese visa, the Board of Special Inquiry of the Immigration and Naturalization Service reopened her case. Through her attorney, Peter A. Lee, Han claimed it had always been her and her husband's intention to return to the islands. In a brief he filed on April 2, 1940, attorney Lee wrote that Han Bong Soon's husband had told his friend Kim Soo Young that he was traveling to Korea only to get medicine, that his intention was not to live permanently in Korea, and that he planned to move back to Hawai'i once he was cured.

This excerpt is from a follow-up hearing on April 2, 1940, that was convened when the board interviewed Han Bong Soon. Her son Henry Lee, who had been born in Hawai'i and was a native English speaker, was present. Han testified to the board through an interpreter. Han's appeal was successful, and she was admitted back into the United States on May 2, 1940.

April 2, 1940

(Case reopened this day by order of the Central Office)

325

Q   What is your name?

A   HAN BONG SOON

Q   Are you the same Han Bong Soon who testified before this Board on March 2, 1940 as an applicant for admission as a nonquota immigrant under section 4 (b) of the act of 1924?

A   Yes

Q   Were all the statements you made during your examination at that time true and complete?

A   Yes

Q   You are advised that by order of the Central Office your case has been reopened to afford you an opportunity to present testimony or evidence supporting your claim of legally admitted returning resident; further to explain discrepancies regarding marriage and places of birth of your children as contrasted with data appearing in the family record attached to the visa presented by you. Do you understand?

A   Yes

Q   Are there any alterations, clarifications or modifications you wish to make in your testimony of March 2, 1940?

A   Yes

Q   Just what do you wish to alter, clarify or modify at this time?

A   When I left Hawai'i my intention was to return to Hawai'i and to live in Hawai'i. In order to come back here I left two girls in Hawai'i, Hannah and Soonhie. At the time of my departure to Korea I thought my husband had applied for a reentry permit.

Q   You were asked whether at the time of your departure for Korea fifteen years ago you or your husband had in your possession permits to reenter the United States to which you answered "I don't know". Is that correct?

A   I thought my husband knew everything and I thought he had applied for a reentry permit. I depended on him. I told him to do so and I thought he would.

Q   I will ask you again do you know whether your husband was in possession of permits to reenter the United States for you and himself at the time of your departure 15 years ago?

A   My husband told me he would apply for a return permit and I thought we had permits. I thought he had the permits so I didn't ask him again.

Q   Did your husband ever tell you he applied for permits to reenter for himself and yourself prior to your departure for Korea?

A   At the time we left for Korea I asked my husband to apply for return permits and he told me yes so I thought he had applied for it. We were busy at that time so I didn't ask him again.

Q   Did your husband show you any permits that he received or might have received from Washington, D.C. enabling you both to return to the United States?

A   No, he didn't . . .

Q   What was the intention of your husband relative to his return to Hawai'i at the time of your departure in 1925?

A   I don't know what his intention was but I told my husband to go to Korea himself but he told me to take the children and go to Korea and see Korea then come back.

Q   Did he mean that you should come back alone?

A   No, we would come back altogether.

Q   At the time he left here in 1925 did he make any indication or tell you the length of time he expected to remain in Korea?

A   No, he didn't tell me how many years; he just told me to go there and see Korea then to come back.

Q   Did he specifically tell you that he would return with you when you wished to come back to Hawai'i from that trip?

A   Yes.

Q   Was it your understanding that your husband had provided himself with permits to reenter the United States for himself and yourself prior to your joint departure in 1925 as you had requested to apply for the same?

A   Yes

Q   When did you first learn that your husband had not provided himself with these papers?

A   When I tried to return to Hawai'i about five or six years ago I went to the American Consulate at Seoul and he told me that I couldn't come to Hawai'i. At that time I suspected that we had no return permits.

Q   That was after you had lived in Korea approximately 9 or 10 years—was it not?

A   Yes.

Q   In all that time had you not asked your husband whether he had provided himself with these papers?

A   No, I didn't ask him . . .

....

Q   The records of this office show that your daughter Hannah departed from here September 6, 1926 and that your daughter Soonhie departed December 28, 1925, and that they both returned together December 7, 1926 on the s.s. "Shinyo Maru". Is that correct as far as you can remember?

A   I can't remember the dates but I know they were in Korea.

Q   But that was very shortly after you had departed with your husband and other children—was it not?

A   Yes, very shortly.

Q Why did you and your husband not return with them when they came back in 1926?

A My husband was very sick at that time. He was sick for a long time and he could not travel; both legs were swollen.

Q Did Hannah ever graduate as a trained nurse from the Children's hospital?

A I don't know.

Q Hasn't she ever told you on the trips she made to Korea?

A I don't know.

Q If she had accompanied you to Korea in 1925 would that have interrupted her training as a nurse at the hospital?

A I don't know.

Q And you maintain that your trip to Korea constituted a temporary absence because your daughters Hannah and Soonhie remained in Hawai'i?

A Yes, it was my intention to return so I left my two girls in Hawai'i.

Q If that was the intention of your husband to return also why did he dispose of all his homes in Hawai'i?

A My husband sold the business because there was not much business and when someone wanted to buy the property he wanted to sell it so he sold it.

Q What did he do first—make up his mind to sell the property or make up his mind to go to Korea?

A He intended to sell the business first; so many people wanted to buy and my husband couldn't make money with the business so my husband told me he wanted to sell it.

Q Did either you or your husband have any ideas as to what time you intended to stay in Korea when you departed in 1925?

A We intended to return within one year so I left my daughters here.

Q Were your daughters self-supporting at that time?

A When we left Hawai'i we gave them about $80 a piece and told them to work part of the time until we returned.

Q At the time you first came to Hawai'i in 1904 was Korea a self-governing nation?

A Yes.

Q At the time you returned in 1925 Korea was under Japanese control—was it not?

A Yes . . .

Q Did your husband ever apply at any American Consulate abroad for papers to return to Hawai'i?

A I don't know.

Q Did he ever talk to you about returning to Hawai'i?

A He told me many times he wanted to come to Hawai'i. He told me many times "I too wish to return to Hawai'i."

Q Why didn't your husband, if that was his intention, ever make any effort to return here?

A I don't know.

Q When did you next apply for a visa before an American Consulate after you were refused one about five years ago?

A About a year ago.

Q And this is the visa you received as a result of that application?

A Yes.

Q Attached to the visa presented by you is a certified copy of a Japanese family census. Can you read anything in this family census?

A No, I cannot read.

Q From whom did you receive that family record?

A My daughter Soonhie obtained it from the Japanese village officer.

Sources: 4395/414 [HAN Bong Soon]; Box 3: Appeal Case Files of Japanese and Korean Aliens Denied Entry by Boards of Special Inquiry, compiled 1917–1940 (ARC 628461); Records of the Immigration and Naturalization Service, Record Group 85; National Archives and Records Administration-Pacific Region (San Francisco); Peter A. Kim, "Brief in Behalf of Applicant After Case has been Reopened and Admission Denied"; 4395/414 [Han Bong Soon]; Box 3: Appeal Case Files of Japanese and Korean Aliens Denied Entry by Boards of Special Inquiry, compiled 1917–1940 (ARC 628461).

Lucy, "'Lucy' Sails for 'Frisco"
(1954)

Published in the early to mid-1950s, the Korean Messenger *was the first English-language Korean American newspaper in the United States. K. W. Lee, the first Asian American journalist to work at a mainstream daily in the United States, began the paper while studying journalism at West Virginia University and the University of Illinois. He graduated from the University of Illinois in 1955 and went on to cover the civil rights movement for small papers in the South during the 1960s. However, Lee is most well known for his investigative work on the conviction of Chol Soo Lee (no relation) for a San Francisco gangland murder in 1973. Lee also founded the* Koreatown Weekly *in 1970 and continues, well into his 80s, to work as an activist in the Asian American community. In this article from the March 1954 edition of the* Korean Messenger, *an anonymous Korean woman recounts the story of leaving for the United States to continue her studies. During this time, many Koreans came to the United States to pursue undergraduate and graduate degrees. Some remained after they completed their studies, becoming an important anchor for the post-1965 Korean immigrant community.*

Ed: For some convincing reasons, the writer wishes to remain anonymous.

There is mounting excitement as the day draws near for you to take off by plane or ship to the dreamed-of land of the United States. When everything is prepared and you have met all the requirements, surmounted all the difficulties of examinations, money exchange and governmental red-tape and hold your visa and the ticket in your hand, you relax and sigh with satisfaction that a challenge has been met and won.

Tearful Good-byes

The day for departure is here and the whole family is out to see you off. There are friends and relatives, too, who look upon you as either merely lucky or God's chosen. There are tearful good-byes. Mother weeps unashamedly, perhaps clinging to your hands telling you to return soon. If you're still single, the advice to return soon is more urgent and you know that you'll be getting letters from mother when you are in the States, telling you about this or that eligible boy or girl whose life will go to waste if you don't return soon. And father—you know he would weep, too, if he could—shakes your hand proudly, wishes you godspeed and tells you to study hard in America.

Cry a Little

Then you are on the boat or plane, filled with a mixture of sadness and excitement and frantically wave good bye until the familiar faces and figures become indistinguishable by distance and a sudden mistiness over your eyes. If you are on a ship, you stand at the rails as long as you can see the pier you have just left, or even longer, before you go to your cabin to sit on the edge of your bunk and find nothing to do but cry a little. If you are on a plane, you sit back on your seat and also cry a little.

Destination Nears

But soon, whether you cry long or short, your destination and the great adventure about to begin takes complete control of your thoughts. You're really on your way to America.

But, was it really true? Was it really me who was sitting in a cabin on a ship bound for "the States?" Was the ship moving? And in the right direction?

Lucy Prefers Ship

I came by ship and I would choose that way again because the days that bring you nearer to your goal are not empty but full of the joys of anticipation. Flying leaves you no time to taste these joys but brings you too quickly and suddenly into an unfamiliar land among strangers before you even have time to adjust from a good-bye feeling to a greeting feeling.

Emotions Irrepressible

The irrepressible emotions of those days which began when you first started procedures to come to America are climaxed by the sight of the Golden Gate Bridge. In readiness to land, you have packed your bags the night before leaving out your best suit which you will wear when you land. You don this best but crumpled suit and go out on deck early the next morning to scan the horizon for the first shoreline of America.

"Land, Land!"

You peer into the barely visible dawn like an explorer and exclaim, like Columbus, "Land," as if it wasn't something you've been expecting to see about this time. You run from starboard to larboard as other passengers exclaim, "land," "land," from all sides, wishing to see all you can of America from the first day.

Out of Fog, Golden Gate

There's really nothing much to see but some blurred pieces of land jutting out from a big mass of sea. There's a heavy fog and the morning is cold, colder than you'd expected for the time of the year in early spring. But never for a moment do you leave the deck for fear of missing something. Then someone, excited, shouts, "The Golden Gate." Where, where? You thought the Golden Gate was only in Heaven or perhaps you were just getting it confused with the Pearly Gates. Anyway, maybe this was the gate to Heaven.

Heart Thumps

Your heart is thumping and the excitement is enough to make you burst out of your skin. You look, you stare, and soon, discernible through the fog is the Golden Gate—a bridge.

The ship is almost beneath it when you see it. You wonder whether the bridge is high enough to let the ship pass unscathed. You wonder if the bridge is going to open.

Memory Bursts into Melody

Then, suddenly snatches of words and melody of a song you heard long ago in an American movie come to your memory and you begin to hum like mad . . . "San Francisco, Open Your Golden Gate, Open Your Golden Gate . . . " You keep repeating like a broken record.

Gate Did Not Open

The Golden Gate did not open but the ship passed under it safely. You were then summoned to the ship's lounge where U.S. immigration and quarantine officers awaited you.

Source: "'Lucy' Sails for 'Frisco." *The Korean Messenger,* March 1954. Reprinted with permission.

Chong Chin Joe, "This Life of Mine"
(1967)

After Japan made Korea a protectorate in 1905, the Japanese kept tight control over the country, limiting educational and career opportunities for Koreans. Some Koreans hoped to move abroad to continue their education, find a better living, and work for Korean independence. The Japanese kept lists of people they considered to be dangerous elements, especially those who had joined patriotic organizations. Although they tried to prevent such people from leaving, fearing they would try to support the independence movement from overseas, the United States became a base for exiled Korean independence leaders like Dosan Ahn Ch'ang Ho, Syngman Rhee, and others who followed them. Rhee fled to the United States in 1912, launching an international campaign for Korean independence. In 1919, he was elected the first president of the Shanghai-based Korean provisional government in exile. He would later become the first president of the Republic of South Korea.

The following excerpt tells the story of Chong Chin Joe, born in Korea during the late 19th century. Because Joe's grandfather had served as an adviser to the Korean king during the mid-19th century, it is apparent that he came from a family of some means. Joe first met Rhee in Seoul, Korea, when Rhee was working as a teacher and missionary for the YMCA. Rhee inspired Joe to join the independence movement and move to the United States, which he did in 1911. In these excerpts from his autobiography, Joe discusses his immigration story, his involvement with the overseas Korean independence movement, and his early life in the United States.

I studied Mandarin in a school in Seoul for a few years, then went to Shanghai and entered an English boarding school named the Hanbury School, located on Schun Road. The owner and principal was a Mr. Price, a middle-aged English gentleman with a wife, two daughters and a son. It was the year 1907. I stayed at this school for about two years and then went back to Korea to attend Pai Chai High School which at that time taught more English than any other school in the country. Mr. Cyn Hung-Woo, the principal, was the first Korean graduate of the University of California at Berkeley, in 1903. At this time I also frequented the Y.M.C.A on Chong-No in Seoul; Chong-No is one of the largest streets in the city. Dr. Syngman Rhee was head of the Y.M.C.A and every Monday and Friday he held classes in international law for young Koreans. It was very interesting to me and during this time I decided that I wanted to come to the U.S.A. I found that not only I but the other young Korean men and women had the same feeling of wanting to go to America to prepare for their future. I felt I had come here to secure a higher education or to make a large sum of money—one or the other—to help Korea attain independence. However, for a long time the Japanese had had my name on their blacklist as a member of a Korean patriotic society and so refused to grant me a passport. The young Koreans who did manage to reach the United States felt they had arrived in Heaven. At this time I had a Korean friend who had received a good education in Tokyo and was now working at the Japanese passport office in Inchon. One evening I invited him to a good Korean restaurant in that city and asked him to help me get a passport to Shanghai as an Insum root (ginseng?) salesman; this root is a type of mountain grown herb which, according to old Chinese custom, if eaten will ward off death. I knew the Japanese would never issue a passport in my name as a student. About two weeks later, my friend Kim Koo obtained the passport for me so in that year, 1904, I went to Shanghai—the largest seaport city in Asia, as a first step on my way to the U.S. . . .

Here I met a man named Chang Kyung from Chicago. He was also a member of the patriotic society (hoi) which we organized and had called the "Great United Korea Protection Society"; it had about ten thousand members outside Korea from China to Europe and America and we did many different things for the good of Korea. Mr. Chang Kyung was a good patriotic speaker who brought in many members and soon the organization became infiltrated by the Japanese secret police. They grew to hate us more and more each day and finally after three years after we founded the hoi, the Japanese dissolved our organization as we could no longer stand the force of the secret police. They did not, however, dissolve the determined spirit of Korea. Mr. Chang Kyung had to return to Chicago by himself because of his American passport limitations and I still had only my Korean passport to Shanghai . . .

[Joe eventually made his way to the United States.]

After a few days in New York I did go on to Chicago to meet my friend Chang Kyung and other members of the Society. Soon I started to look for work. My first job was at Willard Hall, in Evanston, about 25 miles from Chicago. This was a women's residence for Northwestern University which housed about 250 persons at that time, with a Miss Libby in charge. Half a year later I worked for a Mr. Lemen, owner of the Fair store, one of the largest department stores in Chicago. He had a nice summer home at Lake Villa, about 50 miles from Chicago. About four months later I was working for Ogden Armour, owner of the largest packing house and stockyards in Chicago, then for a banker named J.C. Thompson who lived near 63rd Street and Cottage Grove Avenue in Chicago. I moved around in jobs so much that I was not able to save much money. Next I found work at a Chinese restaurant; surprisingly, there were many large and attractive Chinese restaurants in Chicago and New York—almost as many as Greek ones. Both Chinese and Greeks made large sums of money in America, and still do, because the Americans

generally overlook this business due to the long hours. This gave the Chinese, Greeks and others the opportunity to do well in this area.

All these years I worked as a common laborer since I had no special trade or profession. In any case, seven years after arriving in Chicago, I sent my father the sum of $10,000 for I owed my father more than any other son in the world because of my lengthy illness and because, while I lived at Inchon, Seoul and in Shanghai he sent me money for schooling regularly, never failing even once. He was a kind-hearted gentleman, highly educated in both Korean and Chinese. He loved me more than any other father under the sky, but to tell the truth, my mother of course loved me more. After I paid off the debt to my father I again started to save every cent I earned. I started a small cafeteria on the north side of Chicago, called the A.C. Inn and served both Oriental and American food. It was not a success. After that I bought a small restaurant, again serving Chinese and American foods, in Detroit, Michigan, on Woodward Avenue. After a few months I had problems with partners and closed up the business. I bought a small number of stocks in a farming company in Colorado and in the Franklin State Bank of Chicago; a few years later the bank went broke due to what they called "bad management". Then I bought some stock in the Cooperative Society of America when it was being organized in Chicago; I thought their principle of selling to poor people and limiting sales to rich people was very good. However, the struggle for organizing was not quite even since the rich were against this venture so it failed. This was in 1915 and none of the stock business did me any good. Now, as I write this, I see many of the Co-op stores in the Bay Area as a large chain and remember the Cooperative Society of America which went broke three times before opening for business successfully. Next I went to Chicago Business College on Wabash Avenue the owner of which was a Mrs. B. Verden. After attending school there for one year I was forced to withdraw because of my difficulties with the English language; many of our foreign students who first came to American schools had much trouble securing a higher education for the same reason. It seemed to me like trying to bore a hole in a stone wall with toothpicks. During this time I met Mr. Y.M. Chang who was another member of the patriotic society and I brought over my sister Dotham from Seoul in a "picture marriage" to Mr. Chang. They lived in Chicago and Evanston, Illinois and eventually had three children. The daughters, Cora and Lilly and the son, Samuel, were all born and raised in Chicago. They are all married, have their own families and now live in Los Angeles . . .

When I had left Korea I decided in my mind that if I reached the U.S.A. I would secure a higher education, make a large sum of money and do something really significant for our country before it was all swallowed up by the Japanese. I am sorry to say I did not accomplish this. I am still working in different places for very small wages.

Source: Joe, Chong Chin. "This Life of Mine." August 15, 1967. From the Korean American Digital Archive. Digitally reproduced by the University of Southern California Digital Archive. http://digitallibrary.usc.edu.

Sook-ja Kim, Interview by Myong-ja Lee Kwon (February–April 1996)

Sisters Sook-ja, Ai-ja, and Mia Kim began their musical careers in Korea, where they sang for American GIs deployed during the Korean War. After an agent discovered them, the girls came to Las Vegas in 1959. They were very young when they arrived in the United States—Sook-ja, the oldest, was eight years old—and their parents and four other siblings remained in Korea. After nine months performing in Las Vegas hotels, the Kim Sisters were spotted by Ed Sullivan, who gave them their big break when he invited them onto his show. Over the next two decades, the Kim Sisters performed around the country. They sponsored their three brothers to come to the United States in 1963; the Kim Brothers then started their own singing group, following in their sisters' footsteps.

Sook-ja married John Bonifazio, an Italian American casino manager, in 1968, and over the course of the next few decades, she and her husband sponsored more than 40 of her relatives to come to Las Vegas. In this excerpt from her

1996 interview with Myong-ja Lee Kwon, Sook-ja Kim talks about the early days of the Kim Sisters, their struggle to survive on their own in the United States, and how they introduced traditional Korean instruments and clothing to their American audiences. Kim also talks briefly about racism in the United States, saying that although she was aware of its presence, she never experienced it herself.

So, did you bring Kayakeum [a 12-string board zither] here too?

Oh, yes and chang-ku and seungmoo-book [both drums], we brought all that. So, beginning of the show, we would wear Korean costume which I will show you in that picture. We would wear the Korean costume. Inside we had a Chinese gown, so, after Kayageum we'd take it off and then we'd do American songs. It looked really different. That's how our career started to begin. So, my mother was right. When we were in the Stardust Hotel, eight and one half months, we learned different instruments. Now, we learn banjo. Now, we learn marimba. Now, we learn different instruments, one by one that we rehearse. We did six shows, sleep, eat, we carry our own lunches in a make-up case. We didn't know what to make. Ai-ja got yellow hwang-dal [jaundice].

Oh, jaundice.
Because we could not have kimchee. The food was a big battle. We could not get kimchee in those days. We could not make it, we could not buy it. So, we were literally sick about our food. We used to pick up the phone and cry to our mother. We needed kimchee. She [Ai-ja] got sick, very bad. So, we would carry her on stage because if she doesn't perform then we have to pack up and go back. We had no choice. You know, the show must go on in show business. You know why? There's no substitute in show business. It doesn't matter, you're sick or not, you got to be on. So this is why a lot of people asking me today, how could you be so mentally, physically strong. It made me strong through the years. My business did.

Tell us, just to continue on, how you begin with the Stardust and what next? How you grew up? You were a child, you were children.
We were children, but, you know, we really, I don't even know how we grew up. I don't even remember. All I know, the year that we worked 365 days, except for traveling. We couldn't afford to stop working. While we're in the Stardust, now we're going back, eight and one half months, Ed Sullivan came in. That was the big break for us. At that time he had an international show. Every country, he bring people. We were at the right time, right place and timing was great. So, he saw our show. I'd like to have these girls on my show. First show we did with Ed Sullivan, he brought all the crews to the Stardust Hotel at the main showroom. That's where we performed. It was immediately, we were a hit. Ai-ja played the base [sic], but standard base. I played the tenor sax and Mia played the drums. We sang, song the Maguire Sisters made the biggest hit, "Sincerely." We sound just like them. You

could not even tell, the sound was so much like them, Maguire Sister. Even now, I hear our tape and I say to myself, gosh, we sound just like them. This is beginning of our career, yes. So, when we got on Ed Sullivan Show, naturally, those days, everybody close down the door and watch Ed Sullivan.

That's right. Even in Korea we used to watch Ed Sullivan Show.
Right, so, whole country were nationwide watching Kim Sisters, just name spread. Vancouver, Chicago, all these cities, "we want the Kim Sisters," so, booking was coming in. From Stardust we went to Lake Tahoe. We performed at Lake Tahoe. From Lake Tahoe to Chicago. Now, no airplane, we drove. We drove, our road manager drove, we sat in the car for three or four days. That's how we used to travel . . .

Yes, we were teenagers. So, all right, now Kim Sisters has a ponytail and they were really, truly, American people didn't know from kimono, the Chinese dress, to Korean dress. They all call it kimono, whatever we wore, you know that. So, we used to wear Korean costume, 120 degrees in Las Vegas, 'Boson kaji sinko' [even wearing cotton padded Korean socks] walking down trying to advertize [sic], we are from Korea. But you know what people said? "Oh, what a beautiful kimono!" "It's not kimono, it's a Korean dress!" [we told them.] Nobody knew where Korea was at that time. So, you know what we said as we become famous, they will know automatically where we're from. That's exactly what happened. See, even in the beginning, we could tell them 100 times, this is not kimono. They would not know. They keep calling it kimono until we appeared in Ed Sullivan Show with Korean costume, with Korean instrument, then they start to seeing it, oh, that's Korean. O.K. So, one Korean called us like, we did more than even Korean Ambassador for the country at that time. So, this is what they were saying.

We understand back in the olden days, black entertainers have a different entrance to go into and they were only allowed to certain areas. Did you experience any kind of discrimination because you were Asians or how would you describe your experience or what you have perceived?

I heard, I saw history of what black people went through and I sympathize with them. It was tough, but fortunately, we never, ever had that experience. Number one why, we are performers. You know, it's a strange thing that when you perform on stage and people are sitting there, watching you, they are so, how do you say, into plain language, into what you're doing. Their image, now we're talking about image of thinking of us one step higher. How could these girls, how could they have so much talent? Now, I cannot even fry, frying pan or make a sound [A Korean expression to describe something very easy. When you have two frying pans together you can make sound or noise without trying very hard], this is the majority of people talk after our show. So, we were just singing, standing and singing and they sit there hour about we're singing and they go, oh, that was O.K. Maybe there were some people, prejudice people, would say something, but when we finish our act, one hour, they don't even have time to breath. Then, when we get off stage, they're overwhelmed. People just overwhelmed. So, we never, ever had any of that type of, you know, that racial problem, anything like that.

But, have you witnessed it, any . . . ?
Never.

O.K.
That's the very lucky part. I said, I don't think I could handle it, but I do know all my family, the majority of family, came here. I brought them one by one. We have like 45 relatives living in Las Vegas.

Have you now?
Yes, from family to family to family. Everyone [sic] of them got a job through my husband. See, he was vice-president of Sahara Hotel for twenty years. So, through him, all of them got as dealing jobs and he said out of all the people working for him, Korean people is the hardest worker. They all want to better themselves. I surely believe that, but through all of these people working at the casino, yes, I heard so much about it, racism going on. They were told, "where you come from? why don't you go back from where you come from," things like that. When they lose money, so, I heard so many times . . .

But you think because you are entertainers . . . ?
Personally, we never, ever had experienced it which I was very, very grateful. I don't know how I would react if that happened to me. But, I never had that experience. I never had anybody saying nasty about Korean War, which I was very surprised. Somebody would have lost their son, you know, but I never had that experience. I was very fortunate on that.

Source: "An Interview with Sook-ja Kim: An Oral History Conducted by Myong-ja Lee Kwon," February–April 1996, 10–12, 13, 28–29. Las Vegas Women in Gaming and Entertainment Oral History Project, Department of History, University of Nevada, Las Vegas. http://www.library.unlv.edu/oral_histories/addl_pages/kim_sisters.html. Used with permission of the Oral History Research Center at UNLV.

Sonia Sunoo, Interview by Anna Charr Kim
(January 17, 2001)

The first Koreans in Hawai'i arrived in 1903, as their country increasingly became the focus of Japanese imperial ambitions. Historically, China had been the most influential foreign presence in Korea. However, Japan began targeting Korea in the 1870s and forced Korea into signing the Treaty of Kanghwa Island in 1876. This treaty sparked tensions between Japan and China, and the two countries vied for control over Korea for almost 18 years. The conflict finally came to a head in the Sino-Japanese War of 1894. China lost, and Japan increased its grip over the Korean peninsula.

The war and corresponding Japanese incursion into Korea destabilized the Korean economy, society, and culture. This situation made emigration more appealing, creating a favorable atmosphere for the recruiting efforts of the Hawaiian Sugar Planters Association (HSPA), which commenced in 1902. The HSPA was aided by local American missionaries who encouraged members of their congregations to apply for labor contracts, assuring them that their children would get an education and learn Western ways. Within three years, approximately 7,000 Koreans had left for Hawai'i. However, Japan declared Korea its protectorate in 1905. To prevent Koreans from competing for plantation jobs with Japanese immigrant laborers, Japan halted Korean emigration to Hawai'i.

Five years later, Japan annexed Korea. Japanese colonialism in Korea was brutal. In an attempt to extinguish all traces of the Korean culture, the Japanese outlawed the Korean flag and language, imprisoned and tortured political dissenters, and allowed Koreans only limited educational opportunities. Korea remained under Japanese rule until Japan was defeated at the end of World War II.

This is an excerpt of an interview with Sonia Shinn Sunoo, a second-generation Korean American born in San Francisco in 1915. Sunoo's father came to Hawai'i to work on the sugar plantations when he was 18 years old. After two years, he transmigrated to California, a common move among Asian laborers in Hawai'i. Sunoo's mother came to the United States as a picture bride in 1914. In 1975, Sunoo began interviewing elderly picture brides and published their stories in an anthology, Korean Picture Brides: A Collection of Oral Histories *(2002). The following short article, based on a 2001 interview, gives a brief history of Sunoo's own life.*

Sonia Shinn Sunoo was born in San Francisco in 1915. Her father, Shinn Han, had left Korea for the U.S. in 1903 at the age of eighteen during a famine in Korea. He worked on a sugar cane plantation in Hawaii for two years before moving on to California where the wages were higher. Sonia's mother, Park Kang-Aie, had left Korea at the age of nineteen in 1914 as a picture bride. Perhaps it is for this reason that Sonia became so interested in those Korean picture brides in her later scholarship. According to an article Sonia wrote for WE (Ouri) magazine in 1995, adolescent Korean girls began emigating to the U.S. as picture brides beginning in 1910. Eventually, there were 2,000 arranged marriages in the U.S. between older Korean men and their younger brides. The Japanese were anxious to defuse the hostility of the Korean men who had emigrated to the U.S. and allowed the young women to follow them into matrimony.

Sonia began to interview these picture brides between 1975–77. By then these women were all in their 80's and widowed. Their stories of their struggles to survive and support their families were gradually weaned out of them by Sonia after establishing their trust in her. These women were courageous pioneers who sought an escape and freedom from the Confucian strictures of their homeland. Sonia captured these stories on tape and hopes that these interviews will soon be published. Not surprisingly, Sonia also went through struggles to reach her goals, many of them never realized. Though her situations were not on isolated farms like many of these picture brides, they were equally difficult and debilitating.

As the oldest child in her family, Sonia was often given the task of caring for the barber shop her father ran in San Francisco's Chinatown. Her role, according to her article, was to appraise her mother that a break in clients was approaching, so that her mother could warm up her husband's meal. As is required in Confucian teaching, her mother favored her brothers over her. However, this was more than made up for by the attention she received from her father. He even fashioned a notebook for her so that he could teach her the Korean alphabet. He also taught her how to be ladylike, something mothers, usually do, while also instructing her on the conditions in Korea and the occupation by the brutal Japanese.

Sonia attended Jean Parker grade school in 1920 when it was only for girls. Seven years later, boys were allowed to enroll. Sonia attended Galileo High School in North Beach which was located in "Italian" town north of Chinatown. Other students attending the same high school were Henry and Hannah Moon and Frank Choi, both men who later became doctors. Sonia continued to live in Chinatown through her college years. She attended San Francisco State for college and majored in English and Biology. She later earned an M.A. Human Development and Early Childhood Education.

Sonia met Harold Sunoo, her husband, in San Francisco in 1941, Harold having arrived in 1938 from Japan where he had attended Ah O Yama Gaku In [Aoyama Gakuin] University, a Methodist institution. They were married in 1943 at the San Francisco Methodist Church.

Toward the end of World War II, the U.S. government decided it needed to teach the Korean language to those soldiers and officers who would be occupying Korea. As Harold was working on his doctorate at the University of Washington in Seattle, he was asked to head up a department to teach Korean. When the war ended and the language work for the army was no longer needed, Harold was still pursuing his graduate work. He went to England in 1948 to attend the London School of Economics, but was unable to find a job. When an opportunity to attend a conference in Prague came up, Harold decided to go. While there he was offered the chance to finish his Ph.D. while teaching history and the Korean language at King Charles University. He was thus able to complete his doctorate in two years in 1950, after which he returned to the U.S.

In the meantime, Sonia had continued to teach the Korean language at the University of Washington from 1943–49. She later received a summer scholarship to attend Stanford in 1951 for graduate work. She had completed all her work except for her dissertation, but she had to abandon her studies because Harold was unable to get a teaching job upon his return. Although they had interviewed early Koreans in California, Oregon, Washington, Kansas, Colorado and Washington D.C. for one year, no grants for research were available. Finally a grant came from HANA (Methodist Church) and her husband was able to publish a book on their interviews.

Despite his doctorate, or because it came from an Eastern bloc country, Harold was still unable to find a teaching job. He was forced, instead, to operate a grocery store in San Francisco for over ten years. Naturally, Sonia had to help with his business, just as she had previously helped her father with his.

Sonia has found other outlets for her energy and talents. Her walls are covered with her photographs; she also sews. Although Sonia appears to be disappointed that she was denied the chance to finish her doctorate studies, her greatest wish now is to have her book on Korean picture brides published. These picture brides were often misrepresented about the advantages of marrying a stranger in the U.S., but they were usually seeking freedom and an education. They were symbols of feminists, even serving as couriers during the war.

All in all, Sonia is proud of her family which focuses on humanitarian causes. Korean Reunification still causes Harold to lead many committees and conferences on this effort, including having President Carter go to North Korea when tensions were high. Now in their retirement, Harold and Sonia see their children every week. Sonia can be proud that she herself was a pioneer in attempting to preserve the early history of Korean Americans in the United States.

Source: Kim, Anna Charr. Interview with Sonia Sunoo. January 17, 2001. From the Korean American Digital Archive. Digitally reproduced by the University of Southern California Digital Archive. Available: http//digitallibrary.usc.edu.

Phil Yu, "Keepin' It Real with the Rice Fields"
(2001)

Historically, popular culture depictions of Asian American men have not been positive. Characters in early Hollywood films veered between the stock stereotypes of the evil and conniving Fu Manchu and the bumbling, aphorism-spouting Charlie Chan. Although filmmakers and television producers today seem to be making an attempt to include more nuanced characters in the media, people from within the Asian American community have taken it upon themselves to point out racism in pop culture and provide alternative perspectives.

Phil Yu was born in Philadelphia, grew up in Silicon Valley, and now lives in Los Angeles. He started his blog Angry Asian Man *in 2001 as a private venue to express his feelings about racism in the United States. Today,* Angry Asian Man *is one of the most widely read Web sites in the Asian American community. Yu keeps his readers abreast of Asian American issues in popular culture and politics. In the following short piece, Yu talks about how he started writing* Angry Asian Man *and his realization that making fun of racism could play a part in exposing and denouncing it.*

"Keep it real with the rice fields."

Some friends and I made it up in college sitting around over ice cream and Korean food. It started out as a joke, as a mock catchphrase of Asian empowerment. Picture it: Asian Americans everywhere, connecting with their roots and finding pride in the famed rice fields of the Orient. Can't you visualize the Chinamen? Wearing those funny hats. Holding a stick or something. Squatting. It also makes no sense at all. Perhaps that's why we made it up. Actually, that's exactly why we made it up.

That's the way I usually approached most issues of Asian American pride. Facetiously. Mostly by becoming "Angry Asian Man," a persona I had adopted that represented all things loud and proud about Asian America. My purpose was to acknowledge and encourage our yellow struggle against The Man, who in turn was determined to keep us in our bamboo cages and hold us down. I was angry. I was Asian. And I wasn't going to stand by and watch idly as my people were unknowingly subjugated!

And the racism! Man, was everything just RACIST. I threw the word around left and right. Angry Asian Man had developed the special gift of hypersensitivity towards Racism and could detect it anywhere and everywhere. I took the liberty of calling attention to the surrounding Racism for all to see! The picture of the Asian in this magazine ad? Racist. The word 'Chinese' on page 1022 in

Dostoevsky's Brothers Karamazov? Racist. The yellow traffic signal light? Racist. It was all Racism with a capital 'R'. The rest of the world was unaware, but Angry Asian Man had been given the power to see!

Mind you, as I mentioned before, it was all very facetious. A big joke about hyperbolic, misguided Asian pride. And most people knew I was joking, save for a few who just got annoyed at my "zeal," or those who were truly concerned that I might actually lead some sort of dangerous Asian uprising. Watch out for that angry Asian guy—he's really vocal.

However, in time it became apparent to me that I was actually only half-joking. The concerns I was raising were funny because there was truth to them. Because racism does exist, and because Asian Americans still do struggle with issues of acceptance in this country. My context for discussing these problems often came from comic exaggeration, because at times, it was the only way to make such ugly issues open and approachable.

So Angry Asian Man became a cause. And just like Angry Asian Man, the views expressed in the contents of this website will inevitably be ridiculously zealous and exaggerated. Of course, it's all in fun, but just like the persona of Angry Asian Man, rooted in truth.

So stay strong, and support the struggle. Keep it real with the rice fields!

Source: Yu, Phil. "Keepin' it Real with the Rice Fields." 2001. http://www.angryasianman.com/about.html. Used with permission of the author.

Jenny Ryun Foster and Jae Ran Kim, Korean American Adoption (2002 and 2006)

Transnational adoption began in the 1950s, when Americans worked with Christian adoption agencies like Holt and the Christian Children's Fund to adopt children from Korea and China. Initially seen as a way to combat communism abroad, Americans first gave charitable donations to support orphanages overseas, and eventually moved to adopt the orphans themselves. Since the end of the Korean War in 1953, more than 160,000 Korean children, primarily orphans and children of single mothers, have been adopted internationally. More than 100,000 of these children have been adopted by Americans, primarily into white middle-class families; they are the largest percentage of transnational adoptees in the United States.

Until fairly recently, the prevailing wisdom called for quick and thorough assimilation: adoptive parents were discouraged from talking to their children about race or ethnicity, cultural differences, or Korean history or identity. This philosophy is changing, as the first generation of adoptees, now adults, speak about their often confusing and alienating experiences of growing up Asian in white families and communities. The following two writers, both Korean American adoptees, give their perspective on the challenges they faced growing up, and as adults.

1. JENNY RYUN FOSTER, "ONCE UPON A TIME IN AMERICA: AN INTRODUCTION" (2002)

Jenny Ryun Foster was adopted by an American family when she was six months old. The family lived in rural Indiana for six years; when her parents divorced, Foster, her brother, and their mother relocated to Michigan, where she grew up. After graduating from college, Foster moved to Korea to teach English. Here, she confronted her feelings of being "other" in both her native and adoptive countries. In her personal essay "Once Upon a Time in America," originally published in MANOA: A Pacific Journal of International Writing, *Foster shares her perspective on growing up in the American Midwest and her growing awareness of her Korean American history and identity.*

My arrival in the U.S. was without my knowledge. It happened to me. In the spring of 1974, I landed with thirty other Korean infants at Chicago's O'Hare Airport, where we were handed over to our adopted parents. Then, like seeds blown on the breeze, each of us was carried away, scattered in all directions across the wide expanse of America.

Fate dropped me in a small industrial city in Michigan, where I grew up. As a child, I learned what it meant to be Korean very much the way one becomes aware of things in a dream. Ethnicity entered my consciousness at first only in odd and indirect ways. I hardly knew what being Korean meant, but I remember nevertheless being proud of it. It made me different from every other person in my small town: my classmates, my teachers—even my parents. Still, I never felt isolated or disadvantaged because of my differences. In fact, they allowed me to associate with everyone, of whatever race or color, and to have all the normal experiences of a small-town girl in America: a working mom, after-school rehearsals for the school play, diving practice for the swim team, a part-time job at the ice-cream parlor.

And so I grew up dreaming—and living—in two worlds, and was never forced to choose between them. Slowly, though, I began to wonder what exactly it was that made me different and special. I graduated from high school and moved away to college, and it was then that my awareness changed. The large university I attended brought me in contact with people from all over the country, whose experiences were entirely different from my own small-town childhood. In learning about

the great variety of family backgrounds, ethnic origins, mixed-up identities, and passionate points of view, I began to awaken to the world. Oddly, however, as a Korean I was still a singularity, and still found it difficult to learn very much about what it meant to be Korean American. I felt there was only one thing to do: go to Korea and live there.

Soon after college, I landed in Kimp'o Airport in Seoul with one suitcase and no return ticket. I was uncertain what to expect. Nevertheless, I was thrilled with the sense that this was what I was meant to do. I was meant to be standing here, making my way through customs, staring curiously at the airport's military guards—young soldiers no older than I, each carrying a rifle or machine gun, striding sternly along the linoleum walkway and among the passengers. I was meant to find a bus to Taejon, by using sign language and broken Korean from a phrase book. I was meant to travel for an hour and a half away from Seoul, wondering if I was on the right bus. And I was meant to encounter, at the end of that bus ride, the most wondrous, exciting, adventurous year of my life, to be welcomed warmly by Korea and the many new friends that I was destined to make.

In the Korean provinces, I found to my surprise that being American was much more important to the way I was perceived than being Korean—just the opposite situation to the one in America, where being Asian had made me stand out from the majority of Midwesterners, and being Korean had made me stand out from other Asian Americans. Whenever I had had to fill out a form in America, there was always a box to check indicating my ethnicity. The only one that seemed to fit me was ASIAN/PACIFIC ISLANDER, although at times this question would appear as "optional." I wonder if the people that ask such a question think that to be Asian/Korean is optional.

At the end of my year in Korea I recognized the irony of being an "American" in Korea and an "Asian" in America. I realized there is no easy answer to what being Korean means, or to what anyone's life and identity means. Though there were so many things that I found I didn't know, I cherished many of the simple things that I did: how to converse with a traveler underneath the setting sun at Taech'on beach, the taste of *makkolli* (mountain wine), the beauty of cherry blossoms in the spring beside Ch'ungnam National University—like snow petals covering the walkway as far as the eye can see.

I had been given new eyes while I was away, and coming home to the United States was a shock. I thought about how insignificant one person is in our vast world, swirling with cultures and life situations that shift at the whim of gravity and time. Before going to Korea, I had felt that I could merge and submerge into my American surroundings—alternately Korean, Asian, American. But on my return, I felt my differences were more specific. Being Korean meant having a certain cultural history that carried me back through time, a heritage made up of countless experiences, events, and people who were part of me and who continued to form who I was and would become. At the same time, I was even more aware that in this fast-paced world, one's history is difficult to hold on to and remember.

I have journeyed from Korea to the Midwest, back to Korea, and now to Hawai'i; I am still discovering who I am as well as who I am not. My passage has led me to the words on this page. My work with the *Century of the Tiger* filled my mind with compelling and adventurous stories of Koreans who sailed to Hawai'i and made the U.S. their home—these stories are also part of me. I am amazed to think that my story is just one of hundreds of thousands, each different and yet somehow familiar. I am celebrating.

Source: Foster, Jenny Ryun. "Once Upon a Time in America: An Introduction." In: Century of the Tiger: One Hundred Years of Korean Culture in America, 1903–2003, special issue, *MANOA* 14, no. 2, (Winter 2002–2003), 154–157. http://www.jstor.org/stable/4230107. Reprinted with permission.

2. JAE RAN KIM, "COOKING LESSONS" (2006)

Jae Ran Kim is a social worker, teacher, and writer. Born in Daegu, South Korea, she was adopted by Americans in 1971 at the age of three. The following essay is from Kim's blog, Harlow's Monkey, *in which she talks about international and transracial adoption from the perspective of an adoptee— a voice often missing in these discussions. In this excerpt from "Cooking Lessons," Kim discusses the complex nature of adoptee identity, particularly when it comes to cultural and racial needs.*

KIMBAP

"I understand . . . why so many Americans of various ethnic origins have chosen, over the last generation, to adopt a one-size-fits-all 'Asian American identity'" . . . In a way I envy those who choose to become wholeheartedly Asian American: those who believe. At least they have a certain order to their existence. I, on the other hand, am an accidental Asian. Someone who has stumbled onto a sense of race and wonder now what to do with it."
    —Eric Liu, *The Accidental Asian: Notes of a Native Speaker*

A big bowl of steaming rice sits before me, another batch is cooking in the rice cooker. Seolmei instructs me on the fine art of seasoning the rice. A small grater distributes round, roasted sesame seeds over the top of the rice. "Keep it in the freezer," she says. A drizzle of dark, rich sesame oil, a dash of salt, a sprinkle of vinegar. Mix it well and set it aside. Bong is opening the packages of sliced scrambled egg, pickled radish, carrots, spinach and imitation crabmeat.

The seaweed is laid on the bamboo mat, and rice is spread on the lower half. Like a typical American, I put on way too much. "No, no, like this" they scold, scraping the excess off. We lay the strips of crab and vegetables on the bed of rice, roll the end a little and squeeze. Roll some more and squeeze.

On the first day of my son's pre-school Parenting classes, they arrived together. They are Korean. I know this, not because I understand what they are saying, but because I recognize the names as Korean. During parent-sharing time, Seolmei hesitates, apologizing for her English. Though heavily accented, we all understand her. All the other mothers go into brag mode, describing our kids, their ages, what we do for fun in our spare time. Seolmei says, "I am so lonely. I miss my family." She begins to cry. No one knows what to do or say. I hand her a tissue, but don't know what to say either. After class, she and Bong huddle together, gather up their kids and leave quietly. All week I think about her and worry. I feel bad for not saying anything.

The next week I hand each of them a Korean Quarterly. I know nothing about them, whether they are involved in the Korean community here. It is the only thing I feel I can do, to let them know there are other Koreans here in the Twin Cities.

"I'm Korean too," I tell them, and their eyes widen in recognition. "I'm adopted though, so I don't speak Korean." I give them my phone number. "If you'd like to get together, the kids can play. If you're really brave, maybe you can try and teach me a few Korean words."

That is why they are here now, in my kitchen. That is why we are elbow deep in rice, seaweed and vegetables. We are making kimbap, the Korean version of a California Roll. I already know how to make it. They misunderstood; I'd said it was the only Korean food I know how to make; they thought I was asking them to teach me how to make it.

They arrive at my house with everything: rice cooker, rice, seaweed, all the vegetables thinly sliced, crab meat and eggs, scrambled and sliced. They are surprised that I have most of the ingredients we need. They "ohhh" over each item I pull from my cupboards. I have nori. I have sesame oil and toasted sesame seeds. I have a bamboo roller.

As we begin the preparations, inhibitions fall away and personalities peek out. Bong is outspoken. Although I have everything needed to make kimbap, Bong corrects me. "This seaweed is Japanese. Use Korean" she says. "Your rice, it is too long." She gives me a big bag of short grain rice. Seolmei is more sensitive with a sneaky sense of humor. The first kimbap I make is crooked. Instead of being in the middle, the ingredients are

lopsided. "Who made this one?" she laughs, holding the offending kimbap. I show them the scrapbook I made of my trip to Korea two years ago. They are excited to see that I've been to their hometowns.

Seolmei and Bong try to teach me the words for each item we use. I dutifully repeat, trying hard to get the pronunciations correct and I fail miserably. All my small attempts to be more Korean seem completely inadequate now that I have two genuine Koreans in my kitchen. I will always be a kyopo, a foreign-born Korean. Trying to be Korean is like being a little girl playing dress-up with my mother's prom dress; it doesn't fit, but I can see little glimpses of what the future will look like, once I begin to grown into it.

I've spent 90% of my life being American, yet when I think "American" I think of white people, and I don't include myself. But I've been in Korea. If I spent the rest of my life there, I would never be able to call myself a Korean either.

Which country do I choose? The one who appeals to me by the basest aspects of my nature, the one in whom I recognize myself, those who come from the same dust of many trodden feet, the ones whose sorrow and collective soul are the same as mine?

Or the one who has grown me from a transplanted seed, an out of place plant without the ability to spread roots into this soil. The best I can hope for is to thrive as well as I can in a borrowed pot and borrowed soil—but that is all right. I can move myself around, as I have in the past, and thrive anywhere. I've learned to do so.

I struggle to find a place for people like myself, for the person I was not long ago. I don't believe any of us are "Accidental" Asians. That is like saying we're a cosmic or physical mistake. Perhaps we are hesitant or uncertain; the many of us spread out over the world due to war, economic opportunities or adoption. Seolmei and Bong are living the opposite experience as me; they are hesitant Americans. They want to be Americans, but they don't want to lose their Korean culture. They know people here do not know much about Korea, that everyone thinks Korea is poor, "like Mash-ee" says Seolmei, "You know that T.V. show, M-A-S-H."

"Americans" Bong asks, "They only know Hmong? They all ask, are you Hmong?"

I am a bit too American to make kimbap in the correct way. Each time I make it different, depending on my mood and the ingredients I happen to have in my kitchen at any given time.

Sitting at the table Bong, Seolmei and I taste the results of the afternoon. I can honestly say that although I've used the wrong seaweed, stored my sesame seeds incorrectly and left out the vinegar—overall, I can not tell the difference between Bong and Seolmei's version and my own.

But I know that by rinsing the rice first, and using the short grain instead of long has indeed made better rice for kimbap. Americans like their rice Uncle Ben's style—as individual as themselves, each grain standing alone, fluffy, and apart.

I'm seeing the value of Korean rice—stuck together, bonded. Maybe kimbap is like my America. In my world, each of us is the lone ingredient. Spinach may be too bitter for some palates, radish too tart and seaweed too salty. I may not think much of the thick, glutinous white rice that surrounds us, but it does make our individual flavors stand apart. We enhance the flavors of each other. Rolled together, we can make a beautiful balanced dish.

Source: Kim, Jae Ran. "Cooking Lessons." 2006. First published in *Korean Quarterly* 5, no. 4 (Summer 2002). http://harlowmonkey.typepad.com/harlows_monkey/2006/04/cooking_lessons.html. Used with permission of author and *Korean Quarterly*.

You Mi Kim, "Diary of a Sex Slave" (2006)

According to the U.S. State Department's 2006 "Trafficking in Persons" report, between 14,000 and 17,000 people are trafficked to the United States every year. International crime organizations forcibly move their victims from one country to the next, threatening their families, trapping them in mounting debt, and taking advantage of their fear of local authorities to keep them in modern-day slavery. Most of these people are women and girls from Southeast Asia, South America, and Eastern Europe, and most of them are sold into the commercial sex trade.

San Francisco has become one of the nation's top destinations for sex traffickers. Women are brought in from all over the world, often believing they have come to take legitimate jobs. Instead, once they arrive they are taken to massage parlors, strip clubs, and brothels and forced to work off their traveling debts. However,

ever-increasing fees for tickets, food, clothes, and housing trap them in a system of indentured servitude. This contemporary immigration experience, as horrific as it is, has a long history: Asian women have been trafficked into the United States since the mid-19th century.

You Mi Kim was a college student in Busan, South Korea, one of the main hubs for international sex slavery. By the time she was 22 years old, Kim had run up an enormous credit card debt. Desperate for a job, she answered an ad for a hostess in a drinks salon in Koreatown in Los Angeles. In 2003, her broker flew her to Mexico, obtained false documents, and smuggled her into the United States, where Kim discovered that she was actually going to be working at a brothel. Kim worked for a year, first in Los Angeles and then in San Francisco, before she could pay back her "immigration fees" and credit card debt. In 2005, as part of a 10-month investigative journalism project on sex slavery, the San Francisco Chronicle'*s Meredith May interviewed Kim, with the help of an interpreter. The following excerpts chronicle Kim's harrowing experiences in the California brothels and her attempt to create a normal life after her escape from the sex-trafficking industry.*

Over the next two months, You Mi watched a flow of women come and go through the apartment, paying off their trafficking fees in a matter of weeks.

But You Mi couldn't get out. She didn't realize that the way call girls pay off their debts quickly is by developing a list of regulars. By flirting, by specializing in various sexual techniques.

Customers said You Mi made them feel uncomfortable. She wouldn't smile. She insisted on using the most formal of the three Korean syntaxes when addressing men, not the casual kind reserved for friends and lovers. She was stiff, detached.

You Mi didn't know what to do. She called her sister, borrowing a call girl's cell phone. The news wasn't much better back home.

Samsung had sent a letter to You Mi's parents, threatening to repossess the house. You Mi's mother had taken out a bank loan to pay off the credit card, but the moneylenders were still calling, demanding tens of thousands.

"You'd better not come home for a while," You Mi's sister said. "Mother is incredibly angry with you. She told the moneylenders you are dead."

By April 2003, You Mi still owed $6,000 to the traffickers. They were getting impatient, too.

So her boss sold her. Another broker in Koreatown bought her for $7,200—the amount of her trafficking debt plus interest. The sale added $1,200 to her trafficking debt, and she hadn't even begun to address her $40,000 shopping debt from Korea.

You Mi's new owner drove her to San Francisco, explaining there was a massage parlor near the North Beach strip clubs that accepted only Asian girls with trafficking debts.

His plan was to sell You Mi to the madam for more than $7,200. You Mi would then owe her trafficking debt to the massage parlor. The broker told You Mi that massage work would be good for her because the turnover was faster and she'd pay off her debt sooner than if she stayed in outcall.

The broker made his way toward the flashing peep-show marquees of Broadway, and pulled over by an adult video store. He led You Mi next door to a tiny white awning with two surveillance cameras, and pressed the buzzer on a metal security door leading to a two-story staircase.

You Mi was wary. Once inside, she was horrified. She saw the red lights, women in heavy makeup and lingerie, and immediately thought of the glass house districts of Busan and Seoul.

"Don't leave me here," she begged the broker.

The owner of the massage parlor asked You Mi whether she had ever worked in such a place before.

You Mi, head down, shook her head no.

The owner asked the broker to step into the hallway, and told him she didn't want You Mi. She was too immature and wouldn't be a good investment.

The broker was furious. He drove You Mi back to Los Angeles, hardly speaking the whole trip. The next day, he handed her off to a third broker, a friend in the sex-trafficking ring who owed him a favor.

The third broker, also Korean, said his name was Tony. He drove her to a residential house in Inglewood, a brothel without any signs out front. Its lobby was decorated as an aromatherapy center.

Tony handed her a neon-orange tube top that covered only her breasts and a matching micro-mini skirt, and sped away. The owner of the brothel led her inside.

You Mi's mind raced through what was becoming a familiar cycle of panic:

What should I do? Should I just sit down and refuse to work? Should I run? How would I run? Where would I run? If I escape, what about my debt? Do traffickers really find women in South Korea and kill them?

The brothel had five rooms, each with a bed and a shower. There was a separate, larger shower where women bathed customers.

The owner showed You Mi the kitchen at the end of the hall, and the empty milk carton in the fridge where she was told to hide the used condoms.

"Each customer gets 30 minutes," the owner said.

A second woman scheduled to work that day had called in sick, and men were already lining up in the lobby. The two-minute tour was over.

"You're on your own," the owner said . . .

[You Mi eventually paid off her trafficking 'debt,' and moved from Los Angeles up to San Francisco.]

Navigating past the junkies and hustlers in San Francisco's Tenderloin district, You Mi Kim found the metal security door she was looking for, and pressed the buzzer.

Inside Sun Spa massage parlor, the manager saw You Mi on the surveillance camera and threw some sea salt over the threshold—a Korean practice to ward off bad luck.

It was July 2003. It had been five months since You Mi was lured from her home in South Korea by international sex traffickers, who had tricked the debt-ridden college student with promises of a high-paying hostess job in America.

After forcing her into sex work to pay them nearly $20,000, the traffickers had finally let her go. But freedom was elusive.

Traffickers had taken all her earnings, yet she still faced a $40,000 shopping debt back home— the reason she left for an American job that promised big pay. Now, no fewer than six creditors were circling her family in South Korea.

Any kind of job she could get as an illegal immigrant—cleaning homes or washing dishes in a restaurant—wouldn't pay her debts in time. She wanted to protect her family from the shame of bankruptcy. She wanted her life back.

You Mi felt she had no choice.

On her first day of freedom, she took an unlicensed Korean taxi from Los Angeles to another illicit massage parlor in San Francisco.

The door of the Sun Spa opened. The manager, a Korean woman in her 50s, led You Mi inside and quickly handed her off to the masseuse with the most seniority.

For the next four months, You Mi would become a person she never imagined. She and five other sex workers would share a dingy apartment on O'Farrell Street across from the Mitchell Brothers O'Farrell Theatre. She'd spend her waking hours at Sun Spa, having sex with more than a dozen men a day, six days a week, and scurrying into secret hideaways during police raids.

She would find the rumors about San Francisco to be true: It was a booming stop on the international sex-trafficking route. There was lots of money to be made. Customers plentiful, tips great.

But first, she would have to surrender her last shred of dignity.

The first stop on the Sun Spa tour was the five rooms on the bottom floor, used for the regulars. They were tiny, less than 50 square feet and bare except for a cot with one white sheet, a shower and a small painted nightstand in one corner. A mirror covered most of the wall near the bed. A fluorescent ceiling light cast a pallid green glow over the room.

Upstairs, You Mi saw four rooms decorated to look like legitimate Chinese acupressure and massage rooms. They were cleaner, with massage tables instead of beds. The condoms were hidden.

"This is where we bring the new customers," You Mi's guide explained.

Next was the kitchen. The woman showed You Mi an empty water cooler bottle where she was to dispose of the used condoms.

Off the kitchen there was a changing room with lockers. You Mi put on a long, sleeveless Korean dress that sex traffickers had made her wear in Los Angeles.

"That's not sexy enough," her new co-worker said, instructing her to put on a bikini top and a sarong slit all the way to the waistband.

The last stop on the tour was the bell, in a back room off the kitchen, used to summon the women when customers arrived. Within earshot, You Mi saw a half-dozen Korean women lounging, watching TV and eating.

Suddenly, a loud ring cut through the noise of the TV. The women dropped their chopsticks and hustled out to the lobby, arranging themselves on an L-shaped sofa so the customer could make his choice. You Mi followed the pack.

She sat on the sofa, feeling like a dog that had responded to its master's whistle . . .

[Eventually, You Mi earned enough money to pay off her debt to the traffickers and pay back her creditors in Korea. She escaped the sex industry, and went to live with her boyfriend, a man she'd met while working at Sun Spa.]

Epilogue

Inside a Korean restaurant in San Francisco, You Mi ran between the kitchen and the tables with little white bowls of appetizers.

Korean dinner always starts with numerous small plates: kimchi, fish cake, daikon radish, black beans, anchovies, sesame-soaked cucumber and acorn jelly. It's sweaty apron work for minimum wage.

With the Korean custom of not tipping, she was lucky to take home $30 a night from the customers.

But she was free.

It was June 2006. It had been a little over two years since she stepped out of Sun Spa for the last time.

Source: May, Meredith, and Fitzmaurice, Deanne. "Diary of a Sex Slave." *San Francisco Chronicle*, October 6, 8, 9, 10, 2006. http://www.sfgate.com/sextrafficking/. Reprinted with permission of the *San Francisco Chronicle.*

Letters on the Korean "Lost Colony"
(2009)

The following letters were written in response to an article, "Dinuba/Reedley: The Korean 'Lost Colony'," published online in the Information Exchange *for Korean-American Scholars on January 7, 2009. The article, written by Dr. Moo-Young Han, editor-in-chief of the Society of Korean American Scholars and professor of physics at Duke University, traced Dr. Han's trip to Dinuba/Reedley, the site of one of the earliest Korean settlements in California.*

When Koreans first migrated to the United States from Hawai'i in the first decade of the 20th century, many sought work in Dinuba and Reedley, two farming communities about 15 miles southeast of Fresno, California. Koreans began arriving in 1909, and they soon founded a small community that revolved around the Korean Presbyterian Church they established in 1912. As in other Korean communities in the United States, the church became not only a place of worship but also the site of community efforts to free Korea from Japanese colonialism. The most prosperous Koreans were the Kim Brothers (business partners, not related), who owned and operated orchards and a fruit-packing business in Reedley. The Korean community in Dinuba/Reedley built another church on land donated by the Kim Brothers in 1938. Although some of the Korean settlers eventually left for places unknown, many married Mexican farm laborers in the area; some second- and third-generation Korean residents assimilated into the towns' mostly Latino community. The following letters were submitted by former Kim Brothers employees who had read Han's article and wrote to share their memories.

LETTER 1

Dr. William T. Chu
Participating Scientist, Accelerator and Fusion Research Division
Ernest Lawrence Berkeley National Laboratory
Managing Editor, SKAS

I spent the summer in 1954 in Reedley. I just finished my freshman class at Carnegie Institute of Technology in Pittsburgh (now Carnegie-Mellon Univ.) and came to Los Angeles for a summer job arranged by an acquaintance. But unluckily the LA public transit was on strike, and there was no way for me to commute. So, instead I went to Reedley to join about 40 Korean compatriot students working on various fruit farms there.

We picked peaches, nectarines, and apricots, for which we were paid the minimum wage that was below $1 per hour. Picking the grape was more difficult, as your picks were examined for the fruit's sugar content. If you are an experienced picker, you could make almost three times the minimum wage as the job was piece work, that is, paid according to the amount of the picked grapes that passed the sugar test. Many of us novices could not make even the minimum wage, and after a few days we went back to picking peaches.

We worked for the Kim Brothers, who were the richest men in town. They made fortune by developing and patenting fuzzless peaches, hybrid fruits of peaches and nectarines. Both Kims were Korean patriots who worked for the independence of Korea from the Japanese occupation. One of them, Kim Hyungsoon (Harry) returned to Seoul after the liberation in 1945 to organize a political party, but returned to California as a bitter loser to Syngman Rhee.

The other Kim was Kim Ho (Charles), who drove us, the poor students, to work hard for very long days. Some busy days, we had only 2 hours of sleep to pack the fruits to be shipped to the East Coast. Kim brothers lectured us how lucky we, the newly arrived young Korean students, were as there is the Social Security System, which his generation did not enjoy.

Reedley was the center of the Ahn Dosan followers (Hungsa-dan), who were longtime enemies of the Syngman Rhee supporters (Kookmin-dang), who were concentrated in nearby Parlier. We were told that these two groups do not sit in the same room, and their offsprings do not marry offsprings of the other side.

Aside from the young Korean students working in the summer, there were several dozens of advanced-age permanent residents with Korean ancestry in Reedley. They were mostly male and lived in rooming houses. They told us that they could not return to Korea, as they were descendants of Korean criminals, who were sold to foreign merchants by the Chosun Dynasty.

The Korean Consul General (Choo Youngwhan, no relation to me!) from San Francisco, obviously one of the Rhee followers, would come to Parlier, and some Korean students from Reedley went to the party. The Consul General Choo proudly showed us an old photo that depicted the restaurant that he ran in Hawai'i before 1945, which prominently displayed a sign declaring that "We do not serve Japanese." He was a real Japanese hater, and did not know a single word in Japanese. In jest, some of us sang Japanese pop tunes (e.g., anoko kireiyo kan kan musume) saying that the tunes are Spanish. The Consul General loved the songs.

I visited Reedley in the early '80s and could not find the old places in the newly developed town.

LETTER 2

Dr. Maxmillian Whang
Retired Aerospace Engineer
NASA/JPL, TRW Systems, Hughes Aircraft
An OKSPN member

I am glad you visited Reedley, California. I came to America in 1955 with a student visa. During the summer of 1956 I worked for Kim Brother's Ranch in Reedley picking fruits in 100 degrees heat. Kim Brothers inherited from Japanese when the Japanese were shipped to concentration camps. There were about 50 Korean students, including 7 of us from the LA area.

Life style on the farm was exactly the same as that of current migrant farm workers. The old Kim personally directed group of students what to do every morning. We slept all together under a huge tent on floors and ate Korean breakfast at 5 AM. Then, a truck carried a group to fruit fields and we picked peaches. Assembly workers at the packaging assembly lines were all female Mexican migrants. Some students packed the fruit boxes onto railroad carts to be shipped all over the US. Wages were 50 cent per hour. Those days, it was difficult to find a full time job only for three month. I attended Los Angeles City College (LACC) as Pre-Engineering major for 2 years. The tuition at LACC was $6 per semester.

Source: The Information Exchange for Korean-American Scholars, Society of Korean-American Scholars (SKAS), Issue 09-02 (No. 518), January 21, 2009. Reprinted with permission.

Interview with Ou Chiew Saetern; Letter from His Sister (2003)

Ou Chiew Saetern was 17 years old when he was sentenced to 13 years in prison for gang violence. Saetern and his family had moved from Laos to California when he was child, part of the last wave of refugee immigration after the Vietnam War. The Saeterns are Mien, a small ethnic Chinese group living in the mountains of Laos, primarily subsistence farmers. Like the Hmong, many Mien fought alongside the United States as part of the secret army recruited by the Central Intelligence Agency, and they faced similar obstacles once arriving in the United States: poverty, extreme cultural dislocation, and language and literacy barriers.

In this 2003 interview with Eddy Zheng, Saetern talks about the ways his history and culture inform his identity. His words also implicitly reflect the marginal place Asian American prisoners occupy in their communities. The letter from his sister illustrates their family's dislocation and the tragedy of their unfulfilled American dream. Shortly after this interview was conducted, and the day before Saetern was supposed to be released from prison, the Department of Homeland Security detained him for deportation back to Laos.

INTERVIEW WITH OU CHIEW SAETERN (2003)

Eddy: How old are you?

Ou: I'm 26 years old.

E: How long have you been locked up?

O: For over nine years. I started when I was in CYA (California Youth Authority) in Preston (Youth Authority in Ione, California). I was 17 years old. I was transferred from YA to DVI (Deuel Vocational Institution, California Department of Correction's reception center) because I got into a couple of fights with rival gang members. I still had a gang banging mentality. If I'd stayed out of trouble, I would've stayed in YA until I'm 25.

E: What are you in prison for?

O: Gang related shooting. Me and my boys came out of a club, this girl I used to know, one of her friends brought her over. I realized it was a rival gang member. One thing led to another and we started shooting. We had the upper hand because we got access to the gun fast.

E: Why did you want to shoot him?

O: I'm asking the same question myself. I guess I found it necessary at the time. If I don't shoot him, they'll shoot me. I shoot seven times. The guy was paralyzed, couldn't walk no more. He's 18 years old, a gang member too. I asked them whether they bang, he walked up and said what's up blood. I could see the look in his eyes he was scared. He didn't mean to say what's up blood.

E: **What gang were you in?**

O: The Asian Boyz. It's a Crip gang.

E: **How long was your sentence?**

O: They gave me 13 years with 85%.

E: **How did you feel when you knew that you'll be going away for a long time?**

O: I was too young to realize at that time what that meant. I didn't know how long I was going to do. I thought I was going to do a couple of years only.

E: **Did you speak English?**

O: A little bit, limited. I went to school from 4th grade to 7th grade, then I quit. Why? I wanted to get the things my friends got, things my family couldn't provide for me. I gang bang, hustle on drugs for clothes. I got a big family. Most of my clothes were hand-me-downs. My friends got new clothes. They picked on me. I started cutting classes, grades dropped. They sent me to continuation school for a year to pick up my grades and go back to Junior High, but I never did. Kick it on the streets.

E: **What about your parents? How did they feel about it?**

O: Dad was mad. He said if I didn't go to school, don't come home no more. I went to my homeboy's house and hang out on the streets. I didn't go home no more, only once every two months. Since then my Dad don't talk to me no more. To this day, he still doesn't say nothing to me.

E: **How do you feel when your Dad doesn't say anything to you anymore?**

O: As for that, he did me a favor. I don't have to hear from him yell at me anymore. As time went on, I don't know he care anymore. Now, he did his best to keep me out of trouble. He may felt he'd fail, but he didn't. Now I want a relationship with him. Whatever happened in the past is over.

E: **Why do you want a relationship with him?**

O: So I can let him know he didn't fail. I chose to live that life. Now I'm older, I get wiser. Hopefully I can prove to him that I'm a better man and move forward. I want to be there for him when he needs me. He's getting old.

E: **Do you think your Dad loves you?**

O: Back then, no. But now I think so. Back then, I asked him for money, but he didn't give it to me so I thought he didn't love me. Now I know it's not that he doesn't want to give it to me, it's he doesn't have the money.

E: **Who supports you while you're in prison?**

O: I couldn't think of anybody except Mom. I don't ask her for anything because I know she has to take care of my little sister and brother. I want to make sure they have what I didn't have.

E: **How do you survive?**

O: Draw cards, tattoo. I don't get a lot but I can get by. I hustle. I learned how to draw in jail. I need shampoo and soap. I don't want to ask people. I be myself. Keep my nose out of other people's business, by listening to the older ones, learn from them, how to carry myself. When I first came, a lot of older brothers taught me the things I needed to survive.

E: **Who do you miss?**

O: My family, especially my Mom and Dad. They're getting old. I don't know what, how long they have. I want to be there for them.

E: **What do you miss?**

O: Freedom to do whatever.

E: **What would you like to do?**

O: Go fishing, camping, be with my family. It's been a long time, but I want to go to a Broadway play. I don't care what people think, square-ass goes to plays. Homeboys, I kick it with them, but they weren't there for me, not even a letter to say fuck you. I spent all my teenager life for being down with them boys. I want to work, be with family.

E: **How many tattoos do you have? What are they? Why do you have them?**

O: I got a lot. I got like the whole right arm filled up. It got violent pictures on it and troublesome. It symbolizes my past life on the outside. I got three Mongolian nomad warriors on my back symbolize my ancestors. I got Mien pride on my chest, it represents my people. I two guns up there guarding my pride. I also got some gang graffiti.

E: **Why did you decide to get them?**

O: I guess at the time it looked cool. As time go by I see it as how I look at life. Life is like a piece of paper. I can draw anything on the paper to represent myself. You put in hard work on something things will come out good. It's like life. If you work hard, you'll succeed in the long run. If you get it fast, it doesn't last. No payoff. I guess I lived a fast life.

E: **How do you think the tattoos are going to affect you on the outside?**

O: I think it's going to affect me a lot. People look at me as a gang banger, negative affect on me.

E: What do you think would've helped you from going to prison?

O: If my family was able to give me what I wanted so I won't be laughed at. That would've helped.

E: What's the biggest lesson you've learned being in prison for nine years?

O: That your family is the most important thing in the world. Because me and Mom has a good relationship. She's always been there for me. At the time I didn't know what I put her through. Now I know I put her through a lot of pain.

E: What's the hardest thing you have experienced in prison?

O: I guess, I don't know. I think it's waking up not knowing what's going to happen to me. Maybe someone has a bad day and want to take it out on me and become a victim. I seen it happen before. Cellie woke up and beat the shit out of him.

E: Do you regret what you did to the victim?

O: I don't think I have regret for my victim. I have remorse for his family because he can't walk anymore. They have to take care of him. As for him, I don't shoot him, he would've shot me.

E: Who are you?

O: I see myself as very respectful, polite, a guy who knows he made a lot of mistake and tried to change them.

E: Do you think the community should fear you?

O: No, they should have no reason to be, because I'm not the same guy I was nine years ago.

E: How do you make sure that you won't come back to prison?

O: First thing, I have to remember prison. Now I have to take care of myself. I'll go to work, be patient. Hopefully I'll get support from my family. I can't get sidetracked by all the negative stuff. No fast money. If I keep my mind to it, anything's possible if I work hard.

E: What are you going to do after you get out?

O: I have some experience in carpentry. I'll try to open my business so I can sell my artwork. I have a lot of plans and goals, but I can't reach them because I have to finish parole. Hopefully I can get into a Boys and Girls club to talk to teenagers, offer my experience and guide them to be better individuals. I want to help them.

E: What would you say to them?

O: My message to them is I know Asian people don't have a lot, just be patient. Go to school, it'll pay off in the long run. You'll get all that. All the gang banging will get you nowhere but jail. Once you're in jail, nobody cares about you. Never forget where your family come from. They work hard to put food on the table and they came to U.S.A. to get us a better chance.

My grandfather always tell me this, "Every boy will become a man one day, but the real man is determined by how he gets up when he falls." What that means to me is every man gonna make some kind of mistakes in his life. A real man is someone who could live up to his mistake and better himself from it.

Endnote: Saetern was expected to go home on his release day. However, the day before he was to go home, Homeland Security put an immigration hold on him. Instead of going home, Saetern was picked up from prison by Homeland Security agents detained in their facility.

LETTER FROM SAETERN'S SISTER (2003)

February 19, 2003

Dear Ou,

Dearest brother, be very good. You are so bad that mom and dad are not very happy about you. When are you coming out? I love you. Be good, ok, brother. I did see you before. Send me a picture of you. Ou, your big sister has two baby. They oldest is six years old youngest is three year old. Be good so you could come out. Mom love you so much. Be good so you could come out and see mom and dad and us. I am nine years old. Be good. Not long you are going jail. Do not fight other people so you could come out. I just hope you don't do anything bad again like last time you did. Do very very good so you could come out and see us.

I love you.
Write back as soon as possible.
Your sister.

Source: Zheng, Eddy. "Interview with Ou Chiew Saetern." Originally published in *Other: An Asian and Pacific Islander Prisoners' Anthology,* a project of the Asian Prisoner Support Committee, 2007, 133–141.

Bryan Thao Worra, "Asian-Americans Must Speak Up"
(2005)

Chai Soua Vang, a naturalized Hmong American who emigrated from Laos in 1980, was convicted in 2005 for the murder of six deer hunters after a confrontation in the northern Wisconsin woods. The trial and verdict drew national attention. It also divided the Asian American community; some decried the violence and distanced themselves from Vang, whereas others claimed that the trial highlighted racism in the United States and the particular obstacles faced by Hmong American immigrants.

In his 2005 op-ed piece in St. Paul, Minnesota's Pioneer Press, *Bryan Thao Worra links Chai Soua Vang's story to a broader history of anti-Asian violence and criticizes Asian American leaders for not educating the American public about this history. Worra is a Laotian American, adopted by a U.S. pilot in 1973; he is a writer, a poet, and a community activist.*

In the wake of the Chai Soua Vang verdict, now, more than ever, Asian-Americans need to talk candidly about race and racism, or the American dream shall never truly be ours. Throughout the trial, Asian-American leaders uttered little more than politically correct, safe pronouncements hoping for fairness and justice, but said little to help others understand: Yes, racism against Asian-Americans is serious.

The fear Asian-Americans have for their life is connected to a long history of racism we have every reason to take seriously. When Vincent Chin was murdered in 1982 in suburban Detroit, his white killers never served a day in prison. They paid only a fine of $3,000. They called him a "Jap," caving his skull in with baseball bats. The scant punishment implied a license to kill Asians.

In 1998, a 13-year-old Hmong girl, Panhia Lor, was gang-raped, beaten and murdered, her battered corpse left to rot in a Minnesota park like a pile of trash. Her killers called her "gook" and "chink" as they raped her. We were told it was not a hate crime. It was not a racist act.

In 2001, Thung Phetakoune, a 62-year-old veteran from Laos, died after Richard Labbe cracked Thung's skull open on the sidewalks of New Hampshire. Labbe told police, "What's going on is that those Asians killed Americans and you won't do anything about it, so I will. Call it payback." Phetakoune risked his life for Americans stationed in Laos. Trying to rebuild his life, this is how it ended.

In January 2005, 36-year-old Tou Yang, a father of three, was shot at home by the Milwaukee police seven times, including three times in the head because the police could not find a nonviolent resolution, like tear gas or a stun gun. Tou Yang's case was eerily similar to that of Tong Kue, another 36-year-old Hmong man who was shot at home in Detroit in June 1998 by police.

We're told: "There isn't a pattern. It's just a fluke." We're told to turn a blind eye to a culture that consistently depicts us as aliens, foreigners and the enemy. Every time someone calls us a "gook," "chink" or "Chinaman," ignore it like good Uncle Toms.

Why can't we laugh it off? Because words that demean us pave the way for greater violence. Filmmaker Gode Davis, researching "American Lynching: Strange and Bitter Fruit," estimates as many as 200 Chinese, Japanese and Filipinos died from American lynchings, yet we never confront this.

It's time we call things as we see them, because things only get worse, not better, from our silence. Whether it's politically correct can no longer matter. We must hold America accountable for how it treats Asians, or else the dream will fail us just as it failed the Chinese laborers who died ignominiously constructing the American railroad, or the Japanese unjustly forced into internment camps during World War II while German- and Italian-Americans were not.

After 30 years, most of the U.S. remains unaware of the Southeast Asians who died to protect Americans during the Southeast Asian wars of the 20th century.

The culture we get is the culture we make. So, someone needs to say it: Asian-Americans are sick of the slurs, ignorance and stereotypes. We're fed up with injustice against our community. We want life, liberty and happiness as much as anyone else.

And if that means speaking up, so be it. Because this is our country, too.

Source: Worra, Bryan Thao. "Asian Americans Must Speak Up." Op-ed originally printed in the *St. Paul Pioneer Press.* https://www.blogger.com/comment.g?blogID=295 24574&postID=116603477079261448. Used with permission of the author.

Xuliyah Potong, "Adopted American"
(2007)

In 1996, the United States passed the Illegal Immigration Reform and Immigrant Responsibility Act, which mandated deportation for noncitizens who committed felonies and expanded the definition of felony to include many nonviolent crimes. This and subsequent legislation disproportionately affects Southeast Asian communities, where the elevated crime rate reflects the aftermath of violent refugee experiences, a high incidence of posttraumatic stress, pervasive poverty, and intergenerational relationships stressed by language and assimilation differences.

Xuliyah Potong was born in the Thai refugee camp where his parents had fled during the war in Laos. Five months later, his family immigrated to California. Although he was raised from infancy in the United States and is classified as a permanent resident, Potong never became a naturalized American citizen. Therefore, when he was arrested and convicted of an aggravated felony, he was vulnerable to deportation to his native Laos. Potong was under the mistaken impression that he would be deported once his jail term was completed (currently, Laos does not have a repatriation agreement with the United States). His essay, included in Other: An Asian & Pacific Islander Prisoners' Anthology, *illustrates the anguish and uncertainty Potong feels about his future and his national identity. It also highlights the precarious place inhabited by many immigrants in the United States. The editors of* Other *included an addendum at the end of Potong's essay, providing more information on the United States' evolving repatriation agreements with Southeast Asian countries and their effects on Asian American communities and the prison population.*

I often wonder what it would feel like to roam on the soil where my ancestors bled. If the air I breathed in would smell sweeter or if I'd experience a transformation rushing through my entire being. This moment has always only been as elusive as a mirage to me up to this point in my life; a distant illumination that dissipates like misty fog whenever I claw futily [*sic*] to grasp a hold. As I sit in this cage and no longer actively participate in life but merely observe the surreal circumstances that propel me forward, it has become clear that the scenery I've only beheld in my reverie will now take physical shape and await my entrance. Life as I used to know it is over. The carefree days on American streets will now give way to uncertain nights in a foreign country that is to be my new home, Laos.

After seven arduous years of incarceration, I am finally on the cusp of my emancipation. Unfortunately, this freedom that I have been patiently suffering to embrace does not come without a price. Upon completion of my sentence, I will immediately be transferred from State Prison into Federal custody where proceedings concerning my residency status in the United States will begin. Because of my criminal conviction, I am now facing imminent deportation.

Officially, there are two options available to me: I can decide on future litigation and fight to stay in America, or I can waive this right and agree to be deported. Practically speaking, I have no choices. The crime I am convicted of is categorized as an "aggravated felony," and if designated as such, is almost iron-clad in precluding one from averting deportation through judicial means. Although I have accepted that my days in America are numbered, I can't help but hang on to the hope that maybe, I will once again be accepted for the flawed person I always was.

Ever since the 18th century, Laos has been subjected to foreign colonial rule. It was first victimized by its larger neighbor to the west, Thailand, which in turn was succeeded by France and then Japan. Not until 1954 was Laos granted autonomy under the Geneva Accords. This newfound independence only brought to light the ensuing scramble for power that would unfold between competing political factions the world over. It was right around this time that the Communist and non-Communist blocs of the Cold War era were beginning to take shape. The United States, as the leader of the non-Communist countries, was particularly concerned with limiting the advances of Communism in Southeast Asia. Despite the contentious political climate swirling all around them, the Communist Pathet Lao, neutralists, and pro-Western Lao government officials still managed to compromise and set up a coalition government.

However, due to American paranoia and instigation, this tentative arrangement did not last for long. Opposed to any accommodation of the Communist Pathet Lao, the U.S. actively sponsored and encouraged an anti-Communist group to overthrow the existing government. This blatant disregard for Laos sovereignty compelled the Pathet Lao and neutralists to turn to Russia and its Communist allies for aid in resuming guerrilla warfare. Eventually, after more than twenty years of intermittent civil war, the Pathet Lao finally seized power as America pulled out from the region and all of Southeast Asia fell like dominoes to Communism.

After establishing control, the Pathet Lao did not automatically cease their campaign of bloodshed. They continuously hunted and sought to eliminate any remaining soldiers that had opposed them. My father was one of these soldiers. Left with no other alternative but to escape, he— together with my pregnant mother and eldest sister—led the way through treacherous terrain and land mine-laden jungles. They had to gingerly navigate their way into Thailand, fearfully evading detection by the Pathet Lao and getting cut down by machine-guns. Awaiting them in Thailand were refugee camps set up to accommodate the hundreds of thousands of displaced citizens from Laos, Cambodia, and Vietnam. While residing at these camps, refugees were not permitted to travel freely beyond the confines of their designated area. Integrating into Thai society was prohibited. This was merely a temporary layover, pending permanent resettlement in the U.S. or any other Western country willing to accept them. As chance would have it, I was conceived and given birth to during our stay in the refugee camp. On January 17, 1980, when I was at the age of five months, my family and I arrived in California.

Life in America has not always been easy. Growing up in an ethnic enclave with parents who couldn't speak English presented barriers I failed to fully appreciate until I reached adulthood. In spite of this, I have always been aware of how blessed we were to be living in America. My parents never let me forget the trials they had to endure in order to get us here, just so we would not be exposed to the harsh realities of life in Laos. Because of these admonitions, I knew that simply being in America was a privilege that would afford me the opportunities to overcome whatever obstacles I may encounter. With the education I received in school and the abundant resources available for furthering my education, as an adolescent I believed the possibilities for my life were limitless. I had dreams of succeeding in any number of professions, and even dared to envision that I might one day help find a cure for asthma; a disease that claimed the life of my mother and has ailed me since childhood. These ambitions were driven by my motivation to instill pride in my parents by displaying that all their sacrifices were not made in vain.

I cannot recall exactly when it was that I started to stray from the path that was paved for me. Going against everything I was taught, I engaged in behavior that would have appalled my mother were she ever to discover. I joined a gang and did things that adversely affected the lives of countless people. This downward spiral continued until it landed me where I am today. During the entire time that I was facing a life sentence, the one thing I longed for most was a second change to make amends for all my former misdeeds. It was during this period that I realize how destructive I had been. I had complete disregard for how precious life is—the lives of those within my community and my own. This is something shamefully demonstrated by the crime I committed. The punishment I received was more than just. I deserved to serve every last day of my sentence. Throughout this entire tragedy, never was I the victim. The victims are those who have irrevocably changed by my actions. If only it were possible to undo all that has transpired. . . .

I love America. Although I was not born here and am not officially a citizen, it is still the only home I've ever known. I am grateful that America adopted me and provided salvation for my family at a time when death lurked ominously behind every turn. The thought of making a life anywhere else has never even entered my mind. It was not until after my arrest that I became aware of my vulnerability to deportation. This myopic ignorance is the main culprit behind why I never took advantage of my many chances to become a citizen. The reality of not ever being able to call America my home again is very difficult to digest. It feels as though my adoptive parents are banishing me from the home I've spent my entire life in and sending me away to biological parents who are virtual strangers. All because they cannot forgive me. If it is indeed true that it takes a whole village to raise one child, then what village is ultimately responsible for rehabilitating its wayward youth? This assignment should not be delegated to a third party. I am the product of American society, not Laotian. My expulsion will not only create an irreparable disconnect with America, it will also separate me from my family. How can I be expected to survive in a country where I am illiterate and am all by myself? The authoritarian regime that tried to exterminate my family is still entrenched in power. The very same government that America saved us from is now the one it wants to deliver me to?

I never fathomed that this could be my fate. I have already forfeited my youth because of a tragic mistake that I made. Now I must serve another sentence of being barred from America for life. Like a desperate child who has lost his way, I just want to go home. Instead, it is with profound sadness that I return to my ancestors in disgrace.

Addendum

At the time that the writer wrote this piece, he was under the false impression that he would be deported to Laos. Xuliyah was taken immediately into Homeland Security/Immigration & Custom Enforcement's detention facilities (formerly INS) after he completed his prison sentence, but because Laos does not currently have a repatriation agreement with the United States to take back people who are deported, he was NOT deported to Laos. After several months of detention, Xuliyah was released and is now in the process of incorporating back into his commu-nity. However, in order to be released from deten-tion, Xuliyah did sign an order of removal. What this means is that if Laos ever signs a repatriation agreement with the U.S., Xuliyah will be put on a list to be deported back to Laos.

Many API prisoners face the same difficult questions that Xuliyah encountered: do they fight their deportation order and remain imprisoned in an INS jail for an indefinite amount of time, with no guarantee of winning their case? Or do they sign their order of removal and face being deported to a country that they barely have any memory of, don't know the language, and have limited family support for? The high cost of lawyer fees to fight a case leaves most people with no other choice but to sign their order of removal.

The passage of anti-immigrant legislation in 1996 and the heightened paranoia against non-citizens since September 11, 2001, have set the stage for the increased deportation of our commu-nities. Noncitizen, legal residents who have

committed an "aggravated felony" are not manda-torally [sic] deportable and have lost the right to an independent judicial review in the immigration courts. An aggravated felony can include any crime that was given a sentence of one year or more (down from five years pre-1996)—even non-violent crimes such as shoplifting and auto theft.

A large number of non-citizen Cambodian Americans who signed their orders of removal, thinking that an agreement would never be signed, were forcibly deported after the U.S.-Cambodia repatriation agreement of March 2002. Many Laotian and Vietnamese Americans with orders of removal fear they will be next. Laos and Vietnam are the only two Asian countries at this time [2007] that do not have a repatriation agreement with the United States.

Source: Potong, Xuliyah. "Adopted American." Originally published in *Other: An Asian and Pacific Islander Prisoners' Anthology,* a project of the Asian Prisoner Support Committee, 2007, 9–15.

Takashi Matsumoto, "Finding Takashi"
2008

Takashi Matsumoto's family escaped Laos during the Vietnam War, moving first to a refugee camp in Thailand and then to Japan, where he was born. His parents named him Vang Thalangsy, but his name was changed to Takashi Matsumoto when he became a naturalized Japanese citizen. Later, the Matsumoto family immigrated to the United States. In his essay, written for Bakka Magazine, *Matsumoto talks about the ways his family's history has influenced his identity as a Southeast Asian American. His story illustrates the fluidity of ethnic and national identity, especially for transnational immigrants with ties to many different countries.*

A few weeks ago, my cousin, Kouang and I were jokingly discussing how we should start a Laotian group on campus since there are none as of now. We laughed at how it would be funny if someone named Takashi Matsumoto started it. We wouldn't even know where to begin; I don't know anything about Laotian culture and the only words I know are *sabaidee* and *tam mak hung*.

Takashi Matsumoto is the name I use frequently, but my cousins and family all call me Gao. It just feels weird if they call me Takashi. Matsumoto is the last name I use when I write my papers and submit a resume, but my birth certificate says "Vang" and "Thalangsy". Wang is the last name my relatives refer to when addressing my family and me, but I've never used it in the public sphere.

I remember when I entered first grade in Japan; my name tag read "Wang/Vang Gao Zhi" as my classmates tried to pronounce my name with difficulty. I was the only non-Japanese kid in the room. A few seconds later, the teacher quickly called me out and said that there was a mistake in my name tag: It should have read "Takashi Ou", which was my last name at that time.

My last name "Matsumoto" was given to me 14 years ago when we finally became naturalized Japanese citizens. It was chosen so we could be more Japanese. It just became one form of assimilation to the dominant society. At that time, I didn't even question why my name kept getting changed and didn't bother to care; I just wanted to go home and read manga from the nearby bookstore.

Growing up in the US, I always thought I was Japanese. I had a Japanese name,

I spoke Japanese and I was from Japan. So doesn't that automatically make me Japanese?

I remember a time in middle school when racist white and Mexican boys called me and other Asians "nip" while at the same time asking me for help with their homework. I remember the time when my friends were confused because my cousins were not Japanese. Or the time when my ultra-conservative high school history teacher kept looking at me when we discussed Pearl Harbor and how dropping the bomb on Hiroshima was a "good" thing since it ended the war, while tokenizing me to be the expert on Japan just because she thought I was Japanese.

Sometimes I wonder if it was destiny that brought most of my family out of Laos to be reunited once again in the US. Did Nixon order the dropping of over a million tons of bombs in Southeast Asia so that my family can escape to the refugee camps in Thailand? Was my family destined to resettle in Japan instead of the US just like every other refugee we pretend to know about? Were my sister and I supposed to be born in Japan?

Although I was glad that I took Professor Yen Espiritu's Ethnic Studies class this quarter at UCSD, and for the first time in 21 years I felt like I was learning something directly related to my identity, I still feel I know nothing about Laos and Southeast Asia. I respect her for acknowledging that in the context of Southeast Asian studies very few books have been written about Cambodia and Laos compared to Vietnam. So far, the only books I've read about Laos and the Hmong are written by white authors, who exoticize the culture into something that only caters to the white public. It's just so frustrating to see how the memories and histories of Laos are erased in the US. At the same time, I am glad that there are scholars out there in those fields like Seng and Ma Vang.

I always admired and envied the different Asian Pacific Islander (API) organizations at the UC San Diego campus that collectively work to raise cultural/social/political awareness of their own ethnic identities. I know that the Vietnamese Student Association, Kaibigang Pilipino, Nikkei Student Union, Chinese American Student Association, Thai Culture Club, Cambodian Student Association, Sangam and other API organizations put on amazing cultural shows every year. Maybe that's why I wanted to help create Southeast Asian Collective (SEAC) with the other students at UC San Diego—not for the sake of cultural shows, but to address the important issues that Southeast Asians have been facing.

"So, what's your ethnic identity?" This was the question that I got asked so many times while I was at the Southeast Asian intercollegiate summit in January 2008. I don't blame people for asking me this since that summit was meant for Southeast Asian-identified peoples and my name tag didn't clearly reflect that identity. Honestly, I don't know how to answer that anymore.

My ethnic identity is fluid and always seems to be changing. Over the years, when filling out the race/ethnicity box, I've checked: Japanese, Chinese, Laotian, Chinese-Laotian or sometimes just all three. I always hated filling out my race/ethnicity category. I feel like I have to be limited only to these boxes. By just claiming myself as Japanese I ignore the important memories and stories of my family.

My transnational or transethnic identity has shaped me for who I am to this day. Like what Bryan Thao Worra, the Laotian-American writer, said, "If we don't write or leave anything behind, then nothing will be found."

Source: Matsumoto, Takashi. "Finding Takashi." *Bakka Magazine,* April 2008. http://www.bakkamagazine.com/site/articles/finding_takashi/. Reprinted with permission from *Bakka Magazine.*

Malaysian Americans

Shymala Dason, "Outside His Window"
(2010)

Asian immigration always has been complex and multidirectional. Some 19th-century immigrants, unwilling to live in a land that did not accept them, returned to their homeland. Others went back for short periods of time to get married and then returned to the United States, leaving their wives and children behind in Asia. American-born children of immigrants, realizing that equal access to education and employment were not available to them as Asian Americans and availing themselves of their bilingual skills, moved to their parents' native countries in hopes of expanded opportunities. Family and extended family networks took on even more importance in this transnational context; maintaining strong ties in both countries was crucial.

Immigration today is equally complex. Many Asian countries, India in particular, suffered from a "brain drain" in the 1970s and 1980s; thousands of educated professionals, primarily computer industry workers, moved to the United States in search of work. However, in the early 21st century, the financial crisis in the United States and the burgeoning economic growth in Asia, coupled with the enormous backlog of visa applications and the corresponding difficulty in obtaining permanent status in the United States, have resulted in reverse migration becoming increasingly common among Asian Americans. The "returnees" are permanent residents, naturalized citizens, and American-born Asian Americans; they are primarily in their mid-thirties, have graduate degrees, and work in the science and technology fields. They live lives in multiple countries, and their identity in Asia is often complicated by previous adaptation to American culture, American citizenship, and close family members remaining in the United States.

Shymala Dason is a first-generation Indian Malaysian immigrant, fiction author, and poet. She grew up in Malaysia and came to the United States for college. Before becoming a writer, she worked at NASA's Goddard Space Flight Center as an atmospheric scientist. Her writing explores how immigration and transnational experiences affects diasporic families. The following short fiction piece, "Outside His Window," imagines a father's perspective on the phenomenon of reverse migration after he moves his family from California's Silicon Valley back to India.

Google goats were flowing up the hills overlooking the San Francisco Bay, leaping from rock to rock with no visible hesitation, as if they were not risking falling hundreds of feet and dashing their brains out on stony ground. They worked for Google—a company so rich it could afford to own goats whose only job was to eat grass, and own real-estate in the most expensive place on earth that it could simply give over to goats.

He was looking out the giant glass window-wall at the edge of the sea of cubicles in an office much *less* than any at the Googleplex.

In the corner of the room, soccer players in a World Cup game were running and leaping across a large screen, a cluster of expat engineers watching intently; all wishing they were *there,* rather than here.

He had grown up kicking a soccer ball too.

The soccer players were setting up for a penalty kick. He looked out the window again. Rock outcroppings, deep grasses, bare sand and pebbles up on those hills: he had never seen the goats fall. Easy for them.

No Google mountain, anchored to bedrock, under his feet; only—like all small players in hard times—constant little earthquakes. A stone's throw away was the Calaveras fault. A little further, Loma Prieta, and San Andreas. A litany of hypnotic names. A litany of falling stock prices and layoffs.

Come an earthquake big enough to drop a chunk of California and Silicon Valley into the Pacific Ocean, the Google mountain would be okay.

Come an economic tsunami, the little company that paid his salary and let him pay his mortgage and buy his family food would be swept away. . . .

On the screen, his World Cup favorites were getting massacred.

On the hill, he saw a goat jump, apparently into thin air, and—miraculously—find a boulder to land on.

He hadn't seen the boulder, but it must have been there.

Footsteps passing back and forth behind him. The hum of machinery, air conditioning and computers. Keys clattering softly, punctuated by soft beeps, quacks, pings and other custom noises: programmer ambient music. Someone whistling softly. An exclamation of: "*Dude!*" A man's laugh. A woman's. Happy code people. Whispered curses and sounds of coffee pouring. Sad code people. He himself was neither happy nor sad, just weirdly hyper-alert and zoned out at the same time.

How to find another boulder to jump to? Another job, another life?

The goat bent its head and started eating. Grass there, apparently, even though all he could see from his angle was rock.

Where to find fresh grass for himself?

***

After work, walking with his family. A park by the bay. Bicycles and walking paths, joggers and dog-walkers. Sea-birds flying overhead. He had looked up the names so he could tell his children when they asked. A touch on his shoulder, his wife hand. Fragrant, fragment of pure pleasure in an otherwise increasingly pleasure-less life. He turn his head, inhaled—discretely—children might be watching. His wife said, "Do you remember walking near the seaside, back home?" Eyes smiling.

Her hand carried her smell, unique, special. Also a layer of curry spices, she had been cooking before they left the house. Smell and question dislocated him, he felt a moment of *here* and *there*; kerosene lamps where there were no kerosene lamps, vendors singing their wares, cowry shells and glass animals filled with colored water, foaming mugs of 'pulled' tea, the boiling liquid poured back and forth between two super-sized mugs held several feet apart until the liquid filled with bubbles of air: like ice-cream, only hot.

Here: his three-year-old daughter ran off the path after a squirrel and had to be picked up and brought back. Squirrels had bitten children in the park.

His son, seven years old, walked quietly. Already understanding enough to be soberly serious.

Another day, years previously, younger and less serious himself, he had taken his son to the ocean. He had told his son about all the little creatures in the nooks and crannies of the tide pools; saying, "See, that's us right now." Picking up a tiny anemone to show his son, holding it in the palm of his own hand, a strange *wet* feeling, "Look, it's so small it doesn't need a lot of food. But the ocean water is so rich, it will get big and fat." Letting his son stroke the creature, and then putting it back in the water. "I'm only a sea-urchin,"—only an inexpensive, interchangeable code-monkey—"and you're only a baby sea-urchin. But you're growing up here where I grew up far away in a small place, you are going to be like a dolphin, and be able to swim everywhere."

His wife said, her voice calling him back to the present, "Why don't we go back home?"

He said, "You mean to India? For a visit?" She said, "For good." He said, "I don't understand."

His wife said, "Maybe it's not so glamorous at home, but it's more *steady*." He said, "The children . . . ?" She said, "India is also coming up now." A smile crinkling the corners of her eyes, he had married her, over other girls, in the end because she was able to have that little bit of a smile even at the most serious times, "And if anything happens, we'll have our own people around us."

He remembered cousins, and cousins of cousins, hundreds of people in a village all connected. . . .

His son was looking up at him: eyes alert, questioning.

Source: Dason, Shymala. "Outside his Window." 2010. Used with permission of the author. www.shymala.com.

Pakistani Americans

"Salman Ahmad in the News"

(2006)

In addition to playing guitar with Junoon, a popular South Asian rock band, Pakistani American Salman Ahmad also works with various humanitarian organizations in the United States and abroad. He champions moderate Islam and Sufism, particularly in Pakistan (where Junoon was banned for many years). He produced a BBC documentary, It's My Country Too: Muslim Americans, *about being Muslim in the United States after 9/11, combating the pervasive stereotypes he saw around him. Ahmad composed Junoon's first English-language song, "No More," as a denunciation of the terrorist attacks. The following press release provides the backstory to the composition of "No More" and includes a short interview with Polar Levine, a New York City native who collaborated with Ahmad. The press release was published by iSufiRock, an organization cofounded by Ahmad that seeks to educate people about Sufism through music.*

MULTI-PLATINUM PAKISTANI BAND, JUNOON'S FOUNDER AND GUITARIST SALMAN AHMAD HAS JUST RE-RELEASED A SONG BASED ON A POST 9/11 POEM BY POLARITY/1'S POLAR LEVINE

After September 11, Polar Levine wrote a poem called PULVERIZED: I'M BREATHING. He sent a copy to his friend Salman Ahmad of Junoon. Salman wrote NO MORE, the lyrics based on Polar's poem. The song was recorded in Karachi, Pakistan and mixed in New York at producer John Alec's studio in Grandview, New York. Ahmad is re-releasing the song on the 5th anniversary of 9/11 to act as a wake up call for all people who believe in tolerance and cultural harmony. Junoon, South Asia's biggest rock band, has sold over 25 million albums worldwide and "No MORE" was their first English-language single. Standing alongside 9/11 tributes from a host of American musicians, "No More" is the only song denouncing terrorism to come from the region of the world where terrorism has thrived, a unique expression of empathy and solidarity from the other side of the globe. Junoon was the subject of a VH1 News Special which aired just after 9/11 entitled "Islamabad: Rock City." They have been welcomed by audiences around the world from China to England to the US to South Africa and are the first rock band to have performed in the General Assembly of the United Nations. The leading voice for Junoon is Pakistani-American Salman Ahmad, who is also a UN goodwill ambassador for HIV/AIDS. Ahmad explains how the band came to record their first English language song: "Junoon performed a couple of peace concerts in the States right after 9/11. I needed to do something to heal my own wounds and the show we gave near Ground Zero was one of the most deeply moving concerts I've ever experienced. After the show I met Polar Levine, a New Yorker who'd brought his nine year old son to the show. I told him that this Junoon concert had shown to me what America was really all about: unity in adversity." Ahmad continues, "A few days later, Polar presented me with a poem that he had written right after the 9/11 attacks and said, 'you're free to do whatever you want with it'. Until that moment, Pakistan's long history of terrorism, violence and poverty had focused me on writing only in Urdu and Punjabi. 9/11 brought a huge paradigm shift to my consciousness. I now have a reason to write English songs. I want to comment on the flood of paranoia, grief, and crisis of identity that the world is collectively experiencing and "No More" is like a first painting." Ahmad used Levine's poem as the basis for "No More."

NO MORE
©2002 Salman Ahmad & Polar Levine

In my lungs through my windows
on my head on the floor
ashes of falling hope
choking me inside these doors
stormy winds seduce the night
over new york and karachi skies

sinking in a sea of time
mourning since 11/9

No more, I'm breathing you no more, I'm missing you no more, No more

God and money take the blame
for suicidal video games
if all that lives is born to die
love remains I wonder why

black and white tv
red is all I see
I'm sick of spying eyes
wearing suits and secret ties

(Repeat) No More

the dream is not yet over
keep yourself alive
hold on
we may survive
(Repeat) No More
Lyrics by Polar Levine and Salman Ahmad
Music by Salman Ahmad

VATSALA KAUL: That is a really touching poem Salman turned into song. When did you write it? Much after 9/11 or just after? Or did you write the poem at Salman's request?

POLAR LEVINE: Thank you. I live ten blocks from Ground Zero. So when we hear about the attack on America, I also experienced it as an attack on my neighborhood, about two blocks from the field where my son plays soccer. When the dust from the collapsed towers started to collect on my window sills and on my floors it was upsetting in a mundane kind of way. Even war has its mundane side. The ongoing TV coverage had a report on the composition of the dust I'd been inhaling for days that was giving me some respiratory problems. It was mostly crushed concrete and wallboard. Along with that there was plastic from computers and the bones of the people who were in the towers when they collapsed.

I'd been inhaling the remains of the victims of September 11. My lungs were filling up every day with underpaid firefighters, police officers, cafeteria workers, secretaries, mail room workers, word processors, graphic designers and overpaid executives. I had, in my body, Muslims, Jews, Christians, atheists, liberals, conservatives, women and men from hundreds of countries, heterosexuals and homosexuals. I was together with them. We had nothing to disagree or fight about. They were part of my body and came in with the air that keeps me alive. The planet Earth is one body that houses us all in the same way. That realization gave added texture to the whole nightmare. I wrote the poem then, a few days after the attack.

Source: iSufiRock. "Salman Ahmad in the News." http://www.isufirock.com/news/august2006_press_noMore.html. ©iSufiRock.com 2006. Reprinted with permission.

Wajahat Ali, "The Perpoose Story: The Minority Preschool Experience" (2008)

In addition to practicing law, Wajahat Ali, a Muslim Pakistani American, writes essays and plays about religion, culture, and nationality, and he blogs regularly. "The Perpoose Story" recounts one of Ali's experiences as a young child and recent immigrant to the United States, evocatively describing the language and cultural barriers he faced as a "Desi Fob." FOB is the acronym for "Fresh off the Boat," an often uncomplimentary term for new immigrants. Ali, along with many other contemporary Asian Americans, reclaims the term in his humorous and self-deprecating short story.

The Calm before the Storm

Spotlight On: A five-year-old Pakistani American kid speaking Urdu with an assortment of English words to pepper his rhetoric. Those words were limited to three:

1) **"Shut up!":** A phrase commonly deployed by the dictator, my mother, to silence all of my unruly verbal dissent.

2) **"Uh oh Pasghettio":** A fobby butchering of "uh oh spaghettio" by a portly child, which was deemed "cute" during my youth and "disturbing" as I became older.

3) **"Idiot":** A loving term of endearment used by the dictator to admonish the portly Pakistani American child after any and all perceived wrong-doings.

Ascent to Purgatory

I awoke one day to find my parental units, mother and father, casually taking me for "a ride" to a "nice place" . . . or so they said.

Ice cream store? No. Toys R' Us, where a kid can be a kid if he has access to a platinum visa card? No. Comic Book Store? Sorry, but no Spiderman today. Instead, we pull into a foreboding driveway of a large, ominous brown building. Since I was a 5-year-old Fob near illiterate I missed the sign, which glared, "Child's Hideaway."

My spidey sense hits 3.

We leave the womb of comfort, the car, and ascend the cement steps, where sodden footprints of Children's Pay-Less Shoes and Oshkosh Bikosh sandals are noticeable. Spidey sense at 5. We enter into a room of darkness. Slowly, angelic faces marred by sadness and confusion turn toward us. It was the city of lost children. Children whose mirth and merriness was buried deep, deep under their very soul, maliciously robbed by a nefarious evil-doer. My 5-year-old spidey sense kicked up to 7. Something was rotten in the state of Elementary Denmark. A large ogre enters the room. The children inhale fear and exhale hopelessness.

Spidey sense at 8.

The large ogre grunts some inaudible words with the parental units, who will now be referred to as Tyrannical Dictators #1 and # 2 (T.D. for short). The other children sensed dread, like a vulture with an uncanny sixth sense for a dying soul. The 5-year-old portly fobby Pakistani kid smiled like only a 5-year-old portly fobby Pakistani kid could. Oblivious. Confused. Scared. Hungry. Fobby.

Now I'm 4 ft above the ground and I'm flying. I look at the smiling faces of the T.D.'s waving goodbye to me. My poor body is being crushed underneath the fleshy, gargantuan armpit of the large ogre, as she carries me away to what I think is my doom . . . her kitchen. I thought stories of Ogres eating children were mere fairy tales made up by adults to frighten children into submission. I was wrong.

Spidey sense has just hit 9.5.

The conspiracy of adults had resulted in me obliviously being enrolled in "Childs Hideaway" (what an apt name), a pre-school/day care center. Being brown, Muslim, chubby, fobby, dorky but adorable, and not knowing any English save the trinity of "Shut up. Uh oh Pasghettio, and Idiot", I was a minority to say the least. Moreover, my enemies multiplied. It seems not 1 ogre, but 3, ran the dungeon. They will be referred to as Leviathan, Jinn, and Cerberus, respectively.

For the first few hours of that most horrid day, I was convinced my body parts would end up in each of their bellies. These women were HUGE. So huge that I have to spell it again and with emphasis write: H-U-G-E! They were "very very

healthy" as my grandmother lovingly described her overweight grandchild, yours truly, to her friends. Another favorite was, "no, he's not fat, he just has big bones." Or, "no he's not fat, it's just puppy fat." What does that mean? "Puppy fat?" Am I some sort of hybrid canine mutant? And if I'm so healthy, woman, how come I can't run 5 ft without panting like a 90 yr old emphyasemic? Also, do all healthy 5 yr old children wear 10 yr old clothing because their waist size is so "big boned" that no other pant can fit them? I digress. Needless to say, the women were continents unto themselves.

Escape was merely a phantom, a madman's dream. A luxury for those suffering from delusions and overactive imaginations. It was a toddler's Shawshank. We were condemned men and women. Life began anew. Man finds meaning even in empty, meaningless situations such as this one. Usually, mind numbing chores temporarily alleviate the crushing sense of defeat and loneliness. The 3 Dungeon Masters devised a particular sadistic yet effective chore for us. After weeping my last weep, Leviathan grabbed me wholesale, with one fleshly Leviathan arm no less, and forcefully took me outside to "The Wall."

The Wall

The Wall smelled like sand. Desert sand. A vast, endless twilight zone forever trapping the wails and tears of lost men. Our job was to placate the wall. How did the wall feel placated, you ask? Good question. Leviathan instructed me in her Ogre-tongue that "we had to make the wall beautiful by painting it." Of course, these words meant nothing to me since she spoke English and I spoke Fob. Instead, her words came out Charlie Brown Adult style: "Wah wah wah . . . wah wah wah . . . wahwahwah." I understood nothing. But the up and down stroke of her arm made sense. I turned to my left and right and saw patients from "One Flew Over the Cuckoo's Nest." Drooling, vacant eyed children smiling blissfully at the wall. I was convinced the wall is a siren, a beguiling temptress that invites man to his doom through a beautiful song. A vortex leading to perennial brain damage and paste-eating. My dissent was futile. Leviathan grabbed the paintbrush and put it in my chubby hand and commanded me to paint.

Now painting requires paint. Those are the rules. I didn't make it up. It's just how it goes. So, where was the paint? Leviathan placed a large bucket consisting of a watery substance next to me and made hand motions to put brush in said substance, take brush out, and finally paint wall with brush.

I did what I was told. I became enthralled. I was actually "painting" the wall with this mysterious watery substance I assumed was paint. This activity occupied my attention for hours. It was our SOMA. I willingly joined the madmen who occupied my left and right flank. Slowly, however, oh so slowly, doubt crept into my chubby head. Why did the paint disappear? How come the wall stayed the same color? No matter how much paint I put on it still stays dry. Curiosity killed the cat, but not the Desi Fob. I ventured out from my confines to see where Leviathan "refilled" the paint jars. The garden hose served as the source of this mystical paint, which was in actuality . . . water. The sick bastards made us paint a dry wall with water and used Korean Communist brainwashing techniques to convince us Manchurian Candidates that we were actually "painting" and making the hall "happy." If I were that wall, I'd be suicidal.

Sirat al Mustiqim (The Bridge for the Believers)

After dropping my brush in disgust and protest, I needed a new escape. Leviathan, Jinn, and Cerberus knew I was onto their gig. To keep me quiet lest I inspire a Spartacus type revolution, they let me play on the "playground" with the non-minority children. I'm assuming these children spoke English, which served as their passport for some "outdoor" freedom. Surveying the playing field, I quickly chose my avenue of mindless distraction: a bridge. Not a bridge, mind you . . . The bridge. The bridge to end all bridges. The sirat (Arabic for bridge) leading to salvation, as ordained in the Holy Books.

This celestial gift from the heavens illuminated the damp darkness of the dungeoneous outdoor "play area" like a lamp lit from God Himself. It mesmerized me. To my overactive, only child fat brain it represented the ultimate escape. I played endlessly on this mythical landscape, escaping to faraway galaxies and farfetched scenarios where I, the brown fat kid, would be saving my Bollywood heroine from Imperial colonizers. Other times, I just ran back and forth thinking the ogres chased me—training my body for the eventual escape from Alcatraz.

In reality, this was a filthy, limp, wooden ladder raised about 2 feet from the ground and held together flimsily by rope between two tree trunks placed 10 feet apart. To an Einstein "relative" observer, I would be deemed a severely retarded handicapped child running aimlessly like a brown ball to and fro the tree trunks for hours and hours upon end.

Days passed into weeks. There was comfort in the Elementary State of Denmark. Unfortunately, the party pooper, known as "life," can never allow a man to truly enjoy his brief moments of peace. On a glorious, average Fremont California day, as I ran to and fro like a blurry fat brown kebob with pudgy appendages, I felt an unexpected graze. Then, I heard a thump.

A yelp? A scream? Was my mind fooling me? I stopped. I titled my fat head upward. The right shank of my "Husky" sized thigh certainly felt violated. But by whom or what? Alas, as is the way of fat kids, we don't ponder the intricacies of life, so I just resumed my mindless, aimless running. Back and forth. Back and Forth. Back and . . . uh-oh.

A Jinn, one of the unholy triumvirate, blocked my path. Fire came from her nostrils. Steam from her hair. The Jinn was displeased. Next to her, a stereotypical Asian American boy with a Mao bowl haircut stood weeping. Woodchips from the ground cluttered his bowl-cut hair and tears mixed with muddy dirt painted his right cheek.

My husky shank inadvertently and unknowingly destroyed the only other minority on the bridge, causing him to vertically lift upward, and then violently plummet to the floor. I, being fobby, Desi, fat, and fat, ran aimlessly, lost in my hedonistic ways, oblivious to the crime my out-of-proportion, fleshy shank had committed on my behalf. The Jinn muttered nonsensical nonsense to me "Wah wah wahwahwahwah." The Communist smiled revenge. The Jinn leered anger. The Desi Fob yelped hunger.

Finally, the Jinn turned to me square in the face and asks, "Wah Wah Wah, Purpose or Accident?!?" I stand motionless. I stare back into a sea of hideousness.

Spidey Sense is stuck on "horrified."

The Jinn repeats, "Wah Wah Wah Purpose or Accident?!?"

"Hmmn," I muse to myself. "This 'accident' word seems quite familiar. Upon occasion, I reckon I have used it myself." Most tellingly, when I rebelled against my nemesis, the toilet seat, and unleashed hell on the carpet as I ran to freedom, leaving my former nemesis, the diaper, on the toilet floor. When the dictator admonished me, I yelled, "Accident," as was the custom of cartoon characters on TV. This word made some sense. The Jinn shrieks to her minions, summoning them from the pits of hellfire. She snorts. She breathes acid. She asks again, "Wah Wah Wah Purpose or Accident?!?!?"

"Hmmn," I muse to myself. This "Pur pose" word seems alien. "What is it," I wondered? It sounds like "purple," but purple is a color. It also sounded like "purse," the item my dictator spend ridiculous amounts of green Monopoly paper on. Hmnn. Hmnnnnn. Pur . . . pose. Pur . . . .pose. "I wonder." "I wonder."

"WAH WAH WAH WAH!!!! PURPOSE or ACCIDENT?"

The Fat Desi Fob child with dirt on his shank and mud on his knees stares directly into the face of madness. The heart of darkness. His face is solemn and peaceful. He smiles. He asks:

"Per – Poose?"

The Jinn unleashes a Banshee scream that would silence the angels themselves. The Communist grins and rubs his fingers together, relishing his Count of Monte Cristo-esque revenge. The Desi Fat kid looks around confused. He doesn't understand. All he wanted to do was run on his bridge and save Bollywood heroines from colonialist imperialists. He never meant any harm. He was an innocent. A bholoo, as they say in the Motherland. A fat simpleton whose only crime was eating 2 more samosas and kebobs than the other kids. He did not deserve this admonishment. He yearned for days of peace and solitude, but those days, like his innocence, were forever gone.

The Jinn grabbed the Fob's ear, taking him executioner-style to the "Dunce Corner" where he would wait for 5 hours for his 2 TD's to pick him up. Sitting alone in the corner, wailing to himself, not knowing why he was punished. Observing the token Asian minority conquering his once beloved bridge. Being scolded by Jinn, Leviathan, and Cerberus for crimes he unknowingly committed. He sat . . . confused. Then, it all made sense. It was that word. That damn word! Blast that word! What was it, again? Oh, yes. "Per-poose!" The culprit. The femme fatale. The red herring. The bloody glove. The word that serves as the cause and solution to all of life's problems: "Per-Poose."

The Desi Fat Fob Kid sighed. He rolled his eyes. And he said:

"Uh Oh, Pasghettio."

Source: Ali, Wajahat. "The Perpoose Story: The Minority Preschool Experience." 2008. http://goatmilkblog.com/2008/05/31/the-perpoose-story-2/. Used with permission of author.

Asma Hasan, Interview by Nadia Mohammad
(2008)

Asma Gull Hasan, author of Red, White, and Muslim *(2008),* American Muslims: The New Generation *(2000), and* Why I Am a Muslim *(2004), is the daughter of Pakistani immigrants. She has written extensively about Muslim identity in the post-9/11 United States as well as about feminism and Islam. The following excerpt is from Hasan's interview with* Divanee Magazine, *a journal of culture and politics for Desi (South Asian) women. Hasan talks about her nontraditional perspectives on religious and national identity.*

DM: **You've dubbed yourself the "Muslim Feminist Cowgirl." How did you come up with that?**

Hasan: After college I took some time off to write my first book, *Muslims in America*, which was based on my senior thesis. I didn't think that there was anything out that reflected who Muslims really are in America. What was in literature at the time was that they were either these sort of Amish people, sort of alienated—not part of the mainstream, or that Muslims were terrorists. Nothing really described who I felt I was as a Muslim.

For a long time after I wrote my book, I couldn't find a publisher. No one was really interested; in the meantime I thought I'd better go to law school, start looking for a real job. While in law school I still kept pitching my book to publishers. Finally I thought, I need to do something that will get people's attention. So one day while sitting in a cab I thought I should call myself a "Muslim Feminist Cowgirl" because it was a catchy title. Obviously the Muslim part is reflective of my being Muslim, and then the feminist part is my belief that I am a feminist—I believe in equal rights for men and women (sometimes superior for women!)—and then the cowgirl part is from being from Colorado and being independent and self-reliant. I think the American cowgirl is the ultimate symbol of women's freedom in America and of a woman's independence.

I figured it would be a sort of fun thing to put in the cover letters to publishers - "please publish my book . . . I'm a Muslim Feminist Cowgirl . . . " (laughs)

It just turned out to be one to those titles that people seemed to like a lot. I think part of the reason people like it so much is because it debunks so many stereotypes about being a Muslim and a woman at once.

DM: **Growing up as an American, as a Muslim, as a Desi, and as you were saying as a cowgirl and a feminist how have you been able to balance the cultural and ideal differences?**

Hasan: I've had three influences in my life—being American, being a Muslim, and being part of Desi South Asian culture. People could say those three things are in conflict with each other, certainly between Islam and Desi culture there is a lot of disagreement. The religion is very much against patriarchy and treating women unequally, there are many aspects of South Asian culture that favor men and are patriarchal. I think on the other hand though, Islam, in its most ideal form really complements American culture very well—when American culture is living up to its ideal.

Many Americans will ask, how can you possibly say that America is at all like Islam? They see Islam as this religion of tormentors and a religion that justifies violence. What I always say is that there is the best of Islam and there is the best of American culture; as Muslims and Americans we struggle to live to the ideals of our belief systems. Even though America is an egalitarian culture we still have Americans who are racist and sexist and engage in discrimination. Likewise, though Islam is a peaceful and moderate religion, we have Muslims that are extremists.

At first glance when you read that I am an American Muslim of South Asian descent you would think there's lots of conflicting things going on for her. But the thing is I've lived it, and I've come to my own understanding and found my own balance between them. When you get beyond the surface and you get deep into all of the influences in my life the main purpose behind all of it is just to be a good person—Islam wants you to be a good person, America wants you to be a good person and South Asian culture, in the end, wants to make you a good person.

DM: **Have you ever felt any sort of discrimination for being of South Asian descent or being a Muslim woman either here or even, within the Islamic community itself for being too Americanized?**

Hasan: Definitely, I've felt at times I've been discriminated against for being Muslim and because I'm South Asian, more because I'm Muslim. I think most average Americans don't understand the difference between South Asia and the Middle East, so I can't say that I've been discriminated against on that basis because people don't really understand it enough to discriminate . . . (laughs)

Within the Muslim community, I definitely face discrimination, because I don't wear hijab. The vast majority does not wear hijab, nor do they believe that it is required. But a lot of our leadership in our American Muslim organizations do believe that hijab is required. They will only let certain types of Muslim women speak to their organizations. I go to Muslim conventions and events, I look at the speakers and none of them have published two books, none of them have gone to a top five law school, none of them have the resume that I have, not even close. They speak on all kinds of topics, but they would never have me speak in a million years, because I don't wear hijab, because I'm not subscribing to this bare-minimum standard that in their eyes a woman must have. These are usually men making these decisions. It's very

rare that a Muslim woman wearing hijab says anything to me. Muslim women who wear hijab are very open-minded generally, I feel like it's the men that push that [hijab] more. . . .

DM: **Out of all the reasons you spoke about that make you a Muslim what makes you the most proud?**

Hasan: I think I'm most proud of Islam's stance on diversity. The Qur'an was so ahead of its time on so many things. What the Qur'an says about religious and ethnic diversity, it's almost as if portions of the Qur'an were written today. One part of the Qur'an says—if we wanted to we could have made you all speak the same tongue and all have the same law. He purposely made you different because he wanted to test you. I'm very impressed with that, it's very powerful to me, and very appealing to me as an American and as a Muslim. We were purposely meant to be different to see if we could get along, to see if we could be a diverse people and not attack each other all the time.

I also really like my chapter on Sufism, Sufism means to me that you should have no regrets in life and everything happens for a reason. Most Muslims believe that too. Sufis take that to another level. If something bad happens to you, something good is going to happen to you next, and you wouldn't be able to have that good thing happen to you if you didn't have something bad happen to you before that. I get a lot of comfort from that. It makes life a lot easier to handle, when you realize these things are happening for a reason.

Source: Mohammad, Nadia. "Divanee Magazine Interviews Asma Hasan." *Divanee Magazine, 2008.* Reprinted with permission.

Mariam Malik, "We Are All Punjabi"

(2009)

The Punjab is the geographical region spanning northwestern India and eastern Pakistan. The region was split in two along religious lines during the partition of British India in 1947; the

Hindu half went to India and the Muslim half went to Pakistan. In the process, millions of displaced people migrated from one area to the other, enduring riots, horrendous persecution, and massacres on both sides. The Pakistani Punjab contains most of the nation's population. And despite the trauma of the Partition and the emigration of most of the area's Hindus, the Punjab remains a very diverse region, both religiously and ethnically.

Mariam Malik is a recent graduate of the University of California–Berkeley. Although she was born and raised in the United States, Malik's parents are from the Punjab in Pakistan, and they often took their children there to visit family and learn about their cultural heritage. Malik wrote "We are All Punjabi" in response to what she found to be a pervasive lack of knowledge about Pakistan's Punjab region (as opposed to India's). Originally published in UC Berkeley's Asian American student magazine Hardboiled, *"We Are All Punjabi" talks about how the Partition affected the transnational culture of the Punjab and describes Malik's own identity as a Pakistani Punjabi American.*

How being Pakistani and Punjabi has led me to defend my identity

When I tell others where I am from, I often get confused looks. Sometimes, my answer even seems to make people uncomfortable. I was born in the US but I identify myself with what seems to be a misunderstood region: Punjab.

As a first generation US citizen, whose parents were born and raised in the Punjab province of Pakistan, I find it very enriching to embrace my Punjabi culture. Yet, I am disheartened by the general lack of awareness of the richness and cultural heritage of what was once a unified Punjab.

Punjab is an area in South Asia that lies divided by the Radcliffe Line, the border between Pakistan and India that was created in 1947 after partition. This artificial border not only separates Muslims from Sikhs and Hindus, but has also caused people to forget how unified Punjab once was. It saddens me that politics and religious differences have fostered much disagreement and reluctance to acknowledge the Punjabi identity of the other party because the truth is, we Punjabis are all the same.

Frankly, I'm tired of the repetitive "You're Punjabi? I thought you were from Pakistan," or the "So, you're half Indian?", or better yet "I think you're mistaken . . . Punjab is only in India!"

I hear these reactions so often and with such fervor that even I begin to doubt my own identity. At times, my dad had to reassure me that I am "just as Punjabi" as someone from the Punjab province in India. This disconnect sparked my interest in researching why our views have been shaped in such a way that we feel the need to discount the "other Punjab", as if it never existed. I have to remind myself over and over again that these ignorant responses stem from what seems to create many issues around the world: politics.

With that realization, I now respond to these comments with confidence. We may be divided by an arbitrary line, but in reality we sing the same songs, read from the same literature, dance the same dance, live the same lifestyle, eat the same food, speak the same language, and even look the same. We share family members and political leaders, we have roots in the same villages, and our parents went to the same schools together. We have so much in common, but we choose to ignore this because partition sowed the seeds of animosity. Although this animosity has subsided in the last generation, it has been replaced with a general lack of awareness.

I've been fortunate enough to visit my parents' villages in Punjab many times when I return to Pakistan. Therefore, I can personally attest to the beauty and culture of Punjab. It is interesting to me that these villages and cities I visit on the Pakistan side of Punjab are filled only with Muslims because just a few decades ago, before partition, Sikhs, Muslims and Hindus resided together. Religion was an afterthought until the political divide forced it into the consciousness of the Punjabi people. Instead, culture united everyone. In fact, Punjabis were so well integrated that a border drawn anywhere would have been arbitrary.

For generations, Punjabis have lived an agricultural lifestyle due to the lush terrain and five major rivers running through the area, making it the most well irrigated area in South Asia. Therefore, spring has been a time of celebration for centuries that has unified the Punjabi people and manifests itself in two popular forms: bhangra and Basant.

Bhangra is a form of dance that has recently gained popularity in the Western world, but truly dates back to generations ago in the heart of Punjab. The dance began as an agricultural ritual performed by farmers to celebrate the coming of spring. Of course, bhangra has evolved into many different styles and uses today, but it remains a piece of culture that all Punjabis can identify with, no matter their religion.

Likewise, the most popular Punjabi celebration is Basant, a festival that originated as marking the arrival of spring, but today is more commercialized and representative of the strong cultural vibe that runs through the region. During Basant, men, women and children all over Punjab dress up in colorful clothing, compete in kite flying and indulge in authentic music and food. This celebration does not specifically hold to just Pakistan or India; instead, it is something that all Punjabis can relate to because Basant was celebrated by everyone's ancestors. Even after the partition divided the area on the basis of religion, this celebration transcended that division and continues to be celebrated by thousands every year. The only difference today is that Basant is celebrated in an exclusive manner within each country rather than as an overarching and unifying holiday.

This list of similarities can easily go on, but it makes one begin to question: with so much in common between the Pakistan and India sides of Punjab, why is there an ideological disconnect and lack of unity amongst Punjabis?

The partition between the two countries did not occur that long ago, nor did it happen peacefully. The initial reaction to the partition, which forced millions of people to change homes and divided families, was to unify on a political basis by country. From my interactions with both Pakistanis and Indians, I can accurately say that in one generation, we have seemed to forget how much Punjab had in common because we chose to let go of our rich Punjabi culture.

As tempting as it is to get caught up in politics, we must remember that the differences are artificial and politically based, whereas the underlying similarities date back to centuries ago and can prevail if we choose to let go of any political animosity. Luckily, even though recent events have brought the Pakistan-India tension to the eye of the public, we have come a long ways in accepting one another. We are entering a new era of more open minded thinking.

I am confident that we will see a revival of a time where people can be comfortable with their own faith and religion while also allowing themselves to partake in the complete richness of their cultural experience.

I am confident, that with awareness, we can all be Punjabi once again.

Source: Malik, Mariam. "We Are All Punjabi." *Hardboiled* 12, no. 5 (April 2009). http://hardboiled.berkeley.edu/issues/125/125-11-punjabi.html. Used with permission of *Hardboiled*, the Asian American issues newsmagazine at UC Berkeley.

Aman Ali and Bassam Tariq, "Day 30: Celebration" (2009)

In 2009, Aman Ali and Bassam Tariq decided to visit a different New York City mosque every day of Ramadan. They chronicled their journey in their blog, 30 Mosques in 30 Days. *Tariq's and Ali's undertaking, meant to challenge mainstream*

American perceptions of Islam and Muslims, also highlighted the hospitality and generosity they experienced at each of the ethnically diverse mosques they visited. The following entry, from September 21, narrates the final visit of the project, to the Upper Westchester Muslim Society mosque. Here, Ali celebrated Eid, the holiday ending the fasting of Ramadan.

I've seen many spectacular sights in my short lifetime and tonight I have come up with the top four:

1. The ka'bah in Makkah, Saudi Arabia
2. Prophet Muhammad's mosque in Medina, Saudi Arabia
3. Masjid Al-Aqsa in Palestine
4. Seeing a niqabi in Brooklyn get down on Eid

After tonight, I have to bump the birth of my nephew down to number 5. I hope my brother doesn't mind.

Bassam was out of town today spending Eid Al-Fitr, the Muslim holiday celebrating the completion of Ramadan, with his family. Eid is typically a holiday to celebrate among friends and family. But since my family is spread out all over the country, it becomes harder to do that as I get older. Luckily for me, my little brother Zeshawn lives in New York now, so it wasn't too bad celebrating Eid today.

Zeshawn tagged along with me to go to the Eid prayer held by the Upper Westchester Muslim Society. This is a congregation of mostly Arab and South Asian doctor families about 30–45 minutes north of where I live. They held the Eid prayer in a hotel ballroom. . . .

Eid is without a doubt one of my favorite times of the year. It's a day Prophet Muhammad (peace be upon him) said is for rejoicing. So considering that most of my family wasn't with me this year for Eid, I set out on a mission last week to find the most crunk celebration possible that could fill the void of them not being here.

If you listened to the NPR story on 30 Mosques on Friday, you would have learned that I was eager to re-visit Masjid Khalifah in Brooklyn for Eid. It's the mosque Bassam and I visited on Day 24 and we were told the place has an AMAZING live entertainment show during Eid. I was compelled to find out if it was true.

I met up with Sharaf later that afternoon and we rolled through Masjid Khalifah at around 6 p.m. As soon as we stepped inside, all we heard was Michael Jackson music BLASTING through the entire building. I looked across the room I was standing in and saw little kids doing the "MJ kick" and moonwalk. At that moment, Sharaf and I knew we were in store for an interesting evening, so we grabbed some food and sat down at a table in the community hall.

For dinner, I had beef tips, barbecue chicken, baked chicken, lamb, goat and catfish. For sides I had corn, lentil rice and spinach. Masjid Khalifah seriously came correct tonight, I was joking with one of the people that they must have had trouble figuring out what dishes to serve because it looked like they were offering every single halal animal imaginable.

As we were eating, we saw a live band come in and set up on the mainstage. I joked with Sharaf that this band must be legit because some of them were walking around with bookbags to hold their guitars in.

The band started off with some funk instrumentals, to warm the crowd up since people were still coming into the buildings. That's when three Muslim women took the stage to lead the crowd in one of my favorite Motown records, "Stop in the name of love" by the Supremes. THE CROWD WENT NUTS.

The singers were walking up and down the aisles trying to get the audience hyped. All of a sudden I see a woman in black niqab [veil covering the face and hair] get up and bust out moves that I didn't even think were humanly possible.

As soon as I saw that happen, Sharaf and I looked at each other realizing not a single one of our friends would believe what we had just witnessed.

The band continued nailing cover song after cover song from artists such as Tina Turner, Chuck Berry, Barry White and they even busted out with some James Brown . . .

I think it's safe to say that just about every mosque I've been to, the celebration that Masjid

Khalifah had tonight would never fly. Then I started thinking, why not? Let's put the women singing and dancing thing aside, what's wrong with cranking out a few tunes for people to enjoy on one of the most special days of the year to celebrate?

But I don't want to turn this into an argument about the right way vs. wrong way to celebrate Eid. I'm not even remotely qualified to make that argument. But what I saw tonight was spectacular. To see Muslims spend the day of Eid with their friends and family completely energized from head to toe is a sight I haven't seen in a long time.

Most Eid celebrations I have gone to growing up are enjoyable, but fairly routine. You grab a plate of food, sit down with friends and family and talk for a few hours. Still fun to do, but I'd take some James Brown tunes over that any day of the week.

After the celebration, the show's emcees asked everyone to help clean up. They even managed to turn the cleaning instructions into a catchy song. I was like "Wow, they can even get crunk while cleaning."

I helped stack some folding chairs and when I was done with that, I carried over some tables to a nearby wall. As I did that, one of the elderly gentlemen in the community shouted at me not to move the tables.

That's when I ran into one of the women I met when I visited Masjid Khalifah on Day 24. She said "You've prayed with us, had our food, and now you've been yelled at for doing something wrong. Congratulations, you are officially a member of this masjid [mosque]."

Driving back home to Manhattan after the celebration, I started telling Sharaf how hard it was to believe that the 30 Mosques project was coming to an end. That's when we were driving through midtown Manhattan and noticed the green lights coming from the Empire State Building.

Green is a color heavily associated with Islam (Can someone tell me the exact significance of it, I've heard close to 30 different explanations). During the Eid holiday, the city of New York shines green lights on the Empire State Building to let the entire community know it's Eid.

If you ever wondered how strong of an impact Muslims have had on New York City, all you have to do is come visit during Eid and look at the sky.

No person on this Earth could ever replace my family. But tonight I finally realized, the people I've met in this city, especially during this 30 Mosques project, are the next best thing.

Source: Ali, Aman, and Bassan Tariq. "Day 30: Celebration." September 21, 2009. 30 Mosques blog. http://30mosques.com/archive2010/2009/09/day-30-celebration part-1/. Reprinted with permission.

Asma Uddin, "Exploring Gender and Islam"
(2010)

In November 2009, the Center for American Progress's (CAP) Faith and Progressive Policy Initiative, funded by a grant from the Rockefeller Brothers Fund, initiated the Young Muslim American Voices Project. Muslim Americans from across the country convened in Washington, DC, where they discussed the many challenges and opportunities facing their diverse and growing communities.

As part of this project, Sally Steenland, a senior policy adviser at CAP, interviewed Asma Uddin, the founder and editor in chief of Altmuslimah, *an online journal that explores gender-related issues in Islam. Uddin is also a lawyer for the Becket Fund, working on matters of religious liberty. Her parents immigrated to the United States from Pakistan in the 1970s, and she was born and raised in Miami, Florida. In her interview, Uddin speaks about the place of women and gender equality in Islam, the role Sharia law can play in mediating differences within the Muslim American community, and the increasing problem of anti-Islamic rhetoric in the United States.*

Sally Steenland: Asma, let's talk about your work as editor-in-chief of Altmuslimah.com. Tell us why you created it, some of the issues you explore, and your goals for Altmuslimah.

Asma Uddin: Altmuslimah comes out of a very personal experience with gender and Islam. Growing up in America, in middle school and high school, I was very much into religion and religious studies. I had a rosy, warm, and fuzzy picture of religion—something that was without conflict or diversity.

When I entered college, I began to experience more intricacies, including certain interpretations of Islam that didn't fit with my rather simple and rosy version. There were a lot of foreign students at my school, particularly men from Middle Eastern countries, and they had separate organizations from those that Muslim-American students had formed. Their version of Islam was different from ours, most clearly in their views toward women. Of course, none of the foreign students were women. If females wanted to participate in their events, they were required to speak from behind a curtain or not partake in leadership duties. In contrast, the Muslim Student Association had female presidents.

As somebody who is quite proud of her religion, I was shocked to deal with this. It started me on a path of internal reflection and led to quite a bit of turmoil—to what I now call my gender in Islam crisis. It made me question, at a very deep level,

God and Islam and my place in it. I felt so strongly about gender equality and equal identity, but was that just a product of my environment or something that God intended? In other words, how did I fit with this religion that I love so much?

I looked beyond social commentary and what people were saying. I had a tremendous but simple spiritual realization that God wouldn't have created me to be anything but equal—and with equal dignity—so that I could follow a path with complete freedom in reaching him. That is what brought me out of the struggle. And when I came out of it, I was a much stronger Muslim than I had been before.

Since then, my experiences continue to build on that realization, particularly in interactions with various male figures. As I reflected on my previous struggle, I knew there must have been a reason I came out of it with so much clarity and strength.

That is really where Altmuslimah comes from. The actual predecessor to Altmuslimah was a book club I started a few years ago in the tristate area of New York, New Jersey, and Pennsylvania. I invited some young girls and women to get together and we started reading books relating to the question of gender in Islam.

One was *Living Islam Out Loud* and the editor was Saleemah Abdul-Ghafur. She came to one of our meetings, and as the women were reflecting on the book, some became emotional and spoke with absolute honesty. At that moment, it occurred to me that this was a forum so many women needed but few had. I wanted a forum that would be available to women across the country and world. That is why I went online.

In terms of issues, we explore the nature of gender in Islam, relationships and sexuality, beauty, society and politics, mosque, and community. We have a very interesting section called AltVoices, which is our most recent section and one I hope to grow. It comes out of my work at the Becket Fund where I interact with other religious freedom activists. Many of the women have strong views on gender issues within their own faith, and I thought this would be a wonderful area of interfaith dialogue.

Too often interfaith dialogue happens as abstract theology. People agree to disagree, but it doesn't make any deep connection. By having parallel discourses on gender in each of our faiths, we can find commonalities that allow more substantive connections.

S: **So one of your goals is increased interfaith dialogue around issues of gender. Do you have other goals for Altmuslimah? What you would like to see happening in three to five years?**

A: While the online presence is important, we need to support that with real-life events. We have done a little bit of that, but I am looking to do more, especially in the D.C. area. We are planning a roundtable for October 23 on some of the trickier relationship issues that have arisen in our community. We hope to have at these events some of our writers who have developed a following.

A lot of the things we talk about are sensitive. It could be women over 30 having a hard time finding a marriage partner or people considered "too dark" because of subculture racism. People feel strongly about these issues but often don't want to speak in their own name. Some of the best ways to bring out these issues might be in a theatrical presentation, where people take on a different persona to express issues that are personal.

S: **Can you talk about the differences between private conversations where people can be very frank and more public conversations that go beyond the Muslim community? When is a private conversation more important and when is it important to have public conversations?**

A: We straddle the line between the public and the private on Altmuslimah. Many of the discussions, in terms of who's writing and who's commentating, are among Muslims. The discussions are available for public consumption, but the nature of the dialogue is private—referring to things within the community. I think there are spaces for more private, personal discussions. A lot of women have told me that they have small book clubs or groups that discuss content from Altmuslimah. That is happening aside from my involvement, but is something Altmuslimah is leading to.

In terms of the public aspect, a huge part of my creating Altmuslimah came from my realization that the struggle I was going through was very much an issue beyond the community. For instance, the media's portrayal of Muslim women as oppressed and subjugated made my struggle more pronounced. Often when non-Muslims think of Islam, they think of stereotypes very related to gender, whether it be harems or polygamy or the Taliban abusing women in Afghanistan or burqas. The diversity of viewpoints and the intelligent, sincere way we approach issues on Altmuslimah provides nuance to issues that are otherwise seen in black and white.

I want to keep Altmuslimah organic rather than develop or enhance it in an artificial way. I want to maintain a level of sincerity and make sure that whoever writes for the site or comes to it can honestly explore deep issues.

S: **You were talking about the stereotype of Islam. If somebody said to you, "Women are oppressed and subjugated. There is no gender equality within the faith," how would you set them straight?**

A: I think that the easiest way of setting them straight—short of referring them to my website—would be to show myself. Here I am, a Muslim woman. I have a completely supportive husband and an amazing relationship with him and other men in my life. Other than the usual social limitations we all deal with, I have never had my religion limit me and my success. I used to wear a hijab while working as a corporate lawyer. I saw myself as being a representative of my faith to other people—to show all that I was doing. At some point I realized I needed to stop making decisions based only on my role. The examples, whether of myself or the vast majority of Muslim women in this country and across the world, disprove stereotypes.

S: **You work as an attorney at the Becket Fund. One of the issues that you work on is religious liberty. Can you talk about religious liberty and whether you think it is an absolute right or has limits?**

A: Just like all human rights, religious liberty is not absolute in the sense that nothing could ever limit it. I think, however, that the limits are few and must be strictly and well defined. Otherwise they can swallow up the rights.

For instance, religious freedom can be limited for public safety, public order, health and morals, or the fundamental rights of others. But the way that these words are defined is important. Sometimes governments and countries define them in overly broad ways.

In the course of my work, I have seen the "public order exception" be misused. It's the notion that we can't have people criticizing religion or articulating problematic interpretations of it because people who hear that will get upset and be violent. It says that in order to limit potential public disorder, we are going to stop a speaker from speaking in the first place. In U.S. law, a hostile audience should never be able to limit a nonviolent speaker. Ultimately the law is more effective by focusing on the violent actor—that is, the hostile audience that reacts in violence—as opposed to a nonviolent speaker.

Religious liberty is linked to women's rights—in particular, a woman's right to religious freedom. It might be religious garb and the right to wear a headscarf or burqa. It might relate to sharia arbitration or use of sharia law. There was a big debate in Canada when sharia arbitration was being considered. The fear was that it would take away women's rights, and that women would be forced into positions against their will, ending up with fewer rights than non-Muslim Canadian women.

S: **Can you talk about what sharia arbitration might look like? Are there comparables in other faiths?**

A: There are definitely comparables. Orthodox Jews can arbitrate under their own laws, for instance. The disputes are most often family law issues, like divorce or alimony. The interesting thing is that Islam arguably affords greater civil rights than civil laws do. For instance, a Muslim woman's money is always her own and wouldn't be subjugated to division by divorce. That is not the case with civil law.

With sharia arbitration—assuming the parties come together in a completely voluntary way—a panel would decide an issue. In order for a specific decision to be enforced, it would have to go to a civil court, which would check for procedural and substantive fairness. Was the judge fair? Was the arbitrator fair? Was there any inherent bias in the process? In terms of substantive fairness, was the award fair?

These checks by the civil court protect the parties involved. While sharia arbitration might apply to issues of family law, it would not allow parties to circumvent existing laws in the United States. So you couldn't decriminalize something that is criminalized

S: here. Sharia arbitration is not a way of circumventing the law, but of working within the broader framework and finding a space to resolve your disputes through religious law.

S: **You write an "On Faith" column for The *Washington Post*. Recently you talked about those who see the Muslim-American community as monolithic and ignore its diversity. You say that Muslim Americans disagree over a good many issues— both religious and nonreligious.**

A: Altmuslimah is a perfect example of the inherent diversity among Muslims. Its very creation suggests there are many ways to look at things. One question on our site that has gotten quite a bit of attention is the issue of Muslim women marrying non-Muslim men. It's something that was considered pretty black and white for a long time and now is being questioned a little. People are arguing about it. We have debates that we feature, posting an article, and people respond.

On a scholarly level there is a different interpretation for almost every verse in the Koran. There are different methodologies for interpreting the Koran—some take a literal approach, some are more contextual. Some say that each verse should be interpreted within the broader context of the Koran's social justice message.

Muslims are not programmed by the religion to think in one particular way. Whether it's politics or foreign policy, art, literature, or theater, Muslims have different perspectives and tastes. We are just as diverse as every other group.

S: **We have recently seen a dangerous spike in hate speech, not just among extremists but more mainstream conservative politicians like Newt Gingrich and Sarah Palin. In your travels to other countries, how do we stack up in terms of religious liberty and a pluralistic society?**

A: In a lot of other countries, hate speech is thought of as an instigator of public disorder. Even many European countries have laws against hate speech. A danger of these laws is that they can often end up broadly banning all kinds of speech.

In some Muslim countries where the government is in control of speech and religion, it takes it upon itself to define what Islam is and to outlaw everything that doesn't fit that definition. You see mosque sermons being monitored or pre-approved by the government. And of course, what is approved or not approved is often defined by what suits the government's interests. It's a politicizing of Islam.

The process of speaking truth and the spiritual process of discovering Islam and negotiating its relationship with your lived reality is hindered by government intrusions on religious freedom.

In terms of how America stacks up, I don't go out and try to impose our model on other countries. I simply see some of the wisdom that comes from the way U.S. law is set up. I like to see the extent to which those concepts and principles can be implemented elsewhere in particular cultural contexts.

I think America is doing pretty well. Our law is balanced between the very limited categories of restricted speech and allowing for the broad protection of free speech. That means it is not the government telling us what is right or wrong. We are left to determine that ourselves. Ultimately, this is more effective in developing responsible citizenship.

In recent days, there has definitely been a rise in Islamophobic rhetoric. But looking at what other groups in American history have gone through, I think this is just a process every new group has to go through, and I am confident we will get to a better place.

S: **When the extremist Terry Jones was threatening to burn Korans, many people in other countries thought the government approved his actions because otherwise he would be**

arrested. To explain that this was protected speech—how do you sell that?

A: It's very difficult, especially in countries where the solution to problematic speech is to ban it. It is hard to change that way of thinking and say this shouldn't be banned because it leads to other problems. I spend most of my time trying to think up ways to explain why this makes sense in different cultural contexts. Ultimately, I keep going back to the idea of religion as fundamentally a process of inquiry. It is a path we follow, and we have to be able to ask questions. We have to be able to deal with external threats or mockery.

Seeing religion as a spiritual quest is different from seeing it as a social identity that needs to be protected with walls around it or else it will fall apart. As soon as you see religion as something that can deal with obstacles and can come out stronger, I think the less likely you are to be afraid.

S: **When you were talking about the sermons in some Muslim-majority nations needing to be approved by the government, that is a political intrusion, not a religious one. It's not that the government is made up of Islamic scholars—it's really politics they care about.**

A: Yes, they are concerned about the social justice component of Islam—where people find within their faith the ability to stand up against authoritarian governments. That's what the government wants to squelch. Of course, it doesn't make those voices disappear. Like any broad oppression, it drives things underground and takes social justice commentary out of a healthy public debate.

S: **One last question. You're a lawyer with a demanding job, and you're the editor-in-chief of Altmuslimah as well as a wife and the mother of a 3-year-old. How do you balance all of this?**

A: I am very fortunate to have a work situation that is especially attuned to the needs of working parents. Like my other colleagues at The Becket Fund, I have the ability to be quite flexible with my schedule. The fact that I can do all these things is good evidence against people who say there is no gender equality in Islam. I have an incredibly supportive network. I have a husband who bends over backwards to make my goals and dreams possible. Without this network of people in my life, it wouldn't be possible.

I have the incredible luxury of doing what I absolutely love to do. My work comes from a very deep part of me. I think it makes me much happier, and a much cooler mom, and so that's why I do it.

Source: Uddin, Asma. "Exploring Gender and Islam." Interview with Sally Steenland, October 5, 2010. Young Muslim American Voices Project, Center for American Progress. http://www.americanprogress.org/issues/2010/10/uddin_interview.html. Reprinted with permission.

Farha Hasan, "The Decree"

(2010)

Farha Hasan is a Pakistani American writer who lives and works in Boston. She has published several short stories on South Asian American identity. In her following piece, "The Decree," she examines how class played into the expatriate Pakistani community's understanding of the fatwa

Ayatollah Khomeini issued on Salman Rushdie in 1989. "The Decree" illustrates the complicated interplay between class and religious sensibilities that continues to characterize immigrant and second-generation Muslims in the United States.

He was the devil plain and simple.

This was true for our community, for our generation. As I sat in my aunt's good living room in the suburb of Thornhill, my attention focused on Ammar Rizvi, it was the farthest thing from my mind. Us 'kidz' were just lounging. The musicians had not yet arrived, and when they did it would take them some time to tune their instruments and begin the *qawwali.*

Our parents were already in the large finished basement; men on one side, women on the other. They would sit on plush carpet and pillows; laughter and traces of *Urdu* conversation making its way upstairs. Guests trickled into the lobby, their ornate outfits sparkling beneath the large chandelier. People came with their families, and guests let their children go free. Chubby toddlers ran unhindered from the kitchen to the family room, often getting passed from the arms of one child to another. Occasionally, an aunt would pop her head inside, make a polite gesture, or send one of us on an errand.

Our gatherings were rare events and *Qawwali* was the concert of choice for our parents. There was no other music like it, played with traditional instruments like the *tabla* or the harmonium. The artist, or *qawwal,* would recite a *ghazal* . . . a love song infused with mystical poetry and sung in Farsi, Hindi and Urdu; *its purpose to inspire mystical love and divine ecstasy.* A *ghazal*'s deeper meaning was not always apparent, but *ghazals* often had two common themes, intoxication and unrequited love.

Outwardly a *ghazal* may be about the joy of drinking, yet inwardly, the "wine" represented "knowledge of the Divine", the "cupbearer" was God or a spiritual guide, the "tavern" the metaphorical place where the soul may be fortunate enough to attain spiritual enlightenment. Likewise, a *ghazal* may recount the pain of unrequited love

and the agony of being separated from the beloved. Yet in essence, human love was merely a reflection of divine love.

In another couple years this music would take its place in the international arena, but I, finding my parents' music dusty and old fashioned, opted to stay upstairs for as long as possible, vying for Anmar's attention.

Nighat auntie had once been quite a beauty, with skin the color of cream, and hair and eyes like rich maple syrup. She made the raging Indian actress of her time pale in comparison. Ammar had inherited much of his mother's good looks, and although he possessed his mother's eye color, his hair was a shimmery blonde. How could he not stand out, in a sea of brown faces that ranged from as milky as café-au-lait to as deep as chocolate?

I, on the other hand, had been born with more traditional features: skin the color of toasted almonds and dark uncontrollable hair. I felt a little unnerved in the presence of my prettier cousins, and so I sat and listened and hoped that Ammar would notice me. He spoke with all the authority of a precocious eighteen-year-old when he told us about the events of *Juma* (or Friday) prayers. I listened more in awe of the speaker than what was being said.

The Imam had directed his sermon towards a book that had been a point of contention in our community. It was the first time an author, a writer of fiction, had been described as the devil both literally and figuratively, or so Ammar told us.

The author had been accused of blasphemy, and the punishment for blasphemy, according to Islamic law, was death. It was the late eighties, and the Iranian clergy had entered the forefront of literary and political controversy when they issued a death sentence, a decree . . . *a fatwa* over a work of fiction.

Forever this author, this instigator of the *fatwa* would remain a controversial figure in our community. Single-handedly he had initiated a divide between the Muslim and the Western world that would define my generation. At *Juma* (Friday) prayers, the Imam had asked the congregation if anyone agreed with the *fatwa.* Every man had raised his hand. At the time we all agreed with the death sentence . . . believed the fatwa was necessary. Who were we to disagree with an Ayatollah?

It was the last time my life had seemed so clear. Yet it was the clarity that comes with lines drawn in the sand on a windy day. I came back to look for those lines once more, and found I had lost my way, their boundaries blurring before my eyes. Fifteen years later I sat opposite Semena sipping a beverage that was more dessert than coffee. Yet, I was still a blind person groping for solid ground. I found myself easily losing my footing . . . stumbling over my words.

I was talking to a foreigner. Anyone else would have understood my point of view intuitively. Yet, Semena was like no other Pakistani I knew. When she spoke, the lilt of her voice carried a hint of exoticism. Her accent was slightly Pakistani, slightly British, slightly American all rolled into one. It made whatever she said seem richer.

She sat before me wearing a frilly black tank top, designer jeans and a piece of trendy jewelry roped around her throat. I, with my traditional upbringing, would have thought twice about exposing so much skin, but she wore it as naturally as if she had been bred on New York's Upper East Side rather than the subcontinent. My friend was a different species than the Pakistanis I had grown up with in high school.

High school had its own social strata and those of us who were born in the West considered ourselves in a different league than those that were *fresh off the boat*. I remembered these immigrants well, with their thick accents and mismatched clothes. We avoided them in the hallways, called them *FOB*s behind their backs. What we failed to realize was that we had been exposed to only one layer of the onion that is Pakistani society. Only recently had I stumbled upon a segment of the population that I barely knew existed—*the elite*.

"How can you condemn the book if you've never read it," said Semena.

A good point . . .

"*I've read parts of it . . . I've read excerpts,*" I said feeling the weakness of my own argument. In my teens I had attempted to read the entire book,

but could not get past the third chapter. I knew what the controversial parts were about. I had seen them referenced in newspapers and magazines. Yet, I still maintained my resentment of the author. After all this time, I still did not have the words to adequately explain my betrayal. I resolved to read the book again.

I was sixteen when I first visited Karachi. It was a densely packed ghetto filled with traffic and noise, chaos and graffiti. Still, the population barreled onwards, in cars, taxis, rickshaws and scooters. A blanket of dust, pollution and smog coated the city but the natives were as oblivious to it as fish are to water. Pakistan was a mountain, no a heap, or better yet a pile of dung . . . and at the very top of it were the elite.

I was too young to notice them. The fact that my relatives belonged to the professional class blinded me to what existed beyond their plane. They were doctors and engineers and lawyers. They had cars and often drivers, maids to clean their houses. When I visited Karachi I bought tailor-made clothes, went to the beauty parlor and attended wedding banquets at fancy American hotels. I began to think we were the elite. That was how naïve I was. I realized now that we only worked for the elite in hospitals, companies and governments that were run by the upper class.

Religion was everywhere. It was so pervasive than no one noticed it anymore. It made our community slightly Victorian in flavor, as we worried about missing prayers and fasting in Ramadan. Men and women were rarely friends, often favoring arranged marriages with like-minded people from suitable families. In a country where poverty and illiteracy were constant companions, what appeal was there in the material world? It was all about the afterlife.

In contrast the elite were a different species altogether. They had far-reaching wings . . . a jet-setting lifestyle. They were not shackled to the country of their birth. Access to the rest of the world via not only travel, but Internet, satellite and elite schools, meant that the rich were neither constrained by geography nor ideology. In fact, while the rest of the country observed religion, the elite remained comfortably atheist or agnostic.

This was the community that our aforementioned author came from, with his private schools and Oxford education. Like many rulers he failed to see the servant class living around him. Had he come from a more modest background I might have thought he was brave, but our author had no idea the notions his people held dear. He paid for his ignorance.

The common man never had much credence for literary technique. His betrayal was that of a child that has a cherished toy snatched out of his hands, stomped on and thrown into the sewer . . . and they came at him with blows. I understood their outrage . . . I had yet to understand mine.

I read the book again . . . the whole thing, cover to cover. . . . I found the words I did not have when I was sipping coffee with a Pakistani friend one spring afternoon. In *ghazals* a tavern is a place where one receives spiritual enlightenment; *can the same be said for a coffee house?* Here are the pearls that came sweating out of me.

After all these years I realized that my grievances fell in three parts. First, I sympathized with Muslims, whose most sacred figures were contorted and vilified. My second grievance was with the clergy for creating a PR nightmare—*and making us all look like we were crazy*. My third grievance was with the West, for not only defending the writer but glorifying him. It was this glorification that made it seem to Muslims that insensitivity towards our culture was a noble trait.

I understand as I say this that this last statement opens up more doors than it closes, but these are your issues to ponder. As for me, I have done my penance. I am no longer Atlas, with the world upon my shoulders. With a straight back I can re-visit that day where my only ambition was to catch the attention of a handsome boy. I can tell you that eventually I joined the rest of the party, chatted endlessly, and helped served the appetizers, all the while the *qawwal* sang about the pain and bliss of love and intoxication.

Source: Hasan, Farha. "The Decree." 2010. A version of this essay was published by *Asia Writes,* May 31, 2010. http://asiawrites.blogspot.com/2010/05/featured-story-decree-by-farha-hasan.html. Used with permission of the author, www.farhahasan.com.

Sri Lankan Americans

Vasugi V. Ganeshananthan, "It's All in a Name"
(1999)

Vasugi Ganeshananthan, a Sri Lankan American, wrote "It's All in a Name" for The Harvard Crimson, *Harvard University's daily student newspaper. Her essay humorously describes the difficulties people have spelling her name and explains her determination to keep it unchanged, as a symbol of her identity.*

It's all in the name.

Every day of the past 19 years: 10 syllables, 24 letters. My last name alone is five syllables and 14 letters. It's a long time to live with anything, wouldn't you say?

G as in, "God-damn!" A as in, "Are you kidding?" N as in, "No way!" E as in, "Everyone must have a hard time remembering that." S as in, "Seriously?" H as in, "Hell no—I'm calling you by your first name." "Ganesh" is actually the short form of my last name. After the first grade, when I used the short version to make things easier for everyone else—I could handle the whole thing just fine, I figured—I grew angry and thought, "Why should I make things easy for anyone? It's my name and if you can't handle it, that's your problem." I was going all out. As far as my last name was concerned, it was 14 letters or bust.

Even my parents questioned the sudden choice. My brother went all the way through high school "making things easier," despite my arguments. My dad still goes by "Dr. Ganesh." People have suggested various alternatives to me. "Use the first name solo," like Cher, Roseanne or Jackee. I roll my eyes. I don't think I bear any great similarity to any of those people. No, I want to be just like everyone else. First name, last name, middle initial—thank you for coming, thank you for going.

It's been interesting over the years. First grade: People attribute my success with the alphabet to "lots of practice." Second grade: My teacher expresses concern. People wonder if I get less time on tests because I spend so long writing my name. I assure them that my academics have not suffered as a result of my surname. I do, however, learn that if I want my name to fit in the upper right hand corner of a piece of notebook paper, I should start in the middle of the page, not four-fifths over to the

381

right, where everyone else does. Fifth grade: In an unsuccessful bid for school president, I realize that "Vote for Ganeshananthan" isn't exactly, well, pithy. And absolutely nothing rhymes with it. It also makes posters and stickers expensive. I lose. I also begin to realize that when I leave phone messages with people who don't know me, I get the comment "wow" a lot. My mother and I get a similar reaction at the grocery store when she hands over her credit card to pay.

"How do you say that?" the cashier asks politely, eyebrows shooting up.

"Gun-ay-SHAN-an-than."

"Oh." Silence. "I get it. That's long."

Thank you.

Middle school: A bunch of teachers mispronounce my name when I first arrive. They are still mispronouncing it when I leave. "You're missing the second-to-last N," I try to explain to them.

"Are you sure it's phonetic?" they ask.

Yes, I'm sure.

High school: I take the SATs and the APs and similar standardized tests for people with short names. They turn me into "Ganeshananth, Vasug" or variations thereof. Rumor has it that each test-taker gets 200 points for writing his name. Someone asks if I get extra. When I am a sophomore, one of my friends is the editor of the school paper. When stories are a few lines short, she gets her reporters to call me for a quote so they can use my name to take up space. Before graduation, I have to spend extra time with the student announcing my name so she can get it right. I catch her in the bathroom before the ceremony, practicing the fourth and fifth syllables furiously.

College: I comp *The Crimson*. One of my stories runs in *Crimson Magazine*. The column isn't wide enough for my name to fit on one line so I become what is believed to be the first person in history to have a hyphenated byline without a hyphenated name. When I look to purchase a Crimson softball jersey, Crimson President Joshua H. Simon '00 tells me he's pretty sure my last name won't fit above my number. No, not even if

they make the letters smaller and stretch them across the sleeves.

Ganeshananthan. Ganeshananthan-andonand onandonandonandon, as someone once said. But you know what? It's my name and I like it. I even like that some people think it's a pain and that I'm a pain for making them use it.

And we're not even on the topic of my first name yet. Relentlessly misspelled, mispronounced and misgendered, my first name has been an experience. Example 1: A recent job rejection letter addressed to Mr. Sugi Ganeshana- nthan. (It's hanging over my bed, the "Mr." circled in red.) Example 2: This past pre-frosh weekend, I went to dinner with three friends from high school. We were at Uno's, and the hostess had an abnormal amount of energy. The restaurant was crowded with a mixture of what looked like pre-frosh and frosh. It had been a long day and we were hungry. "Four please," I said.

"Name?" the hostess asked, looking up expectantly. I hesitated for a moment, turning back to my friends, tired and not in the mood to be called "Susie." The male among us just laughed, but one of the two women came to my rescue. "Emily," she said, stepping up.

The hostess handed her a timer with a name on it, telling us it would be about 15 minutes. We sat down and Emily shook the timer. Then she laughed. It said, "Elimy." You see my point.

But strangely, my name crops up where you would never expect to find it. Granted, I never find a Sugi mug or keychain or for that matter, a Sugi anything in the card store aisle with all the name merchandise. (There are about a zillion variations of the name Alissa, though. Alisa, Alysa, Alyssa, etc.) But there's a restaurant near Fort Lee, N.J. with my name. I've never actually been there myself, but a friend handed me an advertising card. "Fine Japanese Cuisine ... Sugi features Six Tatami Rooms accommodating up to 20 people." What? There are at least 100 Sugi's on America Online. Sugi.net is a Web site. I hope to buy sugi. org upon graduation. Or maybe ganeshananthan. com. I'm torn. I'm pretty sure no one would ever make it to ganeshananthan.com because they'd forget that pesky second-to-last "n."

So what, in the end, do I think of my name? What should I do when I get married, for example? Keep Ganeshananthan? Change? What if I marry someone with a really long last name? Oooh, I could hyphenate. The excitement!

No, I don't think so. I like my name the way it is.

Vasugi V. Ganeshananthan is a freshman in Holworthy. Have we spelled it right? The key is copy-and-paste.

Source: Ganeshananthan, Vasugi V. "It's All in a Name." *Harvard Crimson,* April 29, 1999. http://www.thecrimson .com/article/1999/4/29/endpaper-its-all-in-a-name/. © 1999 The Harvard Crimson, Inc. All rights reserved. Reprinted with permission.

Poornima Apte, "9/11: A Mother Remembers"

(2004)

The attacks on September 11, 2001, deeply affected Asian Americans. Hate crimes against South Asian Sikhs (often mistaken for being Middle Eastern Muslims) and Asian American Muslims rose dramatically after 9/11. Immigration was restricted, and immigrant rights were curtailed by the Patriot Act. The 2010 controversy over the "ground zero" Islamic Community Center made some Muslim Asian Americans question whether they would ever be accepted as citizens of their own country.

But, even more profoundly, the September 11, 2001, attacks took the lives of hundreds of Asian Americans, including Sri Lankan American Rahma Salie, who was 28 years old and seven months pregnant with her first child when she boarded American Airlines Flight 11. She was also Muslim, as was her husband, Micky Theodoridis, who converted before they were married. In the following article, Haleema Salie talks about her daughter and son-in-law and reminds us that the tragedy of 9/11 affected the entire nation, irrespective of ethnic, religious, and political differences.

NEWTON, Mass.—Three years after the Sept. 11 terrorist attacks, Haleema Salie still finds daily life challenging. Keeping busy is the only way for her to cope with the loss of her daughter and son-in-law, whose memories she is determined to preserve. "It is a normal thing for human beings, as time goes on they forget about things," she said, in the days before the anniversary. "The feelings of people the first year are very different from their feelings now. We must continue to remember the lives lost and the enormous tragedy that it was."

Haleema Salie planned on attending some of the services Boston held to remember the victims of the terrorist attacks, including ones at the Statehouse and the 9/11 memorial in the Public Garden. Her daughter, Rahma Salie, 28, and son-in-law, Micky Theodoridis, 32, were on board American Airlines Flight 11 from Boston, one of the planes that struck the World Trade Center on Sept. 11, 2001. The couple planned to attend a wedding in California, and Rahma Salie was seven months pregnant at the time. Haleema Salie says she is in touch with many of the families in the Boston area that lost loved ones in the tragedy. "They can best understand the pain that we feel," she says.

Recently, Salie got a chance to remember her daughter in a very public way, at the Democratic National Convention in Boston. There, Salie urged the audience to never forget the terrible tragedy, even as they moved forward. "Remember Sept. 11 as the day we were one," Salie urged delegates, "the day we acted as if we valued each other. . . . It was and must remain the defining moment that reminds us that what unites us is stronger than what divides us." Salie, an American citizen of Sri Lankan origin, has a son and grandchildren in Sri Lanka and a daughter here in the United States. She says she is not an outgoing person, but decided to speak at the convention when she was invited to do so by Sen. Ted Kennedy, D-Mass. "Rahma would have liked that," she said. "She liked to participate and be outgoing." Salie was unsure why she was specifically asked to address the convention. "If I didn't speak, somebody else would have," she says. Talking about the tragedy helps heal the enormous pain that it inflicted.

Salie says that families such as hers that suffered personal losses as a result of Sept. 11 were helped out by many local politicians including Senators Kennedy and Kerry. Still, she maintains that the cause is not a political one, but rather a tragedy that unites the country. She saw the attacks being remembered at the recently concluded Republican National Convention and approved of the way it was handled. "The families are just

using the political conventions as a way to remember," she says. Salie's husband, Ysuff, runs a gems business, Lanka Gems, with which Rahma used to help out; its Web site has a special tribute to Rahma and Micky. At the Montessori preschool where Salie works, a special scholarship fund has been created in Rahma's name.

"She is missed very much," Salie says sadly about Rahma. "She was not an ordinary person. She touched the lives of so many people. She was full of energy and spirit and made it a point to keep in touch with people. She was so outgoing and full of life." "I know a lot of parents say this about their children," Salie adds, "but she was very bright. She graduated cum laude from Wellesley, she was articulate and spent a lot of energy in giving her best to everything." When asked how her family copes, she says it is a challenging task. "We keep very busy, we attend to daily things, that is the only way really."

Source: Apte, Poormina. "9/11: A Mother Remembers." *INDIA New England online,* September 15, 2004. http://indianewengland.com/ME2/dirmod.asp?sid=&nm=&type=Publishing&mod=Publications::Article&mid=8F3A7027421841978F18BE895F87F791&tier=4&id=E07D820E7EDB41238A22B48BB602A0BA. Used with permission of INDIA New England.

Dilini Palamakumbura, "My Dream"

(2005)

The Sri Lanka Association of New England (SLANE) was established in Cambridge, Massachusetts, in 1998. Like many other ethnic organizations, SLANE seeks to preserve homeland cultural traditions, historical awareness, and transnational ties for American immigrant communities. When the 2004 tsunami devastated Indonesia and South Asia, SLANE organized a relief effort, sending funds to various

organizations in Sri Lanka. In the 2005 newsletter, schoolchildren in Massachusetts wrote short articles reflecting on the tsunami. Ten-year-old Dilini Palamakumbura's piece highlights the emotional bonds connecting immigrant communities to their homelands.

On December 26, 2004, not just kids, but teenagers and grown ups were swallowed by a monstrous wave that imerged from the little Indian Ocean. Those who survived have their lives, but besides them and their clothes they were wearing, they have nothing else. Some of those survivors are children. After this horrible Tsunami, some were turned into orphans.

A Tsunami (su-na-mi) is a wall of water that can be up to 40 feet. The latest one, which was in South Asia, had even disturbed the rotation of the earth! The areas affected by this disaster in South Asia are Southern India, 2/3 sides of Sri Lanka, Sumatra, Indonesia, and Southern Thailand. There has to be an earthquake to start a Tsunami. This time, the Tsunami started in Sumatra, Indonesia.

I know a town called Galle, which is located in the southern coast of Sri Lanka. I remember a bus station, a train station and lots of buildings in the center of Galle. After the Tsunami, the remains of the railroad looked like a big, twisted ladder. The buildings were either gone or completely destroyed. People who were waiting for buses and trains were swallowed up as well. There was a cricket field near the bus station. It was one of the most picturesque cricket fields in the world. After the Tsunami, the field was flooded and buses were floating at the surface of the water. The players were nowhere to be seen. You might think the Tsunami would have destroyed every thing. But the two Buddha statues that overlook the police station and the train station were left without a scratch while everything around the statues was destroyed.

I feel really bad for the kids affected by the Tsunami, because most of them lost their families and houses. The kids were scared, lonely and confused. They are too small to understand what just happened. Even bigger kids didn't know what a Tsunami was.

Those kids have nothing but themselves. To make it all worse, some don't see any familiar faces in the shelters. Every thing that was part of their lives was washed away by the waves. I feel very sad, so I want to do something about it. I want to get lots of baskets for the kids. In those baskets would be money, clothes, backpacks, pens, pencils and much much more. The only thing I can't give them in their baskets in their parents. With the school supplies, they can go back to school. With the money, they can buy new clothes. I hope they can find some relatives to take care of them or some good families to adopt them.

I think my dream is already coming true. Some organizations like Sri Lanka Association of New England, the New York Buddhist Temple etc. are collecting donations from people in the USA. Another organization made Tsunami key chains and I helped sell them. Some of the members of these organizations have already gone to Sri Lanka with lots of supplies. I am also planning to visit Sri Lanka this summer. I want to go to "Sambodhi Lama Nivasaya"—home for disabled kids, in Galle. The building was flooded and destroyed as a result of the Tsunami, now they are rebuilding it. I want to give a blanket to each of those kids, and then they will feel a little better after losing all their things and some friends. I want to visit other shelters and schools too. After I give a basket to every kid, I hope they will be happy to know that some people care about them. If the kids become happy again, that would surely be my dreams come true.

Source: Palamakumbura, Dilini. "My Dream." SLANE. NOW, Sri Lanka Association of New England, 2005. http://www.slaneusa.org/SLANE.NOW%20Children's %20Page.pdf. Reprinted with permission.

Jeffery Boonmee, Interview by David Tanner
(1995)

Jeffery Boonmee was born in Thailand and lived there until he was an adolescent. His divorced mother met an American serviceman and immigrated to the United States in 1973; two years later, she brought her teenage sons over. The family joined the Church of the Latter-Day Saints (LDS) shortly after the children arrived in Las Vegas. David Tanner, working with Brigham Young University's Charles Redd Center for Western Studies, interviewed Boonmee as part of the LDS Asian American Oral History Project in 1995. In the following excerpts from the interview, Boonmee describes his own conversion experience and provides an interesting reflection on how different Asian and Asian American communities have been involved in the church.

T: Tell me about where you grew up and some of your early family memories.

B: I grew up for the first eleven years in a little village up in Ubon, [Thailand]. My mom got divorced from my dad when I was about seven years old. . . . It wasn't until 1972 or 1973 that she met my current stepfather, David Kapps. She came to the United States through my stepfather. She came in 1973, and then towards the end of 1974 she went back and got my brother and me. . . . We came to Las Vegas at the end of 1975. At that time, we weren't LDS. Once or twice when we were in Thailand the missionaries came over to our house and taught my parents a couple of times. I was still young, so I didn't sit in on it. But I do remember seeing the missionaries coming over. We never joined the Church over there.

We came here in 1975 to Las Vegas. It happened to be that my dad needed some help legally. He went to this law office and met this lawyer. He told my dad that he'd help him out. He learned that my parents had taken a couple of lessons. He made a deal with my dad that if he needed some help that my dad would have to finish up the missionary lessons. They started taking them again. A couple of months later my father, my mom, and my brothers and sisters were baptized. I wasn't. I was twelve or thirteen years old, and I didn't feel like I should. I waited a couple of months before I was baptized . . . .

After we got baptized, we always looked toward Zion. Salt Lake City was the place where we wanted to go. My dad put in a request to see if he could move here to Hill [Air Force Base]. He did receive the order. They came here before I did. I was kind of wild in high school. I basically dropped off from the Church for about a year. They moved

387

here. I found out after about eight months that I couldn't live alone without them, so I moved.

I finished my high school here at Layton High School in 1980. That was when I started going back to church. I wanted to find out exactly what I wanted to do after high school. Like any other high school graduate, I really didn't know what I needed to be doing. I also wanted to find out whether or not I wanted to be a member of the Church. I wasn't really converted at that time.

Three or four months after I graduated I decided that instead of being a fence sitter I wanted to make the real commitment. I told myself that I would read the Book of Mormon and get that finished. If I was going to believe it, I would believe it at that time. If not, I would let it be. I started reading. It only took me a week to finish the Book of Mormon. I actually prayed. The next morning I found out that it was the right church.

I never told anyone this, but I told my parents what had happened after I prayed. I don't know if this should be recorded. It was something that came to me in a dream. It was something that was really impressive. The next morning I woke up. I started crying and screaming at my parents. I ran over and knocked on their door. I told them what had happened. My step dad came running. He asked me, "What happened? Why are you crying?" I started telling him what had happened the night before.

At that time I told my dad that I wanted to go on a mission. That same day we went and got the paper work. We got it sent in. I requested and asked if I could go to Thailand in that paper. I didn't think I could go. My dad warned me that it wasn't necessarily that they would send me to Thailand. That was fine. A couple of months later it came. I was called to Thailand Bangkok Mission . . .

T: What do you see as some of the advantages and disadvantages of a Thai Lao branch?

B: I think an advantage of the branch is for the older generation. What happens is that the older generation knows they need to learn English, but it's not going to happen. With a lot of the things that we teach in the Church, the language that we use is most of the time an old English. They have a hard time understanding English as it is. If we try to teach them doctrine, that doesn't happen. On top of that they're new converts. To get them to really understand and strengthen themselves spiritually, we really need a branch that will teach them in their own native language.

It's a disadvantage for a younger generation. The younger generation needs to get together with the kids their own age that are active in the Church so that they can socialize with the kids that are active in the Church and learn the gospel with those kids. That's the reason why we decided to stay here so that my daughter can go to church and be strengthened by her peers. In the Laotian branch a family doesn't have the strength to support the family as far as spiritual strength. When the children go over there, they really don't have anybody to look up to. Therefore, they just run around the hallway. Then they grow up into teenagers, and they don't go to church anymore.

On the other hand, when my girl goes to church here, she has a friend. I told her, "You've got to find a best friend there and grow up together." That way it's a strengthening thing. The old saying is if you put matches together and try to break it, it's hard. That's what I'm trying to do with my daughter.

As far as values go, I think the Church and the values of Thai culture overlap quite a bit except for multiple marriages. That is a little bit different. The Orient are social people. They don't usually get divorced. The wife understands that for some reason.

T: For the Thai people that join the Church what are some of the biggest challenges they have in staying active in the Church in the United States?

B: Most of the Thai people that come to the United States are really strong. Probably only one-half to one percent go inactive. Maybe it's not relevant for the Thai, but for the Laotians it's relevant. When Thai people came to the United States, they come by choice. They had to work for it. The Laotians or Vietnamese came here because they had no choice. They came here because the United States brought them here because of physical war. They really didn't have the financial support to get here. A lot of them used the Church for physical needs. The reason why they went into the Church is a little different than the way Thai people went into the Church. That makes a lot of difference in how strong they are in the Church spiritually.

T: How have you been accepted by Caucasian Latter-day Saints since you've been in the Church?

B: I have been really lucky in that way. Part of it is because I'm outgoing. Not too many people are that way. I don't let things bother me for too long. A lot of it is my training and my experiences that I've gone through. I've always been very independent. I lived with my grandmother, and my parents were never there for me. I basically took care of my brother after

I was seven years old. My grandmother was already old, and there were just three of us. I don't let things get bogged down and bog me down. I think part of my being here and being successful in the things is that I don't let things bother me.

T: Thanks for sharing your stories and experiences.

Source: Jeffery Boonmee Oral History, interviewed by David Tanner, April 15, 1995, LDS Asian American Oral History Project, Charles Redd Center for Western Studies, L. Tom Perry Special Collections, Harold B. Lee Library, Brigham Young University. Used with permission of the Charles Redd Center.

Pueng Vongs, "Unrest in the Homeland Awakens Thai American Community" (2006)

In the first half of 2006, Thailand's political state of affairs disintegrated. The Royal Thai Army agitated against the populist prime minister, Thaksin Shinawatra—who also had conflicts with King Bhumibol Adulyadej; the urban middle and elite classes vied with the rural poor; and, in September, a military junta staged a bloodless coup and overthrew the government. The unrest reverberated far beyond Thailand. Expatriates and immigrants in the United States closely followed events in their homeland. Political divisions in Thailand were mirrored in the United States, and Thai Americans, fully engaged and invested in Thai politics, protested in Los Angeles and San Francisco. The following article, filed six months before the coup, describes how events in Thailand affected the Thai American community, reviving interest in homeland politics and sparking a new engagement with American participatory democracy.

The relentless protests threatening to topple Thailand's government have triggered public demonstrations by Thai Americans, a departure for a community that tends to avoid conflict and stay out of political affairs in their adopted homeland.

"The (Thai) government thinks they have absolute power, but they have to understand that power comes from the people," says Jiab Tongsopit, a graduate student at UC Santa Cruz who joined a protest in San Francisco last week.

In Los Angeles, more than 100 Thais have gathered at weekly protests in front of the Thai consulate, donning the bright yellow and red sashes worn by their compatriots back home to demand the resignation of Prime Minister Thaksin Shinawatra. Los Angeles is the hub of the Thai immigrant community in America, with approximately 200,000 Thai residents. Similar demonstrations have erupted in Chicago and Las Vegas.

Tens of thousands have taken to the streets in Thailand in the past two months, in Western-style mass demonstrations calling for Shinawatra's ouster. Mounting corruption allegations exploded in January, when the prime minister profited $1.9 billion, tax-free, from the sale of his family's wireless business to a Singaporean company. The protests are the largest the country has seen in 14 years.

Highly visible protests are unusual for Thai Americans, who tend to focus on achieving economic security. Furthermore, when times are tough, Thais' Buddhist nature preaches patience. When other Asian immigrant groups such as Chinese, Japanese and Vietnamese demonstrated for better housing, health care and political rights, most Thai Americans remained on the sidelines.

Behind the scenes, however, is a community actively building temples, proliferating Thai restaurants nationwide and donating quietly to political candidates in the United States.

Now the sale of a top wireless company in Thailand to Singapore appears to have fueled nationalistic fervor in Thais in America.

"We want to see Thai business returned to the Thai people. We want Singapore out," says Montree Chaisorn, head of the new, Westminster, Calif.-based Thai People's Alliance for Democracy. Chaisorn, a nurse who has lived in the United States for 32 years, says he participated in protests against the government as a student in Thailand. According to him, the sale of the wireless company is just the beginning of Shinawatra's illegal activity. Shinawatra also illegally granted Singaporean troops a long-term lease to train in Thailand, Chaisorn says.

But Thais who support Shinawatra are just as passionate as those in the anti-government camp. They too have been staging frequent protests in Los Angeles, and have collected 500 signatures and $4,000 to bolster Shinawatra's campaign. Many fear that ongoing unrest will shake their homeland's economic stability.

"I am concerned about what this will do to the Thai economy," says Rosalynn Carmen, a Thai business owner in San Diego. "Right now Asia is booming. China is doing well and Vietnam is coming back. If Thailand continues to be unstable, it will throw us way out."

"Instead of demonstrating, we should be focused on appointing a council to tackle corruption," Carmen says.

The competition between the two sides is so fervent that at a weekend Buddhist Dharma talk at Griffith Park in Los Angeles, the anti- and pro-Shinawatra camps had an intense standoff and segregated themselves from each other.

Greater access to information outside of government-controlled media in Thailand has also helped galvanize Thai activists in the United States. "The people here look at the Internet, read Thai newspapers published here or watch satellite television every day to get information people do not have in Thailand," says Paison Promnui, editor of Asian Pacific News, a Thai weekly.

Thai Americans are eager to try out new democratic ideals and tools by staging protests and voting. Shinawatra is the first democratically elected leader to last a full term in the country.

On April 2, both sides will weigh in at a provisional election to decide Shinawatra's future. Overseas Thais will be counted in the vote. In a preliminary election on March 17, Thais lined up in front of the Thai consulate in Los Angeles hours before the voting booths were opened.

Some Thai observers in the United States say that the renewed interest in elections in Thailand will encourage more Thais to participate in the American democratic process.

"People from Thailand have two houses. One here and one in Thailand, and when they are 60, they go back. But this will change," Chaisorn says. Thais, he says, are already seeking ways to become more visible. They have created a scholarship fund for a Thai human rights lawyer, and successfully pushed for the appointment of a Thai commissioner as part of Los Angeles Mayor Antonio Villaraigosa's team.

"We pay taxes here for many years and we want to have a greater say in what happens in America," Chaisorn says.

Source: Vongs, Pueng. "Unrest in the Homeland Awakens Thai American Community." March 29, 2006. Imdiversity website. http://www.imdiversity.com/Villages/Asian/world_international/pns_thai_unrest_0306.asp. Used with permission of the author.

Dionne Jirachaikitti, "Thai American Organizing and the Berkeley Thai Temple"

(2009)

Since the early 1990s, the volunteers at the Wat Mongkolratanaram Thai Buddhist temple in Berkeley, California, have run a Sunday brunch to help support the temple. People can buy donation coupons in exchange for hot trays of homemade Thai food. On Sundays, there are already lines outside the temple as early as 9 a.m. Because monks cannot earn money or accumulate wealth, Buddhism calls on the faithful to earn merit and build goodwill for their next reincarnation by supporting monks and temples. For the volunteers, running the brunch is not only a religious duty but also a way to build ties with the local community and maintain cultural traditions. However, some of the temple's neighbors grew tired of the steadily increasing crowds and noise; and tensions mounted further in 2008, when the temple applied for a permit to build a bigger sanctuary and expand buildings and parking on its property. About a dozen angry neighbors soon discovered the temple had an outdated zoning permit that only allowed it to serve food to the public three times a year. They sought to shut down the Sunday brunches. The issue became a rallying point for Bay Area Thai Americans, civil rights organizations, and students at the University of California–Berkeley. After months of public controversy, the Berkeley City Council voted in favor of the Thai temple's right to hold their Sunday brunch.

In the blog post here, Dionne Jirachaikitti, a community advocate in the Juvenile Justice and Education Project at the Asian Law Caucus and an organizer with the Save the Thai Temple collective, recounts how the local Thai American community became galvanized and organized in support of the temple.

On September 22, 2009, the Berkeley City Council voted 9 to 0 in support of the Berkeley Thai Temple. The vote came as a relief to the Thai community in the Bay Area who had been waiting for over a year to know whether they would be able to continue their tradition of merit-making in Berkeley.

The Berkeley Thai Temple is oldest of the three Thai Buddhist temples in the Bay Area. As a second generation Thai American, I spent most of my childhood at Wat Buddhanusorn Thai Temple in Fremont. Most of my weekends and summer vacations were spent at the temple learning Thai language and traditional dance and practicing Buddhism. Like most of my Thai American peers, temple was where we learned about our culture and connected with the Thai community.

It was a shock then to find out that the temple in Berkeley was being threatened. Although I had not frequented the Berkeley temple when I was younger, I was a four year resident of Berkeley where I attended UC Berkeley and was highly involved with city affairs as a student leader. What struck me most about this issue was the blatant contradiction between Berkeley's reputation as a liberal and inclusive city, whose history is full of movements promoting equal rights, and the targeting of a small minority community known for being peaceful.

The neighbors had concerns about parking, noise and odors; all of which the temple tried to address by putting up signs to not block driveways, securing extra parking at a nearby lot, and moving food preparation indoors, just to name a few. It became increasingly clear that neighbors wanted to push the temple out completely when all of the temple's compromises were met with more and more requests. In the four hearings before the Zoning Adjustments Board (ZAB), neighbors complained that our food smells bad, the noise is intolerable and several other comments that have me cringe and question whether Berkeley is as accepting as it is known to be.

At the hearing on September 25, 2008, a woman likened the temple to an "American Capitalist Organization" that expanded like McDonalds and alluded to the temple's Buddhist shrine as the "golden arches." The woman went on to say that the food was "almost addicting like *Supersize Me,* the movie" and asserted that "everybody here [in support of the temple] eats their food and everyone against them doesn't eat their food." In truth, hundreds of supporters signed petitions, wrote letters and called city council members reminding them that the Berkeley Thai Temple is an integral part of the city and provides a service of not just food, but community building and cross-cultural learning for all residents.

To many Thais in the Bay Area, especially first generation Thai elders, the temple is the only place they feel at home, where they can speak Thai, eat Thai food, and practice Thai Buddhism. To a new generation of Thai Americans, this issue marked the first time second generation Thais in America have come together to organize for a cause. The Save the Thai Temple (STTT) collective that came together to advocate for the temple spanned generations and involved community organizations like the Asian Law Caucus.

During a hearing, a Thai woman passionately explained that, "Berkeley is a very unique town. I am *so* proud [to be here]. This city is the center of the universe for me. And Thailand is my home country. To join the two of them together is a blessing."

I feel the same way about the Berkeley Thai temple, except that Thailand was not where I was born and my memories of Thailand are only of a few trips I have had there to see my family. Instead, the Bay Area is my home and Thailand is where my roots are. The Thai temple is where I can connect to my culture and community in a way that I cannot do anywhere else. To have a place like the Thai temple to go to while growing up was truly a blessing in my life and hopefully will be for many young Thai Americans to come.

Source: Jirachaikitti, Dionne. "Thai American Organizing and the Berkeley Thai Temple." *Asian Law Caucus blog,* October 8, 2009. http://arcof72.com/2009/10/08/512/.

Club O'Noodles, "Laughter from the Children of War," Performance Program

(1996)

Founded in 1993, Club O'Noodles is a Vietnamese American theater troupe dedicated to bridging the gap between Vietnamese and other communities and enriching the diversity of American culture through performance art. The group also encourages innovative and socially conscious community involvement through its performance art and strives to nurture and support young performers. The following excerpt is from a program for their show "Laughter from the Children of War," performed at the South Coast Repertory in Costa Mesa, California, from June 21 to 23, 1996. The excerpt introduces Club O'Noodles and gives some background on some of its earliest members.

About Club O'Noodles

Club O'Noodles celebrates the Vietnamese American culture by providing socially conscious, alternative entertainment ranging from hilarious comedy to serious drama, combining music, dance and theatre. Club O'Noodles is insightful, provocative, and outrageous entertainment for the whole family. It also provides opportunities for emerging artists to express their talent in a nurturing environment.

The Noodlers

Chau Dao joined Club O'Noodles while searching to learn more about the Vietnamese culture. Through this process, Chau has realized that young Vietnamese are talented not just academically, but also artistically. "I want people to see me simply as a human being. Life is beautiful when it is not so complicated." Chau is a Math major at Scripps College.

Uyen Huynh is an aspiring actress and singer. She is one of the founding members of Club O'Noodles. She has proven herself to be a "Cam, Ky, Thi, Hoa and Van Vo Ven Toan" kind of woman. Since she liberated herself from slave duties in the U.S. Army, she can do a hundred push-ups easily. Uyen is a Psychology major at UC Irvine.

Tri Le says: "I have no inhibitions when I am playing and rehearsing with friends in Club

O'Noodles. I can be more open and comfortable with the Noodlers." Tri thought that he was going to give up acting to get a real job, but fate has it that he is stuck with Club O'Noodles. "We (Vietnamese) have overcome many obstacles being a minority in this foreign land, and the experience of working on *Laughter* has been like a very fun therapy session for me."

Jay Heip Mai, artist sky ocean blue juice set activist friend lover silence hunger loving thirst brother son green meadow wild sun flowers hot pissing river desert sunset dancing waves potentiality risking HIV-+? pink peace painful wanting fishsauce pho fire kissing queer home flaming body tenderly tough calming roughness fragile smooth shell AIDS Americaness-Vietnamese breathing deep wholeness needing inside-out OUT NOW!

Minh Do Nguyen was born in Saigon in 1975 and lived in Viet Nam for 13 years. Minh came to the United States in 1989 and has lived in Mission Viejo ever since. A graduate of Trabuco Hills High School, Minh is currently attending UC Irvine and majoring in Drama. "I believe Club O'Noodles will provide me the experience I need in my future."

Journey Pham considers himself a modernized and not Americanized person. "Working on *Laughter* has made me more aware of myself and of the Vietnamese culture. I didn't realize how dramatically and profoundly the War has affected me in so many ways." Journey just graduated from CSU Northridge with an Art Degree, with a minor in Biology. "This show is

dedicated to my parents. I will always love you Vicky."

Phuong Pham feels that *Laughter* is a personal, silent movement which converts hidden pains and sufferings into expressions of strength and triumph. Phuong recently graduated from UC Irvine with majors in Women's Studies and Criminology, Law and Society.

Huy Tran feels Club O'Noodles has allowed him to reach deep into his soul and to confront difficult issues about himself and about the Vietnamese community. Huy is a graduate of UC Irvine in Political Science and is currently teaching at a junior high school in Anaheim.

Tuan Tran received his bachelor degree in Theatre Arts at Westmond College in Santa Barbara and is getting his masters in Acting at UCLA. He has appeared in a supporting role in Oliver Stone's *Heaven and Earth,* and in the upcoming Emilio Estevez film *The War at Home*. Tuan also produced and starred in his own feature film called *Bastards*. "This show is dedicated to my Grandmother."

Xuan Vu is a recent graduate from UC Irvine in Political Science and Women's Studies with a minor in Asian American Studies. "I believe in hope, and in changes. I used to repulse from, turn away from talking about the War and its consequences, but through my involvement with *Laughter,* I have learned to deal with these issues in a productive and positive way."

Source: Special Collections and Archives. The UC Irvine Libraries. http://www.calisphere.universityofcalifornia.edu. Reprinted with permission.

Hi-Tek Demonstration Flyer, "America Has Freedom"
(1999)

The largest Vietnamese American protest in U.S. history was sparked in 1999 when Hi-Tek Video owner Truong Van Tran hung a picture of Ho Chi Minh in his store. Vietnamese Americans in Westminster, California, many of whom had fled the communists in the fall of Saigon, were outraged, and the incident sparked massive demonstrations and violence against Tran. Meanwhile, second-generation Vietnamese American students from Irvine had come to protest presidential hopeful John McCain's use of the word gook *to describe his North Vietnamese captors. From the students' perspective,* gook *was a racially charged term applied to all Asians, regardless of ethnicity; they wore shirts reading "American gooks" to highlight McCain's insensitivity. However, the first-generation Vietnamese saw* gook *as a term reserved for communists and were outraged at the students' appropriation of the word. They spit on the students, hit and pinched them, and pushed them out onto the street. These incidents led to a candlelight vigil involving thousands of Vietnamese Americans. Both old and young participated in the event, helping to heal the rifts in the community.*

The following demonstration flyer from the Hi-Tek protest shows that for many Vietnamese Americans, the fear and hatred of communism was still a powerful and motivating force 20 years after escaping the Viet Cong.

***** AMERICA HAS FREEDOM *****

***** YOU (TRAN VAN TRUONG & COMMUNIST GANGSTER) TAKE ADVANTAGE OF THE FREESPEECH OF THE UNITED STATE'S CONSTITUTION. TO HANG THE TRAIDER & KILLER HO CHI MINH'S PORTRAIT AND THE COMMUNIST'S FLAG UNDER THIS FLAG WHICH COST:

+) 58,000 AMERICAN SOLDIERS DIED TO PROTECT THE FREEDOM FOR VIETNAM.

+) MILLIONS AND MILLIONS VIETNAMESES REFUGEES LEFT THEIR HOMELAND.

+) HUNDREDS OF THOUSANDS VIETNA-MESES DIED IN THE OCEAN AND THE JUN-GLE (VIET, CAMBODIA, THAI AND LOAS)

+) THOUSANDS AND THOUSANDS OF INOCENT GIRLS WERE RAPED ON THE WAY TO FIND * FREEDOM *

+) HUNDREDS OF THOUSANDS REPBULIC SOLDIERS DIED IN THE RE-EDUCATION CAMPS WHICH ARE THE NEW NAME "KILLING CAMP" BECAUSE THEY MUST WORK LIKE ANIMAL AND DON'T HAVE ANOUGH FOOD TO EAT.

***** YOU (TRUONG & COMMUNIST GANGSTER) ARE LIER FROM THE BEGINNNING WHEN YOU CAME IN THIS COUNTRY WITH "THE VIETNAMESE REFUGEE." YOU JUST CAME HERE WITH THE ORDER OF THE VIETNAMESE'S COMMUNIST GOVERNMENT *****

***** YOU (TRUONG & COMMUNIST GANGSTER) ARE THE BIGGEST LIER IN THE COMMUNIST THEORY. YOURS ARE JUST REPEATED THE SAME TRICT "ROBBING AND CRYING THE SAME TIME" *****

***** YOU (TRUONG & COMMUNIST GANG-STER) WANT MANY FREE IN THIS FREEDOM

COUNTRY. WE THINK YOURS (TRUONG & COMMUNIST GANGSTER) SHOULD GO BACK VIETNAM AND LET OUR HOMELAND FREEDOM FIRST THEN COME BACK HERE AND WE WILL DISCUSS WITH YOUR *****

***** WE JUST WANT YOU (TRUONG & COMMUNIST GANGSTER) TO BE A NORMAL HUMANITY. NOT SAVAGE SPIRIT IN THE BIG STRONG ANIMAL BODY TO KILLING INOCENT PEOPLE.

+) NEW YEAR 1968 AT HUE (THOUSANDS & THOUSANDS PERSON IN THE SAME GRAVE.

+) SUMMER 1972 ON THE FREEWAY 1 AT HAI LANG, QUANG TRI

+) SUMMER 1975 BAMETHUOT. AND SO ON . . . *****

TO THE UNITED STATE GOVERNMENT

+) FBI, CIA, INS HOW DO YOU THINK THIS SITUATION

FREEDOM & ANTI-COMMUNIST

Source: Special Collections and Archives. The UC Irvine Libraries. http://www.calisphere.universityofcalifornia.edu.

Tuan-Rishard F. Schneider, "Adoptee Connection"

(2001)

In 1975, when he was six months old, Tuan-Rishard Schneider was adopted from Vietnam by a family from Minneapolis, Minnesota. Up until the Vietnam War, most Asian adoptees in the United States came from Korea. In the following excerpt from his essay "Adoptee Connection," Schneider discusses the process of how he gradually came to terms with his identity as a Vietnamese adoptee, culminating with his (former) job at the Children's Home Society of Minnesota.

Saigon, Viet Nam, 1975, and the Communists are taking control of the South. People are fleeing the streets, their homes, and their country. A young infant named Nguyen Ngoc Tuan was being prepared by an adoption agency to leave his country. Only 6 months old, Tuan didn't know what lay ahead of him. He and many other children who were infants during the war were released and placed for adoption by their parents. Some know why they were given up and some don't . . . and never will. But the general purpose was to make sure that the child was given a better chance to survive and live in a country that wasn't as war-torn as Viet Nam. Mothers' hearts were broken, releasing and placing their children up for adoption; records of families were lost, confusion was rampant, and parents were sending their children to a better and safer place, any way they possibly could.

I, Nguyen Ngoc Tuan, now 26-year old Tuan-Richard F. Schneider of Minneapolis, MN, don't remember anything from my months in Viet Nam. The only thing I know now is that my past has many unanswered questions, and I plan on uncovering the answers.

Since my arrival, the most general idea of what people might think of us adoptees is that things are all right now; they aren't. For 25 years I lived in the shadow of adopted Koreans. There were always support groups, weekly summer camps, and other Korean adoptees for others to talk with. Being a

Vietnamese adoptee, I never knew of one other adoptee from Viet Nam. I grew up feeling alone and totally different. I lied about who I was, or what ethnicity I was to fit in. I had on a lot of features that could be described as either Asian, Latin . . . etc. . . .

Growing up, other Vietnamese people didn't really associate me with themselves. I had white parents, white friends, and a sister who was an adoptee from Korea. My facial features aren't exactly similar to my other Vietnamese friends, so the assumption I was Korean was the first prejudgment (thus living in the shadow of the adopted Korean; also, Minnesota has the highest adopted Korean rate in the United States). . . .

Growing up, I was like any other kid. I wanted to fit in and belong. So many times was I teased about my eyes; skin color, straight black hair and anything to get me pissed off. As a little kid, you don't see these things, unless something doesn't look normal. I had white parents, a sister that was Asian looking, and a German last name with my original Vietnamese first name. Put those all together and confuse a little kid and they'll ask a million questions and tease what they don't understand. Growing up I accepted it and dealt with it my own way. I kept the anger inside, but through sports I was able to release the anger. Soccer, martial arts, hockey, rugby, anything basically physical I could do, I would participate in. After awhile I got really good at these sports. As I got into high school, I noticed the other Vietnamese students didn't really have anything to say to me, as I didn't to them. Both our worlds were completely different, white middle class parents raised me. Parents who chose to stay in the inner city of Minneapolis, MN so I would be exposed to the diverse cultures around me. Not knowing that the one culture that now means the most to me wouldn't accept me.

At the time it didn't really bother me until a racial fight broke out in school, the Vietnamese students against the black students. At that time in high school, I was at my peak of performance as an athlete. I was a lot bigger than the other Vietnamese students were, taller, and stockier, which they saw to

an advantage in a fight. As my black friends saw me with the Vietnamese students, and the Vietnamese students seeing me with the black students, I was then confronted. "Whose side are you on!" I was raised to become friends with everyone, and at that time I knew I had to choose. I chose to stay home as the school expelled the fighting students, as it was not safe for me to attend in fear of both sides attacking me. While at home, for the first time I was completely confused and scared. Confused that I let my Vietnamese people down, and also my friends and scared about never choosing the right side. But no one should have to choose for violence. . . .

[Twenty-five years later, at a reunion for adoptees from Viet Nam, Schneider finally felt a sense of belonging.] The cleansing all started from a handshake from a Russell, then Mark, then Chris, then Jono, then Josh, and then others followed. For once in my life, I stood alone, but more loved and accepted than I have ever felt. A feeling I will never forget and a feeling that brings joyful tears to my eyes each time I think of it. . . .

I now have a new job. A job I wake up in the morning and love going to: I work for the Children's Home Society of Minnesota, the same agency that I was adopted through when I was younger. I don't get to work directly with adoption, but as one of the very active and verbally proud Vietnamese adoptees that work there, I do get all the concerns and questions working with Vietnamese adoptees. As the Executive Assistant to the Vice President, I do get to get a better hands-on feeling of what it's like to work for a very successful (NPO) non-profit organization. And from this experience I have been incorporating my knowledge and education to help VAN and the other organizations out. I finally found my ideal job that ties my full time work within my extra-curricular activities and involvement within the Vietnamese and adopted Vietnamese community.

Source: Schneider, Tuan-Rishard F. "Adoptee Connection." 2001. Adopt Vietnam website. http://www.adoptvietnam. org/adoption/babylift-tuanschneider.html. Used with permission of the author.

Anh Do and Hieu Tran Pham, "Camp Z30-D: The Survivors: 1975–2001"

(2001)

Approximately 165,000 Vietnamese citizens—men, women, and children—died in the reeducation camps after the communists took over Vietnam in 1975. The article "Camp Z30-D: The Survivors: 1975–2001," published in the Orange County Register *in 2001, recounts the stories of six former prisoners of reeducation camp Z30-D who later settled in Orange County, California, south of Los Angeles. In the following excerpt, Dong Nga Thi Ha, a resident of Garden Grove and small business owner, tells how she bribed a guard at her husband's prison so they could be together.*

Dong Nga Thi Ha, "Hong Nga"
Age, city: 50, Garden Grove
Family: Widow with two sons
Education: Graduated from high school
Jailed: Four years

Position when entered prison: TV anchorwoman for the South Vietnamese government

Now: Owner of Garden Grove discount goods store. She hopes to make a comeback on Vietnamese radio or TV.

All during that first summer in Camp Z30-D, the female prisoners smile at one another, silently acknowledging the wonderful things about to happen, even amid the horrors of building their own concentration camp.

When will the first one take place? How will they handle it? Is it possible to nurture fragile little lives in the confines of a bamboo jail?

Several of the women around Hong Nga, 24, are expecting—already pregnant when the summons ordering re-education confinement arrived months earlier.

"How do we nurse?" one wonders.

"Where can we find more food?" questions another.

"What names will we give them?" asks a third.

Despite their swelling stomachs, they dig trenches, raise pigs, plant corn under the harsh sun.

Hong Nga, a captain in the South Vietnamese army who anchored the official evening news, watches them in the quiet twilight, wishing for a child of her own. She offers to take on their heavy chores, carrying water buckets and hauling big loads.

Sometimes she thinks of her own childhood, when, born as Dong Nga Thi Ha, she would sit for hours by the radio or television, listening to her favorite stars, mimicking their speech and aspiring to be a face and voice for her nation.

As the hot, long summer days grow shorter, the women start to have their babies. Accompanied by guards, they leave the camp overnight and give birth with the help of midwives. They return with their babies the next day.

New members are not given extra food, but other inmates readily offer theirs. They are allowed one to two months to nurse, and then they return to the fields either taking their babies with them or leaving them in a makeshift nursery.

Hong Nga, one day, gives up her bed slot to a tiny girl with a head of soft curls. She prepares warm vegetable broths, rocks crying babies back to sleep, changes thin cloth diapers. Sometimes, when there is nothing else, they cover the infants' bottoms with the tattered fabric of their own prisoner's stripes or the leaves of a banana tree. . . .

As the years pass, the Camp Z30-D babies grow into toddlers, then young children. Hong Nga feels her life slipping away. Her husband, a once-strong army captain, has written her, saying he is weak and sick in jail in the North. One day, Hong Nga hears from relatives that he has heart trouble. She fears he will die before she can have a baby to carry on his name, Ngot Van Le. She aches for someone to sing to. Then she would have a reason to go on living.

Finally, in 1979, Hong Nga is released from Camp Z30-D. She immediately sets out to fulfill her dream of having a family. But she discovers there is nothing left of her old home. First, she sells scraps on the streets of Saigon to keep a roof over her head and her mother's. Then she pawns all her valuables. After nine months of struggling, she scrapes enough together to buy a ticket to the North to see her husband.

At last, she is on the train to Hanoi. The 40-hour trip gives her time to think. She wonders if her husband, Ngot, still has that broad smile and thick, jet-black hair.

In Hanoi, she boards a bus headed into the mountains. She clutches gifts of rice, medicine, dried fish, sugar—and crumpled bills.

Finally, they gaze at one another across a prison table. He can't stop coughing. She fights back tears.

"He looked like a ghost with his sunken eyes, missing teeth and gray hair," she says. "I had to reach out and touch him, to make sure he was still alive."

After five years of separation, they have 15 minutes to talk. A guard stands at their side. Ngot looks into his wife's face, eyes shimmering with tears.

As the visit ends, Hong Nga makes the move she has been thinking about for years. She slips 10,000 dong, the equivalent of 80 cents, into the hands of the man carrying the rifle. He closes his fist. Hong Nga and Ngot spend the night in a "guest cottage" a few miles from the center of the camp.

The couple shut the door behind them. Hong Nga has carefully timed the trip so she is ovulating. She glances around: dirt floor, bamboo walls, a ceiling of thatched palm fronds . . .

"I want to have a child," she blurts out.

"Are you crazy?" he asks.

"Get your head together. Think of all the reasons not to."

Neighbors will accuse her of infidelity. Even if they believe her story, the baby will bear the stigma of having a prisoner for a father. And just how does she plan to raise a child when she has barely enough money to feed herself?

"But that's why we must take this chance. There might be no second chance. Please don't you remember the dream on our wedding day? We were meant to be a family."

"But what will you do with them when I am gone?"

"I don't know," she replies.

"How can you bear the burden of being an only parent?"

"I don't know. But I don't want to think about that now. I am not changing my mind."

Her husband grows silent. She blows out the kerosene candle . . .

Nine months pass, and Hong Nga gives birth to a baby boy. She names him Khanh. The following year she returns to the prison. The couple conceives another son, Duc.

"When I look at my boys, I remember the irony of hope being conceived in prison, a hopeless place," Hong Nga says. "It reminds me of a poetry collection titled 'Flowers From Hell.'"

In 1993, Hong Nga, her sons—then 11 and 12—and her newly freed husband immigrate to Orange County through a program for former South Vietnamese military veterans.

She borrows money from friends, buys a sewing machine and sets up business in the dining room of their nearly empty apartment in Garden Grove. A statue of the Virgin Mary looks on as she mends old clothes and cuts patterns for new ones.

But the years in prison continue to take their toll. Her husband, Ngot, grows weaker by the month. Hong Nga holds his thinning shivering body, whispering words of encouragement through dark nights. Eventually, he collapses from a heart attack and dies in the hospital six months after setting foot on U.S. soil.

"Khanh, Duc, and I made a vow at his funeral," Hong Nga says. "We promised that his sons would take his place. They would be living memories to the hope that gave them life right in prison."

Two years ago, Hong Nga saved enough money to start her own business, T&N Super Discount, a variety story in Garden Grove. Almost every week, she visits her husband's remains at Westminster Memorial Cemetery. The glass case with his ashes is graced with yellow lilies and a rosary.

Her sons now are working to fulfill one of their father's dreams: that they graduate from college.

Living with their mother and grandmother, they take classes at Orange Coast and Golden West colleges, both pursuing degrees in computer science.

Source: The Orange County Register. April 29, 2004. Special Collections and Archives. The UC Irvine Libraries. http://www.calisphere.universityofcalifornia.edu/.

Trista Joy Goldberg, "Trista"

(2004)

Trista Joy Goldberg, named Nguyen Thi Thu by her Vietnamese birth mother, was born in 1970. Along with thousands of other Amerasian children (whose fathers were U.S. servicemen stationed in Vietnam), Goldberg was adopted by a middle-class American family and raised in the United States. Her biological brother, Nguyen Bic, was adopted by another branch of Goldberg's adoptive family. When she and her brother were adults, Goldberg began studying the Vietnamese language and culture and then began looking for their birth family, which she found in 2001. Inspired by her own experience, Goldberg founded Operation Reunite, a nonprofit organization "providing support and understanding to Vietnamese War Babies." In the following essay, Goldberg talks about the mission of Operation Reunite and describes her own journey to find her Vietnamese family.

I was adopted into a middleclass family. My adoptive father served in the Vietnam War and my adoptive mother was a housewife. They had two biological children and later adopted me and another Amerasian boy. They also sponsored two Vietnamese families. My father would tell me stories of a little Vietnamese girl who sold peanuts in the marketplace of Saigon. The child wore tattered clothes and based on circumstances was forced to peddle small items on the street. He would buy all the items from her each day so she could run off and play with the other kids. Later, he started buying the girl cute little dresses to replace her disheveled clothes. But the young girl would return each day in rags. This continued for about a week until he asked her, "Why don't you wear your new dresses?" The child told my father that her mother sold the dresses so that the family could eat. When he returned to the United States, he decided that he wanted to adopt a baby from Vietnam.

September 9, 2000 was my wedding date. During the planning for my wedding, I began to think about my missing family. I wished my birthmother could be with me on my big day. That's when I decided I wanted to find my birth family. I also wanted to learn my medical history. My younger birth brother was adopted with me but grew up with my aunt. So, we were blessed with the knowledge that we were siblings but happened to be cousins based on our outcome. My brother, Jeff, was also influential in my decision to search. I love him dearly and I am grateful for the day he approached me to ask for help. I might not have done it without him.

In April 2001, I found my birth family with the help of the internet, foster father, adoptive father and numerous other people. The search for my family brought me closer to the Vietnamese Adoptee community which helped support my journey.

I started a non-profit organization that encourages adoptees to search with awareness. Through my network of family and friends we will help Vietnamese adoptees who have any type of information regarding their birth family.

The non-profit organization, Operation Reunite, offers search support to help reunite families separated by the Vietnam War. In addition, we seek to create an awareness and understanding of the Vietnam War era and present an overview of Vietnamese culture, language, customs, and family traditions to help make the journey through time and history more meaningful.

Searching for my birth family was not easy. The process stirs up many issues that are difficult to face. However, I can honestly say that I wouldn't change one thing about my life. I am proud of my choices and hope to help others find closure.

What was the inspiration for starting Operation Reunite?

During the search for my own birth family, I wished that there was more available information that helped with the search. I also didn't find much that dealt with the multitude of feelings and emotions you go through during a search and after a reunion. I hope Operation Reunite will help Vietnamese adoptees all around the world who might try searching in the future to better navigate the journey.

How does Operation Reunite work? Is it a search registry or do you work as a liaison between birth family and adoptee?

Primarily we work as a resource for Vietnamese adoptees that have questioned their past and would like to find out more about their origins. We seek to create an awareness and understanding of the Vietnam War era and present an overview of Vietnamese culture, language, customs, and family traditions to help make sure the journey through time and history is more meaningful. We provide the ideas and imagination for adoptees to start a search on their own. They can contact us if they run into road blocks or just want to connect with adoptee peers. We work as a liaison between the birth family and adoptee. It's kind of like hiring a private investigator to search for clues about your past. We provide specific questions to reflect upon and help adoptees to prepare for a possible reunion. Encouragement is provided to adoptees who might only hear from their families and friends to give up trying. We have developed a support system that is based on trust and understanding. Contact us if you are ready to connect and find out more about us. . . .

In your opinion, what are the positives and negatives of finding birth parents?

I've grown to feel more secure about myself. I have two wonderful children who adore all of their grandparents, aunts and uncles. On one hand having more family is wonderful, but having more family makes it more difficult to balance your time and share yourself and your children fairly. It's nice to know that we have more people to rely on during difficult times. I am also relieved that my search is over and any of my fears can be dismissed. I'm glad that I can look my kids in their eyes and tell them a story about my past and how I was able to overcome a lot of obstacles to get to the place where I am now. To be able to share with them our Vietnamese culture and heritage is something that makes me proud.

Source: Goldberg, Trista. "Trista." 2004. Reprinted with permission of the author.

Diu Hoang, "The Back of the Hand: Vietnamese American Nail Salons" (2006)

Forty percent of the nation's nail salons—and 80 percent of those in California—are run by Vietnamese Americans. This phenomenon is part of a widespread pattern of ethnic specialization and entrepreneurship seen across the United States. Along with Gujarati hotels, Korean dry cleaners, and Cambodian doughnut shops, the proliferation of Vietnamese nail salons highlights the importance of family and social networks for economic development. However, there is an underside to the story of ethnic solidarity. Nail salon employees work long hours in hazardous conditions. Many of them are first-generation immigrants whose language skills prevent them from finding jobs at their Vietnam levels of education and employment. Diu Hoang wrote the following piece describing her family's nail salon while interning at Azine, *the online journal of the Asian American Movement, a network of labor, community, and student activists.*

The holidays are here. Everyone wants to look good and pamper themselves. Customers come in and out of nail salons to get their nails manicured or buy gift certificates for their loved ones.

But what is the price of beauty? For customers, it's $10 for a standard manicure and $25 for a spa chair pedicure. Customers are impatient and often complain about the long wait during holiday season, when everyone is already short of time and temper.

But for the workers and owners of these nails salons—it's long hours, low hourly pay, fierce competition from literally every corner of the block, and health problems from inhaling toxic chemicals such as acetone and acrylic on a daily basis. Let's take a look at what the holidays mean for nail salon workers and owners by looking at my own family's salon. Summer is the busiest season of the year; for the remainder of the year we get by, depending largely on business influx on key holidays and occasions—Thanksgiving, Christmas (where we sell more gift certificates than doing actual nails), New Year, Valentine's Day, prom season and small celebrations in between. My family opens seven days a week from 9am–7pm (except Sundays from 10am–5pm). My mother takes no vacations and closes the salon not more than 3 days a year on Christmas, New Year, and Thanksgiving only because she knows business is poor on these days.

As an owner, my mom considers herself lucky that the business is doing pretty well. The market is already oversaturated with Vietnamese nail salons. Her position is more stable than that of an employee, without salary guarantees and benefits. She is lucky for someone of her age (54), who can no longer keep up with the younger workers. Younger workers do a manicure so fast, she says, they don't even look at their customer's hands. Their eyes are glued to the door, calculating how fast they can finish a manicure to take in the next customer. The competition is fierce outside *and* inside the salon.

Our nail salon is in a white suburban area, an upscale location to all the places my mom used to work at (low income urban neighborhoods where the predominant clientele is black). Her customers here are more affluent and tip better.

The nail salon business is tenuous. While worrying about keeping up with competition and "building our customer base," she also needs to make sure to meet our employees' needs. My mom has to keep employees' salary at a level that would keep them at our salon. In a profession where employees' salaries are based on the number of customers they serve (their earnings is split 6:4 (employee: employer), it means that she can't hire too many workers even if they are stretched too thin during the busy seasons. It means that sometimes they would work straight from 9–7 no break, no lunch. This all evens out during slow periods when we sit around the entire day waiting for customers. My mom also has to worry about building up the skills of her employees as some come in with not much experience; at the same time she has to be careful not to share too much in fear that, when they have a good customer base of their own, they would leave to open up a nearby salon and take away her customers. This has happened in the past. Although this profession is demanding and my mom is always stressed out and has little time to see her family much, it's more than she can make with any other job, given her limited skill set and English ability.

For a nail technician who is younger in her mid 30's, who also has limited English and skills set, doing nails is also an opportunity. She is still young and fast, and has a lot of room to grow and get better in the profession, with hopes of someday owning her own salon. Nails salons, especially bigger ones, like any other workplace, can be a dog eat dog place. You have to join cliques in order to help each other learn and survive; at the same time you can't get too close to anyone because they can and will turn on you at any moment. Their livelihood is dependent on the same hands as your[s].

For an older nail technician in her mid to late 40's or 50's, all she can hope for is keeping their position in the current salon where they are working because no one hires someone past their prime. There is always fresher meat in the market.

My sister grew up in America and has a college degree, but she does nails out of family obligations. She's embarrassed to tell her friends with corporate jobs that she is doing nails. She hates scrubbing other people's hands and feet for the couple of bucks in tips that she gets. The white customers talk down on her, constantly surprised that she can speak English so well or at all. They don't believe that she has a college degree. Why in the world would she being doing nails? She is frustrated that "vacations" and "free time" is almost unheard of and not something important. After all what are we working so hard for if we can't enjoy it (an American mindset my mom says)? But, being the oldest 1.5 generation child in the family, she swallows all this personal shame and helps her family out in this business that definitely can't survive without her. There's all the paperwork and legal matters involved.

There are not many options. In America, it is not a shame for Vietnamese to do nails. But in Vietnam, only the lower group on the ladder would go into any profession that involves touching other people's hands and feet.

In all this, health hazards are always an issue but seem to be the last thing anyone takes into consideration unless he or she gets to the point of physically being unable to continue in the profession. With the sudden influx and saturation of Vietnamese nail salons, how crucial is the profession to the survival of the Vietnamese community/population in the U.S.? What role do nail salons play in shaping the demographics of the Vietnamese community? With such fierce competition, are we driving each other's business and salaries down? These are all food for thought every time you walk into a Vietnamese-run nail salon.

Source: Hoang, Diu. "The Back of the Hand: Vietnamese American Nail Salons." *Azine,* December 15, 2006. http://apimovement.com/vietnamese-americans/back-hand-vietnamese-american-nail-salons. Used with the permission of the author and *Azine*.

Sumeia Williams, "Memorial Inheritance"
(2006)

Born in 1970 in Saigon, Le Thi Buu Tran moved to the United States when she was six months old, adopted by a Texas family who named her Sumeia Williams. Today, Williams writes about her life and identity as an Asian woman and transracial adoptee in the United States. Her work has appeared in the Iodine Poetry Journal *and* The New York Times. *The following piece, "Memorial Inheritance," is not autobiographical; however, it symbolizes Williams's experience as an adopted Vietnamese daughter of an American Vietnam veteran. In reflecting on her poem, Williams explained, "The Vietnam war left its mark on both of us and affects how we view the other. We are not just father and daughter, but share a history that makes us both foreign and familiar, both enemy and ally."*

Mother could not carry all
of herself down into the tunnels
of my mind. She left
the prodigal part behind before fading
into a charcoal sketch on the gray
matter of my memory.

I slept soundly in the arms
of the soldier who carried me
from my birthright. Unborn
embryos in the surrogate belly
of a C-5, we abandoned the loss
on the runway tarmac.
He often shares his memories,
remnants of my inheritance.
Once, we wandered
through Little Saigon and hinted
of our longing to return between
the lines of nylon drawn taunt
against the weight of Ao Dai's
and yellow, red-striped flags.
At a temple, he took snapshots
as I lit incense, lips poised for prayer
in unfamiliar words. Hungry,
we ate at a nearby noodle shop
and indulged ourselves. Carried back
by the smell of fish and sandalwood,
he told me war stories as I chewed
on boneless pieces of meat
spooned from a bowl of pho.

Source: Williams, Sumeia. "Memorial Inheritance." 2006. Reprinted with permission.

Kevin Minh Allen, "Eggroll"
(2006)

According to recent U.S. census reports, nearly 45 percent of Asian American women marry white men. Sociologists, historians, and community activists argue about the impact of gender, cultural, and racial stereotypes on interracial relationships, highlighting everything from colonialist legacies to ingrained social and economic hierarchies and levels of assimilation. In his short poem and accompanying essay, Kevin Minh Allen takes a more prosaic look at sexual politics and race.

Race is something I think about often due to my upbringing and the way I view current events in this country. In a fit of creativity, and with the always-confounding issue of race in the back of my mind, I wrote the following poem a couple years ago:

Never kowtow to the SWM
with his mail-order bride catalog
upon his lap, tapping his pen, double-checking
his checkbook, picking out that rare Thai virgin
who will hang from his arm at the pub, and later
at the club the sight of your Jap ass brings out the
fight in him, and he raises his chin, puffs out his chest
and yells across the bar:
"What are you still doing here?"
Didn't we bomb you VC back to Bombay?
Stay out of my way and pay for my drink, ya chink."
But, don't blink.
Don't even raise your hand against him.
Just hum as you pass him by,
"At least I don't have to pay for sex."

After reading this poem, a casual reader may think to himself, "Well, he definitely overplayed his hand, being all combative and sarcastic. What is he, some kind of racial separatist?"

Hardly, I'd respond. I would explain that the poem is a wry observation on racial and sexual politics that continue to pervade our popular culture and inform the populace as how to think and treat people with Asian physical characteristics. The poem uses the two main stereotypes of Asians in Western culture—the Asian woman as submissive commodity and the Asian man as the perpetual foreign enemy—to criticize this culture's insistence that Asian-Americans are mere props on which to project its fetishes and violent tendencies.

Case in point:

I came across the following two classified ads in the Personals section of the *Northwest Asian Weekly* (July 22–28, 2006):

Single, Caucasian man 50 yrs young. Attractive. Tall, Physically Fit. Business Owner, Financially stable, Would like to meet Asian lady. 35–50. Attractive & physically fit a plus. Honesty & Loyalty a must. Long term relationship. Possible marriage. Little English ok. Language barrier no problem.

JENNY, 36 yr. *5'6"* 120 lbs, Beijing, China. Young Slender and attractive. Looking for 36–50 yr. Caucasian Soul-mate . . . . For more photos: www.SheLoveU.com/ . . . .

It gave me pause to consider why (and how) this sort of solicitation was published in a newspaper dedicated to reporting on issues concerning Asian-Americans, as well as uplifting the Asian-American community.

However, the fact that these two personals appear one right after the other, the male's on top of the female's, and both people appear to be interested in the same age range and race, it seems sweetly fated that they should meet in print. On the other hand, both people are perpetuating the centuries-old racial/sexual dynamic that has continued to poison the self-perceptions of the White male, Asian female and Asian male. The White male's sense of entitlement is strengthened, as well as his emboldened use of White supremacist/White man's burden ideology that (mis)informs him about the people of Asia and their shared history, which ultimately leads him to debase the people's cultural traditions and achievements and strive to "civilize" these people; the Asian female, due to a long process of European colonization and white-washing, strives for a more Western (i.e., "modern") way of life which includes a plethora of beauty enhancement products and, as a last (or first) resort, intermarriage in order to "whiten" the bloodline and forget all about the old ways in the old country; the Asian male is also bombarded with the "white" way of life, but his striving for assimilation is usually thrown back in his face in this society because he has been traditionally viewed as The Enemy, in both actual combat and educationally and economically.

Sounds good in theory, but it's not so simple in reality, says the casual reader. Granted, I tend to agree that human relationships evolve and blame cannot be pinned on someone simply because he/she fits a time-honored paradigm. But, no one can argue that the unfortunate dynamic I just posited above does not persist to exist. Just read the example I took from the newspaper again and ask yourself, "What is it with these two people?"

Source: Allen, Kevin Minh. "Eggroll." 2006. http://www .aamovement.net/viewpoints/2006/eggrolls1.html. Used with permission of the author and *Azine*.

Bác Nguyen Vân Phuong, Interview by Xuan Thanh Le
(2008)

Southeast Asian immigration to the United States exploded in 1975, when hundreds of thousands of Vietnamese, Cambodian, and Laotian refugees fled the ravages of the Vietnam War. In response, Boat People SOS (BPSOS) formed in 1980; originally conducting rescue missions in the South China Sea, BPSOS gradually began shifting its focus to the needs of Vietnamese American immigrant communities in the United States as well as tracking and fighting the trafficking of Southeast Asians throughout the world. In a 2008 interview with BPSOS senior specialist Xuan Thanh Le, Bác Nguyen Vân Phuong talks about his immigration experience and how he painstakingly made a life for himself and his family in the United States.

My name is Nguyen Vân Phuong. I was born in Tân An, miê`n Nam (southern) Vietnam. I came to America in March of 1973 before the fall of Saigon. I ventured to the states with just my family—my wife and four children. *I lost everything . . . and came to America to rebuild my life.* I was a stateless refugee traveling from Northern to Southern Vietnam, "di cu", and it was very difficult to find a job in America without citizenship. I was unemployed for quite some time. American companies were masters at carefully rejecting me . . . every time I tried to show them the degrees I earned in Vietnam and Europe they said it did not meet American requirements. As a result, they didn't allow me to take on senior level positions such as management.

My academic background was in economics— when I tried to search for jobs as a bank teller they said, "I'm sorry, I can't let you take this job because this would be degrading for you. But I can't let you take on management positions either because you don't have the experience to lead in the American system." I had taken some courses on public administration and leadership, but couldn't obtain a bachelor's degree here in the U.S. because it wasn't allowed due to my citizenship status.

"They were kind to me."

I kept searching and searching, and finally stumbled upon a life insurance company that gave me a chance. Up to this point in my professional experience, I had always been on the administrative end of things, and I had never been in sales before. They had a probationary period of 3 months to see if I could make a sale, and if I couldn't sell, then I'd get fired. They knew I didn't have experience so they gave me a starting salary of around $600–700 a month in addition to making commission off of sales. So I did my best to learn about the insurance industry while getting out there and selling policies. They showed me the ropes and gave me a database of potential clients to network and reach out to. I had to call these contacts, set up appointments, come to them, and make a presentation of the products.

My job was also to answer any questions they had about our policies for sale, and ask about their health, well-being, and family. This was our company's way to make our visitations personal, and show that we cared about the client and the future of their children and grandchildren—it made for a good selling tactic, but it was very difficult for me to be in a sales position nonetheless. With every client, I was soft-spoken, never lied, and didn't try to pressure anyone into buying anything.

At the time, I faced a lot of *racial discrimination* as a Vietnamese in the life insurance industry. There were not a lot of Vietnamese in this line of work, and the majority consisted of Whites. But my managers at the company were kind to me, knew that there were obstacles that I had to endure due to racism, and made the effort to enter their social circles and networking meetings to enhance my professional growth. The company taught me to use pressure to make a sale, but I refused and told them that I was unwilling to pressure potential clients. However, my company told me to use a very threatening tactic:

"Tell them that if they don't make the investment to protect themselves now, how are their children and wife going to survive?! They'll end up on the streets!"

They wanted me to put some fire underneath them, but I refused to threaten them by those means to make a sale. My managers and clients understood my style, and I ended up staying at the company for 13 years. They started me out with selling life insurance policies and later on I started selling different types of policies such as health insurance and stock bonds. I earned the different licenses and although I didn't sell that much, the company was kind enough to me to allow me to stay and I received many awards for my work. So when I made the decision to leave, they were very sad.

"For the sake of công dông . . . "

I later found a job with the U.S. Catholic Charities called ROME—they cared for orphans and Amerasians (Vietnamese children of American GI soldiers). Many people there were social workers and a man named Dennis Hunt ran an office of a few dozen staff members in Falls Church, VA. When I came to work for them, they were skeptical of me because I came from an insurance sales background—they warned me that the pay was not going to be comparable to my previous job and wanted to make sure I wasn't going to take the job and quickly quit. I reassured them that I wanted the job because *I wanted to help the* "công dông" *(community)*. They even tried to put me on the job only as part-time just to make sure I was compatible, but I refused because I wasn't going to mess around with a part-time here, and a part-time

elsewhere—I wanted a solid full-time job. So they let me take on a full-time job and gave me a caseload of 16–17 orphans to provide assistance to, and I was quite successful. They had a high school graduation rate of 80–90% and many went on to college thereafter.

"My message to the youth . . . "

In life, you have to set goals, adjust to your surroundings, and continue moving forward. If you don't have *perseverance,* . . . say if you lost your homeland country, everything is stripped away from you, there's no giving up. My wife supported me through thick and thin, and I love her dearly. She helped me in the toughest times. While I was searching for a job and unemployed, she held a stable job as a secretary, and then as an executive assistant at the National Academy of Sciences in Washington, DC. She was working and raising four children, 2 girls, 2 boys. All of them were successful and obtained Master's degrees and above. I have a total of 4 grandchildren—3 "cháu ngoa·i" (maternal grandchildren), and 1 cháu nô·i (paternal grandchildren). My sons and daughters are now in their fifties.

My life is about raising my children and cultivating their values so that in the end, they learn how to love their families and to love others. I always tell them that whatever money you make and earn in this world, to remember to think about those in need and give back to the community, whether that be the American or Vietnamese community.

If you continue having goals in life to obtain material goods . . . *you earn one million, you'll want another million . . . and life becomes meaningless.*

Source: Phuong, Bác Nguyê~n Vân. Interview with Xuan Thanh Le. July 24, 2008. http://chimesofvoices.blogspot .com/2008/07/bac-nguyen-van-phuong.html. Reprinted with permission.

Julie Pham, "Modern Day McCarthyism: The Case of Duc Tan"
(2009)

Thirty years after the Vietnam War, first-generation Vietnamese American immigrants have vivid memories of fleeing their homeland, fearing persecution, reeducation camps, torture, and execution at the hands of the North Vietnamese communists. As a result, many Vietnamese Americans today are still passionately opposed to communism, sparking heated debates within the community over what relationship the United States and individual Vietnamese Americans should have to present-day Vietnam (now governed by the Vietnamese Communist Party).

In April 2009, five Vietnamese Americans successfully sued another Vietnamese American for falsely accusing them of having communist sympathies. Julie Pham, the managing editor of the Vietnamese American paper Nguòi Viêt Tây Bac, *outlines the case in the following article. Pham's parents founded the paper, known in English as the* Northwest Vietnamese News, *in 1986. The longest-running Vietnamese language newspaper in the region,* Nguòi Viêt Tây Bac *strives to build intercultural and intergenerational bridges within and beyond the Vietnamese American community.*

On April 16, 2009, the Thurston County Court ruled in favor of a Vietnamese man who sued for defamation. This case was the first of its kind in the state of Washington.

The court found the five defendants, Norman Le, Dat Ho, Nga Pham, Nhan Tran, and Phiet Nguyen, guilty for wrongly accusing the plaintiff, Duc Tan, and the non-profit organization, the Vietnamese Community of Thurston County (VCTC), of having communist sympathies.

The defendants were fined $310,000. Of this fine, $225,000 was awarded to Duc Tan, the principal of a Vietnamese language school in Thurston County, and $85,000 to VCTC, whose president is Duc Hua. Duc Tan filed the suit in 2004. The defendants published their accusations in mass emails, Internet site postings, and the local Vietnamese press. Defendant Dr. Norman Le said one such newspaper, *New Horizons,* was ordered to pay $25,000 of the $225,000 fine.

A few days later, three of the defendants, Norman Le, Nhan Tran, and Dat Ho, along with plaintiff Duc Tan and Duc Hua, agreed to speak to *Northwest Vietnamese News.*

Chup mũ

Those outside the Vietnamese community may see the defendants' accusations of communist sympathies as modern day McCarthyism. But in this case, both the defendants and plaintiffs fought against communism during the Second Indochina War. All those interviewed invoked a word commonly used within the Vietnamese émigré community to describe the act of wrongly accusing someone of communist sympathies: chup mũ. As this trial brought to light, chup mũ is a widespread practice among Vietnamese community leaders. However, it is very rare for a person who has been chup mũ to sue his/her accusers. "Many people in our community have been chup mũ, but they don't dare go to court," the plaintiff Duc Tan said. "Everyone wants to forget or to make amends instead of going to court. But we couldn't tolerate it any longer. We had to take a stand, to file a lawsuit. Otherwise our consciences would have continued to nag at us."

The defense argued that community leaders should expect to be subject to criticism.

"Even I have been chup mũ," defendant Dr. Norman Le said, "When you are a community leader, you have to be able to swallow the criticisms of your constituents and the public at large."

President of the Vietnamese Community of Tacoma and Pierce County doctor Dung Nguyen disagrees. He served as a character witness for the plaintiff. "I have been chup mũ for over ten years now," said Dr. Nguyen. "With the court ruling in favor of Duc Tan and Duc Hua, I hope this case will set a precedent and force those who chup mũ to be more prudent, more responsible." Duc Tan said that in his case, being chup mũ even led to a death threat.

Fears of communism and being called communists

The defendants expressed real fears of communist sympathizers in their community. "Resolution 36, in which the Vietnamese government funds the propagation of communist propaganda overseas, was released several years ago. We think it's important to watch for signs of communist propaganda and communist activity," said Dr. Le. "We need to fight communism. We left Vietnam to escape communism. We do not want our children to have to leave the US to escape the communists who have come here." Dr. Le himself spent nine years and seven months in a communist re-education camp in Vietnam. In order to determine who is sympathetic to communism, Dr. Le said "We can only use our judgment, because a communist never puts a badge on their chest saying, 'I'm a communist.'" Also real are the fears of becoming vulnerable to chup mũ if one decides to help organize Vietnamese community activities.

Duc Tan said one of the reasons he decided to sue was because he saw that "young people were scared to take part in community organizing, weary of the politics around chup mũ" Duc Hua added, "Those on the organizing committee of VCTC pulled out. They even testified they did so because they were afraid of being chup mũ."

This case has already affected the extent chup mũ" in the Vietnamese community in Washington. Soon after the Thurston County Court ruled in favor of the plaintiff, one group that began sending out email reports accusing dozens of members of the local Vietnamese community of harboring communist sympathies earlier this month drastically shortened its list to a handful of people.

Freedom of speech or freedom to slander?

The defense lawyer Nigel Malden said that his clients were exercising their freedom of speech. "All the statements were presented in a way that any reader could review the material and make their own decisions," said Malden. "They were expressing what they believed to be true and someone else might look at it and have a different opinion." He added, "It's disturbing that an American jury didn't give more latitude to the people who actually lived under communism. They are very sensitive to communist symbols."

The prosecutor Gregory Rhodes said the defendants "presented their opinions as statements of facts." "This wasn't just defamation," said Rhodes. "These were downright lies and for the defendants to do this was so callous and extremely sad for the whole community."

In the trial, the prosecution presented a striking piece of evidence to prove Duc Tan's anti-communism: a photograph of Duc Tan in a rally fighting for the freedom of political prisoners in Vietnam. It was taken when he first came to the US in 1978. Rhodes pointed out the ironic fact that "the people he was fighting for are the same people who are accusing him of being a communist now."

Where to go from here

With the $310,000 awarded by the court, Duc Tan and Duc Hua said they will use it to build up the Vietnamese language school in Thurston County. Thuy Vu, a professor at Evergreen College and the University of Washington, and a long-time resident of Thurston County said, "The case is over now. I only hope that the Vietnamese here can put this behind us and use our energy to build up the community for the future generation."

The trial may be over, but the defense will not rest. "After we heard the court's decision, that we had lost, we viewed it as a single battle in an entire war," the defendant Dat Ho said. "One should not expect that he/she must always win. What is important is that we continue fighting for our good cause and we are confident that we will finally win."

Duc Tan said, "We sued so that we could bring light to this issue and now our work is done. We wait to hear from the other side." In an email dated April 22, Malden said he would file a brief requesting a new trial on April 27 on behalf of the defense. "We will be asking the court to reconsider some of its evidentiary rulings," Malden said.

Source: Pham, Julie. "Modern Day McCarthyism: The Case of Duc Tan." April 24, 2009. http://news.newamericamedia.org/news/view_article.html?article_id=ab9237da2b1347a2f359cf29068b6b8d. Originally published as "Nghe trình bày va^'n d–ê` tù, hai phia liên can sau phán quyê´ t vu· án 'chu·p mu~' của toà án Thurston." *Nguò,i Viê·t Tây Ba˘'c,* April 24, 2009, issue 1812, 4–5, 34–35 (translated into English for New America Media). Used with permission of Julie Pham.

Nguyen Thi Hanh Nhon, Interview by Nancy Bui
(2010)

Nguyen Thi Hanh Nhon was born in 1927 in Hue, the capital of imperial Vietnam. Her father was head of the Central Army Corps and served in the royal army under Emperor Bao Dai. The emperor abdicated in 1945, and Vietnam became engulfed in a civil war between the Viet Minh and the remaining French colonists. The Nguyen family sank into poverty, and Nguyen herself was forced to seek employment. She enlisted in the armed forces, working in the Army of the Vietnam Republic's Corps of Female Soldiers (ARVN). By 1975, nearly 6,000 women were employed in the ARVN. When the communists took over Vietnam, the officers, including Nguyen, were sent to reeducation camps—where, in actuality, they were forced to perform hard labor. Nguyen was imprisoned for nearly five years before she was released and allowed to return to her family.

In 1990, Nguyen, her husband, and five of her children were sponsored to come to the United States by her oldest son, who had escaped during the fall of Saigon. In the following excerpts from a 2010 interview with Nancy Bui from the Vietnamese American Oral History Project, Nguyen talks about her involvement with the Mutual Society of Political Prisoners. The society

was established to help Vietnamese who came to the United States under the Humanitarian Operation program, which ran until 1994 and provided a path for former reeducation camp internees and their family members to immigrate to the United States. Her interview illustrates the ways in which the history of the homeland affects immigrant identity: the continuing effect of the Vietnam War on Vietnamese Americans, the sense of responsibility many Vietnamese veterans feel toward those left behind, and the deep desire to preserve memories and cultural heritage for the next generation in the United States.

TG: How could you start your living here [in the United States]?

NTHN: I was supported by my first son because I was old. The young ones could start with delivering pizzas, or car washing. Some worked as wood-workers for furniture companies. Gradually they grew up and stopped going to school because they got jobs at some companies. One became an engineer. The oldest one was also an engineer. Now they were all settled with their children graduating from college.

TG: What did you think was the most difficult thing to do to integrate into the new way of life?

NTHN: That's the economic aspect. Everyone had a hard living at first and had to work hard. I was old and could not work. I came here in 1990 and was invited in 1991 to serve as a vice president of The Mutual Society of Political Prisoners to help the HOs [Humanitarian Operation immigrants] who came here with no relatives. We sponsored them, helped them to look for employment and housing, got some furniture, and helped them go to school. When the HO plan was terminated, they organized an HO Mutual Society for VN Wounded Veterans to grant assistance to the wounded veterans and widows in Vietnam. Since I had time and found it good so I agreed when invited to serve as President of that Society.

TG: Could you let us know how that Society was formed and what were its purposes?

NTHN: When the first group of HOs came, they knew that there were beggars in Vietnam who were wounded veterans of the former Armed Forces. When they got the money through working, they sent money back there to help those comrades. They were the first organizers. They sent those people the money they earned from work so it would be passed on to others. Since there were so many applications for assistance, the Society was set up to get money to help those wounded soldiers. The numbers were growing fast to more than twenty thousand applications. We thought of having the concerts by various artists who performed for free from ASIA center and SBTN such like the one at Bolsa High School. The first concert got 450 thousand dollars, the second concert brought in more than one million dollars, and the third one in San Jose collected more than 800 thousand. So we had the money to help tens of thousands of wounded soldiers and widows.

TG: So on the average, how much could each person receive?

NTHN: We had some criteria: those who lost both arms, or both limbs, or both eyes could receive two hundred dollars; those who lost one arm, or one leg, or one eye or with internal wound would get 100 dollars; widows got 50 dollars; those widows with cancer could get 100 dollars. In the third phase, we sent money for the years of 2009 and 2010, and this time we stop sending money to those groups so that we could help those who had not received assistance since 2008 and beyond.

TG: How could you contact those people?

NTHN: We could not communicate directly with them in Vietnam. They informed one another to send applications over. Those with incompleted applications were told to complete them. We had to be very careful and detailed, because we had to respect the people's monetary contributions and we had to check very carefully. We could detect all fraudulent applications. Since there were more than 20 people in the society who were also former soldiers so we knew about their ID numbers, what correct forms to be used, in what battle they were wounded, what divisions they belonged to, and in what province they were wounded. Once we knew about their divisions, we knew the correct military clinics where they were treated.

TG: So with cross-checking you knew the figures to be correct?

NTHN: After thorough checking, we made a list of those beneficiaries. We did not have representatives in Vietnam. We sent money through the money transfer services here and we asked them to make sure the money be delivered to the right person with the correct wound at the correct address. The transfer services did not get the ID numbers, but when the money was delivered the receiver had to write his ID on the receipt. In cross-checking again, we knew we had the right person. There were some exceptions when those soldiers wrote to us, they were so scared and burnt all documents and they were in dire conditions.

TG: Who provided you with the ID numbers?

NTHN: We could find it in their documents. For example, the file consisted of their photo showing whether they lost an arm or a limb, a letter mentioning the name of their commanding officer, their ID, their KBC, the description of their body, their address, and the proof of their wound with full details. If those documents were missing, then there should be certifications from the hospital. And this one is missing too, then there should be a report of losses. Some other people could bring back a lot of documents when they returned from Vietnam. There were a lot of files sent to us from other states. We cross-checked them against our files. Those that did match would get assistance. At first, there were only several hundred files then we classified them with our numbers. But now we had more than twenty thousand, we used the military ID numbers listed in several books and those new numbers proved that they had not been helped . . .

TG: Among the 22 thousand people who received help, how many were female soldiers?

NTHN: Female soldiers were not wounded because they did not join fightings [sic], but there were some injured while evacuating or carrying wounded soldiers on the way back. There were only some.

TG: So you helped male soldiers in the past and continued doing so now in their hardships.

NTHN: Yes, that's a big consolation.

TG: What made you happy the most in this job?

NTHN: I am now 83 years old and wanted to retire, but they did not want to let me go because they said I was an honorable person and that people respected and loved me so they donated more money and that they could not match the donations when I retired. I felt happy when I imagined the happiness of the families that received the money. We got letters from them saying that they could never get a millions Vietnamese *piasters* in life. Now that they have the money, they were so happy that they could not sleep. They cried while writing to us. That's my happiness.

TG: Any difficulties that interfered with your job?

NTHN: The obstacle was fraudulent documents by declaring that they were wounded soldiers. Therefore we had to check very carefully. Another problem was receiving the files hand-carried from those who came back from Vietnam. We had tens of thousands of files, but we had lots of work to do so we could remember which was completed and which was not. They complained that we did not do our job several months after they turned in the files. We could not serve everyone at one time. Some people went back to VN, meeting some beggars or some lottery sellers, asking if they had received help. Obviously the response was no, and they gave those people some money. Upon returning here, they said those people had not received help whereas we claimed having sent the money. That's why we felt so sorry, but we felt calm deep in our heart. We did what we had to do no matter what people said . . .

TG: So what did you think about our community in such activities? How to develop the community or just let the younger generations do it?

NTHN: Whenever we organized a concert, we always invited the Students Association to join. They were very energetic in ticket selling, reception, arranging chairs, cleaning and doing lots of odd jobs. Most of them came from the families of veterans. They understood the conditions of their parents and their relatives. Therefore I would like them to replace us. But they had to work elsewhere. Only those retirees could have time to do our job. Some young people came to help us on weekends. They wanted to contribute their help, they joined the students' association, teaching Vietnamese classes. They knew how to maintain the Vietnamese culture and realized their responsibilities. But the older generation should be an example for them.

TG: Did you think it's important to retain the Vietnamese culture here?

NTHN: I always reminded my children and grandchildren that their country was Vietnam on the other side of the Pacific where people were suffering. They should always remember the poor people living there. And later on, when VN could live in freedom and democracy, they should join the young ones to rebuild the country. Now the country was divided and disintegrated.

TG: Did you think that the younger generation here could retain the proper customs and traditions?

NTHN: They knew about that, and their parents knew how to teach them to follow. But we had to adapt to the traditions and habits of this country. They were bi-lingual, so they realized that they were Vietnamese and they should maintain the culture of Vietnam.

TG: You were a woman from a royal family, undergoing through all kinds of ups and downs in life. You had been trying to contribute. What lesson did you want to pass to the younger generations?

NTHN: I wrote an unfinished memoir that I gave it you as a gift, in which I wrote about the life of a woman prisoner. At that time, the *Vien Dong Daily News* asked me to write about the life in prison. You know, when I first came here to work for the Mutual Association of the political prisoners. I was editor-in-chief of a magazine called *Hoi Ngo* (*re-Union*), I asked those prisoners to write for the magazine so that the new comers could read. They wrote about their lives in prison. I also wrote some and then summed them up and sent to *Vien Dong* and won the third prize. In that article, there was one paragraph saying: "In reminiscence of the past, I write here not to call for Pity, and not as a contribution to a period of the history, but with a common wish to help the young and weak women to muster courage to accept all sudden mishaps in life." To the younger generation, I had the following advice: "As former women soldiers and prisoners, after a dark period, we could stand up and go forward, and thus could accept all sorts of hardships."

TG: Did you want to share something else, something that we missed?

NTHN: I barely heard that your purpose of interviewing me was to share with the younger generations in schools. I felt sad that the Americans did not know that a lot of memoirs written by the Vietcong were introduced to the schools, so the students learnt from those history distortions. I therefore wished to have this chance to introduce the translations of the correct memoirs to teach the students about the true history of Vietnam, to make them feel proud of the Vietnamese, intelligent and brave, whose parents and grandparents were good and talented soldiers who had contributed greatly to their country.

TG: Thank you very much. That's the purpose of the society to safeguard the history and culture of the Vietnamese Americans. Throughout the interview, your story revealed a painful period of the Vietnam War and the struggle to survive in this country. Speaking for the Society as well as the young people, thank you so much for sharing your experience.

NTHN: Thank you Ms Trieu Giang and all of you for your kindness in conducting this interview.

Source: Nguyen Thi Hanh Nhon. Interview with Nancy Bui, November 9, 2010, 8–11. Vietnamese American Heritage Foundation and Vietnamese American Oral History Project, University of California, Irvine. http://ucispace.lib.uci.edu/bitstream/handle/10575/5243/VAHF0010_F01_Eng.pdf?sequence=5.

Multiheritage Asian Americans

In 2000, nearly 7 million people in the United States (2.4 percent of the total) reported more than one race on the census, and of these, 1.5 million were Asian American. The continuing evolution of public perception of mixed-race people is evident in the very fact that there was a space on the census for people to identify as multiracial: in effect, establishing an institutionalized legitimization of what historically has been a despised category.

In the 19th and 20th centuries, sociologists came up with several derogatory theories about biracial and multiracial people. The hybrid degeneracy theory, popular in the decades after the Civil War, drew on pseudoscientific and religious racism. Hybrid degeneracy posited that mixed-race children were genetically inferior to both of their parents and displayed physical, mental, emotional, and moral deficiencies that would lead to early death. Although this theory corresponded closely to white Americans' fears of ex-slaves and the racial mixing they believed would result from emancipation, hybrid degeneracy was also applied to mixed-race Asian Americans and other ethnic groups, particularly Native Americans. Other theorists viewed biracial people as marginal men and women, not belonging to either parent's race, culture, or community. They characterized them as confused and torn, mentally and emotionally unstable, and rejected by both their mother's and father's families.

However, attitudes toward mixed-race identity are regionally conditioned and evolving. In Hawai'i, racial mixing has been prevalent for generations. Nineteenth-century Chinese laborers married Native Hawaiians because Chinese women were not encouraged to immigrate, and the close quarters of plantation life, coupled with the successive waves of Asian immigrants who soon made up a majority of the population, made interracial marriages and mixed-race children inevitable. Hapa, the Hawaiian term for "half," soon became used to describe people of mixed Native Hawaiian ancestry; over the years, its definition evolved to signify people of mixed-race Asian heritage. On the mainland, where attitudes toward race were much less progressive, World War II, the Korean War, and the Vietnam War forced an attitude shift. Interracial relationships and marriages between American military personnel stationed overseas and the Asian women they met resulted in mixed-race Asian American children.

Some of these children, Vietnamese Afro-Amerasians in particular, found little acceptance in either their Asian or their American communities. But others, coming of age in the 1980s and 1990s, developed an almost defiant new awareness of and pride in their multiracial identity. In 1992, the Hapa Issues Forum was founded at the University of California–Berkeley. Originally meant to address the Asian Pacific American community's negative stereotypes and comments about biracial people, the Hapa Issues Forum embraced the concept of fluid identity, pioneering the idea that one can define oneself as 100 percent of each ethnicity. In 2005, the forum renamed itself the Multicultural Student Union, moving the focus beyond Asian Pacific Islanders to multiracial people in general and responding to criticism that "hapa" was a colonialist appropriation of Native Hawaiian language and culture. In the meantime, however, other people are navigating mixed-race identity through various media. Kip Fulbeck's multimedia work The Hapa Project *is a book and exhibition*

featuring black-and-white photographs of mixed-race people, along with their handwritten responses to the common question: "What are you?" Filmmaker Yayoi Lena Winfrey is working on Watermelon Sushi, *a feature film about an African Japanese American family.*

Multiracial identity politics remain complicated. Some fear that their ethnic community's government resources will be diluted if people give themselves multiple racial and ethnic labels. Others question the legitimacy of the Asian-ness of mixed-race people. However, the following perspectives are those of multiracial writers themselves. From the 19th century to today, multiheritage novelists, essayists, bloggers, and filmmakers have addressed these struggles, their own search for identity and community, and their refusal to be labeled "other."

Sui Sin Far/Edith Maude Eaton, "Its Wavering Image"
(1912)

Edith Maude Eaton, known by the pen name Sui Sin Far, was the daughter of an Englishman and a Chinese woman. Born in England and raised in Canada, Eaton immigrated to the United States in the early 1900s, living in San Francisco, Seattle, and Boston. Like her sister Winnifred Eaton (who wrote under the name Onoto Watanna), Edith Eaton was one of the first known Asian American authors. She wrote primarily about Chinese American life, and her short stories were often set in Chinatown. They described the interactions between Anglo Americans and Chinese Americans and evoked the cultural dislocation felt by many immigrants, particularly Chinese women, who were isolated in ethnic enclaves while their husbands became more Americanized. Eaton's stories consistently feature sympathetic Asian

American characters, who are just as likely as the white characters—if not more so—to be the moral voice in the stories.

"Its Wavering Image," included in Eaton's 1921 anthology Mrs. Spring Fragrance, *is the story of Pan, the child of a Chinese merchant and a deceased white woman. The plot unfolds in the following excerpt as Pan meets Mark Carson, a newspaperman, who uses their friendship to get the "inside scoop" on Chinatown. "Its Wavering Image" explores biracial identity and the pressure to choose one heritage over another. Eaton locates Pan solidly in the Chinese American community, where she is accepted unconditionally; the unsympathetic Carson, on the other hand, insists that Pan identify herself solely as a white woman.*

I

Pan was a half white, half Chinese girl. Her mother was dead, and Pan lived with her father who kept an Oriental Bazaar on Dupont Street. All her life had Pan lived in Chinatown, and if she were different in any sense from those around her, she gave little thought to it. It was only after the coming of Mark Carson that the mystery of her nature began to trouble her.

They met at the time of the boycott of the Sam Yups by the See Yups. After the heat and dust and unsavoriness of the highways and byways of Chinatown, the young reporter who had been sent to find a story, had stepped across the threshold of a cool, deep room, fragrant with the odor of dried lilies and sandalwood, and found Pan.

She did not speak to him, nor he to her. His business was with the spectacled merchant, who, with a pointed brush, was making up accounts in brown paper books and rolling balls in an abacus box. As to Pan, she always turned from whites. With her father's people she was natural and at home; but in the presence of her mother's she felt strange and constrained, shrinking from their curious scrutiny as she would from the sharp edge of a sword.

When Mark Carson returned to the office, he asked some questions concerning the girl who had puzzled him. What was she? Chinese or white? The city editor answered him, adding: "She is an unusually bright girl, and could tell more stories about the Chinese than any other person in this city—if she would."

Mark Carson had a determined chin, clever eyes, and a tone to his voice which easily won for him the confidence of the unwary. In the reporter's room he was spoken of as "a man who would sell his soul for a story."

After Pan's first shyness had worn off, he found her bewilderingly frank and free with him; but he had all the instincts of a gentleman save one, and made no ordinary mistake about her. He was Pan's first white friend. She was born a Bohemian, exempt from the conventional restrictions imposed upon either the white or Chinese woman; and the Oriental who was her father mingled with his affection for his child so great a respect for and trust in the daughter of the dead white woman, that everything she did or said was right to him. And Pan herself! A white woman might pass over an insult; a Chinese woman fail to see one. But Pan! He would be a brave man indeed who offered one to childish little Pan.

All this Mark Carson's clear eyes perceived, and with delicate tact and subtlety he taught the young girl that, all unconscious until his coming, she had lived her life alone. So well did she learn this lesson that it seemed at times as if her white self must entirely dominate and trample under foot her Chinese.

Meanwhile, in full trust and confidence, she led him about Chinatown, initiating him into the simple mystery and history of many things, for which she, being of her father's race, had a tender regard and pride. For her sake he was received as a brother by the yellow-robed priest in the joss house, the Astrologer of Prospect Place, and other conservative Chinese. The Water Lily Club opened its doors to him when she knocked, and the Sublimely Pure Brothers' organization admitted him as one of its honorary members, thereby enabling him not only to see but to take part in a ceremony in which no American had ever before participated. With her by his side, he was welcomed wherever he went. Even the little Chinese women in the midst of their babies, received him with gentle smiles, and the children solemnly munched his candies and repeated nursery rhymes for his edification.

He enjoyed it all, and so did Pan. They were both young and light-hearted. And when the afternoon was spent, there was always that high room open to the stars, with its China bowls full of flowers and its big colored lanterns, shedding a mellow light.

Sometimes there was music. A Chinese band played three evenings a week in the gilded restaurant beneath them, and the louder the gongs sounded and the fiddlers fiddled, the more delighted was Pan. Just below the restaurant was her father's bazaar. Occasionally Man You would stroll upstairs and inquire of the young couple if there was anything needed to complete their felicity, and Pan would answer: "Thou only." Pan was very proud of her Chinese father. "I would rather have a Chinese for a father than a white man," she often told Mark Carson. The last time she had said that he had asked whom she would prefer for a husband, a white man or a Chinese. And Pan, for the first time since he had known her, had no answer for him.

II

It was a cool, quiet evening, after a hot day. A new moon was in the sky.

"How beautiful above! How unbeautiful below!" exclaimed Mark Carson involuntarily.

He and Pan had been gazing down from their open retreat into the lantern-lighted, motley-thronged street beneath them.

"Perhaps it isn't very beautiful," replied Pan, "but it is here I live. It is my home." Her voice quivered a little.

He leaned towards her suddenly and grasped her hands.

"Pan," he cried, "you do not belong here. You are white—white."

"No! no!" protested Pan.

"You are," he asserted. "You have no right to be here."

"I was born here," she answered, "and the Chinese people look upon me as their own."

"But they do not understand you," he went on. "Your real self is alien to them. What interest have they in the books you read—the thoughts you think?"

"They have an interest in me," answered faithful Pan. "Oh, do not speak in that way any more."

"But I must," the young man persisted. "Pan, don't you see that you have got to decide what you will be—Chinese or white? You cannot be both."

"Hush! Hush!" bade Pan. "I do not love you when you talk to me like that."

A little Chinese boy brought tea and saffron cakes. He was a picturesque little fellow with a quaint manner of speech. Mark Carson jested

merrily with him, while Pan holding a tea-bowl between her two small hands laughed and sipped. When they were alone again, the silver stream and the crescent moon became the objects of their study. It was a very beautiful evening.

After a while Mark Carson, his hand on Pan's shoulder, sang:

"And forever, and forever,
As long as the river flows,
As long as the heart has passions,
As long as life has woes,
The moon and its broken reflection,
And its shadows shall appear,
As the symbol of love in heaven,
And its wavering image here."

Listening to that irresistible voice singing her heart away, the girl broke down and wept. She was so young and so happy.

"Look up at me," bade Mark Carson. "Oh, Pan! Pan! Those tears prove that you are white."

Pan lifted her wet face.

"Kiss me, Pan," said he. It was the first time.

Next morning Mark Carson began work on the special-feature article which he had been promising his paper for some weeks.

III

"Cursed be his ancestors," bayed Man You.

He cast a paper at his daughter's feet and left the room.

Startled by her father's unwonted passion, Pan picked up the paper, and in the clear passionless light of the afternoon read that which forever after was blotted upon her memory.

"Betrayed! Betrayed! Betrayed to be, a betrayer!"

It burnt red hot; agony unrelieved by words, unassuaged by tears.

So till evening fell. Then she stumbled up the dark stairs which led to the high room open to the stars and tried to think it out. Someone had hurt her. Who was it? She raised her eyes. There shone: "Its Wavering Image." It helped her to lucidity. He had done it. Was it unconsciously dealt—that cruel blow? Ah, well did he know that the sword which pierced her through others, would carry with it to her own heart, the pain of all those others. None knew better than he that she, whom he had called "a white girl, a white woman," would rather that her own naked body and soul had been exposed, than that things, sacred and secret to those who loved her, should be cruelly unveiled and ruthlessly spread before the ridiculing and uncomprehending foreigner. And knowing all this so well, so well, he had carelessly sung her heart away, and with her kiss upon his lips, had smilingly turned and stabbed her. She, who was of the race that remembers.

IV

Mark Carson, back in the city after an absence of two months, thought of Pan. He would see her that very evening. Dear little Pan, pretty Pan, clever Pan, amusing Pan; Pan, who was always so frankly glad to have him come to her; so eager to hear all that he was doing; so appreciative, so inspiring, so loving. She would have forgotten that article by now. Why should a white woman care about such things? Her true self was above it all. Had he not taught her *that* during the weeks in which they had seen so much of one another? True, his last lesson had been a little harsh, and as yet he knew not how she had taken it; but even if its roughness had hurt and irritated, there was a healing balm, a wizard's oil which none knew so well as he how to apply.

But for all these soothing reflections, there was an undercurrent of feeling which caused his steps to falter on his way to Pan. He turned into Portsmouth Square and took a seat on one of the benches facing the fountain erected in memory of Robert Louis Stevenson. Why had Pan failed to answer the note he had written telling her of the assignment which would keep him out of town for a couple of months and giving her his address? Would Robert Louis Stevenson have known why? Yes—and so did Mark Carson. But though Robert Louis Stevenson would have boldly answered himself the question, Mark Carson thrust it aside, arose, and pressed up the hill.

"I knew they would not blame you, Pan!"

"Yes."

"And there was no word of you, dear. I was careful about that, not only for your sake, but for mine."

Silence.

"It is mere superstition anyway. These things have got to be exposed and done away with."

Still silence.

Mark Carson felt strangely chilled. Pan was not herself tonight. She did not even look herself. He had been accustomed to seeing her in American dress. Tonight she wore the Chinese costume. But for her clear-cut features she might have been a Chinese girl. He shivered.

"Pan," he asked, "why do you wear that dress?"

Within her sleeves Pan's small hands struggled together; but her face and voice were calm.

"Because I am a Chinese woman," she answered.

"You are not," cried Mark Carson, fiercely. "You cannot say that now, Pan. You are a white woman—white. Did your kiss not promise me that?"

"A white man!" echoed Pan, her voice rising high and clear to the stars above them. "I would not be a white woman for all the world. *You* are a white man. And *what* is a promise to a white man!"

When she was lying low, the element of Fire having raged so fiercely within her that it had almost shriveled up the childish frame, there came to the house of Man You a little toddler who could scarcely speak. Climbing upon Pan's couch, she pressed her head upon the sick girl's bosom. The feel of that little head brought tears.

"Lo!" said the mother of the toddler. "Thou wilt bear a child thyself some day, and all the bitterness of this will pass away."

And Pan, being a Chinese woman, was comforted.

Source: Far, Sui Sin/Eaton, Edith Maude. "Its Wavering Image." In *Mrs. Spring Fragrance.* Chicago: A. C. McClurg & Co., 1912, 86–95. http://www.archive.org/details/cu31924075243513.

Alison Kim, Interview by Jacquelyn Marie
(2001)

Alison Kim was born in Honolulu in 1955 and moved with her military family all over the United States and Europe. Although she came out in high school, she did not become part of a wider lesbian community until many years later, when she began writing for Demeter *magazine. Kim entered the University of California–Santa Cruz in the mid-1980s; while there, she coedited* Between the Lines, *the first Pacific/Asian lesbian anthology to be published in the United States. In this 2001 interview with Jacquelyn Marie, Kim talks about her desire to explore her identity as both a lesbian and an Asian American and the various communities in which she locates herself.*

Marie: Let's start with some questions about you, when and where were you were born, your family background.

Kim: I was born in 1955 in Honolulu. My mom is Chinese and my dad is Korean. On the Korean side I'm second generation born in the United States. On the Chinese side I am second and a half. English is my first language, my mother's first language. She knew just a tiny bit of Chinese, and my dad knew probably equal amounts of Korean. I lived in Hawai'i for nine months. I was a military brat; my dad joined the service. . . .

[After several moves, Kim's family settled in Northern California.] . . . I started working in Monterey, and I worked for a long time before I decided at age thirty to go back to school, to quit my job. I moved back to Hawai'i for a year, to get closer to family. I had come out earlier, but it was a very white community, so I was wanting to reconnect with family and my Asian culture. I knew my grandmother on my Chinese side was getting older, so I moved back to Hawai'i, thinking I was going to live there for awhile, and go to school there, and do some family and Asian lesbian research. But the island was way too small for me.

Marie: Which island?

Kim: Oahu. Small, just because there's so much family. The thing my mom told me when I went was, 'Don't flaunt it.' That's all she said: 'Don't flaunt it.' And that meant, don't let anybody know that you are a lesbian. The islands are so small. I have second cousins, aunts, uncles, the neighbors—you can't really go anyplace without knowing somebody who knows your family. To not flaunt it means don't be seen. So that was a little bit difficult. My aunt and my uncle really welcomed me into their house, and my partner at the time. I lived with them for a few months. But it was like, oh no I can't do this. We got our own place but the islands were just too small. I'm used to California where you drive for ten hours and you're still not out of the state, whereas in Hawai'i you drive for an hour and you're around the island. . . .

Marie: . . . So when you decided to go to Santa Cruz, I wondered whether you thought of it as a more welcoming community to lesbians and gays? What year did you come to UCSC?

Kim: . . . By the time I moved to Santa Cruz, I was really looking at my cultural identity. Different things happened. I wrote one article in *Demeter* about racism, and was feeling kind of isolated. There was in Monterey a hidden women's community. There were three women of color and I was one of them. It was exciting because I could affirm my lesbian identity. But then it started to be where I felt like hey, there's another part. Plus, I was trying to expand my own identity of who I was as being Asian. I've always identified more Chinese than Korean because I've known the Chinese [part of my] family more. I was doing funny little things, like I knew when we used to go to Chinese restaurants they would always hold the bowl of rice by their mouth and just scoop it in. So I started eating my food like that, holding it and just scooping it in. I could down four bowls of rice at one time, thinking okay, now I'm more Chinese because I can do this.

Santa Cruz was that stepping stone to San Francisco where I thought, well there's a bigger Asian lesbian community. The Monterey area has a good-sized Asian community but it's—I don't know how to describe it. In Pacific Grove, in Monterey they had a large Japanese—They were second or third generation, settled in, very comfortable, and very conservative, I would say. I was thinking, I can't be here and be a lesbian and be out. Plus, we knew a lot of people. My mom and my dad were very gregarious. The Hawaiian community, everybody knew who's who. So that was a little hard. I thought coming to Santa Cruz is a stepping stone to be that much closer [to San Francisco].

In that whole period Chris [Kim's housemate and future wife] was exploring her Latina lesbian identity, and I was exploring my Asian lesbian identity. We were housemates. I had moved into this house. It was a lesbian feminist house. It used to be a white lesbian feminist house. Then it transitioned to being a women of color household.

Marie: In Santa Cruz.

Kim: Yes. Chris moved into the house after me. She was a student at UC and I wasn't a student yet. I'd drive to San Francisco every weekend, because I had heard about the Asian lesbian community. I started going to these meetings. The community in San Francisco was still in its beginning stages, especially compared to where it is today. There was a lot of political strife. I jumped in right at the time when a big split was happening. That was a little bit hard, but at the same time I was in a place where I could go in a room and they were not only lesbian, they were all Asian. It was pretty amazing. Chris and I started coming to San Francisco together. She'd go off to her Latina lesbian stuff; I'd go off to my Asian lesbian stuff; and then we'd go back to Santa Cruz. It was a really great time of mutual support and trying to find who we were in the community. . . .

I've come to an identity of being Asian, but even within that I've always struggled about where I fit, because I am Chinese and Korean. I've identified as more Chinese, but now I don't really fit in the Chinese groups because a lot of them are first or second generation and speak the language. I never spoke any of the language, and my family is really from Hawai'i. So I identify with the local people. But then, I've been in California so long. Unless I'm around my mom and family I don't really talk much pidgin. So then I kind of don't fit in there. I am always struggling with my identity, about where do I fit, either within the lesbian community, within family, or within my social community.

Source: Kim, Alison. "Out in the Redwoods." Interview with Jacquelyn Marie. Irene Reti, ed. Regional History Project of the University Library at the University of California, Santa Cruz. 2001. Reprinted with permission.

David Fleming, "Hello, I'm Japanese: Scott Fujita Is Helping to Bring the Saints Back to Life. And That's the Least Surprising Thing about Him"

(2006)

Most stories of Asian American adoption feature white American parents bringing their children from Asia. In the Fujita family, the story is reversed: Rod Fujita, a Japanese American born in the Gila River internment camp during World War II, along with his wife, Helen, who is white, adopted their white son, Scott, and raised him as half Japanese. He and his brother, also adopted, grew up celebrating Japanese cultural traditions with their paternal grandparents, eating Japanese American food, and learning about their family's history.

Scott Fujita was interviewed by ESPN's David Fleming in 2006, after he signed with the New Orleans Saints. In his interview, he talks about how his father's and grandparents' experiences during internment have given him a particular social and political sensibility that carries over into his football career. In addition, Fujita's adoption story brings up fascinating questions about what it means to be an Asian American. How important are physical appearance, biology, and blood lines? Is culture inherited or taught? Is it possible to be adopted into an ethnic community not yours from birth? Is personal identity an internal or external construct? And what happens when family bonds transcend ethnic and racial boundaries?

It's odd at first.

When you push open the massive mahogany door of Scott Fujita's warehouse-style loft in New Orleans, there's a Mardi Gras-style balcony up front and an exposed wall of burned-black bricks near the back. Yet despite how much Fujita says his Japanese heritage means to him, there's no Asian-influenced decor anywhere to be seen. Then he leads you around a corner to his den. And there, sitting on a white metal computer desk (next to Barack Obama's new book) is a stunning blue ceramic recreation of *The Great Wave Off Kanagawa.*

Admiring the piece as he moves, Fujita seems too tall and fluid to be a linebacker. Then he sits down, and his desk—now in the visual frame with his massive shoulders, back and forearms—suddenly looks like a TV tray. Fujita begins opening files on his computer, and with each click he reveals the most cherished artifacts of his remarkable journey, from adopted child to college walk-on to discarded draft pick to centerpiece of the resurgent Saints defense.

He opens a picture of his parents, reaches out to touch their faces on the screen. Given up by his birth mother when he was 6 weeks old, Scott was adopted by Helen and Rod Fujita and raised in Camarillo, Calif. Helen, a retired secretary, is white. Rod, a retired high school teacher and coach, is a third generation Japanese-American. He was born inside an Arizona internment camp during World War II.

Fujita opens more photos. There's one of him holding hands with his wife and college sweetheart, Jaclyn, on Senior Day at Cal; this was a few months before the Chiefs took him in the fifth round of the 2002 draft. There's another one of him playing Pee Wee football, the chubby-cheeked, blond-haired, green-eyed kid with the Japanese name on his jersey. There's another of his paternal grandmother, Lillie, who once overheard him introducing himself like this: "Hi! I'm Scott. I'm 4. And I'm Japanese."

"I swear I'm not delusional," Fujita says, chuckling at the memory. "I know I don't have a drop of Japanese blood in me. But what is race? It's just a label. The way you're raised, your family, the people you love—that means more than everything else."

Many adopted kids grapple to come to terms with who they are and where they came from, especially those raised by parents who don't look like them. But Fujita says he doesn't struggle with his identity, never has. First as a child and now as a football player, his path to success has always been about the same thing: defining for himself who he is. "That's the connection point for Scott," Lillie says. "You choose to be what you are. It's not your location, your obstacles or your skin. You. You choose. He learned that from his family."

Not that he wasn't tested. When his parents took him and older brother, Jason, who was also adopted, to stores, they got the occasional odd looks. Sometimes Scott had to show his ID to substitute teachers who didn't believe that his last name belonged to him. And he ate so much rice with chopsticks that he was 8 before he knew what to do with a baked potato. But he shrugged off most of it, confident in thinking of himself as half Japanese at heart. To his dad, it was even simpler: "American, Japanese. To me he's always just been my son."

Every Jan. 1, the Fujitas celebrated Shogatsu, Japanese New Year's. Every May 5, Rod would raise a koi flag on a bamboo pole in the backyard in honor of the Japanese national holiday of Kodomo-no-hi (Children's Day). But because Rod had become, as he says, "Americanized," most of Scott's knowledge of Japanese culture came from Lillie and Nagao, Scott's grandfather.

The two were extremely strict with Rod when he was a kid, but they spoiled their grandchildren.

Nagao often showed up unannounced at school to take Scott and Jason out for ice cream and to go toy shopping. During these field trips, Scott would sit in the backseat of Nagao's car, gazing at the California coast while listening to tales of great samurai warriors, Japanese art and history, and majestic places like Mount Fuji. "When you've never met a single blood relative in your life," Scott says, "the idea of ethnicity and blood relations takes on a different meaning. I found a very beautiful and interesting culture filled with dignity, respect and honor, and it became mine."

He also connected to his ancestors through his anger about, and empathy for, Japanese-American residents who were interned during World War II. His grandparents had a wrenching story to tell. In 1941, Lillie and Nagao were students at Cal, planning to get married. A few days after the Japanese attack on Pearl Harbor, Lillie was crossing the street in Berkeley when another female student ran up to her, screaming in her face, "You little Jap, why don't you go back home!?" Lillie is a tiny, demure woman. At his wedding reception, Scott got down on his knees to dance with his grandma, only to discover he was still too tall. But that day in 1941, she roared back: "I'm an American too. And a better one than you are!"

Two months later, Franklin D. Roosevelt issued Executive Order 9066: the forcible evacuation of 120,000 American residents of Japanese descent to 10 internment camps. To avoid being separated, Nagao and Lillie married before the order was carried out. Shortly after, they were forced, along with their families, to relocate to an Army barracks in Gila River, Ariz. Unable to pay their mortgage, Nagao's parents lost their farmland in Ventura County.

The government did allow Nagao to leave camp and return to college, but only at a school it approved: BYU. Lillie had to stay behind. Amazingly, after Nagao graduated, he enlisted to fight for the very country that was imprisoning his family. Deployed to Italy, he fought with the all-Japanese 442nd Regimental Combat Team, one of the most decorated battalions of the war. While Nagao was overseas in 1943, Lillie gave birth to Rod at the camp.

On Jan. 2, 1945, FDR revoked his executive order; the last camp closed in early 1946. Nagao attended law school at Cal on the GI Bill, then moved with Lillie and Rod back to Oxnard, where he became one of the first bilingual attorneys in Southern California. He died in 1988. A year later, Lillie received a reparations check for $20,000 and a written apology from then-president George Bush. The letter, which Scott keeps on the computer in his den, says in part: "Your fellow Americans have, in a very real sense, renewed their traditional commitment to the ideals of freedom, equality and justice." Even now, Scott gets angry when he mentions how Japanese internment was never brought up in school. His desktop is full of research on the topic, including photos of the camps and government documents.

Given the depth of his feelings, it makes sense that Fujita has adopted the ideals of perseverance that sustained his grandparents. As a high school freshman in 1994, he was his father's height: 5'6". Over the next three years, he shot up to 6'4" and became a star safety for Rio Mesa High. But lacking mass, he drew meager attention from major D1 schools, and Cal offered him a shot to walk on only a few months before his graduation.

Fujita redshirted his freshman year, but not before blowing away coaches in his first camp by helping out the injury-plagued Bears at safety even though both of his hands were clubbed up with tape—one because it was broken, the other because of a nasty gash. The Bears gave him a scholarship the next spring, and he added 20 pounds to his 6'5" frame while switching from safety to linebacker. But as a sophomore in 1999, he was plagued by nerve stingers in his neck. Following the season, he had career-threatening surgery that put him in the ICU for three days and a neck halo for a week. That was March. By August, he was cracking skulls again in live practice drills. Two seasons later, he was among Cal's leading tacklers. "I call it Pat Tillman syndrome," says former Cal defensive coordinator Lyle Setencich, now at Texas

Tech. "There are a few players you come across who give their heart and soul to the game. That's Pat Tillman, and that's Scott Fujita."

In Kansas City, Fujita's relentless play led his teammates to name him the Chiefs' best rookie of 2002, and he topped the team in tackles in 2003 and 2004. At times, though, he suffered from "walk-on disease." Fearing the next bad play might be his last, he stressed and pressed, not realizing that often the only difference between good and great linebackers is just a stutter step—the split-second difference between thinking through a play and reacting on instinct. "I used to be the guy running around, banging his head on the walls before a game," Fujita says. "Not anymore. Sometimes success is more about relaxing and getting comfortable."

And finding the right fit. After making over their linebacker corps, the Chiefs traded Fujita to Dallas five days before the 2005 season. He started the final eight games for the Cowboys and made enough plays to draw interest, as an unrestricted free agent, from Dallas, Jacksonville, Philadelphia and Oakland. His first trip, though, was to New Orleans, where former Cowboys assistant Sean Payton had just been hired as head coach.

The first time Fujita met with Payton in his office at the team's practice facility (which had been used as a national command center during Katrina), he was struck by how Payton had embraced the Saints' role as sports savior of New Orleans. Sappy or not, Fujita wanted to buy in, if only because he thought that embodying something bigger than the game would bring out his best as a player. "The hurricane, my family's internment, issues of race—I feel like all that is a part of me when I play."

Shortly after his sit-down with Payton, Fujita and Jaclyn were enjoying dinner at Emeril's when Saints GM Mickey Loomis called to thank him for visiting. "I'm ready to sign," Fujita blurted. Ten minutes later, Loomis raced in with a contract in his hands. Fujita got a four-year, $12 million deal for dessert, and the Saints got a key piece for their rebuilt defense without breaking the bank.

On Sept. 25, during the grand reopening of the Superdome on *Monday Night Football,* Saints defensive back Mike McKenzie introduced Fujita to a national TV audience by calling him "the Asian Assassin." On the very next play, Fujita erupted through a crack in the Falcons line and sacked a thoroughly shocked Mike Vick, forcing a fumble and a fourth down. Fujita celebrated with a fist-in palm samurai bow (a move now being mimicked on high school football fields in New Orleans). The Saints then blocked the Falcons' punt and recovered it in the end zone to begin the 23–3 romp.

By the time the Saints reached their Week 7 bye, coming off gritty wins over Tampa and Philly, they had morphed from Katrina recovery mascots to contenders. Most of the hype has centered around the backfield of Drew Brees, Deuce McAllister and Reggie Bush, but the real credit belongs to the Fujita-fueled defense that ranked fourth in the NFC through Week 8. Playing behind a dominant, attacking front four, Fujita is often left unblocked, free to shoot run gaps, roam the deep middle and wreak havoc 80 feet in either direction. He has prototypical size, strength and speed, but it's his lightning-fast presnap recognition that keeps him one step ahead of opponents and all over the stat sheet—a team-high 55 tackles and two picks, plus 2.5 sacks, a forced fumble and five passes defensed. "In the huddle," McKenzie says, "he looks like a missile ready to launch. He's everywhere out there."

Lest anyone want to dismiss Fujita as an overblown do-gooder, note his $7,500 bill for a low hit away from the action on Carolina's Steve Smith in Week 4. Or the red, swollen cleat scars up and down his shins, courtesy of illegal leg whips by blockers—the ultimate sign of respect in the trenches.

Halfway through the Saints' bye week, in fact, Fujita's shins are still so swollen and discolored that he has to gimp the last few blocks home from his favorite sushi joint, Rock-n-Sake (home of the Mt. Fujita Roll). When he gets home, there are half a dozen UPS boxes full of Pottery Barn picture frames waiting for him. One of the candidates for the new frames is a photo of the banner that Fujita's neighbors made for him after the Eagles game. Spread out across his parking space, the sign reads: McNabb Got FUJITA'ED.

It was a nice gesture, and it's a decent enough photo, but the universal truth behind the message is what makes Fujita eager to frame it: the idea that no matter where you're from or how you were raised, no matter what you look like or who you play for, when fans turn your name into a verb, well, you've arrived.

Source: Fleming, David. "Hello, I'm Japanese: Scott Fujita Is Helping to Bring the Saints Back to Life. And That's the Least Surprising Thing about Him." *ESPN the Magazine* (the Content). November 20, 2006. ESPN website. http://sports.espn.go.com/espnmag/story?id=3643439. Accessed October 2010. © ESPN The Magazine, 2006. Article reprinted with permission.

JoAnn Balingit, Three Poems and an Essay
(2007)

JoAnn Balingit is a Filipina American author and Delaware's 16th poet laureate. She teaches poetry in community organizations and schools. "History Textbook, America," "Story I Learn at Forty-Nine," and "My Mother Explains My Father to Her Girls" are reflections on Balingit's Filipino and German American parents. In these poems, Balingit explores how cultures mix in marriage and family and the incomplete ways in which immigrants leave their lives behind. The subsequent personal essay provides additional background information on Balingit's parents' histories and relationship. She also discusses how her father's upbringing in the American-colonized Philippines affected his subsequent decision to immigrate to the United States and turn his back on the language and culture of his homeland.

HISTORY TEXTBOOK, AMERICA

I'd search for Philippines in History class.
The index named one page, moved on to Pierce.
The Making of America marched past
my enigmatic father's place of birth.
The week he died some man we didn't know
called up. *This is his brother,* one more shock,
phoning for him. "He died three days ago."
The leaden black receiver did not talk.

My uncle never gave his name or town,
we never heard from him. Was it a dream?
The earpiece roar dissolved to crackling sounds,
a dial tone erased the Philippines.
And yet my world grows huge with maps, crisscrossed,
my history alive with all I've lost.

STORY I LEARN AT FORTY-NINE

Aunt Rita's lovely cursive
bares its hips, flinging words like
confetti, a story where my mother
delivers herself whole to my father—
elope they called it, a foreigner,
Filipino—old enough to be her
grandfather! Well not quite, Rita,
he was forty-nine and she nineteen
in all, but thirty years is still *one* generation even if
Joan was just a kid, all impulse and beauty, who
knew her mind before he sent the ticket—St.
Louis, a plane fare away! Rising past
midnight she must have worked quickly,
nickels tucked in pleat pockets, must have
opened her bag one last time, called Kitty to
pat the orange glow-in-the-dark before she fled
quietly into one or two a.m. on the moonlit
road. Barely can she make out her house on its hill,
saddle shoes tipping stones like skunks nosing
trash to steal, when Taxi pulls up, its driver, dazed
understudy for tonight's dramatic role,
Viceroy a-dangle as he grunts to slam her door but

"Wait!" she hisses, hand on headrest—as a phantom
X-acto knife slices this life off the next.
"You headed somewhere?" She nods. The Talon
zipper of her good jacket gapes. It's jammed.

MY MOTHER EXPLAINS MY FATHER TO HER GIRLS

    Face from the radiant
other side of the globe. While mine grew dark,
his sky rose tropical, story-book, crammed with color
plates, Marco Polos, Magellans, palaces
    beyond the sea . . .

The Midwest's silver sky looked tarnished.
Some years we had six months of winter.
    Into the office wafts a man
from *the islands with the climate of heaven*
—warmth without heat, coolness without cold—
    who grew up wearing hand-woven linen

all seasons, was weaned by women in white
    gathered lawn and silk sleeves
lit from within like those star-shaped lamps
in festive doorways. What dreams I had
    of him. I painted
mango sunsets in a bowl.

How could a grown man's voice
    be fine as a line cast over water,
land and sink without a ripple? You know
at dusk how sky melts with ocean
    into one aqua plane from your toes
to the world's curve you can't tell

where you are from anything? So I fell
    into your father's voice—
tailored wool, silk tie, fedora. He glowed
like the boss's mahogany. I jumped aboard his liner
into his tiger's eye, his Mariana Trench, his valley
    carved of stone.

No, I do not forget our final disaster.
    I know his silence branded you
as a vine over time will tunnel the bark of a tree.
His beautiful syllables left him when he
came to master English and America
    and me.

    Yet girls, should you find some
few of his words survive your native jungles—
    let them forage like wild pigs!

PERSONAL ESSAY

I am first-generation Filipina-American, the third eldest of 12 children. My father, a Filipino immigrant from Macabebe, Pampanga, left his homeland at the age of 26 and never returned. My mother, a German-American woman from Canton, Ohio, was a Midwesterner whose ancestors fled Alsace-Lorraine in the mid to late 1800's.

My father arrived in San Francisco by ship in May of 1929, with a degree in Engineering from The University of the Philippines and money from his family to attend graduate school. Family lore says that he spent the money but did not complete his schooling. From his photo albums we know he travelled in California, Arizona, Missouri, Tennessee, Mississippi and Louisiana. His photos show pretty American sweethearts, corporate Christmas parties, bowling leagues, city sights—and familiar-looking children we do not know. Likely, long before he met my mother, my father had another family.

Extraordinarily private all his life, indeed taciturn about sharing personal history, Jesus Maglanoc Balingit divulged few details of childhood, friends, family or homeland in response to our questions. I know he became a naturalized U.S. citizen in 1946—the first year he could legally apply. I do not know the names of his parents or siblings.

From the 1930's through 1966, when my father suffered a disabling stroke, he worked for American corporations such as Bechtel, Joslyn & Ryan (Naval Architects), Martin-Marietta and Wellman-Lord. In 1951 he met my mother, Joan Carol Kuntz, at Arthur G. McKee Corporation in Cleveland, Ohio. A talented artist, Joan was 19, a year out of high school, and working at the engineering firm as a drafting apprentice. My father was 49. They married in 1952 and started a family life of moving from state to state, ever southward, babies in tow. They settled in Lakeland, Florida in 1963. I think my father was working all his life to get back to the tropics.

I believe the violent occupation and Americanization of the Philippines transformed my father's psyche even while he was in the womb. After all, he was born in 1903, just eight months after the U.S. government declared the Philippine-American War (1899–1902) officially over. Actually, Filipino armed resistance to the occupation went on for years. Reared and schooled during this era of intense and traumatic cultural change in his native land, my father eventually came to believe that he need not—perhaps must not—perpetuate Filipino culture in his American-born children's lives. For example, my father declined to teach us any of his native language, Tagalog. What little I know about Filipino culture and my particular heritage, I have gathered through research.

Though I am proud to be both Filipina and American, there are times I feel I am not fully either. Perhaps I have inherited from my father, and from my mother too, a dilemma familiar to immigrants. They perpetually search for home—in an effort to define the self.

Source: Balingit, JoAnn. "History Textbook, America," "Story I Learn at Forty-Nine," "My Mother Explains My Father to Her Girls."and "History Textbook, America" originally appeared in *Best New Poets 2007*. Meridian: University of Virginia Press, 2007. Poems and essay used with permission of author (http://joannbalingit.org).

Chloe Sun, "Against Overwhelming Odds: Chinese Women in Ministry" (2007)

Chloe Sun is a professor of Old Testament at Logos Evangelical Seminary in Southern California. Her parents are ethnic Chinese Vietnamese, and Sun was born in China and raised in Hong Kong before she moved to the United States in the 1980s. Sun's essay, calling for the Chinese Christian church to give women a greater voice in ministry, also examines the author's own identity, situated in between first- and second-generation immigrant cultures. In a previous essay, Sun identified herself as a "Third Culture Kid": "the marginalized of the marginalized . . . part of three countries, cultures and languages, but none of them, on their own . . . a perfect fit." The following essay, "Against Overwhelming Odds," originally published on the Asian American Women on Leadership *blog, examines the intersection between religion, gender, and ethnicity.*

Cultural Identity

Let me start by sharing my social location and the struggles that I face as a Chinese woman, both in academia and at church. I am an ethnic Chinese. But since my grandmother is half Vietnamese and half Chinese and my parents were both born and raised in Vietnam, I have some Vietnamese heritage, although I've never been to Vietnam nor speak the language. I lived in both China and Hong Kong before I came to the U.S. and I am fluent in Mandarin and Cantonese. So, the term "Chinese" itself encompasses a diverse background.

Because of this diversity, I struggle with my cultural identity. I am no longer a first generation immigrant because I have embraced the American way of life, but I am not quite an American because the Americans always see me as a "Chinese girl." Within the Chinese context, I am closer to the second generation culture yet not totally belonging to that culture. I am always in the state of "in-between-ness" wherever I go, but I am not a 1.5. I think the acculturation process depends on many factors and not just the age we come to the U.S.

It's been a struggle to teach at a first generation setting during the week and minister to the second generation at church on weekends. On Sundays, I worship God with contemporary music and on Monday mornings, I sing traditional hymns at our prayer meeting at the seminary. I am shifting cultural gear every week, going back and forth, not feeling like I totally belong to either the first or the second generation culture. Although I can read and write in Chinese and English, neither of them is perfect. This state of "in-between-ness" has been disconcerting.

Ministry Identity

I received the call to ministry during my sophomore year in college, so, I went straight to seminary right after college to pursue an M.Div. In several classes, I was the only Chinese woman. However, when I was single, there seemed to be plenty of ministry opportunities. I could serve at a local Chinese church as a woman minister (of course that depended on many factors), or work in a para-church ministry on campus, or as a missionary overseas. But then after I got married to another seminarian, things became different. I was no longer perceived as a minister in my own right, but as a spouse of a seminarian and later as a pastor's wife. I remember when my husband and I were at Dallas Theological Seminary, whenever we visited different churches, people always paid attention to him, asking him, "what year are you in seminary?" "Have you worked with the youth?" And they simply ignored my presence.

The idea of pursuing a Ph.D. arose not only because of my interest in theological education, but also because of the dilemma I was facing: If I wanted to retain my own ministry identity, then I needed to have a different ministry than my husband's. If I wanted to stay with my husband at one church, then I would become a buy-one-get-one-free pastor's wife, since it is very rare for a Chinese church to be willing to have both husband and wife on staff, paying two salaries. Pursuing a Ph.D. seemed like the best possible option to have my own ministry and to stay at the same church with my husband. Another drawback of marrying someone who is also in ministry is that the wife tends to follow the geographical location of her husband's ministry and not the other way around whereas a single woman can go anywhere she wants.

Not all Chinese women who are called to ministry are interested in pursuing a Ph.D., considering the time it takes, the cost it involves and the turmoil it brings. Some of my married Chinese woman students who graduated with an M.Div. who felt called to their own ministries, ended up serving alongside their husbands as spouses only and taking care of kids at home. Some still cannot find a ministry position at Chinese churches after years of graduation. Some are doing clerical work at Christian organizations. The ministry paths for Chinese women are very limited. In general, Chinese churches prefer hiring male pastors. Many denominations such as Southern Baptist and Chinese Missionary Alliance still hold conservative views about the roles of women in ministry. Even though my own denomination (EFC) supports women in ministry and approves of women's ordination (we even have a few women who function as senior pastors), the reservation for women as pastors still persists among pastors and church members. The lack of positions at churches open to Chinese women is disempowering.

The lack of support for women as pastors can come not only from the church but also from parents. My parents never approved of my seminary education or my ministry at church. In fact, it wasn't until I started teaching as a professor that my dad told me "finally, you are more 'normal.'"

Race/Gender/Age Issues

Ministry and theological education are largely male-dominated. When I was at American seminaries, both my race and my gender stood out because there weren't many Chinese women around. Naturally, finding role models was difficult as well, which often resulted in loneliness. At the American seminaries (excluding DTS), race is more of an issue then gender. People always asked me where I came from. Some minority students were treated differently from the white students. At the Chinese seminary, gender seems more of an issue than race. In regard to gender, most of my male colleagues keep a friendly distance from me—reminding me of my "potential danger" to men as a woman. In terms of temperament, as a Chinese woman, if I were tough and outspoken, I would be perceived as a roaring, defensive "lioness." If I remained silent and gentle, I would be considered a "cute little lamb" but would have less credibility to influence. I am yet to find a Chinese woman in ministry who has the toughness of a lioness and the softness of a lamb.

Age is another issue. Grey hair is still a symbol of wisdom in the Chinese culture. When an older Chinese pastor or professor speaks, he seems to gain instant respect. But for a younger female, I have to make extra effort to earn my respect. In Chinese culture as in most Asian cultures, it seems "safer" to be an older woman in ministry. One of the Chinese pastors once told me, "If I want to hire a woman on staff, I will hire an older woman so no one would say anything." It is also "safer" for Chinese women to serve as a children's director or a Christian Education director as opposed to senior pastor. But then not all women have the calling or gifts to work with children or youth. Again, the ministry path for Chinese women is very limited.

Balancing between Ministry and Family

Another struggle that I face as a Chinese woman in ministry is the juggling between multiple roles, particularly between family and ministry. I think this is true for most working women. When Tim Tseng asked me to be on the panel tonight, the first thought that came to mind was "I need to find child care for my son. I need to check with my husband's schedule and with my in-law's schedule." Only then could I consider the possibility of accepting this engagement. And there is always a guilty feeling whenever I leave my child to another care-taker. Men can have both family and ministry at the same time, but it is often difficult for most women in ministry.

For single women in ministry, many of my Chinese women students are in their 40s and still single. What are the chances for them to be married? Very few Chinese men would want to marry women in ministry, especially when these women are over 40.

Physical limitation is another issue. Pregnancy, taking care of young children, menopause and decreasing energy level affect our effectiveness during certain seasons of our ministry experience.

Conclusion

To conclude, as Chinese women in ministry, the odds are against us—from outside factors and from within.

Regarding outside factors, Paul's statements that women should not preach or women should not have authority over men are still etched deeply into the minds of Chinese Christians. The predominant preference for male pastors, the judgmental attitude from those who hold conservative views against women in ministry, the lack of ministry opportunities for Chinese women at church, the lack of role models, the lack of parental support, all contribute to the odds from outside.

From within, our own struggles with cultural and ministry identities, with multiple roles, with balancing between family and ministry, between being a "lioness" and a "lamb," our physical limitations and the sense of loneliness that we are on our own all add to the challenge as Chinese women in ministry.

I can't help but ask God, "Why are you calling us, the marginalized of the marginalized, into ministry?" I think God is doing something unconventional by calling Chinese women into ministry against the cultural norms and traditional expectations. Perhaps God is challenging all of us to break our own stereotypes for Chinese women in ministry and to seek for a better alternative to welcome and to support them for the common good.

Source: Sun, Chloe. "Against Overwhelming Odds: Chinese Women in Ministry." September 23, 2007. Asian American Women on Leadership (blog). http://aawol .wordpress.com/2007/09/23/against-overwhelming-odds-chinese-women-in-ministry/. Reprinted with permission.

Simone Momove Fujita, "Little Momo in the Big Apple" (2008)

Simone M. Fujita is a yonsei hapa (fourth-generation biracial Japanese American) of Japanese and African American heritage. She grew up in Los Angeles, and in 1994, she moved to New York City to attend New York University. Fujita's essay, "Little Momo in the Big Apple," was originally published by Discover Nikkei, a project of the Japanese American National Museum. Here, Fujita describes how her experiences in Los Angeles and New York City influenced her ethnic and racial identity and her sense of belonging in the Asian American community.

The Academy Award-winning 2004 film *Crash* was touted as a painfully honest and true-to-life portrayal of race relations in Los Angeles, but when I viewed the film, there was very little about it that resembled the city that my family has called home for several generations.

(Perhaps this is why the movie is on my list of top ten least favorite movies of all time, but, alas, that is a story for another time.) The interactions in the film were not similar to any that I either experienced or witnessed in Los Angeles. If anything, the film reminded me more of a few bizarre racial incidents I experienced during my college years in New York City, where both ethnic diversity and expansive racial divides exist in abundance—some would argue, much like Los Angeles. This article is my first attempt to synthesize the culture clashes I have experienced in the two American cities that I call home.

Part 1: L.A. Youth

From first through eighth grades (with the exception of fourth), I attended Maryknoll School, a small, Catholic elementary school located in downtown Los Angeles' arts district, nestled between the neighborhoods of Little Tokyo and East L.A.'s Boyle Heights. Intertwined in Maryknoll's history and mine are the stories of Maryknoll's Catholic missionaries to Japan, and the Japanese Americans that settled in Boyle Heights. My *kibei nisei* grandmother was among those converted from Buddhism to Catholicism, and like other Japanese Catholics living in Boyle Heights, she sent my mother and aunts to Maryknoll. Years later, my cousins and I attended Maryknoll too. In 1994, I was among the last students to graduate from the school before it closed down, to later reopen as a Japanese Catholic Center.

By the time I attended Maryknoll, the ethnic demographics of its student population had shifted dramatically from the days when my mother, aunts, and older cousins attended. Once predominantly Japanese, it had since become a commuter school that was home to a mixture of working class Asians and Latinos, with few Japanese families remaining. Its Nikkei roots were still somewhat palpable, but the addition of other cultures made our school feel a bit more international. At one Christmas program, we sang "Joy to the World" in about seven different languages, and it felt as if everyone's heritage was represented. In second grade, a parent taught us an Okinawan folk dance that we later performed at a local mall. My best friends were Kazanna (one of the few students of mixed European American heritage), Jennifer (of Guatemalan and Japanese heritage), and the two Monicas (both Chicana). Although Kazanna was the only Irish American student I knew, Maryknoll's Boy Scout troop held an annual St. Patrick's Day dinner complete with corned beef and cabbage. Many of our classmates and most of the teachers were Filipino. Our potlucks included pancit, lumpia, teriyaki, enchiladas, sushi, chicken adobo, pizza, and various American junk food, and we ate everything without hesitation because it just tasted good. Around Christmastime, we would all go to J-town to take pictures with "Shogun Santa" in Japanese Village Plaza. This was the environment in which I felt most at home—a setting which represented a sampling of Los Angeles' ethnic heterogeneity.

In retrospect, I recognize how significant this time period was in shaping my worldview. Exposure to a variety of different cultures at such a young age was really important to me, as the cultural exchange my friends and I experienced during those years occurred so naturally. My friends and I were open to learning about each other's heritages not because we were being forced to due to a mandate for multiculturalism but instead because we were sincerely curious about each other. As a result of this organic intermingling of cultures and histories both at school and in my multiethnic extended family, I had personal connections with such a wide variety of people that I never grew up viewing other cultures as foreign, weird, or bad. It was not until much later that I learned that this type of openness towards others was something that I took for granted.

After Maryknoll, I left the familiarity of downtown to attend Mayfield, an all-girl, Catholic high school located in an affluent part of Pasadena (a suburb of Los Angeles). Mayfield was composed of dramatically different demographics, predominantly upper income and Caucasian. Coming from a commuter background, with a mother who worked full-time, was a native Angelena, and exposed me to many different parts of Los Angeles, I was surprised to learn that very few Mayfield students had ever ventured outside of Pasadena and its neighboring suburban communities.

Despite this initial culture shock, I eventually made friends with some girls who had similar tastes in humor and music. But unfortunately, all was not good—my identity was challenged on multiple occasions—not by white classmates, but by my Asian peers. Perhaps in reaction to the dearth of ethnic diversity at the school, nearly all of the Asian students belonged to tightly-knit Asian cliques. Although I was accustomed to hanging around other Asians, I felt totally disconnected from those at Mayfield. I attempted to participate in the Pacific Asian Club only to be met with cold stares and ignored during its off-campus outings. This was the first time that I remember my Asianness being questioned so blatantly, and as an introverted and awkward freshman, this rejection really hurt. I actively swore off participation in ethnic activities until a friend of mine became president of the club in our senior year. (I did not participate in the Black Student Union during high school because I was already friends with its three members—that's how small the African American population was!)

My four years at Mayfield provided me with ample learning opportunities both in and out of the classroom. As I rejoined the club from which I was once rejected and connected with a flurry of new friends from other activities, I experienced a zen-like moment of inner peace. Maybe it was a latent effect of our touchy-feeling senior retreat, but a funny thing happened—as graduation neared, I somehow felt a bit closer to all of my classmates, discovering that almost everyone has at least one endearing quality (strange but true). Mayfield was a great growing experience for me because it also challenged me to address my own assumptions about those who I perceived to be very different from me—wealthy white girls. I learned that many of the girls in my class, while undeniably privileged, were relatively down-to-earth and open-minded despite their sheltered upbringings. But perhaps most importantly, Mayfield also taught me that I could create my own sense of home wherever I chose to build it. This particular lesson became even more valuable after my high school graduation, when I moved from California to New York for college.

Part 2: East Coast Style

When I decided to attend college in New York, I knew there would be a period of adjustment after leaving my family and home state of California, but I did not anticipate the type of culture shock that ensued. This culture shock did not arise from becoming accustomed to pedestrian life, from adjusting to life in a densely populated metropolis, or from the challenge of making new friends at a new school. Instead, my culture shock resulted from the realization that New York was indeed diverse, but in ways remarkably different from Los Angeles. The way that people interacted, and more specifically, the lack of meaningful interaction between people of different cultures, felt foreign to me. There was ethnic diversity, but based on my limited experience (as a student, a non-native New Yorker, and as a Manhattan dweller who rarely ventured to other boroughs), each ethnic group seemed segregated from the others. As a result, I could not see where I fit within the culture of New York or its history, and that left me feeling displaced. In an attempt to connect with my new surroundings, I actively sought out community.

I initially felt homesick often. I missed the mishmash of cultures with which I was raised. I had frequent cravings for easily accessible, tasty, and inexpensive Mexican food (L.A.'s soul food). I would fondly remember the familiar faces and foods of the small, family-owned restaurants and stores I frequented in Little Tokyo and in the San Gabriel Valley. Sure, New York accents were fun at first, but after a while, I began to miss the laidback way people talked back home. I even missed the rough-and-tumble cholo culture, nonexistent in New York. Most of all, I missed not having to constantly explain myself—the luxury of having people who understood what I was talking about when I made references to parts of Los Angeles or to local bands that my friends and I followed. I was probably more homesick for an understanding of where I was "coming from" than I was for any actual place.

One day, after having a difficult time locating a Japanese grocery store and realizing I had no "Japantown" to turn to, it suddenly hit me how different the nature of the Nikkei community in New York is, compared with California. While California's Japanese Americans often have roots in the U.S. dating back to the 1800's, many of New York's Nikkei are Shin-Issei (who immigrated to the U.S. in the years following World War II) and their descendants. In New York there is no dedicated Japantown, established in the early 20th century, as there are in multiple locations in California. There are pockets of Japanese businesses and populations, but again, the nature of this community was unfamiliar to me. I did not see where I fit in, and I could not understand how to connect with it. Eventually, a longing for the Japanese American culture I grew up with in addition to my budding curiosity about the history of my Asian ancestors led me to take a few courses in Asian/Pacific/American studies.

The bad memories of my high school experiences with the Pacific Asian Club were still so powerful that when I finally built up the courage to take a course in Asian and Asian American Contemporary Art, I felt shy and awkward, transported back to ninth grade. I self-consciously imagined that everyone was staring at me, wondering, "Why is *she* in this class?" When a professor asked why I chose to take the class, I defensively replied, "because my mom is Japanese American." In time (and after a few more classes), I grew more comfortable and lost the chip on my shoulder. I fed my growing interest in Asian American history and the Asian American community in New York by taking more A/P/A studies classes, eventually earning a minor in the subject.

History became interesting to me when I finally discovered my place within it. My amazing A/P/A studies professors (Margo Machida, Angel Velasco Shaw, Anne-Marie Tupuola, Jack Tchen, Jason Kao Hwang) were not content to simply rehash the past—they strongly encouraged us to create, shape and preserve our own histories. In highly interactive class formats, we were active participants doing in-depth research, meeting with cultural activists, conducting oral history projects, and working on projects of our own. I learned about my Japanese American forebears on the West Coast as I had hoped, but I also gained a better overall understanding of the first waves of immigration, how the Asian American community on the East Coast was formed, the impact of the Asian American Movement, and the vibrant Asian/Pacific/American communities that continue to flourish (from coast-to-coast). As an added bonus, I also met a new group of wonderful, community-minded friends who shared many of my interests. It was a very exciting and inspiring period of time in my life.

My homesick feelings of displacement dissipated once I located untapped sources of community. After becoming more involved with my A/P/A classes, the multiracial student club I started on campus, and the Asian American community in New York, I finally began to feel truly comfortable here. I discovered the warm, welcoming side of the city that I never knew existed. New York had suddenly become my second home, a place where I too belonged.

Source: Fujita, Simone Momove. "Little Momo in the Big Apple." 2008. Japanese American National Museum. Discover Nikkei website. http://www.discovernikkei.org/en/journal/2008/5/16/little-momo/. Used with permission of the author.

Laylaa Abdul-Khabir, "Living the Mixed Life: Growing Up as a Black Chinese Muslim in America"

(2008)

Less than 5 percent of interracial marriages in the United States are between Asian Americans and African Americans. Laylaa Abdul-Khabir's family is in this minority: Her father is African American, and her mother is a first-generation Chinese immigrant. Abdul-Khabir was born in Beijing, China, where she lived with her grandparents for several years. She then moved to the United States and grew up in Hesperia, in Southern California. Her parents converted to Islam, raising their children Muslim. In this excerpt from her essay "Living the Mixed Life," written while she was an undergraduate at the University of California–Berkeley, Abdul-Khabir outlines the various roles played by ethnicity and religion in her personal identity.

Are we defined by our ethnicity?

As a young girl, I thought my ethnic identity was the same as everyone else's. At five-years old, I had just returned to the United States from China after living with my grandparents in Beijing for two years. Starting elementary school in America,

I thought all the kids in my class were the same 'color' as me and it didn't occur to me that anyone had different ethnic or cultural backgrounds. I didn't think at the time that my mom is Chinese, and my dad is African-American; to me, they were just my mom and dad and we were no different from the typical American family. Being raised in a Muslim home, I wore a scarf on my head to school to cover my hair, and when my classmates asked me why, I said, "It's because of my religion." I had a vague sense of being different from the other kids because of this, but otherwise, I was a kid caught up in my own world. In class, I fit my shapes together, organized my Crayolas, and usually finished first in the mini-Math problem set. (Should I have known I was Asian then?) Of course, I counted my numbers in Chinese when learning addition and subtraction, but this didn't bother me; I just did it naturally. I didn't perceive myself to be distinctively different from the standard first-grader.

It was only later, during the last few years of elementary school, when I noticed I had to start defining myself. Since I look more Asian than Black, kids would approach me and ask me things like, "Are you Japanese?" or "What are you?" and, the question that would follow me throughout my middle and high school years, "Why do you wear that thing on your head?" That's when I began identifying myself as "Chinese," in response to those first questions. I did so mainly because it seemed to satisfy others' queries as to my Asian appearance. I'm not sure if I felt entirely Chinese then; for the most part, I still felt like everybody else because I didn't distinguish people primarily by ethnicity. As to the headscarf, I was still part of some vague 'other' religion that identified me as a Muslim, but it was an identity that I myself did not yet quite understand or identify with.

In my family, my mother has always been the one who has emphasized education for me and my sisters, while my father places the focus on religion. My mother is a first-generation Chinese immigrant. She met my father when she went to college in Ohio, where he grew up and became the first in his family to go beyond a high school education. My parents are both converts to Islam. Growing up in our household wasn't easy; both parents had high standards for my sisters and I, in terms of our personal behavior and academics, and this is a mentality that we've carried with us even after leaving home.

In starting community college after high school, I became more connected to my ethnic roots, and more accurately defined myself as "half-Chinese, half-Black." In doing so, I've become accustomed to getting the 'mixed stare', the stare people give after learning someone is biracial in an attempt to figure out how all their physical features fit together. However, when I began defining myself in this broader way, my thinking and my perspective changed as well. Instead of seeing myself as a member of one ethnic group out of the many that exist in this country, I became more cosmopolitan in thinking. I began to feel like I had a little of everyone in me; being Black, Chinese, Muslim, and American all at once, nearly anyone I came across could relate to me in some way after learning my background. Encompassing so many identities allowed many people of various backgrounds to feel an affinity for me. My close friends in community college were of various ethnic stripes; some were Jordanian, Chinese, Korean, Black, Caucasian, and Mexican. I realized the great potential of race, and my racial identity in particular, to serve as a bridge between people of different backgrounds.

On the other hand, however, things weren't always straightforward. I have so many identities that sometimes, growing up, it was difficult deciding who I was. Society tends to propagate certain sets of stereotypes or myths associated with each ethnic group, and although we sometimes write these off, I feel as if they subconsciously affect us, seeping into us when we aren't paying attention. From casual racial jokes to associating qualities with people based on their ethnicity, I feel that we have, perhaps inadvertently, created sets of expectations that are associated with each ethnic identity. For a while as I was growing up, I felt increased pressure, mostly self-inflicted, to succeed in academics in a misguided effort to 'embrace' my Asian identity. Being one of the few Asians at my school, I especially felt I had to prove myself in my math and science courses. I was trying to find my 'niche' and I did so by attempting to live up to a general stereotype of Asians, which in my mind had turned into an expectation. Most of us would agree that race inherently, by itself, does not make anyone smarter, kinder, or more righteous than anyone else. However, associating standards or expectations with certain racial groups can create an environment of stereotypes, even casual ones. While most of us wouldn't outrightly agree with general race stereotypes like, for instance, that Asians are inherently better at the sciences or that African-Americans have innate athletic prowess, the subliminal influence of these messages is often underestimated.

I've grown out of living up to stereotypes now. Since leaving the home of my parents and coming to Berkeley, I've had to forge my own path and identity. I feel that there are many people who go through their lives trying to live up to expectations that they perceive their family, friends, or the larger community to hold for them. Also, I feel that many people take their identity almost as a given, not as something either they themselves have constructed, or that others have constructed for them. I believe in constructing my own identity, based on the values and belief system I hold. My ethnicity speaks to where I come from, the cultures of my parents and grandparents, and also the cultural environment in which I was raised. However, my ethnicity says little about the person that I am, because it does not speak to the morals or beliefs I hold, or even to my personality. My ethnicity, in essence, does not define me; it is simply an ornament to my identity. I love my biracial heritage, and it is interesting and unconventional, but it doesn't enrich my life with deeper meaning. Despite how unique my racial background is, it was not something I had a choice in.

Because I have decided that I don't want my ethnicity to be my primary level of identifying myself, I've had to go on a deeper search in the construction of my identity. In earlier times, my Islamic faith had simply been something I inherited from my parents, not something I found for myself and embraced. Today, I identify myself first as a Muslim, because my faith directs my value system, and gives my life greater purpose and meaning. Faith gives a person an explanation for

why they are here in this world, and what they must do with their lives until they inevitably die, something I couldn't find anywhere else. Since starting community college and later coming to Berkeley, I've learned a lot about other religions and belief systems. I choose my faith, Islam, because it gives me a level of clarity and peace that I don't see anywhere else. My cultural heritage gives me a history, a backdrop upon which to paint the person I choose to be, and the values, beliefs and actions that define me.

Today, I still get asked the same questions about ethnicity as I did when I was a kid, only in a slightly more sophisticated manner. I still grapple with issues of race and identity, and where I fit into this complex puzzle that is American society. When I first came to Berkeley, the great diversity in its people and the range of social and political expressions I observed intrigued me. My initial and lasting impression of Berkeley is that it is a place in which people have great freedom in expression, as evidenced by its history, and it's a place where people are free to define themselves. I've tried to hold on to this sentiment as I struggle to define and give voice to my identity.

Source: Abdul-Khabir, Laylaa. "Living the Mixed Life: Growing Up as a Black Chinese Muslim in America." *Hardboiled* 12, no. 2 (November 2008). http://hardboiled .berkeley.edu/issues/122/122-11-idenity.html. Used with permission of the author and *Hardboiled.*

Jade Keller, "On Being Part Other"
(2009)

Jade-Celene Gjestland Keller, born in Mississippi and raised in California, is the daughter of immigrants: her mother is Thai, and her Norwegian father grew up in South Africa. In addition to her research into political

socialization, Keller writes multicultural and feminist fiction and a blog. In her essay "On Being Part Other," Keller asks what it means to be "authentically" Asian and wonders where she fits as a multiracial woman in Asian America.

"Your daughter is beautiful."

"A little chubby."

"But her face is pretty. She looks like her mom."

"She looks like a person from India."

"True. She's got good skin too."

This conversation about me takes place as I look directly at the smiling faces of those discussing me. They talk as if I'm not in the room, as if I don't understand, as if being part-white means I don't understand Thai. My mother hadn't made a concerted effort to teach me her native tongue, but I was around it enough to pick up a lot of the everyday language. I might not speak it perfectly fluently, but my comprehension works well enough. *Thanks, guys,* I think, as I smile innocently back at them.

In America, I am half-Asian. In Thailand, I am *fahrung*—foreigner (always said with a smile and laugh, so that makes it better, right?). I am classified by my otherness, defined by my whiteness. I am proud of my Asian heritage, but amongst Asian relatives, I feel I am always trying to prove my authenticity. I mimic the accent flawlessly when speaking. Most of my jokes about flatulence and genitalia are expressed in Thai because it's just funnier that way. I know what to do with lemongrass and how to combine chili, shallot, and lime. I grab a mortar and pestle before I'd use a grater. I have a layer of cool reserve towards non-family, whilst full of conscious gratitude for my family cohesion and deep roots. I take off my shoes before entering the home, and I kind of take pleasure in the fact that my house is the one with the funny food smells that reduce you to coughing, sneezy fits when grandmother is roasting the chilies. I *wai* (bow) gracefully, sit properly, show deference to elders, and I cook and eat spicy food—because they always ask: *"gin ben? "Do you know how to eat spicy food?"*

("Do you know how to eat spicy food?" is reduced to "Know how to eat?", as if eating only non-spicy food is, in fact, not eating at all. "Yes," I say, "I know how to eat." See chubbiness for detail.)

And still, I am not fully integrated among them. Do others feel this too: within your own family, even though you are loved, do you feel you sometimes do not belong? Isn't it funny sometimes, how within family, the one place you are loved unconditionally, you feel the strongest need to prove yourself? And for all your effort, pretty much no one notices because 1) they expect it, and 2) they love you anyway. Talk about an exercise in futility. I try to prove my sameness, but what they see is difference. I am one step removed from that part of my heritage. While my cousins just grow up *knowing* certain things, I must make the extra effort to acquire them: the language, the history, the idioms. I feel sorry I never learned to speak fluently as a child, for now, as an adult, language acquisition is much harder. The sayings, the myths, the ways words are strung together, it all shapes and communicates a unique worldview. And really, most importantly, some of the humor just does not transcend cultural lines. You have to belong to understand. (Meanwhile, what I do come by naturally is the bone-deep need for deep-fried coconut snacks. Again, see chubbiness. Thank you, God, for your lovely sense of humor.)

Whatever distance I have now from this part of my identity, I wonder what my own children will feel. I will strive to pass on the tradition of cooking and enjoying food and conversation together. I will pass on whatever ability to speak Thai I have. And I will teach them the value of respect towards elders and responsibility to family and community. But they will never know my grandmother and the depth of her presence. Tales of their great-grandfather will be muted and second- or even third-hand. And I wonder what words of the blood line will I pass on to them? What stories will make up their identities? Where will they feel rooted? Will they find comfort in garlic and noodle soup, or will they turn instead to burgers and spaetzle?

I am proud of my multicultural heritage. I feel it adds color and dimension to an otherwise ordinary life. But I suspect passing it on and keeping it alive will be a challenge. What should be as natural as breathing will be a struggle for us, as a multicultural family: part Thai, part American, part Norwegian, part German, and part South African.

As the varied strands of genealogical influence compete for dominance, I wonder what will persist? And what part of the heritage will fall by the wayside?

Source: Keller, Jade. "On Being Part Other." September 14, 2009. http://jadekeller.com/2009/09/on-being-part-other/. Used with permission of the author (www.jadekeller.com).

Sara Sarasohn, "I Cook Nothing Like My Mother" (2010)

Sara Sarasohn is a Jewish Japanese American who writes about religious and ethnic identity and about the evolution of marriage, family structure, and gender roles. She is an editor for NPR News and lives with her wife, Ellen, and their two children in Berkeley, California. In her essay "I Cook Nothing Like My Mother," Sarasohn describes a distinctive Japanese American community, generations removed from Japan and culturally removed from more recent immigrant institutions. Sarasohn also describes her experiences as hapa—Hawaiian slang meaning half Japanese and half white—and talks about how preparing food can provide an anchor for this sometimes tenuous identity, linking her to her family and her history.

I cook nothing like my mother. We ate Japanese food a lot when I was growing up in central California, but now the Asian ingredients I use are mostly ones my mom didn't use much, like miso and Vietnamese fish sauce. I cook like any old good American cook who has worked some Asian ingredients into her pantry, not like a Japanese-American person who makes the food that her mother and grandmother made.

The only thing I make the way my mother does it is sushi. The first time I wanted to make it myself I was in my 20s and living in Washington DC. There was good restaurant sushi in Washington, but it wasn't what I wanted. I was put off by the idea that sushi was something so precious that you would line it up with fancy garnishes. I was put off by the idea that to eat it you had to sit in a darkened restaurant and pay with a credit card. When I was a child I didn't even know that sushi was something expensive and fabulous that you ate at restaurants.

I wanted the sushi that I ate at family gatherings as a child. We ate it off paper plates with potato salad and teriyaki chicken and washed it down with store-brand grape soda. Sushi was downscale family party food, like the finger jello and macaroni salad we ate with it on New Year's Day. To me, sushi has something to do with the creaky screen door at my great grandfather's house, a football game on an old black-and-white TV and my great-aunts sucking on their dentures. I'd take my plate into the living room to sit on the dirty carpet with my cousin. We played with the Barbies she got for Christmas the week before.

My mother's sushi rolls are thick with rice. At the center they have a small, tight grouping of fillings: shitake mushrooms, red slivers of pickled ginger, dried gourd (kampyo), barbequed eel (unagi), thin-sliced cucumber. My cousins called it "black sushi" because of the nori. There was also "brown sushi," tofu that was deep fried, boiled in broth and stuffed with rice. The kids liked the brown sushi better than the black sushi.

For my mother making sushi is a two-day process. On the first day she preps all of the fillings. On the second day she makes the rice and rolls it up. From the time I was little she let me help her on the second day with the rolling.

During those lessons my mother said nothing to me about the taste of the sushi at all. She did show me with complete care and focus all of the techniques for rolling sushi: how to place the fillings so they would end up in the center of the roll, how to cheat the roll off the edge of the bamboo mat at just the right time. She taught me all the mechanics but she never mentioned the way it tasted.

Most of the flavor in my mother's sushi has very little to do with the rolling on the second day and everything to do with the hours she spends on the prep on the first day. When I was a child that whole first day process was a mystery to me. By the time my mother invited me to roll with her, all the fillings—the kampyo and the egg and the eel—were sliced up and ready to be placed on the rice. So when I was in my 20s and I wanted to make the sushi of my childhood, the kind I ate with macaroni salad and grape soda, I didn't know how to do it.

My grandmother didn't teach her daughters to make sushi either. In the late 70s my mother and her sister followed my grandmother around the kitchen taking notes and sticking a measuring cup under her before she dumped things together. When I wanted to make the sushi of my childhood, my mother could email the documentation to me in Washington DC.

Washington is completely different from the central California where I grew up in so many ways, but to me the most striking was that there were so few Japanese people in Washington. There were even fewer people who were half-Japanese, like me. By the time I was 26 I'd been living in Washington for five years and I was starting to understand nobody in Washington knew what it meant that I was Japanese-American. When my friends saw me, they saw a white girl. If I said, "I'm half Japanese," people would think of the women who greeted you at the door of a sushi restaurant in accented English. It was all wrong.

In central California, being half Japanese meant having a grandmother who spoke a few words in Japanese—no more than a few—because she was born in California. It meant the flat, hot light of the central valley in the summer when you were dragged back to the farm town your grandmother grew up in to see all of your second cousins. It meant that your mother (or your father) was the slightly rebellious one in the family because they married out first. In central California when I see someone who looks like me and we smile a little in recognition, we know that's what it means to be half. The word we use is hapa. It's a Hawaiian word, and when we used it in California it meant half-Japanese-American-half-white, but you can say it without needing all the hyphens and the explanations. Hapa is a thing unto itself. It's not a subset or an exception.

In Washington, if I felt like I needed to connect with being Jewish, I could go to synagogue. If I wanted to be Japanese-American, I couldn't go to a Japanese restaurant because their sushi wasn't my family sushi. If I wanted to feel the part of me that was that central California Japanese-American, if I wanted to feel closer to my cousin eating brown sushi with her Barbie doll on the dirty carpet of my great-grandfather's house, I didn't know where to go. I wasn't sure if I was even that girl anymore, who ate sushi with finger jello. The last three, five, eight times I'd had sushi I'd had it with Absolut vodka tonics. I was beginning to believe that I had lived in Washington so long that I wasn't really hapa anymore.

Then a friend suggested that we have a hang-out-on-Sunday-afternoon kind of party, and I said, "We can make sushi." She loved this idea. I loved it, too. It was so clear in my head. I'd do all of the first-day prep by myself on Saturday. Then on Sunday I could teach everyone to roll. I felt that if I could make my family sushi, I could stay myself even so far from home. I felt that if I did this thing, my friends would see me doing it and they would know me a little bit better. They might understand the word hapa.

My mother's email with the recipes was both carefully detailed and disturbingly vague. Her recipe called for things like "11 little dried fish" and "kombu—cut with scissors" and "shrimp small handful." Was that small shrimp? Or a small handful?

I had no clue where to buy this stuff. I sent an email to the only other Japanese person I knew in

DC. She wrote back that there was no Japanese store but to try a huge Korean supermarket out in the suburbs. The driving directions involved going so far out that I had no idea what she was talking about after the first couple of turns and highway exits.

At the time, my wife, Ellen, and I didn't own a car. We lived in the opposite of the suburbs: a third-floor walkup in the inner city across the street from a drug park. We rode our bikes to work. We hated cars and we hated the suburbs. To make the sushi of my childhood, we had to borrow a car from our neighbor and drive out past the Beltway.

We passed strip malls and roads that had eight lanes of traffic but no sidewalks. We got lost at least twice. The store was a huge concrete box in the middle of a parking lot. Once we got there I got lost again. The sign was in unfamiliar blocky Korean script. The automatic door slid open and I saw aisles of packages and refrigerators, all labeled in Korean. I wandered around the store, unable to figure out what I needed. Ellen watched me poke packages. "What are you going to do?" she asked.

"I don't know," I said. This was in the mid 90s, before there were stricter rules about labels on foods, so the stuff in the store had a Korean label that might (or might not) be transliterated into English, but it was not translated. "I'm really sorry, honey," Ellen said. "I can't help you on this one at all."

This was my project, my party, my friends, my childhood food. I asked a woman who worked there, "Is this unagi?" but she mostly spoke Korean. "Eel?" I tried. She shook her head, not understanding my question. After a while I gave up. I think she apologized but I'm not sure.

I wanted to give up and go home, but I'd told my friends that I would teach them to roll sushi. I had wanted to show my friends what hapa is. I wanted to show myself that I could perform this task that my mother never taught me to do. I wanted to find out if there was still some part of me that was a hapa girl from central California. I was trying to recapture my California childhood in the middle of a Korean grocery store in the farthest, scariest suburb of Washington DC. I knew that everything I needed to make the sushi was in this store

somewhere. I just didn't know which plastic packages and metal tins were the ones I needed.

E walked up behind me with a bag in her hand. "Are these the little fish?" she asked. She handed me the bag and I looked at the fish inside. "Could be," I said. I smelled them.

They smelled old and salty and thin. It was a smell I knew. Even if my mother had never taught me how to make the dashi (broth) to cook the mushrooms and the kampyo, from my childhood bedroom I smelled it cooking. The smell of the little fish Ellen handed to me was one of the threads in the dashi smell. The child in me remembered it, but it took the adult experienced cook in me to identify that small part of the complex dashi smell in the plastic bag. These were the little dried fish. I needed 11 of them.

I went around the store smelling packages of shrimp and seaweed, searching for the smells that would fill out the smell of the dashi I remembered. I stopped looking at the labels. I stopped trying to read the words I'd never decipher and I followed the best guide any cook has: I smelled.

We only taste four or five things on our tongues: sweet, sour, salt, bitter, and some people say also savory. Everything else that we enjoy about the flavor of our food is smell. The subtle notes and complexities are all in the smell. Of all senses, smell is the one that is the most powerful in evoking memory, and smell memories last longer than any others. Scientists think the reason is that when our brains process smells we use both our cortex, our thinking brain, and our limbic system, our animal brain. We smell with the part of us that is older than being human. Standing in a Korean market in the farthest-out suburbs of Washington DC, I did not need to go back to my animal ancestors to remember where I came from. I was just looking across a continent and back a few decades to a little girl with a paper plate and a grape soda. She liked the brown sushi the best, but when I grew up I remembered the smell of it all.

Source: Sarasohn, Sara. "I Cook Nothing Like My Mother." 2010. Used with permission of the author.

Yayoi Lena Winfrey, "Fire Lily"
(2010)

In the aftermath of the American occupation of Japan, and after the passage of the 1945 War Brides Act, nearly 46,000 Japanese women immigrated to the United States as the wives of servicemen. Many faced hostile reactions from both their own and their husbands' families; mixed-race marriages were neither common nor accepted in Japan or the United States, and cultural and language differences often made life very challenging for the war brides.

Yayoi Lena Winfrey was born in Tokyo, the daughter of a Japanese war bride and an African American soldier. Although her own mother and father later divorced, Winfrey is committed to recording the experiences and perspectives of hapas (mixed-race people) and their parents. She moderates watermelonsushiworld.blogspot.com, a forum for mixed-race people, and is directing a feature film, Watermelon Sushi, *about African Asian American identity. Winfrey's essay "Fire Lily" provides a glimpse into her mother's life.*

It's Sunday morning, and I'm sitting in my mother's compact dining room just like I do every week at this time. A hefty, plastic-covered table surrounded by several stiff chairs crowds the space, the focal point of her house where we can eat, talk and watch TV simultaneously.

Stirring a pot of bubbling oatmeal in the adjacent narrow kitchen, my mother barks out orders like a WWII Japanese officer—reminiscent of *samurai daimyo* of feudal Japan.

"Yayoi-san!" she shouts while dropping puckered raisins into the oatmeal. "Make tea!"

Pointing to the gigantic, gurgling electric thermos on the counter, she adds. "Water hot-u!"

Slowly, I rise from my rigid chair, moving leisurely towards the kitchen. If she's going to yell at me, I'm taking my sweet time. My mother's husband, Bob Smith, sits blandly at his place at the table. He's already prepared his coffee, and waits for my mother to serve him breakfast like she always does.

"Yayoi!" my mother roars again, this time gesturing at the toaster. "Toast-u!"

Choosing a plate from the cupboard above her head, I plunk slices of toasted homemade bread onto it. If my mother didn't have a hearing problem, she might not sound so gruff, I think, but then again, she's never been one of those fragile cherry blossoms of Japanese movies and magazines either. Nope. Yuriko, whose name means "lily", is about as delicate as a sword-wielding *ronin* and a firebrand to boot. To be fair, her crustiness is probably due to suffering in her early life, and her husband blames her hearing loss on the explosion of bombs she endured during WWII.

Born in Tokyo, Yuriko was the middle child of parents who owned a salon where they both styled hair. When her father died suddenly, he left his widow without insurance and five children all under the age of 10. Without the benefit of public assistance, my maternal grandmother was forced to travel daily to style *geisha's* hair while leaving her kids to manage on their own. When my mother turned 13, she was sent away to work as the nanny in a doctor's family. There, she often cried; silently questioning why she had to strap a baby to her back while the family's same-aged daughter hoisted a nooksack filled with books onto hers. Every *sen* Yuriko earned was sent home to her mother. At 20, finally freed from indentured servitude, she enrolled in secretarial classes. But shortly afterward, WWII broke out and Yuriko was forced into a factory job. The battle scars she bears are masked by a zany sense of humor, but her brusque demeanor is likely the byproduct of a brutal war she witnessed.

"Yayoi-san!" my mother shrieks, startling me.

"What?" I yell back, unable to control myself.

"Turn on TV," she orders. "*Nodojiman* now."

It's our favorite weekly show on NHK, the Japanese program channel, featuring 20 competing amateur singers and two of Japan's most popular professionals. I listen intently to the announcer as he chats with each contestant. Then, turning to my mother, I relay the English words for any Japanese ones I recognize. Most of the time, it's the contestants' ages that I interpret because the host and guests fuss over any elderly participants. The Japanese treat old folks like demigods.

"Kyuju-ni!" I shout, excitedly pointing to an old man on the screen.

"92?" My mother asks.

"So, desu," I answer, pleased that she comprehends.

"Look like so," she sneers. "He not look young."

At 90, my mother could pass for 70, and acts as if she should be awarded a medal for it.

Afterwards, we watch Japanese news and my mother reads the *kanji* headlines out loud. They are so mild compared to CNN's. A lead-in story is about people who lost money because they were defrauded by ATM machines.

Astounded, I ask my mother, "That's the headlines?"

But she ignores me, seemingly oblivious to the daily violence reported in American news.

Unbelievably, my mother's first U.S. home was a small Texas town where my African American father brought us after they'd married in Japan. My soldier dad joined the military to escape his harsh life in a risky place at a dangerous time. Besides being forced to pick cotton without pay for white farmers, he also suffered atrocities including an uncle who disappeared—possibly a victim of lynching. Jim Crow was tough on my mother, too, who was told by a white bus driver that she could sit up front even though she was traveling with my father's black relatives who were relegated to the back. Surrounded by snakes, tarantulas, mosquitoes and hostile rednecks that had never seen an "Oriental" before, my mother's pleasures came

from learning to cook black-eyed peas and collard greens from my paternal grandmother. Wringing chickens' necks for supper, though, was something else altogether.

When NHK's news is finished, my mother's husband plays the videotape he's made of the *taiga* drama with English subtitles broadcast the evening before. This year, we've been watching the *Tenchijin* series featuring many well-known historical figures that shaped 17th century Japan. While Bob and I love it, my mother waves her hand dismissively towards the TV.

"I not care those things," she scoffs. "That happen long time ago."

I'm puzzled by her lack of interest in her own history because, growing up, I recall her proudly telling many tales of the *Genji* or *Tokugawa Shogunate* or *Tenno*, the Emperor. Indeed, Japanese culture dominated our childhoods. When we lived on military bases, my mother regularly played a card game called *hanafuda* with other Japanese warbrides. And, when we moved to a civilian town, she taught my sister and me so that she could continue playing.

Later, as my mother prepares dinner, I try to become invisible. I don't want her screeching at me to come help wash, cut, chop, slice, dice or prepare anything. I've hated cooking since I was 10 when she made me fry bacon for my sister and I got splattered with hot grease. In later years, my mother made us cool off hot rice for *sushi* by waving paper fans. Cooking is just too labor intensive for me.

One by one, my mother sets dishes on the plastic-covered table. A bowl of shredded cabbage sprinkled with *shiso* seeds appears followed by a plate of steamed spinach with sesame. Sliced dill pickles and tomatoes are placed next to Bob who loves sour flavors. *Miso* soup brimming with homemade *tofu* is served in tiny lacquer bowls. Stinky *natto* (fermented soy beans) is briskly stirred with *shoyu* and mustard. Then, the piece de resistance, a huge pot of steamed rice arrives. Today, my mother's added carrot, *nori* (dried seawood), *shoga* (pickled ginger), *ume* (pickled plum from the tree in her yard) and homemade *age* (fried *tofu*). These are the dishes she serves in honor of my vegan diet.

"Bob, you gonna eat monks' food today," my mother teases, even though most of the time she prepares a separate meal of meat or fowl for him.

After dinner, we watch more TV. If *sumo* is on, my mother hoarsely shouts instructions at the wrestlers as if they could hear her.

When it's time for me to go, my mother packs some of her freshly baked bread, leftovers from our dinner, a four-roll package of toilet paper, and homemade cookies for my Ukraine neighbor, Nadia, who regularly sends her fresh fruit.

At the door, my mother watches intently as I pull on my boots, staring as if it's the last time she'll ever see me. Then, in a voice suddenly gentle as a lily, she advises, "Be careful, okay?"

As I walk outside through the garage, she stands at the utility room window waving like a child. I climb into the car and she continues waving until I'm down the street and can't see her anymore. This vision of Fire Lily will stay with me until next Sunday when I visit her again.

Source: Winfrey, Yayoi Lena. "Fire Lily." 2010. Used with permission of the author.

Paisley Rekdal, "And Now for a Little Biracial Rage"
(2012)

Paisley Rekdal is a multigenre author, poet, and poetry professor at the University of Utah. Her father is Norwegian and her mother is Chinese American. Her writing explores race, ethnicity, and the "betweenness" inhabited in particular by biracial people—the liminal space between self and external representation, which shifts based on physical appearance, location, and proximity. Among other awards, Rekdal has won a Fulbright Fellowship and a Pushcart Prize for her writing.

The following essay is taken from Rekdal's blog, an unpublished account of her year traveling the world. Here, she analyzes an interaction she had in Vietnam with a white American man, who questions her experience, history, and identity based on his own preconceptions and assumptions.

Travel, people like to say, is wonderful precisely because of how much it changes you. Mostly I am changing into something I don't want to be—angry, hot, overwhelmed; one more ex-pat whining in an air-conditioned lounge, unable to ask for the bill in

Vietnamese. Last night, I got to be changed into a hot-headed, self-deluded bitch.

Why, you ask?

Because of my appearance. Let me say that I'm used to people talking about what I look like here. The northern Vietnamese are pretty blunt: they'll tell you if they think you're fat or not, pretty or not, old-looking or young. But the most common comment I get about my appearance here is how I don't quite look like an American. "You look like Asian peoples," is, in fact, what I was just told by a bookshop owner, after having a drink at a bar where the waitress asked me if I was Korean, an hour after my French class in which all the other Vietnamese students asked if I came to Hanoi because I might be part Vietnamese. It's been years since I've had this much continuous speculation about my appearance, a fact I had chalked up to a) increased media attention to mixed race people as a whole in the US and b) just looking really white. I have traveled to a lot of Asian countries over the years (China, Japan, Korea, the Philippines, then-independent Hong Kong, and Taiwan) and what's struck me in each of these places is how obviously the people with more historical exposure to the west are better at identifying mixed-race people. Being mixed race in Asia is not just a marker of a possible foreign nationality but of class status, family history and language. I mean, you don't have two major wars with two major western powers in the course of less than a hundred years, along with decades of colonization, and not have a thing or two that pops into your mind upon seeing a mixed-race person of my particular age in Vietnam.

I haven't met many mixed Vietnamese or Viet Cu here, but that doesn't mean I haven't seen a lot of them. There's a fashion magazine here called Dep which routinely puts mixed-race models on its cover, and a lot of the travel tourism television ads that come out of Malaysia and Singapore feature attractive biracial women running in and out of shopping complexes, eating something barbequed over a pit, flying helicopters and going deep sea diving. The mix of west and east in these models offers the viewers (most of whom would be Asian) their own sense of the "exotic" experience all of us want, with the added comfort of knowing they will never be—or become—too far away from the familiar comforts of home.

An important side note: as you might expect, if biracial women are the female spokesmodel of choice here, white men are the inevitable leads to this eternal costume drama that is the southeast Asian tour brochure. Thus, in an ad for a new swanky Hong Kong hotel, you can see a gorgeous mixed-race woman (possibly full, hard to tell as she's always in half-shadow having a dumpling shoved into her mouth) being clutched near a balcony by a white guy, or sitting down on the chair a white guy is offering to pull out for her, or following a white man into what seems to be a steam room-meets-wedding chapel. The worst ad I've seen that panders to this is a perfume ad in which a white man at an airline ticket counter gets a whiff of the young Vietnamese woman standing next to him in line, falls head over heels and then pursues her maniacally throughout the rest of the airport.

The perfume is called—and you're really going to hate this—"Miss Saigon."

Leaving aside for the moment how "Miss Saigon"/Madame Butterfly Redux finishes, I should say that I'm not as upset by this as you might imagine, largely because it's so familiar to me and because I'm just too damn tired to keep getting worked up about it. This is the background music of Asia—Vietnam's "white noise"—that I've learned to live with (not happily, I'd like to add) and that I think a lot of the smart young Vietnamese students in my class at least are pretty savvy about. I think they see it for what it is—a fantasy that feeds on that complex brew of envy, competition, and—yes—self-hatred, all of which has been injected with an awareness that parts of Vietnam have become more globally changed; if not in the physical make-up of Vietnamese themselves, then at least in its landscape of the business world. To me, "Miss Saigon" isn't just a reference to a bad rock-opera, it's a nice little dig at a changing Saigon itself.

But what does this have to do with me becoming a raging bitch? Well, the other night, I had an odd dinner with a friend's father. This man is a 76 year-old white American, very kind, smart, well-off and certainly well-traveled. He had just read my book *The Night My Mother Met Bruce Lee* which I wrote fourteen years ago (TOTALLY not per my request: he was just curious). The book is about some of these issues I've listed above: the ambivalence I feel about seeing Asian women in relationships with white men considering the persistence of our stereotypes (both positive and negative) about Asian femininity, the confusion of being told that race doesn't matter while at the same time being forced to continually acknowledge the appearance of your difference, the ways in which your "exotic" appearance makes you the object of someone's consumerist fantasy. Anyway, he told me he thought it was very, um, *interesting* (pursing his lips here sourly to let me know he hated it: thanks for that, by the way) but that he wondered about some things.

For instance, he said, he'd just gone to a party in Hanoi with a bunch of young ex-pat couples. All of them were mixed: white husband, Asian wife. The backyard was filled with their happy, mixed-race progeny chasing each other around the grill. As he had just finished my book, he decided to take a little survey, and so went around the party polling people about what they thought about their marriages, about their kids being mixed race, if their children (or they themselves) ever felt confused about it.

"And guess what?" he asked, shaking his head with bemusement. "None of them thought anything LIKE what was in your book!"

"How old were the children?" I asked.

"Six," he said.

Let's pause here to consider the fact that I wrote my book when I was 26. If at age 6 I had felt anything like what I felt about my life at age 26, I can say with some confidence that I wouldn't have made it past my tenth birthday.

And let's *also* take a moment to consider that people at a party might not feel comfortable talking about their identity issues to an unknown American near-octogenarian trying to use them as a basis for a survey.

These things acknowledged, what galled me about this remark, and the conversation we proceeded to have after ("I'm telling you, you don't look Asian at all to me. And I had a wife who was mixed! I have a *very good eye* for these things!") was the fact that I was again being questioned about my appearance (this time, my NOT-Asianness), but this time being implicitly asked to defend not only myself but a book written to explore the meaning of this very betweenness of identity. And what mattered in this debate was NOT the conclusion that I myself had come to about what I was or felt I was, but the conclusion that I could make HIM come to about what I was ("I don't know, those kids seemed fine, and my mixed wife, well, she basically told me it never meant anything. She was, admittedly, an unhappy woman. To be honest, I only married her because I liked her kids."). In short, the book was not about my life or my perceptions of it, they had to be about HIM and HIS perceptions, and if they didn't correspond to things he experienced at an

hour-long barbeque with strangers less than half his age (or, better yet, to an unhappy but brief marriage to a woman he acknowledged he didn't even like), then the conclusions I had reached about what being mixed race meant over the shortish/nasty/brutalish course of my life were essentially negated, ESPECIALLY considering the fact that I didn't look mixed to him at all, thus shouldn't have ever bothered myself writing about this topic.

All of which really made me want to bash his head in with a wine bottle.

What also galled me about the conversation was that, during our meal, the waiter kept looking to me for confirmation of what this man was ordering—in very loud English—and would address all his questions for this man to me: something I notice that happens when I eat with other friends who look more white. Basically, a lot of waiters here seem to think that, between the two pale foreigners sitting before him/her babbling in English, the one most likely to understand Vietnamese in a pinch is the darker-haired, vaguely familiar-looking one. And so while this man is going on and on about how white I seem to him, the waiter is subtly signaling to me (via his visual distress) how Asian I hopefully might be.

For the record, I don't doubt that those children weren't conflicted about their identities. First of all, they're *six*. They're still learning about zoos and *ice cream*. They also, obviously, come from a different generation, one in which the media is—if not exactly saturated then at least burgeoning with images of multiracial people, ambivalent as these images may be. They also live in Vietnam, in an ex-pat enclave that has a VERY healthy percentage of mixed families, and are going to the expensive international school which requires that a certain percentage of its attendees be Vietnamese. In short, these kids are living the globalized, mixed family dream. I won't lie: I had a great childhood, but if I'd had the chance to be among those families at the barbeque when I was a child, I'd have killed for it.

But the thing that enrages me most, that still makes me seethe writing this, is that at stake was the very palpable sense that the only identity at that table that counted, the one truly stable self-consciousness able to make such fine distinctions and judgments, was his: it was only through the surety of his perceptions of me that I could be granted an identity that fit with my own perceptions of myself. In short, only he could decide to confer identity on me. On that level, I had to PROVE something to him: something that he couldn't, or didn't want, to see.

"You know," I said, angrily at one point. "We could flip this whole thing around. We could spend a half hour talking about what I first thought YOU looked like when we met, and then how surprised—or not—I am by the facts of your opinions based on my assumptions."

"I didn't tell you what I thought you looked like when we first met."

"But you're telling me now."

"Yes, because you brought it up!"

It is true that, having published that fucking book, I brought it up. And yet, even without that book, I think it would have come up, and keep on coming up. Because at some point I would have mentioned my family, and maybe mentioned that my mother is Chinese American, and then we'd slip into the quagmire in which we found ourselves last night: the conversation about race that's been going on around all of us, not just in Vietnam, but in the States. Let me be clear: when the Vietnamese (and Cambodians and Laotians) ask me if I'm Asian, it doesn't bother me. If someone from America thinks I'm white, it doesn't bother me. What bothers me—and I've said it before in this blog—is when someone starts to implicitly or explicitly insist that I must curtail myself to certain values and experiences based an identity that he thinks HE gets to confer on me. THAT'S when I get annoyed.

I've had Asian friends who have been just as teeth-gratingly annoying: friends who insist I like food because I'm Chinese, who say I think certain things because I'm Chinese, that I like certain types of men because I'm Chinese. I've had Asian boyfriends who want me to be as Asian as possible in public and as white as possible in the bedroom. (Don't ask how that works: I still don't know.) The thing is, it doesn't work like that. Perhaps it might be nice if we could tie certain personal tics so directly to the genetic, physically expressed invariables of racial appearance. But we can't. We have culture, which explains much, but race itself explains nothing.

It's just one more digit in the ever-expanding equation.

Honestly, I hate the fact that I'm writing—again—about this. But being biracial is like living in a room filled with mosquitoes. Every time you start to drift off to sleep, you get bitten. And I'm sad about the dinner because the friend's father is actually a kind and generous man; it's just a testament to how infuriating the topic of race is, how it turns everyone into cartoon versions of themselves. In all honesty, I understand his argument. I even understand his suspicion and his petulance. I understand these things so well because his perception of and feelings about me are the predominant ones that American culture offers: they are—and this is what I wasn't able to explain to him—the predominant psychic space that has been granted me. I exist, but only as far as I don't insist upon another narrative about my life other people don't recognize or feel uncomfortable about. In this, I'm the one who is asked—constantly—to give something up, to adapt myself to an outsider's way of seeing, rather than the reverse. This man's position is the one we start from, the logical proposition which has to be—through logic and persistent alternative reasoning—negated.

Wouldn't it be interesting if it were actually the reverse? If my identity was the "stable" position we had to start with? In my mind's eye, I go back to that party filled with six-year olds. I don't know what they'll think about race, what they do think already, but in some ways I like to imagine them the way my friend's father saw them: wildly, uniquely indifferent to their meaning in this world. What a change that would be, to be like them. I can hardly begin to imagine it.

Source: Rekdal, Paisley. "And Now for a Little Biracial Rage." May 11, 2012. http://paisleyrekdal.blogspot.com/2012/05/and-now-for-little-biracial-rage.html. Reprinted with permission.

Selected Bibliography

Arts, Media, and Popular Culture

Chang, Gordon H., Mark D. Johnson, and Sharon Spain. *Asian American Art, 1850–1970.* Palo Alto, CA: Stanford University Press, 2008.

Chang, Leonard. *The Fruit 'n Food: A Novel.* Seattle, WA: Black Heron Press, 1996.

Chin, Frank. *Donald Duk.* Minneapolis: Coffee House Press, 1991.

Choi, Annie. *Happy Birthday or Whatever: Track Suits, Kim Chee, and Other Family Disasters.* New York: Harper, 2007.

Choi, Susan. *The Foreign Student: A Novel.* New York: Harper Flamingo, 1998.

Espana-Maram, Linda. *Creating Masculinity in Los Angeles's Little Manila: Working Class Filipinos and Popular Culture, 1920s–1950s.* New York: Columbia University Press, 2006.

Hamamoto, Darrell Y., and Sandra Liu, eds. *Countervisions: Asian American Film Criticism.* Philadelphia: Temple University Press, 2000.

Kim, Suki. *The Interpreter.* New York: Farrar, Straus, and Giroux, 2003.

Kogawa, Joy. *Obasan.* Norwell, MA: Anchor Press, 1993.

Lê, Thi Diem Thúy. *The Gangster We Are All Looking For.* New York: Alfred A. Knopf, 2003.

Lee, Chang-rae. *Native Speaker.* New York: Riverhead Books, 1996.

Lee, Robert G. *Orientals: Asian Americans in Popular Culture.* Philadelphia: Temple University Press, 1999.

Min, Katherine. *Secondhand World: A Novel.* New York: Knopf, 2006.

Mori, Toshio. *Yokohama, California.* Seattle: University of Washington Press, 1985.

Mukherjee, Bharati. *Jasmine.* New York: Grove Press, 1989.

Murayama, Milton. *All I Asking for Is My Body.* Honolulu: University of Hawai'i Press, 1988.

Nadeau, Kathleen. *The History of the Philippines.* Westport, CT: Greenwood Press, 2008.

Nair, Ajay, and Murali Balaji. *Desi Rap: Hip-Hop and South Asian America.* Lanham, MD: Lexington Books, 2008.

Ng, Fae Myenne. *Bone: A Novel.* New York: Harper Perennial, 1994.

Pham, Andrew X. *Catfish and Mandala: A Two-Wheeled Voyage through the Landscape and Memory of Vietnam.* New York: Farrar, Straus and Giroux, 1999.

Phan, Aimee. *We Should Never Meet: Stories.* New York: St. Martin's, 2004.

Roley, Brian Ascalon. *American Son: A Novel.* New York: W. W. Norton, 2001.

Rosal, Patrick. *My American Kundiman.* New York: Persea Books, 2006.

Santos, Bienvenido. *Scent of Apples: A Collection of Stories.* Seattle: University of Washington Press, 1997.

Scripter, Sami, and Sheng Yang. *Cooking from the Heart: The Hmong Kitchen in America.* Minneapolis: University of Minnesota Press, 2009.

Shigekuni, Julie. *Unending Nora.* Granada Hills, CA: Red Hen Press, 2008.

Terada, Yoshitaka, ed. *Transcending Boundaries: Asian Musics in North America.* Osaka: National Museum of Ethnology, 2001.

Tossa, Wajuppa, with Kongdeuane Nettavong. *Lao Folktales.* Edited by Margaret Read MacDonald. Westport, CT: Libraries Unlimited, 2008.

Wong, Deborah. *Speak It Louder: Asian Americans Making Music.* New York: Routledge, 2004.

Wong, Sau-ling. *Reading Asian American Literature: From Necessity to Extravagance.* Princeton, NJ: Princeton University Press, 1993.

Economics, Work, and Education

Bangerter, Amy Nelson. "Chinese Youth and American Educational Institutions, 1850–1881." Diss., George Washington University, 2005.

Bao, Xiaolan. *Holding Up More Than Half the Sky: Chinese Women Garment Workers in New York City, 1948–1992.* Urbana: University of Illinois Press, 2006.

Cariaga, Roman R. *The Filipinos in Hawaii: Economic and Social Conditions, 1906–1936.* Honolulu: Filipino Public Relations Bureau, 1937.

Chan, Sucheng. *This Bittersweet Soil: The Chinese in California Agriculture, 1860–1910.* Berkeley: University of California Press, 1986.

June, Moon-Ho. *Coolies and Cane: Race, Labor, and Sugar in the Age of Emancipation.* Baltimore: Johns Hopkins University Press, 2006.

Kwong, Peter. *Forbidden Workers: Illegal Chinese Immigrants and American Labor.* New York: New Press, 1997.

Light, Ivan, and Steven J. Gold. *Ethnic Economics.* San Diego: Academic Press, 2000.

Ong, Paul. *Beyond Asian American Poverty: Community Economic Development Policies and Strategies.* Los Angeles: Leadership Education for Asian Pacifics, 1993.

Parreñas, Rhacel Salazar. *Servants of Globalization: Women, Migration, and Domestic Work.* Stanford, CA: Stanford University Press, 2001.

Wei, William. *The Asian American Movement.* Philadelphia: Temple University Press, 1993.

Wong, K. Scott, and Sucheng Chan, eds. *Claiming America: Constructing Chinese American Identities during the Exclusion Era.* Philadelphia: Temple University Press, 1998.

Wu, Frank H. *Yellow: Race in America beyond Black and White.* New York: Basic Books, 2003.

Yang, Fenggang. *Chinese Christians in America: Conversion, Assimilation, and Adhesive Identities.* University Park: Pennsylvania State University Press, 1999.

Yee, Alfred. *Shopping at Giant Foods: Chinese American Supermarkets in Northern California.* Seattle: University of Washington Press, 2003.

Yu, Renqiu. *To Save China, to Save Ourselves: The Chinese Hand Laundry Alliance of New York.* Philadelphia: Temple University Press, 1992.

Zhou, Min. *Chinatown: The Socioeconomic Potential of an Urban Enclave.* Philadelphia: Temple University Press, 1992.

History

Anderson, Robert N., Richard Collier, and Rebecca F. Pestano. *Filipinos in Rural Hawaii.* Honolulu: University of Hawai'i Press, 1984.

Azuma, Eiichiro. *Between Two Empires: Race, History, and Transnationalism in Japanese America.* New York: Oxford University Press, 2005.

Barter, James. *Building the Transcontinental Railroad.* San Diego: Lucent, 2002.

Chan, Sucheng. *Asian Americans: An Interpretive History.* New York: Twayne Publishers, 1991.

Chan, Sucheng. *Survivors: Cambodian Refugees in the United States.* Urbana: University of Illinois Press, 2004.

Chang, Iris. *The Chinese in America.* New York: Penguin Group, Inc., 2003.

Chen, Yong. *Chinese San Francisco: A Trans-Pacific Community, 1850–1943.* Stanford, CA: Stanford University Press, 2000.

Choy, Catherine Ceniza. *Empire of Care: Nursing and Migration in Filipino American History.* Durham, NC: Duke University Press, 2003.

Conroy, Hilary F. *The Japanese Frontier in Hawaii, 1868–1898.* Berkeley: University of California Press, 1953.

Daniels, Roger. *Asian America: Chinese and Japanese in the United States since 1850.* Seattle: University of Washington Press, 1988.

Daniels, Roger. *Guarding the Golden Door: American Immigration Policy and Immigrants since 1882.* New York: Hill and Wang, 2004.

Donnelly, Nancy D. *Changing Lives of Refugee Hmong Women.* Seattle: University of Washington Press, 1994.

Dorita, Mary. *Filipino Immigration to Hawaii.* San Francisco: R&E Research Associates, 1975.

Glick, Clarence E. *Sojourners and Settlers: Chinese Migrants in Hawaii.* Honolulu: University of Hawai'i Press, 1980.

Hing, Bill Ong. *Defining America through Immigration Policy.* Philadelphia: Temple University Press, 2004.

Horton, John. *The Politics of Diversity: Immigration, Resistance, and Change in Monterey Park, California.* Philadelphia: Temple University Press, 1995.

Hsu, Madeline Y. *Dreaming of Gold, Dreaming of Home: Transnationalism and Migration between the United States and Southern China, 1882–1943.* Stanford, CA: Stanford University Press, 2000.

Ichioka, Yuji. *The Issei: The World of the First Generation Japanese Immigrants, 1885–1924.* New York: The Free Press, 1988.

Jensen, Joan. *Passage from India: Asian Indian Immigrants in North America.* New Haven, CT: Yale University Press, 1988.

Kurashige, Lon, Alice Yang Murray, and Thomas Paterson, eds. *Major Problems in Asian American History: Documents and Essays.* Florence, KY: Wadsworth, 2002.

La Brack, Bruce. *The Sikhs of Northern California, 1904–1975.* New York: AMS Press, 1988.

Lai, Eric, and Dennis Arguelles, eds. *The New Face of Asian Pacific America: Numbers, Diversity & Change in the 21st Century*. San Francisco: AsianWeek, 2003.

Lai, Him Mark, Genny Lim, and Judy Yung. *Island: Poetry and History of Chinese Immigrants on Angel Island, 1910–1940*. San Francisco: HOC DOI, 1980.

Lee, Erika. *At America's Gate: Chinese Immigration during the Exclusion Era, 1882–1943*. Chapel Hill: University of North Carolina Press, 2003.

Lee, Jonathan H. X., ed. *Cambodian American Experiences: Histories, Communities, Cultures, and Identities*. Dubuque, IA: Kendall and Hunt Publishing, 2010.

Leonard, Karen. *Ethnic Choices: California's Punjabi-Mexican Americans, 1910–1980*. Philadelphia: Temple University Press, 1991.

Lowe, Lisa. *Immigrant Acts: On Asian American Cultural Politics*. Durham, NC: Duke University Press, 1996.

Lydon, Sandy. *Chinese Gold: The Chinese in the Monterey Bay Area*. Capitola, CA: Capitola Book Co., 1985.

Ngai, Mae M. *Impossible Subjects: Illegal Aliens and the Making of Modern America*. Princeton, NJ: Princeton University Press, 2004.

Noda, Kesa. *Yamato Colony, 1906–1960: Livingston, California*. Livingston, CA: Japanese American Citizens League, 1981.

Odo, Franklin, ed. *The Columbia Documentary History of the Asian American Experience*. New York: Columbia University Press, 2002.

Okihiro, Gary. *Margins and Mainstreams: Asians in American History and Culture*. Seattle: University of Washington Press, 1994.

Omi, Michael, and Howard Winant. *Racial Formation in the United States: From the 1960s to the 1990s*. New York: Routledge, 1994.

Osorio, Jonathan Kay Kamakawiwo'ole. *Dismembering Lahui: A History of the Hawaiian Nation to 1887*. Honolulu: University of Hawai'i Press, 2002.

Peffer, George Anthony. *If They Don't Bring Their Women Here: Chinese Female Immigration before Exclusion*. Urbana: University of Illinois Press, 1996.

Pho, Tuyet-Lan, Jeffrey Gerson, and Sylvia Cowan, eds. *Southeast Asian Refugees and Immigrants in the Mill City*. Hanover, NH: University Press of New England, 2007.

Salyer, Lucy E. *Laws Harsh as Tigers: Chinese Immigrants and the Shaping of Modern Immigration Law*. Chapel Hill: University of North Carolina Press, 1995.

Spickard, Pual, Joanne L. Rondilla, and Debbie Hippolite Wright, eds. *Pacific Diaspora: Island Peoples in the United States and across the Pacific*. Honolulu: University of Hawai'i Press, 2002.

Takaki, Ronald. *Strangers from a Different Shore*. New York: Little, Brown and Company, 1989.

U.S. Bureau of the Census. *United States: 2010 Census of Population and Housing*. Washington, DC: U.S. Bureau of the Census, 2013.

U.S. Office of Immigration Statistics. *2012 Yearbook of Immigration Statstics*. Washington, DC: U.S. Department of Homeland Security, 2013.

Yung, Judy. *Unbound Feet: A Social History of Chinese Women in San Francisco*. Berkeley: University of California Press, 1995.

Zhao, Xiaojian. *Remaking Chinese America: Immigration, Family, and Community, 1940–1965*. New Brunswick, NJ: Rutgers University Press, 2002.

Zhou, Min, and James V. Gatewood, eds. *Contemporary Asian America: A Multidisciplinary Reader.* New York: New York University Press, 2000.

Zia, Helen. *Asian American Dreams: The Emergence of an American People.* New York: Farrar, Strauss and Giroux, 2001.

Identity, Culture, and Community

Aguilar-San Juan, Karin. *Little Saigons: Staying Vietnamese in America.* Minneapolis: University of Minnesota Press, 2009.

Aguilar-San Juan, Karin, ed. *The State of Asian America: Activism and Resistance in the 1990s.* Brooklyn, NY: South End Press, 1994.

Ang, Ien. *On Not Speaking Chinese: Living Between Asia and the West.* London: Routledge, 2001.

Bonus, Rick. *Locating Filipino Americans: Ethnicity and the Cultural Politics of Space.* Philadelphia: Temple University Press, 2000.

Brian, Kristi. *Reframing Transracial Adoption: Adopted Koreans, White Parents, and the Politics of Kinship.* Philadelphia: Temple University Press, 2012.

Butcher, Beverly J. *Chinese and Chinese American Ancestor Veneration in the Catholic Church, 635 AD to the Present.* Lewiston, NY: Edwin Mellen Press, 2010.

Chan, Sucheng. *Not Just Victims: Conversations with Cambodian Community Leaders in the United States.* Urbana: University of Illinois Press, 2003.

Cheng, Vincent. *Inauthentic: The Anxiety over Culture and Identity.* New Brunswick, NJ: Rutgers University Press, 2004.

Chun, Gloria H. *Of Orphans and Warriors: Inventing Chinese-American Culture and Identity.* New Brunswick, NJ: Rutgers University Press, 2000.

Chung, Sue Fawn, and Priscilla Wegars, eds. *Chinese American Death Rituals: Respecting the Ancestors.* New York: AltaMira Press, 2005.

Danico, Mary Yu, and Franklin Ng. *Asian American Issues.* Westport, CT: Greenwood Press, 2004.

Espiritu, Yen Le. *Filipino American Lives.* Philadelphia: Temple University Press, 1995.

Espiritu, Yen Le. *Home Bound: Filipino American Lives across Cultures, Communities, and Countries.* Berkeley: University of California Press, 2003.

Fong, Timothy P. *The First Suburban Chinatown: The Remaking of Monterey Park, California.* Philadelphia: Temple University Press, 1994.

Freeman, James A. *Hearts of Sorrow: Vietnamese-American Lives.* Stanford, CA: Stanford University Press, 1989.

Hein, Jeremy. *Ethnic Origins: The Adaptation of Cambodian and Hmong Refugees in Four American Cities.* New York: Russell Sage Foundation, 2006.

Kessler, Lauren. *Stubborn Twig: Three Generations in the Life of a Japanese American Family.* New York: Penguin Books, 1994.

Kibria, Nazli. *Family Tightrope: The Changing Lives of Vietnamese Americans.* Princeton, NJ: Princeton University Press, 1993.

Kwong, Peter. *The New Chinatown.* New York: Hill and Wang, 1987.

Kwong, Peter, and Dušanka Miščević. *Chinese America: The Untold Story of America's Oldest New Community.* New York: The New Press, 2005.

Lee, Jennifer, and Min Zhou. *Asian American Youth: Culture, Identity, and Ethnicity*. New York: Routledge, 2004.

Lee, Jonathan H. X. *The Temple of Kwan Tai—Celebrating Community and Diversity, Mendocino, CA*. Rev. 2nd ed. Mendocino, CA: Temple of Kwan Tai, 2004.

Ling, Huping. *Emerging Voices: Experiences of Underrepresented Asian Americans*. New Brunswick, NJ: Rutgers University Press, 2008.

Lui, Mary Ting Yi. *The Chinatown Trunk Mystery: Murder, Miscegenation, and Other Encounters in Turn-of-the-Century NYC*. Princeton, NJ: Princeton University Press, 2005.

Lukes, Timothy J., and Gary Y. Okihiro. *Japanese Legacy: Farming and Community Life in California's Santa Clara Valley*. Cupertino: California History Center, 1985.

Maria, Sunaina. *Desis in the House: Indian American Youth Culture in New York City*. Philadelphia: Temple University Press, 2002.

Matsumoto, Valerie. *Farming the Home Place: A Japanese American Community in California, 1919–1982*. Ithaca, NY: Cornell University Press, 1993.

Nee, Victor G., and Brett De Bary Nee. *Longtime Californ': A Documentary Study of an American Chinatown*. New York: Pantheon Books, 1972.

Otsuka, Julie. *A Buddha in the Attic*. New York: Knopf, 2011.

See, Lisa. *On Gold Mountain: The One-Hundred-Year Odyssey of My Chinese-American Family*. New York: Vintage Books, 1995.

Shah, Nayan. *Contagious Divides: Epidemics and Race in San Francisco's Chinatown*. Berkeley: University of California Press, 2001.

Yamamoto, Traise. *Masking Selves, Making Subjects: Japanese American Women, Identity, and the Body*. Berkeley: University of California Press, 1999.

Yang, Fenggang. *Chinese Christians in America: Conversion, Assimilation, and Adhesive Identities*. University Park: Pennsylvania State University Press, 1999.

Yeh, Chiou-ling. *Making an American Festival: Chinese New Year in San Francisco's Chinatown*. Berkeley: University of California Press, 2008.

Yoo, David. *Growing Up Nisei: Race, Generation, and Culture among Japanese Americans of California, 1924–49*. Urbana: University of Illinois Press, 2000.

Yoo, David K., ed. *New Spiritual Homes: Religion and Asian Americans*. Honolulu: University of Hawai'i Press, 1999.

Young, Robert J. C. *Colonial Desire: Hybridity in Theory, Culture and Race*. London: Routledge, 1995.

Yu, Henry. *Thinking Orientals: Migration, Contact, and Exoticism in Modern America*. Oxford: Oxford University Press, 2001.

Yung, Judy, Gordon H. Chang, and Him Mark Lai, eds. *Chinese American Voices: From the Gold Rush to the Present*. Berkeley: University of California Press, 2006.

Literature, Memoirs, and Writing

Bacho, Peter. *Dark Blue Suit: And Other Stories*. Seattle: University of Washington Press, 1997.

Bulosan, Carlos. *America Is in the Heart: A Personal History*. Seattle: University of Washington Press, 1974.

Chang, Victoria, ed. *Asian American Poetry: The Next Generation*. Urbana: University of Illinois Press, 2004.

Chin, Frank, Jeffrey Paul Chan, Lawson Fusao Inada, and Shawn Wong, eds. *The Big Aiiieeeee! An Anthology of Chinese American and Japanese American Literature.* New York: Plume, 1995.

Davis, Rocío G. *Begin Here: Reading Asian North American Autobiographies of Childhood.* Honolulu: University of Hawai'i Press, 2007.

Davis, Rocío G, ed. *Ethnic Life Writing and Histories: Critical Intersections.* Münster: LIT Verlag, 2007.

Davis, Rocío G., and Sue-Im Lee, eds. *Literary Gestures: The Aesthetic in Asian American Writing.* Philadelphia: Temple University Press, 2006.

Dinhand, Truong-nhu, and Tran Thi Truong Nga. *The Last Boat Out: Memoirs of a Triumphant Vietnamese-American Family.* Leander, TX: GASLight Publishing, 2006.

Gallo, Laura P. Alonson, ed. *American Voices: Interviews with American Writers/Voces de America: Entrevistas a Escritores Americanos.* Cadiz, Spain: Aduana Vieja, 2004.

Gotanda, Philip Kan. *Fish Head Soup and Other Plays.* Seattle: University of Washington Press, 2000.

Hagedorn, Jessica. *Dogeaters: A Play about the Philippines.* New York: Theatre Communications Group, 2003.

Houston, Jeanne Wakatsuki. *Farewell to Manzanar.* New York: Laurel Leaf Press, 1995.

Huang, Guiyou, ed. *Asian American Autobiographers: A Bio-Bibliographical Critical Sourcebook.* Westport, CT: Greenwood Press, 2001.

Huang, Guiyou, ed. *Asian American Literary Studies.* Edinburgh: Edinburgh University Press, 2005.

Huang, Guiyou, ed. *Asian American Poets: A Bio-Bibliographical Critical Sourcebook.* Westport, CT: Greenwood Press, 2002.

Huang, Guiyou, ed. *Asian American Short Story Writers: An A-to-Z Guide.* Westport, CT: Greenwood Press, 2003.

Huang, Guiyou. *The Columbia Guide to Asian American Literature since 1945.* New York: Columbia University Press, 2006.

Huang, Guiyou, and Bing Wu, eds. *Global Perspectives on Asian American Literature.* Bejing: Foreign Language Teaching & Research Press, 2008.

Huang, Su-ching. *Mobile Homes: Spatial and Cultural Negotiation in Asian American Literature.* New York: Routledge, 2006.

Huntley, E. D. *Amy Tan: A Critical Companion.* Westport, CT: Greenwood Press, 1998.

Huntley, E. D. *Maxine Hong Kingston: A Critical Companion.* Westport, CT: Greenwood Press, 2001.

Hwang, David Henry. *Trying to Find Chinatown: The Selected Plays.* New York: Theatre Communications Group, 2000.

Kim, Elaine H. *Asian American Literature: An Introduction to the Writings and Their Social Context.* Philadelphia: Temple University Press, 1982.

Kingston, Maxine Hong. *China Men.* New York: Alfred A. Knopf, 1980.

Kingston, Maxine Hong. *The Woman Warrior: Memoirs of a Girlhood among Ghosts.* New York: Alfred A. Knopf, 1976.

Lahiri, Jhumpa. *Interpreter of Maladies.* New York: Mariner Books, 1999.

Lahiri, Jhumpa. *Unaccustomed Earth.* New York: A. A. Knopf, 2008.

Okada, John. *No-No Boy.* Seattle: University of Washington Press, 1978.

Sone, Monica. *Nisei Daughter.* 1953. Reprint, Seattle: University of Washington Press, 1979.

Tan, Amy. *The Joy Luck Club.* New York: Ballantine Books, 1989.

Uchida, Yoshiko. *Picture Bride: A Novel.* Seattle: University of Washington Press, 1997.

Wong, Jade Snow. *Fifth Chinese Daughter.* Seattle: University of Washington Press, 1989.

Wong, Shawn. *American Knees: A Novel.* New York: Simon and Schuster, 1995.

Woo, Susan J. *Everything Asian: A Novel.* New York: Thomas Dunne Books, 2009.

Yamamoto, Hisaye. *Seventeen Syllables, and Other Stories.* Piscataway, NJ: Rutgers University Press, 1998.

Yang, Gene. *American Born Chinese.* New York: First Second, 2006.

Zhou, Xiaojing. *The Ethics and Poetics of Alterity in Asian American Poetry.* Iowa City: University of Iowa Press, 2006.

Zhou, Xiaojing, and Najmi Samina, eds. *Form and Transformation in Asian American Literature.* Seattle: University of Washington Press, 2005.

Politics and Activism

Chang, Gordon, ed. *Asian Americans and Politics: Perspectives, Experiences, Prospects.* Stanford, CA: Stanford University Press, 2002.

Cho, Song. *Rice: Explorations into Gay Asian Culture and Politics.* Toronto: Queer Press, 1997.

Espiritu, Yen Le. *Asian American Panethnicity: Bridging Institutions and Identities.* Philadelphia: Temple University Press, 1992.

Ho, Fred, ed. *Legacy to Liberation: Politics and Culture of Revolutionary Asian/Pacific America.* Edinburgh: AK Press, 2000.

Kim, Claire Jean. *Bitter Fruit: The Politics of Black-Korean Conflict in New York City.* New Haven, CT: Yale University Press, 2000.

Kim, Hyung-Chan, ed. *Asian Americans and the Supreme Court: A Documentary History.* New York: Greenwood Press, 1992.

Lien, Pei-ti. *The Making of Asian America through Political Participation (Mapping Racism).* Philadelphia: Temple University Press, 2001.

Lowe, Lisa. *Immigrant Acts: On Asian American Cultural Politics.* Durham, NC: Duke University Press, 1996.

Nakanishi, Don T., and James S. Lai. *Asian American Politics: Law, Participation, and Policy.* Lanham, MD: Rowman & Littlefield, 2003.

Park, John. *Elusive Citizenship: Immigration, Asian Americans, and the Paradox of Civil Rights.* New York: New York University Press, 2004.

Saito, Leland T. *Race and Politics: Asian Americans, Latinos, and Whites in a Los Angeles Suburb.* Urbana: University of Illinois Press, 2001.

Schueller, Malini Johar. *The Politics of Voice: Liberalism and Social Criticism from Franklin to Kingston.* Albany, NY: SUNY Press, 1992.

War and Conflict

Abelmann, Nancy, and John Lie. *Blue Dreams: Korean Americans and the Los Angeles Riots.* Cambridge, MA: Harvard University Press, 1995.

Anthony, Nathan, and Robert Gardner. *The Bombing of Pearl Harbor.* Berkeley Heights, NJ: Enslow, 2001.

Chan, Sucheng. *The Vietnamese American 1.5 Generation: Stories of War, Revolution, Flight, and New Beginnings.* Philadelphia: Temple University Press, 2006.

Commission on Wartime Relocation and Internment of Civilians. *Personal Justice Denied: Report of the Commission on Wartime Relocation and Internment of Civilians.* Washington, DC: Commission on Wartime Relocation and Internment of Civilians, 1982.

Daniels, Roger. *Concentration Camps, North America: Japanese in the United States and Canada during World War II.* Malabar, FL: Krieger, 1981.

Daniels, Roger. *The Politics of Prejudice: The Anti-Japanese Movement in California and the Struggle for Japanese Exclusion.* Berkeley: University of California Press, 1978.

Daum, Andreas W., Lloyd C. Gardner, and Wilfried Mausbach, eds. *America, the Vietnam War, and the World: Comparative and International Perspectives.* New York: Cambridge University Press/German Historical Institute, 2003.

Desai, Jigna. *Beyond Bollywood: The Cultural Politics of South Asian Diasporic Film.* New York: Routledge, 2004.

Fujino, Diane C. *Heartbeat of Struggle: The Revolutionary Life of Yuri Kochiyama.* Minneapolis: University of Minnesota Press, 2005.

Glenn, Evelyn Nakano. *Issei, Nisei, War Bride: Three Generations of Japanese American Women in Domestic Service.* Philadelphia: Temple University Press, 1986.

Harth, Erica, ed. *Last Witnesses: Reflections on the Wartime Internment of Japanese Americans.* New York: Palgrave, 2001.

Harvey, Robert. *Amache: The Story of Japanese Internment in Colorado during World War II.* Dallas, TX: Taylor Trade, 2003.

Hayslip, Le Ly, and Jay Wurts. *When Heaven and Earth Changed Places: A Vietnamese Woman's Journey from War to Peace.* New York: Doubleday, 1989.

Henning, Joseph M. *Outposts of Civilization: Race, Religion, and the Formative Years of American-Japanese Relations.* New York: New York University Press, 2000.

Higashide, Seiichi. *Adios to Tears: The Memoirs of a Japanese-Peruvian Internee in U.S. Concentration Camps.* Seattle: University of Washington Press, 2000.

Inada, Lawson Fusao, ed. *Only What We Could Carry: The Japanese American Internment Experience.* Berkeley: Heyday Books/California Historical Society, 2000.

Ishizuka, Karen L. *Lost & Found: Reclaiming the Japanese American Incarceration.* Urbana: University of Illinois Press, 2006.

Kashima, Tetsuden, and United States Commission on Wartime Relocation and Internment of Civilians. *Personal Justice Denied: Report of the Commission on Wartime Relocation and Internment of Civilians.* Seattle: University of Washington Press, 1997.

McClain, Charles J. *In Search of Equality: The Chinese Struggle against Discrimination in Nineteenth-Century America.* Berkeley: University of California Press, 1994.

Okihiro, Gary Y. *Cane Fires: The Anti-Japanese Movement in Hawaii, 1865–1945.* Philadelphia: Temple University Press, 1991.

Weglyn, Michi. *Years of Infamy: The Untold Story of America's Concentration Camps.* New York: Morrow Quill Paperbacks, 1976.

Yang Murray, Alice, ed. *What Did the Internment of Japanese Americans Mean.* Boston: St. Martin's, 2000.

Yoon, Won-kil. *The Passage of a Picture Bride.* Loma Linda, CA: Loma Linda University Press, 1989.

Yuh, Ji-Yeon. *Beyond the Shadow of Camptown: Korean Military Brides in America*. New York: New York University Press, 2002.

Web Resources

General

Asian American History Timeline (Loni Ding)
http://www.cetel.org/timeline.html

Asian American Voices: Voices from American History
http://www.digitalhistory.uh.edu/voices/voices_content.cfm?vid=1

Asian American and Pacific Islander Faculty Staff Association, Washington State University
http://aapifsa.wsu.edu/

Asian Media Watch
http://www.goldsea.com/Mediawatch/mediawatch.html

Asian-Nation: Asian American History, Demographics, & Issues
http://www.asian-nation.org

AsianWeek (national English-language newspaper)
http://www.asianweek.com/

Association for Asian American Studies
http://www.aaastudies.org/aaas/index.html

Center for Asian American Media
http://caamedia.org/

Divanee Magazine
http://www.divanee.com

Elan magazine, a daily, online publication on global Muslim youth culture
http://www.elanthemag.com/

Hyphen Magazine
http://www.hyphenmagazine.com/

Smithsonian Asian Pacific American Program
http://www.apa.si.edu/

University of California Los Angeles Asian American Studies Center
http://www.aasc.ucla.edu

Wing Luke Asian Museum, Seattle
http://www.wingluke.org/

Census 2000 Briefs

The Asian Population: 2010
http://www.census.gov/prod/cen2010/briefs/c2010br-11.pdf

The Native Hawaiian and Other Pacific Islander Population: 2010
http://www.census.gov/prod/cen2010/briefs/c2010br-12.pdf

Immigration and Refugees

Asian Immigration to Hawaii (Pacific University)
http://mcel.pacificu.edu/as/students/hawaii/index.html

Immigration Records at the Library of Congress
http://www.loc.gov/teachers/classroommaterials/themes/asian-pacific/search-terms.html

U.S. Citizenship and Immigration Services (formerly the Immigration and Naturalization Service)
http://www.uscis.gov/portal/site/uscis

Chinese Americans

Angel Island Immigration Station Foundation
http://aiisf.org/

Chinese American Museum (Los Angeles)
http://www.camla.org/

Chinese Historical Society of America
http://www.chsa.org/

Chinese Historical Society of Southern California
http://chssc.org/

Documents on the Chinese in California (San Francisco Museum)
http://www.sfmuseum.org/hist1/index0.html

Gateway to Gold Mountain Exhibit (Smithsonian)
http://www.wright.edu/admin/ahna/gateway%20pictures.htm

On Gold Mountain Online Exhibit
http://www.apa.si.edu/ongoldmountain/

Filipino Americans

Carlos Bulosan Memorial Exhibit (Seattle)
http://www.bulosan.org/

Filipino American National Historical Society
http://www.fanhs-national.org/

Filipino American Photographs of Ricardo Ocreto Alvarado (Smithsonian)
http://www.tfaoi.com/aa/6aa/6aa220.htm

Filipino Links (Filipino American National Historical Society, Stockton)
http://fanhsstockton.com/

Spanish-American War in Motion Pictures (Library of Congress)
http://www.loc.gov/collection/spanish-american-war-in-motion-pictures/about-this-collection/#overview

Hawaiians and Immigration to Hawaii

Annexation of Hawaii Documents (University of Hawaii)
http://libweb.hawaii.edu/digicoll/annexation/annexation.html

Asian Immigration to Hawaii (Pacific University)
http://mcel.pacificu.edu/as/students/hawaii/index.html

Hawaii Kingdom History
http://www.hawaiiankingdom.org/political-history.shtml

Hawaiian Sovereignty Movement
http://www.hawaii-nation.org/

Hawaii's Story, by Hawaii's Queen Liliuokalani (1898)
http://digital.library.upenn.edu/women/liliuokalani/hawaii/hawaii.html

Women and Work in Hawaii (Hawai'i Women's Heritage Project)
http://www.soc.hawaii.edu/hwhp/hawork/itm.open.html

Japanese Americans

Ansel Adams's Photographs of Internment at Manzanar (Library of Congress)
http://memory.loc.gov/ammem/collections/anseladams/

Documents, Reports, and Letters Related to Relocation on Bainbridge Island, Washington (University of Washington)
http://www.lib.washington.edu/exhibits/harmony/documents/

Hirabayashi v. United States (1943)
http://supreme.justia.com/us/320/81/case.html

Japanese American Citizens League
http://www.jacl.org/

Japanese American Exhibit and Access Project (University of Washington)
http://www.lib.washington.edu/exhibits/harmony/default.html

Japanese American National Museum
http://www.janm.org/

Japanese Americans in San Francisco (San Francisco Museum)
http://www.sfmuseum.org/hist1/index0.1.html#japanese

Kiyoshi Hirabayashi v. United States (1943)
http://caselaw.lp.findlaw.com/cgi-bin/getcase.pl?court=us&vol=320&invol=81

Korematsu v. United States (1944)
http://caselaw.lp.findlaw.com/scripts/getcase.pl?court=US&vol=323&invol=214

Minoru Yasui v. United States (1943)
http://caselaw.lp.findlaw.com/scripts/getcase.pl?navby=search&court=US&case=/data/us/320/115.html

A More Perfect Union—Japanese Americans and the Constitution (Smithsonian)
http://americanhistory.si.edu/perfectunion/non-flash/index.html

Photographs by Dorothea Lange (Library of Congress)
http://www.loc.gov/exhibits/wcf/wcf0013.html

War Relocation Authority Camps in Arizona, 1942–46 (University of Arizona)
http://parentseyes.arizona.edu/wracamps/camplife.html

War Relocation Authority Publication, "The Relocation of Japanese Americans," 1943 (University of Washington)
http://www.lib.washington.edu/exhibits/harmony/documents/wrapam.html

Korean Americans

Korean Adoptee Adoptive Family Network
http://www.kaanet.com/

"Korean Adoptees Remember," in Finding Home: Fifty Years of International Adoption (American Public Radioworks)
http://americanradioworks.publicradio.org/features/adoption/a1.html

Korean American Historical Society
http://www.kahs.org/

Korean American Museum
http://www.kamuseum.org/

Korean Americans: A Century of Experience (Smithsonian)
http://www.apa.si.edu/Curriculum%20Guide-Final/index.htm

Korean Quarterly
http://www.koreanquarterly.org/Home.html

South Asian Americans

Little India
http://www.littleindia.com/

Masala!
http://www.masala.com/

Sikh American Legal Defense and Education Fund
http://www.saldef.org/

Sikh Community: Over 100 Years in the Pacific Northwest (Wing Luke Asian Museum)
http://www.wingluke.org/sikh-community-exhibition/

South Asian Women's Network
http://www.sawnet.org/

Southeast Asian Americans

Cambodian Genocide Program (Yale University)
http://www.yale.edu/cgp/

Hmong Studies Internet Resource Center
http://www.hmongstudies.org/

Hmong Studies Journal
http://www.hmongstudiesjournal.org/

Lao Census Data
http://www.hmongstudies.org/LaoCensusData.html

Lao Language and Culture Learning Resources (Northern Illinois University)
http://www.seasite.niu.edu/lao/lao3.htm

Southeast Asian Archive (University of California–Irvine)
http://www.lib.uci.edu/libraries/collections/sea/sasian.html

Index

About the Editors

Gary Y. Okihiro is a professor of international and public affairs at Columbia University. He is the author of *Pineapple Culture: A History of the Tropical and Temperate Zones,* and *Island World: A History of Hawai'i and the United States*, as well as the *Encyclopedia of Japanese American Internment* (Greenwood, 2013).

Emily Moberg Robinson received a BA in history from Wellesley College, and an MA and a PhD in history from the University of California, Santa Cruz. Her research is in memory studies, and immigrant and national identity. She has taught courses in United States history, religious history, and Asian American studies at UC Santa Cruz and at Menlo College.